TEXAS LABOR HISTORY

Number 119: Centennial Series of the Association of
Former Students, Texas A&M University

Texas Labor History

Edited by

Bruce A. Glasrud

AND

James C. Maroney

TEXAS A&M UNIVERSITY PRESS   COLLEGE STATION

Copyright © 2013 by Texas A&M University Press
Manufactured in the United States of America
All rights reserved
First edition

This paper meets the requirements of ANSI/NISO Z39.48-1992 (Permanence of Paper).
Binding materials have been chosen for durability.
∞ ♻

Library of Congress Cataloging-in-Publication Data

Texas labor history / edited by Bruce A. Glasrud and James C. Maroney. — 1st ed.
    p. cm. — (Centennial series of the Association of Former Students, Texas A&M University ;
no. 119)
    Includes bibliographical references and index.
    ISBN-13: 978-1-60344-944-1 (cloth : alk. paper)
    ISBN-10: 1-60344-944-2 (cloth : alk. paper)
    ISBN-13: 978-1-60344-945-8 (pbk. : alk. paper)
    ISBN-10: 1-60344-945-0 (pbk. : alk. paper)
    [etc.]
    1. Labor—Texas—History—19th century. 2. Labor—Texas—History—20th century. 3. Labor
movement—Texas—History—19th century. 4. Labor movement—Texas—History—20th
century. 5. Labor unions—Texas—History—19th century. 6. Labor unions—Texas—History—
20th century. I. Glasrud, Bruce A. II. Maroney, James C., 1936– III. Series: Centennial series of
the Association of Former Students, Texas A&M University ; no. 119.
    HD8083.T4T356 2013
    331.8809764—dc23

                                                                                    2012044210

Contents

Acknowledgments

Our greatest debt is owed to the contributors to this volume; without their dedication to the cause of the working-class majority of this state and nation, this work would not have been possible. The encouragement, suggestions, and enthusiasm of a number of scholars for this project, including several not among the eighteen authors whose articles are included in this volume, surprised, delighted, and humbled us. Two of our contributors—the Greens—George and Jim, who are related only by their commitment to the cause of those represented in the pages of this work, wisely suggested alternative articles of their own work as well as the work of newer scholars that we should include in order to enhance the volume. We continue to be inspired by the scholarship of, and our friendship with, the practitioners of our art who are represented in these pages.

We also owe thanks to the publishers of the articles, particularly to the *Southwestern Historical Quarterly* from which nine of our selections derived, and the *West Texas Historical Association Yearbook*, which published two of the articles.

We owe an incalculable debt to Mary Lenn Dixon, editor-in-chief of Texas A&M University Press, who offered ongoing enthusiasm, support, and encouragement for the project. Furthermore, the assessment of the outside readers, as well as their support and encouragement for the project, was invaluable.

We would be remiss if we failed to acknowledge the support of the many librarians and archivists at a number of university libraries, archives, and publishing houses, too many in number to name individually. Specifically, however, Jim Maroney wishes to acknowledge the yeoman service provided by Ashley Williams at Lee College for her assistance in securing books and articles through interlibrary loan and Lee College librarian Beverly Li for her assistance in locating other library material. Their contributions to this work are greatly appreciated. Cecilia Gutierrez Venable, at the archives of Texas A&M University Corpus Christi, helped in innumerable ways, including garnering article copies, scanning, and reading.

Also, Jim wishes to acknowledge an ongoing debt to his mentor and friend, the late Tom Morgan, who died far too young, and who initially encouraged him to study and to write about labor and working-class history. Jim wishes to acknowledge the love and support of his wife, Kathleen McEntee Maroney, without whom his contribution to this book would not have been possible. Likewise, Bruce recognizes the continual help from his friend and spouse, Pearline Vestal Glasrud.

Bruce A. Glasrud
James C. Maroney

TEXAS LABOR HISTORY

JAMES C. MARONEY AND BRUCE A. GLASRUD

Introduction

The Neglected Heritage of Texas Labor

The history of organized labor movements in Texas is too often overlooked or ignored by observers and writers of Texas history, many of whom hold inaccurate or false views about Texas unionists. This has led to a number of misconceptions. First is the presumption that a viable labor movement never existed in the Lone Star state. On the contrary, collective action by workers occurred in key areas of employment, although it was frequently sporadic and short-lived. Second is the belief that black, brown, and white laborers—whether male or female—could not collectively work together to achieve even short-term solidarity. Despite differing working conditions and places in society, however, many workers managed to unite, sometimes in biracial efforts, to overturn the top-down strategy utilized by Texas employers. Third, many Texas writers subscribed to a persistent belief that labor unions in Texas remained weak and ineffective because of their inability to successfully confront employers, which in turn accounted for the powerlessness of their organizations. A more accurate explanation, however, acknowledges the unyielding and frequently violent opposition to labor organizations by a critical number of business and political leaders determined to crush any and all union activity on the part of their employees. It also should be pointed out that even when unions achieved limited success, they seemed to generate even more opposition from employers.

A fourth fallacy contends that unions in Texas enjoyed little or no success. This assumption is also inaccurate. Over the years, notable examples of union achievement include the efforts of black and white workers to overcome southern mores and collaborate to successfully organize the Galveston waterfront, and the Brotherhood of Timber Workers' pattern of success in their struggle for self-determination in the early twentieth century. Fifth is the myth that laborers and other progressive groups could not work together. The populist and progressive movements of the late nineteenth and early twentieth centuries, and the election of Ralph Yarborough to the United States Senate in the 1950s, all indicated that unionists, farmers, and other working people could effectively unite in order to achieve common goals. And a final fallacy is the assumption that little has been written or studied about the Texas labor movement. This book, *Texas Labor History*, refutes that belief by presenting eighteen previously published articles that reflect the rich heritage of Texas labor. Also refuting that notion are hundreds of books and other articles on various aspects of Texas labor history, as well as numerous unpublished works by graduate students. This anthology provides access to the articles and works cited in its bibliography to scholars and students of the "neglected heritage" of Texas labor.

Not until recent decades, however, have historians who write about Texas workers and their unions begun any sort of organized study of the topic. Before 1960, most of the historical studies written about labor activity in the state, like those that focused on the national scene, were the products of labor economists led by Richard T. Ely, John R. Commons, and the "Wisconsin School." Only a limited number of historians wrote about labor, and those who did followed the lead of the labor economists and studied the history of specific labor organizations, union federations, jurisdictional disputes, work stoppages, and conflicts with employers and nonunion workers, many of whom were African American or Mexican, either native-born or immigrant.[1]

Although scholars who specialize in the history of African Americans, Hispanics, or other minorities have published meaningful and insightful works on their subjects that include an emphasis on labor, in recent decades practitioners of the "new labor history" have noted that despite their work, little about labor studies has made its way into the nation's textbooks or into the public's consciousness. Since the 1960s, however, younger and often more radical scholars, influenced by British historians E. P. Thompson, Eric Hobsbawm, and others, have focused on a wider canvas in an attempt to understand how the total environment of the worker influenced his life,[2] rather than limiting their investigation to union and other work-related activity. This perspective initiated a new and exciting approach to the study of working people that viewed the working class from "the bottom up."[3] In the United States, this interpretation resonated with Howard Zinn, who soon published the first of many editions of a popular history and widely used text, *A People's History of the United States*.[4] Zinn and other radical historians used the work of Thompson and others to bolster their belief that the overwhelming amount of written history about the working classes in this country prior to the 1960s has reflected almost entirely the point of view of an educated elite. According to this interpretation, individuals such as George Washington, Thomas Jefferson, Benjamin Franklin, Abraham Lincoln, and Franklin D. Roosevelt became presidents, secretaries of state, and opinion leaders who wrote letters, diaries, books, and produced thousands of public and government documents in the course of their very public and influential lives. These individuals created an explanation that shaped the public's understanding, which was that an elite brotherhood "made" our nation's history, and it is this version that accounts for the prominent place of elites in American life and their veneration by the American public.

Scholars of labor, working-class, and gender studies found that the traditional top-down accounts of American history, while sometimes brilliant and enlightening, are woefully incomplete, and they argue that these accounts are responsible for the general public's lack of knowledge concerning the history of middle-class and working-class Americans, who until recently were mentioned only briefly in public school and college history textbooks. One obvious explanation for their invisibility is that "common" folk customarily did not write diaries, books, or letters that survived for the eyes of future scholars. All this began to change, however, in the 1960s with the Vietnam War, protests by the New Left, and, perhaps most importantly, the modern media. Media both enlightened and horrified Americans with daily televised coverage of events such as the excesses of Birmingham's Eugene "Bull" Connor during the civil rights protests, and of the Vietnam conflict, which included the My Lai massacre and disturbing nightly images of body bags returning from the Asian country.

Furthermore, those who produced the "new labor history" fervently believed that throughout human history, common folk served as foot soldiers in the armies of dynamic and influential leaders of epoch-making mass movements like that led by Martin Luther King. In doing so, they became vital and essential participants in historic changes that ultimately made more significant and lasting contributions to history than did any king, president, or dictator. According to this interpretation, ordinary people, then, deserve prominent places in our written history, and their legacies should be studied and treasured. This perspective helped to bring about a virtual revolution in the writing of working-class history.

Before the advent of this "history from the bottom up," labor studies focused on unions, strikes, and other work-based activity, but the practitioners of the new labor history were influenced by insights from the "new social history," and they began to incorporate the pursuits of working people in their daily lives apart from the workplace, including those associated with home, sports, and recreation. In doing so, their research significantly broadened our understanding of the motivation and actions of the working class and their leaders, and other previously "invisible" Americans.[5] Anyone wanting to benefit more fully from the perspectives and methods utilized in the newer scholarship, which incorporates those previously left out of our national story, would do well to carefully study the essays in *The New American History*, an anthology edited by Eric Foner. Although the essays do not focus on Texas, the article by Leon Fink on American labor history is especially strong in explaining how historians of the new labor history incorporate the previously overlooked members of the working class into the story. Also effective are the chapters on the newer scholarship in social history by Alice Kestler-Harris, on African American history by Thomas C. Holt, and on women's history by Linda Gordon.[6]

Texas's great size and its many small, isolated communities, in combination with its lack of industry during the formative years of the nineteenth century, help to explain why the state and its southern and western neighbors developed a suspicious and hostile environment toward labor unions. Numerous employers formed businessmen's organizations and trade associations with the express intent of destroying labor unions, and at the same time they condemned as un-American any form of organization among their employees. Such actions inevitably led to the formation of unions among working people in Texas. Houston witnessed the creation of the first unions as early as 1838, although widespread union activity in Texas did not appear before the great railroad strikes of 1877.[7]

Writing in 1971 on the status of Texas labor history in a brief but perceptive article, University of Texas economist and future US secretary of labor F. Ray Marshall acknowledged that most of the academic writing on labor in Texas and in the South was the work of economists and pointed out that few American historians had produced labor studies. Although the economists' works had been historical in nature, Marshall thought that historians' insights and analysis would contribute a great deal to our knowledge of labor, especially since contemporary economists increasingly were turning to theory and statistical studies. Marshall pointed out that while historians were beginning to write on labor topics in Texas and in the South, no comprehensive history of the Texas labor movement existed.[8]

Almost forty years later, the history of the labor movement in the Lone Star state remains unwritten, although many excellent individual studies by historians of labor in Texas and other southern states advance our understanding of the economic and cultural development of the region. Although we will chronicle a number of these developments in the remainder of this essay, it should be noted that the articles on labor history in the *New Handbook of Texas* are an excellent starting place for an investigation of Texas working-class history.[9]

Also noteworthy are the essays in an important new anthology, *Beyond Texas through Time: Breaking Away from Past Interpretations*, edited by Walter L. Buenger and Arnoldo De Leon, which evaluate current developments in Texas historiography.[10]

One of the earliest scholarly efforts of the Texas labor movement, a contemporary account of "The South-Western Strike," by Harvard economist Frank W. Taussig, denounced demands made by the Knights of Labor as "an arrogant invasion of property rights."[11] Other early works on labor in Texas included investigations of organized labor in Austin by University of Texas graduate student Earle Sparks, of the labor supply in Texas by Townes M. Harris, and of discrimination against African American workers in Texas by Robert Teel.[12] These studies, although required reading even for today's labor historians, did not focus on laborers but on discrimination, institutions, and numbers.

The next scholarly accounts on Texas labor history did not appear until the early 1940s when University of Texas economist Ruth Allen produced two significant works. In *Chapters in the History of Organized Labor in Texas*, she countered Taussig's analysis with a favorable assessment of the Knights of Labor's role in the labor-management conflict on the railroads in the 1870s and gave an overall positive view of organized labor. Subsequent chapters dealt with the unionization of Texas mine and oil workers, the early years of the Texas State Federation of Labor (TSFL), and the involvement of African Americans in the state federation. The work is noted for its coverage of labor activity virtually unknown at the time, even to many Texas historians, and for the inclusion of specific statistics and other pertinent data from TSFL proceedings. The book also reproduced excerpts of scarce union records and actual courtroom testimony in significant labor cases. For these reasons, Allen's *Chapters* remains an essential source for any study of Texas labor during its formative years. Allen's second study on the Texas labor movement, *The Great Southwest Strike*, also included hard-to-find sources and excerpts of courtroom testimony about the epic struggle between Knights of Labor–affiliated railroad workers and the Gould system railroads that began in Marshall, Texas, and exploded onto the national scene in 1886 before its ultimate defeat by powerful railroad barons led by Jay Gould. One of the book's significant contributions was to recognize the leadership of labor leader Martin Irons.[13]

A few studies by graduate students on Texas labor topics covering the late nineteenth and early twentieth centuries appeared soon after the end of World War II. John L. Wortham studied the regulation of labor organizations, Jay L. Todes wrote on organized employer opposition to unions, and John F. Carruthers examined the unionization of oil workers. Todes's thesis in particular provided great assistance to future scholars who studied antiunion activity by the Texas business establishment.[14] The decades following Ruth Allen's publications in the early 1940s also witnessed a growing number of significant scholarly works on the Texas labor movement. Grady Mullenix wrote a history of the Texas State Federation of Labor, based in part on interviews with key participants and hard-to-find union records, Murray E. Polakoff investigated the Texas CIO Council, Harold A. Shapiro studied the labor movement in San Antonio, and James V. Reese and Allen Taylor investigated Galveston's Screwmen's Benevolent Association.[15]

Reese also studied statewide union activity in the nineteenth century in depth, providing what became essential sources for scholars concerned with the origins of Texas labor history and revealing largely unknown union ventures and a treasure trove of sources.[16] He pointed out that the earliest organized activity came in Galveston, Houston, and communities with large numbers of German immigrants, many of whom were skilled artisans whose work enabled those communities to support wage earners with specific economic specializations. Surprisingly, Reese found that the Congress of the Republic of Texas enacted a mechanics' lien law in 1839, although the measure had little immediate or lasting effect, and it attests more to the existence of at least some level of organizational activity among workingmen than to any degree of real concern among the general population or the government of the Republic. Reese's article, "The Early History of Labor Organizations in Texas, 1838–1876," appears as the first essay in this anthology.

An insightful article by Robert Shelton in the *Journal of Social History* on casual and slave labor in pre–Civil War Galveston revealed a great deal about interracial arrangements among enslaved and poor white casual laborers. Shelton found that these individuals sometimes worked in segregated groups, but at other times toiled alongside one another on the waterfront at construction sites as well as in other low-wage jobs. Furthermore, he found that Galveston brothels employed white and black women who lived and worked together. The African American women included free and enslaved prostitutes, and the brothels in which they worked accommodated both black and white males. Shelton concluded that on-the-job contact seemed to foster social arrangements leading to after-hours social relations that the city's white establishment found completely unacceptable. Similar to actions by white elites in other parts of the South, Galveston's leaders took steps to curtail such activity that they believed posed a serious threat to the established southern social structure. Shelton's article, "On

Empire's Shore: Free and Unfree Workers in Galveston, Texas, 1840–1860," is the second in this anthology.[17]

Additional works on nineteenth-century labor conflict in Texas include a recent study by David Urbano on the "cart war" of 1857, in which Anglo merchants harassed a Tejano monopoly of overland traffic between the port of Velasco and San Antonio. The Tejano teamsters' use of oxcarts enabled them to transport goods more rapidly and economically than their would-be Anglo competitors. Intimidation, destruction of property, and reports of physical violence led the Mexican minister in Washington to protest the affair, which ultimately led to federal pressure on Texas governor Elisha M. Pease to end the conflict despite widespread public antagonism toward Tejano domination of the trade. Among white Texans, only German settlers expressed any degree of sympathy with Tejanos.[18]

Perhaps the most unusual work stoppage in Texas during the nineteenth century, however, was the cowboy strike of 1883. According to Robert E. Zeigler, the unsuccessful conflict, which lasted more than two months, began as a protest by cowboys over perceived domination of the cattle business in the Texas panhandle by profit-driven corporate-owned ranches. Although the failed walkout had little lasting influence on either cowboys or ranchers, it became part of Texas labor folklore and served notice that unrest was more widespread than previously assumed. Zeigler's article, "The Cowboy Strike of 1883: Its Causes and Meaning," is the third article in *Texas Labor History*.

Theresa A. Case's recent investigation of free labor involved in the Gould system strikes moved beyond Ruth Allen's analysis in *The Great Southwest Strike*, a frontier-based and somewhat romantic "them vs. us" understanding of the conflict between railroad barons and unionized railroaders at the grassroots level. In her book *The Great Southwest Railroad Strike and Free Labor*, Case discovered significant tensions among black and white workers over their understanding of the very meaning of "free labor," as well as evidence of a fierce struggle within the Knights of Labor between its leadership and its workers at the local level.[19] Case's analysis of the Knights' role in the conflict with Gould, "The Radical Potential of the Knights' Biracialism: The 1885–1886 Gould System Strikes and Their Aftermath," appears as our fourth article. In a second important article, "Blaming Martin Irons: Leadership and Popular Protest in the 1886 Southwest Strike," Case also strengthens knowledge of the role that Martin Irons played in the railroad conflict.[20]

In the early twenty-first century many conservative Texans associate Washington, DC, with liberalism and their state government as the defender of states' rights and conservatism. They might be surprised to learn, however, that Texas, along with Louisiana, Arkansas, Oklahoma, Kansas, and a number of other states, was in the forefront of the progressive reform from the late nineteenth century through the progressive era. It was reform that represented discontented farmers and members of the working class, even in a comparatively unindustrialized state like Texas. Farmer discontent during the post–Civil War era, the great upheaval on the railroads beginning in 1877 and culminating with the Great Southwest Strike in 1886, perceived excesses of Reconstruction, along with widespread corruption in government and in the business community, all led reformers to believe that influencing their state legislatures and municipal governments through the ballot box, public protests, and other forms of collective action were the most promising avenues for change. At various times reformers looked to the Greenback Party, the Farmers' Alliances, the Farmers' Union, the Populist Party, the Texas Socialist Party, and organized labor as possible vehicles for change.

The literature on reform activity in Texas includes surveys by George N. Green on the Texas labor movement from its beginnings in the nineteenth century through the progressive era. Green's articles investigated the railroad strikes of the 1870s and the subsequent rise of the Knights of Labor, the growth of the railroad brotherhoods and other unions, the impact of the Farmers' Alliance, and the rise of Jim Hogg as the spokesman for reform. Green examined the role of employer tactics, which have played such a major role in the development of collective action by workers in the mining, maritime, and railroad industries, as well as management's treatment of minorities. He also evaluated the rise of collective action by means of frequent collaboration among farmers' organizations, the railroad brotherhoods, and the rise of the Texas State Federation of Labor (TSFL).[21]

A number of other historians besides Green have added to the literature of reform from the late nineteenth century through the progressive era in Texas. Those that contributed significantly to our understanding of the state's labor history included the previously cited works of Ruth Allen, James V. Reese, Robert E. Zeigler, and Theresa A. Case. In other studies, Charles Mac Gibson chronicled organized labor activity in Texas during the 1890s, Zeigler published an article on Houston's streetcar employees and their battles with "alien" corporations from the late 1890s to 1905, and Jonathan Garlock contributed a valuable volume that provided specific data on Knights of Labor assemblies in Texas and in the United States. Other works that investigated labor in Texas cities included an article by James C. Maroney on Houston workers from 1900 through the 1920s, and several chapters in Patricia Evridge Hill's *Dallas: The Making of a Modern City.*[22]

Before the discovery and widespread use of oil in Texas, coal was a major source of fuel, and the mining of "black gold" in communities like Thurber, Strawn, Lyra, and Bridgeport played a major role in the state's economy. Ruth Allen and Mary Jane Gentry published colorful accounts of the company town of Thurber, the state's most important coal-producing community, and their works became essential sources for future scholars in Texas labor history. Later studies included investigations by James C. Maroney, Michael Hooks, and Roberto R. Calderon, but Marilyn D. Rhinehart has produced the most complete and scholarly works on Thurber, an isolated company town composed largely of immigrant workers. After early battles with autocratic management, Thurber became a staunchly unionized community that for the most part maintained harmonious relations with management for many years. Rhinehart's article "'Underground Patriots': Thurber Coal Miners and the Struggle for Individual Freedom, 1888–1903," originally published in the *Southwestern Historical Quarterly*, is the fifth essay in this anthology.[23]

The colorful history of the Brotherhood of Timber Workers, their battles with lumber barons, and their affiliation with the Industrial Workers of the World (IWW) have drawn considerable attention from historians. The Brotherhood of Timber Workers was a militant and biracial labor organization in which African Americans comprised about half. Neither its black nor white members wanted the other to be used as strikebreakers. Robert S. Maxwell studied East Texas lumbermen, while James R. Green, Jeff Ferrell, Charles R. McCord, and George T. Morgan Jr. analyzed the lumber barons' excessive exploitation of their employees, especially union members. More recently, Thad Sitton and James Conrad contributed to the literature of labor-management conflict with their book on Texas sawmill communities, *Nameless Towns: Texas Sawmill Communities, 1880–1942.* The owners used harsh and violent tactics to defeat the Brotherhood of Timber Workers. George T. Morgan's article "The Gospel of Wealth Goes South: John Henry Kirby and Labor's Struggle for Self-Determination, 1901–1916" reveals much about John Henry Kirby and the oppressive labor policies and devices of the Southern Lumber Operators Association (SLOA) in their epic struggle with the Brotherhood of Timber Workers and the IWW, and is the sixth article in this anthology.[24]

At the dawn of the twentieth century, overall conditions for many Texas workers remained grim, particularly for the unskilled, but Texas unionists saw reason for optimism. Many skilled workers had gained union membership and looked forward to the prospect of cooperation with downtrodden farmers. However, while organized labor succeeded in its efforts to forge bonds of friendship and mutual support with the numerically superior Farmers' Union, it initially failed to unite divisive forces among workingmen. The failure to get concessions from the Texas legislature in 1901 resulted in large part from a lack of cooperation between the railroad unions and the TSFL. After learning their lesson, the TSFL and the railroad brotherhoods forged a meaningful partnership in cooperation with the Farmers' Union from 1903 until about 1910. That example of working-class solidarity produced significant results for both Texas progressives and the working class, and it came about largely because of effective lobbying on the part of the Joint Labor Legislative Board.[25]

Thus, even before the election of a governor favorably inclined toward progressivism, a reform coalition in Texas had produced significant legislative gains, including a child labor law, safety measures for workers in mines and on railroads, and a bill that limited consecutive work hours for railway employees. Even greater gains came as a result of Joint Labor Legislative Board action during the administrations of Thomas M. Campbell (1907–11), including an anti-blacklisting bill and an anti–loan shark law, among other measures. The board also achieved further gains for labor during the administration of Oscar B. Colquitt (1911–15) despite the board's criticism of Colquitt's hostile attitude toward labor. After the governor vetoed several worker-friendly laws, labor nonetheless achieved a measure of success with the passage of additional child labor and safety legislation, including a law that limited women's working hours to ten hours per day and fifty-four hours per week and a bill giving state employees an eight-hour workday. Throughout these years, the work of the Joint Board benefited from letter-writing campaigns and other forms of lobbying by local unions and citywide trades councils at the grassroots level. Studies of the Joint Board by T. P. O'Rourke, of the TSFL by Grady Mullenix, of organized labor by James C. Maroney, of the progressive movement in Texas by James A. Tinsley, and of Texas Democrats during the administration of Woodrow Wilson by Lewis L. Gould, all dealt effectively with the Joint Board's impact during the Campbell and Colquitt administrations. The outstanding work of the Joint Labor Legislative Board, made possible by the newfound unity among working-class representatives during the early years of the new century, represented the high point of Texas progressivism.[26]

With the fall of populism and the farmers' alliance movement, along with the effects of economic depression in the 1890s, many small farmers in Texas and throughout the South lost their land and were forced to become tenant farmers.

Entangled in the twin evils of the share-crop and crop-lien systems, some tenants sought relief through the Farmers' Union as their champion. Earlier, its strength had proved so valuable to the TSFL and the railroad brotherhoods in their collaboration on the Joint Labor Legislative Board. Near the end of the initial decade of the new century, however, the Farmers' Union came under the spell of the business-oriented Commercial Secretaries Association, and its coopera-tion with the TSFL and the railroad brotherhoods collapsed. Traditionally not affiliated with labor unions, farmworkers and depressed tenants began to look at the emerging socialist movement, and were sometimes joined by their coun-terparts among unskilled urban laborers. Peter H. Buckingham's essay on the Texas Socialist Party, and James R. Green's article, "Tenant Farmer Discontent and Socialist Protest in Texas, 1901–1917," effectively discuss the appeal of the Socialists, whose agenda was proclaimed forcefully in the pages of Thomas A. Hickey's *The Rebel*. Green's essay is the seventh article in *Texas Labor History*.[27]

Soon after the discovery of oil in 1901 at Spindletop, near Beaumont, fren-zied wildcatters descended upon the area, and a boomtown atmosphere soon led to land speculation, lawlessness, gambling, and prostitution as well as to overnight profits and losses. Following a pattern begun in other industries, oil field workers soon suffered from the exploitation, long hours, and inadequate wages commonplace for working-class Texans of the time. Harvey O'Connor discussed such conditions in his history of the Oil Workers International Union, while Ruth Allen and Grady Mullenix studied labor during the early days of the Texas petroleum industry. James C. Maroney and William Lee Greer analyzed the Texas-Louisiana oil field strike of 1917, a major confrontation during World War I between major oil producers, oil field workers, and the administration of Woodrow Wilson.[28] Maroney's article, "The Texas-Louisiana Oil Field Strike of 1917," is the eighth essay in this volume.

While James Reese pioneered studies of the Screwmen's Benevolent Associa-tion, James C. Maroney, Eric Arnesen, and others investigated the International Longshoremen's Association (ILA) on the Gulf Coast as well as in Texas. Gilbert Mers provided a fascinating account as a participant who at various times was affiliated with the ILA, the Communist Party, and the ILA rival and short-lived Maritime Federation of the Gulf Coast, which he organized in 1937 before fi-nally becoming a member of the IWW in the 1940s. A number of excellent and detailed scholarly works on union activity among waterfront workers and African Americans have been authored by Robert Shelton, Clifford Farrington, Ernest Obadele-Starks, Gregg Andrews, and Joseph Abel. "Opening the Closed Shop: The Galveston Longshoremen's Strike of 1920–1921," by Joseph Abel, is the ninth article in this volume. These works on labor, anti-unionism, and legislative action in the form of the Open Port Bill and its impact have enriched our understanding of waterfront workers, their unions, and race relations.[29]

The status of Texas workers during the 1920s is discussed in previously cited works by Grady Mullenix, James C. Maroney, James V. Reese, Ernest Obadele-Starks, and others. Norman D. Brown's book on Texas politics during the 1920s and recent articles in David O'Donald Cullen and Kyle G. Wilkison's *The Texas Left* have dealt effectively with the fate of Texas labor during that decade. These investigations revealed that the wartime cooperation with the Wilson administration evaporated in 1919 amidst a series of chaotic events. The Red Scare and rapid inflation following the end of wartime price and wage restrictions led to a series of strikes after manufacturers increased prices but not wages. Not unexpectedly, a conservative reaction soon followed at both national and state levels. After the Texas legislature enacted an Open Port Bill following the longshoremen's strike of 1920, business leaders created the Texas Open Shop Association (TOSA). Thus, organized labor faced unconcealed and sustained hostility throughout the decade from the state legislature and the majority of the Texas populace, as well as from governors William P. Hobby and Pat Neff. Union membership declined dramatically, and the State Federation, composed almost entirely of AFL-affiliated craft unions, assumed an increasingly conservative stance that for the most part abandoned unskilled and semiskilled workers to fend for themselves. The TSFL membership of 50,000 in 1920, as reported in the proceedings of its annual convention, fell to half that by 1927.[30]

As noted above, valuable new dimensions have been added to the literature of Texas labor historiography in recent decades by in-depth investigations of Tejano, Mexican, and African American workers, who for the most part had remained invisible in earlier historical accounts. Emilio Zamora produced several significant studies of Mexican and Tejano labor in Texas, including *The World of the Mexican Worker in Texas*, which focused on the first two decades of the twentieth century, an article investigating Mexican workers in the oil industry, and a book concerning job politics during World War II. The tenth chapter of this volume is Zaragosa Vargas's "Tejana Radical: Emma Tenayuca and the San Antonio Labor Movement during the Great Depression," an intriguing and thought-provoking article on the Chicana labor organizer and folk heroine Emma Tenayuca. Irene Ledesma, Mario T. Garcia, Julie Pycior, Arnoldo De Leon, and David E. Vassberg among others, have contributed studies of Mexican American workers in Texas that broaden our understanding of the contributions and employment problems of the Tejano community.[31]

After the onset of the Great Depression and following the presidential election of 1932, Franklin D. Roosevelt's administration inaugurated the New Deal, which benefited both the nation and American workers. George Norris Green and Michael R. Boston Jr. surveyed the resulting renaissance of Texas workers and found that New Deal legislation, along with the CIO and its Texas branch, the Texas State Industrial Union Council, led not only to membership gains for Texas unions but also to electoral success in municipal elections in Fort Worth, Port Arthur, and Beaumont, and even a measure of favorable legislation from the state legislature. Grady Mullenix and Murray Polakoff chronicled the roles of the TSFL and the Texas CIO Council during these years, Gilbert Mers wrote on the struggles of maritime unions, and Michael Botson analyzed labor and civil rights issues at the Hughes Tool Company. The eleventh contribution to *Texas Labor History* is Gregg Andrews's remarkable essay "Unionizing the Trinity Portland Cement Company in Dallas, Texas, 1934–1939," in which he dissects the long and violent struggle to unionize the Trinity Portland Cement Company in Dallas. George N. Green revealed Henry Ford's morbid fear of unionism that was enthusiastically endorsed by the reactionary Dallas business community; Green's enlightening article, "Discord in Dallas: Auto Workers, City Fathers, and the Ford Motor Company, 1937–1941," is the twelfth in our anthology.[32]

These scholars were not alone in pointing to the labor discord of the 1930s. Texas A&M University professor Julia Kirk Blackwelder expanded the approach of Texas labor historians in her investigation of Mexican and Tejano homeworkers in San Antonio and Laredo. Revealing both deplorable working conditions and wages, Blackwelder found that women workers spent long hours engaged in pecan shelling and garment sewing in their homes, conditions that accelerated already wretched living conditions. Her article "Texas Homeworkers in the Depression" is the thirteenth in this collection. George Norris Green's classic *The Establishment in Texas Politics* evaluated the role of conservatives' dominance of Texas politics from 1938 to 1957, and other publications by Green, Polakoff, Mers, and Botson described the struggle between communist and anticommunist factions within the state's CIO-affiliated unions from the late 1930s and into World War II.[33]

In addition to the previously cited studies of dock workers, lumber workers, and those on railroads, streetcars, and the mining and oil field industries, other studies with coverage of African American workers include an article by Bruce A. Glasrud and Gregg Andrews on the African American confrontation with white supremacy from the 1870s to the 1970s, several significant publications by Mi-

chael R. Botson Jr., and studies on black police unionism by W. Marvin Dulaney. Gregg Andrews published a book with the University of Missouri Press
on Texas-raised Thyra Edwards, an important black labor activist and leftist.
Glasrud's historiographical article "Literature of Black Labor Unionists in Texas"
is included in the inaugural issue of *Lone Star Legacy: African American History
in Texas*.[34]

While most of the literature on the black working class has focused on the unskilled, Ernest Obadele-Starks studied the development of two African American craft-oriented locals in Dallas and Houston that represented an important
beachhead for blacks into theater craft unionism. His noteworthy article "Black
Texans and Theater Craft Unionism: The Struggle for Racial Equality," the four-
teenth in this collection, assesses black participation in the theater crafts from
the beginning of the twentieth century through the 1960s, and discusses racism,
conservative unionism, and the challenges posed by the Red Scare, television,
and the modern civil rights movement.[35]

World War II restored full employment after the nightmare of the depression years. With millions of American men in the military, many jobs became
available to women and other minorities, including Mexicans admitted under
provisions of the bracero program. Furthermore, Texas unions assumed a more
moderate stance during the war, thereby avoiding the more radical positions supported by the CIO in the late 1930s. George Green wrote on antilabor politics
in Texas from the late 1930s to 1957, Ray Marshall surveyed labor during the war
years, and both Green and Murray Polakoff studied the Texas State Industrial
Union Council (TSIUC) and its activities during the war and in subsequent
years to 1956. Labor in the oil industry received scrutiny from Harvey O'Connor,
Emilio Zamora, and Ray Marshall. Gilbert Mers evaluated conditions confronting the maritime unions, Michael Botson investigated black workers and dual
unions in the steel industry, and Ernest Obadele-Starks surveyed the status of
black workers in the maritime, steel, and oil industries. Long-time labor activist
Clyde Johnson provided a participant's account of the CIO oil workers' organizing campaign in Texas during World War II, in which he played a major role.
The Fair Employment Practices Commission (FEPC) and its wartime work received scrutiny from Zamora, Obadele-Starks, and Joseph Abel. Abel's article,
"African Americans, Labor Unions, and the Struggle for Fair Employment in
the Aircraft Manufacturing Industry of Texas, 1941–1945," contributed to our
understanding of race and labor in the war years. So does Emilio Zamora's article
on Mexican labor in the oil industry, "The Failed Promise of Wartime Opportunity for Mexicans in the Texas Oil Industry," the fifteenth essay in this book.

It is a prominent example of new techniques and interpretations in studying Texas labor history.[36]

The lifting of wage and price controls following the end of World War II resulted in rapid inflation and political challenges for progressives. These factors played a major role in the failure of the CIO's Operation Dixie. Texas unions faced united opposition from state and local government officials, conservative businessmen, and antilabor legislation, mainly a 1947 Texas "right-to-work" law and the US Congress's Taft-Hartley bill. Nonetheless, against all odds the TSIUC remained strong into the 1950s, and Texas workers, bolstered by the AFL-CIO merger in 1955 (1957 in Texas), helped to elect the liberal Ralph Yarborough to the US Senate and fellow liberal congressmen Bob Eckhardt and Henry B. Gonzalez.[37] Against these same and even more formidable odds, black workers achieved a significant victory in the Hughes steel plant as Michael Botson details so well in his excellent "No Gold Watch for Jim Crow's Retirement: The Abolition of Segregated Unionism at Houston's Hughes Tool Company," the sixteenth article in this anthology.

The decade following World War II witnessed several developments affecting Texas labor, including a strike by Houston municipal workers in early 1946 that resulted from stagnant wages in a period of postwar inflation. Although both parties claimed victory in a walkout supported by more than seven hundred of some thirty-eight hundred city workers, Marilyn Rhinehart found that the strike produced only meager results. While workers did receive a small wage increase, city fathers, supported by state and local officials and business leaders, adamantly refused to extend recognition to a labor union that sought to represent their employees.[38]

Perhaps the most historic event of the decade involving Texas workers was the strike and 390-mile march by Tejano and Mexican farmworkers from South Texas to Austin in 1966–67. "La Marcha," with widespread media coverage, focused nationwide attention on the plight of migrant workers. The upheaval in fact dramatically proclaimed a new threat to the white male establishment: a Tejano presence in a nation still struggling unsuccessfully to cope with and to understand the meaning of black power. Indeed, this new Hispanic presence had unleashed a "brown power" movement that posed a powerful and provocative challenge to the middle-class Mexican American community similar to the threat posed to middle-class African Americans by the black power movement.[39] Not surprisingly, then, the probable historic impact of the campaign by South Texas farmworkers soon attracted the attention of not only a number of scholars and journalists but also those who opposed any challenge to the status quo.

Three graduate students, Jan Hart Cohen, Charles Carr Winn, and Richard R. Bailey, chose the farmworkers' struggle as the subject of their research. Bailey published an article, "The Starr County Strike," in an academic journal, as well as an entry on the strike in the *New Handbook of Texas*.[40] In an account published soon after the event, Texas Christian University history professor Ben H. Procter recognized that an essential goal for the Texas Rangers was to improve relations with the press in order to avoid the appearance of remaining, in the public's mind, the establishment's enforcers of the status quo, consistently hostile to all minorities. Procter's assessment, while acknowledging serious areas of concern and a definite need for Ranger ranks to become more inclusive, nonetheless represented an overall positive evaluation of the Rangers that emphasized their skill as exceptional modern law enforcement officers, as well as recognizing their heroic heritage.[41]

Published at the same time but with a different interpretation was *Gunpowder Justice: A Reassessment of the Texas Rangers*, by Julian Samora, Joe Bernal, and Albert Pena. It provided a favorable account of the farmworkers' struggle and an extremely critical assessment of both Governor Connally and the Texas Rangers. "John Connally's Strikebreakers," the book's chapter on La Marcha, documented a number of civil rights violations by the Rangers and emphasized Connally's adamant refusal to grant any concessions to the farmworkers, even to the point of refusing to recommend any measure of reform to the legislature. The book also traced the federal investigation of wrongdoing and the seven-year history of state and federal litigation, which culminated in the *Allee et al. v. Medrano et al.* decision by the US Supreme Court in 1984 that struck down five Texas antilabor laws and offered vindication for the farmworkers by restraining Ranger harassment and intimidation.[42] Needless to say, these events also received daily coverage in the state's major newspapers and in the liberal *Texas Observer*. Recently, Mary Margaret McAllen Amberson published a less interpretive but detailed and thorough coverage of the entire event in the *Journal of South Texas*. Her study, which provides essential data and guidance for future researchers, is intriguingly titled "'Better to Die on Our Feet than to Live on Our Knees': United Farm Workers and Strikes in the Lower Rio Grande Valley, 1966–1967," and is the seventeenth article in *Texas Labor History*.[43]

Another historical account of the farmworkers' struggle is a perceptive essay in the *Houston Review* by Marilyn D. Rhinehart and Thomas H. Kreneck, which analyzed Houston's ties to the minimum wage march and its role in the development of Mexican American politics and identity.[44] Historian Robert M. Utley, in the second volume of his history of the Texas Rangers, recognized significant challenges that the farmworkers' episode posed for the Rangers, including widespread public hostility and years of state and federal litigation that ultimately resulted in censure by the US Supreme Court. Utley also contends that publicity surrounding civil rights violations and the lack of diversity among the Rangers served to polarize public opinion, and once again led to calls for reform and to renewed demands to disband the Rangers.[45] Recently, Texas labor historians George Green and Michael Botson have provided a cogent assessment of the strike's legacy in the aforementioned *The Texas Left*.[46]

South Texas was not the only region affected by labor's struggles during the 1960s. In the final article in this anthology, "*Adelante Compañeros*: The Sanitation Worker's Struggle in Lubbock, Texas, 1968–1972," Yolanda G. Romero evaluated the effect on West Texas of continuing Mexican American influence resulting from the 1968–72 struggle of sanitation workers in Lubbock. Of their partial victory, Romero notes, "the sanitation workers succeeded in bringing the message to the Mexican American community that rather than looking back, their *compañeros* should look *adelante* to the future."[47]

The West Texas Mexican American community, as well as their counterparts in other regions of the state, heard the message and continued the struggle for labor solidarity over the succeeding forty years, demonstrating that they had internalized lessons learned during the nearly 175 years of organized labor activity. The Texas labor movement existed, sometimes under the radar, amidst intense opposition from industrialists, politicians, and the general populace unabated into the twenty-first century, a hostility that has proved impossible to eradicate. Historians and other scholars have captured much of the story, although portions of Texas labor history remain untold.

As the editors of this anthology, we hope that the articles and bibliography herein will provide encouragement to future scholars and students in their quest to continue the study of Texas labor history. In our view, there are several specific areas worthy of further study, not only because the field lacks published works on these topics but also because of the besieged state of the working class in both contemporary Texas and in the nation at large. The great majority of working people, men and women, skilled and unskilled, of all ethnic groups, whether in public or private sectors, remain unorganized. Specific groups worthy of attention include teachers and those in other underpaid jobs such as the health-care industry, the restaurant and hospitality professions, public service workers, and employees of national, state, and local governments. Government workers at the beginning of the twenty-first century represent a rare beacon of relative union strength, but they currently face a determined attack by Tea Party activists and their supporters. Also demanding specific attention are the conditions and deficiencies in pay of female workers at all levels of experience and skill and in all occupational areas. It is our hope that new investigations will not only more fully reveal the current conditions of these workers but also enable us to better understand the causes and to identify possible avenues through which labor organizations might work more effectively to improve the lot of the working-class majority.

Lastly, we believe that a key lesson that has emerged from the history of the Texas working class is that labor's greatest success came in the years from the 1870s to about 1910. During those agrarian and populist years the reform impulse melded with the contributions of the men and women in the state's somewhat nebulous and unstable progressive coalition. Representatives of TSFL craft unions and the railroad brotherhoods, in cooperation with the numerically superior Farmers' Union, were able to take advantage of a synchronicity of events and to seize the opportunity to assume an important role in the progressive coalition that accomplished truly impressive legislative gains. Today, many believe labor's achievements have been relegated to the distant past with few, if any, future prospects. It is possible that today's highly partisan political climate, which coexists with the most serious economic crisis since the 1930s, represents a contemporary chain of events similar to that of a century ago. Once again, working people may have the opportunity to collaborate with other reformers and successfully organize a reform coalition directed against those who would eradicate the very foundations of the reforms begun during FDR's New Deal and LBJ's Great Society. If this is so, the study of history could once again demonstrate its utility.

Notes

1.   Richard T. Ely, *The Labor Movement in America* (New York: T. Y. Crowell, 1886); John R. Commons and Associates, *History of Labor in the United States*, 4 vols. (New York: Macmillan, 1918–35). Also see Selig Perlman, *A Theory of the Labor Movement* (New York: Macmillan, 1928); Perlman, *A History of Trade Unionism in the United States* (1922; repr., Ithaca, NY: Cornell University Press, 2009); Phillip Taft, *The A. F. of L. in the Time of Gompers* (New York: Macmillan, 1957); Taft, *The A. F. of L. from the Death of Gompers to the Merger* (New York: Harper, 1959).

2.   We use the pronoun *his* because scholars, for the most part, wrote about white males only, as if women and minorities, other than slaves, indentured servants, or convicts, either did not exist or were not a significant part of the workplace.

3. E. P. Thompson, *The Making of the English Working Class* (1963; repr., New York: Vintage, 1966); Eric J. Hobsbawm, *The Age of Revolution* (1982; repr., New York: Vintage, 1996); Hobsbawm, *The Age of Empire* (1975; repr., New York: Vintage, 1989).

4. Howard Zinn, *A People's History of the United States*, 2nd. ed. (New York: Norton, 1996).

5. For a sampling of the historiography of the "new labor historians," see David Brody, "The Old Labor History and the New: In Search of an American Working Class," *Labor History* 20 (Winter 1979): 111–26; Brody, "Reconciling the Old Labor History and the New," *Pacific Historical Review* 62 (February 1993): 1–18; Thomas A. Krueger, "American Labor Historiography, Old and New: A Review Essay," *Labor History* 20 (Winter 1979): 276–85; Eric Arnesen, "Up from Exclusion: Black and White Workers, Race, and the State of Labor History," *Reviews in American History* 26 (March 1998): 146–74; and Venus Green, "Race on the Line: Gender, Labor, and Technology in the Bell System, 1880–1980," *Reviews in American History* 31 (March 2003): 80–86.

6. Leon Fink, "American Labor History," in Eric Foner, *The New American History*, rev. and expanded ed. (Philadelphia: Temple University Press, 1997), 333–52; Alice Kestler-Harris, "Social History," ibid., 231–56; Thomas C. Holt, "African American History," ibid., 311–52; Linda Gordon, "U.S. Women's History," ibid., 257–84.

7. Ruth A. Allen, *Chapters in the History of Organized Labor in Texas* (Austin: University of Texas Press, 1941); James V. Reese, "The Early History of Labor Organizations in Texas, 1838–1876," *Southwestern Historical Quarterly* 72 (July 1968): 1–20.

8. F. Ray Marshall, "Some Reflections on Labor History," *Southwestern Historical Quarterly* 75 (October 1971): 137–57.

9. Ron Tyler, Douglas E. Barnett, Roy R. Barkley, Penelope C. Anderson, and Mark F. Odintz, eds., *The New Handbook of Texas*, 6 vols. (Austin: Texas State Historical Association, 1996).

10. Walter L. Buenger and Arnoldo De Leon, eds., *Beyond Texas through Time: Breaking Away from Past Interpretations* (College Station: Texas A&M University Press, 2011).

11. Frank W. Taussig, "The South-Western Strike of 1886," *Quarterly Journal of Economics* 1 (January 1887): 184–222; Michael James Lacey and Mary O. Furner, eds., *The State and Social Investigation in Britain and the United States* (New York: Cambridge University Press, 1993), 209. This account includes the fascinating explanation that Taussig's father "had an interest in a route shut down by the strike."

12. Earl Sylvester Sparks, "A Survey of Organized Labor in Austin" (master's thesis, University of Texas at Austin, 1920); Townes Malcolm Harris, "The Labor Supply of Texas" (master's thesis, University of Texas at Austin, 1922); Robert Eli Teel, "Discrimination against Negro Workers in Texas: Extent and Effects" (master's thesis, University of Texas at Austin, 1947).

13.   Ruth A. Allen, *The Great Southwest Strike* (Austin: University of Texas Publications, 1942).

14.   John L. Wortham, "Regulation of Organized Labor in Texas, 1940–1945" (master's thesis, University of Texas at Austin, 1947); Jay L. Todes, "Organized Employer Opposition to Unionism in Texas, 1900–1930" (master's thesis, University of Texas at Austin, 1949); and John F. Carruthers, "The Influence of the Oil Workers International Union in Port Arthur, Texas" (master's thesis, University of Texas at Austin, 1950).

15.   Grady L. Mullenix, "A History of the Texas State Federation of Labor" (PhD diss., University of Texas at Austin, 1955); Murray E. Polakoff, "The Development of the Texas CIO Council" (PhD diss., Columbia University, 1958); Polakoff, "Inner Pressures on the Texas State CIO Council, 1937–1955," *Industrial and Labor Relations Review* 12 (January 1959): 227–42; Harold A. Shapiro, "The Labor Movement in San Antonio, Texas, 1865–1915," *Southwestern Historical Quarterly* 75 (October 1971): 160–75; Shapiro, "The Pecan Shellers of San Antonio, Texas," *Southwestern Social Science Quarterly* 32 (March 1952): 229–44; James V. Reese, "The Evolution of an Early Texas Union: The Screwmen's Benevolent Association of Galveston, 1865–1891," *Southwestern Historical Quarterly* 75 (October 1971): 158–85; and Allen Taylor, "A History of the Screwmen's Benevolent Association from 1866 to 1924" (master's thesis, University of Texas at Austin, 1968).

16.   James V. Reese, "The Worker in Texas, 1821–1876" (PhD diss., University of Texas at Austin, 1964).

17.   Robert Stuart Shelton, "On Empire's Shore: Casual Laborers and Enslaved African-Americans in Galveston, Texas, 1840–1860," *Journal of Social History* 40 (Spring 2007): 717–30.

18.   David Urbano, "When the Smoke Lifted: The 1857–1858 'Cart War' of South Texas" (PhD diss., University of Houston, 2009); also see Arnoldo De Leon, *They Called Them Greasers: Anglo Attitudes toward Mexicans in Texas, 1821–1900* (Austin: University of Texas Press, 1983); Ellen Schneider and Paul H. Carlson, "Gunnysackers, *Carreteros*, and Teamsters: The South Texas Cart War of 1857," *Journal of South Texas* 1, No. 1 (Spring 1988): 1–9; Andrew H. Young, "Life and Labor on the King Ranch: The Early Years, 1853–1865," *Journal of South Texas* 6, No. 1 (Spring 1993): 54–71.

19.   Theresa A. Case, *The Great Southwest Railroad Strike and Free Labor* (College Station: Texas A&M University Press, 2010); Case, "Black and White Railroaders Join the Texas Knights of Labor" (paper presented at the annual meeting of the Texas State Historical Association, March 6, 2003).

20.   Theresa A. Case, "The Radical Potential of the Knights' Biracialism: The 1886–1887 Gould System Strikes and Their Aftermath," *Labor: Studies in Working-Class History* 4 (Winter 2007): 83–107; Case, "Blaming Martin Irons: Leadership and Popular Protest in the 1886 Southwest Strike," *Journal of the Gilded Age and Progressive Era* 8 (January 2009): 51–82.

21.   George N. Green, "The Texas Labor Movement, 1870–1920," *Southwestern Historical Quarterly* 108 (July 2004): 1–25; Green, "Texas . . . Unions . . . Time:

Unions in Texas from the Time of the Republic through the Great War, 1838–1919," in *The Texas Left: The Radical Roots of Lone Star Liberalism*, ed. David O'Donald Cullen and Kyle G. Wilkison (College Station: Texas A&M University Press, 2010): 92–111; Green, "Crucial Decade for Texas Labor: Railway Union Struggles, 1886–96," in *Seeking Inalienable Rights: Texans and Their Quests for Justice*, ed. Debra A. Reid (College Station: Texas A&M University Press, 2009): 17–35. On Socialist Party activity in Texas, see Peter H. Buckingham, "The Socialist Party," in *The Texas Left*, 74–79.

22. Charles Mac Gibson, "Organized Labor in Texas from 1890 to 1900" (master's thesis, Texas Tech University 1973); Robert E. Zeigler, "The Limits of Power: The Amalgamated Association of Street Railway Employees in Houston, Texas, 1897–1905," *Labor History* 18 (Winter 1977): 32–46; Jonathan Garlock, *Guide to the Local Assemblies of the Knights of Labor* (Westport, CT: Greenwood Press, 1982); James C. Maroney, "Labor's Struggle for Acceptance: The Houston Worker in a Changing Society, 1900–1929," in *Houston: A Twentieth Century Urban Frontier*, ed. Francisco A. Rosales and Barry J. Kaplan, (Port Washington, NY: Associated Faculty Press, 1983): 225–30. Expanded and revised version, *Houston Review* 6, No. 1 (1984): 5–24; Patricia Evridge Hill, *Dallas: The Making of a Modern City* (Austin: University of Texas Press, 1996).

23. Allen, *Chapters*; Mary Jane Gentry, *The Birth of a Texas Ghost Town, 1886–1933*, edited and with an introduction by T. Lindsey Baker (College Station: Texas A&M University Press, 2009); James C. Maroney, "The Unionization of Thurber, 1903," *Red River Valley Historical Review* 4 (Spring 1979): 27–32; Michael Q. Hooks, "Thurber: A Unique Texas Community," *Panhandle-Plains Historical Review* 56 (1983): 1–17; Roberto R. Calderon, *Mexican Coal Mining Labor in Texas and Coahuila, 1880–1930* (College Station: Texas A&M University Press, 2000); Marilyn D. Rhinehart, "'Underground Patriots': Thurber Coal Miners and the Struggle for Industrial Freedom, 1888–1903," *Southwestern Historical Quarterly* 92 (April 1989): 509–42; Rhinehart, *A Way of Work and A Way of Life: Coal Mining in Thurber, Texas, 1888–1926* (College Station: Texas A&M University Press, 1992).

24. Charles R. McCord, "A Brief History of the Brotherhood of Timber Workers," (master's thesis, University of Texas at Austin, 1959); Melvin Dubofsky, *We Shall Be All: A History of the Industrial Workers of the World* (Chicago: Quadrangle Books, 1969), 209–20; James R. Green, "The Brotherhood of Timber Workers, 1910–1913: A Radical Response to Industrial Capitalism in the Southern USA," *Past and Present* 60 (August 1973): 161–200; Jeff Ferrell, "The Brotherhood of Timber Workers and the Culture of Conflict," *Journal of Folklore Research* 28 (1991): 163–77; Ferrell, "East Texas/Western Louisiana Sawmill Towns and the Control of Everyday Life," *Locus* 3, No. 1 (1990): 1–19; George T. Morgan Jr., "No Compromise—No Recognition: John Henry Kirby, the Southern Lumber Operators' Association, and Unionism in the Piney Woods, 1900–1916," *Labor History* 10 (Spring 1969): 193–204; George T. Morgan Jr., "The Gospel of Wealth Goes South: John Henry Kirby and Labor's Struggle for Self-Determination,

1901–1916," *Southwestern Historical Quarterly* 75 (October 1971): 186–97; Thad Sitton and James H. Conrad, *Nameless Towns: Texas Sawmill Communities, 1880–1942* (Austin: University of Texas Press, 1998). Membership data for the Brotherhood of Timber Workers frequently is not specific, and differs according to the above sources. James R. Green's article, "The Brotherhood of Timber Workers, 1910–1913" cites breakdowns of skilled and unskilled black workers and includes charts. Green also makes clear that the majority of unskilled sawyers were African American. The 50 percent black membership figure in the Brotherhood is cited by Dubofsky.

25.   Maroney, "Organized Labor in Texas, 1900–1929" (PhD diss., University of Houston, 1975), 58–59.

26.   T. P. O'Rourke, *A Brief History of the Union Labor Legislative Movement in Texas* (1909; repr., Ithaca, NY: Cornell University Press, 2000); Mullenix, "A History of the Texas State Federation of Labor"; Maroney, "Organized Labor in Texas," 50–89; James A. Tinsley, "The Progressive Movement in Texas" (PhD diss., University of Wisconsin, 1953); Lewis L. Gould, *Progressives and Prohibitionists: Texas Democrats in the Wilson Era* (1973; repr., Austin: Texas State Historical Association, 1992).

27.   The Commercial Secretaries Association was later known as the Texas Business Men's Association. Buckingham, "Texas Socialist Party" in Cullen and Wilkison, *The Texas Left*; James R. Green, "Tenant Farmer Discontent and Socialist Protest in Texas, 1900–1917," *Southwestern Historical Quarterly* 81 (October 1977): 133–54.

28.   Harvey O'Connor, *History of Oil Workers Intl. Union (CIO)* (Denver: Oil Workers International Union, 1950), 4–5; Grady L. Mullenix, "A History of the Labor Movement in the Oil Industry" (master's thesis, North Texas State Teachers College, 1942), 10; Allen, *Chapters*, 222; James C. Maroney, "The Texas-Louisiana Oil Field Strike of 1917," in *Essays in Southern Labor History*, edited by Gary M. Fink and Merl E. Reed (Westport, CT: Greenwood Press, 1977), 161–72; William Lee Greer, "The Texas Gulf Coast Oil Strike of 1917" (master's thesis, University of Houston, 1974); Clyde Johnson, "CIO Oil Workers' Organizing Campaign in Texas, 1942–1943," in *Essays in Southern Labor History*, 173–87.

29.   James C. Maroney, "The International Longshoremen's Association in the Gulf States during the Progressive Era," *Southern Studies* 16 (Summer 1977): 225–30; Maroney, "The Galveston Longshoremen's Strike of 1920," *East Texas Historical Journal* 16, No. 1 (1978): 34–38; William D. Angel Jr., "Controlling the Workers: The Galveston Dock Workers' Strike of 1920 and Its Impact on Labor Relations in Texas," *East Texas Historical Journal* 23, No. 2 (1985): 14–27; Eric Arnesen, *Waterfront Workers of New Orleans: Race, Class, and Politics, 1863–1923* (New York: Oxford University Press, 1991); Gilbert Mers, *Working the Waterfront: The Ups and Downs of a Rebel Longshoreman* (Austin: University of Texas Press, 1988); Cliff Farrington, "The Galveston Waterfront and Organized Labor, 1866–1900" (master's thesis, University of Texas at Austin, 1997); Farrington, *Biracial Unions on Galveston's Waterfront, 1865–1925* (Austin: Texas

State Historical Association, 2007); Ernest Obadele-Starks, "Black Labor, the Black Middle-Class, and Organized Protest along the Upper Gulf Coast, 1883–1945," *Southwestern Historical Quarterly* 103 (July 1999): 53–65; Robert Stuart Shelton, "Waterfront Workers of Galveston Texas, 1838–1920" (PhD diss., Rice University, 2000); Shelton, "Slavery in a Texas Seaport: The Peculiar Institution in Galveston," *Slavery and Abolition* 8 (August 2007): 155–68; Shelton, "On Empire's Shore": 717–30; Abel, "Opening the Closed Shop: The Galveston Longshoremen's Strike of 1920–1921," *Southwestern Historical Quarterly* 110 (January 2007): 317–47; Gregg Andrews, "Black Working-Class Activism and Biracial Unionism: Galveston Longshoremen in Jim Crow Texas, 1919–1921," *Journal of Southern History* 74 (August 2008): 627–68.

30.   Grady Mullenix, "A History of the Texas State Federation of Labor"; James C. Maroney, "Organized Labor in Texas, 1900–1929"; Ernest Obadele-Starks, *Black Unionism in the Industrial South* (College Station: Texas A&M University Press, 2000); Norman D. Brown, *Hood, Bonnet, and Little Brown Jug: Texas Politics, 1921–1928* (College Station: Texas A&M University Press, 1984); George Norris Green and Michael R. Botson Jr., "Looking for Lefty: Liberal/Left Activism and Texas Labor, 1920s–1960s," in Cullen and Wilkison, *The Texas Left*, 112–32; Bruce A. Glasrud and Gregg Andrews, "Confronting White Supremacy: The African American Left in Texas, 1874–1974," in Cullen and Wilkison, *The Texas Left*, 157–90.

31.   Emilio Zamora, *The World of the Mexican Worker in Texas* (College Station: Texas A&M University Press, 1993); Zamora, *Claiming Rights and Righting Wrongs in Texas: Mexican Workers and Job Politics during World War II* (College Station: Texas A&M University Press, 2009); Zamora, "The Failed Promise of Wartime Opportunity for Mexicans in the Texas Oil Industry," *Southwestern Historical Quarterly* 95 (January 1992): 323–50; Irene Ledesma, "Texas Newspapers and Chicana Workers' Activism, 1919–1974," *Western Historical Quarterly* 26 (Fall 1995): 309–31; Ledesma, "Unlikely Strikers: Mexican American Women in Strike Activity in Texas, 1919–1974" (PhD diss., Ohio State University, 1992); Mario T. Garcia, "Obreros: The Mexican Workers of El Paso, 1900–1920" (PhD diss., University of California, San Diego, 1975); Garcia, *Desert Immigrants: The Mexicans of El Paso, 1880–1920* (New Haven: Yale University Press, 1981); Julie Leininger Pycior, "La Raza Organizes: Mexican American Life in San Antonio, 1915–1930" (PhD diss., University of Notre Dame, 1979); Arnoldo De Leon, "*Los Tasinques* and the Sheep Shearers' Union of North America: A Strike in West Texas, 1934," *West Texas Historical Association Yearbook* 55 (1979): 3–16; Zaragosa Vargas, "Tejana Radical: Emma Tenayuca and the San Antonio Labor Movement during the Great Depression," *Pacific Historical Review*, 66, No. 4 (1997): 553–80; David E. Vassberg, "The Use of Mexicans and Mexican Americans as an Agricultural Work Force in the Lower Rio Grande Valley of Texas" (PhD diss., University of Texas at Austin, 1967).

32.   Green and Botson, "Looking for Lefty"; Mullenix, "A History of the Texas State Federation of Labor"; Polakoff, "The Development of the Texas State CIO Coun-

cil"; Mers, *Working the Waterfront*; Michael R. Botson Jr., *Labor, Civil Rights, and the Hughes Tool Company* (College Station: Texas A&M University Press, 2005); Gregg Andrews, "Unionizing the Trinity Portland Cement Company in Dallas, Texas, 1934–1939," *Southwestern Historical Quarterly* 111 (July 2007): 31–49; George N. Green, "Discord in Dallas: Auto Workers, City Fathers, and the Ford Motor Company, 1937–1941," *Labor's Heritage* 1, No. 3 (July 1989): 21–33.

33.   Julia Kirk Blackwelder, "Texas Homeworkers in the 1930s," in *Homework: Historical and Contemporary Perspectives on Paid Labor at Home*, ed. Eileen Boris and Cynthia R. Daniels (Urbana: University of Illinois Press, 1989), 75–90; George Norris Green, *The Establishment in Texas Politics: The Primitive Years, 1938–1957* (Norman: University of Oklahoma Press, 1979).

34.   Glasrud and Andrews, "Confronting White Supremacy"; Botson, *Labor, Civil Rights, and the Hughes Tool Company*; Botson, "Jim Crow Wearing Steel-Toed Shoes and Safety Glasses: Dual Unionism at the Hughes Tool Company, 1918–1942," *Houston Review* 16, No. 2 (1994): 101–16; Botson, "No Gold Watch for Jim Crow's Retirement: The Abolition of Segregated Unionism at Houston's Hughes Tool Company," *Southwestern Historical Quarterly* 101 (April 1968): 497–521; W. Marvin Dulaney, "Texas Negro Peace Officers' Association: The Origins of Black Police Unionism," *Houston Review* 12, No. 2 (1990): 59–78; Gregg Andrews, *Thyra J. Edwards: Black Activist in the Global Freedom Struggle* (Columbia: University of Missouri Press, 2011); Bruce A. Glasrud, "Literature of Black Labor Unionists in Texas," *Lone Star Legacy: African American History in Texas* 1 (2011): 45–55.

35.   Ernest Obadele-Starks, "Black Texans and Theater Craft Unionism: The Struggle for Racial Equality," *Southwestern Historical Quarterly* 106 (April 2003): 533–50.

36.   George Green, "Anti-Labor Politics in Texas, 1941–1957," in *American Labor in the Southwest: The First One Hundred Years*, ed. James C. Foster (Tucson: University of Arizona Press, 1982), 217–27; Green and Botson, "Looking for Lefty"; F. Ray Marshall, *Labor in the South* (Cambridge: Harvard University Press, 1967); George Green, "Texas State Industrial Council," *Handbook of Texas Online*, http://www.tshaonline.org/handbook/online; Polakoff, "The Development of the Texas State CIO Council"; Obadele-Starks, *Black Unionism in the Industrial South*; Ernest Obadele-Starks, "The Road to Jericho: Black Workers, the Fair Employment Practice Commission, and the Struggle for Racial Equality on the Upper Texas Gulf Coast, 1941–1947" (PhD diss., University of Houston, 1996); Clyde Johnson, "CIO Oil Workers' Organizing Campaign in Texas, 1942–1943"; Botson, *Labor, Civil Rights, and the Hughes Tool Company*; Botson, "Revisiting the Battle of Baytown: Unions, Reds, and Mayhem in a Company Town," *East Texas Historical Journal* 49 (Fall 2011): 9–23; Botson, "We're Sticking by Our Union, 1942–1943," *Houston History Magazine* 8 (Spring 2011): 8–14; Joseph Abel, "African Americans, Labor Unions, and the Struggle for Fair Employment in the Aircraft Manufacturing Industry of Texas, 1941–1945," *Journal of Southern History* 77 (August 2011): 595–638; Zamora, "Failed Promise of Wartime Opportunity."

37. Green, *The Establishment in Texas Politics*; Green and Botson, "Looking for Lefty," 123.

38. Marilyn D. Rhinehart, "A Lesson in Unity: The Houston Municipal Workers' Strike of 1946," *Houston Review* 4, No. 3 (Fall 1982): 137–53.

39. The militant Malcolm X considered conservative middle-class African Americans to be part of the "white establishment," and derisively referred to them as "Negroes."

40. Jan Hart Cohen (Jan Hart), "To See Christ in Our Brothers: The Role of the Texas Roman Catholic Church in the Rio Grande Valley Farm Workers' Movement, 1966–1967" (master's thesis, University of Texas at Arlington, 1970); Charles Carr Winn, "The Valley Farm Workers' Movement, 1966–1967" (master's thesis, University of Texas at Arlington, 1970); Winn, "Mexican Americans in the Texas Labor Movement" (PhD diss., Texas Christian University, 1972); Richard Ray Bailey, "Farm Labor in Texas and the Starr County Strike" (master's thesis, Texas Christian University, 1969); Bailey, "Starr County Strike," *Red River Historical Review* 4 (Winter 1976): 42–61; Bailey, "Starr County Strike," *New Handbook of Texas*, http://www.tshaonline.org/handbook/online.

41. Ben H. Procter, "The Modern Texas Rangers: A Law Enforcement Dilemma in the Rio Grande Valley," in *Reflections of Western Historians*, ed. John Alexander Carroll (Tucson: University of Arizona Press, 1969), 215–33.

42. Julian Samora, Joe Bernal, and Albert Pena, "John Connally's Strikebreakers," in *Gunpowder Justice: A Reassessment of the Texas Rangers* (Notre Dame: University of Notre Dame Press, 1979). Samora was a University of Notre Dame professor of sociology and anthropology, Bernal, regional director of Action and former Texas state senator, and Pena, a political activist and municipal judge in San Antonio.

43. The *Texas Observer* provided regular and extensive coverage, and the special issue of September 9, 1966; Mary M. McAllen Amberson, "'Better to Die on Our Feet, Than Live on Our Knees': United Farm Workers and Strikes in the Lower Rio Grande Valley, 1966–1967," *Journal of South Texas* 20, No. 1 (2007): 56–103.

44. Marilyn D. Rhinehart and Thomas H. Kreneck, "The Minimum Wage Mark of 1966: A Case Study in Mexican-American Politics, Labor, and Identity," *Houston Review* 11, No. 1 (1989): 27–44.

45. Robert M. Utley, *Lone Star Lawmen: The Second Century of the Texas Rangers* (New York: Oxford University Press, 2007), 238–47.

46. Green and Botson, "Looking for Lefty," 127.

47. Yolanda G. Romero, "*Adelante Compañeros*: The Sanitation Worker's Struggle in Lubbock, Texas, 1968–1972," *West Texas Historical Association Yearbook* 69 (1993): 82–88, quote on 88.

JAMES V. REESE

The Early History of Labor Organizations in Texas, 1838–1876

Until the development of effective railway transport in the 1870s, there was little in the Texas economy or society conducive to the development of labor organizations. Outside the port towns of Galveston and Houston, which developed relatively diversified economies even before the Civil War, the economy of Texas remained one of self-sufficient agriculture until the railroad broke the frontier pattern of isolated communities seeking to supply most of their own basic needs. The growth of labor organizations in Texas, like the development of the state's economy, lagged far behind the nation. Unionization accelerated in the 1870s, climaxing in the widespread and violent strikes of 1877, which apprised Texans, for the first time, of the confusing problems and conflicts wrought by industrialization.

In that year Texas experienced not only extensive railway strikes and major work stoppages among the dockworkers of Galveston and the building trades in several cities, but also scores of minor labor troubles. These strikes came as Texas started on the road to a modern, if still primarily agricultural, economy and marked the arrival of militant, if still weak, unionism.

Although the history of modern organized labor in Texas really began with the strikes of 1877, antecedents existed. Where and when the most rudimentary conditions for labor organizations existed and where the number of wage earners and the amount of economic specialization were sufficient, Texas workers, like their eastern counterparts, organized.

These early labor organizations, some dating from the era of the Texas Republic, did not all take the classic form of unions, nor did many of them endure more than a few months or years. Yet they were important as early examples of the Texan worker's attempts to meet through collective action the particular problems of an isolated agrarian society. Such action might take a variety of forms, usually spontaneous. Workers, both craftsmen and common laborers, who were temporarily engaged to erect desperately needed buildings on Thomas Affleck's

East Texas plantation, threatened to walk off the job if a certain unpopular fore-man were not fired. In this, as in most like incidents, the threat failed, because no matter how great the need, the owner refused "to be dictated to by a group of common laborers."[1] Yet, on occasion, such outbursts might prove successful. Late in the era of the Republic, Galveston seamen took advantage of a shortage of qualified seamen and a Republic of Texas law requiring that three-quarters of the crew of ships flying "Texian Colors" be citizens of Texas to wrest increased wages from its owner on threat of leaving the craft unmanned.[2] In these and similar cases, no organization existed before, during, or after the action took place. Indeed, most of the group activity on the part of workers in the antebel-lum days was hardly more than immediate action designed to meet a specific problem or take advantage of a promising situation, characterized by little prior organization or planning and with no attempt to maintain the group when the situation passed. In the kind of economic institution most common in Texas—small enterprises with no stable labor force—unions, as such, could not exist. The most common way to gain recourse from a grievance was a threat to quit—a threat the worker would have to be prepared to make good because he usually would be fired for such insubordination.

Not all spontaneous group action by workers was motivated by on-the-job grievances. At a time when the public meeting to protest this or that was al-most a reflex action, it was only natural that workers would adopt this method to comment on issues that affected them. When a mechanics' lien law was be-fore the Congress of the Republic of Texas in January 1839, "a meeting of the master-workmen and mechanics generally of Houston" was called "to discuss some matters relating to the LIEN LAW." It is not known what action the meet-ing took, or if it had any effect on the final passage of the law, one of the first such laws in North America, but apparently there had developed a group of five or six "workingmen" fond of calling the "Mechanics and Workingmen" of Houston together to make a group statement on various issues.[3] Prior to the election of county officials in 1845, they called a meeting of workingmen, who passed a resolution noting that one section of the county was controlling county government to the detriment of the other sections, and placed before the vot-ers the names of three men as candidates for the county court. When the new county court met, all three held seats, indicating that the "workingmen," if not powerful, were prudent in choosing sides.[4] When annexation was the question of the day, the same group of men dominated a meeting of "Harris County Me-chanics" that endorsed annexation and called for the election of at least a few mechanics to the convention to write a new state constitution. To attain this end they named Alexander D. McGowan, a tinsmith, as "the nominee of the Mechanics' and Working Men's ticket." McGowan, who later served as mayor of Houston for three terms and held several county offices, received 340 votes, and thus was one of the representatives from Harris County to the Convention of 1845.[5] There is no indication that this workingmen's group had any permanent structure, and like so many such groups of the Jacksonian era, it included more successful tradesmen and shopkeepers than wage earners.

Another favorite means of exhibiting "public opinion" in this era was the petition, which workingmen occasionally used to make known their desires. For example, in 1841 a group of twenty-eight blacksmiths in Nacogdoches County petitioned the Congress of the Republic of Texas for an extension to the mechanics' lien law allowing them to take liens on property, as they claimed to be losing money by their inability to force payment of bills.[6] Likewise, just prior to the Civil War, thirty-two mechanics from Marshall petitioned against "being put in competition With Negro Mechanicks who are to rival us in the obtaining of contracts [for buildings] . . . or any other of the Mechanical Branches that are taken by contract." The petition called for a law to keep "Negroes in their places (Vez [sic]: in Corn and Cotton Fields)."[7] While such actions as mass meetings and petitions can hardly be considered "organizations" (except in the sense that they represent the attempts of individual workmen to gain a more responsive ear for their desires through collective actions), this type of action precedes more permanent organizations.

A substantial portion of the wage earners in Texas were of foreign birth, with the result that ethnic organizations drew workers into their orbit.[8] These groups provided social, benevolent, and educational services to those of a common national origin. In Texas towns ethnic groups were strong and numerous, and as each national group gained relative importance, an ethnic society developed. In Houston, in addition to the several "singing societies," there were the German Union (established in 1841), the Scandinavian Club (begun shortly after the Civil War), and the Irish Texan Society (founded in 1871).[9] In Galveston, where the German clubs were quite active before the war, the Irish Benevolent Association (organized in 1871) and the Spanish Benevolent Association (started about 1874) provided social services to the underprivileged and unfortunate.[10] Club Reciproco, established in Corpus Christi in 1873, was the first of numerous benevolent societies for Latin Americans established particularly in South Texas during the late nineteenth century.[11] All these groups were quite active, and while not barring foreign-born workers from union activity, their vitality surely retarded the development of similar societies for workers alone by providing the foreign-born wage earner with services he might have otherwise sought in workingmen's associations. There was also a secondary consideration. Occupational benevolent societies had a tendency to evolve into something like true labor unions; ethnic groups did not.

The 1850s saw the beginnings of such benevolent societies. If not truly unions, at least they had some permanence and structure. These emerged mainly under the influence of the Germans, who had brought to their new home a strong belief in group action and associations for self-betterment. In addition to the singing clubs, immigrant aid societies and other "uplift groups" were active in the establishment of workingmen's associations in several towns. These associations were a first step toward bona fide labor unions.

An unsigned letter to the editor of the *Texas State Gazette* proposing the establishment of a "Mechanic's Association" perhaps best describes the reasoning behind the organization of such groups. Suggesting that the prosperity and comfort of any community depended upon "industrious, intelligent mechanics," the writer asked, "Do they occupy among their fellow men, in a social point of view, that position to which their intrinsic merit should entitle them?" They do not, he went on to explain, because "no one, however exalted in intellectual endowment, can expect to rise to eminence among his fellowmen, who does not apply himself to study and store his mind with useful knowledge." The mechanics had the time to do this, he asserted, "as is apparent every day and night in our streets or houses of amusement and dissipation." What was needed was group action, and the writer called for a meeting "to form a Mechanic's Association, and to project measures for the general welfare and benefit of the brotherhood." The proposal bore fruit, for on November 16, 1850, in the state capitol, a Mechanics' Association was organized, with agreement to meet every Saturday thereafter in the Sons of Temperance Hall.[12] That the new association attained its high goals is doubtful; evidence that it lived more than a short time is lacking.

Similar organizations were established in New Braunfels, which was almost exclusively German in population. In 1854 two clubs for workingmen were begun: the Tradesmen's Club and the Workingmen's Club. The former hoped to encourage the development of the several trades by further reading and study in agricultural and technical journals, while the Workingmen's Club had broader aims, including instruction in English, arithmetic, essay writing, and other skills in addition to the maintenance of a sick fund and providing for social gatherings.[13]

Workingmen's associations were begun in Galveston and Houston in June 1857. A joint meeting of mechanics from the two cities, held in Houston, took up "matters pertaining to their mutual aid" and decided on the creation of me-chanics' reading rooms and mechanics' clubs "for mutual aid and protection." As a result, the Houston Mechanics' Association was born. Several meetings were held in late June, and the mechanics took part in the Fourth of July parade. The Galveston association, on the other hand, seems not to have passed the organizational stage at this time.[14] Nor does it appear that these kinds of groups were organized in other towns prior to the Civil War. The San Antonio Labor-ers' Association, the first such labor group in that city, for example, was not established until 1865.[15]

Several factors retarded the growth of organized labor in the prewar period. Most assuredly the small number of workers, the absence of industrial develop-ment, and the corollary absence of concentrations of labor were of major im-portance. Isolation likewise played a key role. Texas workers seemingly had little contact with or knowledge of labor organizations in other areas, even those as near as New Orleans. Texas newspapers rarely carried items about labor activi-ties in other states, except those of the most spectacular nature. The extent of outside contact was limited to the individual worker who moved to Texas with some prior contact with organized labor. No outside union, national or local, gave any aid to organizational efforts in Texas before about 1870. Texas work-ers did know of other labor unions, but distance and poor transportation and communication placed them almost in another world, beyond the influence, exuberance, or stimulation of a common cause. The frontier nature of Texas society, with its stress on individual action, surely played an important role. Group discontents found little outlet on a frontier, and class identification, weak enough elsewhere in nineteenth-century America, was especially weak on the frontier.

Still another factor working against the growth of labor organizations was the growing sectional crisis. The 1850s were a time of rebirth of unionism in the East. New Labor organizations, espousing "pure and simple" unionism, were making rapid strides, and although in southern cities such as New Orleans and Balti-more several labor unions were established, on the whole the number and size of these groups were smaller than might have been expected.[16] As one scholar has observed, to most southerners "labor organizations and strikes were 'Yankee in-novations' and 'abominations.'"[17] At a time when all social reformers in the South were looked upon as possible abolitionists, anyone with "radical" ideas about labor relations and workingmen's rights would be suspect. In Texas the strong unionist and antislavery sentiments of the Germans, who were so closely identi-fied with labor organizations, undoubtedly hurt the chances for the growth of unionism. Especially important in this connection was the Texas State Convention of Germans held in San Antonio in 1854, where a platform of proposed reforms was drawn up, including a strong statement condemning slavery and demanding its removal by state action. The continual agitation for abolition by the *San Antonio Zeitung* under its radical editor Adolf Douai was another disturbing element. Meetings and resolutions by numerous German groups condemning the views of Douai and the *Zeitung* failed to quiet fears about the antislavery leanings of the Germans, and the specter of "radical Germans" remained in the forefront of Texan thinking throughout the 1850s.[18]

Yet very few organizations that might pass as labor unions were begun prior to the Civil War. The two earliest known labor unions in the state were in fact established as early as the time of the Texas Republic. In April 1838 journeymen printers of Houston organized the Texas Typographical Association, "to promote the interests of the Craft throughout the Republic." At its initial meeting the group proposed a uniform wage scale, elected officers, adopted a constitution and bylaws, and invited all printers in the Republic to become members of the association.[19] The Typographical Association, which had no direct ties with the Printers Union in the United States, was very active during its first year. Meetings were held each month, and seemingly several new members were "elected" and "qualified."[20] In September or October 1838, in the first organized strike in Texas, the association in Houston struck and received a 25 percent wage increase.[21] Nothing in the few mentions of the association gives any idea of the size of its membership, although it must have been rather small. Nor is there any indication how long the Texas Typographical Association continued in existence past the last mention of it by a British observer in late 1839, though it would seem that if it had continued long in existence some notice would have appeared in the newspapers.[22] Undoubtedly it died in the 1840s.

The carpenters of Houston organized in 1839. Justifying their agreement to establish uniform wages, they affirmed that "we exact no more than our services justly deserve, believing that the mechanic is worthy of his hire."[23] Their success in enforcing the agreement and the endurance of the organization are unknown. More likely than not, there was no real organization but rather a single meeting, the resolutions and agreements of which were soon forgotten by all involved.

These two early unions were clearly exceptional cases because no evidence exists of any labor union active in the state from 1839 to 1857. In March 1857 the printers on the two Galveston newspapers founded a union in an effort to gain wage increases that the newspapers claimed they could not afford to pay. When negotiations failed to gain the desired raise, the printers did not try more drastic action.[24] The union continued, nevertheless, as it sent a delegate to the meeting of the National Typographical Union in 1857, and in November 1860 affiliated with that union as Local No. 28. By 1866 the Galveston local had forty-five members and five years later became a member of the International Typographical Union.[25]

In 1860 the carpenters of Galveston organized what was to become one of the oldest local unions in the United States never to undergo reorganization. Carpenters Local No. 7 was to be part of almost every major national union from its founding—being in turn a member of the National Labor Union, the Knights of Labor, and the American Federation of Labor. German tradesmen were the major group in the local throughout its early years, to the point that its records were kept in German through much of the late nineteenth century.[26] Like the printers' union, the carpenters' seemingly engaged primarily in benevolent activities until the 1880s. Thus, Galveston had the only two legitimate labor unions active in Texas at the outbreak of the Civil War.

During the war there is no evidence of organized labor activity. As the call to arms took most workers from their jobs, the economic stagnation of the war years provided no stimulus to the development of business or labor organizations. That much of the failure of organized labor to make inroads into Texas in the immediate prewar period was emotional seems to be borne out by the rapid growth of such organizations as soon as the war was over, when there was still relatively little industry and equal isolation.

The printers led in the development of unions after the war just as they had done before. In 1866 the Houston local of the Typographical Union was established as Local No. 87, holding its meetings in the city council chambers once a month. This union remained relatively active from that time on, although it floundered for a few years. In 1872 a reorganization of the local was necessary.[27] No information as to the size of the union in its early days is available, and its activities seem to have been limited to persuasion of employers and benevolent initiatives such as burials and sick benefits.[28]

In April 1870 the printers' union invaded the state capital. After a disastrous strike the next year that resulted in the "blackballing" of its members, Austin Local No. 138 of the Typographical Union went into a decade of decline. George S. Smith, who after the strike was forced to leave Austin to obtain employment, found the Galveston printers' union also in low estate. Local No. 28 was so inactive that affiliation was unnecessary to get work in Galveston.[29] This local, one of the two unions active before the war, was reorganized in 1872 when it became affiliated with the International Typographical Union.[30] In 1872 the Typographical Union continued its pioneering ways in Texas with the establishment of the first true union in San Antonio. Local No. 172 was small, weak, and inert during its first twenty-five years, with a membership varying between fifteen and fifty members, but it maintained its rather precarious existence, grew, and endured.[31]

Since the printer was usually a highly skilled and in Texas a somewhat scarce craftsman, he was among the best paid and most secure of workers. Because of the nature of his work, the printer was for the most part much better read and more abreast of current happenings than other workers, and thus more likely to know about labor unions and their activities. Although printers occasionally made use of the union to gain higher wages or redress grievances, the union always served other important purposes—primarily the training of apprentices and the maintenance of craft standards. Like other skilled crafts, the printers organized as much to control these two facets of their trade as to gain protection and bargaining power.

Yet, being highly skilled in the ordinary sense of the word was not an absolute prerequisite for successful organization if other conditions were favorable. Perhaps the most successful of all the early Texas labor unions was not that of a highly skilled trade, but rather of the screwmen in the port of Galveston. The work of screwmen, who, using screwjacks, packed cotton bales in the holds of ships, did not require long training or apprenticeship as did that of skilled artisans. A few weeks was all that was needed to learn the basics of their job. Established on September 11, 1866, the Screwmen's Benevolent Association during the first decade of its existence was plagued by those problems common to so many nineteenth-century labor unions. Flirtation with ritual and social activities threatened at one time to turn it into a kind of hybrid Masonic order. Older members sought to limit membership through the "blackball" and high initiation fees, hoping thereby to keep death and sick benefits at a higher level. There were pressures both inside and outside the organization to have it become active in politics. The race question reared its head on more than one occasion, always to be resolved by keeping the association all white. From the very first the association was more than its name indicated. Beginning in 1867, it periodically attempted to regulate working conditions, hours, and wages in the port through perseverance and a sort of limited boycott. The lack of early success only seemed to increase militancy. By 1883 it was strong enough to use the strike for the first time, winning improved working conditions and increased wages.[32]

Several other unions were established in the postwar years. The Houston telegraphers organized sometime prior to January 1870, and the brickmasons in Galveston had a union by late spring of that year.[33] In neither of these cases is information available about the union. Nor is anything known about the Texas Engineers' Association, which held a meeting in Houston in July 1870, or the Machinists and Blacksmiths' Union No. 1 of Texas, which was organized in the same city the following year.[34] The Longshoremen's Benevolent Association, established in 1870 by the black longshoremen of Galveston, was probably similar to the Screwmen's Benevolent Association in its activities. In 1877 the Longshoremen's Benevolent Association worked in conjunction with the Screwmen's Association in a dispute over wages that resulted in a most difficult, yet partially successful, strike.[35]

The Longshoremen's Benevolent Association was the first of a small number of black labor groups organized in the early 1870s. Attempts to organize black labor were made, with varying success, throughout the South during Reconstruction. In December 1869, the National Labor Convention of Negroes began in Washington, DC, as a reaction to the failure of white labor organizations, especially the National Labor Union, to give sufficient attention to black labor. Texas was represented at this convention, which sought to stimulate the organization of labor unions especially among African Americans in the South, although the nature of the representation is not clear.[36] The convention adopted a resolution urging all delegates to aid in the organization of state labor associations to seek solutions to the problems of black labor through cooperation with the National Convention and the National Labor Union.[37] By January 1871, some kind of unofficial organization of the National Labor Union (Colored) existed in Houston, because in that month the Houston group sent a representative to the national convention, where the Texans were officially empowered to establish a branch of the National Labor Union (Colored) in Texas.[38]

The organizational campaign that grew out of this action by the National Labor Union was the first such undertaking in Texas by any national body. Prior to this, the impetus for organization came from the individuals involved, and affiliation with a national organization was a sign that the local group had reached some degree of maturity and stability. The results of the drive of the national Labor Union in Texas provide an excellent example of why national groups might well consider organizational efforts in Texas a waste of time and money.

The organizational drive began with the call for a convention of "the Laborers' Union Association of the State of Texas" issued by Robert Nelson, the Texas agent of the National Labor Union. Both white and black laborers were urged to attend the meeting in Houston on June 8, 1871, although it appears only blacks attended.[39] Unfortunately for the union, the Republican Party was having a meeting in Houston the same week, and the labor convention became involved in the intraparty struggles of the Republicans.[40] Many of the same individuals involved in the Republicans' troubles attended the labor convention, and since the National Labor Union (Colored) met its demise by becoming involved in national Republican politics, it was not out of character for politics to enter into the labor convention. Nonetheless, the organization of a National Labor Union (Colored) branch in Houston was completed at the Houston meeting, and by the end of the year there was a similar group in Galveston. Delegates representing Texas were again sent to the national convention in late October, but no more was heard of the union in Texas after December. Its life as a national organization was not much longer.[41] The evidence indicates that the attempt to organize black labor met with only discouragement and failure.

If the organization of black labor was unusual, the establishment of a section of the International Workingmen's Association was equally surprising. In February 1872, at a meeting held in Galveston, what was later to be Section 44 of the International was organized. Under the leadership of John McMakin, whose oratorical abilities were the source of rapturous newspaper comment, Section 44 grew from twenty-five members in the beginning to about two hundred in April, before a rapid decline. Though clearly guilty of deviationism—Section 44 was so moderate in its proposals that a local editor thought it by no means dangerous to society—it was race rather than radicalism that led to its demise.[42] When it became clear that the International would invite black laborers to affiliate, most of the workers seemingly agreed with Bernard Lochrey that if "the colored man is to be taken into full fellowship in this society, socially and politically, I must decline to become a member." As if the race issue were not enough, an attack on the International by a local priest, charging it with responsibility for the Paris Commune, was answered to the effect that while the crimes of the commune were the outgrowth of passion, "the crimes of the Church of Rome were cool and deliberate, requiring years for their accomplishment."[43] By June 1872 the International passed out of local influence if not existence.

In the early 1870s organized labor began to grow at a comparatively rapid rate. Galveston remained the center of labor activity. The organization of a Carpenters and Joiners' Union in July 1872 and of a Hack-Drivers' Association in October brought the number of labor organizations in the city to over a dozen.[44] In addition to the two new unions, these included a Painters' Union, Plasterers' Union, Screwmen's Benevolent Association, Longshoremen's Benevolent Association, Typographical Union, Brickmasons' Union, National Labor Union (Colored), Carpenters' Local No. 7, International Workingmen's Association, and the Galveston Workingmen's Association. The rest of the state was hard pressed to equal Galveston in number of labor organizations. Houston had a Typographical Union, National Labor Union (Colored), Railway Trainmen Local No. 87 (organized in 1872), Machinists' and Blacksmiths' Union, and a new Workingmen's Association.[45] San Antonio and Austin both had locals of the Typographical Union, and the latter had a local of the Railway Trainmen; Fort Worth had a local of the Railway Engineers. Dallas did not have her first labor organization for another decade.[46] This rather rapid growth of labor unions suffered a serious setback in the Panic of 1873. Between 1873 and 1876 only a handful of new unions were begun in the state, including the Stone Cutters and Masons' Association in Austin (1873), Brotherhood of Locomotive Engineers in Houston (ca. 1876), Railway Firemen in Galveston (1876), and the Pilot Association of Galveston (1875).[47] The great breakthrough in labor organizing in Texas did not come until the early 1880s.[48]

In spite of the growth of labor unions there were few work stoppages in Texas before 1877. Outbursts, provoked by injustice, real or imagined, were the cause of most of the disturbances, and no labor union was needed for this type of action. Such spontaneous demonstrations continued after the Civil War just as they had before.

In March 1870 it was rumored that 150 men quit a Houston and Texas Central Railway Company construction job because they refused to work with the Chinese coolies brought in from the West Coast. Whether this particular incident did occur cannot be ascertained, but it is clear that there were numerous complaints on the part of construction workers against Chinese labor.[49] In November 1870 a large group of workers on the Houston and Texas Central, including engineers and brakemen, left their jobs, demanding a fifty-cents-per-day wage increase "on account of the extra night work." The company refused even to consider a wage increase. All employees who had taken part in the ill-conceived walkout were immediately dismissed and it ended almost before it began. There was no union among the Houston and Texas Central employees.[50] Draymen in Galveston, in December of the same year, refused to haul goods, demanding higher prices for carrying a load from the docks to downtown. The stoppage was short-lived. It was perhaps more like a fit of temper than a strike.[51] In April 1873 there was a classic example of unorganized workers solving a grievance. Nine men who worked for the Houston and Texas Central appeared at a farm outside Denison, where mules belonging to their employer were being kept, and demanded the animals and a bill of sale. Having been unable to collect their pay in money, they rode away on their "wages."[52] Such actions by workers were not the least uncommon, even if real strikes were.

Few, if any, of the labor organizations in Texas prior to 1876 had the strength to sustain a successful strike. They were weak, small, and usually without the outstanding kind of leaders so important to the success of the early labor movement. Only two strikes involving a union have been discovered. The first was that of the telegraphers in Houston, who joined in a nationwide strike against Western Union in January 1870. It was short-lived: within a few days most of the workers had begun to return to work and by the middle of the month the union admitted defeat. In May of the same year the brickmasons of Galveston struck for a wage increase from five to six dollars a day. Although an attempt by contractors to bring masons from New Orleans to break the strike failed because the Bricklayers' Union in that city refused to allow any of its members to be a party to strikebreaking, the Galveston masons were unsuccessful in obtaining their raise and went back to work in about a week.[53]

The only large-scale strike that occurred in Texas prior to 1877 was on the Houston and Texas Central in June 1872. It was only proper that the first important strike in Texas be on a railroad, for as Ira G. Clark has pointed out, "Railroads introduced complicated labor problems into the Gulf South-west, never before fully cognizant of the revolutionary social and economic implications of the industrialization and urbanization of the East. In practically the entire area, railroad employees were more nearly the counterpart of industrial labor than any other group."[54]

No union was involved in the strike. The organization of the railway brotherhoods had just gotten under way in Texas, and the Houston and Texas Central employees were not as yet unionized. Around June 1, 1872, the Houston and Texas Central announced a wage increase for all employees—tied to the signing by each employee of an agreement that the company would not be held liable for injury or death suffered while at work. Only a few of the operating employees signed the agreement, which the men termed the "Death Warrant." At a hastily called meeting on June 4, workers passed resolutions condemning the agreement as "unjust and uncalled for" and reaffirmed their refusal to sign it. They resolved not to return to work until the agreement was withdrawn. Some employees had already begun to leave work when the meeting was held, and by the next morning most were staying away from work.[55]

During the first full day of the strike, June 5, only one complete train made its run on the H &TC tracks; it was carrying only mail to Houston and was operated by the strikers. The northbound train from Houston was stopped at Hempstead and all cars except the mail car were placed on a siding before the train was allowed to continue.[56] On the afternoon of the fifth, the strikers stopped another train, offering to let it continue carrying only mail, an offer the company rejected. No violence was involved in stopping these trains, nor was any property damaged. Several engines had been disabled by the removal of the steam plugs from their boilers, but nothing was damaged.[57] No doubt the arrival of Capt. L. H. McNelly and the state police discouraged the use of force.

On the following morning the company announced that all men who refused to sign the agreement were fired and began attempts to get the trains running again. In spite of the company's success in putting the line into partial operation, the strikers remained adamant. Approximately four-fifths of the workers stationed in Austin held a meeting and reaffirmed their demand that the Death Warrant be withdrawn.[58] By June 10 passenger service had been restored almost to normal, although only one freight train ran that day.[59] Two days later it was reported that all passenger trains were running on time and that eight freights had run that day. New employees rapidly took the strikers' jobs, although some of the striking engineers were rehired by the company. The strike was clearly broken. Not all employees were as irreplaceable as the engineers. Approximately half the strikers were replaced, either because they refused to go back to work for the company or because the latter would not hire them back. In the end the strike had been a partial victory for both sides, as the company withdrew the Death Warrant but not until it had demonstrated that it would not be forced into any action by the workers.[60]

The growing number of unions and labor disputes in the early 1870s brought the first considerable public comment by Texans on labor organizations. For the most part, Texas newspapers had been somewhat condescending toward labor and labor organizations prior to this. As early as 1838, labor disturbances had drawn comments from editors, usually in the manner of the editor of the *Telegraph and Texas Register* who condemned murders and property destruction on the part of striking Irish shipbuilders but assured readers that American workers, "while enforcing their own rights, will respect those of others."[61] Papers often had noncontroversial articles on the "dignity of the laborer" or in praise of "our industrious and enterprising mechanics."[62] "Away then with this sickening foolery of fashionable life, that puts a mark of reproach upon the honest laborers and mechanics of the country," because, as the same editor said later, "American mechanics and artisans have proved to be . . . among the principle [*sic*] agents affecting American greatness."[63]

While Texan editors expressed little support for unions, they were not strongly antilabor. Most saw little reason for labor to organize, and their major fear seemed to be that violence would result. Yet in 1857, when the printers of Galveston organized, one historian of the island city found "the editorial comment on the Gulf Coast as to the printers' right to organize was respectful and, in the case of the Galveston and Houston papers, cordial."[64] On occasion, labor enjoyed considerable public approval and support. Such had been the case in the 1872 Houston and Texas Central railworkers' strike.

Public opinion seemingly favored the strikers from the first. The passengers, stranded as a result of the disagreement, held a meeting and passed a resolution asking the company to withdraw the Death Warrant, even threatening to hold the company responsible for damages incurred because of the delay. The editor of the *Austin Statesman* expressed sympathy for the strikers and averred that the company was wrong to ask to be released from liability. In Corsicana several individuals offered to pay the board bills of the strikers in that town because of the injustice of the company's demands. "The sympathy of the town [of Brenham] seems unanimously in favor of the Engineers," wrote a correspondent to the *Galveston News*, so much so that after the strike failed, citizens "raised a fund . . . for the benefit of the Engineers and other employees, late of the Central Railroad."[65] The editor of the *Galveston News* on another occasion indicated "every sympathy with the man who asks for more wages, [although] we have none at all with him or for him that asks to reduce the hours of his labor to eight. A lazy man is an abomination only tolerated by an inscrutible [*sic*] Providence."[66] Most Texas newspapers continued to give fair coverage to labor stories into the 1880s in spite of a tendency for newspaper editorials to exhibit growing distrust of labor unions.[67]

This changing attitude came primarily as a result of violence, which became more frequently a part of work stoppages. "In the struggle between capital and labor," warned the editor of the *Houston Weekly Telegraph*, "labor must find some more skillful strategy, or the battle will invariably go against it. Force is the last resort of the wise General; the champions of labor seem inclined always to make it the first."[68] While some Texas editors limited their criticism to such mild rebuffs, others began to express hostility toward the whole idea of labor unions. "We have watched with much sorrow the gradual, nay rapid spread of Labor Organizations, the beginning of which we are now seeing," the editor of the *Galveston News* wrote. "The beginning is here—the little rippling stream, so weak as to be insignificant—the end is like that of Paris. It is the Commune with its sea of blood and its ocean of fire." Labor organizations were, he continued, based on three false principles—that labor and capital are at odds; that there is a class of men who will remain workers all their lives; and that there is not labor enough for all ... therefore, no man ought to do all of which he is capable. ... The freedom of labor, free education, the cheapness of land, and a hundred other considerations, render it easy for the laboring man to raise [*sic*] to a position of greater ease, if not of greater respectability. ... Yet, demagogues intervene in the natural process and seek to form labor unions, all of which have a history of violence, a history of social disturbance, and a history of social degradation. Every labor association we have ever known has been composed of two classes, industrious laborers, who supported idling demagogues.[69]

Unions and strikes were, declared the same editor later, contrary to economic laws:

The wages of labor, as well as the prices or values of all articles ... should be left to themselves to be regulated by demand and supply, and ... all attempts, either by legislation or by strikes, to interfere with the prices as established by that law of trade are attended sooner or later by a reaction against the very parties intended to be benefitted.[70]

A simple sentence in one report on the 1872 H&TC railroad strike hinted at another cause of this change in the attitude toward unions. "The public are suffering greatly from the present misunderstanding," reported the *Houston Union*.[71] By the 1870s the Texas economy had developed to the point that a strike affected more Texans than just the workers and manager involved, especially if it was a railroad strike. As the railroad became the very life of the state, when every merchant in every town became dependent on the railroad to get his goods and every farmer needed the rails to transport his bulky cotton to market, then the public would take a very different attitude toward railroad strikes, no matter what their cause. And the railroad strikes of the 1870s were the first personal contact with labor disturbances for most Texans.

Previously, in fact, few Texans, workers or not, had had any firsthand experience with labor organizations and their activities. In the stage of economic development which characterized Texas to the mid-1870s, conditions conducive to labor organizations of any type existed almost exclusively in the larger towns. It was here that the early labor organizations had developed. These had been for the most part benevolent societies. The few true unions that had been established, primarily after the Civil War, were weak, and most failed to survive more than a few months. As a result, organized labor had little impact on the worker or the public. Work stoppages had seldom occurred, and when they did, most often represented the spontaneous reaction of unorganized laborers rather than the actions of organized unions. The successful strike was extremely rare.

As the railroad came, breaking the state's isolation and stimulating its economy, the character of the labor movement changed. Railroad laborers, the first large group of industrial workers, brought militant unionism to Texas. The history of labor in the state was entering a new phase, and the strikes of 1877 marked the change.

Yet what had been the contributions of the meager attempts at organization during the years 1838 to 1876? Their major importance was not so much in accomplishment, which was all but nil, but rather as an indication—a sign that even in Texas's agrarian society labor problems existed and that at least some workers experienced these problems to the point of seeking to improve their lot through labor organizations.

Notes

This chapter originally appeared in *Southwestern Historical Quarterly* 72 (July 1968): 1–20, and is reprinted with permission.

1. Fred C. Cole, "The Texas Career of Thomas Affleck" (PhD diss., Louisiana State University, 1942), 137–38. Thomas Affleck, well-known agricultural reformer and editor of several agricultural papers, moved from his native Mississippi to near Brenham in 1858. There he operated a large plantation and established one of the earliest nurseries in Texas. Walter P. Webb and H. Bailey Carroll, eds., *Handbook of Texas* (Austin, 1952), 1:11.

2. R. P. Jones to [the] Congress of the Republic of Texas, January 11, 1845, Memorials and Petitions, Congress of the Republic of Texas, Archives, Texas State Library, Austin; N. H. P. Gammel, comp., *The Laws of Texas, 1822–1897* (Austin, 1898), 2:479–82.

3. *Telegraph and Texas Register* (Houston), January 2, 5, 1839. The lien law was passed January 23, 1839. Gammel, *The Laws of Texas, 1822–1897*, 2:66–67.

4. *Telegraph and Texas Register* (Houston), September 3, 1845; Minutes [of the] Commissioner's Court [of Harris County, Texas], Office of the Clerk of the County Court, Houston, A:127.

5. *Telegraph and Texas Register* (Houston), May 21, 1845; *Biographical Directory of Texan Conventions and Congresses* (Austin, 1941), 131–32; Record of Board Commissioners and Election Returns [of Harris County, Texas], Office of the Clerk of the County Court, Houston), 1:208.

6. S. M. Orton[?], John H. Wilson, H. K. Carson . . . [and others] to the Honorable Congress of Texas, November 8, 1841, Memorials and Petitions, Congress of the Republic of Texas.

7. A petition of Sundry Citizens of Harrison Co[unty], Marshall, Texas, January 19,

1861, Memorials and Petitions, Legislature of the State of Texas, Archives, Texas State Library, Austin.

8. James V. Reese, "The Worker in Texas, 1821–1876" (PhD diss., University of Texas, 1964), 19–33; Ralph A. Wooster, "Foreigners in the Principal Towns of Ante-Bellum Texas," *Southwestern Historical Quarterly* 66 (October 1962): 209, 213–14.

9. Rudolph L. Biesele, *The History of the German Settlements in Texas, 1831–1861* (Austin, 1939), 41; *Telegraph and Texas Register* (Houston), December 9, 1840; *Galveston Daily News*, June 6, September 2, October 18, 1871.

10. *Galveston Daily News*, January 5, 1872; John H. Heller, *Heller's Galveston City Directory, 1876–7* (Galveston, 1876), 161.

11. Paul S. Taylor, *An American-Mexican Frontier: Nueces County, Texas* (Chapel Hill, 1934), 173–75.

12. *Texas State Gazette* (Austin), November 9, 23, 1850.

13. Biesele, *History of the German Settlements in Texas*, 210.

14. *Houston Telegraph*, June 15, 24, July 2, 1857; *Galveston Tri-Weekly News*, June 16, 1857.

15. Harold A. Shapiro, "The Labor Movement in San Antonio, Texas, 1865–1915," *Southwestern Social Science Quarterly* 36 (September 1955): 160.

16. Herbert Aptheker's view that workers were "markedly militant during the 1860's in several Southern states" certainly does not apply to Texas. Nor, one might add, does Aptheker's evidence seem to justify such a judgment. Herbert Aptheker, *The Labor Movement in the South during Slavery* (New York, 1955), 12.

17. E. Merton Coulter, *The Confederate States of America, 1861–1865* (Baton Rouge, 1950), 236.

18. Biesele, *History of the German Settlements in Texas*, 198–204.

19. *Telegraph and Texas Register* (Houston), May 2, 1838.

20. Ibid., May 5, June 30, October 20, 1838.

21. The exact date, events, and causes of the strike are unknown. The *Telegraph and Texas Register* of December 15, 1838, has a notice that "the recent advance made by the typographical association upon the wages of journeymen printers" had made necessary an increase in "the rates of advertising and other printing" by the publishers in Houston. Samuel Whiting, who held the contract for government printing, wrote to Pres. Mirabeau B. Lamar on May 3, 1839, that since the contract for government printing had been made, "the Journey men [*sic*] printers have struck for higher wages, and we now have been facing for the last 8 mos 25 pr ct more [wages]." C. A. Gulick et al., eds., *The Papers of Mirabeau Bonaparte Lamar* (6 vols.; Austin, 1921–1927), 5:281.

22. William Kennedy, *Texas: The Rise, Progress, and Prospects of the Republic of Texas* (Fort Worth, 1925), 767.

23. Quoted in *Houston: A History and Guide*, compiled by Workers of the Writers' Program of the Works Projects Administration in the State of Texas (Houston, 1942), 153.

24. *Galveston Tri-Weekly News*, March 7, 21, 1857.

25. W. Richardson and Co., *Galveston Directory for 1866–67* (Galveston, 1866), 91; *Galveston Daily News*, October 27, 1872; Ruth Allen, *Chapters in the History of Organized Labor in Texas* (Austin, 1941), 136.

26. Allen, *Chapters*, 136.

27. *Houston City Directory for 1866* (Houston, 1866), 84; *Houston City Directory for 1867–8* (Houston, 1867), 177; *Houston City Directory for 1873* (Houston, [1873]), 88; Texas State Bureau of Labor Statistics, *First Biennial Report, 1909–1910* (Austin, 1910), 137; Preliminary Sketch of the History of the Labor Movement in Texas, Labor Movement in Texas file, University of Texas Archives, Austin. The present Houston printers union traces its beginning to the 1872 reorganization.

28. Ibid.; *Galveston Daily News*, April 20, 1873.

29. Texas State Bureau of Labor Statistics, *Second Biennial Report, 1911–12* (Austin, 1912), 167; Earle Sylvester Sparks, "A Survey of Organized Labor in Austin" (master's thesis, University of Texas, 1920) , 10. The Typographical Union was reorganized in 1882.

30. *Galveston News*, August 15, 1939. This local has remained active since 1872.

31. Shapiro, "Labor Movement in San Antonio," 160.

32. Screwmen's Benevolent Association of Galveston, Records, University of Texas Archives, Austin, 1:1–245, passim; W. Richardson and Co., *Galveston Directory for 1866–67*, 20, 28; *Flake's Bulletin* (Galveston), December 4, 1869. The SBA remained active as a labor union until 1914, when it became a local in the International Longshoremen's Association.

33. *Houston: A History and Guide*, 85; Ulriksson Vidkunn, *The Telegraphers: Their Craft and Their Union* (Washington, 1953), 28; *Galveston Daily News*, May 24, 1870.

34. *Galveston Daily News*, July 1, 1870; *Houston: A History and Guide*, 155.

35. Allen, *Chapters*, 137; *Galveston Daily News*, October 11, 1871, March 6, June 1, 1873, June 17, 24, August 5, 1877; Maud Cuney Hare, *Norris Wright Cuney: A Tribune of the Black People* (New York, 1913) , 23–24; Robert V. Bruce, *1877: Year of Violence* (Indianapolis, 1959), 263. The Longshoremen's Association joined the national longshoremen's union in 1913.

36. Charles H. Wesley, *Negro Labor in the United States, 1850–1925: A Study in American Economic History* (New York, 1927), 177–78.

37. Wesley, *Negro Labor*, 179.

38. Wesley, *Negro Labor*, 182–83; *Houston: A History and Guide*, 172.

39. Wesley, *Negro Labor*, 184; *Galveston Daily News*, June 6, 9, 1871.

40. *Galveston Daily News*, June 13, 1871.

41. Ibid., December 1, 1871.

42. Ibid., February 20, 28, March 3, 11, 21, April 14, 1872.

43. Ibid., May 5, 29, 1872.

44. Ibid., July 14, August 25, October 22, 23, 1872.

45. Texas State Bureau of Labor Statistics, *First Biennial Report, 1909–1910*, 137; *Galveston Daily News*, August 16, 20, 23, 1872.

46. Texas State Bureau of Labor Statistics, *Second Biennial Report, 1911–12*, 166;

Jack Rivers Strauss, "Organized Labor in Dallas County" (master's thesis, Southern Methodist University, 1948), 36.

47. *Galveston Daily News*, May 11, 1873; *Mooney and Morrison's Directory of the City of Houston for 1877–78* (Houston, 1877), 44; Texas State Bureau of Labor Statistics, *First Biennial Report, 1909–1910*, 136; W. A. Fayman and T. W. Reilly, *Fayman and Reilly's Galveston City Directory for 1875–76* (Galveston, 1875), 66.

48. Allen, *Chapters*, 19–24.

49. *Galveston Daily News*, March 10, 1870.

50. *Houston Weekly Telegraph*, November 27, 1870.

51. *Galveston Daily News*, December 4, 1870.

52. Ibid., April 25, 1873.

53. Vidkunn, *The Telegraphers*, 28; *Galveston Daily News*, May 24, 1870.

54. Ira G. Clark, *Then Came the Railroads: The Century from Steam to Diesel in the Southwest* (Norman, 1958), 215.

55. *Galveston Daily News*, June 6, 1872.

56. Ibid.; *Tri-Weekly State Gazette* (Austin), June 7, 1872.

57. *Galveston Daily News*, June 6, 12, 1872; *Austin Statesman*, June 11, 1872.

58. *Galveston Daily News*, June 7, 1872.

59. Ibid., June 11, 1872.

60. Ibid., June 12, 14, 16, 1872; *Austin Statesman*, June 13, 1872.

61. *Telegraph and Texas Register* (Houston), May 16, 1838.

62. Ibid., September 14, 1839, May 4, 1842.

63. *Northern Standard* (Clarksville), May 27, 1846, August 3, 1850.

64. Earl Wesley Fornell, *The Galveston Era: The Texas Crescent on the Eve of Secession* (Austin, 1961), 101.

65. *Galveston Daily News*, June 7, 13, 1872; *Austin Statesman*, June 8, 1872.

66. *Galveston Daily News*, June 25, 1872.

67. John S. Spratt, *The Road to Spindletop: Economic Change in Texas, 1875–1901* (Dallas, 1955), 233.

68. *Houston Weekly Telegraph*, September 5, 1867.

69. *Galveston Daily News*, June 7, 1871.

70. Ibid., May 18, 1872.

71. *Houston Union*, June 8, 1872.

ROBERT S. SHELTON

On Empire's Shore

Free and Unfree Workers in Galveston, Texas,
1840–1860

During the summer of 1854 the editor of a Texas newspaper wrote in anguish
that dances attended by blacks and working-class whites were common in the
state's larger cities and that anyone observing such an event "almost imagines
himself in the land of amalgamation, abolition meetings, and women's rights
conventions." The illegal but common practice of allowing slaves to hire out
their own labor and find their own housing, the editor complained, had led
them to "impudence" and the taking up of such alarming habits as smoking,
gambling, drinking, and carousing with "low, unprincipled white men," who
"because they are conscious that they do not deserve the respect of decent persons of their own color . . . resort to Negrodom for society and sympathy." If
such practices were left unchecked by proper authorities, the editor warned, "we
will ere long have a Southampton insurrection, or a general Negro stampede for
Mexico." The editor then urged the board of aldermen to enact stricter ordinances to control the behavior of slaves—and of "low, unprincipled" whites.[1]

As the editor's observations suggest, in antebellum southern cities such as
Galveston—the small but thriving seaport that served as Texas's commercial
emporium—poor whites and enslaved African Americans at times interacted
in ways uncommon in southern slave society and unsettling to the slaveholders whose economic, social, and political dominance required a unified white
commitment to black inferiority. Social interaction among enslaved black and
"common" white people, who shared few of the material advantages of white supremacy, represented a dangerous blurring of established racial lines and posed
a potential threat to the social control of slaveholders and to the rigid hierarchy
of southern slave society. Such relations did indeed develop, however, as African
American slaves and white casual laborers in Galveston spent much of their wak-
ing hours together working at the most menial and arduous tasks; living side
by side in cheap houses, shacks, and shanties; and socializing in homes, liquor
stores, brothels, saloons, and on beaches away from the immediate supervision

of authorities. As in other antebellum port cities, the degree of interracial social-ization in Galveston worried the slaveholding elite to such an extent that the city repeatedly passed laws carrying increasingly harsh penalties designed to draw more clearly the color line between black and white workers.[2]

Historians have long recognized that the urban landscape proved inhospi-table to the kind of slavery found on the South's plantations. In southern cities, common practices such as allowing slaves to find their own jobs, earn their own wages, rent their own dwellings, and manage their own time bred an in-dependence that eroded the discipline of slavery. Moreover, as scholars have abundantly documented, and slaveholders frequently lamented, free black city-dwellers further undermined slavery by providing enslaved African Ameri-cans with information, domestic partners, temporary and permanent refuge, and sources and markets for illicitly traded goods.[3] Perhaps what distinguished Galveston among southern urban areas, however, was the virtual absence of free persons of color—only two by 1860—owing to state and local laws that drove free blacks out of the state, into hiding, or back into slavery. Consequently, in Galveston, slaves had far more contact with poor white casual laborers than with free black people. Yet even in areas of the South with large free black popula-tions, varying degrees of interaction between enslaved African Americans and poor, nonslaveholding white people have been discovered by scholars studying northern colonial cities and the antebellum southern countryside.[4] Further-more, scholarship of Atlantic seamen in the eighteenth and nineteenth centuries has revealed a rough equality, albeit frequently marked by racism and white su-premacy, that existed in the maritime world on ship and shore.[5] These findings modify the conclusions of historians who have argued that the legal segregation that emerged at the end of the nineteenth century originated during Recon-struction as an alternative, accepted by African Americans, to the exclusion of black people from public accommodations and services that had prevailed dur-ing the period of slavery.[6]

Certainly, during the antebellum period tradition and habit, if not law, ex-cluded free blacks and slaves, except as servants, from institutions used by the South's white elite and middle classes. In Galveston, for example, there were few municipal or state laws that specifically prohibited African Americans from establishments frequented by white people, yet it is clear that black residents of the city did not attend balls thrown for the elite, eat in the restaurants fre-quented by middle- and upper-class diners, drink in gentlemen's clubs or taverns, or patronize most businesses. One of the few institutions that did allow black participation was the Methodist Church, which in the 1840s began providing separate services for African American worshipers.[7] Such racial exclusivity no doubt conditioned Euro-American workers to the practices of white supremacy. Despite the racism that pervaded all strata of southern cities such as Galveston, on the margins of society such exclusion, while perhaps traditional, was not habitual. This chapter furthers the excavation of a little-worked field of inquiry by focusing on the interactions between black slaves and the poorest of the South's urban whites—casual laborers who worked at whatever low-paying, low-skilled jobs they could find—and by suggesting why such benign interactions developed in a region where social relations based on domination, fear, and repression usually prevailed.

In 1846, after a decade of desultory independence, Texas joined the United States, expanding the South's cotton-slave frontier westward and promising to take its place as the most bountiful plantation region in the country. From 1850 to 1860 the state rose to become the fifth-leading cotton producer in the nation, and observers predicted even more spectacular growth as more slaves and better transportation opened up more of Texas's fertile lands to agriculture. As the editor of Austin's *Texas State Gazette* prophesied, Texas was destined to become the "Empire State of the South."[8] On the shores of this potential empire of cotton and slaves, Galveston also awaited the fulfillment of its promise. Located on a barrier island about three hundred miles west of New Orleans, the city possessed one of the best natural harbors on the Gulf of Mexico, and its boosters crowed that if Texas became the South's Empire State, Galveston would be its New York City. Galveston, another editor predicted, "will undoubtedly, at no distant day, become the center of commerce rivaling in extent that of many of the first commercial cities of the world. The products of many millions of acres of the most fertile lands on the globe, and of many rich mines of gold, silver, and iron, will necessarily be wafted to this spot, rendering Galveston City the commercial emporium of Texas."[9]

Although the city eventually lost its commercial preeminence to Houston, such predictions seemed justified in the antebellum era. The state's richest plantation districts lay in the counties surrounding Galveston, making the city a natural egress for slave-grown produce. By 1860 Galveston had become the state's second-largest city with more than seven thousand residents, its cultural center, and its leading commercial hub.[10] Most of the state's cotton, sugar, and rice exports passed over the city's wharves, and ships from Europe, the Caribbean, and South America as well as New York, Boston, Baltimore, and New Orleans regularly called on the port.[11] Galveston's leading businessmen—cotton commission agents and speculators, slave traders, and absentee plantation owners—were among the wealthiest men in Texas, shaped the state's policies, and dominated the city politically, economically, and socially.

At the bottom of Galveston society, however, resided two groups of people who possessed little wealth, few prospects, and, for some, not even themselves. The first of these groups, white casual laborers, constituted perhaps one of every five residents who listed occupations in the 1850 and 1860 censuses. Casual laborers worked at low-paying jobs that could not be counted on as regular sources of income and were perceived as requiring little skill to perform. Such jobs included working as unskilled labor on construction sites, collecting and dispersing oyster shells for the city's streets, rolling cotton at the cotton presses, keeping the streets clear and in repair, hauling fill for low spots in the city, digging cisterns, cleaning privies, performing domestic labor, taking in washing and sewing, selling sexual services, hauling cargo to and from warehouses, working on Galveston's wharves loading and unloading the ships calling at the port, and carrying passengers through shallow water to and from ships anchored in the harbor awaiting their turn at the wharves.[12] The other group, enslaved African Americans, constituted as much as 17 percent of the city's antebellum population. As in other southern cities, enslaved black people often found their own lodgings and employment, which not only provided them with greater freedom than plantation slaves but also brought them into daily, close contact with poor white workers. Although many bondsmen found work in various skilled trades—it was frequently reported by observers that skilled work in Galveston was performed by slaves and European immigrants—most worked at the variety of tasks performed by white casual laborers, often working at these tasks together.

In 1854, for example, a visitor to the city noted that slaves joined white men lightering cargo from ships anchored outside the sandbar that prevented the deepest draught vessels from entering the harbor. One visitor to the city remarked that the slaves and casual laborers sang together as they loaded and unloaded vessels tied along the city's wharves. Enslaved black men also worked as cotton screwmen alongside white men. Working in gangs of four or five men, the screwmen, or cotton jammers, used large jackscrews to compact cotton bales into the holds of ships. The work was hard and dangerous and required coordination and cooperation among the gang members. Longshoring work for shipping companies and individual ships' captains employed men of both colors. When the schooner *Nameaug* arrived in Galveston in 1856, for example, white "steveders" helped the crew, which included black seamen, load cotton bales, molasses, sugar, and tanned hides for its return voyage to Boston.[13] Both cotton jamming and longshoring paid better than other forms of casual labor but were seasonal and thus perhaps more irregular in nature. Another dangerous task shared by enslaved and free workers involved salvage operations. The cargoes of ships grounded on Galveston Bay's numerous sandbars or sunk by storms were retrieved by African Americans and poor whites hired by the ships' owners or the commission house responsible for the cargo.[14] It could be dangerous work that not infrequently resulted in drowning. In 1856, for example, a white man identified as F. Schoenenfield drowned in the harbor when he became trapped in a sunken vessel despite the efforts of several slaves and other white men also working the salvage to save him.[15]

Enslaved black people and free white people also found themselves working and sometimes living side by side as domestic servants. Slaves and white servants not only mingled while performing such tasks as shopping at the city's markets and groceries but also occasionally lived with one another in the same house and sometimes even the same rooms. The 1850 and 1860 census shows that approximately one-quarter of households had a young adult of a different name and often of different nationality living in them. Evidence suggests that at least some of them performed domestic duties in return for room and board.[16]

Slaves hiring their own time or hired out by their masters often worked with poor white men for the city. In 1851, for example, the city contracted with John S. Sydnor to fill low spots throughout Galveston. The city regularly contracted for this work in an effort to prevent the accumulation of standing water that they and other nineteenth-century Americans vaguely associated with deadly yellow fever outbreaks. Sydnor, who operated the largest slave auction in town and frequently rented out his inventory before their sale, billed the city $1.25 per day for use of a slave and $1.50 for a white man. In 1849 E. O. Lynch, one of the largest slaveholders in the state, billed the city for repairing streets and digging a cistern. His bill for the work showed that he had employed his own slaves and white men. At construction sites enslaved black men and poor whites also worked together as common laborers.[17] In a lawsuit filed in 1848 Sydnor sought remuneration for the hire of a slave and white man for helping a white carpenter build shelving in a grocery store. Gilbert Winney, owner of a livery stable in 1850, owned a thirty-year-old male slave who worked with his two white livery keepers, French immigrant Lewis Boneall and a middle-age Pennsylvanian named John Magill. Court records from the 1840s and 1850s occasionally mention white and black people working together to perform such tasks as moving outbuildings, cutting firewood, pressing cotton, constructing buildings, filling land, digging ditches, and draying goods from warehouse to wharf.[18] This is not to suggest that relations between black and white workers were free of animosity stemming from job competition or white racism. Although there is little documented evidence of conflicts between enslaved black people and casual white laborers during the antebellum period, no doubt insults flew, fights erupted, and racial antagonism festered at work and in social situations. During the Civil War, for example, Irish casual laborers from Galveston pledged support for the Confederacy and slavery and formed their own company that saw action in Louisiana. Furthermore, in the years following emancipation, longshoremen and cotton screwmen, who constituted a large segment of the casual labor force in antebellum Galveston, attempted to ban blacks from waterfront work, which was the most reliable and highest-paying labor in the port city. The dramatic changes wrought by emancipation, beyond the scope of this study, increased economic and political competition between black and white workers and no doubt thereby increased incentives for Euro-Americans to embrace white supremacy. The ease at which they did so indicates that racism figured significantly in antebellum relations as well. It is worth noting, however, that it was not until late 1869 that white waterfront workers excluded black workers from their unions and attempted to do so from the docks, suggesting the new competitive environment and the possibility that racial exclusion was not an automatic, unconsidered reaction to emancipation. Furthermore, Galveston's antebellum white elite considered working-class saloons and brothels lawless and dangerous owing to the brawling that broke out between patrons—certainly sometimes because of racial enmity.

Yet brothels, as historian Ira Berlin has noted, were perhaps among the most integrated places in the South. In Galveston, enslaved and free black women and white women lived and worked under the same roof in the city's houses of prostitution. On the city's east and west sides and in the alleys a few blocks off the waterfront stood several houses of prostitution such as Fanny Hill's "house of ill fame," whose "fancy girls" were enslaved black women and free white women. According to the *Galveston Weekly News*, the brothels catered to "the rougher element" of men of all colors, who could drink alcohol, gamble, and "carouse loudly throughout the night."[19] Attempting to remove such establishments from commercial and residential areas, the city council in 1857 restricted the operation of houses of prostitution to the far western end of the city among the cotton presses and warehouses. White men or women operating a brothel anywhere else in the city faced a one-hundred-dollar fine and fifteen days in jail; free women of color risked being hired out for six months to the highest bidder; free men of color, six months' hard labor working under the direction of the city marshal.[20]

The city's response to the carousing at brothels demonstrates that Galveston's slaveholding elite intended to prevent interracial association outside the work-place—in brothels, saloons, pool halls, grog shops, alleys, and private homes.[21] Yet legal and illegal associations between black slaves and white workers occurred frequently. In Galveston, biracial social interaction often occurred because slaves who lived apart from their owners often lived in the neighborhoods where most of the city's casual laborers dwelled. On the west side of the city these neighborhoods lay near the cotton presses and warehouses; on the east side, beyond one of the main markets. In the center of town, the extensive alleyways often became virtually impassable owing to the number of ramshackle homes erected in them. Together these neighborhoods enclosed the commercial center of town on the waterfront. The Galveston City Company, which had title to all the unsold land in the city, owned many small houses in these neighborhoods that were rented to laborers, to slaves or slaveholders, or to free persons of color. Boardinghouses that in the late 1850s charged $2.50 to $4 per week for a room with multiple occupants could be found here.[22] Some laborers owned small houses, most of which were valued at less than a quarter of even the least-valued homes in other portions of the city. One worker recorded that a house measuring sixteen by twenty-four feet and occupied by nine people sold along with its furnishings for five thousand dollars—a figure far beyond the means of most unskilled workers who typically earned no more than thirty dollars per month.[23] The slaves in these areas lived apart from their owners, who usually resided in the more upscale portions of town. In the 1840s and 1850s, local newspapers often complained about the "pest houses," inhabited by enslaved black people, that infested various parts of the city. In April 1854 the city council's report on city-owned property found that city property along Broadway had been "seized upon by three trespassers on the North side who have erected 'hovels' that are for rent." The other portion of the property "seems to be in the occupancy of a negress with an old hovel-like building." The city passed ordinances to clear the alleys of "hovels" and other structures that grew up to provide accommodations for poor whites and living-out black slaves.[24]

Most slaves, however, lived with their owners, or rather behind their owners, in slave houses that often lined the city's alleyways in the more prosperous Second Ward. Yet even slaves who lived on their masters' premises frequented the saloons and shops in the less reputable neighborhoods. As one observer noted, the slaves of Galveston could be seen in all parts of the city going on various errands for their masters or at their leisure. The city's newspapers repeatedly expressed dismay at the number of slaves and "poorer sorts" of whites who congregated around grog shops, groceries, gambling tents in the alleys, and pool halls.

The city council, at the urging of Galveston slaveholders, repeatedly increased the severity of punishments for slaves buying liquor or whites selling liquor to slaves. "Let anyone travel through the suburbs of our city and note the number of our little whiskey shops (called groceries to give them more respectability) out and into which he may see negroes coming and going at night, and on Sundays, and he cannot fail to be satisfied that this negro traffic is carried on most systematically."[25] In 1857 the city raised the licensing fees for the operation of groceries, beer halls, grog shops, and saloons and increased the fines and jail time for anyone operating one without a permit. At the same time the city council increased the penalties for white people who allowed enslaved black people to drink or gamble in private homes, enacted harsher measures against slaves who hired their own time or found their own living arrangements, and raised the fines for slaveholders who permitted their slaves to do so and for anyone who rented or hired a slave without the permission of his or her owner.[26]

Dances also occurred fairly regularly and were of great concern to slaveholders. In 1852, for example, the slaves of Joseph Bates held a ball that was attended by "negros finely turned out" and a smattering of less well-appointed white people.[27] Such balls prompted the city council in 1854 to require slaveholders to obtain permission from the city council before holding any sort of entertainment for groups of five or more slaves. The same ordinance increased the punishment from ten to thirty-nine lashes for slaves who congregated without their masters' permission and provided for jail time for whites who allowed slaves to congregate in their homes without the permission of the slaves' owners.[28]

The waterfront also provided slaves and laborers who worked along it opportunities for socializing. Visitors in the 1840s and 1850s noted that black and white people frolicked on the beach, "making the air sound with their songs and shouts of revelry." Other visitors noted that even on the wharves during the summer men of both colors could be seen swimming, diving, and horse-playing together in the harbor with what one observer called a "disgraceful lack of decorum and an obscene lack of dress." In 1857 the city passed several ordinances proscribing this activity, making it illegal for men or women to "divest themselves of their clothing for the purpose of, or under the pretense of, bathing" on the beaches of the bay or gulf or along the wharves. The wording—"under the pretense of bathing"—suggests that perhaps more than skinny-dipping was occurring. Virtually no hard evidence exists that interracial sex occurred between casual workers and slaves, or between slaveowners and slaves, for that matter. The number of people census enumerators classified as "mulattoes" represented about 25 percent of the slave population in 1850 and 20 percent in 1860. In 1850, about 36 percent of "mulattoes" were young enough to have been born in the city; in 1860, 64 percent. So assuming that census enumerators and slaveholders knew and accurately represented the racial background of slaves—a very large assumption—it seems clear that though the percentage of mixed-race individuals decreased during the decade, the number born in the city may have increased substantially. Nevertheless, the lack of information about the provenance or parentage of the enslaved people in Galveston makes it all but impossible to reliably infer from demographic statistics the extent of interracial sex. Certainly, no evidence remains to suggest that interracial sexual relations occurred beyond the walls of brothels.[29]

By 1861 the city had enacted a rigorous slave code that prohibited slaves from hiring their own time, finding their own dwellings, buying or drinking liquor, gambling, congregating in groups of five or more without permission, holding dances without permission, and going about on their own after sunset without a pass from their owners. White people who inveigled slaves to break these laws faced fines and jail time. The city also enacted in the late 1850s a strict vagrancy law that made it a crime to be unemployed and not looking for work. Enslaved and free men and women found loitering on the sidewalks were to be arrested and put to work on the city's streets under the direction of the marshal. This law was so successful that the *Galveston Daily News*, the voice of conservatism in the city, recommended an amendment to it to relieve overcrowding in the city jail by inmates who "would work when work was at hand." The ordinance, however, remained in place until the end of the Civil War.[30]

Clearly, black and white Galvestonians formed associations at work that carried over to social interactions after the workday was done. Why did such interaction occur and why did it worry slaveholders in the city? The daily interaction between white workers and enslaved African Americans noted above, the composition of the white casual workforce, and the circumstances of their lives must figure prominently in any explanation. Among white people, recent arrivals overwhelmingly performed casual labor in Galveston. During the 1840s and 1850s, a steady stream of immigrants from the United States and Europe flowed through the city. Although most of the newcomers stayed only a short time before striking out for the interior, where cheap and abundant land beckoned would-be farmers, many others remained for years or stayed permanently, boosting the city's population during the decade before the Civil War from 4,177 to 7,328. Native-born Americans dominated the skilled trades and white-collar jobs in small business, medicine, the law, and government, and those who worked at casual labor did so only for a short time as a step up the economic ladder. "Many of our most prominent residents earned their first money by carrying passengers and freight to and from vessels on their strong shoulders," one nineteenth-century writer noted about a job commonly available before the construction of wharves from shore across the shallows to the harbor channel.[31]

Casual labor, on the other hand, rarely provided a basis for social mobility. Many casual laborers were immigrants—in 1860 nine out of ten of men listed as "laborers" were foreign-born—and frequently stayed only a short time in Galveston before moving on. "There are more men in this town who are dissatisfied and wish to get out of it than in any town I was ever in before," stated a workingman from Minnesota who spent the winter of 1859 in Galveston. This transience, typical of the antebellum American urban poor, makes it difficult to determine from the federal censuses the persistence of casual labor. Of the more than one thousand Galvestonians with occupations enumerated in the 1850 federal census, for example, only two hundred also appeared in the 1860 census. Of these, fewer than ten had been listed as "laborers" in 1850; all were engaged in casual labor in 1860 as well. Some who remained casual laborers, however, prospered. For example, Antone Herman, an immigrant from Prussia who arrived in Galveston in 1848, listed his occupation in 1850 as "hunter"—probably stalking the wild game of Galveston Island and Southeast Texas to sell in the city market. By 1860 he was listed in the census as a laborer, but he probably continued to supplement the family income through hunting since in 1870 he again claimed hunting as his main occupation. By that time, however, he was also a member of the Screwmen's Benevolent Association, an organization of longshoremen whose specialization in packing cotton into the holds of ships made them among the highest-paid unskilled workers in the last decades of the nineteenth century. Herman by 1870 had also managed to purchase a home and several other houses in Galveston and amassed personal property valued at four thousand dollars. Other laborers did not fare so well. Frederick Brandies, for example, remained a laborer during the decade of the 1850s, and though he managed to acquire a house, its value of five hundred dollars represented one of the poorest such properties in the city. For casual laborers—frequently immigrants who had not been brought up to the social etiquette of slavery—the material benefits of white supremacy were not apparent.[32]

Their poverty and lack of a political voice in local affairs no doubt also made it clear to poor white Galvestonians that their material condition lay closer to that of the slaves than to the middle and upper classes in the city. In 1850, for example, 45 percent of the city's families possessed no real property, and another 25 percent owned less than a thousand dollars' worth of property. Thus more than three out of four working families in Galveston owned nothing or only small homes. On the other hand, 5 percent of heads of families possessed more than ten thousand dollars' worth of real estate, and the wealthiest 4 percent of heads of households—those with more than ten thousand dollars in real estate holdings—owned 59 percent of all real estate in the town. Slaveholders, though representing only 4 percent of the total white population in 1850 and only 3.9 percent in 1860, owned 51 percent of all real property in 1850 and 64 percent in 1860. Slaveholders' share of personal property, which included slaves, was even greater—77 percent in 1860.[33] Such disparity of wealth was clearly apparent. The fine houses of the elite and the modest but relatively spacious homes of the emerging middle class lay toward the gulf side of city, away from the noise and smells of the port. Most of the poor white and living-out enslaved black people, on the other hand, lived in one- or two-room houses, shanties, or shacks along the streets and alleys surrounding the port. Visitors noted that the wealthy not only dressed in the finest clothing themselves but strove on special occasions to outdo one another in dressing their bondspeople in the most extravagant clothing.[34]

Municipal politics, another avenue of opportunity that had opened for workingmen during the Jacksonian period, was not available in Galveston.[35] Few if any working-class men ever held state or federal office in Texas during the antebellum period, and even at the local level, officeholding was dominated by slaveholders and their wealthy allies. During the antebellum period, for example, 62 percent of elective and appointive municipal offices were held by slaveholders. In 1860, 96 percent of officeholders owned slaves even though only 17 percent of all families held bondsmen. Frequently a single slaveholder held numerous municipal offices over the years. Lent Hitchcock, for example, served as alderman, harbormaster, and treasurer from 1839 through 1852 and was succeeded as treasurer by his son, Frank Hitchcock. Frank Hitchcock served as treasurer or port warden, an office with responsibility for examining ships for signs of disease, free black sailors, and runaway slaves, for almost a decade during the antebellum period.[36]

From Galveston's founding, slaveholders took for granted their political domination of the city. The town's first charter, approved by the Republic of Texas Congress on January 28, 1839, provided for a city council of eight aldermen, a mayor, and a recorder and required all officeholders to possess at least five hundred dollars' worth of real estate within the corporate limits.[37] In consequence of the property requirements, only about thirty-five of Galveston's three thousand residents possessed sufficient property to qualify for office. A charter revision in 1840 required voters to own at least five hundred dollars' worth of real estate.[38] In February 1844 yet another new charter eliminated the property qualifications for voting, but instituted a property requirement of one thousand dollars for aldermen.[39] In 1856 the charter was amended again. The number of wards was increased to four and the number of aldermen was increased to twelve. Responding to agitation by white artisans, the city now allowed white males twenty-one and older who had rented at least twelve months previous to the day of the election and paid all poll taxes to vote. Property requirements for officeholding, however, remained at one thousand dollars for mayor and aldermen.[40] As a result of the property requirements, in 1850 only 20 percent of the white males twenty-one years or older qualified for officeholding. In 1860 the percentage of white adult males eligible for office had increased to 36 percent of all white males older than twenty-one. Coincidentally, approximately 36 percent of Galveston's eligible residents actually voted in Texas's 1861 secession referendum, which passed in Galveston County 765 to 33, perhaps indicating a citizenry habituated to avoiding political affairs.[41]

Mired in poverty with few opportunities to improve their economic condition, so unmoored from the community that they eagerly sought their fortunes elsewhere, and virtually barred from political participation because they owned no property, Euro-American casual laborers clearly had little stake in the democracy of whiteness that racially cemented the white South together. Casual laborers, furthermore, worked with enslaved African Americans at arduous, dangerous, and poorly paid jobs for hours and days at a time and often continued their associations beyond the workplace, giving rise to a benign association, if not an affinity, with the enslaved people with whom they worked, lived, and caroused. Consequently, as scholars of "whiteness" assert, Galveston's casual laborers did not seize upon the "white identity" that shaped the attitudes of free workers in the antebellum North.[42] While Galveston's white workers no doubt knew that slavery legally placed black bondspeople below them in the South's social hierarchy, the common experiences they shared with enslaved African Americans suggests that at times, at least, they recognized their common humanity. The enslaved people, practiced at maintaining wary relations with white folk, nevertheless psychologically benefited from the acceptance implicit in their interactions with white workers and recognized that such relationships could prove materially beneficial in their struggle with slavery. Despite the dearth of evidence of the attitudes of white and black laborers toward each other, and despite the certainty that animosity and suspicion characterized some or even most of the relationships between them, a rough equality not uncommon among denizens of

Atlantic port cities existed at times that undermined the rigid white supremacy expected by slaveholders and others who supported the southern slave regime. It is clear from the repeated efforts of the city's slaveholding elite to curb biracial interaction and forestall relationships from developing that they recognized the threat such relations posed to slavery and the social system based upon it. Slaveholders never questioned the "whiteness" of casual laborers, but rather regarded them with contempt for occupying a low social strata that brought them into daily interaction with slaves and that thereby led them to forsake the principles and moral duties of white supremacy. Such racial apostasy, slaveholders believed, upset the social order by encouraging otherwise docile black people to strain against the bonds of slavery. "It is no easy matter," wrote one slaveholder, "to estimate the influence a few vulgar, unprincipled white men can, in a short time, exert over a large community of ignorant negros, who, if not tampered with, would remain quiet, inoffensive and dutiful."[43]

Notes

This chapter originally appeared in *Journal of Social History* 40 (Spring 2007): 717–30, and is reprinted with permission.

1. *Austin State Gazette*, July 22, 1854.
2. Ira Berlin and Herbert Gutman, "Natives and Immigrants, Free Men and Slaves: Urban Workingmen in the Antebellum South," *American Historical Review* 99 (December 1983): 1177. See also Timothy Lockley, *Lines in the Sand: Race and Class in Low Country Georgia, 1750–1860* (Athens, GA, 2001), chapter 3; Michele Gillespie, *Free Labor in an Unfree World: White Artisans in Slaveholding Georgia, 1789–1860* (Athens, GA, 2000), 131–34; John Gjerde, "'Here in America There Is Neither King nor Tyrant': European Encounters with Race, 'Freedom,' and their European Pasts," *Journal of the Early Republic* 19 (1999): 673–90; John Bezis-Selfa, "A Tale of Two Ironworks: Slavery, Free Labor, and Resistance in the Early Republic," *William and Mary Quarterly* 56 (1999): 677–700; Randall M. Miller, "The Enemy Within: Some Effects of Foreign Immigrants on Antebellum Southern Cities," *Southern Studies* 24 (Spring 1985): 30–53.
3. John Hope Franklin and Loren Schweninger, *Runaway Slaves: Rebels on the Plantation* (New York, 1999), 69–71, 109–11, 130, 278–79. Three of the most important studies that document the corrosive effects of city life on slavery are Ira Berlin, *Slaves without Masters: The Free Negro in the Antebellum South* (New York, 1974); Richard C. Wade, *Slavery in the Cities: The South, 1820–1860* (New York, 1964), 250–52; Barbara Jeanne Fields, *Slavery and Freedom on the Middle Ground: Maryland during the Nineteenth Century* (New Haven, 1985), 3–4, 28–38.
4. David T. Gleeson, *The Irish in the South, 1815–1877* (Chapel Hill, 2001),

124–29. See also Fred Siegel, "Artisans and Immigrants in the Politics of Late Antebellum Georgia," *Civil War History* 27 (September 1981): 21–30; Jeff Forret, "Slaves, Poor Whites, and the Underground Economy of the Rural Carolinas," *Journal of Southern History* 70 (November 2004): 783–824. Several excellent studies of African Americans in the antebellum South discuss the relations among waterfront workers in port cities, which shared with northern ports an open, cosmopolitan character that militated against strict racial hierarchy. For southern ports, see David S. Cecelski, *The Waterman's Song: Slavery and Freedom in Maritime North Carolina* (Chapel Hill, 2001), 37–39; Christopher Phillips, *Freedom's Port: The African American Community of Baltimore, 1790–1860* (Urbana, 1997), 30–113; Fields, *Slavery and Freedom on the Middle Ground*, 40–62; Bernard E. Powers Jr., "Black Charleston: A Social History, 1822–1885" (PhD diss., Northwestern University, 1985), 20–22; Whittington Bernard Johnson, *Black Savannah, 1788–1864* (Fayetteville, AR, 1996), 85–132; Betty Wood, *Women's Work, Men's Work: The Informal Slave Economies of Lowcountry Georgia* (Athens, GA, 1995), 81–121; Graham Russell Hodges, *Slavery, Freedom, and Culture among Early American Workers* (Armonk, NY, 1998), 127–44. For northern port cities, see for example, Paul A. Gilje, *Liberty on the Waterfront: American Maritime Culture in the Age of Revolution* (Philadelphia, 2004), 25–27, 63. Other historians have argued that for political, social, economic, and psychological reasons, European American workers in the antebellum North embraced a "white identity" that precluded the development of cordial relations with African Americans and bolstered white supremacy. See David R. Roediger, *The Wages of Whiteness: Race in the Making of the American Working Class* (New York, 1991); Matthew Frye Jacobson, *Whiteness of a Different Color: European Immigrants and the Alchemy of Race* (Cambridge, MA, 1998); Noel Ignatiev, *How the Irish Became White* (New York, 1995). For cogent criticism of "whiteness" studies as an interpretive framework, see Arnesen, "Whiteness and the Historians' Imagination," *International Labor and Working Class History* 60 (Fall 2001): 3–32; and Peter Kolchin, "Whiteness Studies: The New History of Race in America," *Journal of American History* 89 (June 2002): 154–73.

5.   Marcus Rediker, *Between the Devil and the Deep Blue Sea: Merchant Seamen, Pirates and the Anglo-American Maritime World, 1700–1750* (New York, 1987), 29, 62–63, 68, argued that seamen in the eighteenth century represented a maritime proletariat whose cosmopolitan perspective, shared experiences, respect for nautical skills, and common exploitation created a rough equality at sea and on shore. W. Jeffrey Bolster, on the other hand, argued that racism and white supremacy pervaded this maritime world. Yet Bolster noted that at sea, respect for nautical skill often muted racism and that African American seaman often identified themselves and were identified according to circumstances by race, class, or skill. Bolster, *Blackjacks: African American Seamen in the Age of Sail* (Cambridge, MA, 1997), 35.

6.   Howard N. Rabinowitz, *Race Relations in the Urban South, 1865–1890* (Athens, GA, 1996), 97–98, 128. Rabinowitz, however, does admit that enslaved and free

black people found opportunities in southern cities, 62–63. Howard N. Rabinowitz, "From Exclusion to Segregation: Southern Race Relations, 1865–1890," *Journal of American History* 63 (1976): 325–50.

7.   W. A. Droddy Diary, transcript, Center for American History, University of Texas at Austin, June 7, 1846. There was also an "African church" in Galveston in the mid-1840s. Fanny O. Trueheart, Galveston, to Kitty T. Minor, Thompson's Cross Roads, Virginia, August 21, 1846, Trueheart Family Papers, 1822–1904, Rosenberg Library, Galveston, TX.

8.   Earl Fornell, *The Galveston Era: The Texas Crescent on the Eve of Secession* (Austin, 1961), viii, 23; Randolph B. Campbell, *An Empire for Slavery: The Peculiar Institution in Texas, 1821–1865* (Baton Rouge, 1989), 4.

9.   *Houston Telegraph*, August 19, 1837.

10.   Kenneth W. Wheeler, *To Wear a City's Crown: The Beginnings of Urban Growth in Texas* (Cambridge, MA, 1968), 120.

11.   Fornell, *Galveston Era*, 24; Charles W. Hayes, *Galveston: History of the Island and the City from Discovery of the Island in 1526, from the Founding of the City in 1837, down to the Year 1879* (Cincinnati, 1879; repr., Austin, 1974), 1:322–23; Richard G. Lowe and Randolph B. Campbell, *Planters* and *Plain Folk: Agriculture in Antebellum Texas* (Dallas, 1987), 18.

12.   Antebellum census enumerators listed the occupation of workers so employed as "laborers," though other job descriptions such as draymen, cotton press operators, and boatmen also fall into the category of casual labor.

13.   Hayes, *Galveston*, 1:322–23; Log 284, Manuscripts Collection, G. W. Blunt White Library, Mystic Seaport Museum, Inc. Also see *Galveston Weekly News*, December 21, 1858.

14.   Fornell, *Galveston Era*, 115–25; Paul D. Lack, "Urban Slavery in the Southwest" (PhD diss., Texas Tech University, 1973), 42–45; Mrs. Frederick M. Burton, *History of Galveston, Texas*, typescript, Letter #10, p. 5, Southwest Collection, Texas Tech University; *Galveston Weekly News*, December 21, 1858; Wheeler, *To Wear a City's Crown*, 120.

15.   *Galveston Weekly News*, September 25, 1853.

16.   Manuscript returns of the Seventh Census and Eighth Census of the United States, Galveston County, Schedule I, *Free Inhabitants*, Schedule II, *Slave Inhabitants*, 1850 and 1860, microfilm, Fondren Library, Rice University, Houston (henceforth cited as Seventh Census or Eighth Census with appropriate schedule).

17.   Proceedings of the Mayor and Board of Aldermen for the City of Galveston, 1849–1855, City Secretary's Office, City Hall, Galveston, August 30, 1850, September 30, 1851, February 3, 1849.

18.   Seventh Census, *Population, Slave Inhabitants*; John Sydnor v. C. C. Moore, et al., 1849; also see Thomas J. Lewis v. Joseph Bates, 1849, Thomas Lewis v. Elanor Spann, 1853, Charles Schaeffer v. Elisha O. Lynch, 1852, Records of the County Court, Galveston County Courthouse, Galveston.

19.   *Galveston Civilian and Gazette*, October 20, 1857; *Galveston Weekly News*, April 18,

1855; *Charter and Revised Code of Ordinances of the City of Galveston*, 1856–1857, Rosenburg Library, 83.

20. Berlin, *Slaves without Masters*, 265; *Revised Code of Ordinances*, 81.

21. For elsewhere on the south, see Timothy J. Lockley, "Crossing the Race Divide: Interracial Sex in Antebellum Savannah," *Slavery and Abolition* 18 (1997): 159–73; Timothy J. Lockley, "Trading Encounters between Non-Elite Whites and African Americans in Savannah, 1790–1860," *Journal of Southern History* 66 (2000): 25–48; also see Michele K. Gillespie, "Artisan Accommodation to the Slave South: The Case of William Talmage, a Blacksmith, 1834–1847," *Georgia Historical Quarterly* 81 (1997): 265–86; Gillespie, "Planters in the Making: Artisanal Opportunity in Georgia, 1790–1830," in *American Artisans: Crafting Social Identity, 1750–1850*, ed. Howard B. Rock, Paul A. Gilje, and Robert Asher (Baltimore, 1995), 33–47.

22. Eugene Marshall Papers, Diary, Special Collections, Duke University, Durham, NC, 4:4, 8, 90.

23. Reports of the Comptroller of Public Accounts, Ad Valorem Tax Division, Galveston County Real and Personal Property Tax Rolls, 1837–88, Texas Room, Houston Public Library, Houston, 1855–60 (henceforth referred to as Tax Rolls with appropriate year); Marshall Diary, 4:90.

24. *Civilian and Galveston Gazette*, November 2, 1844; *Galveston Weekly News*, September 20, 1853; Minutes of the City of Galveston, 1849–1955, Galveston City Clerk's Office, April 1, July 14, July 20, 1854.

25. *Galveston Weekly News*, June 10, 1856, October 2, 1856; March 6, 1860.

26. For editorials against the selling of liquor to slaves, see *Galveston Civilian*, April 9, 1856; *Galveston Daily News*, March 21, 1857; November 7, 1859; *Revised Code of Ordinances*, 23.

27. *Galveston Civilian*, May 7, 1849, and November 12, 1852.

28. *Galveston Civilian and Gazette*, July 22, 1851; *Revised Code of Ordinances*, 26, 57, 23.

29. Emmanuel Henri Diedonne Domeich, *Missionary Adventures in Texas and Mexico: A Personal Narrative of Six Years' Sojourn in Those Regions* (London, 1859), 223; Hayes, *Galveston*, 1:335, 347; *Revised Code of Ordinances*, 83.

30. *Revised Code of Ordinances*, 79–85, 45; *Galveston Daily News*, July 12, 1859.

31. Hayes, *Galveston*, 1:322.

32. Federal Censuses of 1850, 1860, 1870; Galveston County Tax Rolls; Marshall Diary, 4:30. For the transience of Americans and the working class in particular during the nineteenth century, see Stephen Thernstrom, *Poverty and Progress: Social Mobility in a Nineteenth Century* (Cambridge, MA, 1964); Michael B. Katz, Michael J. Doucet, and Mark Stern, *The Social Organization of Early Industrial Capitalism* (Cambridge, MA, 1982); Clyde Griffen and Sally Griffen, *Natives and Newcomers: The Ordering of Opportunity in Mid-Nineteenth-Century Poughkeepsie* (Cambridge, MA, 1978).

33. Wealth-holding figures for Galveston derive from Campbell and Lowe and from

samples from the 1850 and 1860 federal population census. Seventh Census, *Slave Inhabitants*; Eighth Census, *Slave Inhabitants*.

34. Seventh Census, *Slave Inhabitants*; Eighth Census, *Slave Inhabitants*; Fornell, *Galveston Era*, 116–17.

35. For more on antebellum Texas politics, see Walter L. Buenger, *Secession and the Union in Texas* (Austin, 1984); Robert Kingsley Peters, "Texas: Annexation to Secession" (PhD diss., University of Texas at Austin, 1977); Ernest Wallace, *Texas in Turmoil: The Saga of Texas, 1849–1875* (Austin, 1965). For Jacksonian democracy, see Arthur M. Schlesinger Jr., *The Age of Jackson* (Boston, 1945); Marvin Myers, *The Jacksonian Persuasion: Politics and Belief* (Stanford, 1957); William J. Cooper, *Liberty and Slavery: Southern Politics to 1860* (New York, 1983).

36. Richardson and Richardson, *Galveston Directory for 1859–1860*, 33–35; Seventh Census, *Slave Inhabitants*; Eighth Census, *Slave Inhabitants*.

37. H. P. N. Gammel, comp., *Laws of the Republic of Texas*, 1839 (Houston, 1839), 4:94–99.

38. Tax Rolls, 1840; Gammel, *Laws of the Republic of Texas*, 1840 (Houston, 1840), 266–73.

39. Ibid.

40. H. P. N. Gammel, comp., *Special Laws of the State of Texas* (Austin, 1898), 4:154.

41. Tax Rolls, 1840; Seventh Census, *Free Inhabitants*; Eighth Census, *Free Inhabitants*; Earnest William Winkler, ed., *Journal of the Secession Convention* of Texas (Austin, 1912).

42. For criticisms of the concept of "whiteness" and identity as a category of historical analysis, see Arnesen, "Whiteness and the Historians' Imagination," and Barbara J. Fields, "Whiteness, Racism, and Identity," *International Labor and Working Class History* 60 (Fall 2001): 48–56.

43. *Austin State Gazette*, July 22, 1854.

ROBERT E. ZEIGLER

The Cowboy Strike of 1883

Its Causes and Meaning

In the two decades that followed the Civil War, the open-range cattle industry dominated the Great Plains, then died and was replaced by enclosed range ranching and stock farming. In Texas the movement to enclose the range began in earnest in the early 1880s and was completed by 1890. During this transitional period there was also a great upsurge in European and Eastern investment in cattle, bringing owners who viewed ranching primarily as a profit-making enterprise rather than as a way of life. Cattle raising, like other businesses in the Gilded Age, was becoming a corporate affair.[1] Growing corporate activity resulted in problems for the cowboy similar to those faced by workers in other industries during the same period.[2]

In addition to having problems in common with other workers, the cowboy, in some rare instances, reacted by forming cooperatives to protect himself from the capricious whims of employers, and on occasion, he went out on strike.[3] One such incident was an 1883 cowboy strike in the Texas Panhandle. A group of dissatisfied hands demanded wage increases and launched a protest that lasted two-and-a-half months before ending in failure.

The strike has been treated by other scholars who mention that ownership changes occurring in the Panhandle region helped to bring on the conflict. However, these scholars do not consider the causes of the strike or its failure in detail. It is the purpose of this chapter to examine these factors in the hope that such an examination will help to put the cowhand in better prospective as a workingman.[4] Such a study does substantiate Kenneth Porter's recent assertion that the infrequency of cowboy strikes cannot be solely attributed to the independent, carefree, and free-spirited nature of the cowhand.[5] Indeed, a realistic examination of the various determinants leading to the outbreak of the Panhandle walkout creates serious doubts about the validity of any romanticized picture of the cowboy.[6]

There were five ranches involved in the 1883 strike—the LIT, T-Anchor,

LE, LS, and the LX.[7] All were controlled by large corporations or by individuals whose actions indicate an interest in ranching largely as a speculative venture for quick profit. The LIT was owned by a Scottish syndicate, the Prairie Cattle Company.[8] The T-Anchor was controlled by the Gunter-Munson Company, which was involved in land speculation as well as ranching.[9] The LE was owned by the American-based Reynolds Land and Cattle Company. This firm had some financial backing from John M. Bond of the Alliance Trust, a Scottish company.[10] The Lee Scott Company owned the LS.[11] The LX brand was brought to the Panhandle in 1877 by two Boston men, W. H. Bates and David T. Beals, who sold out in 1884 to the American Pastoral Company. All these ranches grew rapidly. Typical of the growth was the LX. After an initial concentration on cattle buying, LX representatives in 1882 began to accumulate land and by 1885 had purchased 123,680 acres.[12] The large ranches had, by 1883, also established the practice of fencing as a means of safeguarding their lands and protecting their cattle.

This trend in the Panhandle ranch industry in the 1880s toward corporate activity and large landholdings had a tremendous effect on the status of the cowboy. The man engaged in working cattle had traditionally viewed a brand mark as the demonstration that property concentrated itself in herds. The cowboy had been devoted to his job of protecting the cattle, and among the hands there had developed a high sense of group solidarity. Also, the owners had usually been in constant touch with their employees, thereby establishing the feeling of a common interest between workers and boss. As holdings became larger it proved much more difficult for a cowboy to feel personal fealty to the new symbol of property concentration, the fenced range and the corporation.[13]

As Tascosa Sheriff Jim East explained in 1884, loyalty was breaking down because "the cow business is not what it used to be. You take such men as John Chisum or Charley Goodnight. They were real people. . . . Their cowboys would have died in the saddle rather than have complained. See what we have now; a bunch of organized companies. Some of them are foreign and have costly managers and bookkeepers who live on and drink the best stuff money can buy and call their help cow servants."[14] Not only was there a breakdown of loyalty, there was a definite feeling of resentment toward those outsiders who, out of ignorance or arrogance, failed to recognize that in ranch country, titles and inherited wealth meant little. Rather, status had to be achieved.[15] Thus, John McNalty, a director of the Spur Ranch who insisted that he be driven around his Texas holdings in a buggy with an umbrella to shield him from the sun, very nearly had his hat and buggy shot full of holes by disdainful ranch hands. Likewise, Mrs. John Adair, the wife of the eastern partner of the Panhandle rancher Charles Goodnight, had to be protected from a kidnapping planned by sensitive westerners.[16]

This feeling of alienation on the part of the cowboy was, according to Lewis Atherton, intensified by the establishment of stockmen's organizations such as the Panhandle Plains Stock Association, which was formed in 1881.[17] These groups consisted of owners and managers, not of hands. While the meetings of stockmen's associations did not deal with such matters as wages or working conditions, the fact that cowboys were not represented helped to break down the common bond between employer and employee.[18]

The large companies made other changes that adversely affected the position of the small owner as well as the common hand. In the 1870s the ambitious Texas cowboy could become a small owner by taking part of his pay in calves and by branding mavericks (unbranded calves).[19] He was usually allowed to pasture his cattle along with his employer's. As alien and unsympathetic ranchers moved into the Panhandle region, these practices were eliminated. The cattle baron was interested in expanding his own holdings and refused to help in elevating his employees to the status of owner.[20] Additionally, rising land prices increased the difficulty faced by the hand who desired to become a land owner.[21]

Moreover, working conditions were not improving even though it was evident the cattle industry was booming.[22] The Panhandle cowhand's work consisted primarily of riding fence line, branding cows, and doctoring sick animals. He usually slept in a dugout or tent, and lacking dishes, often ate out of a common pot. His life was lonely and hard, wholly lacking in glamour and romance.[23] The best-known aspect of ranch work, the roundup, was held twice a year, in September and April, and required a relatively large work force. Once the roundup was completed, one-half to three-fourths of the men were discharged, each employer keeping only a small group of regular workers to man line camps and to perform assorted menial tasks around the ranch.[24] The hand's pay varied according to his dependability and skill. An ordinary ranch worker usually made from $30 to $40 a month, a top hand received $40 to $45, while a wagon boss might draw as much as $125 monthly.[25] The pay was definitely earned, for during the busy roundup periods the cowboy worked a grueling 105-five hour week.[26]

This wage scale compares favorably with that of other workers. For a sixty- to seventy-two-hour week the average industrial employee in Texas earned only twenty-three dollars a month. In counties that were actively engaged in manufacturing, the pay was thirty-three dollars a month. Thus a cowboy who was a permanent and not just a roundup hand earned a relatively good wage.[27]

The lack of year-round demand for employees meant, however, that cow-boys were essentially a seasonal work force with little job security. Adding to the insecurity of employment was the existence of a ranch labor surplus in Texas during the 1880s.[28] Also working against the development of job security was the very nature of ranch work itself. While requiring a knowledge of stock and a measure of horsemanship, the job was not so skilled as to be exclusive. This is evidenced by the lack of any effective division of labor and by the fact that employers placed a higher premium on loyalty and reliability than on any par-ticular skill.[29] The tradition of loyalty, combined with the oversupply of labor, made protest on the part of the hand who was fortunate enough to have a steady job both difficult and hazardous. In spite of the difficulty and hazard involved, some Panhandle cowboys did decide to use the only real weapon the working man possessed, the strike.

In late February or early March of 1883, the LIT, the LS, and the LX ranches had "floating outfits" that followed drift cattle.[30] The wagon bosses were Waddy Peacock for the LIT, Tom Harris for the LS, and Roy Griffin for the LX. The three crews were camped at the LS supply depot, near the mouth of the Frio Creek and east of the present location of Hereford, Texas.[31] These men, dis-tressed by the changing conditions in the ranching industry, drew up an ulti-matum to be submitted to the ranch owners. They demanded a raise in pay to fifty dollars a month for regular hands and cooks, and seventy-five dollars for a range boss. The men set March 31 as their strike date and ended their declara-tion with the vague warning "anyone violating the above obligations shall suffer the consequences."[32] The ultimatum was signed by twenty-four discontented hands.[33]

The real leader of the strike was Tom Harris. In addition to being a wagon boss he was the owner of a small herd of cattle—a man of ability who was gen-erally respected.[34] Indeed, most of the original strikers were a stable group of small owners or permanent hands. These men, working in a relatively small area the year round, would obviously be most likely to organize. Also, they were the ones most affected by the increasing difficulty of economic advancement. They hoped to improve their worsening position through higher wages. In spite of the increasing difficulty of economic advancement it is doubtful that the hands accepted their wage-earner status as permanent. Money represented a means of becoming an independent entrepreneur, a dream that the cowhands still clung to and that urban workers were only beginning to abandon.[35] Also, higher wages would appeal to all hands and was the concession the owners were most likely to grant. Therefore, while the cowboys were being threatened by the new business developments, they did not try to halt progress, they simply followed the example of other American workers and asked to share its fruits.

This hard-core group of organizers hoped, of course, to unite a sufficient number of hands to force the owners into submission, and various efforts were made in this direction. Harris and his twenty-three companions established a small fund to provide financial aid for needy strikers and attempted to convince all cowboys in the area of the five ranches to refuse to work for less than the hoped-for scale.[36] The success of these organizational efforts was limited. Reports on the number involved in the strike vary from 325 down to a handful of twenty-five or thirty.[37] Available evidence indicates that the number involved was never stable; rather, it changed as hands joined and deserted the organizers. Hence, it is possible that at one time 325 men were involved.[38]

Regardless of the size of the strike, it did pose enough of a threat to cause both ranchers and nonstriking hands to fear violence. The strikers had of course threatened in their ultimatum that "anyone violating the above obligations [wage demands], shall suffer the consequences."[39] This rather vague statement could well have meant that coercive action would be taken against strikebreakers or ranchers—or both. Actually there were only isolated attempts to intimidate noncomplying hands. Individuals argued over the merits of the strike, and on one occasion strike leader Harris warned Kid Dobbs, who had taken a job on the LS, "If you want to keep a whole hide, and know what's good for you, quit the LS at once."[40] Dobbs refused, and Harris, due to judiciousness or timidity, did not follow through on his threat. In fact, there are no reports of injury, and it appears that organized sanctions of hands who violated strike rules were not seriously considered.[41]

Ranchers possibly had more to fear than did nonstriking workers. Newspapers reported that the strikers were planning fence burnings, attacks on ranchers, and indiscriminate killing of cattle.[42] The same reports warned, however, that a company of the Texas Rangers under Lt. John Hoffer was camped and ready for action in nearby Mobeetie.[43] Since no attacks were made on cattlemen, extreme action was unnecessary. There probably were some threats made by overzealous hands, but Harris, in an April 25 letter to the *Texas Live Stock Journal*, denied any plan of organized violence: "I will say that it is not the intention of the cowboys to resort to any violence or unlawful acts to get adequate compensation for their services, but to do so by all fair and legal means in their power."[44] In spite of the absence of violence and the presence of Texas Rangers, Jules Gunter, a T-Anchor owner, prepared for trouble. He had the promise of additional men from Charles Goodnight should it be necessary. Gunter, however, seemed quite able and willing to punish unruly hands. He and some of his nonstriking men filled a nail keg with horseshoes and dynamite, connected a fuse, and placed this homemade land mine near a storehouse where it was thought striking cowboys might take refuge to fire upon the house. A strike delegation did come to the T-Anchor to discuss demands, but nothing more serious than vehement insults and loud profanity occurred.[45]

This sort of preparation was the exception. The ranchers found means of dealing with the strikers that were less eruptive and more effective than dynamite. The T-Anchor, after its initial preparation, merely replaced striking employees.[46] On the LS, L. E. McAllister, the foreman, offered the hands forty dollars a month. It was refused. W. M. D. Lee, the owner, came in from Leavenworth, Kansas, and reprimanded McAllister for not meeting the strikers' demands. Lee's concern, however, was not with the welfare of the men; instead, he reportedly felt a wage increase would keep the cowboys at work until he could secure new ones at the old prices.[47] Lee did hold a conference with Harris, offered him an opportunity to keep his one-hundred-dollar-a-month job, and promised to pay fifty dollars to all top hands recommended by Harris if they would remain on the job. The organizer refused and was promptly fired along with every striker on the LS payroll.[48] In the case of the LIT, thirty-five dollars a month for regular hands and a minimum of sixty-five dollars for wagon bosses was the first and only offer made.[49] The LE manager refused the strikers' demands and discharged his hands.

The ranchers' general attitude toward the strike was one of disbelief, a feeling that their men would not refuse to work. If they did, they should be fired. This attitude did not, of course, prevent at least two of the owners, regardless of their motives, from offering some concessions, which were quickly refused by the strikers. Harris and his followers seemed determined to bring all the ranches involved to terms; they were not willing to accept a compromise from only two. This decision was obviously an error; the cowboys were in no position to force further concessions. Moreover, a partial victory might have made organization more attractive to other hands; defeat merely discredited the entire effort.

Press opinion tended to favor the owners.[50] The attitude was that the hands had a right to ask for the wages they wanted and even had a right to resort to group action. There was general agreement, however, to the qualification expressed by the *Texas Live Stock Journal*. The *Journal* argued that some cowboys were worth "almost any money as *faithful servants*" (italics added) and that these cowboys were entitled to all ranchmen[could] "*afford* to *pay*" (italics added).[51]

Presumably the owners were thought to be the best and fairest judges of what they could "afford to pay."

The news reports spoke of violence being threatened by the hands, referred to Harris as "bold and bad," and viewed the availability of state forces with obvious relief. Yet there was no criticism of the owners and no hint that the hands had just complaints. The consensus was that the employee should seek the goodwill of his employer and that any improvement in pay or conditions should be left to the discretion of the owner.[52]

A rare bit of objectivity was expressed by the *Trinidad Weekly Advertiser.* After reporting that the hands were proposing "to burn the ranches, confiscate the cattle, and kill the owners" the *Advertiser* concluded that "an ordinary cowboy is as explosive as a nitroglycerin bomb, and a good deal more dangerous. We shall watch the war with interest, not caring much which side whips or gets whipped."[53] The ranchers, even while negotiating, expressed confidence in their ability to secure enough new workers to break the strike and, acting on this confidence, made no change in roundup plans.[54] However, at least one ranch, the T-Anchor, found it necessary to pay new hands the fifty-dollar-a-month rate on the understanding that a twenty-dollar wage cut was a distinct possibility.[55] This qualified submission bears out newspaper reports that stressed the seriousness of the strike. It also explains a report by the US Commissioner of Labor that categorized the walkout a success.[56] Any success was somewhat short-lived—the higher wage lasted only a month.[57]

The owners certainly had the advantage. Only a few hands initiated the strike, and with a transient labor force, any type of sustained effort was quite difficult. Moreover, even local cowboys were not unanimous in their views on the revolt, some remaining loyal to the owners rather than joining the walkout. Also, a serious lack of discipline existed among the boycotters. Contemporary accounts indicate that many strikers went to Tascosa, drank up their funds, and then decided to go back to work. Indeed, the pleasures of a town that boasted hospitable saloons and the entertainments of such ladies as "Rocking Chair Emma" were enticing enough to break any strike.[58] The owners' practice of firing recalcitrant cowboys and of hiring those who were sufficiently dutiful certainly helped to break the spirit of the strikers.[59] In the absence of strong class consciousness, effective organization, and sufficient funds, the temptation to seek the owners' favor was understandably strong.

Thus, the actual strike failed after approximately two-and-a-half months.[60] This, however, was not the end of the episode. Following the strike, the Panhandle region was plagued with an outbreak of rustling that most contemporary accounts link with the initial revolt. While it is not true that all strikers became thieves, there is evidence that at least some of the discontented hands, after failing in legitimate labor action, gave vent to their frustration in an illegal manner.[61]

The Panhandle Plains Stock Association, in an effort to stop rustling, in July 1883 officially adopted the practice of blackballing any man fired because of "complicity in any illegal branding."[62] Attempts to bring rustlers to trial failed because, according to the Oldham County grand jury of 1884, investigation revealed "in some instances that witnesses either from fear or moral turpitude are exceedingly loath to give any information and from this cause our investigations have not been so satisfactory to ourselves as could be desired."[63] The stock association also hired Pat Garrett to organize a force to stop the thieves, and began to assign inspectors the job of watching markets and trails for stolen cattle.[64] These actions, combined with the election of responsible public officials, made rustling hazardous.[65] Thus, if strikers were involved in cattle stealing, they soon drifted to other ranches or to other occupations.

Even though they failed to attain their objective, striking hands had responded to the changes brought by industrialism in a manner similar to workers in other sections and in other industries. Cowboys were, to be sure, individualistic and undisciplined—traits that certainly contributed to the walkout's failure. However, the individualism of American workers was not restricted to cowhands; workers in other sections and in other industries also experienced organizational difficulties. Nor does the strike prove that cowboys were more naturally anticorporation than were other groups in American society.[66] Instead, the hands, like many other American workers, opposed some aspects of corporate activity but were nonetheless interested in participating in the economic benefits of a growing industrial society. Higher wages could buy the status and provide the opportunity to advance that the large owners were destroying. However, it must be remembered that the organizers and permanent employees were the elite of the workers and as such were not representative of all hands. That all cowhands did not share the strikers' aspirations is partially proven by the failure of the strike.

It is also true that all cowboys were not agreed on the effectiveness of strikes as a method of obtaining benefits. The power of the owners, plus the labor surplus, made participation in a strike a short cut to unemployment. These conditions, and not merely the unique character of the cowboy, served to split the ranks of the hands and were instrumental in making organization difficult and failure imminent. The ranch worker was truly a victim of the progress that was changing the complexion of the cattle business. He was losing his traditional position, yet he was almost powerless to improve his situation by labor action. In this one instance, and probably others, the hand did not effectively organize, not simply because he was more independent than other workers, but because he was unable to overcome the obstacles thrown up by the conditions that prevailed in the cattle industry.

Notes

This chapter originally appeared in *West Texas Historical Association Yearbook* 47 (1971): 32–46, and is reprinted with permission.

1. Ray Allen Billington, *Westward Expansion: A History* of *the American Frontier* (New York, 1967), 684–85; Rupert N. Richardson, Ernest Wallace, Adrian N. Anderson, *Texas: The Lone Star State* (Englewood Cliffs, 1970), 263–66.

2. See Ruth Allen, *Chapters in the History of Organized Labor in Texas* (Austin, 1941), 33–42.

3. See John Clay, *My Life on the Range* (Norman, 1962), 123, 135; Dulcie Sullivan, *The LS Brand: The Story of a Panhandle Ranch* (Austin, 1968), 69; Kenneth W. Porter, "Negro Labor in the Western Cattle Industry," *Labor History* 10 (Summer 1969), 364–65; and Clifford P. Westermeier, comp. and ed., *Trailing the Cowboy: His Life and Lore as Told by Frontier Journalists* (Caldwell, ID, 1955), 131, 135, for references to other strikes and to the cooperative efforts. The following newspaper citations were taken from the Westermeier Collection: *Texas Live Stock Journal*, *Caldwell Commercial*, *Trinidad Daily Advertiser*, *Fort Collins Courier*, and *Trinidad Weekly Advertiser*. The inaccessibility of the originals made this use necessary. Where it was possible, Mr. Westermeier's reproductions were checked and always proved to be correct.

4. For other, earlier accounts of the strike, see Allen, *Chapters*; John L. McCarty, *Maverick Town: The Story* of *Old Tascosa* (Norman, 1946).

5. Porter, "Negro Labor," 364.

6. It is necessary to keep in mind that this strike involved ranch hands, not drovers. Drovers might work on ranches between drives as roundup hands, but there were three classes of cowboys: regular hands, roundup hands, and drovers.

7. This information is based partially on Allen, *Chapters*. She mentions a list of ranches but gives no citation. Also John Carty, "The History of Tascosa, Texas" (master's thesis, West Texas State University), attributes the strike to the above-mentioned ranches. His information was obtained by individuals who were witnesses to the strike. However, an official government rep said seven ranches were involved but does not name them. Where possible, the list has been verified by checking names with list of ranch workers.

8. Walter P. Webb and H. Bailey Carroll, eds., *Handbook of Texas* (Austin, 1952), 2:1.

9. Ibid., 250, 686, 748–49; Laura V. Hamner, *Short Grass and Longhorns* (1943), 174–75.

10. Harley True Burton, *A History of the J. A. Ranch* (New York, 1966), 28; Hamner, *Short Grass and Longhorns*, 168.

11. Sullivan, *The LS Brand*, 27–33.

12. Webb and Carroll, *Handbook of Texas*, 2:1.

13. Lewis Atherton, *The Cattle Kings* (Bloomington, 1961), 181.

14. Colonel Jack Potter, *The Lead Steer* (Clayton, NM, 1939), 32.

15. Atherton, *Cattle Kings*, 120; Frederick Bechdolt, *Tales of the Old Timers* (New York, 1924), 113–14; R. E. Baird, interview by Western History class at West Texas University, August 23, 1933. Class member's notes are in the Panhandle Plains Museum, Canyon, TX. See also Robert V. Clemer, "British Controlled Enterprise in the West between 1870 and 1900 and Some Agrarian Reactions," *Agricultural History* 27 (1953): 132–41; Charles Goodnight, interview by J. Evetts Haley, July 24, 1925, Panhandle Plains Museum, Canyon, TX; Philip Ashley Rollins, *The Cowboy* (New York, 1922), 88.

16. Atherton, *Cattle Kings*, 120.

17. J. Evetts Haley, *Charles Goodnight: Cowman and Plainsman* (Norman, 1949), 3; Atherton, *Cattle Kings*, 182.

18. Atherton, *Cattle Kings*, 82. See Haley, *Charles Goodnight*, for an example of large company efforts to take over the Panhandle Plains Stock Association.

19. Fred A. Shannon, *The Farmers' Last Frontier, 1860–1897*, vol. 5 of *Economic History of the United States* (New York, 1966), 222; McCarty, *Maverick Town*, 108; LaWanda Cox, "The American Agricultural Wage Earner, 1865–1900: The Emergence of a Modern Labor Problem," *Agricultural History* 22 (1948): 104.

20. Baird interview; *Amarillo Globe News,* 1938 Centennial Edition, 25D; C. May Cohea, "The Cowboy Strike," WPA Project, Panhandle Plains Museum, Canyon, TX, 1; McCarty, *Maverick Town*, 108; Allen, *Chapters*, 36; Sullivan, *LS Brand*, 64–65.

21. Haley, *Charles Goodnight*, 303–4; Lester F. Sheffy, *The Francklyn Land and Cattle Company* (Austin, 1963); Estelle D. Tinkler, "Nobility's Ranche: A History of the Rocking Chair Ranche," *Panhandle Plains Historical Review* 15 (1942): 16.

22. For evidence of the striking cowboy's knowledge of this change in relative position, see Potter, *Lead Steer*, 32; Allen, *Chapters*, 40; *Caldwell Commercial*, March 29, 1883, and *Texas Live Stock Journal*, April 23, 1883, cited in Clifford P. Westermeier, *Trailing the Cowboy* (Caldwell, ID: Caxton, 1955), 124, 128–29.

23. Billington, *Western Expansion*, 684; Shannon, *Farmers' Last Frontier*, 207–8; Rollins, *The Cowboy,* chapter 10; Clifford P. Westermeier, "The Cowboy in His Home State," *Southwestern Historical Quarterly* 58 (October 1954): 228–29.

24. Harley True Burton, "A History of the J. A. Ranch," *Southwestern Historical Quarterly* 22 (April 1928): 363; Cox, "American Agricultural Wage Earner," 103; W. C. Holden, "The Problems of Hands on the Spur Ranch," *Southwestern Historical Quarterly* 35 (January 1932): 198.

25. Holden, "Problems of Hands," 195; Payroll Ledger, April 1885–November 1893, in Spur Records, Southwest Collection, Texas Tech University; Payroll Ledger, 1883–1892, in Alamositas Division, Matador Land and Cattle Company, Ltd., Records, Southwest Collection, Texas Tech University.

26. US Commissioner of Labor, *Strikes and Lockouts, 1887,* Serial No. 2546, Doc. No. 1, 580–83.

27. US Census 1880, vol. 2, *Report on the Manufacturers of the United* States, xvi, 176–79. The panhandle counties reported no manufacturing establishments, thus comparison with industrial workers in the panhandle area is impossible.

28. Holden, "Problem of Hands," 198–99; John S. Spratt, *The Road to Spindletop* (Dallas, 1955), 229.

29. Holden, "Problem of Hands," 196. The unskilled nature of ranch work is borne out by Holden's study of Spur labor, and it is likely that the situation was similar on other ranches in the same area in the same period.

30. This date is approximate. The US Commissioner of Labor places the date of the strike at March 23. The first known newspaper report is on March 12 and indicates the hands had already asked for wage increases. See US Commissioner of Labor, *Strikes and Lockouts, 1887,* 580–83; *Texas Live Stock Journal,* March 12, 1883, in Westermeier, *Trailing the Cowboy,* 125–27.

31. McCarty, *Maverick Town,* 109–10; Allen, *Chapters,* 37; John Arnot, "My Recollections of Tascosa Before and After the Coming of the Law," *Panhandle Plains Historical Review* 6 (1933): 69.

32. "Cowboy Strike Ultimatum," Southwest Collection, Texas Tech University, Lubbock. The original is located at the Panhandle Plains Museum, Canyon, TX. There are reports that better food, larger winter crews, and permission to own and run cattle on the owners' land were also strike demands. However, the ultimatum and newspaper reports mention only wages.

33. The list of names is as follows: Thomas Harris, Roy Griffin, J. W. Peacock, J. L. Howard, W. S. Gaton, J. L. Grissom, S. G. Brown, W. B. Borina, D. W. Peeples, Jas [*sic*] Jones, C. M. Hullett, V. F. Martin, Harry Ingerton, J. S. Morris, Jim Miller, Henry Stafford, Wm. F. Kerr, Juan A. Gomez, Bull Davis, T. D. Holliday, C. F. Goddard, E. E. Watkins, C. B. Thompson, G. F. Nickell.

34. Jack Potter quotes Sheriff Jim East as giving this description of Harris. Potter, *Lead Steer,* 32. This view is substantiated by Harris's conduct during the strike.

35. *The Western Range Cattle Industry Study: Outline of Project* (Denver, n.d.), 9. For an astute survey of the worker's dream of entrepreneurship and its abandonment, see Gerald N. Grob, *Workers and Utopia* (Chicago, 1961).

36. *Fort Collins Courier,* April 12, 1883, in Westermeier, *Trailing the Cowboy,* 124–29; *Denver Republican*, March 27, 1883; US Commissioner of Labor, *Strikes and Lockouts, 1887,* 580–83, for seriousness of the strike. "Cowboy Strike Ultimatum," Southwest Collection; Bechdol, *Tales of the Old Timers,* 1–15; Sullivan, *LS Brand,* 65; Allen, *Chapters,* 36.

37. See US Commissioner of Labor, *Strikes and Lockouts, 1887,* 580–83; *Fort Collins Courier,* April 12, 1883; *Texas Live Stock Journal,* April 28, 1883, in Westermeier,

Trailing the *Cowboy*, 125, 128–29; *Fort Worth Daily Gazette,* March 29, 1883, for varying reports on the number of hands actually involved.

38. This figure is based on the US Commissioner of Labor, *Strikes and Lockouts, 1887*. This report was derived from newspaper accounts and interviews by government representatives; therefore, the figure could be inflated.

39. "Cowboy Strike Ultimatum"; Baird interview.

40. Quoted in Sullivan, *LS Brand*, 68.

41. Nowhere in the news coverage or in memoirs is there the charge that strikers actually injured hands who continued to work. The *Houston Daily Post*, April 24, 1883, reported that the adjutant general had received no reports of "impending serious trouble." There are statements to the effect that trouble was feared or that an individual threatened another. See *Ford County Globe*, May 1, 1883, for an example of this sort of report.

42. *Texas Live Stock Journal*, March 12, 1883; *Caldwell Commercial*, March 29, 1883; *Fort Collins Courier*, April 12, 1883, in Westermeier, *Trailing the Cowboy*, 124–25; *Denver Republican*, March 27, 1883.

43. *Texas Live Stock Journal*, April 28, 1883, in Westermeier, *Trailing the Cowboy*, 127, 129; *Denver Republican*, April 25, 1883.

44. T. B. Harris, Tascosa, TX, to the editor, *Texas Live Stock Journal*, April 25, 1883, in Westermeier, *Trailing the Cowboy*, 125–26.

45. "Judge" L. Gough, "Memoirs," typed manuscript, Panhandle Plains Museum, Canyon, TX, 1935, 203; "The 'T-Anchor,'" *Amarillo Sunday Globe News*, clipping, n.d., Panhandle Plains Museum.

46. Gough, "Memoirs"; Gough, "Reminiscences," typed manuscript, n.d. Panhandle Plains Museum, Canyon, TX; *Graham Leader*, April 21, 1883.

47. Sullivan, *LS Brand*, 66–67; McCarty, *Maverick Town*, 111.

48. McCarty, *Maverick Town*, 111.

49. Sullivan, *LS Brand*, 65; McCarty, *Maverick Town*, 111.

50. The *Fort Worth Gazette*, March 22, 1883, erroneously reported that smallpox in Mobeetie prevented press coverage, but some papers, both in and outside Texas, did cover the strike.

51. *Texas Live Stock Journal*, March 12, 1883, in Westermeier, *Trailing* the *Cowboy*, 124.

52. *Dodge City Times,* April 26, 1883, in *Panhandle Plains Historical Review* 40 (1967), collected by Lonnie J. White; *Texas Live Stock Journal*, March 12, 1883, April 21, 1883, April 28, 1883, in Westermeier, *Trailing the Cowboy*, 124, 126, 130; *Denver Republican*, April 25, 1883; *Fort Worth Gazette*, March 25, 1883; *Graham Leader*, April 21, 1883.

53. *Trinidad Weekly Advertiser*, April 25, 1883, in Westermeier, *Trailing the Cowboy*, 127.

54. *Fort Worth Gazette*, March 25, 1883; *Ford County Globe*, May 1, 1883.

55. Baird interview.

56. For newspaper accounts, see *Fort Collins Courier*, April 12, 1883, in Westermeier, *Trailing the Cowboy*, 125; *Denver Republican*, March 27, 1883; *Denver Republi-*

can, April 25, 1883. On the success, see US Commissioner of Labor, *Strikes and Lockouts, 1887*. This report calls the strike a complete success, which is obviously in error. However, it does seem logical that the report refers to the period when higher wages were being paid. Since the report puts the dates of the strike from March 23 to April 4, it is probable that the higher wages were decided upon early in the strike.

57. Baird interview.
58. For the delights of Tascosa, see Baird interview; Cohea, "The Cowboy Strike," 2. An examination of the 1880–90 minutes of the district court of Oldham County reveals numerous convictions for "vagrancy" and "gaming," thereby indicating a thriving business in prostitution and gambling. Ladies charged with vagrancy usually pled guilty, were fined five dollars and court costs, and went back to work. See Oldham County District Courts, Minutes, vol. 1. These may be found in the County Courthouse, Vega, TX.
59. Potter, *Lead Steer*, 31, 75; McCarty, *Maverick Town*, 117, 123; *Dodge City Times*, May 10, 1883. Waddie Peacock, one of the original strikers, is listed as foreman on a list of employees of the LS in 1898. This list may be found in the Panhandle Plains Museum, Canyon, TX. The Oldham County District Court minutes show J. L. Grissom as being a juror on several occasions in 1884 and 1885.
60. The government reported the strike over on April 4, but newspapers did not mention it ending until late April. The *Houston Daily Post* reported it over on April 25, but the April 28, 1883, *Texas Live Stock Journal* reported the strike sufficiently strong to endanger the success of the May 10 roundup. The *Graham Leader*, April 28, 1883, reported one hundred cowboys on strike. The last press mention was in the *Dodge City Times,* May 10, 1883. Thus the strike ended sometime between April 25 and May 10.
61. Baird interview*;* Sullivan, *LS Brand*, 67. Potter, *Lead Steer*, 30, quotes Sheriff Jim East as saying the strike was still going on in September of 1884, which indicates some trouble was still occurring. Louis Bousman, "Reminiscences," prepared by the personnel of the WPA, Panhandle Plains Museum, Canyon, TX, 1934); Fred Post, "He Escaped Boot Hill to Help Capture Billy the Kid," *Amarillo Globe News,* 1938 Centennial Edition, 12E; Haley, *Charles Goodnight*, 376. The "Hoggie" that Haley holds responsible for much of the rustling was Tom Harris's brother-in-law. See McCarty, *Maverick Town*, 112–13. Although some strikers probably resorted to rustling, it hardly seems accurate to assume rustling was actually a part of the strike. Instead, it is more likely that some or many strikers refused to back down, were fired, and became rustlers.
62. Panhandle Stock Association Constitution and Minutes, 1883, Panhandle Plains Museum, Canyon, TX.
63. Oldham County District Court, Minutes, 1:92.
64. McCarty, *Maverick Town*, 129; Panhandle Plains Stock Association Constitution and Minutes, 1883.

65. Haley, *Charles Goodnight*, 380; *Ford County Globe*, April 19, 1883.
66. See Allen, *Chapters*, 33, for the account that cowboys and corporations were naturally antagonistic. See the essay "The Robber Baron in the Gilded Age: Entrepreneur or Iconoclast?" in *The Gilded Age*, ed. H. Wayne Morgan (Syracuse, 1963) 14–37, for a good summary of the attempts on the part of American society to adjust to the corporation.

THERESA A. CASE

The Radical Potential of the Knights' Biracialism

The 1885–1886 Gould System Strikes and Their Aftermath

In 1941 an elderly white socialist named Patrick Cassidy wrote to Ruth Allen, a historian of the Southwest railway strike of 1886. Cassidy had participated in that strike under the leadership of District Assembly 101 of the Knights of Labor, along with thousands of other railroad workers on Jay Gould's Southwest system of railways in Kansas, Texas, Arkansas, Missouri, and Illinois.[1] The walkout involved a broad spectrum of railway occupations, from unskilled trackmen to semiskilled switchmen to skilled shop workers. In his letter, Cassidy mentioned that at the beginning of the conflict, the Knights had taken over the railroad yards in Palestine, Texas, and had made the railway coaches their meeting place. Then he supplied one of the few surviving bits of evidence by a Knight on race relations and the strikes:

> The two coaches we got for the whites and the one for the colored people. We had lots of fun going from one car to another . . . that lasted about three weeks. Then the company got out injunctions on us all to keep us from going on the railroad, so that kept us busy running. . . . I believe we sent a colored Blacksmith from Palestine to represent us at the first K. of L. Convention in St. Louis in 1886, and we got credit for sending one of the best delegates at the convention.[2]

Does Cassidy's recollection of interracial camaraderie reveal more about the "interests of the teller"—perhaps a unite-and-fight romanticism—than black-white interactions more than a half century prior in a Texas town with deep roots in the Old South?[3] Two sources, also distant in their own ways, confirm his memory of significant black involvement, but in contradictory ways. In June 1886, *John Swinton's Paper* described Palestine's black Knights as "among the most loyal" to the order. Yet, alongside this picture of enthusiastic black support stands the testimony of a railroad contractor who described the same scene in Palestine as Cassidy but who intimated that hierarchy and separation rather than familiarity and cooperation characterized the order's cross-racial alliance. He testified that one coach "was full of negroes, from twenty-five to thirty of them . . . and in another coach, *in the other end of the yard* [my emphasis], there was [the Knights'] general headquarters, and they were claiming that they were protecting the company's property."[4]

What, then, was the nature and significance of the Knights' cross-racial alliance on the Gould system? What experiences, assumptions, worries, and hopes did black and white workers share? In what ways did the structure of work and the racial meanings attached to different kinds of railroad labor divide them? Answers to these questions do not come easily, in part because accounts of both walkouts on the Gould system do not dwell on the issue of race. The strikes never devolved into "race strikes" nor did the railroads or the local press make much mention or use of race until late into the 1886 conflict. Before this point, much of what is documented was said in passing. This was so despite the fact that the racially inclusive Knights organized in a region and era in which racial strife, racial exclusion, and racial violence were endemic. Moreover, although southern Knights typically organized locally on a biracial rather than interracial basis, meaning that black members sought equal or greater power in the workplace but joined separate assemblies from whites, this instance of biracial unionism occurred in an otherwise intensely segregated industry. This raises a further question: why did near silence on the issue of black-white relations, instead of controversy over the specter of social equality, greet Knights' efforts for most of the upheaval?

Historians have long wrestled with interpretations of race and labor. In regard to working-class history, New Labor historians have emphasized the strength of class feeling and their critics the overriding significance of race, or "whiteness," to the history of American workers. More recently, studies of New Orleans dockworkers and Alabama miners have pointed to the complexity and ambiguity of these relations, the gradations between the two extremes of race and class, and eschewed the dichotomy altogether.[5] The latter school has rightly moved the field away from the glass-half-full or nine-tenths-empty approach to understanding working-class race relations.[6] As various scholars have noted, that approach risks missing the degree to which biracialism opened up space for cross-racial activism, and in abstracting social movements from their historical context, it minimizes the power of employers and the state to limit a movement's strategies and aspirations.[7]

On the face of it, a focus on gradations and ambiguity seems ill suited to a history of race and labor on the railroads, where black laborers held considerably less power in the workplace than on the waterfront of New Orleans or the mines of Alabama. Yet "boomer" railroaders on the Gould system, who experienced their workplace as a bastion of racial subordination, managed somehow to establish a connection across the racial divide. Cooperation was rooted in the promises and costs of railroading and in some common notions of manhood and citizenship. White and black racial identities shaped these efforts in contradictory and likely explosive ways, with whites often understanding the alliance within the mythic framework of southern "redemption" at the same time that blacks sought ways to reclaim the political leverage and relative autonomy they had known under Reconstruction. Anti-eastern and anti-Gould sentiment held the coalition together during the strikes, backed up to varying degrees by the threat of racial violence. The bonds that Knights forged were sturdy enough to inspire a wave of black activism that spilled over beyond the railroads into urban politics and the cotton fields of Texas and Arkansas. To a surprising extent, given the context, the story of the Gould system strikes confirms the complex nature of racial identities and suggests the unpredictable and potentially far-reaching outcomes of cross-racial organizing.

Race and Gilded Age Railroading

Certain enduring elements of railroad work opened up the possibility for biracial cooperation. It was generally an unstable and dangerous occupation, whether one was a trackman, trainman, or shopman, but railroaders of various skills, ages, and heritage also shared, albeit to varying degrees, in the social and cultural benefits of railroad work. Their reminiscences often depict railroad labor as, in the words of Paul Michel Taillon, a "heroic, manly confrontation with the task." The task involved performing one's job well, coping with or toughing out even the worst conditions, and doing everything possible to avert disaster. A railroader's manhood, in his own eyes and in the eyes of others, often hinged upon how well he responded to a crisis, the skill with which he executed his job, his reliability or "steadfastness," or simply his tenacity in facing the elements, though the fear of accidents often accompanied occupational pride. Railroading offered the youthful and untried a social ladder to manhood as well. When economic times were good, a black or white youth could easily move from place to place to find work, earn relatively high wages, and come of age. Although the image of railroaders as "men in motion" is overdrawn, a significant number were "boomers," whom economist Victor Clark described as "train hands who drift about the country, working for first one road, and then another." During the 1860s and 1870s, these railroaders found their services most needed, and therefore better compensated, in western areas only recently linked to the East by rail.[8]

Still, despite these shared hazards and benefits, most white railroaders, whatever their skill level, held in common strong racial assumptions about black workers. Whites' cumulative experience on the roads, and in society at large, encouraged them to equate black men and women with poorly paid work or work considered undesirable in general. Their popular slang reveals this: "nigger local" was a brief trip with numerous stops, while "niggertrack" referred to rarely traveled track in an isolated area.[9] A strict racial code reflected these prejudices and governed working relationships. Until the late 1960s and early 1970s and across the United States, the most desirable positions of locomotive engineer and train conductor were reserved for whites only, and in shops and roundhouses throughout the South, whites relegated blacks to the lowest occupational rungs. Exclusion of blacks from the running trades may have been even stricter in the 1870s and 1880s than in the heyday of Jim Crow. Eric Arnesen has described the white backlash to blacks in firing and braking positions on southern railroads at the turn of the twentieth century, but in 1880 few African Americans engaged in this kind of work in Dallas, Texarkana, Marshall, or Little Rock, four major sites of labor unrest on the Gould system. Those who hired on as firemen likely worked for less pay, performed extra duties, and were never promoted to engineer. Railroad work was far more segmented racially than the coal mines of Alabama, which Daniel Letwin finds were "racially mixed from the beginning," with blacks in skilled as well as unskilled occupations.[10]

Black workers, then, faced a stark contradiction on the railroads. At the same time that the occupation provided a chance to affirm ideas about their manhood—to provide for a family, gain some measure of self-sufficiency, and move about—it required black men to conceal these independent and worldly traits from whites. The cultural resources of black workers express frustration with this dilemma. Songs dedicated to the black steel driver John Henry, for example, found widespread appeal among black laborers of all kinds, whose work was otherwise uncelebrated and denigrated by whites and many middle-class black leaders. But what Robin G. Kelley might call a "hidden transcript of resistance" is revealed in less epic tales as well. Unlike John Henry, ex-slave Steve Brown was an ordinary man forced to draw upon all of his skill and courage, the same "manly virtues" white railroaders claimed only for themselves, in avoiding a disaster not of his own making. To an interviewer for the Works Progress Administration, Brown related a story that offered a black "hero of the rails," a fireman who must think and act quickly in a battle against not only technology but also an incompetent white engineer, thereby inverting the famous picture presented on the cover of an 1873 issue of *Harper's Magazine* of a brave white engineer "sticking to his post," with his faithful black helper at his side.[11]

In 1883 Brown found a job as a section man on the Missouri, Kansas and Texas railway. He learned how to fire an engine and worked as a fireman between 1887 and 1895. While in Mississippi on a passenger run, Brown was nearly involved in a terrible wreck. The train was running late. The engineer ordered Brown, "Boy, bear down on dat shovel," because he planned to beat the express train. "He don't have to tell dis nigger to bear down on de shovel, 'cause Ise know weuns have to make de lake sidin' or Ise a gone nigger," Brown recalled. However, the engineer inexplicably pulled the throttle "wide open an' leves it thar," placing the burden upon Brown to "make de steam to get de speed." He had to deposit the coal more carefully than usual so as to maximize its use by the engine. The speed of the train and the low areas in the track led Brown to fear that the train would jump the track, and the rocking of the train across low spots made it difficult to feed the coal. Despite the train's high speed, the engineer never pushed in the throttle. Just as they pulled onto the sidetrack and cleared and closed the switch, the express train "thundered by." Brown's achievement went unrecognized by the company. Though the engineer was discharged for bypassing a stop, Brown was given a thirty-day layoff.[12]

Brown's narrative dramatizes the strength of racial hierarchy on the roads. What it does not reveal is that whites' association between blackness and subordination did not conform to social reality: the unskilled labor force was of mixed ancestry. In 1880 in Little Rock, Arkansas, it was not unusual for both whites and blacks to work as porters, car cleaners, trackmen, and laborers. Forty percent of all laborers in Dallas, Texas, in 1886 were white, and although native-born whites "avoided section work at all costs," a number of white laborers, both native and foreign-born, worked in railroad construction crews and as section hands.[13]

The presence of laborers from varying traditions and backgrounds did not necessarily fracture white racial identity on the roads. According to Walter Licht, ethnic hierarchies among railroaders were declining in significance. While the available evidence on the Gould system relates more to exterior circumstances than to railroaders' interior sense of identity, the 1880 census data for two Texas towns on Gould's Southwest system bears Licht out. In both Marshall and Texarkana, Irish immigrants frequently held skilled positions as engineers, boilermakers, firemen, machinists, and blacksmiths. That a Scottish-born machinist named Martin Irons could readily find skilled railroad employment and lead the 1886 Great Southwest Strike further suggests that the line between immigrant and native-born was less important in railroad work than it once had been.[14]

Combined with a relatively cohesive white racial identity, social mobility limited the extent to which the unskilled identified with one another. White "boomers" could reasonably expect to climb to a more skilled position, and they tended to associate their own dreams of social mobility with control over black labor. Upon meeting a conductor for the first time when he was twelve years old in East St. Louis, Harry French admired the man's immaculate clothes, his self-assurance, and his ability to pay a black man to shine his shoes and "negro waiters in spotless white garments" to serve him dinner. Had French journeyed to Marshall or Texarkana, he almost certainly would have been impressed by the number of conductors and engineers who hired black cooks, washerwomen, and nurses for their families and by the fact that boardinghouses frequently employed black servants to wait on white railroaders.[15]

However, certain conditions cut against racial identities. Unskilled blacks and whites lived in a particular working world, for example. They labored in close proximity to one another, often in remote locations, were more vulnerable to the arbitrary rule of foremen and the vagaries of the labor market, and despite the risks of their work, suffered social stigma, unlike the engineer, whom the public celebrated in story and song as a "hero of the rails" and a pillar of the community.[16] Moreover, the specific work routines of nonbrotherhood men gave rise to distinctive work cultures that made cross-skill and even cross-racial organizing imaginable. Unlike skilled trainmen, who were more isolated and itinerant, skilled shopmen worked in one place and among men of diverse skills and occupations. Not coincidentally, these workers played a leading role in the 1885–86 strikes and identified strongly with the more inclusive Knights, in contrast to conductors, engineers, and firemen, who generally belonged to the craft-based, racially exclusive, conservative brotherhoods. Switchmen and brakemen also played a prominent role in the strikes. Due to their frequent contact with men in the yards of other railroads, the running trades, meatpacking, and freight handling, these semiskilled railroaders traditionally acted as a "natural bridge between workers employed on different roads" and were particularly inclined to engage in sympathy strikes. Finally, however many skilled trainmen looked down on brakemen and switchmen, these railroaders tended to celebrate their reputation as footloose, rowdy risk takers whose precision and nerve were critical to railroad operation.[17]

The power of white workers and railroad officials intertwined to form a taut knot that held Steve Brown and other black workers in place at the bottom of the railroads' social and economic ladder, binding black to black and white to white. Yet another bond pulled brotherhood men in one direction and skilled shopmen, the unskilled, and semiskilled in another. The conditions that western railroaders met with in the 1880s and the Knights' "producer" ideology slackened these knots, allowing a broad coalition to gather against Jay Gould's railroad empire.

A "Union of Producers"

By the 1880s, black and white workers on Gould's Southwest system of roads saw the benefits of railroading endangered. Large-scale migration intensified labor competition, reducing western railroaders' prospects for advancement. At the same time, the railway industry experienced growing financial instability. Increasingly confident in the available labor supply, managers pushed for reductions in labor costs. Companies changed the work rules of brotherhood men, attacked wages, resisted extra payment for overtime and special conditions, and tried to get by with smaller crews. Such was the state of affairs on the system of roads controlled by Jay Gould when in 1884 and 1885, the Wabash, St. Louis & Pacific and the Missouri Pacific railways ordered a series of wage cuts for shopmen, engine wipers, and laborers. Fireman Charles Maier remembered that the news of one of the cuts came to shop employees in midwinter, when "actual privations stared them and their families in the face."[18]

For boomer railroaders, these cost-cutting policies threatened to introduce the same sort of conditions that many had left behind in the East. Slashed and depressed wages meant hardship for railroaders and their families, which in turn frustrated individual and collective efforts to escape dependence—to roam in search of a better situation, contribute to a mutual association, take up collections for injured coworkers, or save to buy a farm or shop. Skilled trainmen faced increasing competition with "extras," or part-timers. Reduced crews labored at a frantic pace that placed an enormous strain on men engaged in what was already a highly dangerous occupation. Such disregard for safety upset the very notion that railroading was a test of manliness.

Between March 7 and 11, 1885, some forty-five hundred railroaders walked off their jobs across the Gould system of roads, principally in Illinois, Missouri, and Texas. The strike won wide public support, as antimonopoly sentiment ran deep in railroad communities, and the conflict's short duration did not seriously strain the resources of farmers, merchants, and other townspeople. Skilled train-men left their posts when prostrike crowds blocked their trains at public cross-ings. Smarting from the depth of strike sympathy and the standstill in freight traffic, representatives from the Missouri Pacific and the Texas & Pacific railway companies met with state leaders in St. Louis on March 15 and agreed to most of the strikers' demands as well as a separate agreement with engineers.[19]

In the aftermath of the March 1885 victory, the Knights of Labor "sprung up overnight" and "took like wildfire" among black and white workers in towns along the Gould system, particularly among railroaders.[20] When the national Knights forced Jay Gould to promise reinstatement of locked-out Knights on the Wabash in September 1885, the order experienced another massive wave of growth.[21] However, managers routinely violated the provisions of the 1885 agreements, particularly in regard to the semiskilled and unskilled. Most of the locked-out Wabash Knights were never rehired as promised. More alarming still, company officials argued that the March 1885 settlement applied only to shopmen, which was clearly not the case. Finally, by December, the Texas & Pacific, like the Wabash, was under receivership and therefore enjoyed special legal protections against strikes. Its new managers told the Knights commit-tee that the March 1885 agreement was null and void. In this context, the dis-missal of T&P Knights leader C. A. Hall following his attendance at a district assembly meeting signified to many Gould system Knights a clear attack on their organization.[22]

The breaking point came in early March, first in railway towns in East Texas and north-central Texas and then in Arkansas, Missouri, Kansas, and Illinois. On March 8, a Missouri newspaper headline read, "Traffic Throttled: The Gould System at the Mercy of the Knights of Labor." Although the situation initially seemed hopeful, ultimately strikers in 1886 could not sustain the level of unity of purpose and action expressed the previous year. Engineers and firemen withdrew from the conflict, because their brotherhoods advised it and because Gould system managers had largely lived up to their agreement with skilled la-bor. Moreover, a rift developed between the walkout's leader, Martin Irons, and national Knights leader Terence Powderly over the strike's tactics and legitimacy. Most important, the courts placed the Texas & Pacific under the control of a US marshal and enjoined strikers on the Missouri Pacific to end their takeovers of shops and yards, blockades of freight traffic, removal and disablement of criti-cal equipment, and interactions with nonstrikers. Some Knights turned to vio-lence as a means of enforcing the walkout, and bloody confrontations between prostrike crowds and company-hired deputies in Fort Worth and East St. Louis brought state troops in to protect freight traffic. By mid-April, the walkout was effectively over.[23]

In 1885 black strikers found a space for themselves alongside whites as part of a local community under attack by a powerful and unpopular outsider. Thus, the *Dallas Daily Herald* reported in clearly approving terms a story about a black strikebreaker who had "returned to the rural district" after receiving "twelve stem-winders with a barrel stove" at the "hands of his own race." But the reluctance of skilled trainmen to participate in the 1886 strike convinced the Knights to appeal directly to unskilled laborers with a list of demands that called for wage increases for all laborers, including section men, trackmen, and crossing watchmen.[24]

Upon examining events in Marshall, Texas, casting white-black participation in 1886 as a biracial alliance seems perverse. The East Texas town was located in a black majority county that only recently had come under Democrats' control. The *Marshall Tri-Weekly Herald* embraced at once "redemption," the Knights, and a murderously antiblack credo. Reporting on the city's July Fourth picnic and barbecue, which area Knights organized and Palestine, Texarkana, and Longview Knights attended, the editor described the procession of the Marshall Knights as a "sturdy patriotic set of men" but ridiculed the "colored brass band" as "out of tune" despite its "airs." An "old time barbecue" followed, the "first . . . spread in this place since antebellum days." The *Herald*'s vision of community was one unsullied by powerful eastern outsiders, whether Republicans, the Union army, or monopolizing railroads. The degree to which this vision relied upon racial terror is revealed in its comments, published several weeks later, on a lynching in nearby Elkhart of five black people who, along with other black townspeople, were rounded up and threatened by a mob until the five "confessed" to raping and killing the young white wife of a local law official. While Texas newspapers often sympathized with lynch mobs, the *Herald*'s warning was unusual among those I surveyed in its venom and sweep: "The lonely grave by the roadside is a warning that colored people would do well to heed."[25] To be fair, the local paper did not necessarily represent the sentiments of white Knights in Marshall, but in this context, for black strikers, the line between coercion and cooperation was likely a thin one, as a Marshall Knights' handbill intimates: "We have resolved to come to the rescue of our downtrodden brethren, known as unskilled laborers. . . . We call upon all laborers, trackmen, engine wipers, coach cleaners, baggage and freight hands, and coal heavers, to lend us their aid. . . . Trackmen, get clear out of sight of the track until we gain your victory."[26] Authored by an overwhelmingly skilled and semiskilled white leadership and addressed to a racially mixed, unskilled workforce, it sympathizes but also instructs and subtly threatens.

As the key spectacle of the 1886 conflict confirms, race was central to white Knights' conception of their struggle all along the Gould roads. In contrast to the March 1885 walkout, in which they had relied upon moral suasion to stop engineers and firemen from running the trains, in 1886 strikers at numerous points immediately and in large numbers overpowered trainmen manning freight engines, took possession of shops and roundhouses, and "killed" or disabled locomotive engines as a means of stopping freight traffic. Some evidence exists of black participation in the first two actions but none survives of the last.[27] The *Waco Daily Examiner*'s description of one very public display of engine sabotage offers us a clue as to why:

> A bold Knight . . . mounted the steps and stood in the cab. Opening the fire doors, he flung in a pocket of water on the fire, and kept it up by drawing water from the tender and throwing it in the fire doors. . . . Soon a brother knight . . . came down, and shoving the throttle valve down against an upright pipe, he tied it fast there . . . and taking a hammer he struck the "connecting link" which holds the hose together [and] runs water from the tender to the engine. . . . Then the big fellow . . . disconnected some more links. . . . [I]n about thirty minutes the engine was dead.[28]

The practice represented a key means by which strikers exerted their power on the roads, since the Knights learned, probably even before the strike commenced, that they could not count on the support of engineers and firemen. But it also communicated white strikers' strong occupational and therefore racial identity, as killing or disabling an engine displayed technical know-how, muscle, determination, and cooperation, the same "manly" qualities that skilled and semiskilled white railroaders most associated with whiteness.

Despite the association between the major symbol of the strike and whiteness, black workers took part in significant numbers. Black strikers were arrested and jailed at Marshall, Palestine, Paris, and elsewhere in Texas. Although exceptional, a more vivid scene of black involvement emerges from a report on crowd action in Palestine that derailed an engine: "Engineer Jack Kimbrough knocked one of the colored strikers from the engine with a hammer, but was soon overpowered by numbers." Moreover, Patrick Cassidy's forty-five-year-old memory that black participation extended to leadership roles is corroborated by other examples. The receiver for the Texas and Pacific, John Brown, met with one black and two white Knights from Denison on the eve of the strike to discuss grievances, and Dallas black leader and Knights supporter Melvin Wade spoke before a mass meeting of fifteen hundred people at the height of the conflict. At the statewide level, David H. Black of Dallas served as an executive board member. He was a key negotiator for Galveston Knights, who had launched a boycott and then strike against the Mallory Company and also spoke in Fort Worth on behalf of the Knights.[29]

Beyond the visibility of Wade and Black, which surely attracted black support to the order, the Knights represented a unique opening for black workers, who were often either dissatisfied with the Republican Party or demoralized by its declining fortunes in southern politics, or both. The Greenback cause had come and gone in Texas and Arkansas.[30] In addition, no other union or fraternal order, and no farmers' organization, allowed black participation, much less leadership. The brotherhoods made whiteness a requirement for membership. The Freemasons, Knights of Pythias, Odd Fellows, and others had long banned black members, forcing parallel organizations to form that went unrecognized by white ones. The Knights admitted all workers, with the significant exception of the Chinese, signaling some white acceptance of the idea that African Americans held economic rights and that they too were "producers" and possibly "brothers."[31] Certainly, some black members saw the organization as a vehicle for racial equality. A number of black newspapers urged readers to participate in the Knights, the only major biracial organization on the horizon willing to challenge the "color line." One white organizer in Indiana complained to Powderly of the efforts of black Knights to integrate a local assembly. One reportedly told him, "This is the only organization in which we stand on an equal footing with the whites, and it is a big thing, and unless we can work here we will work nowhere."[32]

In forming separate assemblies, the Knights both accommodated to and reflected the realities of southern race relations. As Eric Arnesen has noted, biracial unionism "barely required comment, much less debate" in late-nineteenth-century America given the pervasiveness of the color line. The national Knights accepted segregated locals because to require integration at the local assembly level would alienate not only southern whites but also many southern blacks who saw all-black local assemblies as a refuge from white domination. However, in order to satisfy the demands of those black Knights who saw the order as a force for equality, assemblies at the state, district, and national level were integrated. The Knights' white leadership realized that to appeal to African Americans on purely an economic basis would limit the order's ability to organize in the South.[33]

Black Knights who sought equality or at least greater leverage within the labor movement rather than the more controversial, difficult, and often undesired course of integration found in the Knights an appeal to a rough "stomach equality," not civil or political equality. Although Powderly made public allusions to his belief in racial equality, most of his pronouncements and the Knights' literature stressed the common economic interests of black and white working people.[34] Gould system strikers made a similar appeal: the railroad had forced labor "to the wall of subjection" where they could "lay hold of nothing but the bare necessities of life."[35]

Biracialism proved largely uncontroversial for much of the mid-1880s conflict on the Gould system, because the exigencies of economic crisis relaxed the importance strikers attached to racial fraternalism in the same way that it did for Populists. Strikers' communities, whose residents had long seen themselves as victims of eastern capital, easily took up the call to defend the mutual self-interest of local blacks and whites against Gould.[36] Thus, black and white Knights found in the order's appeal to a "union of producers" a broad and elastic ideology that left room for a host of different interactions, goals, and strategies on the part of black and white members. In addition, in organizing across racial lines, white Knights provided unambiguous signs of white control. The public display of engine sabotage expressed white racial identities but also communicated to the public white domination and authority, so that when black striker Wyatt Owens was arrested on trespassing charges, his white jailer did not see him as the source of the trouble; it was "those white son of bitches" he was after.[37]

In regard to C. Vann Woodward's classic thesis that southern white workers swung ambivalently between exclusive and inclusive approaches to black workers, Leon Fink has observed that in Richmond, Virginia, the fact that "black and white workers were not actively competing for the same jobs . . . presented southern white labor leaders with a strategic choice. . . . In short, [they] need not have greeted blacks directly as competitors or as brothers." The situation was comparable for skilled shopmen and semiskilled trainmen. Whites filled these positions, whereas blacks were virtually always regulated to unskilled work. Also, as in Richmond, the Knights in no way explicitly challenged the racial hierarchy at work. However, a greater percentage of whites labored at the bottom of the occupational ladder in Dallas than in Richmond, 40 percent as opposed to 20 percent.[38] Probably it was the need in 1886 to attract a base of unskilled workers, who experienced labor competition across racial lines, that explains why a further element binding black and white Knights proved so important: the demand to drive convict and Chinese labor from the Gould system roads.

How Free Is Free?

Anti-Chinese and anticonvict labor sentiment came in large part from the bottom up. Strikers in numerous Texas towns, and trackmen at the January 1886 Knights state district assembly meeting, related that one of their major grievances was employment of "Chinamen" and convicts on the road.[39] At first glance, neither group worked on the railroads in large enough numbers to warrant strikers' attention. In 1886 only 293 convicts worked on all of Texas's railroads, and the Gould system employed but a hundred or so Chinese in West Texas, far from the scene of the strikes.[40] Still, strikers had some reason to fear that the seemingly all-powerful Jay Gould, whom Knights condemned as "the arch-monopolist of the world," might dramatically and suddenly multiply those numbers. Local newspaper reports fanned fears of economic competition. Railroaders perhaps recalled the Southern Pacific's use of Chinese labor to construct its roads in West Texas in the early 1880s and conjectured that the state might easily and quickly shift the majority of convicts from agriculture to railroad labor.[41]

The conditions that convict laborers experienced more than their numbers help to explain railroaders' alarm. In both Texas and Arkansas, convict leasing received a great deal of bad press and was generally considered barbaric, corrupt, and antagonistic to the interests of free laborers. The large number of successful escapes intensified this opposition. Though a mainly white workforce performed convict labor on the railroads, reports of harrowing conditions frequently surfaced.[42] That the lives and well-being of convict laborers were of so little value to employers beyond their productive capacity likely reminded railroaders of how uncertain and ill-defined the relationship was between free and unfree labor. Black itinerants, who often combined waged agricultural and railroad work in order to make ends meet, likely saw multiple hazards in convict labor: the threat of labor competition on the roads and on the farms but also the threat of arrest and imprisonment for some alleged crime, which could well erase all remaining boundaries between free and unfree labor.

On the Southern Pacific, Chinese workers were paid about half the wages of others, and they were reportedly "treated more like slaves than anything else, they are drove [*sic*] round and sometimes used severely, if they don't work to suit the bosses." However, it is unclear whether strikers were widely aware of the hardships that Chinese workers encountered. This raises the question: why did Gould system railroaders focus on the Chinese when their experiences with these workers were so remote? Beyond the not-irrational concern with Gould's power to rapidly import Chinese, strikers likely sensed in the anti-Chinese cause a means to gain community sympathy and to unify an otherwise racially divided unskilled workforce.[43]

Both strikers and railroad managers appealed to the apparently widespread assumption that, at least in relation to Chinese workers, black and white workers shared a common citizenry. When the receivers for the Texas & Pacific defended the employment of Chinese workers in West Texas, one claimed he would prefer white and black labor because, in his words, "I am an American." The other insisted that Chinese workers were kept at "the lowest grade of labor" and that they were "not worked together with white men or with Negroes either."[44] Black Knights leader Melvin Wade hit upon a similar theme in his March 1886 speech before a gathering of hundreds of strikers and their supporters in Dallas. When asked why the Knights admitted black workers but not Chinese, he replied:

> The Negro never came to this country of his own volition, the white man brought him here and it was only right that he should be cared for and given labor that he was a citizen of this country, but the Chinese never became citizens. . . . Negroes had more rights than the Chinese from the fact that they were brought here not of their own accord, while the Chinese came of their own accord, and that whereas when a negro gets $5, he puts it into a lot. . . . [T]he Chinese would not give $15 for all the lots in America unless he could ship it back to China.[45]

While the practical need to build a biracial alliance probably encouraged strikers' anti-Chinese demand, Chinese laborers may have also symbolized to strikers, as David Gouter has put it, "the excesses of industrialism." For white Canadian workers, he has argued, "while American blacks were associated . . . with the 'old' slavery, the Chinese were models of industrial wage slaves," because their migration coincided with the largest spurts of industrial growth in Canada. In the context of western railroading in the United States, one result of unrestrained industrialism was a growing association between itinerancy and cultural degradation. This was less the case in regard to white "boomers" in the era of railroad expansion, when social mobility was closely tied to geographic mobility. But rising labor competition and thus the possibility of "tramping" in search of work made the social status of Gould system railroaders more vulnerable. Focusing on the Chinese, who had long suffered condemnation for their perceived lack of attachment to family and to a fixed geographic location, allowed strikers to posit themselves as stable community members and to deflect attention from their own fears of falling into dependency and rootlessness.[46]

The social dangers of labor mobility held different implications for black and white railroaders, however. The arrival of a young black man in a small town, without any identifiable link to family or to a person who could vouch for his character, proved unsettling to many whites. White apprehension quickly turned murderous against black strangers who violated "some invisible and shifting line of permissible behavior," especially in areas of low rural population density and rapid black population growth. One such area was the cotton uplands that spread across central Mississippi, northern Louisiana, southern and central Arkansas, and eastern Texas; this region had the second-highest rate of lynching during the late nineteenth and early twentieth centuries.[47] The latter two areas were sites of intense strike activity. Perhaps it was this highly charged context that led Wade to stress not the transience of the Chinese but their self-imposed foreignness. Wade likely felt that a safer, more convincing anti-Chinese argument was not that the Chinese were "nomads" but that they had no loyalty, or more importantly, no history or future in the United States, whereas black Americans most assuredly did.

Ultimately, Chinese and convict laborers raised a discomfiting question for strikers: "How free is free?" The Civil War had abolished chattel slavery, but the insecurities, inequalities, and dependence many free railroaders experienced, especially the unskilled, existed uneasily alongside the claims of free labor ideology, which promised to the thrifty, industrious man social mobility, an income adequate to support a family, and an absence of coercion.[48] While Wade's speech suggests the racial fault lines under the surface of strikers' anti-Chinese demand, that demand, along with the call for a ban on convict labor, represented an economic, cultural, and psychological bridge across racial lines among the less skilled. Upon this fragile bridge the Knights built a biracial political movement in Texas and Arkansas that was radical for its time in its ability to pull some white Knights away from the Democratic Party and further embolden black Knights to organize. As one midwestern black newspaper wrote, "Southern whites may well look with apprehension upon the spread of the order of the Knights of Labor among the colored people of their section, and yet it may prove in the end the long sought wedge which shall split the solid South—industrially, socially, and politically."[49] At the same time, the pragmatism behind the Knights' cross-racial organizing continued to curb the degree to which blacks and whites challenged racial hierarchies and identities.

Poststrike Biracialism

For the first full month of the 1886 Gould system strike, the main public criticisms levied against the Knights involved not race but strike tactics, which included crowd blockades of the tracks, engine sabotage, intimidation of returning workers, and in early April, armed confrontations with local authorities. In this context of growing hostility to the strike, the first reports surfaced that associated Knights with racial troubles. The *Texarkana Independent* warned, "Adventurers and meddlers are at work organizing some kind of secret societies amongst the colored men in the country." Texarkana whites reportedly feared that the "half a dozen Negro assemblies of the Knights of Labor" in the area might "become the blind instruments of some bold Communist," in which case "their proverbial cunning and impenetrable superstition would render them an element far more dangerous in the estimation of law-abiding citizens than the white brotherhood of the Knights." Almost simultaneously, talk spread of Austin Knights allegedly organizing black cotton pickers along the Colorado River to "strengthen the hands of the strikers."[50] One might dismiss these charges as paranoid and opportunistic, as they came in the aftermath of both the Gould Knights' defeat and the Haymarket bombing. However, events in Pulaski County, Arkansas, tell another story.

About two months after the 1886 railway strike's official end, on a plantation outside Little Rock, black men and women struck for a wage increase from seventy-five cents to one dollar a day and for payment in cash rather than scrip. County sheriff Robert "Wat" Worthen and his posse moved in to arrest the alleged strike leader, Hugh Gill, at this home. Gill was shot in both arms for allegedly resisting arrest and brought with another strike leader to a plantation house, which was soon surrounded by about 250 armed black strikers. About one hundred had come from local Knights assemblies in the surrounding area. Deputy Sheriff Ham Williams organized a group that engaged in a brief skirmish with strikers to aid Worthen, but Worthen's pledge to not take Gill and Larkin to Little Rock to stand trial diffused the crisis. Once back in the city, Worthen reneged on his promise and called for reinforcements to put down what he claimed was a wider revolt by black laborers on area plantations. Reports of an impending race war followed in the *St. Louis Post-Dispatch* and the *Dallas Morning News,* the latter of which estimated that one thousand well-armed rebels were threatening to "burn crops, barns, and houses." Although the strikers returned to work the next day and Gill was later tried and acquitted, "peace" did not "prevail," as the *Arkansas Gazette* declared. Within days a local planter discovered this note: "As you think it is Best for the Knights to keep off ov [*sic*] your Place . . . if you Don't want us to talk to hands you had Better turn them of, if we take you in han it will Bee [*sic*] to Late for Wat Worthen to Come to help you and we wont Bee Long about it."[51]

The connection between the farm laborers' strike and the 1886 walkout on the Gould system has not gained previous historians' attention. The pro-Democrat *Arkansas Gazette* charged that white Knights had "told [the Tate plantation strikers] lies and tried to array them against the white citizens as a class." "Republican politics are at the bottom of the whole matter," it concluded. While vastly underestimating black Knights' leadership in the conflict, the paper rightly feared that a biracial labor coalition was in the making against the Democratic Party. The Tate plantation strike had attracted the aid of the city's Knights, a fact that Worthen recognized when he allowed two Little Rock Knights leaders, a black member reported only as "Merriman" and Don Tomson, the state assembly organizer, to go try to "control the colored men" at Tate plantation. The two intervening Knights did seek to calm the waters, but Tomson clearly opposed Worthen's measures. Shortly thereafter he wrote in the Arkansas Knights organ that Worthen and his men had committed "outrages" at Tate "in the hope that the colored people, being organized, would resist, and that this would serve as a pretext to break up organization among them." At the same Little Rock meeting on the cotton pickers' strike, planter Col. Anderson Mills rose to condemn the poor wages and scrip payment on Tate plantation, and Dr. F. M. Chrisman, whose son was a fireman, concurred. E. A. Fulton, a black speaker, then charged Democrats with stirring up the trouble at Tate for political reasons. In the September elections, Chrisman ran for county judge as a Republican candidate with the Knights' endorsement, as did prolabor Republican Colonel Oliver. Oliver ran for county sheriff against Worthen, who had come to office in the wake of the state's "redemption" in 1875.[52]

The Pulaski County Republican Party made a concerted effort to appeal to Knights with a platform that easily could have been taken up across racial lines by both railroad and cotton plantation strikers. Democrats, it charged,

> have made judges of a few men and compelled us to depend upon their will for the tenure of their offices. They have sent officers to harass and disturb good, honest working people, and by bad laws and worse officers eaten up the substance of the people. They have without cause or shadow of law in time of peace kept standing armies as so called posse comitatus, and sent them out without the consent, even of our legislature. They have made the military independent of and superior to

the civil power. They have sent armed troops among us and protected them by mock trials from punishment for assaults and attempted murders committed on the inhabitants of this state and county. . . . They have sent armed men, without the shadow of law or authority, without even a warrant, into peaceable neighborhoods and performed acts of cruelty and perfidy.[53]

The condemnation of judges grew out of Gould system Knights' experience with injunctions and their efforts after the walkout's failure to push for a federal arbitration bill, but Sheriff Worthen and Deputy Sheriff Williams were the unstated targets of this platform, for it was they who had led the aggressive attack on the cotton picker's strike, and, two months earlier, the Great Southwest Strike—delivering writs, taking out freight trains, and protecting strikebreakers and railroad property.[54]

Support for the prolabor Republican slate was far from universal among either Knights or Republicans. Democrats charged Oliver with corruption, a theme that white Knight Jasper N. Ferguson also took up. "Though he is in earnest sympathy with the working classes," Ferguson gave a "stirring address" to the "working men of Pulaski County" to see that the election's central issue was "honesty or dishonesty" and not "personal grievances," presumably against Worthen and Williams. At the same time, some discontent existed among black Republicans. In June 1886 the *Arkansas Gazette* relayed that the *Sun*, "which speaks for a large number of colored Republicans of this county," had attacked the Republican Party's white leadership for "taking all of the best paying and most honorable offices and the majority being placed on the tail and where worth, intelligence et al. are equal."[55]

However, some basis existed for the Democrats' fear of defeat in the September 1886 elections. The *Arkansas Democrat*'s shrill charges of corruption against Oliver, its mixture of threats and entreaties to black voters, and its oft-repeated plea, "Every Democrat to the polls," belied the editor's confident insistence that the county's comfortable white majority ensured a Democratic victory. In the end, the ballot count gave Democrats a solid majority, but at least seven out of twenty-three townships and wards voted Republican. Reports of election fraud raise the question as to whether Republicans had more support than the official tallies recorded. In Eastman Township, for example, Chrisman met with black voters about "not having access to the poll." A number wanted "to force their way in and see the vote counted."[56]

Despite defeat in Pulaski County, the Knights went on to play a key role in the Populist movement in the state over the succeeding years. The Agricultural

Wheel, which at an 1886 meeting with Knights had only begrudgingly agreed to accept blacks in "separate and distinct" assemblies, met with a staggering electoral defeat that convinced white members to expand the wheel's appeal across racial and economic lines. In 1888 the state's farmer and labor movements formed the biracial Union Labor Party, which won considerable backing from disenchanted Republicans and Democrats statewide, and in Pulaski County, 52 percent of the vote went to the party's gubernatorial candidate and 60 percent to its congressional candidate, ex–railroad shopman Isaac McCracken. Democrats secured their victory in 1888 largely through fraud and violence and in subsequent years by meeting some of the farmers' demands and passing disfranchisement laws aimed at black voters, who had voted for the Union Labor Party in significant numbers.[57]

A biracial working-class political coalition also emerged to challenge Democratic dominance in Dallas, a politically key Texas city. In combination with a business element that hoped to reduce the class animosities exacerbated by the Southwest strikes, black and white workers supported locally independent Winship C. "Bud" Connor in the 1887, 1889, and 1891 mayoral races. Although Connor steadfastly voted Democrat at the state and national level, in Dallas he proclaimed himself free of partisan politics. His appeal to the city's laboring element was chiefly economic. Beyond his prolabor and pro-Knights rhetoric, his administration's generous public spending on infrastructure and improvements created jobs for workers in the city. Wards that included the railroad yards and the warehouse districts were wells of pro-Connor sentiment. Indeed, in 1887 labor issues animated the election debate, with Connor and one opponent, Ed Smith, wrangling over which candidate was truly the "workingman's friend." Black Knights actively campaigned for both Smith and Connor, but by 1891, one prominent Dallas Democrat lamented, "The negroes, the Trafic [sic] men—gamblers & saloon men were practically solid for" Connor.[58]

As in Arkansas, third-party gains prompted Democrats to intervene. The Texas legislature passed the Kimbrough election law, which required that disputed electors provide a witness who was a "well-known resident of the ward that he is a qualified voter at such election and in such ward." The policy disenfranchised many itinerant or newly settled laborers who made up much of Connor's coalition. In a large sample of votes challenged in Dallas's 1891 election, Alicia E. Rodriquez has found that most were cast by black citizens but that the "challenges also had a class dimension. The majority of the challenged men, black as well as white, whose occupations were listed in the city directory, were employed as laborers, porters and in other unskilled or semiskilled jobs. . . . They fit the profile of men supporting W. C. Connor's challenge to the Democratic party, and thus their race and class made them targets."[59]

The class dimensions of the Democrats' attack notwithstanding, the strength of black working-class activism in these poststrike independent political movements highlights the degree to which the Knights' cross-racial organizing was biracial rather than interracial. In terms of everyday interactions, racial separation and racial identity dominated. Pro-Connor black activists seem to have agitated among black voters, and in both Pulaski County and Dallas, black Knights represented the most solid and aggressive block in the prolabor party's ranks, suggesting the same spirit of political brokering that Leon Fink found among black Knights who backed a prolabor ticket in Kansas City after the March 1886 strike. Indeed, in both locales probably only a minority of white Knights left the Democratic Party to join the prolabor ticket with black voters. During the railway strikes, too, black Knights apparently took responsibility for persuading or intimidating black strikebreakers to cease work. Biracialism in the Little Rock area and in Dallas weathered longer than in Richmond, where, Peter Rachleff has argued, black and white Knights never generated an interracial culture that could withstand the dominant parties' attempts to play upon racial fears and mistrust. It helped that neither city was the site of northern Knights' direct and dramatic challenge to southern segregation, as was Richmond. Even Fink's conclusion that Richmond Knights were "together but unequal" seems generous in regard to the race-conscious Gould system Knights and their poststrike coalitions.[60] The expedient motives for these alliances, along with the broader context of segregation in the railroad industry, in southern life, and in the Knights' own assemblies curbed the extent to which those alliances encouraged egalitarianism and communalism among workers.

Given the power of racial hierarchies and ideas, any other outcome was unlikely. It is all the more extraordinary, then, that Knights in Arkansas and Texas exhibited some small measure of the "genuine fellowship" that Daniel Letwin discovered among Alabama miners. Beyond Patrick Cassidy's recollection of interracial comradeship in the railway yards of Palestine, a small but significant distance developed between the racism espoused by some white supporters of biracialism and white Knights who remained within the fold of the Democratic Party. One can discern the former position in a report published in the Arkansas Knights organ, the *Industrial Liberator*, by Don Tomson, the white leader of the state assembly who had so resolutely defended Tate plantation strikers. While Tomson cast the order's role as an educator of "illiterate, ignorant, even superstitious" ex-slaves who were "entirely without culture" and "sadly lacking that independency characteristic of an American citizen," he departed from this uncomplicated language of white supremacy to emphasize that these traits had a historical rather than natural explanation: southern blacks were the victims of slavery, war, and the "adventurers, renegades and scoundrels" of the Reconstruction era. "Thousands," he went on, "could be found among their ranks who were capable of exercising their power with the caution enjoined by the Order . . . [and benefiting] others, less fortunate of their race." He saluted Tate plantation strikers for remaining lawful, "even under such trying circumstances," and looked forward to the day when "colored men . . . with their white brothers" would "march onward in the army of progress and eventually raise themselves to that high and efficient standard of industrious and dignified citizenship that must be obtained before the masses can assert and maintain their right to the full product of their labor." Tomson's racial views included at once a fairly orthodox version of white paternalism and, paradoxically, a faith born of experience in black Knights' abilities. That ideological amalgam stood in stark contrast to the Democrats' creed, which, even when it sought black votes, allowed little to no room for black "producers" or citizens. White Knights who, along with the Farmers' Alliance, made their "fight in the Democratic party" of Dallas County typified the latter outlook. The county's Knights and Farmers' Alliance held a Fourth of July picnic in 1886 that stayed safely within the racial boundaries of "redemption" politics. No allusions were made to black participation or leadership. Instead, to frequent applause and Confederate yells, Col. W. L. Crawford pledged that Dallas County Knights and Alliance members would "retake possession of the heritage that was given them by their patriotic ancestry. . . . There was a time when the government of the United States protected the States and the people, and the people hardly knew that there was a federal government. Are you ready to bring back those good old times?"[61]

Conclusion

The historiography on race and Populism mirrors to some degree the debate over race among labor historians. For example, Gregg Cantrell and D. Scott Barton have maintained that white Texas Populists "had traveled further toward racial equality than the Democrats had, but even the Populists had gone only part of the way." In 1894, for example, they endorsed "equal protection of the law" but not black officeholding, and in 1896 overwhelmingly voted Democrat rather than fuse with Republicans and risk the charge of racial treason. Lawrence Goodwyn was more hopeful. He largely dismissed the importance of white Populists' motivations in his examination of Garrett Scott, a white Populist leader of Grimes County, Texas, and concluded, "The political realities that undergirded the majority coalition and Scott's ability to respond to those realities shaped a course of government conduct under the People's party that was demonstrably of more benefit to Negroes than was the conduct of other administration before or since."[62] In light of the history of the Knights' biracialism here, neither interpretation satisfies. The first tends to discourage exploration of the many forms of biracial relationships that existed short of biracial support for the Republican Party. The second underestimates the role of ideas—about race, skill, citizenship, and monopoly, for example—in animating, expanding, and also limiting biracial movements. In this case, the Knights' biracialism developed hastily and expediently under crisis circumstances: a tightening labor market on western railroads, a popular walkout in 1885 against starvation wages, railroad managers' violations of the 1885 agreements, and the collapse of the 1886 railway strike. The last of these drove a number of black and white workers to expand the alliances that they had initiated with the Gould system strikes to include working-class and pro-business urban communities and also black laborers and labor activists in rural areas outside railroad towns. It also developed partially, with the strike in Marshall, for example, representing perhaps the most cynical form of the Knights' biracialism. During these conflicts, racial hierarchies on the railroads and the chief ritual of the strike, engine killing, mitigated the degree to which whites saw the Knights as a threat to the developing Jim Crow system. However, shared principles also propelled these coalitions and gave them new shape. In 1885 common cause promised a triumph of "producers," black and white, over "monopoly." The intense and communitywide resentment of Jay Gould and eastern capital, the considerable risks and hardships associated with railroad work, the qualms surrounding Chinese and convict labor, and state intervention on behalf of railroads and planters gave rise to a class identity, although this identity was felt and articulated unequally, uncomfortably, and ambiguously. The Knights' broad language allowed this diverse coalition of boomer railroaders, cotton pickers, and urban workers to form a range of associations, all of which accommodated in some way the realities of racial hierarchy and separation, the threat of racial violence, and white paternalism. Yet, in the end, the Knights created a workable, albeit fragile, rhetorical bond between black and white workers.

In cooperating even in limited ways across racial lines, Knights opened up political and cultural space for local challenges to Democratic control and contributed to a larger wave of third-party politics. Black Knights used this space as a wedge to create new opportunities and alignments in a society that had closed most of its doors to them and was fast closing more. Hence, in 1891, longtime Republican Melvin Wade lent his critical support to the developing independent political party in Texas, which many black voters associated with the Knights, and which eventually promised not civil equality but reforms of the convict lease system, an eight-hour day in industry, and black control over black public schools. As elsewhere in the South, black workers "adopted the Knights" rather than the other way round.[63] In doing so, they forged a different path from most traditional black leaders, who had not concerned themselves much with the interests and ideas of the unskilled and itinerant.

The nature of biracial working-class cooperation in Arkansas and Texas requires further study, to be sure, as do the connections between black rural and railroad workers and between black Knights and black Populists.[64] But this examination of the links between the Gould system strikes and local political challenges to "democracy" suggests the potential radicalism of the Knights' biracialism. This radicalism did not involve a sweeping transformation in racial ideologies or racial hierarchies, nor did it inspire daily or even frequent organizing across racial lines. Instead, it entailed a partial yet palpable shift in the allegiances of a significant number of white and black workers, away from the customary leadership and networks that had long divided them and toward one another as participants in a cross-racial alliance. This step seems unremarkable only if we forget its origins and context—a highly segregated industry operating in the post-Reconstruction South and in the aftermath of two failed strikes—and if we overlook the fierce reaction it brought from the Democratic Party. Finally, for Tomson, and perhaps others, the Knights' biracialism opened a door to a more elastic, mixed, alterable, and empathetic understanding of race—a development that both black and white advocates of pragmatism must have feared but never fully anticipated.

Notes

This chapter originally appeared in *Labor: Studies in Working Class History* 4 (Winter 2007): 83–107, and is reprinted with permission.

1. By the mid-1880s, the Gould railway system included the Missouri Pacific, the Texas and Pacific, the International and Great Northern, the Wabash, St. Louis and Pacific; the St. Louis and Iron Mountain; and the Missouri, Kansas and Texas. It linked eastern Kansas, St. Louis, Little Rock, Dallas/Fort Worth, and El Paso to the northeast via the Wabash. Maury Klein, *The Life and Legend of Jay Gould* (Baltimore: Johns Hopkins University Press, 1986), 304.

2.   Patrick Cassidy to Ruth Allen, February 5, 1941, Box 2E303, Labor Movement in Texas Collection, Center for American History, University of Texas at Austin (hereafter cited as LMTC).

3.   Quoted in Allesandro Portelli, *The Death of Luigi Trastulli and Other Stories: Form and Meaning in Oral History* (New York: State University of New York Press, 1991), 2.

4.   US Congress, *Investigation of Labor Troubles in Missouri, Arkansas, Kansas, Texas, and Illinois,* 2 pts., 49th Cong., 2nd sess., Report No. 4174 (1887), 2:75; *John Swinton's Paper,* June 13, 1886. I found no black delegates representing Palestine in the records of the Knights' General Assembly meetings from 1885 to 1890. Knights of Labor, *Record of Proceedings of the General Assembly of the Knights of Labor* (Reading, PA: The Assembly), and *Proceedings of the General Assembly of the Knights of Labor of America, 1887–1913* (Minneapolis: The Assembly). Cassidy may have meant a regional meeting, but I could not locate a record of this.

5.   Two important articles in this debate are Herbert Hill, "Myth-Making as Labor History: Herbert Gutman and the United Mine Workers of America," *International Journal of Politics, Culture and Society* 2, No. 2 (1988): 132–200, and Stephen Brier, "In Defense of Gutman: The Union's Case," *International Journal of Politics, Culture, and Society* 3, No. 2 (1989): 382–95. Eric Arnesen provides a valuable evaluation of this debate in "Up from Exclusion: Black and White Workers, Race, and the State of Labor History," *Reviews in American History* 26, No. 1 (1998): 146–74. Examples of the more recent trend are Daniel Letwin, *The Challenge of Interracial Unionism: Alabama Coal Miners, 1878–1921* (Chapel Hill: University of North Carolina Press, 1998), and Eric Arnesen, *Waterfront Workers of New Orleans; Race, Class, and Politics, 1863–1923* (New York: Oxford University Press, 1991).

6.   Eric Arnesen, "'Like Banquo's Ghost, It Will Not Down': The Race Question and the American Railroad Brotherhoods, 1880–1920," *American Historical Review* 99, No. 5 (1994): 1603.

7.   Arnesen, "Up from Exclusion," 146–74.

8.   Walter Licht, *Working for the Railroad: The Organization of Work in the Nineteenth Century* (Princeton, NJ: Princeton University Press, 1983), 182–86, 216–21; Paul Michel Taillon, "Culture, Politics, and the Making of the Railroad Brotherhoods, 1863–1916" (PhD diss., University of Wisconsin at Madison, 1997), 74–75; Susan Curtis, *Dancing to a Black Man's Tune: The Life of Scott Joplin* (Columbia: University of Missouri Press, 1994), 34–35, 40–41; Shelton Stromquist, *A Generation of Boomers: The Pattern of Railroad Labor Conflict in Nineteenth-Century America* (Chicago: University of Illinois Press, 1987), xiii (quotation), 101, 193–97. Taillon subsequently contributed two more specific studies that analyze the ways in which gender shaped brotherhood men's views of their work and their unions. See "What We Want Is Good, Sober Men: Masculinity, Respectability, and Temperance in the Railroad Brotherhoods, c. 1870–1910," *Journal of Social History* 36 (2002): 319–38; and "'To Make Men Out of Crude Material': Work Culture, Manhood, and Unionism in the Railroad Running Trades,

c. 1870–1900," in *Boys and Their Toys? Masculinity, Technology, and Class in America,* ed. Roger Horowitz (New York: Routledge, 2001), 33–54.

9. Taillon, "Culture, Politics, and the Making of the Railroad Brotherhoods," 78; Eric Arnesen, *Brotherhoods of Color: Black Railroad Workers and the Struggle for Equality* (Cambridge, MA: Harvard University Press, 2001), 16–17.

10. Arnesen, *Brotherhoods of Color,* 24–26; Sterling D. Spero and Abram L. Harris, *The Black Worker: The Negro and the Labor Movement* (1931; repr., New York: Atheneum, 1968), 308; Letwin, *Challenge of Interracial Unionism,* 77–78; US Census Office, *Tenth Census: 1880* (Washington, DC: US Government Printing Office, 1883–1888); *Directory of the City of Dallas, 1886* (Dallas: Galveston, Morrison, and Fourmy, 1886); *Shole's Directory of the City of Little Rock and Argenta, 1883–1884* (Little Rock, AR: A. E. Sholes, 1884).

11. George P. Rawick, gen. ed., *The American Slave: A Composite Autobiography,* supplement, ser. 2, vol. 3: *Texas Narratives,* pt. 2 (Westport, CT: Greenwood, 1979), 489, 492–94; Robin G. Kelley, "'We Are Not What We Seem': Rethinking Black Working-Class Opposition in the Jim Crow South," *Journal of American History* 80, No. 1 (1993): 75–112; Arnesen, "'Like Banquo's Ghost,'" 1612, 1613. Scott Nelson recently unearthed evidence of the real John Henry in *Steel Drivin' Man: John Henry; The Untold Story of an American Legend* (New York: Oxford University Press, 2006).

12. Rawick, *American Slave,* 489, 492–94.

13. Arnesen, *Brotherhoods of Color,* 6 (quotation); *Directory of the City of Dallas, 1886; Shole's Directory of the City of Little Rock and Argenta*; Rawick, *American Slave,* supplement, ser. 2, vol. 8: *Texas Narratives,* pt. 7, 2965–66; Alton King Briggs, "The Archeology of 1882 Labor Camps on the Southern Pacific Railroad, Val Verde County, Texas" (master's thesis, University of Texas at Austin, 1974), 31, 33–34.

14. Licht, *Working for the Railroad,* 223: US Census Office, *Tenth Census*; Martin Irons, "My Experiences in the Labor Movement," *Lippincott's Monthly Magazine,* June 1886, 625–27. Kevin Kenny emphasizes the importance of immigrants' self-identification in *The American Irish: A History* (Essex, UK: Pearson Education Limited, 2000), 69–70.

15. Chauncey del French, *Railroadman* (New York: Macmillan, 1938), 3–5. Similarly, black cowboys' skill and courage won them the respect and admiration of white coworkers but no blurring of the color line. See Kenneth W. Porter, "Negro Labor in the Western Cattle Industry," *Labor History* 10, No. 3 (1969): 346–74.

16. See representations of the unskilled in *Fort Worth Gazette,* February 25, 1882, and *St. Louis Post-Dispatch,* September 25, 1884, for example.

17. Taillon, "Culture, Politics, and the Making of the Railroad Brotherhoods," 79–80, 376–77, 387–89; Stromquist, *Generation of Boomers,* 55–56, 64–65, 110 (quotation).

18. Stromquist, *Generation of Boomers,* 101, 116–17, 124–27, 132–33; Maier, "The Realization of My Boyhood Dream," Box 2E302, Folder 2, pp. 8–9, LMTC.

19. See Theresa A. Case, "Free Labor on the Southwestern Railroads: The 1885–

1886 Gould System Strikes" (PhD diss., University of Texas at Austin, 2002), 160–210.

20. Maier to Ruth Allen, November 18, 1939, and "The Realization of My Boyhood Dream," 9–10, Box 2E302, Folder 2, LMTC (quotation); Jonathan Garlock, *Guide to the Local Assemblies of the Knights of Labor* (Westport, CT: Greenwood, 1982), 86–89, 130–31, 138–39, 148–49, 240–59, 491–507.

21. Craig Phelan, *Grand Master Workman: Terence Powderly and the Knights of Labor* (Westport, CT: Greenwood, 2000), 161.

22. Moberly to Terence Powderly, September 23, 1885, and Jay Gould to Terence Powderly, October 11, 1885, Incoming Correspondence, Reel 10, Terence Vincent Powderly Papers (cited hereafter as TVPP); US Congress, *Investigation of Labor Troubles*, 1:378, 434–35, 448, 450, 466–67, 478, 486, 553.

23. Case, "Free Labor on the Southwestern Railroads," 250–302.

24. *Dallas Daily Herald*, March 14, 1885; US Congress, *Investigation of Labor Troubles*, 1:378–79.

25. Randolph B. Campbell, *A Southern Community in Crisis: Harrison County, Texas, 1850–1880* (Austin: Texas State Historical Association, 1983); *Marshall Tri-Weekly Herald*, June 25, 1885; Isaac T. Davis, "Interview of Pioneer by Isaac T. Davis, Elkhart, Texas," *American Life Histories: Manuscripts from the Federal Writers' Project, 1936–1940*, memory.loc.gov/ammem (accessed November 2005).

26. *Fort Worth Gazette*, March 4, 1886.

27. US Congress, *Investigation of Labor Troubles*, 2:301; *Waco Daily Examiner*, March 26, 1886, and *Austin Statesman*, April 27, 1886, typed copies in Box 2E 303, LMTC; Ruth Allen, *The Great Southwest Strike* (Austin: University of Texas, Bureau of Research in the Social Sciences, 1942), 87.

28. *Waco Daily Examiner*, March 9, 1886, quoted in Allen, *The Great Southwest Strike*, 73.

29. US Congress, *Investigation of Labor Troubles*, 2:182; *Dallas Morning News*, March 23, 1886; *Galveston Daily News*, March 5, 9, 12, 13, 27 (quotation), 31; April 1, 10, 27, 1886.

30. Alwyn Barr, *Black Texans: A History of African Americans in Texas, 1528–1995* (Norman: University of Oklahoma Press, 1996), 72–73; Gerald T. Hanson and Carl H. Moneyhon, *Historical Atlas of Arkansas* (Norman: University of Oklahoma Press, 1989), 135.

31. Arnesen, *Brotherhoods of Color*, 26–27; Mary Ann Clawson, *Constructing Brotherhood: Class, Gender, and Fraternalism* (Princeton, NJ: Princeton University Press, 1989), 123, 131–35; Robert Weir, *Beyond Labor's Veil: The Culture of the Knights of Labor* (University Park: Pennsylvania University Press, 1996), 49–51.

32. Philip S. Foner and Ronald L. Lewis, eds., *The Black Worker during the Era of the Knights of Labor*, vol. 3 of *The Black Worker: A Documentary History from Colonial Times to the Present* (Philadelphia: Temple University Press, 1978), 52, 104, 105.

33. Arnesen, "Following the Color Line of Labor: Black Workers and the Labor Movement before 1930," *Radical History Review* 55 (Winter 1993): 68; Melton

McLaurin, *The Knights of Labor in the South* (Westport, CT: Greenwood, 1978), 134–39.

34. Foner and Lewis, *The Black Worker*, 3:72, 242–43, 252–53. At the October 1886 Richmond convention, a racially mixed group set off a storm of racist protest when it challenged the order to take a stand against southern segregation. See Leon Fink, *Workingmen's Democracy: The Knights of Labor and American Politics* (Urbana: University of Illinois Press, 1983), and Peter Rachleff, *Black Labor in Richmond, 1865–1890* (1984; repr., Urbana: University of Illinois Press, 1989).

35. "An Address," Reel 10, TVPP; US Congress, *Investigation of Labor Troubles*, 1:378, 553; *Marshall Tri-Weekly Herald*, March 3, 1885.

36. Edward L. Ayers, *Promise of the New South: Life After Reconstruction* (New York: Oxford University Press, 1992), 273–74. Alabama coal miners made a similar distinction between regional and northern capital. See Letwin, *Challenge of Interracial Unionism*, 75.

37. US Congress, *Investigation of Labor Troubles*, 2:115–17.

38. Fink, *Workingmen's Democracy,* 150, 171 (quotation).

39. *Fort Worth Gazette*, March 4, 1886; *Galveston Daily News*, March 5, 10, 25, 1886; US Congress, *Investigation of Labor Troubles*, 1:378–79; 2:104, 159, 165, 206; "Proceedings of First Annual Session at Galveston, District Assembly No. 78," January 1886, Reel 66, pp. 52–53, TVPP.

40. L. L. Foster, *Forgotten Texas Census: First Annual Report of the Agricultural Bureau of the Department of Agriculture, Insurance, Statistics, and History, 1887–88*, ed. Barbara J. Rozek (Austin: Texas State Historical Association, 2001), 290; Edward J. M. Rhoads, "The Chinese in Texas," *Southwestern Historical Quarterly* 81, No. 1 (1977): 2, 5–8; US Congress, *Investigation of Labor Troubles*, 2:206.

41. *St. Louis Globe-Democrat*, March 26, 1886; *Arkansas Gazette*, September 5, 1885; Foster, *Forgotten Texas Census*, 290. While the 1882 Chinese Exclusion Act slowed Chinese immigration to a trickle, the belief that the law was inadequate was widespread. See Erika Lee, *At America's Gates: Chinese Immigration during the Exclusion Era, 1882–1943* (Chapel Hill: University of North Carolina Press, 2003), 44.

42. Matthew J. Mancini, *One Dies, Get Another: Convict Leasing in the American South, 1866–1928* (Columbia: University of South Carolina Press, 1996), 117, 121–22, 125, 172–74, 175, 177; David R. Walker, *Penology for Profit: A History of the Texas Prison System, 1867–1912* (College Station: Texas A&M University Press, 1988), 57.

43. Rhoads, "The Chinese in Texas," 10 (quotation); Briggs, "Archeology of 1882 Labor Camps," 34, 198. Similarly, political expediency drove support for the 1882 Exclusion Act among eastern workers. Andrew Gyory, *Closing the Gate: Race, Politics, and the Chinese Exclusion Act* (Chapel Hill: University of North Carolina Press, 1998), 222, 228–29.

44. US Congress, *Investigation of Labor Troubles*, 2:183–84, 206.

45. *Dallas Morning News*, March 23, 1886.

46. Gunther Peck, *Reinventing Free Labor: Padrones and Immigrant Workers in the*

North American West, 1880–1930 (Cambridge: Cambridge University Press, 2000), 166; David Gomer, "Drawing Different Lines of Colour: The Mainstream English Canadian Labour Movement's Approach to Black and the Chinese, 1880–1914," *Labor: Studies in Working-Class History of the Americas* 2, No. 1 (2005): 69. Turn-of-the-century brotherhood members expressed similar fears in their rhetorical assaults against new immigrants, who posed little direct economic threat to them, as they found their own autonomy undermined and social status deteriorating. Arnesen, "'Like Banquo's Ghost,'" 1617.

47.   Ayers, *Promise of the New South,* 22, 156, 157 (quotation).

48.   Leon F. Litwack addresses this question in regard to the status of freed people in *Been in the Storm So Long: The Aftermath of Slavery* (New York: Vintage, 1980).

49.   Reprint of an article from the *Leader* in the *Cleveland Gazette,* July 17, 1886.

50.   *Texarkana Independent,* April 19 and 21, 1886; *Louisville Commercial,* April 21, 1886; *Galveston Daily News,* April 6, 1886.

51.   *Arkansas Democrat,* July 6, 8, 1886; *Dallas Morning News,* July 6, 1886; *Arkansas Gazette,* July 7, 10, 1886; William Warren Rogers, "Negro Knights of Labor in Arkansas: A Case Study of the 'Miscellaneous' Strike," *Labor History,* No. 3 (1969): 498–505.

52.   *Arkansas Gazette,* July 6, 8, August 31, September 5, 10, 1886; US Census Office, *Tenth Census;* Carl H. Moneyhon, *Arkansas and the New South, 1874–1929* (Fayetteville: University of Arkansas Press, 1997), 3; *Journal of United Labor,* September 25, 1886.

53.   *Arkansas Gazette,* September 1, 1886.

54.   *Arkansas Democrat,* March 11, 18, April 9, 1886; Matthew Hild, "Labor, Third-Party Politics, and New South Democracy in Arkansas, 1884–1896," *Arkansas Historical Quarterly* 63 (2004): 31.

55.   *Arkansas Gazette,* June 22, August 29, 31, September 7, 1886.

56.   *Arkansas Democrat,* August 25, 1886; *Arkansas Gazette,* September 7, 8, 10, 1886; *Daily Texarkana Independent,* September 14, 1886.

57.   *Arkansas Gazette,* August 29, 31, September 8, 1886; Moneyhon, *Arkansas and the New South, 1874–1929,* 82, 85–86, 90–91; Hild, "Labor, Third-Party Politics, and New South Democracy in Arkansas," 28, 30, 34, 36, 38; Hanson and Moneyhon, *Historical Atlas of Arkansas,* 135. The Knights represented one of many protest organizations in which black agrarians participated. The networks that emerged from these efforts laid the basis for black populism. See Omar H. Ali, "Black Populism in the New South, 1886–1898" (PhD diss., Columbia University, 2003).

58.   Alicia E. Rodriquez, "Disfranchisement in Dallas: The Democratic Party and the Suppression of Independent Political Challenges in Dallas, Texas, 1891–1894," *Southwestern Historical Quarterly* 108, No. 1 (2004): 46, 52, 63, and "Urban Populism: Challenges to Democratic Party Control in Dallas, Texas: 1887–1900" (PhD diss., University of California, Santa Barbara, 1998), 57; *Dallas Morning News,* April 2, 6, 1887.

59.   Rodriquez, "Disfranchisement in Dallas," 50–51.

60. *Dallas Morning News*, April 6, July 5, 1886; *Arkansas Gazette*, August 31, 1886; Rachleff, *Black Labor in Richmond*, 200–201; Fink, *Workingmen's Democracy*, 121, 129, 142; Rodriquez, "Urban Populism," 64–66.

61. Letwin, *Challenge of Interracial Unionism*, 6–7; *Journal of United Labor*, September 25, 1886, 2178; *Dallas Morning News*, July 5, 1886. The following inspired my analysis of the nuances of Tomson's racial views: Gunther Peck, "White Slavery and Whiteness: A Transnational View of the Sources of Working-Class Radicalism and Racism," *Labor: Studies in Working-Class History of the Americas* 1, No. 2 (2004): 41–63.

62. Gregg Cantrell and D. Scott Barton, "Texas Populists and the Failure of Biracial Politics," *Journal of Southern History* 55, No. 4 (1989): 659–92; Lawrence Goodwyn, "Populist Dreams and Negro Rights," *American Historical Review* 76, No. 5 (1971): 1450. To be fair, Gregg Cantrell subsequently went on to explore the tensions and ambiguities in black–white relations among Populists in Gregg Cantrell and Kristopher B. Paschal, "Texas Populism at High Tide: Jerome C. Kearby and the Case of the Sixth Congressional District, 1894," *Southern Historical Quarterly* 109 (July 2005): 30–70, and Gregg Cantrell, *Kenneth and John B. Rayner and the Limits of Southern Dissent* (Urbana: University of Illinois Press, 1993).

63. Cantrell, *Kenneth and John B. Rayner and the Limits of Southern Dissent*, 203, 205, 213–15; Fink, *Workingmen's Democracy,* 169 (quotation).

64. Joe William Trotter Jr. recommends such a course in "African-American Workers: New Directions in US Labor Historiography," *Labor History* 35 (1994): 495–523.

MARILYN D. RHINEHART

"Underground Patriots"

Thurber Coal Miners and the Struggle for
Individual Freedom, 1888–1903

In January 1945, as Allied forces pushed into Germany, Gomer Gower reminisced about his turn-of-the-century experiences as resident, worker, and labor activist in Thurber, Texas, a coal-mining town owned and actively operated by the Texas and Pacific Coal Company from 1888 through the 1920s. Alluding to resistance fighters in war-torn Europe, Gower wrote: "We in Thurber, too, had our underground forces . . . in supposedly free America ." He continued, "[I]t was due to the silent and patient activity of this band of underground patriots that Thurber was transformed from a 'Bull-Pen' in its early history, into one of the most . . . pleasant mining communities in the entire country."[1]

To accomplish this transformation, Thurber's miner labor activists emphasized such traditional forms of collective action as unionization, work stoppages, and solicitation of funds and aid from local and distant allies. But it was the employment in 1903 of a device that the company could not outmaneuver—worker/resident emigration—that forced officials to recognize that not only were workers dependent on the company, but the company needed its workers. In the end, this success resulted, as Ruth A. Allen has accurately concluded, in the appearance of "a powerful and militant organization" that enforced the closed shop in the Texas mining district for over twenty years.[2] It also provided a bridge for Texas labor between the militant, but often unsuccessful, strike activity across the state in the 1880s challenging emerging industries' monopolistic control over markets and workers and the move in the early twentieth century, which James C. Maroney's work on organized labor in Texas identifies, toward labor's steady growth, public acceptance, and effective use of legislative lobbying as an additional means of achieving the movement's goals.[3]

The factors that incited Thurber's ethnically and racially mixed coal miners to the underground agitation that resulted in total unionization of the town in fifteen years included coal-weighing procedures, wage scales, and working hours deemed unfair by the workers, as well as difficult and dangerous work conditions. Equally significant in generating resentment among the population, however, were features of company-dominated life that limited personal freedom. Paternalistic and autocratic under the management of Col. Robert D. Hunter, a native of Scotland who made his fortune in the American West as a prospector, cattleman, and mining entrepreneur, the company owned and administered almost all community enterprises. It thus touched every aspect of its workers' lives from working conditions to entertainment and, under Hunter, its first president and general manager, created a virtual serfdom.[4] As a result, in action strikingly similar to that of miners in southern Illinois whose early twentieth-century activism Eric D. Weitz has analyzed, Thurber's native and foreign-born miners, motivated by an individualist urge that the solitary nature of their underground work and preindustrial habits encouraged, and united by shared grievances that overcame ethnic, racial, and religious divisions, turned to union organization as the collective expression of their individual aspirations.[5] Although management's capitulation to the miners' demands in 1903 did not terminate the company-town concept in Thurber, it facilitated the introduction of a strong counterforce to bring "democracy to the mines" and to give the workers a greater measure of control over their daily lives.[6]

Thurber Village developed in the far northwestern corner of Erath County in the arid, infertile western reaches of north-central Texas along the line of the coal-dependent Texas and Pacific Railroad. In the mid-1880s Harvey E. and William W. Johnson discovered evidence of coal deposits there and established the original mining camp, known simply as Johnson Mines, within a surrounding wall of small hills covered in low vegetation.[7] The "pencil" vein of bituminous coal that the Johnson brothers struck and on which Thurber's future would depend, averaged eighteen to twenty-eight inches in thickness and extended some sixty-five miles, varying in width from five to ten miles. In 1886, with little fanfare, the Johnson Coal Mining Company opened Mine No. 1 to tap that vein and to supply Jay Gould's railroad line with steam-producing coal.[8]

When the Johnsons prepared to open Mine No. 1 in 1886, they recruited miners from nearby Coalville, where from 1884 to 1886 the Gould interests had attempted to operate two mines, with little success, to provide fuel for the Texas and Pacific Railway. For two years the Johnson Coal Mining Company struggled to fill the void left by Coalville's demise, but railroad complaints about low production levels and poor-quality coal, and financial difficulties generated in large part by insufficient capitalization, prompted the company to sell its properties and assets to a newly incorporated coal operation, the Texas and Pacific Coal Company, presided over by Colonel Hunter and funded by investors from the

Northeast. In 1888 the company purchased the twenty-three hundred acres and improvements owned by the foundering Johnson Coal Mining Company along with twenty thousand adjacent acres. By November 1888, when the Texas and Pacific Coal Company actually took possession of the property, two hundred to three hundred residents already lived and worked in the village that "T&P" (or the TP), as its employees would call the company, named Thurber to honor one of the company's major stockholders.[9]

As the Texas and Pacific Coal Company expanded its investment in the coal deposits, opening nine new mines by 1901, Thurber's population increased correspondingly.[10] The 1890 federal census reported the population of Thurber Village as 978.[11] The 1900 federal census recorded 2,559 residents in Thurber, of which 828, or 75 percent, of males listing occupations identified themselves as coal diggers or coal miners. Two-thirds of this population, representing sixteen different nationalities, claimed foreign birth.[12]

Countywide figures compiled in 1890 and 1900 show that the importation of immigrants to Thurber to work the mines, and their migration from other coal-mining regions around the country, played a significant part in Thurber's population growth in the late nineteenth century. The *Compendium of the Eleventh Census* for 1890 reported only 351 (1.6 percent of a total population of 21,594) foreign-born residents in Erath County, but by 1900 the number of immigrants had nearly tripled to 955 (and doubled in percentage of the county population of 29,966).[13] In ledger books that the Johnsons maintained before sale of the coal property and in Texas and Pacific Coal Company payroll records for 1890, English, Irish, Scots, and Welsh names predominated.[14] By 1900, however, 41 percent of Thurber's coal miners listed Italy as place of birth, making Italians the most numerous of the alien population.[15] The trend toward hiring Italian miners began with company recruiting trips to Indiana, Illinois, Kentucky, and Missouri necessitated by labor difficulties that had virtually halted coal production.[16] Poles—who numbered forty-seven among the mining population in 1900 and constituted the second most numerous alien group—along with Mexicans, Germans, Austrians, Hungarians, Irish, Scots, Russians, Welsh, Belgians, French, Bohemians, English, Swedes, and Swiss joined the Italians in establishing a cultural diversity that lent Thurber one of its most distinctive qualities.[17]

Studies by Mary Jane Gentry and Michael Q. Hooks have shown how Thurber's ethnically diverse population created a social setting where Old World traditions and customs filled the ethnic neighborhoods into which the various groups tended to segregate themselves or into which economic condition, social position, or the availability of housing led them.[18] Southern and eastern Europeans generally populated Hill No. 3 on the town's west side, the residential area closest to mining operations by 1930, which included some of the least expensive housing with the fewest amenities. Many Irish lived at the base of Stump Hill nearby. The 1900 census and company rent books suggest that American-born and English, Scots, and Welsh miners and brick plant workers tended to live in close proximity to one another, perhaps on Park Row, another low-rental area near the baseball park to the north and east of town, which residents regarded as a somewhat more desirable neighborhood because of its greater distance from the mines.[19] Although residents noted that the ethnic groups interacted well and spoke with appreciation of the special cultural events that were so much a part of Thurber's social life, Thurberites also reported few "intermarriages," a certain "clannish" tendency, and little effort on the part of immigrants to learn English. Of the foreign-born coal miners from non-English-speaking nations listed in the 1900 census taken at Thurber, 95 percent did not speak English. However, over 80 percent of Thurber's coal miners, both foreign-born and native, reported themselves as literate in their own languages.[20]

To cope with the large foreign-speaking element in the coal town, the company retained at least one interpreter who spoke seven languages and who conducted English lessons in the evening, particularly for those seeking naturalization. The 1900 census recorded 31 percent of the foreign-born coal miners as naturalized citizens and another 15 percent as having filed the first papers for citizenship. Only a minority of these were Italian; less than one-third of the Italian miners held naturalization or pending citizenship status. The recent immigrant status of the Italian miners, 82 percent of whom had resided in the United States less than ten years—as compared, for example, to the Polish (45 percent), the Mexicans (56 percent), the English (0 percent), and the Irish (0 percent)—at least partially explains this situation.[21] Also, the intention among Italian immigrants in particular to return to their homelands to buy land and improve their economic and social status reduced Americanization and naturalization to secondary considerations.[22]

In the community's work life, coal mining clearly predominated, and the number of foreign-born employed as miners exceeded that in any other major occupation represented in the community. The second largest single industry, the brick-making plant, which opened in 1894, employed fifty-four workers in 1900, only two of whom were foreign-born—one English and the other German. The only occupations other than coal mining in which the foreign-born found employment in significant percentages were saloon keeping (out of five, two were from Italy and one from Scotland), sewing (of two, one was from Scotland), cooking (of three, one was from Italy and one from China), and preaching (of four, one was from Italy and one from Holland). Only one salesman and one manager listed themselves as foreign-born. No store clerks, mine or shop foremen, or company executives—Thurber's white-collar population—claimed foreign birth for themselves or their fathers or lacked the ability to read, write, and speak English. One can conclude, therefore, that country of origin (or ethnicity) and related language capabilities constituted important determinants of occupation, housing patterns, and social/economic position in the community.[23]

Racial diversity also characterized Thurber's coal-mining population. During the company's early labor difficulties, from late 1888 to the middle of 1889, Hunter recruited an estimated 100 to 150 black miners from Indiana. Importing the workers as strikebreakers, Hunter complicated an already tense situation by injecting the racial issue. Outside of occasional fights and threats of violence, however, no massive organized racial disturbances erupted. Hunter kept racial problems, minor or major, to a minimum, as he did various other forms of disruption, by simply removing the "troublemakers."[24] In 1900 the mining company still employed 107 black miners, the largest group of black workers in the community; 87 percent of blacks who resided in Thurber and listed an occupation in the 1900 census held jobs as coal miners. Other occupations open to blacks included positions as boardinghouse keepers, teamsters, day laborers, brick plant workers, servants, launderers, and preachers. Blacks constituted the largest percentage of servants (40 percent) and boardinghouse keepers (46 percent).[25] Race, then, in addition to ethnicity, was an important factor in dictating occupation and socioeconomic position.

Segregation of the races typified Thurber's social life, as reflected in the company's sponsorship of separate Christmas barbecues for black and white residents in 1889, as well as in the existence of separate housing, educational and religious facilities, and fraternal clubs. Yet blacks apparently shopped with whites at company stores, patronized a company saloon where the races imbibed together, and in isolated cases lived in apparent proximity to whites.[26] Furthermore, at the workplace the races toiled together, faces so blackened by coal dust at the end of the day that observers could hardly distinguish the races, and black and white miners earned wages based on the same scale. Once labor agitation began in earnest, it even became biracial and multiethnic. Despite strong animosity toward the black miners imported in 1888 and 1889 to operate mines being struck by former Johnson employees, labor agitators—who by 1894 had identified as adequately as the company the special problems of an ethnically and racially mixed population—had integrated their underground. Of three labor agitators arrested in that year for unlawful assembly, one was black.[27]

Despite their diverse ethnicity and racial makeup, Thurber's coal miners shared the characteristic of youth. The average age for a miner was thirty-one. The 1900 census reported the youngest "miner" as seven, the oldest as seventy-two; 65 percent of these miners fell between the ages of twenty-one and forty, were single, and lived with relatives and fellow countrymen or in boardinghouses the company operated. A significant minority, 30 percent, however, were married heads of households living with their spouses; 80 percent of these homes also had an average of three children in them, lending a family atmosphere to the community that the company encouraged from the time it acquired the property to assure stability in the workforce.[28]

Even with the large number of single coal miners, a group-living experience, made possible by boarding in the homes of married miners, was the norm.[29] Significantly, such living arrangements afforded these miners the opportunity to share their experiences and establish what James R. Green has called "bonds of companionship" so important to the development of a group consciousness.[30] One of the topics that must have filled their conversations was the unique and often frustrating experience of residing and working in a community totally owned and controlled by a business corporation.

Company towns like Thurber commonly existed in the mining industry because of the isolation of deposit sites. In its construction and operation, Thurber exhibited few distinctions from other such company-owned communities within or outside the coal-mining industry.[31] When the corporation acquired the Johnson property and adjoining acreage in 1888, it immediately purchased the few shacks on the property, some owned by Johnson Company miners, to prevent any "outside" ownership on its acreage and denied anyone else the right to construct private buildings on the property. While the inherited labor difficulties slowed production in the mines, the company constructed a general store and warehouse, drugstore, hardware store, boardinghouse, offices and shops, stables, schools, church buildings, and two hundred L- or T-shaped wooden buildings painted the red, green, yellow, or gray typical of early company towns. Containing five or fewer rooms, the houses rented for eight dollars or less a month; the company charged four dollars for the first two rooms, one dollar a month for each additional room, and varying amounts for amenities such as a finished ceiling or a porch. Most of the houses sat on rocky soil that never produced much greenery. As the company's rapid growth demanded more miners and additional housing in a short period of time, neighborhoods closest to the increasing number of producing mines developed a chaotic appearance with haphazard planning leaving the front doorway of one house opening onto the side or back door of another. Inside, dust from coal stoves blackened ceilings and walls, and the view from the unscreened windows rarely changed. The mine dump, the shale dump, and the railroad spur always dominated the scene.[32]

Shortly after acquisition of the site, Hunter supervised erection of a six-foot, four-wire barbed fence that enclosed the nine-hundred-acre tract. Three locked gates controlled access on the south, east, and north sides until a legal confrontation between area residents and the colonel resulted in removal of the locks. Even so, armed guards—including Texas Rangers periodically requested by the company when labor disputes threatened tranquility there—checked outsiders entering the compound.[33] One resident claimed that "an old, gray whiskered man . . . rode these gates, and believe me, nobody got past him."[34] Actually, peddlers and farmers regularly sold goods to residents, but Thurberites complained that men on horseback followed "unwelcome peddlers" inside and recorded the names and house numbers of those who purchased goods from them. This in turn resulted in ingenious methods to escape detection, such as hiding goods under a woman's skirts after a buying trip outside the camp.[35] Hunter testified in an unrelated trial that everyone who lived "by [his] permission" in the enclosure generally traded at the stores, but denied that the company compelled residents to buy there. Nevertheless, a resident claimed that threats of dismissal sometimes followed too many outside purchases by employees, although in reality the company, so hard-pressed for labor in the first years of operation, could hardly afford to release employees for such an insignificant reason.[36] Whatever the company's policy may have been, residents associated the fence with company limitations on freedom of movement and action and detested it as the symbol of Hunter's control over them.

In 1894 the Texas and Pacific Coal Company stockholders chartered a new subsidiary, the Texas Pacific Mercantile and Manufacturing Company, to operate the company stores. One of its most important functions was the issuance and acceptance of scrip as goods payments by employees who found themselves short of money in the thirty to thirty-one days between paydays. The company held two weeks' wages for each employee to guarantee he could pay his rent and utilities charges, but anything above that amount employees could draw as scrip or checks before payday. For example, in January 1900, out of a miner's average gross salary of $43.09, the company deducted an average of $19.95 for scrip purchases. The Texas and Pacific Coal Company issued the coupon checkbooks in denominations of one to ten dollars with five-cent to fifty-cent coupons inside.

Residents used them to purchase everything from groceries, tools, and blasting powder to caskets. If the store did not have a requested item, the company would order it.[37] With the widespread use of the scrip system, debits sometimes outnumbered credits, since the company also deducted fees for rent, utilities, medical care, transportation, blacksmithing, and even special services of a priest. In August 1903, for example, out of nearly 900 miners on the payroll, 135 owed the company money at payday in sums from 24 cents to $26.50.[38] New employees especially faced indebtedness because the company provided credit upon their employment for tools, household goods, furniture, and other necessities. Usually these newcomers began their employment twenty to fifty dollars in debt, gradually working off the balance in the first few months unless extraordinary expenses prevented it.[39] The company typically continued carrying an indebted employee on the account books, maintaining his line of credit until he could earn enough to eliminate his debt. Occasionally miners left the company's employ with a debt outstanding, but these isolated cases had little apparent impact on the company's financial health.[40] The once-a-month payrolls and the scrip system, however, had significant effects on the company's employees and proved to be a source of considerable irritation.

In the interest of public health and safety, the Texas and Pacific Coal Company employed two doctors in the camp's early days and in 1893 constructed a nine-room building to serve as a hospital. Each company wage earner contributed fifty cents per month to a hospital fund, over which the town's superintendent exercised discretionary power, to pay for medical care, supplies, and burial costs.[41] Although wage earners and all family members could receive immediate medical care (and doctors treated an average of twenty patients a day), there were some who feared the doctor's opportunity, once inside the worker's home, to serve as a company informant and who also expressed doubt as to the adequacy of medical care, preferring to choose their own physicians.[42] Minutes from a store managers' meeting proved the former concern was not unfounded. To meet customers' needs more adequately, it was proposed that if, in making their rounds, the doctors saw a peddler at a house, they should inquire as to why the family preferred purchasing from him and report the response to the store's general manager. The physicians apparently agreed.[43] As for the question of the quality of medical care, the company physicians had adequate training and experience and were, according to Gomer Gower, "of a high type."[44] At least one miner, however, who had been injured in a mine blast and treated by company physicians, successfully filed suit against the company, claiming he had received negligent care. He won his case despite the company's appeal that it provided its employees medical treatment as a charity, thus absolving it of any responsibility for possible negligence. The court rejected the company's position on the grounds that the Texas and Pacific Coal Company was "a monopoly with accrued profits in taking care of the sick."[45] Even in the provision of medical care, then, the question of adequacy aside, the company maintained a profitable monopoly. This, above all, residents apparently resented.

The miners further suspected that the company profited from the monthly dollar deduction for railroad transportation to the mines, since the company charged each miner even if he lived close enough to walk. In addition, the miners complained, the railroad operated the mine spur at the company's convenience and at the employees' inconvenience, often delaying the miners' return home at the day's end and limiting their output when an insufficient number of coal cars prevented workers from filling as many cars as they normally could. In retaliation, some miners refused to work the day following such an occurrence. Even company officials complained about the lack of cars, because inadequate numbers of railroad cars hurt production in general.[46]

Although residents objected to company policies and conditions they felt adversely affected their work and personal lives, they also recognized and appreciated the benefits of having the only public library in the county, rent-free church facilities and housing for ministers, a public school for which no one paid school taxes and a private Catholic school with inexpensive tuition, and electrical service after 1895, to which few West Texans had access. An opera house built by the company presented traveling and local shows, and the company encouraged the numerous cultural events central to the lives of the various ethnic groups represented in the community. The coal company also operated two saloons, moving one across the county line when Erath County voted dry so the residents could continue to imbibe and the company could continue to sell them wine, beer, and whiskey. The company supported resident sports activities—Thurber's baseball team, the Thurber Colts, won the state amateur championship in 1896.[47] Robert Goldman and John Wilson have argued that companies sponsored such leisure activities to make workers happier and thus more efficient, hence providing or endorsing the activities to extend the company's control over employees. James R. Green and Herbert G. Gutman, among others, have pointed out that the type of after-work events that Thurber residents enjoyed—family, religious, and national holiday celebrations, sports contests, formal and informal musical productions, fraternal organization meetings, and relaxation at the company saloon or in backyard arbors—constituted more than a simple diversion from work. These activities also afforded residents the opportunity to assert some control over their lives, feel a sense of independence from the company, and participate in events that often crossed ethnic and cultural barriers, thus helping to seal bonds within the working-class population.[48] Even with all the services the company provided and the social opportunities that gave workers a measure of control over their lives, one basic condition still aggrieved them. As Hunter reported in his 1889 report to stockholders, "The management of all affairs of the town is in the hands of your general manager."[49]

The general manager's power extended even to the dispensing of justice. The company, through its general manager, employed all police officers and often hired or asked for county appointment of special constables or other special peace officers to maintain order and to supplement forces already there. Although Hunter denied any knowledge of it, one resident claimed that the local justice of the peace, who was on the company payroll, also lived in Hunter's house during his absence, was wined and dined by company officials, and conducted court in a back room of the saloon. At one point in Thurber's early history, a justice of the peace managed the drugstore for the coal company.[50] Such a close relationship with the company must have dictated the officers' position when problems between employees and employer developed. Additionally, the synonymity of company rules with local law and job dismissal with removal from the camp must have deterred disruptive activity of all kinds. During a protracted fight with saloon lessees, Hunter gave orders, "on pain of discharge" for noncompliance, that his shopkeepers were to refuse service, water, cash for scrip payment redemption, and even ice cream at the parlor to saloon employees. "I didn't want them in the village," he bluntly stated. A very personal form of "justice" thus permeated the camp.[51]

Hunter regarded the most serious disruptions in the community as those inspired by unwanted labor activity. Labor organizations near the site of the Texas and Pacific Coal Company mining operations had a history at least six years longer than that of the coal company itself. Jonathan Garlock's *Guide to the Local Assemblies of the Knights of Labor* lists three locals in Erath County between 1885 and 1888 (none specifically for coal miners), four in nearby Eastland County between 1883 and 1887, and nine in Palo Pinto County, of which one at Gordon, adjacent to Thurber, represented coal miners from 1882 to 1889. In 1886, the same year the Johnson mine began operation, the Gordon local recorded over two hundred members in an area having a population under one thousand.[52]

The members of this local assembly most likely worked for the Gould interests at Coalville until operations ceased in January 1886. When the Johnson brothers recruited the unemployed miners there, they offered the workers a mining rate of $1.50 a ton, twenty-five cents lower than what they had received at Coalville.[53] Under the best conditions, mining coal was difficult and dangerous, but the mining situation around Gordon hardly could be termed ideal. "Low" coal veins required twice as much effort as ordinary mining to produce a ton of coal. The typical miner undermined the vein of coal by hand, then drilled two-inch holes at the top of the deposit, in which he placed blasting powder. With the coal loosened by the explosion of the powder, he then crawled into the narrow working place necessitated by the thin vein and, lying on his side while working, kicked the coal back with his feet until he filled the nearby railroad car. Without electricity, the miner had only the light from an oil lamp positioned in front of his pit cap to guide him. Rats roamed the mines, and the fear of explosion, fire, injury, cave-ins, and suffocation constantly confronted him. Thus, considering the adversities of mining such veins, the Johnson Mining Company's offer fell on deaf ears.[54]

For two months the miners remained idle until the company accorded the local Knights of Labor Assembly the right to appoint a mine committee to negotiate with management in settling disputes and agreed to remunerate the miners at the wage scale paid at Coalville. From that point, good relations between the miners' local and the company continued until the Johnsons announced in 1888 that they could not meet the September payroll. Payment for seven weeks' work was at stake, so a strike with far-reaching consequences resulted. The company's financial distress precluded a satisfactory settlement for either side, and so Johnson completed negotiations begun with the Texas and Pacific Coal Company months earlier for sale of the property and company assets.[55]

Hunter attributed the Johnsons' "financial embarrassments" to "refugees from justice and Mollie MacGuires" [*sic*] who had "taken possession of the new enterprise of the Johnson Company," a charge which Gomer Gower, who with his father was among the original Johnson employees, adamantly denied. He instead attributed the troubles to the untimely death of the more capable Harvey Johnson and the financial demands of digging a new mine.[56] Robert W. Spoede, William Johnson's biographer, has speculated that Hunter, though already in the process of acquiring the company, allowed its financial collapse to occur in September, thus deceiving the miners into leaving the shaft so he would "have the opportunity to make new arrangements with them at a lower wage scale."[57] Whatever the cause of the Johnsons' problems, Hunter refused to recognize the existence of the strike he inherited from the former owners since the miners had never worked for T&P. For four years, however, the situation proved to be an expensive frustration for him.

Hunter held no affection for assertive, organized workers, and as he established his domain in Thurber, refused to negotiate on any terms but his own. When T&P took possession of the property on November 13, 1888, he told his stockholders he had "found . . . three hundred men of all nationalities in control."[58] He immediately posted notices in the camp announcing more than a 30 percent cut in the mining rate and almost a 10 percent reduction in the day wage the Johnsons had paid. He further stated that the mining rate would be paid on the "screened coal basis." By this method the coal, before being weighed, was dumped over a six-by-twelve-foot screen with one-quarter-inch spaces between the bars. The miners received nothing for the nut and pea coal that fell through the bars, which the miners believed the company used to fire its boilers and to trade for some of the beer sold at the company-owned saloons. Since the Johnsons had paid the men on the "mine run basis" for the full weight of the coal mined, worker acceptance of the screening method would have reduced wages another 12 to 13 percent, an impossible concession. Further alienating the Johnson miners, the T&P general manager demanded that employees "renounce their allegiance to the Knights of Labor and refrain from joining or otherwise assisting in the formation of a union of any sort." This demand for a yellow-dog contract, Gower said, was like the "shaking of a red shawl in the face of a bull." When a miners' committee sought a meeting with Hunter, he received them cordially but could not conceal his disdain for them. As they left, having gained no concessions, Gower recalled that Hunter admonished them: "I will make a dollar look as big as a wagon wheel to you S-O-Bs before I get through with you."[59] No one subsequently applied for Hunter's jobs, forcing him to send his confederates on recruiting tours to mining camps in Indiana, Illinois, Pennsylvania, Kentucky, Missouri, and Kansas.[60]

In a remarkable display of unity, the Johnson miners in concert with Knights of Labor locals in various mining districts across the country managed to impede company recruiting efforts for almost three months. Their means of operation were simple but effective. Gomer Gower wrote, "There was a sufficient number of us who sought employment in various parts of the country . . . to advise unsuspecting miners of the conditions in Texas. I, myself, though but an eighteen year old boy at the time, was assigned to the Belleville field in southern Illinois for that purpose."[61] Thurber miners also filed reports on conditions around the Thurber mines for publication in the *Journal of United Labor*, news organ of the Knights of Labor. In December 1888 the paper carried an item requesting miners "to stay away from the Johnson mines near Gordon, Texas as there is a strike of the men at that point." In January Dan McLauchlan, secretary of the

Knights of Labor local near Thurber, wrote a lengthy letter explaining that T&P wage cuts had precipitated the crisis and that all the miners wanted was a chance to be heard and to receive fair arbitration of the wage issue. He concluded with the warning: "This is a poor place to come to for work at present, and all miners are requested to keep away until the matter is settled."[62] McLauchlan sent similar letters to another labor newspaper, the *National Labor Tribune*, news arm of the National Progressive Union of Miners.

Such publicity in the areas where the company sought recruits and speech making by Knights of Labor leaders to miners upon their arrival in Texas kept the mines practically shut down until February 1889. Furthermore, to Hunter's dismay, the striking workers congregated only a mile from company headquarters on land that the Knights of Labor had purchased in 1887. When the company demanded that the miners with homes on the Johnson property remove or sell them, many transported the shacks to the labor union's ten-acre tract nearby. There the Knights Assembly had constructed a two-story meeting hall that doubled as a community center in the isolated campsite. As the troubles with the Texas and Pacific Coal Company began, the hall became a setting for considerable commiseration and agitation.[63] The saloon on the Johnson property also provided the strikers with a place to meet and to plan their activities, further arousing Hunter's ire.[64]

Moral support and financial assistance from the Knights of Labor, supplemented by food supplies contributed by local Farmers' Alliance members and assistance from a sympathetic county sheriff, seriously impeded Hunter's effort to start production. Knights of Labor locals throughout the nation's mining districts contributed funds and information to the Thurber miners as they dispatched their representatives to apprise potential T&P recruits of the situation around the mines. When company trains arrived in these areas, local assembly members infiltrated the meetings, learned the time of return to Texas, and passed the information to Thurber's local. When the trains arrived in Fort Worth, a Knights delegation waited to persuade the potential strikebreakers to leave, and with Farmers' Alliance and Knights of Labor national assembly aid, to fund their return.[65] In February, however, T&P officials and Texas Rangers (who had arrived in Thurber around Christmas) duped labor activists waiting for the train in Fort Worth, and 172 miners arrived in Thurber to begin work. Even so, one-third of them subsequently refused to enter the mines and joined the Knights of Labor after hearing speeches at the Labor Hall. The rest commenced work, their numbers supplemented by other recruiting trips. By March 1889 the mines were producing two hundred tons of coal per day; by July production had increased to over three hundred tons and was expected to reach as much as eight hundred tons by September.[66]

Frustrated in his initial attempts to import new employees, operate the mines, and maintain absolute control, Hunter resolved to crush the striking miners. By Christmas 1888, after gunfire showered the store and office where Hunter and his lieutenants had ensconced themselves, the general manager appealed to state officials for a contingency of Texas Rangers to be sent "to protect life and property at the mines."[67] The *Dallas Morning News* reported on December 23 that ten of Captain S. A. McMurry's company of Texas Rangers had arrived at the mines three days earlier to handle a disturbance caused by striking miners. Five days later, the paper noted, McMurry wired Adjutant General W. H. King in Austin that all was "quiet and orderly" around the mines.[68] McMurry reported that thirty to forty strikers continued their agitation and were "very much annoyed on a/c of a number of them having been arrested for Rioting, Intimidation, [and] Carrying Pistols."[69] On July 8 McMurry noted that John Clinton, a member of the miners' strike committee, had penetrated the enclosure and beaten two white miners, for which he was promptly detained.[70]

Although Mary Jane Gentry contends that the Rangers acted as "referees to see that no foul punches were administered,"[71] it is clear that the primary reason the adjutant general ordered the Rangers to Thurber was to remove the agitating miners or to maintain control over them for the company's benefit. As long as the Rangers remained, the striking miners knew they had little chance to succeed. Shortly before the Rangers left Thurber, McMurry told King, "the strikers still remain in force on the outside, praying for the Rangers to be moved away. They claim that they could soon get clear of 'old Hunter' & the Negroes, were it not for the Rangers."[72] Although Covington A. Hall, general lecturer for the Knights of Labor, claimed that a "peaceful law abiding lot of citizens" at Thurber were "being abused, imposed upon and mystreated [*sic*] by a company of State Rangers," Gomer Gower described them overall as a "pretty decent bunch of fellows."[73] Whatever their demeanor, however, their purpose was indisputable. When they departed, Hunter held the upper hand. In the process he expended thirty thousand dollars in company funds. He also took advantage of a situation that Gentry and others who have written on Thurber's early labor difficulties have only hinted at—the acute problem of dual unionism then complicating organizational efforts in American mining districts. Apparently recognizing the competition for jurisdiction occurring between the fledgling Knights of Labor District Assembly 135 and the National Progressive Union, Hunter convinced representatives of the latter, which in 1890 formed the United Mine Workers, to declare the strike over.[74] The organization's willingness to do so reflected its leaders' reasoning that the possible employment of miners in Texas would open the district to them.[75]

In December 1888, Hunter contacted the *National Labor Tribune*, which by then already had run several T&P recruitment advertisements as well as letters from Dan McLauchlan charging the company with "trying to get men who cannot talk English to come here" and with employing tactics that "would bring the blush of shame to the cheek of the worst landlords that ever Ireland saw."[76] Hunter requested that a Progressive Union representative investigate conditions at the mines. The union complied; after arriving on Christmas Day 1888, William Rennie reported to the *Tribune* at the conclusion of meetings with Hunter and the miners' committee, and upon an examination of the camp, that the company had not misrepresented to potential employees the physical conditions around the mines. He concluded with the comment that he knew of "no mining camp where a miner can enjoy more advantages than at the mines of the Texas and Pacific Coal Company." His denunciation of and personal attack on McLauchlan reflected consolidationists' frustration with Knights of Labor locals, which, they contended, acted too brashly and without the sanction of district leaders. "It is no wonder the K. of L. has got into bad repute," Rennie concluded.[77]

Shortly after Rennie's trip, the *National Labor Tribune* declared that under union rules a strike did not exist, opening the way for workers to accept employment in Thurber. This, the paper stated, would preserve the Texas coalfield for unionization and save it from being overwhelmed by cheap Mexican labor.[78] The local strikers, however, rejected the *Tribune's* decision and wrote letters to the *Journal of United Labor* requesting continued support. The Knights of Labor newspaper subsequently called for the *Tribune's* condemnation but took no further action.[79] Finally, in the fall of 1889, apparently after submission of the local's case to the General Executive Board of the Knights of Labor, Terence V. Powderly sent an aide, executive board member James J. Holland, to meet with Hunter (who refused to "treat with him"), resulting in abandonment of the fight and a declaration that the strike was "off."[80] Many of the strikers drifted to other parts of the country, but problems remained and underground activism continued.

In July 1890, the same year that the newly formed United Mine Workers (UMW) assumed jurisdiction over District Assembly 135 miners, Hunter asked the Rangers to return to Thurber "to prevent race troubles," which, he claimed, the "old strikers" were fomenting. Fence cutting was the principal manifestation of the "considerable disorder," Captain McMurry reported. With Ranger assistance, however, Hunter and the fence held their ground; within a month normal coal-mining operations resumed.[81] Even so, Gower recalled, though Hunter had discharged union members and blacklisted former Johnson employees, the colonel agreed in 1892 to employ some of them if they refrained from organizing activity. Whatever short-term promises they may have made to Hunter, the organizational activity did not end.[82]

In June 1894 General Manager Hunter again wrote Ranger Adjutant General W. H. Mabry for assistance: "Owing to the troubled condition among the miners of the United States at this time, I ask you to appoint about five special rangers to assist in keeping peace at the mines." Hunter refused to admit that a strike had occurred in his mines, though the *Dallas Morning News* reported a work stoppage, but he contended striking miners elsewhere "are sending their walking delegates in here in a clandestine manner." All would be peaceful in Thurber, he concluded, if "let alone by these agitators."[83] Not only did the Rangers arrive in Thurber, but a mounted police force also patrolled the mines. Company spies reportedly infiltrated miner groups and reported "troublemakers" to Hunter, who called them in for questioning by himself and a coterie of lawyers. However, even the "untutored miners," Gower claimed, were "well versed in the art of dealing with spies and evading the hypothetical questions of the inquisitors" and "baffled the Colonel."[84] Even so, after a strike meeting at a darkened Knights of Labor Hall, peace officers detained the participating parties, apparently on the word of the special undercover officer in attendance.[85] The *Dallas Morning News* reported the arrest of three "outsiders," two white and one black, on the charge of unlawful assembly for organizing the "riotous meeting." "No further trouble is anticipated," the Dallas paper optimistically announced, "as the miners here refuse to come out at the solicitation of agitators sent here by outside parties."[86]

In 1899 Hunter retired, his son-in-law Edgar L. Marston replacing him as president of the company. William K. Gordon, a former railroad surveyor, geologist, and assistant manager under Hunter, assumed Hunter's duties as general manager. Considerably more sensitive and sympathetic to the miners and enlightened in his management of the town, Gordon was well liked by residents. Nevertheless, he inherited Hunter's labor problems and continued the company's antiunion policy, to which he was personally sympathetic.[87] This change in management occurred as the United Mine Workers of America began making important inroads in the organization of miners in the Southwest.

By 1899 UMW organizers, emboldened by their successes in organizing the nation's central mining district, had moved west of the Mississippi and received recognition in parts of the Southwest Field (including Arkansas, Indian Territory, and Texas).[88] By 1900, for example, the mines at Lyra, Strawn, Rock Creek, Alba, and Bridgeport could be counted as union camps. Gordon wrote Marston in January of that year that things were "quiet" with his miners after a spate of difficulty with the drivers, but he expressed disappointment that "Bennett over at Strawn is allowing the Union to get a very strong foothold there. . . . Besides, it gives this organization a starting point in Texas, which could have been so easily prevented had he opposed it in its infancy."[89] Thurber was one of the holdouts in the area, but the history of labor agitation there, the intensive organizational activity apparently realizing success in nearby mining camps and across the Southwest, and mine operators' recognition that districtwide union agreements could actually help stabilize an industry plagued by cutthroat competition and falling prices paved the way for Thurber's succumbing to the inevitable.[90] Furthermore, though company officials may have felt some security in the large number of non-English-speaking immigrants in Thurber, whom employers typically regarded as docile and less inclined to join unions, the UMW early recognized the reality of multiethnic and multiracial mining populations and quickly adapted to them. In 1891, when the *United Mine Workers Journal* began publication, it printed its weekly editions in a number of foreign languages. Organizers who spoke foreign languages worked areas with a high concentration of immigrant workers. The UMW also actively organized mixed locals to include not only immigrant but black laborers as well.[91]

With the intensification of organization activity in Texas by 1900, union organizers were working the Thurber mines surreptitiously, some even donning disguises to penetrate the fenced compound. The company ordered activists discovered inside the town to vacate the premises, but smoldering discontent and "secret preparations" produced well-organized collective action by Labor Day 1903.[92] The union's stepped-up activity prompted the company to post an announcement dated August 23, written in four languages, that—effective October 1—the Texas and Pacific Coal Mining Company would increase the mining rate from $1.00 to $1.05 a ton and pay bonuses for production of anything over the miners' average monthly production of thirty tons. Additionally, the company proposed to delay the early-morning train departure time from 6:30 to 7:00 and granted the miners a nine-hour day. Few miners failed to recognize what was afoot. A September 3 notice confirmed this perception: "For the information of all employees, notice is given that Thurber will remain a nonunion camp." Anyone who disagreed could "get a settlement at any time."[93] The miners took these notices as a direct challenge. Fanning the fire were reports of the disappearance of a Mexican organizer and rumors of the discovery of a murdered Mexican, his identification withheld by the company, in the area.[94] Sensing the tension, Gordon took action.

On August 30, 1903, the general manager wrote Governor Samuel Willis Tucker Lanham for a contingent of Rangers. Claiming that 98 percent of the workers wanted no union, he charged UMW activists with "endeavoring to create discontent amongst our people." The first group of Rangers arrived on September 5 after the mine workers' union had announced plans for a three-day picnic to begin on Labor Day.[95] To defuse the union's plans, Gordon announced that the Thurber Club, a private social organization not normally open to the miners, would be the site of a grand barbecue in celebration of Labor Day. Not to be outdone, the UMW seized the opportunity of having the miners all together—some eleven hundred persons assembled there—and instructed a miner's son to ride among them spreading the word that a UMW organizer waited at Lyra to induct them into the union.[96] About sixty miners immediately left Thurber and joined the organization. Peter Hanraty, president of UMW Union District 21, which covered the Southwest Field, William M. Wardjon, international organizer of the UMW, and C. W. Woodman, secretary of the Texas State Federation of Labor, received the new members and sent them back to the company town to "work quietly and wait." To the surprise of even the organizers, "the work of the sixty bore immediate fruit."[97]

On the following day Thurber's as yet largely unorganized miners presented Gordon with a set of demands calling for a mining rate of $1.35 a ton, an increase in day wages, an eight-hour day, biweekly paydays, and recognition of the United Mine Workers of America. Although it was not among their written demands, the miners also made clear their sentiment that the fence and armed guards should be removed.[98] When Gordon refused to meet the demands, the miners boycotted the mines the following day and marched to Lyra to meet UMW representatives. "There the men ... congregated in a grove awaiting [Wardjon]—waiting for some one [*sic*] to tell them how to become union men." Seven hundred miners joined the union on the spot, and organizers called another meeting to be held at the Palo Pinto Bridge. On Friday unionized miners from Lyra led the procession and upon their arrival at the bridge "found fully 1800 men and women," representing not only miners and their families but brick workers, clerks, carpenters, teamsters, and laborers, all interested in unionization. As a posse of Rangers approached, the crowd surrounded the speakers, fearing confrontation. None occurred; the peace officers simply requested that the miners not set off any blasting powder, as was the custom during celebrations, and departed. The organizers, with benefit of translators, proceeded to swear in the union's newest converts and to initiate steps to organize all the other company employees.[99] Wardjon counseled the miners not to return to work, draw any pay, or remove their tools from the mines until Hanraty arrived to advise them further, because under company rules workers had to vacate their homes one week after drawing their final pay. The miners then created a relief committee with all "races" represented, opened a commissary to aid those in need, and promised shelter to anyone forced out of his home.[100]

On Hanraty's arrival, the district president told the strikers that if they did not want to work for the company under existing conditions, they should pick up their tools and leave the property. Hanraty explained: "If the company will not treat you as human beings, then leave them in peace. . . . If you are denied the right to have a voice in what your wages will be, then you are not free men." So emerged the union's plan of action—an exodus, a massive "going away."[101] To succeed, the exodus had to be a peaceful one. "If anyone imposes upon you, let us know and we will see that you are protected under the law. But, let me tell you," Hanraty continued, "if you do any one [sic] wrong, I will be the first to see that you are sent where you belong."[102] The workers complied without exception. No violence or drunkenness aggravated the tense scene. To those ready to depart Thurber, the UMW offered shelter, assistance, new employment, and transportation and even promised to supervise the stock of those leaving if quarantine laws at their destinations would affect them. Gordon offered the miners train service to the mines, accompanied by Rangers, to collect their tools. All miners who requested their pay received it in cash. Tools that the company offered to purchase and personal property too cumbersome to transport sold cheaply.[103]

All together some five hundred miners left Thurber, most being single Italian men who sought new employment elsewhere in the United States or returned to Italy. The dramatic departure crippled the company, since only eight or nine men refused to strike, and the limited recruitment efforts initiated by the company failed miserably. In one case eighteen miners from Pennsylvania imported by the company marched to Lyra as soon as local residents described the situation to them. Once there, union organizers convinced them to leave and paid their return passage.[104] Almost two weeks into the strike, Edgar L. Marston arrived in Thurber in his private railroad car and met with Hanraty, Wardjon, and Woodman to request that the mine workers' union not call out the miners at Rock Creek, where a subsidiary of T&P employed 150 men. In return he agreed to recognize the union at Rock Creek. The company having taken the first step, UMW officials promised not to transport any more workers from the area, inferring that Marston would recognize the union in Thurber if the employees halted their departures. Marston then agreed to participate in an upcoming Fort Worth meeting between Southwest coalfield operators and union representatives.[105]

From September 23 to September 26, Marston met with national, regional, and local UMW leaders, finally signing an agreement granting the workers a 15 percent raise, a biweekly payroll, and the eight-hour day. The company also agreed to collect union dues, assessments, fines, and initiation fees, an agreement that subsequent payroll records confirm. The miners further received the right to have a check weighman oversee the weighing of each miner's output, and although the screened mining system continued, the miners gained company acquiescence in a narrowing of the bars that determined the amount of coal retained for weighing. In return, the union promised to return the men to the mines and to solicit four hundred to five hundred miners if needed to replace employees who had departed permanently.[106]

Not only did the negotiations successfully address the miners' concerns about their work, but the strike also influenced company policy in regard to those features of a company town that had continued to frustrate residents, even with the change in management after Hunter's retirement. The fence surrounding Thurber, the symbol of an autocracy that even in its paternalism affronted human dignity, came down.[107] John S. Spratt's recently published reminiscence about life in and around Thurber indicates that in the post-1903 period T&P acquiesced in allowing employees to live outside the town, tolerated outside merchants and peddlers who began to advertise freely and to sell their goods in the camp, and accepted residents' requests to seek the care of physicians other than those employed by the company if they so chose. Spratt's father, who brought his family to the area in 1904 and established his medical practice in nearby Mingus (Thurber Junction), actually had a larger practice in Thurber than in Mingus.[108] Additionally, Marston's annual report for 1903 proposed that the mercantile company be operated more independently of the coal company since the company stores served as a perennial topic at union meetings.[109]

Fifteen years of activism produced by Hunter's repressive operation of Thurber and its residents' attendant desire for greater control over their work and personal lives, the history of labor activism in the area before Hunter began his enterprise, the influence of a strong national labor organization, and the need for greater stability in coal-mining operations nationwide produced a victory in which every resident in Thurber would share. The company won as well, for few labor difficulties threatened the mines' operation during the next twenty years. Both Marston and Gordon, whom union organizers praised as gentlemen and recognized as considerably more enlightened than Hunter in their relationship with company employees, faithfully fulfilled the contracts that the UMW negotiated.[110] However, by the 1920s, as demand for coal declined with the railroads' increasing use of fuel oil, the Texas and Pacific Coal and Oil Company increasingly shifted its attention to oil deposits that Gordon had discovered on company property in nearby Ranger.[111] Under such conditions, Thurber's coal-mining population became expendable when the union demanded a wage increase in 1921. A subsequent strike resulted in a permanent exodus that left Thurber a virtual ghost town within fifteen years. This time the company also departed, no longer dependent on its coal-mining population for financial success, and the United Mine Workers Union disappeared.[112]

Although Mary Jane Gentry is partially correct in her description of Thurber's labor problems as peculiar and unique, the events that occurred in Thurber between 1888 and 1903 were played out similarly in other bituminous and anthracite coal-mining areas across the United States as the United Mine Workers sought and won official recognition. In Texas, Thurber's miner activists constituted only one group of numerous labor agitators who were protesting working conditions. Longshoremen, railroad workers, cowboys, cotton handlers, streetcar workers, and miners all expressed their discontent.[113] What did make Thurber unusual was the complete success of unionization efforts among an ethnically and racially mixed population by 1903. Before the strike there were only three hundred organized miners in Texas. By 1904 the closed shop operated in Texas mining districts. As of April 1909 the total United Mine Workers Union membership in Texas locals was twenty-two hundred.[114] Beyond the community's significance to an organized mining industry, James C. Maroney has added that the victory in Thurber enabled organized labor in Texas to persevere in the face of the early twentieth-century open shop movement.[115] Leading this defense was the Texas Federation of Labor, in which the United Mine Worker locals—including the two at Thurber, which were among the largest in the country—played an influential role until their decline in the mid-1920s.[116] The state organization at this time not only endorsed labor's traditional tactic, the strike, but also mobilized organized labor's resources to lobby successfully for legislation to protect Texas industrial workers. Laws that the state legislature passed in the early 1900s, under pressure from organized labor, included prohibition of the use of coercion against employees who did not patronize company stores, institution of safety standards in mines, establishment of sixteen as the minimum age for mine workers, a declaration that scrip payment to employees was illegal, and passage of an antiblacklisting law.[117] Gomer Gower claimed: "Labor . . . was in the saddle in Texas."[118] The transition that labor activism underwent from reliance primarily on the strike in the late nineteenth century to a combination of organization, striking, and concerted legislative lobbying by a more united labor movement in the twentieth century was furthered by the success of organization efforts such as those in Thurber. Thus the significance of events there—a victory of the individual and of a union—extended well beyond those community boundaries that the old fence had once marked.

Notes

This chapter originally appeared in *Southwestern Historical Quarterly* 92 (April 1989): 509–42, and is reprinted with permission.

1.   Gomer Gower to M. J. Gentry, January 18, 1945, in Mary Jane Gentry, "Thurber: The Life and Death of a Texas Town" (master's thesis, University of Texas at Austin, 1946), 236–37.

2.   Ruth A. Allen, *Chapters in the History of Organized Labor in Texas,* University of Texas Publication No. 4143 (Austin: Bureau of Research in the Social Sciences, University of Texas, 1941), 91.

3.   James C. Maroney, "Organized Labor in Texas, 1900–1929" (PhD diss., University of Houston, 1975), 50, 57, 59, 92–93.

4.   "Thurber, Texas . . . TP's Birthplace," *TP Voice* 2 (May–June 1966): 6; Miscellaneous File, Texas and Pacific Coal Company Records, 1887–1969 (Southwest Collection, Texas Tech University, Lubbock, cited hereafter as Texas and Pacific Coal Company Records); Jimmy M. Skaggs, "To Build a Barony: Colonel Robert D. Hunter," *Arizona and the West* 15 (Autumn 1973): 245. The *TP Voice,* a publication of the Texas and Pacific Oil Company, stated: "Thurber was virtually his [Hunter's] serfdom."

5.   Eric D. Weitz, "Class Formation and Labor Protest in the Mining Communities of Southern Illinois and the Ruhr, 1890–1925," *Labor History* 27 (Winter 1985–86): 88–91. Carter Goodrich examines the "freedom" of miners' work in *The Miner's Freedom: A Study of the Working Life in a Changing Industry* (Boston: Marshall Jones Co., 1925), 31: "There is in fact a strong feeling in the industry . . . that the miner is a sort of independent petty contractor and that how much he works and when are more his own affair than the company's." Robert F. Foerster, *The Italian Emigration of Our Times* (1919; repr., Cambridge, MA: Harvard University Press, 1924), 351, writes: "The North Texas Community, at Thurber, is also of Sicilians [southern Italians]." Most of those emigrating from southern Italy were agricultural day laborers, but they also included some artisans, miners, and small proprietors. Ibid., 104. See also Herbert G. Gutman, "Work, Culture, and Society in Industrializing America, 1815–1919," in *Work, Culture, and Society in*

Industrializing America: Essays in American Working-Class and Social History, ed. Herbert G. Gutman (New York: Vintage Books, 1977), 6, 22–24.

6.   Mr. and Mrs. Robert W. Spoede, interview with Lawrence Santi, August 1, 1967, in Thurber, Texas Collection, 1897–1980 and undated, Southwest Collection, Texas Tech University, Lubbock (cited hereafter as Thurber Collection).

7.   Gentry, "Thurber," 1–4.

8.   Data submitted by W. K. Gordon, secretary, vice president, and general manager, for the Texas and Pacific Coal Company's Twenty-Fifth Anniversary Souvenir, Thurber, TX, July 4, 1913, pp. 1–4, Miscellaneous File, Texas and Pacific Coal Company Records; data submitted for Twenty-Fifth Anniversary by T. R. Hall, Thurber, TX, July 30, 1913, p. 1, Miscellaneous File, Texas and Pacific Coal Company Records.

9.   Annual Report of the Texas and Pacific Coal Company, 1889, pp. 1–3, 6, Miscellaneous File, Texas and Pacific Coal Company Records (cited hereafter as Annual Report, 1889); John C. Brown to Johnson Brothers Coal Mining Company, March 24, 1888, William Whipple Johnson Papers, 1855 (1870–1904), 1908, Southwest Collection, Texas Tech University, Lubbock (cited hereafter as Johnson Papers); Document of Sale, Johnson Coal Mining Company and Texas and Pacific Coal Company, October 6, 1888, Johnson Papers. Hunter stated that he chose the name Texas and Pacific for his coal company simply because of the proximity of the railroad to the purchased site. The Texas and Pacific Company and the Texas and Pacific Railroad were separate companies with no corporate link.

10.   Data submitted by W. K. Gordon, p. 30, Texas and Pacific Coal Company Records.

11.   US Department of the Interior, Census Office, *Compendium of the Eleventh Census: 1890* (Washington, DC: US Government Printing Office, 1894–1897), pt. 1, 391.

12.   US Department of the Interior, Census Office, *Twelfth Census of the United States* (1900), Thurber, Erath County, TX, Population Schedules, microfilm of original MS, Clayton Genealogical Library, Houston (cited hereafter as *Twelfth Census* MS); Dr. Vernon L. Williams, History Department, North Harris County College, Houston, provided me with invaluable assistance in applying computer-based quantification methodology to this project. The History Department, University of Houston, facilitated my access to the university's computer system. All analyses of *Twelfth Census* data in this study are based upon information provided in the census on all 2,559 residents in Thurber. My conclusions are based not on random sampling but on an analysis of the total population.

13.   *Compendium of the Eleventh Census*, 508; US Department of the Interior, Census Office, *Twelfth Census of the United States Taken in the Year 1900* (Washington, DC: US Government Printing Office, 1902), 784, 787.

14.   Ledger, 1887, Johnson Papers; Mine Payrolls, 1890–1899, Financial Material, Texas and Pacific Coal Company Records.

15.   *Twelfth Census* MS.

16.   Gomer Gower to Ben L. Owens, November 4, 1940, Mine Workers, Gower Let-

ters [folder], Labor Movement in Texas Collection, Barker Texas History Center, University of Texas at Austin (cited hereafter as Gower Letters); see Journal A, October 1888–June 1893, pp. 8, 18, Financial Material, Texas and Pacific Coal Company Records.

17. *Twelfth Census* MS. The designation "Polish" in table 1 refers to census respondents who listed country of birth as Poland Austria, Poland Germany, Poland Russia, or Russia Poland. Similarly, the designation "Hungarian" applies to those who described themselves as being from Hungary-Austria.

18. Gentry, "Thurber," 185–200; Michael Q. Hooks, "Thurber: A Unique Texas Community," *Panhandle-Plains Historical Review* 56 (1983): 1–17.

19. Biographical Information Sheets, Earl Brown, Sammie F. Booth, Ruth Elaine Calloway Costa, Sadie Markland Plummer, John Franklin Jordan, William K. Gordon Jr., Thurber Collection (cited hereafter as Biographical Information Sheets); *Twelfth Census* MS; Gentry, "Thurber," 135, 141–42, 187–88; Rent Book, Texas and Pacific Coal Company, 1900–1901, Financial Material, Texas and Pacific Coal Company Records.

20. *Twelfth Census* MS; Biographical Information Sheets, Costa (quotations).

21. *Twelfth Census* MS; Biographical Information Sheets, Plummer, Pauline Anna Havins, Hut Brock; Gomer Gower to Ben L. Owens, November 12, 1940, Gower Letters.

22. See Betty Boyd Caroli, *Italian Repatriation from the United States, 1900–1914* (New York: Center for Migration Studies, 1973), v, 85, 93–94.

23. *Twelfth Census* MS. By 1900 Hunter, who was foreign-born, had retired from the company, leaving its control in the hands of his son-in-law Edgar L. Marston, who was American-born. Marston resided in New York. In an environment such as Thurber, with workers being recruited for particular occupations, there was obviously less "natural" competition initially for certain types of jobs. This, however, does not diminish the significance of the occupational composition of the population, housing patterns, and social position as related to ethnicity, race, and gender.

24. Annual Report, 1889, p. 4; *Texas and Pacific Coal Company vs. Lawson*, p. 300, Case #346, Supreme Court of Texas Records, 1838–1945, Lorenzo de Zavala State Archives, Texas State Library, Austin (cited hereafter as *Texas and Pacific vs. Lawson*).

25. *Twelfth Census* MS.

26. *Fort Worth Gazette,* December 27, 1889, copy in Mine Workers, United, 1889–1940, Labor Movement in Texas Collection (cited hereafter as Mine Workers, United). The *Texas Miner*, a weekly publication of the Texas and Pacific Coal Company, January 27, 1894, mentioned the existence of two public schools for Thurber's school-age children, one "colored and [one] white." White children attended the Thurber School; black children attended the Hunter School, according to County Superintendent's School Record, 1890–1891, Erath County Records, Special Collections, Tarleton State University, Stephenville, TX; Bio-

graphical Information Sheets, Costa, Gordon; Gentry, "Thurber," 139. The *Texas Mining and Trade Journal* (which the Texas and Pacific Coal Company previously had called the *Texas Miner*), September 16, 1899, included a "General Directory" for the community that listed a "colored" church, the Hunter Morning Star Church, and seven "colored" lodges (as well as several Italian lodges).

27.　*Dallas Morning News*, June 5, 1894; Ann Clark interview with Daisy Conn, August 8, 1967, Thurber Collection; Biographical Information Sheets, Jane Graham Terry, Lorene Smith Dobson.

28.　*Twelfth Census* MS; advertisement placed by the Texas and Pacific Coal Company in the *National Labor Tribune*, December 8, 1888, for two hundred miners, "married men preferred."

29.　*Twelfth Census* MS; Rent Book, 1900–1901, Texas and Pacific Coal Company Records. A nuclear family is defined as parent(s) and child(ren); an extended household as parent(s), child(ren), and other relatives; and an augmented household as parent(s), child(ren), and nonrelatives. The Fantini home, for example, housed seven boarders in addition to four family members. Alex Fantini paid the company six dollars a month in rent. The four-room house with washhouse that the Morietta family rented contained seven boarders in addition to two family members. The company charged Morietta seven dollars a month. Five boarders lived in the Gerrotti residence with four family members. The house had four rooms and a washhouse.

30.　James R. Green, *The World of the Worker: Labor in Twentieth-Century America* (New York: Hill and Wang, 1980), 15.

31.　See, for example, James B. Allen, *The Company Town in the American West* (Norman: University of Oklahoma Press, 1966), 6–7, 13, 80–137; David J. Saposs, "Self-Government and Freedom of Action in Isolated Industrial Communities," 1–47, microfilm set of 15 reels, Reel 11, University of Houston Library, Houston, in material submitted by John R. Commons of the US Commission of Industrial Relations to the State Historical Society of Wisconsin from US Senate, *Industrial Relations: Final Report and Testimony Submitted to Congress by the Commission on Industrial Relations Created by the Act of August 23, 1912*, Document No. 415, 64th Cong., 1st sess., 1916 (cited hereafter as State Historical Society of Wisconsin microfilm set, Reel 1); US Department of Labor, Bureau of Labor Statistics, *Housing by Employers in the United States*, Bulletin No. 263 (Washington, DC: US Government Printing Office, 1920).

32.　Biographical Information Sheets, Havins; Gentry, "Thurber," 133–34; Gower to Owens, November 4, 12, 1940, Gower Letters; Annual Report, 1889, pp. 5–6. See Rent Book, 1900–1901, Financial Material, Texas and Pacific Coal Company Records, for charges for amenities.

33.　Annual Report, 1889, pp. 5–6; Gower to Owens, November 4, 12, 1940, Gower Letters; *Texas and Pacific vs. Lawson,* 268; Gower to Gentry, January 18, 1945, in Gentry, "Thurber," 235–36.

34.　George Carter, "The Thurber Story," Miscellaneous File, Thurber Collection.

35. Gower to Owens, November 12, 1940 (quotation), Gower Letters; Gentry, "Thurber," 106; *Texas and Pacific vs. Lawson,* 261, 271, 531, 562; *Texas Miner,* January 27, 1894; *Stephenville Empire,* July 16, 1892.

36. *Texas and Pacific vs. Lawson,* 269, 271 (quotation); Biographical Information Sheets, Brock.

37. Gentry, "Thurber," 105; *Texas and Pacific vs. Lawson,* 334–35; Gower to Owens, November 12, 1940, Gower Letters. Richard Mason, a field representative at the Southwest Collection, Texas Tech University, compiled a Statistical Sample of Miners' Pay, a copy of which is in my possession. See also Texas Pacific Mercantile and Manufacturing Company Records, Texas and Pacific Coal Company Records, for variety of goods sold.

38. Mine Payrolls, August 1903, Texas and Pacific Coal Company, Financial Material, Texas and Pacific Coal Company Records.

39. *Texas and Pacific vs. Lawson,* 347–48, 353.

40. Mine Payrolls, September, October, 1903, Texas and Pacific Coal Company, Financial Material, Texas and Pacific Coal Company Records. See Gentry, "Thurber," 121, for table showing consistently profitable operation of the mercantile company from 1900 to 1923.

41. *J. W. Connaughton vs. Texas and Pacific Coal Company*, trial transcript, Clerk's Office, Texas Court of Civil Appeals, 2nd District, Fort Worth, 85, 96, 100, 114; *Texas and Pacific vs. Lawson,* 269, 271.

42. Gower to Owens, November 12, 1940, Gower Letters; Gentry, "Thurber," 159.

43. Gentry, "Thurber," 110.

44. *J. W. Connaughton vs. Texas and Pacific Coal Company*, 95, 101, 120, 123; Gower to Owens, November 12, 1940 (quotation), Gower Letters.

45. *The Texas Civil Appeals Reports: Cases Argued and Adjudged in the Courts of Civil Appeals of the State of Texas during the Months of December, 1898, and January, February and March, 1899* (Austin: State of Texas, 1900), xx, 642–45, 646 (quotation); see *J. W. Connaughton vs. Texas and Pacific Coal Company.*

46. *United Mine Workers Journal,* September 24, 1903 (excerpt from "Thurber on Strike") in Mine Workers, United; Gentry, "Thurber," 33–34. General Manager William K. Gordon wrote Edgar L. Marston that the transportation tax was "a source of serious discontent with our employes [sic] and in fact is the only onjectionable [sic] feature of our village." Gordon acknowledged that the miners objected to the "six in the morning until six-thirty in the afternoon" workday, but proposed that offering them free transportation, while not reducing the length of time spent at the mines, would nevertheless make the situation "more satisfactory" to the miners. William K. Gordon to Edgar L. Marston, December 21, 1899, Personal Papers, William K. Gordon Jr. [Fort Worth] (cited hereafter as Personal Papers, William K. Gordon Jr.). Concerning the problem with railroad cars, Gordon wrote Hunter: "You already know of the trouble and expense we are having on account of scarcity of empty coal cars. As matters now stand, we are unable to keep the miners we now have steadily employed, and unless we are to be better supplied with cars, transportation men are certainly not needed." Wil-

liam K. Gordon to Colonel R. D. Hunter, November 17, 1896, Personal Papers, William K. Gordon Jr.

47. Gentry, "Thurber," 128, 160–61, 164, 174; Rent Book, 1900–1901, Texas and Pacific Coal Company Records, shows no charge "by order of W.K.G." for pastors' housing. The *Texas Miner,* January 20, 1894, mentions a free public library in Thurber with fifteen hundred volumes.

48. Robert Goldman and John Wilson, "The Rationalization of Leisure," *Politics and Society* 7 (1977): 167, 183; Green, *World of the Worker,* 8, 16; Gutman, *Work, Culture, and Society,* 43.

49. Annual Report, 1889, p. 6.

50. *Texas and Pacific vs. Lawson,* 328–29, 334, 420. See Mine Payrolls, 1903, for example of payment to peace officers; see also R. D. Hunter to W. H. King, February 17, 1889, July 3, 1890, General Correspondence, Adjutant General Records, Lorenzo de Zavala State Archives, Texas State Library, Austin (cited hereafter as Adjutant General Records); R. D. Hunter to W. H. Mabry, June 5, 1894, General Correspondence, Adjutant General Records; Appointment of William Lightfoot as Special Ranger, March 10, 1899, General Service Records, Adjutant General Records; Monthly Return of Company C Ranger Force, State of Texas, for the Month Ending October 31, 1903, Frontier Battalions Monthly Returns, Adjutant General Records; *Dallas Morning News,* September 18, 1903.

51. *Texas and Pacific vs. Lawson,* 284, 285 (2nd quotation), 286 (1st quotation), 328, 333, 335.

52. Jonathan Garlock, comp., *Guide to the Local Assemblies of the Knights of Labor* (Westport, CT: Greenwood Press, 1982), xxiv, 495–96, 505, 636; Gower to Owens, April 12, 1940, Gower Letters.

53. Gower to Gentry, August 14, 1944, in Gentry, "Thurber," 228.

54. Gomer Gower to Ben L. Owens, November 4, 1940 (quotation), January 28, 1941, Gower Letters; Biographical Information Sheets, Brock, Booth, Franklin; Carter, "The Thurber Story," Thurber Collection.

55. Gower to Owens, April 12, November 4, 12, 1940, Gower Letters; Gower to Gentry, August 14, 1944, in Gentry, "Thurber," 228; Legal Document—Option to Buy, Johnson Coal Mining Company to R. D. Hunter, May 7, 1888, Legal Documents, Johnson Papers; Robert William Spoede, "William Whipple Johnson: An Enterprising Man" (master's thesis, Hardin-Simmons University, Abilene, TX, 1968), 57–59.

56. Annual Report, 1889, p. 2 (quotations); Gower to Owens, November 4, 12, 1940, Gower Letters.

57. Spoede, "William Whipple Johnson," 59.

58. Annual Report, 1889, p. 3.

59. Gower to Owens, November 4, 12, 1940, Gower Letters; Gower to Gentry, August 14, 1944, in Gentry, "Thurber," 229 (3rd–5th quotations), 230 (1st and 2nd quotations).

60. Annual Report, 1889, p. 3; *Texas and Pacific vs. Lawson,* 301, 318, 397–400; Journal A, Financial Material, Texas and Pacific Coal Company Records.

61. Gower to Owens, November 4, 1940, Gower Letters.
62. *Journal of United Labor*, December 13 (1st quotation), 20, 1888, January 3, 1889 (2nd quotation).
63. Gower to Owens, November 4, 1940, Gower Letters.
64. *Texas and Pacific vs. Lawson,* 282, 286.
65. Gower to Owens, November 4, 1940, Gower Letters; S. A. McMurry to W. H. King, April 6, 1889, General Correspondence, Adjutant General Records; Annual Report, 1889, p. 3; Gower to Gentry, August 14, 1944, in Gentry, "Thurber," 230–231. The *Journal of United Labor*, January 10, 1889, includes a letter of thanks for donations to the local.
66. S. A. McMurry to W. H. King, February 17, 1889, April 6, 1889, July 2, 1889, General Correspondence, Adjutant General Records; Annual Report, 1889, p. 4.
67. Annual Report, 1889, pp. 3, 4 (quotation).
68. *Dallas Morning News*, December 23, 28 (quotation), 1888.
69. McMurry to King, April 6, June 6 (quotation), 1889, General Correspondence, Adjutant General Records.
70. McMurry to King, July 8, 1889, General Correspondence, Adjutant General Records.
71. Gentry, "Thurber," 53.
72. McMurry to King, July 2, 1889, General Correspondence, Adjutant General Records.
73. C. A. Hall to Attorney General J. S. Hogg, June 2, 1889 (1st and 2nd quotations), Mine Workers, United; Gower to Owens, November 4, 1940 (3rd quotation), Gower Letters.
74. Annual Report, 1889, p. 5.
75. *National Labor Tribune*, January 12, 1889. "With so many miners needing . . . employment is it not shameful that our efforts to secure a new union district should meet with obstruction among miners?"
76. *National Labor Tribune*, December 22, 1888 (2nd quotation); see also October 20, December 8, 15 (1st quotation), 25, 1888.
77. *National Labor Tribune*, January 5, 1889.
78. Ibid.
79. *Journal of United Labor*, January 17, 1889.
80. Annual Report, 1889, p. 5; *National Labor Tribune*, January 19, 1889; *Proceedings of the General Assembly of the Knights of Labor of America Thirteenth Regular Session, November 12–20, 1889* (Philadelphia: Journal of United Labor, 1890), 9 (quotations).
81. Telegram, R. D. Hunter to W. H. King, July 5, 1890 (2nd quotation), General Correspondence, Adjutant General Records; note, S. A. McMurry, July 7, 1890 (1st quotation), General Correspondence, Adjutant General Records; S. A. McMurry to W. H. King, July 12, 1890 (3rd quotation), General Correspondence, Adjutant General Records.
82. Gower to Owens, April 12, 1940, Gower Letters.

83. R. D. Hunter to W. H. Mabry, June 5, 1894 (quotations), General Correspondence, Adjutant General Records; *Dallas Morning News,* June 4, 5, 1894.

84. Gower to Owens, November 12, 1940, Gower Letters; Gower to Gentry, August 14, 1944, in Gentry, "Thurber," 233 (quotations).

85. Copy of affidavit filed by William Lightfoot, June 18, 1894, General Correspondence, Adjutant General Records.

86. *Dallas Morning News,* June 6, 1894.

87. Biographical Information Sheets, Gordon; Gower to Owens, January 28, 1941, Gower Letters; James C. Maroney interview with William K. Gordon Jr., June 15, 1985, Fort Worth. The *Dallas Morning News,* September 13, 1903, used the term "going away" to describe the situation in Thurber.

88. Arthur E. Suffern, *Conciliation and Arbitration in the Coal Industry of America* (New York: Houghton Mifflin, 1915), 50–51, 53–54.

89. W. K. Gordon to E. L. Marston, January 10, 1900, Personal Papers, William K. Gordon Jr. C. W. Woodman, secretary of the Texas State Federation of Labor, wrote J. E. Enness in Bridgeport, TX, in 1902 asking the union there to assess its members twenty-five cents to help support a lobbyist in Austin. Enness apparently refused, prompting Woodman to respond with some understanding: "[A]s you say," he wrote Enness, "the drain on your treasury to support the miners has been heavy." This letter indicated both the existence of a state-affiliated miners' union near Thurber in 1902 and labor upheaval necessitating some financial response by the local union. In his letter Woodman also acknowledged receipt of $1.80 for the per capita membership assessment. The federation's annual tax was six cents per member. C. W. Woodman Papers, Box 2, Collection 163, Special Collections, University of Texas at Arlington.

90. Suffern, *Conciliation and Arbitration,* 45; Chris Evans, *History of United Mine Workers of America from the Year 1860 to 1890* (n.p., n.d.), 1:639, 641.

91. "Black Coal Miners and the American Labor Movement," in Gutman, *Work, Culture, and Society,* 31, 124, 157–58; Suffern, *Conciliation and Arbitration,* 39.

92. Gower to Owens, April 12, 1940 (quotation), Gower Letters; *United Mine Workers Journal,* September 24, 1903; Report to the Sixth Annual Convention of District 21 (n.d.), Statements/Speeches P. Hanraty, Peter Hanraty Papers, Oklahoma Historical Society, Oklahoma City. James C. Maroney, "The Unionization of Thurber, 1903," *Red River Valley Historical Review* 4 (Spring 1979): 27–32, most recently chronicled the 1903 strike utilizing sources such as the *United Mine Workers Journal,* the Gower Letters, the John Mitchell Papers, Samuel Gompers Letterbooks, and state labor sources not used by previous authors on the subject. I have described the labor unrest preceding the 1903 strike in greater detail than Maroney, relying on sources such as the *National Labor Tribune* and *Journal of United Labor* as well as proceedings of the Knights of Labor General Assembly and the personal papers of William K Gordon Jr., C. W. Woodman, and Peter Hanraty, which no other author has researched in terms of events transpiring in Thurber. Unlike Maroney, Ruth Allen, and myself, Gentry (and most other writ-

ers on the subject) did not describe the 1903 strike within the context of the labor movement in the state.

93. *Dallas Morning News*, September 11, 1903.
94. *United Mine Workers Journal*, September 24, 1903; *Dallas Morning News*, September 18, 1903.
95. W. K. Gordon to S. W. T. Lanham, August 30, 1903, General Correspondence, Adjutant General Records.
96. Gower to Owens, April 12 , 1940, Gower Letters.
97. *Dallas Morning News*, September 11, 1903.
98. Ibid.
99. *United Mine Workers Journal*, September 24, 1903.
100. *Dallas Morning News*, September 11, 1903.
101. *Dallas Morning News*, September 13 (1st quotation), 20 (2nd quotation), 1903.
102. *Dallas Morning News*, September 12, 1903.
103. *Dallas Morning News*, September 13, 14, 15, 18, 1903.
104. *Dallas Morning News*, September 17, 18, 29, 1903.
105. *Dallas Morning News,* September 20, 1903; C. W. Woodman to Ben Owens, April 22, 1940, Gower Letters.
106. *Dallas Morning News,* September 27, 1903; *United Mine Workers Journal*, October 1, 1903 (a photocopy of the October 1, 1903, *UMW Journal* article can be found in "Thurber Strike," part of material compiled by Dr. Ruth Allen and Mr. Ben L. Owens), Labor Movement in Texas Collection; copy of Agreement between Miners and Operators in the Bituminous Mines of Texas, September 26, 1903, Personal Papers, William K. Gordon Jr.
107. Woodman to Owens, April 22, 1940, Gower Letters.
108. Harwood P. Hinton, ed., *Thurber, Texas: The Life and Death of a Company Coal Town* by John S. Spratt Sr. (Austin: University of Texas Press, 1986), 6–7. Gower's account in Gower to Owens, November 12, 1940, Gower Letters, supports Spratt's recollection.
109. Gentry, "Thurber," 110.
110. Woodman to Owens, April 22, 1940, Gower Letters. Gower stated: "Mr. Gordon went more than halfway in many instances in demanding that his mine foremen observe the terms of the agreement in their dealings with the miners." Gower to Owens, January 28, 1941, Gower Letters.
111. Gower to Owens, April 12, 1940, Gower Letters; Richard Mason, "Ranger and the First West Texas Drilling Boom," *West Texas Historical Association Yearbook* 58 (1982): 54–59.
112. Gower to Owens, November 4, 1940, Gower Letters; Gentry, "Thurber," 99; Allen, *Chapters*, 100.
113. Gentry, "Thurber," 100. See Allen, *Chapters*, for a full description of militant labor activity in late nineteenth-century Texas. *Sixteenth Annual Report of the Commissioner of Labor, 1901*, "Strikes and Lockouts" (Washington, DC: US Government Printing Office, 1901), 108, 252, 348, demonstrates the extent of strike activity in Texas in the last two decades of the nineteenth century as

well as strikes and lockouts in the coal mining industry in various parts of the country.

114. Texas State Federation of Labor (TSFL), *Proceedings*, 1904, p. 17, Gower Letters; *Fort Worth Union Banner*, April 10, 1909. The representative of Thurber miners at the 1904 TSFL meeting claimed the community was "the most thoroughly organized city of Texas. . . . The entire town is closed shop, not being more than five residents in the entire town who are not union men."

115. Maroney, "Unionization of Thurber, 1903," 2; Maroney, "Organized Labor in Texas," 121.

116. Maroney, "Organized Labor in Texas," 52; Allen, *Chapters*, 98, 137. As Ruth Allen notes, legislative activity by Texas unions predated the TSFL, but with the federation's participation in lobbying efforts that railway unions had initiated as early as 1889, the more united legislative activism produced greater results (Allen, *Chapters*, 131–34).

117. Maroney, "Organized Labor in Texas," 59, 62, 65; Woodman to Owens, April 22, 1940, Gower Letters; Gower to Owens, April 12, 1940, Gower Letters.

118. Gower to Owens, April 12, 1940, Gower Letters.

GEORGE T. MORGAN JR.

The Gospel of Wealth Goes South

John Henry Kirby and Labor's Struggle for
Self-Determination, 1901–1916

In his *American Conservatism in the Age of Enterprise, 1865–1910*, Robert G. McCloskey contends that society's acceptance of the doctrines of Social Darwinism and laissez-faire economics ultimately and inevitably turned the democratic faith upside down. That is, property rights supplanted human rights as the primary tenet of democracy; in the process capitalism and democracy became synonymous terms and the excesses committed by the business community aroused negligible criticism in a society consumed by materialism.[1]

Some members of the business elite, however, sought a more self-satisfying rationale for their actions than could be found in the bleak atmosphere of William Graham Sumner's survival-of-the-fittest postulates. Out of the tortured conscience of Andrew Carnegie came the "gospel of wealth" which glorified youthful poverty, hard work, thrift, success, and organized philanthropy indulged in during the wealthy man's lifetime. Thus possessors of wealth became stewards of the people, whose superior abilities obligated them to use their fortunes to uplift their fellow men.[2]

Imitators of Andrew Carnegie, conscious and otherwise, included John Henry Kirby, the East Texas lumberman, whose life and career in many ways paralleled that of the Pennsylvania ironmaker. Like Carnegie, Kirby grew up in modest surroundings, worked hard, and reaped his first financial successes through fortunate connections with already established men of wealth. Like Carnegie, too, John Henry Kirby sincerely believed he was a just, compassionate employer and a charitable, patriotic citizen. "I try," he wrote to an intimate in 1910, "to do my duty as a citizen, build up the country, create opportunities for men, promote the prosperity of communities, [and] add to the taxable wealth of the country." Kirby then listed what he considered most praiseworthy among his actions as a responsible businessman and patriot: reduction of the working day of his employees from eleven to ten hours without a decrease in wages, provision of free house rent and supplies to needy workers when the Panic of 1907 forced a closing of Kirby Lumber Company operations, leadership of the Texas Five Million Club and cash contributions amounting to over $10,000, assumption of the presidency of the Texas Commission at the St. Louis World's Fair and donations in excess of $10,000, and a $5,000 contribution for a monument to Hood's Texas Brigade, "as gallant a fighting organization of citizen soldiers as ever drew a blade or ever spilled patriotic blood in behalf of liberty."[3]

Kirby's public charities—directed in good "gospel of wealth" style toward social uplift of the less fortunate—provided him with equal personal satisfaction. His listing in this regard included commentary through which there runs a strong strain of the philosophy of stewardship: provision of funds for teachers' salaries for a night school program at Kirbyville, "so as to give opportunity to the children of the poor that they could not otherwise enjoy"; donation of twenty-five hundred dollars to help Methodist University at Georgetown build a dormitory "for the accommodation of the poor boys in attendance . . . who were not otherwise able to secure its advantages"; maintenance over an eight-year period of from five to nine boys and girls attending institutions of higher learning throughout the state, many of whom were offspring of "dead ministers whose wives were unable to educate their children"; and donation of five thousand dollars for a Young Men's Christian Association building in Houston "to provide entertainment, education and culture for ambitious young men, most of them the sons of mechanics and people in moderate circumstances."[4]

Throughout a long life John Henry Kirby remained proud of these and other philanthropies, but like so many of his fellows he failed to realize that self-seeking even if screened by paternalism often leads the well-intentioned astray and results not in benevolence but repression. Thus Andrew Carnegie defended the right of workers to organize and join unions, yet in the Homestead strike of 1892 his company used the lockout, blacklist, scab labor, and armed Pinkerton detectives to break the strike and reduce the steel workers' union to an impotency from which it did not recover until the 1930s.[5] John Henry Kirby, while he never recognized unionism as a legitimate or beneficial goal for the workers, likewise employed standard antiunion tactics to deny his laborers the advantages provided by collective bargaining. A short memory permitted him to defend himself in 1915 against a newspaper attack upon him as the "leading Texas representative of the exploiters of labor" with the statement that during his years in the lumber industry "I have never had a strike or any disagreement with my employees. On the contrary, every dollar my company has earned has been distributed in wages to my pals who toil about [my] mills."[6] The sobriquet "the Peon's Pal," given Kirby by at least some of the workers, indicates that not everyone in the Piney Woods shared his interpretation of his relations with employees of the Kirby Lumber Company, nor does the record bear him out.[7]

After forming the Kirby Lumber Company in 1901, Kirby not only reduced working hours in his mills without decreasing wages but also, for a time at least, paid his workers on a weekly basis. Financial difficulties stemming from Kirby's connection with the Houston Oil Company reached serious proportions by the summer of 1903 and led to the first stirrings of unrest among workers employed by the Kirby Lumber Company.[8] Leaving his assistant, B. F. Bonner, in Houston to supervise overall operations, Kirby hurried to New York City and other eastern financial centers to obtain funds. In the meantime, payrolls went unpaid and failure to meet credit obligations resulted in curtailment of commissary purchases except on a cash basis. The workers, unpaid except for the customary commissary checks, remained quiescent until mid-September 1903, when men at the company's Beaumont plant walked out because of nonpayment of the payroll and demanded that a weekly payday be honored.[9] The strike, if indeed the walkout of only a few hours' duration can be so dignified, resulted in no gain for the workers and elicited expressions of public sympathy only for the company. The *Beaumont Enterprise* commented that the strikers "acted hastily in quitting their work merely upon the behest of an agitator or two" and warned that the "good people of Beaumont cannot afford to see the Kirby Lumber Company treated unkindly." Responsible citizens, the paper continued, should act to prevent further disturbances because the company could easily move its mills to the pineries at no loss to itself but at a considerable loss of income to the city.[10] The *Industrial Era*, a local black newspaper, reported that according to the company's Beaumont manager, the weekly payday demand came from "negro gamblers and a parasite class which does not thrive on monthly payments." Like the *Enterprise*, the black paper warned its readers of the danger that the company might move out of Beaumont to a point where it could "live cheaper, get labor cheaper, sell . . . lumber for more money, [and] get . . . logs at the mills." Kirby, the paper finally admonished, "is looking to see where the Negro stands in this strike and who he is and who belongs to the gang. We are all known and don't forget that."[11]

Not all the seventy-three men involved in the walkout were allowed to return to their jobs, and company officers later commended the manager's blacklist with the observation, "If in this you are persecuting some innocent parties who were not in the cause, it could not be helped and will put them to thinking about labor unions."[12]

Labor difficulties continued to plague the company, however, and a number of workers at Silsbee and Bessmay left their jobs because wages earned in August remained unpaid by the first days of October. While company officials were irritated by the necessity of running shorthanded, they remained relatively complacent until a union agent organized the employees of the Trinity Lumber Company at Groveton on October 8, 1903. Five days later, Kirby Lumber Company workers at Beaumont again walked out because the company failed to meet the promised payday. As before, the walkout lasted only one day and the mill immediately returned to full-scale operation, an occurrence that led B. F. Bonner to the opinion that "passing this pay day has been a blessing in disguise not only at Beaumont but at all other points. It has demonstrated the fact that not only is there plenty of labor, but that it is a tolerably easy matter to retain it." Bonner also informed Kirby that "when you return and finances will admit of a regular payday . . . I am fully confident it will be an easy matter not only to reduce the wages we are paying, but to put them back on the eleven hour basis."[13]

As October turned into November, lagging production, attributed to continued failure to meet the payroll and consequent "soldiering" by the workers, brought increased pleas from Bonner to Kirby for immediate financial aid. The laborers, Bonner again advised Kirby, "are controlled much more easily than you would imagine, and you will find that when we catch up with our payroll that we will be able to reduce the wages or increase the hours at ease."[14]

For the next few weeks, however, Kirby's fund-raising efforts met with only limited success and Bonner found it increasingly difficult to satisfy the demands of creditors. "I am," he wrote to Kirby in early November, "paying out almost our entire receipts each day, and therefore cannot accumulate anything." He also warned that Kirby's return without having obtained funds would be disastrous because "I have been feeding not only our creditors but our laborers on the story of your successfully carrying out your plans . . . and that when you did return it would mean the safe arrival of the big ship.[15] The "big ship" did not arrive and at the end of November, Bonner informed Kirby, "We have been entirely out of groceries at the stores. . . . Our credit is so impaired that we cannot buy anything except for cash, and when we run out of groceries and meat at the stores it hurts worse than the delayed payroll." If financial help did not arrive immediately, Bonner warned, "we will be in the midst of another storm." To stave off the predicted trouble, Kirby acquired fifty thousand dollars, which, when added to the company's meager cash reserves, enabled only a feeble gesture toward meeting the August and September payrolls.[16]

The New Year brought relief neither to the company nor to the unpaid workers. The company's difficulties increased in fact as each passing day brought a parade of employees demanding their wages; some departed satisfied with token payments, others became, according to Bonner, "so ugly" that the mill managers discharged them—a procedure that required payment in full and made further inroads into already inadequate daily receipts. The depths of the company's insolvency and disregard of unpaid wages is reflected in a request from one long-suffering employee dated September 27, 1904, that he be paid wages earned for the eight-month period from June 1903 through January 1904—a sum of four hundred dollars.[17]

Court litigation between the Houston Oil Company and the Kirby Lumber Company resulted in the appointment of receivers for both companies in March 1904. Although workers for the latter enterprise at first regarded the receivership "as a New York job to swipe everything," they soon realized an improvement in their financial lot with the change of administration. On the other hand, the continuing attitude in administrative echelons toward walkouts resulted in the observation by one of their number that the receivership had resulted in "even the sore-head leaders . . . trying to make peace and get on the Pay Roll again. Those in my department are not and never shall be on a Pay Roll again. They are dead ones."[18]

John Henry Kirby did not regain full control of his company until the summer of 1909. During the intervening five years, the receivers significantly reduced the company's indebtedness and increased annual production. Also, the period from 1905 to the fall of 1907 witnessed improved lumber prices, and in an era of general prosperity workers forgot past grievances. Good times ended, however, with the Panic of 1907, and as lumber prices plunged downward the Kirby Lumber Company reacted in October by putting its mills on a four-day work week—a reduction soon imitated by the majority of operators in the Texas-Louisiana pinelands. Reduced output failed to stem the tide of recession, and in mid-November the Kirby mills began total cessation of operations. Other companies in the region continued on a short-week basis, cut wages 10 to 20 percent, and resorted completely to commissary checks in lieu of cash in order to provide the workers with the "necessities of life."[19]

Kirby publicly laid the blame for depressed conditions at the doors of unwise legislators. "We have," he explained, "repealed the laws of industry in our efforts to suppress the trusts. If these enactments do not prove efficacious and [if] our leaders continue to lead, we shall next repeal all the laws of property. We shall then have sufficient chaos to gratify all our politicians."[20]

Depression lingered on in the Piney Woods throughout the remainder of 1907, and the following year brought only partial recovery. Workers from time to time resisted wage cuts, hour reductions, and commissary check payments, but resistance only resulted in strengthening management's control and the laborers sank deeper and deeper into apathy.[21] During the winter of 1910, however, workers in East Texas and western Louisiana cast off their lethargy and launched a campaign for alleviation of corporate abuses and recognition of their right to membership in a union. Led by Arthur L. Emerson and Jay Smith, who organized a first local at Carson, Louisiana, in December 1910, the laborers sent delegates to a convention in Alexandria, Louisiana, in June 1911 and formally established the Brotherhood of Timber Workers.[22]

In language reminiscent of the defunct Noble Order of the Knights of Labor, the brotherhood proclaimed, "It is our aim to elevate those who labor — morally, socially, intellectually, and financially. . . . It is our purpose to use every legitimate effort to remove and correct such obvious and patent abuses as compulsory doctor's fees, hospital dues, and unfair insurance system . . . the inordinately high commisary [*sic*] prices, the long and trying hours of labor, the high rents . . . and any and all other unfair and unjust impositions."[23] John Henry Kirby, who publicly commented in 1908, "I would never be president of any corporation which . . . underpaid those who work for it, or limited the opportunity of any man," never recognized the validity of the brotherhood's complaints and considered the union's leaders anarchists, criminals, or worse.[24]

The Socialist press, on the other hand, described the system wherein an East Texas lumber worker was "born in a Company house; wrapped in Company swaddling clothes, rocked in a Company cradle. . . . At five years of age he goes to the Company school. At eleven he graduates and goes to the Company woods. At sixteen he goes to work in the Company mill." Years of labor did not improve his condition, and "at forty, he sickens with Company malaria, lies down on a Company bed, is attended by a Company doctor who doses him with Company drugs, and then he draws his last Company breath, while the undertaker is paid by the widow in Company scrip for the Company coffin in which he is buried on Company ground."[25] Covington Hall, Socialist and Industrial Workers of the World organizer, passionately declared that "the revolt is economic to the last degree, a thing the brutal bosses of the Lumber Trust seem absolutely unable to comprehend, for, like the Manchu mandarins they have literally driven the workers into rebellion."[26] William D. "Big Bill" Haywood, Wobbly secretary-treasurer, described in greater detail the conditions that precipitated rebellion: "[M]iserable shacks [and] exorbitant rents; sewerage there is none; there is no pretense at sanitation; the outhouses are open vaults. For these accommodations families pay from $5 to $20 a month. . . . Insurance fees are arbitrarily collected from every worker, for which he receives practically nothing in return. . . . The same is true of the doctor fee, and the hospital fee, which, in all places, is an imaginary institution."[27]

Unmindful of the truth of the brotherhood's list of abuses and oblivious to the bitterness expressed by the Socialist press, Kirby and his colleagues, confident that unionism could only "breed pestilence and trouble," quickly took steps to destroy the brotherhood. At Kirby's insistence the lumbermen revitalized the Southern Lumber Operators' Association, an antiunion organization established in 1906, and the association immediately ordered a lockout at union-controlled mills.[28]

Undaunted by economic coercion, the brotherhood successfully continued its organizational activity, attaining a peak membership of between eighteen thousand and thirty-five thousand.[29] Union successes were short-lived, however, as Kirby and his associates patiently perfected machinery, including paid labor spies, blacklists, yellow-dog contracts, and shutdowns, to force the brotherhood to its knees. During the winter of 1911–12, report after report confirmed the inevitable. Penniless workers throughout the timber belt fell behind in their dues, and rather than submit to total destruction, union leadership resorted to subterfuge. In January 1912 brotherhood members received instructions to destroy their membership cards, sign the required yellow-dog contracts, return to work, and *pay their dues*. At the same time, Emerson, after a hurried trip to Chicago, began to hint of possible affiliation with a national organization—the Industrial Workers of the World (IWW).[30]

Relative peace and quiet prevailed during the first months of 1912 while the Brotherhood of Timber Workers labored underground, apparently unaware that strategically located secret agents reported its every action to the Operators' Association. Scattered warnings of successful organizational activity in western Louisiana alarmed some lumbermen, particularly those in East Texas, but in fact the brotherhood bided its time and prepared for affiliation with the IWW. On May 7, 1912, after hearing impassioned speeches by Big Bill Haywood and Covington Hall, the brotherhood voted to merge with the national group on the following September 1.[31]

Quickly seizing the tactical advantage presented by this amalgamation, Kirby and his fellows wasted no opportunity to turn the IWW's reputation to their ends. A circular addressed to managers of the Kirby operations announced the intended merger of the brotherhood with "an organization that is known throughout the country as being largely composed of desperate and unreasonable men; men who make no claim to confining their demands to what is right but who recommend ... to their followers to not be satisfied when they are getting what is right, but to take by force, what they want. ... You will understand that the only flag Haywood and his associates recognize or follow is the red flag of anarchy and destruction." The company recognized and appreciated past resistance to unionism, but now the managers had to "redouble efforts realizing ... that the new factors we have to deal with are the most dangerous in the industrial or public life of this Republic."[32]

Two months later, Kirby personally outlined the tactics he expected his managers to employ. Upon learning of an intended speech by Haywood at Kirbyville on July 4, 1912, he advised his superintendent, C. P. Meyer, to "do everything ... to prevent our boys attending. ... We do not want to put it to them that we are opposed to them doing as they please ... but we do want to put it up to them that Haywood is a dynamiter and a lawless character; that he breeds disturbance and anarchy wherever he goes and that all he is here for is the purpose of precipitating trouble and getting some money out of the boys." No better or "more effective way of interrupting his progress" existed, Kirby concluded, "than to keep the men away from his meetings. ... It seems to me that merchants and general citizenship of Kirbyville should be discreetly interviewed by some discreet man and ... any attendance ... be prevented."[33] Haywood later canceled his scheduled appearance; his replacement, Covington Hall, spoke to a small gathering, but according to reports, "created no enthusiasm whatsoever."[34]

In the same vein, Kirby informed a close friend and business associate in Woodville of the impending arrival of George Creel in that community to speak on socialism: "I think you and other law-abiding citizens who believe in the church, the maintenance of a family relation, the preservation of property and the stability of American institutions, ought to see to it that this wolf is not permitted to use the people's courthouse in a Christian law-abiding community." Soon afterward Woodville's sheriff informed Creel that the courthouse was closed for repairs.[35]

These and other tactics took a gradual but heavy toll upon the vitality of the brotherhood. Its ebbing strength suffered still further as a result of the Grabow Massacre (or Riot) on July 7, 1912, and the heavy expenditures subsequently required to defend nine union members against conspiracy to murder charges. A few tenacious members fought on until early 1916, but in fact the brotherhood, now officially the National Industrial Union of Forest and Lumber Workers, did not exist as a viable organization after January 1913.[36]

The defeat of the brotherhood, the tactics used, and the rhetoric employed throughout the years of labor–management strife underscore the continuing conflict between human and property rights. The workers, reduced over the years to little more than pawns to be manipulated at will by economic masters who excused their actions in the name of "God's law" of supply and demand and capitalistic progress, sought to attain recognition by the lumbermen of a long-affirmed tenet of the democratic faith—the right of the individual to control his own destiny.[37] John Henry Kirby and his fellow lumbermen, confident that all the blessings of democracy automatically flowed from capitalistic progress, denied the workers that essential human right.

Born nearly a generation apart, Andrew Carnegie and John Henry Kirby rose to wealth and prominence in a society that held the "captain of industry," his acts, and his opinions in high esteem. Carnegie did not live into the 1930s when his kind would be labeled "economic royalists." Kirby did, and found himself almost totally estranged from a society that no longer esteemed nor honored his opinions. Frustrated and embittered by a political-economic milieu which he could neither understand nor accept, Kirby, with the aid of Vance Muse and Austin Callan, organized the anti–New Deal Southern Committee to Uphold the Constitution. He also became a contributor to the American Liberty League and attended the August 1936 Detroit convention that founded the National Jeffersonian Democrats. His reputation by that time, however, had degenerated to the point that the politic Jeffersonian Democrats failed to include him in the list of official delegates, and Congressman Maury Maverick described Kirby as the "trigger man of special interests that destroyed the timber resources of the people of Texas and Louisiana . . . an old bore . . . who doesn't control ten votes in the whole United States."[38]

Notes

This chapter originally appeared in *Southwestern Historical Quarterly* 75 (October 1971): 186–97, and is reprinted with permission.

1. Robert G. McCloskey, *American Conservatism in the Age of Enterprise, 1865–1910: A Study of William Graham Sumner, Stephen J. Field, and Andrew Carnegie* (Cambridge, 1951), 1–20, 168–74.

2. Andrew Carnegie, "The Gospel of Wealth," in *The Gospel of Wealth and Other Timely Essays* by Andrew Carnegie (Garden City, 1933), 1–39.

3. Kirby to "Dear Friend," January 24, 1910, John Henry Kirby Papers, University of Houston.

4. Ibid.

5. McCloskey, *American Conservatism*, 148–50.

6. *Winters (Texas) Tribune,* April 23, 1915; Kirby to M. Lester Chambers, May 21, 1915, Kirby Papers.

7. Ruth A. Allen, *East Texas Lumber Workers: An Economic and Social Picture, 1870– 1950* (Austin, 1961), 181. The Industrial Workers of the World press lampooned Kirby as "Con H. Jirby, president of the Hotair Lumber Company." See *Industrial Worker* (Spokane, WA), May 30, 1912.

8. The Houston Oil Company of Texas and the Kirby Lumber Company were chartered in 1901 as the result of a complicated promoters' agreement between Kirby and Patrick Calhoun of New York City. Under the terms of the agreement, Kirby agreed to convey to the oil company title to some 1.1 million acres of timberland which he either owned or "controlled" through options to purchase. The oil company then executed an agreement with the Kirby Lumber Company allowing it to conduct cutting operations on the conveyed lands. The contract also specified stumpage rates and annual production quotas. The purchase of sawmills and equipment required to implement the agreement placed a severe financial burden on Kirby, and in fact, the Kirby Lumber Company never succeeded in meeting the payments required by the contract. Meanwhile, Calhoun's attempts to obtain adequate financing for the Houston Oil Company, and thus provide some indirect relief for Kirby, failed due to eastern coolness toward proposed Texas petroleum ventures. The history of the Houston Oil Company and Kirby's involvement with it is ably and thoroughly told in John O. King, *The Early History of the Houston Oil Company of Texas, 1901–1908* (Houston, 1959).

9. F. M. Aldridge to Kirby, September 23, 1903, Kirby Papers.

10. *Beaumont Enterprise*, September 17, 1903.

11. *Industrial Era* [September 1903], undated clipping in Kirby Papers.

12. Aldridge to J. F. Stunkel, September 23, 1903, Kirby Papers.

13. Bonner to Kirby, October 5, 8, 14, 15, 1903, Kirby Papers. Quotes are from letter of October 14.

14. Bonner to Kirby, November 2, 1903, Kirby Papers.

15. Bonner to Kirby, November 11, 1903, Kirby Papers.

16. Bonner to Kirby, November 24, 28, 1903, Kirby Papers. Quotes are from letter of November 24.

17. Bonner to Kirby, January 8, 1904; T. J. McNeill to Kirby, September 27, 1904, Kirby Papers.

18. S. A. McNeely to Kirby, March 21, 1904, Kirby Papers.

19. *Beaumont Enterprise*, October 20, 27, November 9, 11, 12, 13, 27, 1907; *Beaumont Daily Journal*, November 11, 1907. The *Daily Journal*, November 19, 1907, editorialized that although about ten thousand workers in East Texas were out of work the reduced production would be of benefit to manufacturers and "insomuch as it benefits the manufacturers it benefits the workmen." One observer explained that the Central Coal and Coke Company's adoption of "clearing house

checks" in lieu of cash would "do away almost entirely with the migratory spirit which possesses so many of the mill men. . . . Another thing, they will be physically in better condition, as the temptation to squander their money for 'booze' will be removed." *Beaumont Enterprise*, November 25, 1907.

20. Kirby to A. L. Harris, in *Beaumont Enterprise*, November 24, 1907.

21. *Beaumont Enterprise*, April 4, 7, June 18, July 21, August 27, 30, September 18, 1908.

22. For a detailed account of the Brotherhood of Timber Workers and the role played by management in the destruction of the union, see George T. Morgan Jr., "No Compromise—No Recognition: John Henry Kirby, the Southern Lumber Operators' Association, and Unionism in the Piney Woods, 1906–1916," *Labor History* 10 (Spring 1969): 193–204.

23. *Constitution and By-Laws of the Brotherhood of Timber Workers* (n.p., n.d.), 1. A copy of this constitution is available in the Kirby Papers.

24. *Beaumont Enterprise*, June 21, 1908. On the same occasion Kirby asserted, "I had rather be president of the Kirby Lumber Company and enable it to give profitable employment to the people of East Texas, paying the highest wages and giving the shortest hours ever afforded in this or any other country, bringing sunshine and comfort into the homes of these fathers and mothers and opportunity to these boys, who are to be the husbands and fathers of the future, than be president of the United States."

25. *Rebel* (Hallettsville), February 17, 1912, quoted in Allen, *East Texas Lumber Workers*, 155.

26. Covington Hall, "Revolt of the Southern Timber Workers," *International Socialist Review* 13 (July 1912): 52.

27. William D. Haywood, "Timber Workers and Timber Wolves," *International Socialist Review* 13 (August 1912): 106.

28. Kirby to R. M. Hallowell, August 3, 1911, Kirby Papers.

29. Morgan, "No Compromise—No Recognition," 197–98; Allen, *East Texas Lumber Workers*, 182.

30. M. L. Alexander to M. L. Fleishel, December 1, 1911, January 3, 1912; Alexander to All Members, December 30, 1911, Kirby Papers; Morgan, "No Compromise—No Recognition," 200–201.

31. Morgan, "No Compromise—No Recognition," 200.

32. C. P. Myer to All Managers and Superintendents, May 25, 1912, Kirby Papers.

33. Kirby to Myer, June 26, 1912, Kirby Papers.

34. Alexander to C. D. Johnson, July 6, 1912, Kirby Papers.

35. Kirby to J. A. Mooney, July 16, 1912; Mooney to Kirby, July 18, 1912, Kirby Papers.

36. Morgan, "No Compromise—No Recognition," 202–4.

37. In a speech before the Texas Lumberman's Association, Kirby commented that "Lumber values are regulated solely by the law of 'supply and demand'—a law having origin in the divine economy of God and therefore higher than the act of

legislatures and not affected by the roar of the demagogues." *Beaumont Enterprise*, April 11, 1907.

38.   Kenneth G. Crawford, *The Pressure Boys: The Inside Story of Lobbying in America* (New York, 1939), 164. See also George Wolfskill, *The Revolt of the Conservatives: A History of the American Liberty League, 1934–1940* (Boston, 1962), 175–76, 234, 240–42, for an account of Kirby's anti–New Deal activities.

JAMES R. GREEN

Tenant Farmer Discontent and Socialist Protest in Texas, 1901–1917

The tenant farmer discontent and socialist protest that developed in Texas during the 1910s grew out of the terrible depression of the early 1890s, which caused thousands of small farm owners throughout the South to lose their land and fall into tenant farming. At first, academic experts thought this situation to be temporary. They developed a useful theory of social mobility, in which laborers and tenants were supposed to climb an "agricultural ladder" to farm ownership. After the turn of the century, however, the facts of rural life in Texas and other cotton states conflicted with the theory of the agricultural ladder.[1]

Indeed, by the turn of the century it was clear that many tenants could not work their way back up the ladder to farm ownership in spite of the return of prosperity. Yet the tenancy problem remained largely unrecognized. The Farmers' Alliance, which originated in Texas, slighted the issue even though it contained large numbers of white tenants and allied itself with a Colored Farmers' Alliance composed largely of black sharecroppers. Also, as Paul Wallace Gates explains, the Populist party, which was especially militant in Texas, "offered no aid . . . to tenants struggling to retain their step on the ownership ladder." Despite their radicalism, the Texas Populists displayed little interest in Henry George's ideas about placing confiscatory taxes on land that was rented and held for speculation. Passionate apologists for "agrarian individualism," like Thomas E. Watson of Georgia, ignored the growing dichotomy between "dispossessed farmers and possessing farmers." The call for the unity of rural society toward increasing tenancy was fraught with fatal implications for the "ideology of populist agrarianism."[2]

The decline of Populism and the return of prosperity in the early 1900s left the tenant farmer a marginal figure "on the lowest rung of the economic ladder." He "could well pose as the Forgotten Man," C. Vann Woodward writes, because "he shared little of the new prosperity and continued a relic of the depressed nineties in the new century." In fact, the situation worsened as the boll weevil blight caused more small farm owners to lose their land and fall into tenancy. At the same time the growth of absentee ownership and new forms of land speculation inflated the price of homesteads beyond the means of those tenant farmers who wanted to own their own places.[3]

The Farmers' Union, a more moderate form of the Farmers' Alliance, was born in Texas around 1902 as the agricultural expression of progressivism. But the "old Populist formula of agrarian solidarity to which the Farmers' Union appealed was put under increasing strain by the burden of rising tenancy," Woodward explains. "While the Union occasionally passed a resolution of sympathy with the tenant, the order was predominantly of landowner leanings, and there were plenty of signs that conflict between landless and landed" would not be resolved in the "new fraternity."[4]

The most important sign of tenant farmer discontent was the outbreak of night riding that erupted when cotton prices dropped in 1907–8. The Farmers' Union crop-withholding schemes failed to bolster the plunging market. In response to the crisis, frustrated bands of renters terrorized farmers who refused to hold their crops from the market. Following this debacle, membership in the Farmers' Union declined precipitously as did the progressive impulse which it had fostered. In 1907 Taylor McRae, editor of a Farmers' Union newspaper in Fort Worth, wrote Tom Watson to explain that many of the younger farmers were "sliding into the Socialist Party," which had started organizing in Texas after the turn of the century.[5] When the old Populist newspaper, the *Southern Mercury* of Dallas, stopped publication in 1907 and the weakened Farmers' Union fell into the hands of business interests, the way was open for the young Socialist Party to win recruits among discontented Democrats and ex-Populists.

The growth of Socialism in the Lone Star State during the early twentieth century was directly related to the rise of tenancy, which increased from 37.6 percent of all farmers in 1880 to over 52 percent in 1910. During this time, the Socialist vote grew rapidly in the fertile "black waxy" cotton belt of East Texas and in the newer cotton counties north of Abilene, where land speculation caused a rapid increase in tenancy.[6] In 1900 Eugene V. Debs only polled 1,841 votes in Texas on his first run for the presidency, despite the efforts of William E. Farmer, a radical Populist who had merged his own Texas Social Democratic Party with Debs's in 1899. After the founding of the Socialist Party of America in 1901, party organizers established locals in various counties, wooing trade union leaders and ex-Populists. In 1904 Debs polled a few thousand votes in his second Socialist presidential campaign, but failed to win as many votes as the popular agrarian, Tom Watson, who was running as the candidate of the Allied People's Party. In 1908, after the *Southern Mercury* folded and the Farmers' Union collapsed, however, Debs exceeded his 1904 vote by a noticeable margin, polling close to eight thousand votes and easily outdistancing Watson, who ran a token campaign for the moribund People's Party. The Texas Socialist vote increased to eleven thousand in 1910 despite the effects of off-year election apathy and rising cotton prices.[7]

The growth of tenancy continued. "There was a marked tendency for farm lands to be consolidated into the hands of fewer owners, many of them business or professional men who had foreclosed on mortgages or had invested their profits in farm lands," wrote the historian of one Texas cotton county. "These large owners usually held the lands for a rise in value and rented them to immigrant farmers from the older southern states." While land values were rising, however, owners still gained the same returns on their land from the tenants (one-third of the grain and one-fourth of the cotton), so they began charging extra rent to bring them a larger return on land that had increased in value. "This caused much resentment among the tenant farmers" and became one of the Socialists' main organizing issues.[8]

These developments resulted in protests from the tenant farmers who were paying the price for the absentee landlords' increased profits. "Land is getting high," wrote one frustrated renter in 1907. "Lots of it [is] being sold and [it is] advancing fast in price.... If we could keep the capitalists out of the country it would be good. They buy up land and hold it in large tracts for high prices."[9] The capitalists were there to stay. Indeed, they had been in Texas for some time, but now they were applying new corporate business methods to landholding.[10]

According to an investigator for the US Commission on Industrial Relations, which conducted hearings on the land question at Dallas in 1915, the migratory white tenants were beginning to resemble "casual workers" who worked for wages. While the tenants were moving further away from their goal of landownership, the wealthier landlords were moving to town, creating a greater distance—physically, economically, and socially—between the landed and the landless.[11] By 1910 the class differences were becoming obvious. As the son of one Texas cotton renter recalled, even poor white children perceived the division. "The landlord's children were commonly called the 'rich chillern' by us in renter families. We were called 'poor children' by those who really felt their aristocracy.... The attitude of the rich and poor groups was set by our economic gap, or difference. This was a ratio of 'sixteen to one.' That is, a landlord with sixteen renters, who paid him half of all crops, had sixteen times as much income as a renter family."[12]

Despite this widening social and economic distance between poor white tenants and propertied townspeople, agricultural experts still insisted that the tenancy problem was temporary: any hardworking renter could advance up the ladder to ownership if he was thrifty and businesslike. But when the 1910 census statistics showed that over half the Lone Star State's farms were operated by tenants, the credibility of the agricultural ladder theory began to crumble. For example, in 1910 the *Dallas News* admitted that "nine in ten of the tenants today, probably nineteen out of twenty, are destined to remain tenants."[13]

The Texas Socialists responded to this growing consciousness of the tenancy problem by taking two ambitious steps: they helped to organize a renters' union and they started publishing a weekly newspaper called the *Rebel.* The newly formed Renters Union of America convened its founding convention at Waco and declared that "use and occupancy" was the "only genuine title to land." The one hundred delegates supported a "confiscatory tax" on idle land and voted to exclude the landowners and businessmen who had co-opted the Farmers' Union. Most important, they decided to follow the route taken by industrial labor unions. Just before they organized the Renters Union, the Texas Socialists printed the first issue of their newspaper. The *Rebel* was published and edited by Thomas A. ("Red Tom") Hickey, who was then working as the Socialist Party's state organizer.[14]

"Red Tom," an Irish revolutionary, had organized for the Knights of Labor, the Socialist Labor Party, and the Western Federation of Miners before coming to Texas. A militant admirer of the Irish Land League, Hickey inherited his hatred of landlords from the "auld sod." He was determined to make the *Rebel* the heartbeat of renter radicalism in the Southwest and to make the "land question" the "paramount issue" in Texas politics. Within six months, a Houston paper observed, Hickey had "scored a striking success" with his weekly paper, which already had a circulation of over eighteen thousand. In the next half year the number of subscribers increased to twenty thousand.[15]

Every week the *Rebel* lashed out at landlordism in the idiom of the southwestern poor whites. The "five-minute sermon" column, in which radical preachers used the Good Book to condemn land engrossment, appealed to fundamental Christian standards of right and wrong. Hickey's sensational exposés and editorials took a more political approach; they revealed the miserable conditions in which tenants lived and worked and insisted that the landlords, merchants, and businessmen were responsible for the plight of the landless farmer. In the summer of 1911 the *Rebel* editor attacked the agricultural ladder theory as a cruel myth designed to deceive tenants who were heading for peonage, not landownership. "The tenants," Hickey declared, "have been going steadily down hill and they will be dumped in the ditch of despair if they don't look out."[16]

Exploiting the growing alarm in the established press over the rising rate of tenancy revealed in the 1910 census, the *Rebel*'s editors reprinted an editorial from the *Galveston News* questioning the conventional notion that the tenant would be able to amass "a small amount of money" and "inevitably [be able to] buy a place of his own and leave the landlord." Clearly, the *Rebel* continued, a permanent tenant class existed in Texas under conditions that "even the tenants of poor old Ireland scorned 100 years ago."[17]

What would the renters of the Lone Star State do about these conditions? As the article concluded confidently, the desire of landlord, banker, and merchant was still clear "[that the] tenant . . . be a nice subservient menial who will meet the land lord cap in hand and confer with him as to how much of his hide shall be taken and under what conditions shall the skinning be done. . . . The Texans are going to submit to these degrading Europeans [*sic*] condition of life long tenantry is a proposition so ridiculous that it would only occur in the mind of a vaudeville clown or a land lord editorial writer."[18]

The *Rebel* also publicized the platform of the Texas Socialist Party designed to appeal especially to tenants with grievances. The Socialists made three basic demands after 1908: a new state land policy to expand the public domain for tenant use and occupancy; a graduated land tax to eliminate the profits in speculative landholding; and a system of state-sponsored cooperatives designed for production as well as exchange. Other planks demanded government ownership of transportation, manufacturing, and marketing facilities; free agricultural education; and a state-owned farm insurance program. This platform continued to win converts to Socialism in Texas in the years after 1908, but it was not endorsed by the national party convention until 1912. The Texan delegates came to that meeting from the state with the fastest-growing Socialist Party in the country; they had chartered 181 new locals in the Lone Star State during the spring months of 1912. More important, the Renters Union had organized forty-five locals during its seven months of activity. This achievement helped to convince orthodox Socialist delegates that the southwestern movement was recruiting potential proletarians, not petty capitalists. After defeating a left-wing demand that all land be collectivized immediately, the convention adopted the main planks of the Texas program as part of its national platform.[19]

During the summer of 1912, the Socialists waged their most ambitious campaign in the Lone Star State. Debs again brought his presidential candidacy to the Southwest. He toured Texas in September, speaking at camp meetings that drew thousands of farmers and their families. He was followed by Hickey of the *Rebel* and by the famous radical labor agitator William D. ("Big Bill") Haywood. In August the Socialist editor of the *Dallas Laborer* enthusiastically reported that the party had twenty-four "regularly routed organizers" in the field besides "a host of volunteers"; it had scheduled thirty "big camp meetings" and recruited six thousand dues-paying members, "most of them tenants." The *Rebel* had twenty-two thousand subscribers, and the *Appeal to Reason*, the national Socialist weekly published in Kansas, had forty thousand Texas readers.[20]

The militancy of the southwestern Socialists' campaign was enhanced by the outbreak of a "lumber war" in the Piney Woods of East Texas. The Brotherhood of Timber Workers, an independent union based in Louisiana, affiliated with the Industrial Workers of the World (IWW) in May of 1912 and immediately faced a lockout, an action organized by the Southern Lumber Operators' Association and its leader, John Henry Kirby, who effectively kept the brotherhood out of most of his East Texas mills. Some of the smaller operators were less successful, however. After the brotherhood affiliated with the IWW, it became a more equalitarian industrial union, and during the lumber war it continued to sign up black mill hands who actually held a majority of the pine industry's jobs. When company guards shot into a crowd at Grabow, Louisiana, on July 7, 1912, union men returned their fire, killing one of the assailants. In a few days, lawmen put most of the brotherhood leadership in jail on murder charges, and the Piney Woods was on the brink of open rebellion. In the midst of this widening class conflict, IWW leader Bill Haywood returned to the Sabine lumber region and toured the camps speaking for Debs and raising money for the Grabow defendants. After challenging Kirby to a debate in Kirbyville, Texas, Haywood moved into the cotton country to the west and spoke at a number of large encampments, urging the Renters Union to come to the aid of the Brotherhood of Timber Workers. Hugh Moore, a Texas tenant union leader, echoed these pleas and declared that he was deeply indignant over the treatment meted out to his brothers in the Piney Woods. He vowed that the members of his organization would stand behind the brotherhood because, in his view, the "interest of the Timber Workers was identical with that of the renters."[21]

As Charles W. Holman observed, there was a growing similarity between the transient tenant farmers of Texas and the "casual workers" who comprised the state's unskilled rural and industrial proletariat. Texas tenants who joined the Socialist Party were thinking more in terms of class and less in terms of individualism. The Socialists were more forward-looking than the Populists; they were willing to accept the need for collective farms. But they were not about to

alienate potential agrarian supporters by demanding the immediate collectiviza-
tion of *all* farms. The small farmer's natural right to retain individual use and
occupancy of the land was guaranteed not only by the Bible and common law
but also by the Socialists' labor theory of value. Those working farmers who used
their land for production and not for speculation or for the exploitation of hired
labor would be guaranteed the use, occupancy, and fee simple ownership of their
land in the Cooperative Commonwealth. In the short run, the Texas Socialists
based their attack against landlordism on immediate demands for confiscatory
land taxes, an idea borrowed from Henry George, whose "single tax" plan had
been ignored by the Populists.[22]

Those Texas tenants who joined the Socialist Party to defend their natural
rights against absentee landlords and speculators responded primarily to the
Socialists' fundamental moralistic appeal. Radical revivalists, like the Reverend
M. A. Smith, author of the *Rebel's* weekly "sermon" on the evils of capitalism,
added biblical support to the cotton tenants' grievances against the landlords.
Tom Hickey and the more "scientific" Socialists sought to transform this moral
sense of grievance into a materialist sense of class consciousness. They were partially successful, because they blended the traditional moralistic appeal with a
materialist class analysis, especially in their popular summer encampments that
replaced religious revivals in the yearly ritual of most Socialist renters. After
its investigation of the southwestern land question at Dallas in 1915, the US
Commission on Industrial Relations concluded, in the words of its historian,
that "militant class consciousness" was not "limited only to industrial communities"—it "now threatened sweeping social change in one of the most exclusively
agrarian regions of America."[23]

In the years after 1908, when the Farmers' Union declined into a businessmen's interest group, tenant farmers expressed their new class consciousness
forcefully in party publications. As one radical renter said after leaving the old
Farmers' Union for the new socialistic Renters Union: "The poor renter has
found he is in with the wrong crowd." Being in the same organization with rich
farmers and landlords "has made him. . . . fit for a class conscious organization."
A *Farm and Ranch* report on the Union's 1912 convention clearly indicated
that renters were developing a collective anticapitalist consciousness that was
directed not only at landlords but also at merchants, bankers, lawyers, and the
larger corporations. Only the "radicals" of "strong socialist sentiment" prevailed
at the Waco convention, according to the alarmed report, and "only resolutions
emphasizing bitter relations between landlords and tenants" passed. The delegates denounced the eviction of tenants for their political beliefs. They also

endorsed the need for parallel black renters unions and identified their cause with the land revolution of the Mexican insurgents under Zapata and with the labor revolt of the timber workers against the lumber trust.[24]

This growing radical consciousness, coupled with a new decentralized organizing campaign, allowed the Socialists to make significant gains at the polls in 1912, even though Woodrow Wilson ran extremely well in Texas. Eugene V. Debs, once again the Socialist Party's presidential candidate, polled 25,743 votes, or 8.5 percent of the total cast; this represented an impressive threefold increase over his 1908 vote. There were few states, with the exception of Oklahoma (which claimed the largest dues-paying membership in the country), where the Socialists made such striking gains in the 1912 election.[25] But then there were few states experiencing anything like the land struggle that polarized the Texas and Oklahoma cotton country after 1910.

The Socialist Party's voting strength was concentrated mainly in the northern and eastern sections of Texas. The party's candidates won very few votes in the vast reaches of West Texas and South Texas, where the population was sparse and the visits from party organizers were rare. The new party also suffered from its lack of poll watchers in these sections, where Democratic "courthouse rings" controlled most counties with an iron hand.[26]

Socialist Party candidates ran more successfully in the Piney Woods counties of East Texas where Debs averaged 17 percent of the vote, and the party's gubernatorial candidate, Reddin Andrews, an ex-Populist, outpolled his Republican and Progressive rivals. Socialist support in this section came largely from indebted ex-Populist farmers who worked the poor sandy soil, but the Debs ticket also received the support of younger tenant farmers and lumber workers who had not previously supported the People's Party. Roscoe C. Martin has documented the strong correlation of Populist and Socialist voting in a few East Texas precincts, but there are other precincts (including many in the lumber counties and in areas where tenancy became predominant after 1910) in which the Socialists were relatively strong and the Populists were weak.[27]

The Socialists polled rather low percentages (7 percent on the average) in the black prairie counties, which contained the state's largest level of tenancy, but the party did enjoy significant support in the state's leading cotton counties. In fact, Debs's raw totals in these "black waxy" counties vastly exceeded his statewide county average. Debs received *lower percentages* in these high tenancy counties, however, because his rural vote was offset by big Wilson totals in prosperous commercial cities like Fort Worth, Dallas, Sherman, Denison, Corsicana, Cleburne, and Temple (all with populations in the range of ten thousand and over). The Socialist Party campaign of 1912 also yielded significant results in the old Populist counties of the Western Cross Timbers section and in some of the newly settled counties north of Abilene where land values and tenancy rates increased after the turn of the century.[28]

After two more years of organizing under the leadership of Tom Hickey and party secretary Ed Green, the Texas Socialists launched another energetic campaign, hoping to take advantage of the new discontent caused by the 1914 cotton crisis. The party's 1914 platform reiterated the demand that "occupancy and use" be the only title to the land: it also called for taxing of idle lands, for repeal of the poll tax and vagrancy laws, and for state ownership of mineral and lumber industries.[29]

In 1914 the Texas Socialists continued to politicize the "wonderful unrest" that one Democrat observed in the depressed cotton country. While the Democrats locked into their perennial issues, "Baileyism" and prohibitionism, their radical critics were busy making the land question the paramount issue in their campaign. The Socialists were undermined, however, by an ambitious political upstart from Temple named James E. Ferguson, who declared for the democratic gubernatorial nomination. While the Wilsonians and the old regulars continued to ignore the tenancy problem, Ferguson dismissed the liquor issue and proposed a land plank to hold rent shares at the customary one-third grain and one-fourth cotton. Ferguson was a banker who was "not unfriendly to corporate wealth and industrial enterprise," but he aimed his colorful campaign at tenant farmers, and won his primary campaign against a more conservative opponent.[30] In the general election Ferguson "stole the Socialist Party's thunder" and prevented the radicals' vote from increasing in 1914. The Socialists polled a higher percentage of the vote than they did in 1912, but the increase came about because the overall turnout declined.[31]

The Texas Reds carried on their campaign enthusiastically because of the popular response the Socialists received in spite of Ferguson's "demagoguery" on the land question. When Debs toured the Texas Socialists' encampment circuit during the summer of 1914, he was tremendously impressed at the size and enthusiasm of the crowds who came long distances in the heat to attend these protracted radical revivals. "These farmers have the true Socialist spirit," he exclaimed. "Many of them have scarcely a crop between themselves and destitution and yet they are the most generous, whole-hearted people on earth, and for Socialism they would give the last of their scant possessions."[32]

Debs could not foresee the retarding effect that Ferguson would have on the movement's growth, nor could he foresee the breakdown of the party's discipline and the emergence of violent forms of social protest. The Socialists worked energetically to mobilize tenant discontent in the cotton country, but after 1914 they could not channel all this protest into the party or the tenant unions.

Although the Socialists failed to increase their statewide strength in 1914, they polled a substantial vote in some areas, notably in Rains and Van Zandt Counties, the area that supported the annual Grand Saline encampment, the first and foremost event of its kind. In 1914 the Socialists polled one-third of the vote in these two counties that bordered on the "black waxy" belt, and they joined a remarkable anti-usury movement that erupted in this region during the cotton crisis.[33]

In 1914 renters in Rains County, the birthplace of the Farmers' Union, brought suit against a bank accused of violating the state anti-usury law. The bank had "caused much public resentment" by foreclosing on a number of farmers during the cotton crisis. When the directors' threats failed to intimidate the tenants who filed the suit, they settled out of court. The news spread rapidly and "set the county wild." Within a few weeks several Socialists collected compensation from usurious bankers, though party leaders opposed the suits, fearing that they would put the banks out of business and leave the farmers no alternative but the credit merchants. In any case, the revelation that many banks in the area charged an "extortionate rate of interest" of up to 35 percent per annum was grist for the Socialists' propaganda mill.[34]

In addition to usurious interest rates, demands for increased rents angered southwestern tenants. After the United States comptroller revealed in 1915 that 450 bankers in Texas and Oklahoma *admitted* charging more than the legal rate of interest, a survey conducted by the University of Texas showed that many landlords in the cotton country, mainly absentee, charged extra rents on their plantations; in some cases, they even asked their indebted tenants to pay in cash. These actions, like those of the bankers who charged unfair interest rates, provoked angry protests from Texas tenants against the landlords who were violating what was called the customary or natural rent of one-fourth cotton and one-third grain. The Socialists organized petitions and mass meetings to denounce these offenses. Some militant renters took to night riding and sowing Johnson grass in the cotton fields of landlords who charged bonus or cash rents.[35] Many of these men belonged to a secret insurrectionary union called the Farmers and Laborers' Protective Association that was formed after the original Renters Union was weakened by landlord blacklists. This secret organization, called the FLPA, soon made contact with the Working Class Union (WCU), another secret organization of tenants and laborers then waging a violent struggle against usury north of the Red River in Oklahoma.[36]

Although Ferguson won many tenant votes by criticizing the curse of absentee landlordism and by proposing a law to limit rents to a third and a fourth, he did not halt the deterioration of landlord-tenant relations in Texas. The Socialists were still winning support for a confiscatory land tax designed to attack the system at its roots by taking the profit out of absentee and speculative landholding. The *Rebel* defended tenants' rights more strenuously than ever, attacking journals of the landlord class like *Farm and Ranch*, which criticized the renters' shiftless, thriftless traits as the cause of their failure. "My renter friend," Monroe Jones proclaimed in the *Rebel*, "you are poor and homeless, not because you are lazy and extravagant but because you have been and are being robbed by what our present society calls 'good managers.' They are robbing you with interest, rent, and profit."[37]

After more than a decade of Socialist propaganda, more and more tenants blamed their impoverished condition on speculation and land hoarding rather than on hard luck. Early in 1915 renters interviewed in the leading Texas cotton county agreed that the failure of the tenancy system resulted from the high cost of land and credit as well as from "hard times and oppression . . . by land owners." Most landlords, bankers, merchants, newspaper editors, and university professors still insisted that the agricultural ladder existed and that the failure to climb up to ownership resulted from laziness and lack of thrift, but "even the most ignorant and conservative landowners" agreed that there was "discontent."[38] A few even admitted that rising land values and the "curse" of absentee ownership were creating a "dangerous condition" in rural Texas. A banker-landlord from the Panhandle knew a surprising number of farmers who were "imbued with Socialism and anarchy." He warned that an increasingly "dangerous state of opinion" existed in that region, especially among the young tenant farmers.[39]

Some outspoken landlords blamed the Socialists for instilling radical discontent in the farmers, but one large landowner from the Brazos Bottom blamed property owners themselves for the "dangerous" antagonism of tenants toward the landlords. He believed that landlords would have to start treating their renters better, or "serious harm" would come to the cotton country. Many property owners, however, were "hostile" to discussing land reform because they thought it would "put devilment in the heads of tenants."[40]

Another Brazos Bottom landlord who lived in Waco was less conciliatory. His attitude illustrates that although the frustration and resentment of the landless was easily stirred up into class hatred, fear and resentment characterized the response of the propertied as well during these troubled times. He declared:

> White tenants are a worthless, lazy, lying, anarchist lot. I have kicked every one of them off my farm except one and replaced them with negro laborers, whom I can boss and who will do as I tell them. My experience with white tenants was disastrous. They will lie, steal, and cannot be depended on to take care of property entrusted to them. I do not know what is to become of this country so long as this class continues to increase, for they are socialists at heart—everyone of them.[41]

Scores of letters written by radical Texas tenants in late 1914 and early 1915 to the editors of the *Rebel*, who solicited documents to present to a government commission, reflected a widespread mood of anger, frustration, and increasing radicalism. Some renters said they were near starvation and had to leave their farms to cut railroad ties and work in the sawmills. Others talked of moving on to escape the hard times. And some even vowed to take armed action. They were skeptical about Ferguson's land plank, but they retained their faith in the Socialists who had finally made tenancy a key political issue in the state. Many of these renters hoped that they would finally get their say before a national audience when the Commission of Industrial Relations opened its hearings on the land question at Dallas in March 1915.[42]

After hearing testimony for four days, the US Commission on Industrial Relations concluded that "a state of acute unrest" existed in the Southwest as a result of usurious interest rates, bonus rents, blacklists, and other forms of "oppression" inflicted on tenants; these conditions created an "organized resistance which may result in civil disturbances of a serious character."[43]

The commission's chief field investigator, Charles Holman, testified at the start of the hearings: "A very large per cent of the tenant farmers have slipped away from the old feudal conception of being tenants of the soil, and have dropped into the modern condition of being laborers in fact." The cotton tenants were "very closely akin to the casual laborers" who worked in the extractive industries. Holman stated the transformation caused by the speculative increase in land values and the concentration of land ownership in the cotton region had produced a "rising absentee landlord class and a descending tenant farmer class."[44]

The commission's investigations in the Southwest gave the Socialists and their cause a great deal of publicity in 1915 and embarrassed some of the most powerful men in Texas, notably Governor Ferguson and Postmaster General Albert S. Burleson. Its recommendations on the land question appeared partially in the Rural Credits Act, which passed through Congress, and after the president's objections were met, emerged in the Federal Farm Loan Act of 1916; but the single-tax proposal was all but ignored in Washington.[45] In Texas the commission's report aroused the opposition of businessmen and landlords. The president of the Texas Bankers' Association, for example, attacked the commissioner's findings on usury, a potent political issue in the region. He affirmed the honesty of the bankers and blamed the state's tenants for their problem, which resulted from the farmers' thriftlessness; there was nothing "radically wrong" with the system.[46]

In fact, many Texas tenants still believed something was radically wrong with the system, especially when Governor Ferguson's reforms failed to solve the poor farmers' problems. The *Rebel*, boosted by the publicity of the Commission on Industrial Relations, still enjoyed a large circulation. And the new Land League (formed in 1915 out of the remnants of the old Renters Union) recruited new supporters by raising the old demand for a confiscatory land tax based on Henry George's single-tax ideas.[47]

Like most Socialist parties, the Texas organization voiced official support for Socialist activity among racial minorities. In practice, the support given by Texas Socialists to building Mexican American tenants' unions was often "ambiguous and inconsistent." Spanish-speaking farmers and workers, influenced by the tenets advanced during the Mexican Revolution, found Socialist doctrine appealing. In 1915 Socialist founders of the Land League, led by F. A. Hernandez, organized several locals of Mexican American tenants in South Texas with about one thousand members. When Hernandez was arrested for making allegedly seditious remarks in San Antonio, the Socialist Party mobilized a vigorous defense committee for the Mexican organizer, who was acquitted later in 1915. In spite of the party's defense of Hernandez, many individual members were indifferent or actively hostile to the Mexican American locals. Although the Socialists published a few Spanish-language newspapers in San Antonio, their most influential organ, the *Rebel*, never printed articles in Spanish. Furthermore, this newspaper did print letters that revealed the racism of the party's Anglo rank and file. The Mexican American effort remained, therefore, isolated from its Anglo counterpart both by the divisive effects of language differences and by active discrimination on the part of most Anglo members.[48]

White supremist attitudes within the Socialist Party were probably aggravated by landowners who used black sharecroppers and brown migrants to replace troublesome white tenants. Needless to say, these attitudes inhibited efforts by Socialist Land League organizers to form separate locals for black sharecroppers in 1915.[49] Many progressive party members shared Eugene Debs's militant opposition to racial discrimination, but even these advanced radicals helped to limit the Socialist Party's attraction to the oppressed minorities of Texas by refusing to make "special appeals" to any "section" of the working class.[50]

In early 1916 the Socialists of Texas had not lost any significant support to President Wilson's progressivism or Governor Ferguson's agrarianism. In fact, they hoped that the Democratic reformers' dubious record would win the Socialist Party new supporters from the party of Jefferson and Jackson. During this period, an editorial in Governor Ferguson's hometown newspaper indicated that the issues raised by the radicals were still very much alive. "The socialist party of Texas will make a campaign this year in the proposition of usury and the land question," remarked the *Temple Telegram*. "They want usurers sent to the penitentiary and they desire that use and occupancy shall be the sole title to land. It may be said in passing that the propaganda is winning converts every day."[51]

Furthermore, the Socialist Party of Texas was winning converts to a newer propaganda campaign—its outspoken opposition to military preparedness and intervention in the European war. The Socialists added a radical anticapitalist caste to the popular antiwar views already being expressed by Texas congressman Oscar Calloway and other southwestern politicians who followed William Jennings Bryan in opposing President Wilson's armed neutrality polity.[52]

As a result, the 1916 presidential campaign seemed to present great opportunities for the Socialists. But by the time the elections rolled around, it was clear that the party would suffer disappointing losses. The setback occurred partly because Debs, one of the most popular figures in America, refused to run for president and was replaced by a lackluster antiwar propagandist named Allan Benson. But the Socialists also lost votes to Wilson's highly successful "peace and prosperity" campaign. The War Issue pushed aside the land question and many other concerns raised by the Texas Socialists and forced the radicals into a bitter confrontation with opponents who were preparing, in the name of patriotism, to destroy the Socialist Party in the years between 1917 and 1919.[53]

It is interesting to note that after the United States declared war, Postmaster General Burleson, a Texan, chose the *Rebel* as his first victim under the newly enacted but unsigned Espionage Act. Tom Hickey, after being kidnapped by Texas Rangers and then held several weeks by federal agents for allegedly organizing an antidraft uprising, sent a flyer to the weekly's subscribers to explain why he had been falsely arrested and why his paper was the first in the nation to be banned from the mails. Both actions were the result of wartime "hysteria," Hickey explained, but they were directed against the *Rebel* and its editors because Hickey and E. R. Meitzen had exposed the mistreatment of tenants on Burleson's plantation. In singling out the *Rebel* for immediate prosecution, the Wilson administration showed that it was under the influence of "Texas politicians of the landlord and banker stripe such as E. M. House, Albert Burleson, Morris Sheppard et al." They were taking "advantage of the national crisis," Hickey declared, in order "to crucify a political opponent they could not bribe or control."[54]

When the *Rebel* was suppressed, the heartbeat of the Texas Socialist movement stopped. During the war, militant leaders of tenant protest were silenced and the organizers of the Socialist Party were arrested. Many of these radicals surfaced again in the short-lived Nonpartisan League movement, led by Hickey and Meitzen, and in the socialistic Farm-Labor Union that increased its membership of agricultural workers from 45,000 to 160,000 between 1921 and 1925. The old Reds also participated in the surprisingly strong Nonpartisan League campaign waged by Fred S. Rogers in the 1922 Democratic gubernatorial primary against incumbent Governor Pat Neff. Tom Hickey and others were also active opponents of the Ku Klux Klan during its heyday. But they were eclipsed by their old rival Jim Ferguson and his wife, "Ma." Furthermore, the land struggle they tried so hard to politicize in the 1910s receded into the background as renters grew more resigned to their permanent poverty.[55]

In the 1920s the tenant farmer was once again a forgotten man, despite the publication of moving sharecropper novels by Ruth Cross and Dorothy Scarborough, who tried to enkindle some sympathy for the Texas tenants. This situation prevailed until the mid-1930s when a new generation of Socialists led by H. L. Mitchell, Howard Kester, and Norman Thomas organized the Southern Tenant Farmers' Union and brought the plight of the sharecropper to the nation's attention with the help of kindred spirits like Paul S. Taylor, Dorothea Lange, John Steinbeck, James Agee, Carey McWilliams, and Maury Maverick. But the rediscovery of the tenant problem came too late to save the renters and their families who were "tractored out" during the Great Depression, forced out of the dust bowl and onto Route 66, which was supposed to take them to a new promised land in California.[56]

Notes

This chapter originally appeared in *Southwestern Historical Quarterly* 81 (1977): 133–54, and is reprinted with permission.

1. LeWanda Fenlason Cox, "Tenancy in the United States, 1865–1900: A Con-

sideration of the Validity of the Agricultural Ladder Hypothesis," *Agricultural History* 18 (July 1944): 98–100.

2. Paul W. Gates, *Landlords and Tenants on the Prairie Frontier: Studies in American Land Policy* (Ithaca, NY, 1973), 324; C. Vann Woodward, *Tom Watson, Agrarian Rebel* (New York, 1938), 404 (2nd, 4th, and 5th quotations), 405, 406 (3rd quotation).

3. C. Vann Woodward, *Origins of the New South, 1877–1913* ([Baton Rouge], 1951), 407 (quotations), 408, 410; W. E. Leonard and E. B. Naugle, "The Recent Increase in Tenancy, Its Causes, and Some Suggestions as to Remedies," in *Studies in the Land Problem in Texas,* ed. Lewis H. Haney, University of Texas Bulletin No. 39 (Austin, 1915), 12–33; T. J. Cauley, "Agricultural Land Tenure in Texas," *Southwestern Political and Social Science Quarterly* 11 (September 1930): 144.

4. Woodward, *Origins of the New South,* 413, 415 (quotations). See also Robert Lee Hunt, *A History of Farmer Movements in the Southwest, 1873–1925* (College Station, TX, 1935), 27–40.

5. James A. Tinsley, "The Progressive Movement in Texas" (PhD diss., University of Wisconsin, 1953), 63–67, 164; Taylor McRae to Tom Watson, January 23, 1907, Thomas E. Watson Papers, Southern Historical Collection, University of North Carolina, Chapel Hill.

6. Leonard and Naugle, "Recent Increase in Tenancy," 12, 14–15, 18.

7. On the early development of Socialism in Texas see Howard H. Quint, *The Forging of American Socialism: Origins of the Modern Movement* (Columbia, SC, 1953), 331–32. Also see William Farmer's articles in the *Social Economist* (Bonham, TX), January 13, March 1, 19, 1899. Voting returns are from *World Almanac* (New York), 1901, 437; 1905, 488; 1909, 617; 1910, 695. For cotton prices, see Hunt, *History of Farmer Movements,* 41–42.

8. George W. Tyler, *The History of Bell County,* edited by Charles W. Ramsdell (San Antonio, 1939), 329.

9. J. F. O'Connor to editor, March 28, 1907, *Hallettsville New Era,* June 14, 1907. This statement is corroborated in a detailed academic survey by Leonard and Naugle, "Recent Increase in Tenancy," 14–15, 28–29.

10. C. W. Holman, "Landlord and Tenant: White Tenants versus Black Tenants," *Farm and Ranch* 30 (November 4, 1911), points out the difference between the black sharecropper and his traditional "master" (one that had changed little since slavery) and the new relationship between white tenants and landlords.

11. Charles W. Holman, "Probing the Causes of Unrest: The Tenant Farmer, Country Brother of the Casual Worker," *The Survey* 34 (April 17, 1915): 62–63.

12. G. L. Vaughan, *The Cotton Renter's Son* (Wolfe City, TX, 1967), 41–42.

13. *Dallas Morning News,* November 13, 1911 (quotation). Also see Cox, "Tenancy in the United States," 97–100; and Shu-Ching Lee, "The Theory of the Agricultural Ladder," *Agricultural History* 21 (January 1947): 53.

14. T. A. Hickey, "The Land Renters Union in Texas," *International Socialist Review* 13 (September 1912): 243 (quotations), 244; *Houston Chronicle and Herald,* Feb-

ruary 12, 1912. In addition to the *Rebel*, the most important Socialist newspaper was *The Laborer*, edited in Dallas by George Clifton Edwards. In all, at least forty Socialist papers were published in Texas between 1900 and 1917, ranging from J. C. Thompson's *Texarkana Socialist*, which reached several hundred subscribers to tiny local newspapers like the *Mt. Pleasant Eye Opener*, the *Grand Saline Vanguard*, and the *Palestine Worker's Warrior*. Foreign-language Socialist newspapers were also published in San Antonio (three Socialist-oriented Spanish-language sheets and, briefly, the anarchist paper *Regeneracion)* and in Hallettsville where the *Rebel* publishers produced weeklies in German (*Habt Act*) and Bohemian (*Pozor*). On G. C. Edwards, who edited the *Laborer* after being fired from his job as a schoolteacher in Dallas, see the *Laborer* (Dallas), January 6, 1912, and on J. C. Thompson of Texarkana, who, like Edwards, remained a radical long after the Socialist Party declined, see W. F. Wiltse to Carl D. Thompson, June 4, 1913, Socialist Party Papers, Duke University. James Weinstein, *The Decline of American Socialism, 1912–1925* (New York, 1967), table J, p. 101, lists seventeen Socialist newspapers published in Texas between 1912 and 1918. Neil Basen, beginning his search in 1900, has discovered references to forty-three such papers published in the state prior to 1917. On the Spanish-language papers published in San Antonio, see Emilio Zamora Jr., "Chicano Socialist Labor Activity in Texas, 1900–1920," *Aztlan* 6 (Summer 1975): 228; and on the European language papers published in Hallettsville, see Paul C. Boethel, *The History of Lavaca County* (Austin, TX, 1936), 134–36, and the *Rebel*, July 1, 1911.

15.   Ruth A. Allen, "Thomas A. Hickey and *The Rebel*," 6–9 (1st, 2nd, and 3rd quotations). This unpublished manuscript is quoted with permission of the author. *Houston Chronicle and Herald*, February 12, 1912 (4th quotation).

16.   *Rebel*, July 15, 1911.

17.   *Rebel*, November 18, 1911 (3rd quotation); *Galveston News*, November 8, 1911 (1st and 2nd quotations).

18.   *Rebel*, November 18, 1911.

19.   *Rebel*, May 4, 25, June 29, 1912; *Appeal to Reason* (Girard, KS), August 31, 1912; John Spargo, ed., *National Convention of the Socialist Party Held at Indianapolis, Ind., May 12 to 18, 1912* (Chicago, 1912), 64–70, 73–79, 81–85, 192–93.

20.   *Rebel*, May 25, June 29, August 17, September 14, 1912; *Appeal to Reason*, August 31, 1912 (quotations). On the importance of the *Appeal* and the activists who "hustled" it, see James R. Green, "The 'Salesmen-Soldiers' of the *Appeal* 'Army': A Profile of Rank-and-File Socialist Agitators," in *Socialism and the Cities,* ed. Bruce M. Stave (Port Washington, NY, 1975), 13–40.

21.   *Rebel*, July 6, 20, 27, August 17, September 7 (quotation), 14, 1912; *Houston Chronicle and Herald*, June 26, 1911. On Haywood's activities, and Kirby's refusal to debate him, see Covington Hall, "Labor Struggles in the Deep South," typescript in Tulane University Library, n.d., pp. 150–55. Also see James R. Green, "The Brotherhood of Timber Workers, 1910–1913: A Radical Response to Industrial Capitalism in the Southern USA," *Past and Present* 60 (August 1973): 161–200; and George T. Morgan, "No Compromise-No Recognition: John

Henry Kirby, The Southern Lumber Operators' Association and Unionism in the Piney Woods, 1906–1916," *Labor History* 10 (Spring 1969): 193–204.

22.   Holman, "Probing the Causes of Unrest," 62 (quotation), 63; "State Platform of the Texas Socialist Party, 1912," Socialist Party Papers. Also see *Rebel*, July 1, September 2, October 7, 1911; and on the single tax, *Rebel*, July 6, 1912, January 3, 1914.

23.   Graham Adams Jr., *Age of Industrial Violence, 1910–1915: The Activities and Findings of the Commission on Industrial Relations* (New York, 1966), 203 (3rd, 4th, and 5th quotations). On the Socialists' moralistic appeal, especially in the encampments, see Tom Hickey's comments in *Rebel*, August 10, 1912, November 7, 1914; and for an example of M. A. Smith's "sermons," see *Rebel*, July 29, 1911.

24.   *Rebel*, October 7, 1911, November 16, 1912; *Laborer*, November 8, 1911 (1st and 2nd quotations); "Land Renters' Convention at Waco," *Farm and Ranch* 31 (November 16, 1912): 21 (3rd, 4th, and 5th quotations).

25.   *World Almanac*, 1913, 763; *World Almanac*, 1909, 617. On the Oklahoma Socialist Party, see Garin Burbank, *When Farmers Voted Red: The Gospel of Socialism in the Oklahoma Countryside, 1910–1924* (Westport, CT, 1976).

26.   E. E. McKee to Ethelwyn Mills, March 12, 1913, Socialist Party Papers.

27.   Roscoe C. Martin, *The People's Party in Texas: A Study in Third-Party Politics* (Austin, 1933), 60, 79–81, 185–86. For a more extensive analysis of the 1912 Socialist vote in Texas and Oklahoma, see James R. Green, "Socialism and the Southwestern Class Struggle, 1898–1918: A Study of Radical Movements in Oklahoma, Texas, Louisiana and Arkansas" (PhD diss., Yale University, 1972), 200–32.

28.   Statistics on voting are from *World Almanac*, 1913, 762–63. Statistics on population are from US Department of Commerce, Bureau of Census, *Thirteenth Census of the United States, Taken in the Year 1910* (Washington, DC, 1913), 3:795–96. Statistics on tenancy and land values are from University of Texas, Department of Extension, Division of Public Welfare, *Farm Tenancy in Texas*, University of Texas Bulletin No. 21 (Austin, 1915), 18–21; Leonard and Naugle, "Recent Increase in Tenancy," 14.

29.   *Rebel*, May 6, 1914.

30.   Sam Hanna Acheson, *Joe Bailey, the Last Democrat* (New York, 1932), 376 (1st quotation); Lewis L. Gould, *Progressives and Prohibitionists: Texas Democrats in the Wilson Era* (Austin, 1973), 119 (2nd quotation), 120–21, 125–44; Ernest William Winkler, ed., *Platforms of Political Parties in Texas* (Austin, 1916), 590–96; Rupert Norval Richardson, *Texas, the Lone Star State* (Englewood Cliffs, 1958), 275 (3rd quotation). "Baileyism" referred to the policies of conservative US senator Joe Bailey.

31.   *Rebel*, November 28, 1914 (quotation); *World Almanac*, 1916, 766; *World Almanac*, 1913, 763.

32.   Eugene V. Debs, "Revolutionary Encampments," *National Rip-Saw* (St. Louis), September 1914, 12.

33.   *World Almanac*, 1916, 766.

34. Texas Agricultural and Mechanical College, *Farming Credit in Texas*, Extension Service Bulletin No. B-34 (College Station, Texas, 1917), 33–34, 37 (3rd quotation), 38, 39 (1st and 2nd quotations), 40–42. This bulletin is cited hereafter as Texas A&M, *Farming Credit in Texas*.

35. *Appeal to Reason*, October 16, 1915; *Daily Oklahoman* (Oklahoma City), October 27, 1915; *Rebel*, September 19, November 28, 1914; Haney, *Studies in the Land Problem in Texas,* 89–96; Holman, "Probing the Causes of Unrest," 63.

36. US Department of Labor, Bureau of Labor Statistics, *Labor Unionism in American Agriculture*, by Stuart Jamieson, Bulletin No. 836 (Washington, DC, 1945), 260–64.

37. *Rebel*, February 1, 1913 (quotation), December 26, 1914. On Ferguson's tenant support, see Acheson, *Joe Bailey*, 376–77.

38. Texas A&M, *Farming Credit in Texas,* 60 (1st quotation), 61–63, 68, 73; US Commission on Industrial Relations, "The Land Question in the Southwest," in *Industrial Relations: Final Report and Testimony . . .* (Washington, DC, 1916), 9:9051 (2nd and 3rd quotations). This report is cited hereafter as CIR, *Testimony*. For further information on the farm experts' views of tenancy, see George C. Osborn, "The Southern Agricultural Press and Some Significant Rural Problems, 1900–1940," *Agricultural History* 29 (July 1955): 120–21.

39. Texas A&M, *Farming Credit in Texas*, 73.

40. Ibid., 54 (quotations), 55.

41. Ibid., 55.

42. CIR, *Testimony*, 10:9264–83.

43. Ibid., 1:86–87.

44. Ibid., 9:8952 (1st and 2nd quotations), 8953, 8954 (3rd quotation). Also see Holman's comprehensive "Preliminary Report on the Land Question," February 17, 1915, CIR Records, National Archives; Holman, "Probing the Causes of Unrest," 63.

45. In his testimony, E. O. Meitzen, whose exposes had appeared in the *Rebel*, presented evidence to show that in previous years Governor Ferguson's bank in Belton charged usurious interest rates and that Postmaster General Albert Burleson's plantation in the Steiner Valley forced the old tenants off with convict labor. CLR, *Testimony*, 9:8958, 8965, 10:9144–45, 10:9288–89. On the Wilson administration's response, see Adams, *Age of Industrial Violence*, 222.

46. *Texas Bankers' Record* 4 (June 1915), 2 (quotation), 12, 15.

47. *Rebel*, April 3, 1915.

48. Zamora, "Chicano Socialist Labor Activity in Texas," 226–28, 229 (quotation), 230.

49. For Socialist appeals to blacks, and positions on the race question, see the *Rebel*, April 24, August 28, October 23, 1915. Also see Donald Graham, "Red, White and Black: An Interpretation of Ethnic and Racial Attitudes of American Radicals in Texas and Oklahoma, 1880–1920" (PhD diss., University of Saskatchewan, 1973), 114–21, 219–28, and passim.

50. Debs actually made a point of denouncing racial discrimination on one of his trips to Texas. See Ray Ginger, *Eugene V. Debs: The Making of an American Radical*, 2nd ed. (New York, 1966), 276–77.

51. *Temple Telegram* quoted in the *Rebel*, January 29, 1916.
52. *Rebel*, October 28, 1916; Thomas Lloyd Miller, "Oscar Callaway and Preparedness," *West Texas Historical Association Yearbook* 43 (1967): 80–93.
53. David A. Shannon, *The Socialist Party of America: A History* (New York, 1955), 34–36.
54. *Rebel*, June 2, 1917; T. A. Hickey, circular addressed "To the Friends of *The Rebel*," June 30, 1917 (quotations), Thomas A. Hickey Papers, Archives, University of Texas, Austin.
55. Weinstein, *Decline of American Socialism,* 144, 161–62; H. C. Peterson and Gilbert C. Fite, *Opponents of War, 1917–1918* (Madison, 1957); Nonpartisan League Circular, December 22, 1917, signed by Thomas A. Hickey, Hickey Papers; Hunt, *History of Farmer Movements in the Southwest*, 159–60, 184–85; Richardson, *Lone Star State*, 314; Lowell K. Dyson, "The Red Peasant International in America," *Journal of American History* 58 (March 1972): 962–65. On the Ku Klux Klan in Texas, see Charles C. Alexander, *The Ku Klux Klan in the Southwest* ([Lexington], KY, 1965); and on the Socialists' attack on the Ku Klux Klan, see Tom Hickey's columns in the *Calliham Caller and Three Rivers Oil News*, February 8, 15, 1925, in Hickey Papers.
56. C. L. Sonnichsen, "The Sharecropper Novel in the Southwest," *Agricultural History* 42 (April 1969): 250–53. On Mitchell, Thomas, and the Socialist-led sharecropper movement of the Southwest, see Howard Kester, *Revolt among the Sharecroppers* (New York, 1936); Donald H. Grubbs, *Cry from the Cotton: The Southern Tenant Farmers' Union and the New Deal* (Chapel Hill, 1971). Also see Dorothea Lange and Paul Schuster Taylor, *An American Exodus: A Record of Human Erosion in the Thirties* (New Haven, CT, 1969); Carey McWilliams, *Ill Fares the Land: Migrants and Migratory Labor in the United States* (Boston, 1942); Maury Maverick, *A Maverick American* (New York, 1937); Walter J. Stein, *California and the Dust Bowl Migration* (Westport, CT, 1973), 22, 23 (quotation), 25–26.

JAMES C. MARONEY

The Texas-Louisiana Oil Field Strike of 1917

By World War I, labor unions were beginning to make significant progress in the South, an area experiencing dramatic developments in manufacturing. Although most Americans balked at mass unionism until the 1930s, skilled craftsmen in the South, like their counterparts in the rest of the nation, frequently attained middle-class status during the initial decades of the new century and thereby shared in the fruits of prosperity. Too, during World War I, the American Federation of Labor (AFL) achieved the benefits accompanying an unprecedented degree of collaboration with government and business. As the 1917 strike of Texas and Louisiana oil field workers vividly illustrates, however, some employers remained inexorably opposed to organized labor and greatly resented all concessions made to labor by the administration of Woodrow Wilson.

Labor unions initially came to the East Texas oil fields in the wake of the mighty Spindletop gusher in 1901.[1] Jay H. Mullen of Bowling Green, Ohio, secretary of the International Brotherhood of Oil and Gas Well Workers, indicated to Samuel Gompers his organization's interest in the East Texas workers as early as February 1902. Gompers sent an organizer into the fields, and locals soon appeared at such sites as Spindletop, Batson, Sour Lake, Saratoga, and Humble. In 1905 the J. M. Guffey Petroleum Company—later to become the Gulf Oil Corporation—reduced wages for the standard twelve-hour day from $3 to $2.50. Widespread dissatisfaction led to rapid union growth, and workers chose an executive board to act on behalf of the Spindletop, Saratoga, Batson, and Sour Lake locals. Although a ten-day strike preserved the three-dollar wage scale, union membership soon declined.[2]

A new attempt by operators to cut wages in the spring of 1907 revived union membership. Employers initially refused all sixty-two demands, including union recognition, and another ten-day strike followed. Upon notification of the "critical" situation in Batson, AFL organizer James Leonard rushed to the scene and helped negotiate a settlement in which the union won all but its most important demand—union recognition.[3]

Oil workers, however, remained committed to unionism only during periods of crisis; with little prior knowledge of organized labor, "they could see no need for paying dues to union unless they were in immediate distress and needing strong assistance." This lack of interest, along with the effects of the 1907 panic, virtually eliminated unionism in the Texas oil fields until World War I.[4]

Wartime demands during the presidency of Woodrow Wilson, however, led to the development of close ties between the national government and the American labor establishment. The US Conciliation Service, established within the Department of Labor and strongly supported by President Wilson and secretary of labor William B. Wilson, a former official of the United Mine Workers Union, was created to mediate labor disputes.[5] During World War I, the Conciliation Service overcame much of the initial suspicion on the part of both business and labor. Ultimately, wartime collaboration of government, business, and labor resulted in an industrial code administered by the War Labor Board, which recognized labor unions but forbade strikes or lockouts.[6]

Disputes between employers and organized labor in Texas referred to the Conciliation Service after failure to achieve settlement locally included a 1918 streetcar strike in Waco and disputes with shipbuilding contractors in Orange, Beaumont, and Houston. The latter disputes arose over the practice of contractors paying carpenters, electricians, caulkers, and other skilled tradesmen from 5 to 20 percent below the prevailing area wage rate, even though organized labor previously had been assured by representatives of the secretary of the navy and other government agencies that the local wage scale would be paid. Former Texas labor commissioner C. W. Woodman, serving as a commissioner of conciliation for the Department of Labor, helped to adjust the shipyard disputes whereby all employees received the union scale retroactive to the beginning of the controversy.[7]

The promise of a new era of labor-management accommodation offered by successful conciliation of these disputes proved illusory, however, when would-be conciliators confronted the united opposition of oil producers during the Texas-Louisiana Gulf Coast oil field strike of 1917–18.[8] In their adamant stand, the producers not only undermined attempts at conciliation but also inflicted a defeat upon organized labor from which it did not recover until the 1930s.

Rising costs of living, poor working conditions, and paternalistic company policies prompted Goose Creek oil field workers, aided by the Texas State Federation of Labor and the Houston Trades Council, to form a local in December 1916. By the spring of 1917, oil field workers throughout the Texas-Louisiana Gulf Coast area had established locals affiliated directly with the AFL since no national union for oil workers existed.[9]

When Gulf Coast locals invited producers to meet with them in Houston to discuss worker grievances on October 15, 1917, the producers refused and sent letters of explanation to their employees. Representative of the employer stance, Ross Sterling, president of the Humble Oil and Refining Company, wrote in part: "We see no reason why we should confer with outsiders or strangers upon matters which concern our employees and ourselves." In regard to union labor, Humble Oil expected "from every employee loyalty to the company and conscientious and competent performance of his duty. So long as membership in a labor union does not in any way interfere with or prevent an employee from rendering this character of service," Sterling continued, "we have no objection to his being a member of such labor union." However, "this company will continue to exercise the right to select its own employees and to deal with them directly and not through the medium of a 'labor union' or other organization."[10]

Such an unequivocal declaration of employer position prompted the union to issue a set of formal demands and to call a strike vote. The demands included replacing the standard twelve- to fourteen-hour day with an eight-hour day, a minimum daily wage of four dollars, a revision in the bonus system, and union recognition.[11] In the strike vote that followed, 5,992 of the oil field workers, representing 97 percent of those participating, voted to strike, and on November 1, 1917, approximately ten thousand men in some seventeen oil fields in Texas and Louisiana walked out.[12]

When the strike was more than a month old and US commissioners of conciliation James J. Barrett and George W. Musser were unable to effect a settlement, the President's Mediation Commission, a specially created branch of the Conciliation Service, previously assigned to deal with a similar dispute in California and headed by President Wilson's personal representative, Verner Z. Reed, arrived in Houston, charged with responsibility to bring about a settlement. A number of factors, however, worked against an equitable solution for the oil field workers. Basic to all else was tenacious employer opposition to unionism. Management tactics included a determination to defeat worker solidarity, featuring the full use of economic resources at their disposal and an identification of the workers' cause with radicalism and disloyalty. Associated producers initially denied workers the same right of association they enjoyed themselves by refusing to meet with representatives of the Gulf Coast oil field workers, although each individual company proclaimed a willingness to meet with its own employees. Furthermore, the producers subsequently displayed an ill-concealed contempt for the agents Barrett and Musser of the US Conciliation Service. Finding himself unable to establish a basis for negotiations with "the chief officer of one of the largest [oil] companies," Musser offered to send for labor secretary Wilson. The oil man, however, quickly replied with utter disdain that even if Musser secured the services of President Wilson, the producers fully intended to run their own businesses. Barrett reported that he was being followed, presumably by agents of the companies, and that producers had spread the word among the workers that he was affiliated with the Industrial Workers of the World (IWW).[13] With the onset of the strike, certain producers informed Attorney General T. W. Gregory that IWW agents and German spies representing the "mailed hand of [the] enemy" had secretly infiltrated the union and suggested that Gregory send Justice Department agents to ferret out the enemy agents.[14] The *Gulf Coast Oil News*, a mouthpiece for the producers, claimed that the "average American workingman," making up 80 percent of the oil field workers, had enunciated no real complaints until the arrival of outside agitators several months before and that ordinary American workmen, now bitter toward union leaders, feared to return to work in the oil fields because of a "reign of terror" imposed by a "vicious class" that included "the arch enemy of our Nation, the IWW."[15] Employer propaganda notwithstanding, the men continued to support the union leadership. Little evidence of IWW influence during the strike exists; moreover, the union firmly denounced the IWW on numerous occasions.[16]

The none too subtle propaganda disseminated by the producers found a sympathetic ear in the person of Texas governor William P. Hobby, who requested that the army send troops into the oil fields to guard company property "from enemies and trouble makers."[17] While some evidence exists to indicate that the army initially maintained an impartial stance, the very presence of government troops could not help but lend credence to employer claims of subversive influence within the ranks of the strikers.[18] Furthermore, some military officials displayed a hostile attitude toward the strikers. Colonel D. J. Baker, of the Fifty-Seventh Infantry, characterized the majority of the strikers as "Americans of the irresponsible type which, when it feels itself aggrieved is prone to violence and disorder." While recognizing little violence had actually taken place, Colonel Baker warned that "there is much latent hostility to the operators which, whatever the outcome of the strike, . . . must be for some time taken into account and guarded against." Complaints against troops came not only from strikers but from local citizens who charged soldiers with indiscriminate destruction of property, slaughtering of stock, and a cavalier attitude toward disturbing citizen sensibilities.[19]

Influenced by the producers' insistence that IWW agents and German spies infested the union, and constantly reminded that the nation was at war, public opinion remained hostile to the strikers. The *Houston Post* branded the wartime strike "a blow below the belt," and Sydney J. Smith, chairman of the Exemption Board of Appeals for the Selective Service's Southern District of Texas, threatened to use his position to induct strikers into the army.[20]

The ready availability of strikebreakers, resulting in part from a lengthy drought affecting West Texas farmers and ranchers, an influx of job applicants from across the state attracted by the $3.60 daily wage, and the importation of skilled drillers from other states, severely damaged the strike's effectiveness. Within two weeks, producers were maintaining near normal production levels, which convinced them the strike would soon be over.[21]

In dramatic contrast to the unity of purpose achieved by the producers, the inability of the oil field workers to win the support of the refinery workers in Texas and Louisiana sealed the fate of the strike; only by enlisting the support of the refinery workers could production be significantly affected, a necessary condition for union victory. While expressing sympathy for the strikers' cause and undoubtedly influenced by producer propaganda and public opinion and more firmly entrenched in middle-class society than the itinerant roughnecks, Beaumont and Port Arthur refinery workers voted against a sympathy strike on November 26, 1917.[22]

These, then, were the conditions greeting Verner Z. Reed and his colleagues comprising the President's Mediation Commission upon their arrival in Houston on December 17, 1917. After several hurried meetings with representatives of management and labor, Reed issued the commission's findings on December 21 after wiring Felix Frankfurter, counsel for the commission, that he would suggest government takeover of pipelines and refinery properties if the operators "continue in their arbitrary and autocratic attitude."[23]

While rebuking the strikers for walking out before granting the government an opportunity to mediate, the findings approved most of the union demands and, in doing so, infuriated the producers. The findings of the commission called off the strike "without prejudice" on or before December 24, 1917; approved the eight-hour day in all branches of the industry effective March 1, 1918; granted immunity against intimidation or discrimination to members of any AFL-affiliated union; and charged representatives of operators, employees, and the Texas and Louisiana state federations of labor to devise a uniform minimum wage scale for the entire Gulf Coast district by February 1, 1918. If they failed to reach a settlement, the matter should be decided by a government-appointed board of arbitration.[24]

Apparently unaware of the limits of the commission's authority, Reed appeared to dictate the terms as he "respectfully requested and directed [both parties] to accept the . . . findings without delay."[25] While operators registered an official complaint with Reed, a committee representing the Louisiana and Texas oil workers endorsed the commission's findings and declared the strike over. His task apparently accomplished, Reed left for his Colorado home.[26]

On January 2, 1918, some 241 producers, representing 95 percent of area production, met in Houston, organized a formal association of oil and gas producers of Texas and Louisiana, arrogantly questioned Reed's authority, and refused to accept the findings of the President's Mediation Commission. In a letter to Reed, the producers took exception to the wording in the commission's findings "directing" them to comply: "If we may do so with courtesy, permit us to suggest the limits of your authority. . . . The President never intended that your Commission should undertake to order the settlement of strikes, but merely to negotiate between the parties and endeavor to get them to dispose of the differences by agreement; his purpose is manifest from the name — Mediation Commission — which he gave to your body."[27] The producers' rebuttal to the findings of the Reed Commission argued the following points. First, an eight-hour day, reducing the labor supply and increasing production costs, would be "unpatriotic" in wartime. Second, union demands represented the work of outside agitators who claimed a strike would force the government to compel the producers to grant the union demands, and to give in at this point would represent an endorsement of such tactics. Third, oil field workers already received better pay than other workingmen, although "[i]f we could believe that an increase in this minimum wage would be of benefit to our Nation, we would cheerfully add this to the other ever growing burdens of enhanced cost . . . from which the oil industry now suffers." Fourth, the companies presently employed a sufficient labor force to maintain normal production, rendering government interference unnecessary — in fact, implementation of the commission report would require the dismissal of current employees "to make room for the strikers." Finally, the producers appealed to the Department of Labor for a hearing before the full mediation commission to protest the Reed Commission's report.[28]

Between January 21 and January 28, representatives of the producers' association and the union men met with the officials from the Department of Labor in negotiations leading to an agreement that "superseded" Reed's report. With all parties ultimately signing the new agreement, albeit with reluctance on the part of the union men, the settlement, announced on January 30, 1918, by the secretary of labor, vetoed the eight-hour day and left a decision on wages and hours up to a proposed committee on complaints of the oil and gas producers' association. Only employees—not "paid agitators" or union organizers—could present grievances to the committee on complaints. No current employees would be dismissed to make room for strikers, but former employees would be shown preference when openings occurred. But "[i]t is understood . . . that no employer shall be expected to re-employ any man who is personally objectionable to the foreman or superintendent of the employer under whose direction such applicant would have to work if so employed." Provision was made whereby either party could appeal a decision made by the complaint committee to a three-man board of appeals composed of a producer representative, an appointee of the secretary of labor, and the federal district judge of the Southern District of Texas. In practice, however, the board proved totally ineffective. At the producers' insistence, the final settlement took the form of an agreement between the producers' association and the government in order to avoid recognition of the oil workers' union.[29]

The final settlement represented almost a total victory for the producers and killed union effectiveness. Approximately one-fourth of the strikers lost their jobs as a result of the strike, including R. E. Evans, president of the Goose Creek local and one of the union's guiding lights. Within two months of the settlement, Gulf and Humble granted wage increases equivalent to the union request, and the executive committee of the employer association recommended another increase a short time later which became effective on June 1, 1918. Furthermore, several of the oil companies soon inaugurated housing programs and stock-purchasing plans for employees, all of which thoroughly undermined any effective demand for unionism. Such activity represented an adaptation of the so-called Rockefeller Plan, which has been called "a hybrid form of organization somewhere between the various alternatives of a company union, open shop, and union shop."[30]

Failure to win the support of refinery workers and the success of employer solidarity convinced members of the Gulf Coast oil field locals and their counterparts in California of the necessity to form a national union. Upon application, the 1918 AFL convention issued a charter in June to the International Association of Oil Field, Gas Well, and Refinery Workers of America (OFGWRWU), with the full understanding that the charter did not entitle the new organization to infringe upon the jurisdiction of any existing craft union.[31]

Continued division in the ranks of union members, in stark contrast with employer unity, remained abundantly clear in the sixteen-day organizational convention of the OFGWRWU, which began late in November in El Paso. Sharply divided between moderate and radical factions, the convention enacted a resolution demanding nationalization of the oil, railroad, communication, shipping, coal, water, and electric power industries, but it elected R. E. Evans, representing the moderate faction, as president by a slim three-vote margin. While the new international grew rapidly for a time, the combined effects of the failure to attract refinery workers because of craft union hostility, internal conflicts, employer-initiated benefits, and a new open shop offensive led to a near total decline of the OFGWRWU until its reincarnation under the New Deal.[32]

Notes

This chapter originally appeared in *Essays in Southern Labor History*, edited by Gary M. Fink and Merl E. Reed (Westport, CT: Greenwood Press, 1977), 161–72, and is reprinted with permission.

1. On the beginnings of the Texas oil industry, see John O. King, "The Early Texas Oil Industry: Beginnings at Corsicana, 1894–1901," *Journal of Southern History* 32 (November 1966), 505–15; and Seth S. McKay and Odie B. Faulk, *Texas After Spindletop* (Austin, 1965), 1–16. For colorful glimpses of life in oil field camps, see Mody C. Boatright and William A. Owens, *Tales from the Derrick Floor: A People's History of the Oil Industry* (Garden City, NY, 1970); and Charlie Jeffries, "Reminiscences of Sour Lake," *Southwestern Historical Quarterly* 50 (July 1946): 25–35.

2. Samuel Gompers to George J. Jordan, February 14, 1902, and Gompers to E. P. Lord, January 30, 1906, in Samuel Gompers Letterbooks, Manuscript Division, Library of Congress, Washington, DC (hereafter cited as Gompers Letterbooks); *Dallas Laborer*, December 16, 1905; and *American Federationist* 13 (February 1906): 107.

3. Telegram, Samuel Gompers to James Leonard, April 27, May 1, 1907, Gompers Letterbooks; and Ruth A. Allen, *Chapters in the History of Organized Labor in Texas* (Austin, 1941), 222.

4. Grady L. Mullenix, "A History of the Labor Movement in the Oil Industry" (master's thesis, North Texas State Teachers College, 1942), 10; and Harry O'Connor, *History of Oil Workers Intl. Union* (CIO) (Denver, 1950), 4–5.

5. The Conciliation Service was officially established in 1917, although Secretary

Wilson put Department of Labor mediators into the field early in President Wilson's administration. The US Conciliation Service, within the Department of Labor, was a forerunner of the Federal Mediation and Conciliation Service, established as a separate government agency in 1947 by the Taft-Hartley Act. Popular usage during the World War I era, however, commonly referred to the US Conciliation Service as the "Federal Mediation Commission" or the "Federal Mediation Service."

6.   John S. Smith, "Organized Labor and Government in the Wilson Era, 1913–1921: Some Conclusions," *Labor History* 3 (Fall 1962): 265–86, sees the wartime collaboration as beneficial to organized labor. For a much different view, see Ronald Radosh, "The Corporate Ideology of American Labor Leaders," in *The Twenties: The Critical Issues,* ed. Joan Hoff Wilson (Boston, 1972), 73–83.

7.   Federal Mediation and Conciliation Service Records, files 33/1068 and 33/1634, Record Group 280, National Archives (hereafter cited as Federal Mediation Records). *Proceedings*, Texas State Federation of Labor, 1918, 34.

8.   The best account of the strike is William Lee Greer, "The Texas Gulf Coast Oil Strike of 1917" (master's thesis, University of Houston, 1974). See also Allen, *Chapters*, 221–48; O'Connor, *History of the Oil Workers Intl. Union*, 5–8, 204; Henrietta M. Larson and Kenneth W. Porter, *History of Humble Oil and Refining Company: A Study in Industrial Growth* (New York, 1959), 66–71; and Harold F. Williamson et al., *The American Petroleum Industry: The Age of Energy, 1899–1959* (Evanston, IL, 1963), 831–35.

9.   *Proceedings*, Texas State Federation of Labor, 1917, 16, 112–13; ibid., 1918, 4; and O'Connor, *History of the Oil Workers Intl. Union*, 204.

10.   W. A. Campbell to Oil Producers and Operators of Texas and Louisiana, October 2, 1917, Federal Mediation file 33/754; *Gulf Coast Oil News*, October 20, 1917.

11.   The wage demands demonstrated that neither the earlier employer action instituting the bonus as a solution to the rising cost of living nor the increasing of the minimum wage rate from $3.40 to $3.60 per day satisfied worker demands.

12.   *Oil and Gas Journal*, November 1, 1917, 18; *Houston Labor Journal*, November 3, 31, 1917.

13.   James J. Barrett to E. J. Cunningham, November 2, 1917, Federal Mediation Records, file 33/754; Barrett to H. L. Kerwin, November 12, 1917, ibid.; Barrett to Kerwin, October 31, 1917, ibid., file 33/754A; G. W. Musser and Barrett to William B. Wilson, December 8, 1917, ibid.

14.   F. C. Proctor to T. W. Gregory, October 29, 1917, ibid., file 33/754; telegram, J. B. Rogers to Gregory, November 6, 1917, ibid.

15.   *Gulf Coast Oil News*, November 3, 1917, 1, 4, 31; December 1, 1917, 1.

16.   E. P. Marsh to James L. Rodier, February 24, 1918, Chief Clerk's Files, file 130/14A, Department of Labor Records, National Archives; Greer, "Texas Gulf Coast Oil Strike," 40–41; Allen, *Chapters*, 224–25; *Houston Labor Journal*, August 25, November 31, 1917.

17.   Hobby acted after receiving an appeal from Houston sheriff M. Frank Ham-

mond, who telegrammed Hobby that he could not protect nearby oil fields from "I.W.W. or alien enemies." Telegram, Hammond to Hobby, October 31, 1917, US Army, Southern Department, Records, file 370.6, Record Group 393, National Archives, Washington, DC (hereafter cited as Southern Department Records). Telegram, Hobby to Commanding General, Southern Department, Fort Sam Houston, TX, November 2, 1917, ibid.; Brigadier General H. L. Todd to Commanding General, Southern Department, Fort Sam Houston, November 2, 1917, ibid., file 370.61; Hobby to Major General John J. Ruckman, November 16, 1917, ibid.

18.   Greer, "Texas Gulf Coast Oil Strike," 44; O'Connor, *History of the Oil Workers Intl. Union*, 6.

19.   Colonel J. D. Baker to Commanding General, Southern Department, Fort Sam Houston, December 22, 1917, and March 13, 1918, Southern Department Records, file 370.61; F. M. Jordan to Hon. J. B. Daily, February 8, 1918, ibid.; Sheriff W. C. Jordan to General Ruckman, February 11, 1918, ibid.

20.   *Houston Post*, October 30, 1917; Minutes, Houston Labor Council, November 6, 1917, January 15, February 5, 1918, Division of Archives and Manuscripts, University of Texas at Arlington.

21.   Allen, *Chapters*, 223; Williamson et al., *American Petroleum Industry*, 833–34; *Oil and Gas Journal*, November 15, 22, 1917, 16; Greer, "Texas Gulf Coast Oil Strike," 59.

22.   Greer, "Texas Gulf Coast Oil Strike," 29, 47–51, 86–87; *Gulf Coast Oil News*, November 3, 1917, 3.

23.   Allen, *Chapters*, 225; telegram, Verner Z. Reed to Felix Frankfurter, December 21, 1917, Federal Mediation Records, file 33/754B.

24.   "Findings of the President's Mediation Commission," December 21, 1917, Federal Mediation Records, file 33/754B.

25.   Ibid. On Reed's authority, see Greer, "Texas Gulf Coast Oil Strike," 55–58; Allen, *Chapters*, 225.

26.   R. E. Brooks, Underwood Nazro, W. S. Farish, and F. C. Proctor to Hon. Verner Z. Reed, December 21, 1917, Federal Mediation Records, file 33/754B; telegram, Reed to Felix Frankfurter, December 22, 1917, ibid.; Charles T. Connell to H. L. Kerwin, December 22, 1917, ibid., file 33/754; *Houston Labor Journal*, December 29, 1917.

27.   Oil Producers to Verner Z. Reed, January 2, 1918, Federal Mediation Records, file 33/754.

28.   Ibid.

29.   "Report of the Executive Committee of Texas Gulf Coast and Louisiana Oil and Gas Association and Agreement with the President's Mediation Commission," February 12, 1918, ibid., file 33/754C; *Gulf Coast Oil News*, February 2, 1918, 3–5.

30.   Larson and Porter, *History of Humble Oil*, 70–71; O'Connor, *History of the Oil Workers Intl. Union*, 7. Quote from Williamson et al., *American Petroleum Industry*, 832.

31.   Williamson et al., *American Petroleum Industry*, 834; O'Connor, *History of the Oil Workers Intl. Union*, 13.

32.   The decline can be followed by OFGWRWU membership: 1919—4,500, 1920—20,900, 1921—24,800, 1924—2,000, 1929—1,100, 1933—less than 300. Williamson et al., *American Petroleum Industry,* 834–35; O'Connor, *History of the Oil Workers Intl. Union*, 15–21, 29–35; *Oil and Gas Journal*, December 20, 1918, 51, 58.

JOSEPH ABEL

Opening the Closed Shop

The Galveston Longshoremen's Strike of 1920–1921

On June 25, 1920, an anonymous writer submitted this poem to the *Union Review* in Galveston:

> Forth went the Hobby mandate / Throughout this Texas land
> To mobilize the National Guard / That was his stern command. Ho!
> Martial law and war declared / "By my halidom," said he,
> "I'll humble that Galveston / Galveston by-the-Sea."
>
> In olden days in Ancient Rome / When Carthage did annoy
> The Romans sent their Scipio / That Carthage to destroy.
> A modern pigmy Scipio / This Hobby, he would be,
> And make a modern Carthage of / Galveston by-the-Sea.
>
> Several pompous Generals / And Colonels too galore,
> And Majors bold and Captains / And Lieutenants by the score,
> All riding fast and furious / With eagerness and glee
> To capture poor old Galveston / Galveston by-the-Sea.
>
> But what of those, the rank and file / Those Texas' mothers' sons
> Who must obey this mandate / And handle murderous guns?
> Have they forsworn their manhood? / Must they automatons be?
> And murder men and mothers / In Galveston by-the-Sea.
>
> "Oh, Liberty! Oh, Liberty!" / Once cried a famous dame; "Alas! Alas!
> The awful crimes / Committed in thy name!"
> 'Tis thus may cry Galveston / As to tyranny she bends her knee
> For outraged homes and human rights / Galveston by-the-Sea.[1]

These stanzas illustrate the frustration of the island's coastwise longshoremen in late June 1920—on strike for a 25 percent wage increase since March 19. Day after day, hundreds of strikebreakers worked an increasing number of ships tied up along the docks of the Morgan Line and Mallory shipping companies. No strangers to conflict, the longshoremen were used to such tactics, but the event that inspired these verses caught them completely off guard.

On June 7, the "modern pigmy Scipio," Gov. William P. Hobby declared martial law and took control of the strike situation in Galveston. Within days, more than one thousand soldiers occupied the island, and for the next four months the striking dockworkers indeed bent their knees to what they believed was tyranny, watching as "pompous Generals" and "Majors bold" trampled upon their rights. By the time the troops left in October, the union stronghold of Galveston bore at least a metaphorical similarity to ancient Carthage—although the city remained physically intact, its entire organized labor movement lay in ruins, especially the longshore unions. Much like their Roman predecessors, business leaders and their allies in Austin hoped to prevent future annoyances from this modern Carthage. Rather than salt the earth, however, these men planted and nurtured the antiunion doctrines of the open shop. Ultimately, the Galveston longshoremen's strike was a major turning point in the history of the Texas labor movement. Supported by bayonets and rifles, Texas's business interests joined the nationwide assault on the American working class and launched the capital-state alliance that would prove so disastrous for organized labor through the 1920s.[2]

When the sixteen hundred members of the International Longshoremen's Association (ILA) Locals 385 and 807 walked off their jobs on March 19, 1920, they had no idea that their actions would have such dramatic repercussions. The weeks and months leading up to the strike had demonstrated the longshoremen's continued faith in the wartime bargaining power granted them by the federal government through the National Adjustment Commission (NAC). The origins of the strike lay in two hearings held between ILA representatives, the shipping companies, and the NAC in October and December 1919. Presented with a demand for higher wages, the shipping representatives stubbornly refused, arguing instead that Congress must first allow an increase in freight rates. The newly reorganized peacetime NAC, meanwhile, backed off, stating that the privately owned shipping companies bore full responsibility for resolving the wage dispute, thus effectively eschewing its functions as arbitrator. By March 1920 the longshoremen had had enough of this back and forth. Following the lead of locals in New York, the Galveston longshoremen "woke up to the fact that their loyalty to the city and country had caused them to allow their employers to play with them for a period of six months" and voted to go out on strike.[3]

As frustrated as they were by their companies' intransigence and the NAC's impotence, the longshoremen nevertheless exercised great restraint in their strike activities, confining themselves primarily to peaceful picketing. Although local papers reported minor incidents, the only violence of any mention took place on May 11, when a police officer accompanying strikebreakers on an interurban rail car bound for Houston received a bullet wound in his shin.[4] The striking unions quickly condemned the incident and denied any responsibility. Further investigation by the Galveston police supported the longshoremen's innocence—police chief W. J. Sedgewick blamed the affair on "disturbers."[5] Bolstered by such official support, J. H. Fricke, president of the South Atlantic and Gulf Coast District of the ILA, would later call the strike "the most peaceful, law-abiding controversy in history."[6]

Though Fricke's words may be something of an exaggeration, the strikers' overall passivity was indeed noteworthy, especially when one considers their racial composition: of the sixteen hundred men on strike, the nine hundred members of Local 385 were white, while the remaining seven hundred members of Local 807 were African American. Since 1912, Galveston's longshoremen had maintained a fragile and frequently contested fifty–fifty agreement in which whites controlled all the jobs on the Southern Pacific docks and blacks monopolized those of the Mallory line. Modeled after similar arrangements in New Orleans, this biracialism was based strictly on pragmatic considerations.[7] Whether they liked it or not, white longshoremen simply could not overlook the large numbers of African Americans in their industry. In 1920 blacks made up well over 50 percent of the waterfront workforce in Texas.[8] If either race hoped to improve its position on the docks, it would have to ally with the other. This did not mean, however, that social equality was ever a goal. Both unions were careful to avoid raising this specter, since doing so would have called down upon them the wrath of the entire racist society in which they lived. The strike was no exception to this. Both black and white longshoremen realized, especially after their employers began importing strikebreakers in late April, that if they hoped to bring the strike to a successful conclusion, they would have to maintain at least the semblance of economic cooperation across the color line.

What, then, was the motive behind Hobby's otherwise unprovoked declaration of martial law? As the few minor incidents above indicate, it would have severely strained the governor's credibility to claim violence as the underlying cause. Hobby also could not truthfully say that the dockworkers sought a new racial order. In any case, if social equality had been one of the strikers' goals, white Galvestonians would likely have taken care of the matter themselves. While the answers to such questions may seem elusive to historians, contemporary observers and participants had no doubt what Hobby's motives were. In the headlines of its June 7 issue, the *Houston Press* articulated perhaps the most succinct explanation of the governor's actions: "Open Shop War Is On."[9] Simply put, Hobby's aim in declaring martial law was the establishment of an open shop in Galveston. His decision to do so followed a nationwide trend that reached its peak in the early 1920s. During the first five years of the decade, strike duty accounted for about 90 percent of all National Guard activity throughout the country.[10] Whether or not Hobby was aware of such events outside Texas is unknown; suffice it to say, however, that his actions placed the organized longshoremen of Galveston in the same position as many other union members across the country. Combined with the forces of the open shop, this martial activism did not bode well for the Galveston longshore unions.

Largely dormant since their initial crusades at the beginning of the century, proponents of the open shop reemerged in late 1919, and their ideas quickly became popular among American businessmen. Feeding off the patriotism fostered by World War I, the open-shop advocates of the 1920s attempted to hide their antiunion message in the guarantee of all men's right to work regardless of whether or not they paid union dues. These crusaders even went so far as to euphemistically name their movement the American Plan. In Texas, the Beaumont Retail Merchants' Association became the first group to declare itself in favor of the open shop in April 1919. Soon thereafter, its members helped form the Southwestern Open Shop Association, and within two months the entire city of Beaumont operated on such principles. As a clearinghouse for local groups in Texas, New Mexico, Arkansas, Oklahoma, and Louisiana, the Southwestern Association became particularly successful at spreading its antiunion doctrines. Supported by civic leaders, municipal governments, and businessmen of all stripes, other organizations soon emerged throughout the state. In Dallas, for example, the chamber of commerce sponsored the city's new Square Deal Association. By the beginning of 1920, the open shop was indeed a force to reckon with in Texas.[11]

It was under the influence of such ideas that Galveston's business interests viewed the longshoremen's struggle. On May 6, the conflict assumed a new level of urgency for these men when Mallory line officials announced that two steamers that had departed from New York had changed course to dock in the rival city of Port Arthur rather than Galveston. Soon thereafter, several ships already in port left to receive their cargo elsewhere. Eight days later, agent F. T. Rennie further complicated the situation when he declared that the Mallory line intended to cease operations in Galveston indefinitely and move its offices and terminals to Port Arthur. J. B. Denison, vice president of the company, stated, "I don't know if the Mallory line will ever return to Galveston, but in case it does, conditions making it possible for vessels to be worked unhampered by strikers must prevail." Morgan officials held their tongues, but on May 17, rumors leaked into the press that they too might relocate their affairs to either New Orleans or Sabine. Perhaps trying to capitalize on this fear, the Southern Pacific's general agent H. M. Wilkins refused to either confirm or deny the reports.[12] Such fears were made worse by Houston boosters' efforts to attract the Morgan and Mallory lines to their city. On May 31, various Houston civic clubs, including the Young Men's Business League, the Salesmanship Club, the Advertising Association, the South Texas Automobile Association, and the Retail Merchants' Association, issued a resolution denouncing Galveston as a longshoremen's town and suggesting a local bond issue to secure funds for new dock facilities on the Houston Ship Channel. Houston labor, they claimed, remained satisfied, and shipping companies would not have to worry about strikes and unrest.[13] The prospect of losing two of Galveston's most important shipping concerns made the island's businessmen eager to end the strike and no doubt did much to enhance the appeal of the open-shop movement in their eyes.

For their part, the state's open-shop crusaders were only too willing to help Galveston's beleaguered business interests. Breaking the power of organized labor in such a strongly unionized town would be a spectacular victory for their movement. Beginning with the formation of the Screwmen's Benevolent Association in 1866 and continuing with the introduction of the ILA in the early 1900s, Galveston's waterfront had been a bastion for unions, who in turn provided their members with a great deal of power in the city's affairs.[14] On May 22, the Southwestern and Square Deal open shop associations announced that they would offer whatever assistance they could in relieving the freight congestion. In pledging their aid, these two groups claimed to have the cooperation of similar organizations in twenty-one cities across the state. One week later, F. O. Thompson, the head of the Southwestern Association, arrived in Galveston with the goal of adding another city to this list. In a closed-door meeting with local civic and business leaders, the open-shop leader outlined plans for inaugurating a new movement on the island.[15]

The Texas Chamber of Commerce was quick to throw its support behind the open shop as well. At a May 29 meeting, the board of directors adopted a resolution opposing strikes, picketing, the minimum wage, boycotts, and "class rule by either labor or capital." On Wednesday, June 2, the chamber took matters a step further and sent a committee to Austin to meet with Governor Hobby. Three business representatives from the Island City—H. A. Treat, John Jacobson, and Peter Cummings—together with Louis Lipsitz of Dallas, H. H. Haines, general manager of the Galveston Commercial Association, and chamber president J. G. Culbertson of Wichita Falls presented the governor with a petition asking him "to provide adequate protection to citizens of Texas in the port of Galveston while in the pursuit of their work, even to the extent of declaring martial law." Thanks to the "utterly inadequate" and fully unionized police force, assaults occurred on an almost daily basis against these nonunion American citizens. Repeated petitions to local authorities for protection had yielded no help, causing a congestion of goods the chamber committee valued between 5 and 7 million dollars. As a result, the inventories of many mercantile establishments in Texas and the Southwest had grown short, and the downward trend in prices seen elsewhere in the United States was not present in Texas. The committee also attempted to appeal to the governor's racial prejudices, reporting that blacks controlled the powerful Dock and Marine Council in the port, a charge that was adamantly denied by the white longshoremen. Hobby, they concluded, had a constitutional duty to exercise his authority and offer state protection so that the operation of the docks could proceed in "a systematic, lawful, comprehensive fashion in the interest of the city, state, and nation."[16]

Throughout their meeting, these representatives of Texas business interests repeatedly expressed their belief that the open shop was the only way to end the strike and prevent future conflicts. Lest there be any confusion about where they stood, the chamber committee declared, "In line with the conclusion reached by New York interests and the steamship concerns engaged in coastwise traffic, Galveston has determined to organize and operate an open-shop policy on these coastwise docks as the only solution to a serious and expensive obstruction to traffic and commerce." Still on the island, F. O. Thompson supported this declaration, stating "the only solution of the strike situation at Galveston as at other ports where the union men have quit work lies in the establishment of open-shop conditions."[17]

These business leaders were quite fortunate to have a man like William Pettus Hobby in Austin. A native of East Texas, the governor had made a name for himself at the age of twenty-nine as editor of the *Beaumont Enterprise*. Hobby used the paper to promote civic improvement and commerce in his adopted

city, championing everything from a deepwater port to improvement of the surrounding roads. Such actions led his overly admiring biographer to conclude
that Hobby believed "Transportation . . . was the key to human progress." In
1914 the young editor made the transition into politics as the state's lieutenant governor. Following Gov. James Ferguson's impeachment in 1917, Hobby
became Texas's supreme executive authority on September 25. The election of
1918 returned Hobby easily to office in his own right. A dynamic political leader
by Texas's standards, Hobby threw his gubernatorial weight behind such issues
as women's suffrage, prohibition, and education reform. He also placed the
foundering highway department on its feet, an indication that his biographer's
assessment contained some validity.[18] Given his penchant for transportation and
economic improvement, it was little wonder that Hobby responded to the strike
as he did. The governor's reputation for progressivism did not easily extend to
striking workers in an industry so intimately connected to his obsession with
commerce.

Even more important than his boosterism and political record, however, was
Hobby's demonstrated willingness to use force in maintaining law and order
throughout his term. The governor's first experience with martial law occurred
during the Texas–Louisiana oil field strike that began in November 1917. Although evidence indicated that the strike was proceeding peacefully, Hobby
succumbed to reports of radical activity and requested federal troops in the area
around Humble. With the army's help, the oil producers crushed the strike in
January 1918.[19] Hobby also played the role of commander in chief during the
Red River War between Texas and Oklahoma in mid-1919. Hoping to assert the
state's claim to oil found in the riverbed, the governor sent Rangers to the North
Texas town of Burkburnett. Before leaving office in 1921, Hobby placed nearly
the entire state police force along Texas's northern frontier.[20] Like his actions
in the Gulf Coast oil fields, Hobby's role in the Red River affair illustrated his
propensity for using force when he perceived the state's economic interests to
be in danger. His experiences seem to have made him quite susceptible to the
propaganda and appeals for military intervention presented by the open-shop
chamber committee and its allied business interests throughout Texas.

Upon hearing the committee's requests, Hobby immediately sprang into action, issuing a telegraphic ultimatum to Mayor H. O. Sappington and Galveston
County sheriff Henry Thomas on June 3. "[The strike] has reached proportions
affecting the business interests and material welfare of Texas and the property
rights of citizens to such an extent," said Hobby, "that unless police protection is
given . . . I shall, under the constitution and the laws of Texas, assume control."

Setting the deadline for action on Saturday, June 5, Hobby then ordered Adj. Gen. W. D. Cope of the Texas National Guard to proceed at once to Galveston. His directions were "to take such action as will be necessary to enforce the laws of the state without partiality, and to keep open those arteries of trade which are essential to the prosperity and uninterrupted conduct of business in Texas." Twenty-nine units of the National Guard, including three machine gun companies and four troops of Houston cavalry, assembled in their armories to await instructions from Austin.[21]

Organized labor responded indignantly to the business committee's widely publicized pilgrimage and Hobby's subsequent actions. At a mass meeting held on June 4, a mixed crowd of fifteen hundred union members, including between three hundred and four hundred African Americans, adopted a resolution protesting the governor's intention of sending troops to Galveston and the chamber committee's misrepresentation of the facts. The *Union Review* argued that these "union labor haters" misrepresented the Galveston conditions to the governor, citing as an example the committee's assertion that the strike delayed delivery of 15 million bushels of grain. "Any one [*sic*] who knows anything about the coastwise traffic out of Galveston," argued the journal, "knows that the coastwise ships of the Mallory and Morgan line carry no grain and never have." Responsibility for holdups in the port's grain traffic rested entirely upon the deep-sea shipping companies and the rail lines that served them. I. M. Barb, president of the Galveston Labor Council, seconded this, saying that Hobby and the Austin committee overlooked the lack of arrests since the strike began. Barb stated that the actions of the governor were "wholly uncalled for and entirely unnecessary."[22]

The citizenry and municipal officials of Galveston generally echoed much of this criticism. The *Galveston Daily News* reported that "several prominent business men of the city"—though they refused to be quoted—expressed their disapproval at the threatened use of troops. Less guarded action emanated from the city commission. On June 3 its members unanimously approved a resolution protesting Hobby's actions. According to the commissioners, the strikers had proven themselves, with few exceptions, as law-abiding and peaceful citizens. For this reason, the strikebreakers did not need protection. If problems did arise, the local police force could deal with them itself. The commissioners also called a mass meeting for that evening at the city auditorium. In front of a crowd of fifteen hundred, city attorney Frank S. Anderson and several labor leaders repeated the message contained in the city's resolution: Galveston would view a declaration of martial law as an insult to its citizenry.[23]

The city commission's indirect support for the strikers remained a recurrent theme throughout the conflict. Elected in 1919 with the backing of organized labor, the so-called City Party had wrested control of the municipal government from the hands of the Citizen's Party, the representative of Galveston's aristocratic interests. Since its election, this new administration had offered a serious challenge to elite control of Galveston, even going so far as to secure a series of amendments to the city charter in early May 1920 that were hostile to the interests of the island's leading businessmen. These amendments included such progressive provisions as the recall of city officials, eminent domain, and authorization for the city government to purchase and sell up to two-thirds of the powerful, elite-controlled Galveston Wharf Company's total value.[24] At least one scholar has argued that the City Party's victory in the bitter amendment battle was a direct cause of martial law.[25] Although it is difficult for historians to conclusively draw a straight line between the two events, there is still much in this thesis to recommend it. As subsequent events would demonstrate, such class tensions were fundamental to understanding the events of the strike and the declaration of martial law.

Such political currents notwithstanding, however, not even the city commission's protests prevented Hobby from moving forward. On the morning of June 4, Cope arrived in Galveston accompanied by Maj. Gen. John Hulen and Ranger Capt. Joe Brooks. After meeting with city officials in a closed-door session, Cope and his entourage attended a public hearing presided over by the mayor and commissioners. The hearing, which featured speeches by Fricke and fellow labor activist M. J. Gahagan of Local 385, presented Cope with the facts of the strike, reemphasizing its peaceful nature and the ability of the local police force to handle any situation that might arise. Mayor Sappington admitted denying police protection on two occasions, but justified these refusals with the argument that an armed presence would have only stirred up greater trouble. Commissioner A. P. Norman spared no words, branding the charges against his police force as "damn lies." When Cope finally spoke, he neglected to mention the strike at all. Instead, he stressed that his only reason for visiting Galveston was to see the freight moved. Following this statement, the adjutant general left the meeting and proceeded to the docks for an investigation. The fate of the city and the strike now rested entirely in Cope's hands.[26]

Galvestonians breathed a collective sigh of relief when the June 5 deadline passed without a declaration of martial law. After appearing on the docks that morning and observing the situation, Cope stated, "Freight is moving at the Mallory wharf and switchmen are at work moving empty freight cars and pulling out loaded ones. Additional workers are employed on the docks. The mayor and the chief of police have assured me that the fullest police protection will be given workers on the docks and going to and from their homes."[27] Soon thereafter, the adjutant general received a telegram from Hobby. The governor requested that Cope remain in Galveston and hold in readiness such troops as might be necessary to deal with any further holdups or threats of violence. According to H. H. Haines, this announcement pleased the business community. He believed that the threat of martial law would provide a sufficient guarantee of improvement in the port's operations. With the recruitment of additional labor, normal conditions would return shortly.[28]

Haines's words carried a grain of truth. The day after Cope's announcement, reports indicated that approximately eighty nonunion men had shown up on the Mallory docks to move and load freight. The *Daily News* reported that this was "due solely to the presence of General Cope and a group of rangers" and optimistically estimated that accumulated freight would be cleared within three or four days.[29] Even more telling, on June 2, Southern Pacific agent C. J. Blackwell wrote a letter to Cope in which he claimed that everything was running smoothly on the docks. His company employed about 150 laborers and brought in new hands every day. Blackwell also discussed the local police, saying, "There seems to be quite a lot of Dissatisfaction against the Police Department here, but all that we talked to seemed anxious to do anything they can to prevent any trouble."[30] Blackwell's superior, H. M. Wilkins, stated the following day that increasing numbers of dockworkers came in voluntarily and that the company was having no trouble procuring inland labor.[31]

Year-end shipping totals uphold these claims and indicate that freight was moving even before Cope arrived in the city. Contrary to the concerns of Hobby and his supplicants, commerce through the port increased substantially during 1920. Figures indicate that $3.2 million and $27.8 million in imported and exported goods, respectively, passed over Galveston's wharves during May 1920, two months into the strike. These figures represented an increase over the previous May, when only $2.1 million and $27.5 million in merchandise visited the city.[32]

Taken together with the increased activity on the Mallory and Morgan docks, these numbers would seem to have satisfied the demands of Hobby and his visitors. Whether they attributed this improvement to Cope's presence or some other factor, none of these men could deny the movement of freight through the port of Galveston. Given such improved conditions and the overall peacefulness of the strikers, there is only one satisfactory explanation for Hobby's abrupt declaration of martial law on June 7. When Brig. Gen. Jacob F. Wolters,

Galveston's new military commander, disembarked at the head of one hundred cavalrymen that morning, he did so with the intention of breaking the strike and inaugurating an open shop on the island. By the evening of June 8, Wolters commanded 947 enlisted men and 71 officers from across the state. The military district that these troops controlled included the entire island and its waterfront, as well as Pelican Island, portions of Bolivar Peninsula, and the mainland lying within Galveston County. All the soldiers were either dismounted cavalrymen or infantry assigned to provisional duty. Ominously, military officials also designated three troops of cavalry as machine gun squads and equipped each with an amazing five hundred thousand rounds of ammunition.[33] The National Guard left nothing to chance.

Intended to divide the strikers and bring the public's wrath upon them, the arrival of troops actually seemed to toughen the longshoremen's resolve. The strikers' solidarity was further strengthened by the shipping companies' decision to begin hiring Mexican strikebreakers in the days following Hobby's declaration. Both races stood to lose when a third group of competitors appeared on the docks. Neither black nor white showed much respect for the members of this alleged "in-between" race. To whites, Mexicans represented the further deterioration of already sagging wages and conditions. For African Americans, these Mexicans were competitors standing in the way of economic and social advancement; their economic exclusion from the docks reinforced white and black biracial solidarity. In the wake of the companies' announcement, the *Union Review* declared, "We are for America first, last, and all the time, and the best is not too good for Americans and we say send these people back where they belong until they are willing to uphold what we have fought many years to gain, and not allow themselves to be used as tools by some money-grabbing corporation to the detriment of American citizens." Coinciding as it did with the shipping companies' decision, martial law could easily be seen by the longshoremen as a tactic for replacing unionized American workers with nonunion foreigners.[34]

On the evening of Hobby's announcement, the Galveston Labor Council and the Dock and Marine Council organized a joint session. This "indignation meeting" resulted in a sharply worded resolution accusing Hobby of being misinformed of the facts in the strike. "We resent with all the manhood we possess," the resolution stated, "the humiliation and insult which we have been forced to suffer through the action taken by the governor." The joint meeting astutely charged the troops with assisting in the establishment of an open shop in Galveston.[35] The local labor press and its supporters abroad offered the same assessment of Hobby's action. Most carried headlines declaring the open-shop motives behind martial law. The *Union Review* stated that "the reputation of our city has been assassinated, the character of its citizenship besmirched, and the fair name of Galveston prostituted before the world by the actions of the smallest governor of the largest state in the nation." The Houston Labor Council went so far as to call for Hobby's impeachment once an independent investigation could confirm that he abused the power of his office by aiding business over labor. Not surprisingly, these denunciations were largely ignored by those at whom they were directed.[36]

Wolters and his commander in chief were, however, forced to pay at least token attention to the protests of the longshoremen's supporters in the municipal government, a fact that would have repercussions in the months ahead. Shortly after receiving word of the martial law declaration, Galveston city officials telegraphically denounced Hobby's actions as "the biggest outrage ever to be perpetrated on a peaceful community."[37] On the commission's instructions, city attorney Anderson began injunction proceedings against the National Guard to prevent it from bivouacking in Menard Park. Located within sight of beachfront attractions and the most popular bathing areas, the commission was concerned that a military camp in the park would adversely affect the busy summer tourist season. Hoping to appease his less-than-cordial hosts, Wolters voluntarily removed the camp to a vacant property farther down the seawall, donated for his use by several unacknowledged private parties. One commentator joked that the beautiful beachfront location of the new Camp Hutchings, as it was called, "will to an extent compensate [the guardsmen] for the enforced military duty that they are under."[38]

Although the state legislature ultimately sided with Hobby and appropriated the one hundred thousand dollars needed for this action, their support was not unanimous, as a handful of representatives took the opportunity to denounce the governor and his business allies for their actions on the floor of the House. "I resent the subsidizing of state troops of this state [*sic*] to jog down the throats of its citizens the Open Shop Association," cried Rep. Lee Brady of Galveston County. Brady went on to denounce the chamber of commerce committee that visited Hobby, stating that its members did not represent city, county, or state officials. Rep. Don H. Biggers of Eastland County affirmed, "I am not dominated by union labor. I am standing here as a free American, or as free as John D. Rockefeller and that bunch will let me be. I vote this way because I do not want to be dictated to by a bunch who have not given a reason for their so doing."[39]

Many individuals uninvolved with the labor movement joined these legislative outcasts to voice their disapproval of both the martial law declaration and its open-shop motives. G. V. Sanders, editor of the *Houston Press*, opined, "Governor Hobby has been led into a number of bonehead plays during his administration, but his declaration of martial law is by far the worst of all."[40] In Galveston an anonymous "large businessman" stated that 90 percent of the city's employers were satisfied with their workers and opposed the open shop. They had no desire to stir up labor trouble. Even some of the National Guardsmen appeared to be dissatisfied with Hobby's decision. In Houston, officials issued arrest warrants for forty-nine soldiers who refused to report for duty in Galveston. When asked why, many of the men stated they had signed up to fight overseas, not against strikers in their own state.[41]

Hobby and the state's business interests were apparently unimpressed by these protests. Not only did the governor refuse to lift his orders, but on June 10, Galveston businessmen chartered the city's first Open Shop Association. The announcement finally confirmed the suspicions of organized labor and the opponents of martial law. Although it refused to make public the names of its members, the new association included approximately one hundred businessmen. The directors inaugurated the open shop with a telegram to Lt. Gov. W. A. Johnson announcing their opposition to "autocracy . . . of labor or capital." The indiscretion of this wire helped reveal the economic interests that business and state leaders shared.[42] Strengthened by this support, the shipping companies of Galveston gained the upper hand in their battle against the striking longshoremen.

Wolters's first action in Galveston involved securing the city and its waterfront. After a quick survey, the troops established several outposts, two of which commanded a direct view of all activity on the Morgan and Mallory docks. Three officers, fifty enlisted men, and two machine guns garrisoned each outpost, maintaining communications with Camp Hutchings by telephone. Military police under the command of the new provost marshal, Col. Billie Mayfield, began patrolling day and night. An intelligence department consisting of several plainclothes officers supplemented this police force. Wolters also ordered the construction of a bullpen surrounded by double barbed wire in which to keep anyone arrested by the Guard.[43]

General Order No. 1, declared by Wolters immediately after his arrival, ensured that this bullpen would soon contain prisoners. Among its several provisions, the order forbade all interference with persons in pursuit of work, loitering by crowds of more than two people, and public assemblies. Wolters also declared that "Any person found on the streets who appears to be habitually idle and without visible means of support will be placed under arrest." Although

General Order No. 1 applied to the entire city, Wolters clearly had the strikers in mind when he issued it. Denying them the right to assemble, converse with strikebreakers, or even remain unemployed, Wolters severely circumscribed the longshoremen in their campaign against the shipping companies. His order attempted to make the strike illegal within the military district of Galveston.[44]

Dock activity responded quickly to the military presence. Within days, the coastwise shipping companies each employed several hundred Mexican workers who, despite their inexperience, moved freight with little interruption. Given these circumstances, many were optimistic when the governor's personal secretary Ralph Soape made a trip to the island on June 15. Authorized by Hobby to call off martial law if conditions warranted, Soape interviewed strikebreakers, company officials, and military authorities. Apparently refused an audience with Soape, the striking longshoremen were conspicuously absent from these meetings. The pro-business interviewees he did meet provided the secretary with predictable assessments of the situation, charging that conditions did not warrant the removal of soldiers. Soape responded to this evidence by declaring the indefinite continuation of martial law.[45]

Soape's visit coincided with an even more important event. On the morning of June 15, assistant judge advocate Maj. C. H. Machem began hearing testimony from dozens of witnesses, mostly strikebreakers and company representatives, repeating reports of violence and intimidation against nonunion workers. These hearings did not bode well for the longshoremen or their supporters. Machem's final report noted at least thirty-five instances of intimidation directed at strikebreakers, shipping officials, and open-shop advocates ranging from verbal threats to physical assaults and property damage. The most damaging of these incidents were those that appeared to pit interracial groups of strikers against whites. According to one account, "a crowd of men—black and white—beat up a young white man. He was knocked to the ground by two negroes while fifteen or twenty of the crowd stood by and saw it done. Asked by a citizen what the trouble was, one of them replied, 'Just beating up one of the scabs coming from the Mallory Line.'" By publishing these findings, the National Guard attempted to use postwar racial anxiety to its advantage in ending the strike. Machem's commission also hurled charges at the police, accusing them of neglecting their duty and taking the longshoremen's side in the conflict. Together with Soape's visit, the investigative commission conferred legitimacy on Hobby's actions and Wolters's continued presence in Galveston.[46]

In spite of this ex post facto propaganda effort—or perhaps because of it— the National Guard soon became quite unpopular throughout the city. Wolters's draconian orders did not serve to improve public relations. Besides interrupting regular meetings of labor organizations, the commanding general also refused to allow a mass protest meeting called by the city commissioners. Similarly, Wolters paid little attention when city attorney Anderson declared that General Order No. 1 violated the guarantee of peaceful assembly, leading the *Union Review* to declare "Why Have a Constitution?"[47] Local merchants and the police force railed against the Guard's presence as well. Responding to reports that shopkeepers along the waterfront and in Galveston's downtown business district refused to deal with the hundreds of strikebreakers residing on the island, Wolters issued General Order No. 6 on June 14. Besides making it unlawful for individuals to refuse service to nonunion workers, the order also declared that "Any person who by words spoken or written, or by any act, token or sign, attempts to intimidate, or place in fear or terror of any bodily harm, or injury to the business of, any person in the territory affected by martial law . . . will be arrested by the military authorities."[48] The first person arrested under General Order No. 6 was police officer William Mihovil, who stood accused of telling a group of strikebreakers that they would be dealt with after the troops left. The guardsmen turned the patrolman over to civil authorities, who revoked his commission. Wolters's victory proved brief, however; one week later the same officials acquitted Mihovil and reinstated him onto the force.[49]

The National Guard received even more opposition from local Galvestonians when it attempted to control the tourist-filled beaches. On June 15, a group of businessmen and ministers approached police chief Sedgewick and police commissioner Norman to request the closure of beachfront concessions, citing their use for gambling purposes. Both officials denied this appeal. Although there is no direct evidence, it appears that the rejected petitioners then approached and enlisted the support of Wolters to their cause. On June 18, the commanding general shut down all concessions and midway games along the beachfront. Reaction to these high-handed tactics came swiftly. W. L. Roe, secretary of the Galveston Beach Association, indignantly expressed, "Since the troops have been here the city's business has been cut down to one fifth of normal. People are afraid to come here with these men butting into everything we do. . . . Galveston is being used as a political football by a crowd of politicians who are attempting to put the city administrators in bad." The following day, Wolters capitulated and reopened the concessions, but not before issuing new orders closing all bars, brothels, and gambling houses.[50]

Roe's concluding statement was indicative of the attitude many middle-class Galvestonians and small business owners had toward the powerful Galveston

Wharf Company and the aristocrats that controlled it. These protesting citizens believed that local elites had enlisted Wolters and the National Guard to reestablish themselves as the city's undisputed rulers. Although the Galveston Commercial Association had traditionally supported the aristocratic Citizen's Party, events such as the strike and martial law tended to undermine its members' economic interests and led them into short-lived understandings with the working class.[51] The general's new moral crusade indicated that these suspicions had some basis in reality. By labeling Galveston a "wide open city," Wolters created a powerful piece of propaganda against his opponents on the city commission. In a July 4 announcement dismissing 525 officers and enlisted men needed at home for the upcoming harvest season, Wolters declared, "It is necessary to keep [the remaining five hundred troops] here because the city officials are backing up the strikers. . . . If we leave[,] every nonunion man here will either be run out of town or killed." Wolters went on to claim that the administration owed its election to the city's African American voters, who he called "the worst and most insolent in Texas."[52]

As this last statement shows, Wolters was not above race-baiting the longshoremen. On June 29 the general made a stunning announcement. Intelligence indicated that Galveston's black residents had recently begun gathering weapons and ammunition in large quantities. In light of this discovery, Wolters ordered the removal of all ammunition from the city's pawnshops. Galveston's African American population responded indignantly, denouncing the general for his attempt to "stir up race trouble" and vehemently denying all accusations. Although local citizens could not have known it at the time, the findings of federal investigators, themselves on the lookout for signs of African American radicalism in the postwar South, indicate that Wolters probably exaggerated these claims. Their reports show that many blacks in Houston attempted to buy ammunition, but make no mention of similar purchases in Galveston. While it is impossible to tell whether Wolters sincerely believed the reports he heard, there can be no denying that his decision to make them public was calculated to drive a series of wedges between the biracial longshoremen and their supporters in the community.[53]

The seeds of these propaganda campaigns against the city commission and black Galvestonians soon bore bitter fruit, confirming the suspicions of many that in addition to establishing an open shop, Wolters also hoped to displace the labor-backed municipal government. One scholar has gone so far as to argue that "the troops were only surrogates for Galveston's aristocracy in a conflict that had been in progress since 1840, but had intensified with the election of the City Party [in 1919]."[54] Although this conclusion is somewhat overwrought, there is little doubt that the city commission stood in the way of the shipping companies' success in the strike. Hobby recognized this, and on July 15 he upped the ante by suspending all civil authority in Galveston. Making specific reference to Mayor Sappington, all four commissioners, city attorney Anderson, the judge of the city court Henry Odell, and the entire police force, the governor's order "suspended and restrained [all officials] from performing or discharging any duty appertaining to their respective offices, with respect to enforcing the penal laws of the State of Texas and the City of Galveston, during the pendency of martial law."[55] "The laws of this state are not being faithfully executed," proclaimed Wolters, "nor can they be . . . so long as the above named city officials are permitted to remain in their respective offices and use the power and influence of their official position in aiding and encouraging the lawless element of the city." On Wolters's orders, Colonel Mayfield and the provost guard took control of police headquarters and all police functions for the city. Tellingly, the shipping companies' private guards retained their positions as "special marine policemen" under military jurisdiction. Violators of state laws would receive trial in a competent civil court, and Capt. O'Brien Stevens, provost judge for the military, would try violations of all local ordinances.[56]

Galveston's official response to this new insult was predictably indignant. In a statement released the same day and signed by everyone but the mayor, the commissioners charged that their displacement and the declaration of martial law were political moves "for the avowed purpose of establishing the 'open shop,' destroying union labor and taking over the city government." These men also hurled countercharges of repression and autocratic treatment at the guardsmen. "Any further encroachment upon the right of the people of this city to govern themselves," warned the commissioners, "will be resisted by application to the federal courts, where we may reasonably expect the constitutional guarantees to be respected and enforced."[57] Two weeks later, city attorney Anderson followed through on this threat, filing a suit to enjoin Hobby and Wolters from any further maintenance of martial law. Robert G. Street, presiding judge of the Fifty-Sixth District Court, rejected the injunction application, upholding the constitutionality of martial law and declaring the governor to have exclusive jurisdiction in the matter.[58]

The suspension of civil authority prompted Hobby's first and only visit to Galveston on July 21. Accompanied by Soape, Adjutant General Cope, and Atty. Gen. C. M. Cureton, the governor met behind closed doors with a small group of local judges and lawyers to discuss a plan for ending the occupation.

The *Daily News* speculated that the proposal involved setting up the local judiciary as a central committee, which would then direct the efforts of Texas Rangers and a new citizens' police force in protecting strikebreakers, but could not confirm these reports. Whatever the topic of discussion, Hobby apparently left the meeting unimpressed. When asked what it would take to have the troops removed, he responded, "I must have absolute assurance—no, to put it stronger than that, an absolute demonstration that Galveston can care for the situation here so as to insure the uninterrupted movement of freight through this port and the protection of all workers connected with shipping."[59]

Wolters's assumption of civil authority quickly changed what had been an otherwise peaceful atmosphere. Throughout the first month and a half of martial law, the state troops stationed in the city remained on good behavior. The inactivity and silence of the striking longshoremen mirrored this. Unable to picket, most of the men found temporary jobs on deep-sea piers, and strikebreaking activity went on at the Morgan and Mallory docks with little interruption. Following the July 15 declaration, however, the actions of the National Guard began to generate a great deal of negative publicity. Whether accidental or intentional, these events adversely affected the way most people viewed the occupation. The first such incident occurred on July 30 when Pvt. J. C. Tyer shot and killed Capt. Herbert A. Robertson for refusing to stop at an outpost. Justice of the Peace E. B. Holman issued a civil warrant charging Tyer with murder, but Wolters refused to turn him over. After a court martial had acquitted him of all charges, Tyer was removed from Galveston County to face civil charges.[60]

The subsequent fate of Private Tyer was less important than the effect that his actions had on public opinion. Robertson's shooting was the most recent in a string of accidental deaths known or suspected to have been associated with the National Guard. Days before, Pvt. Abe Ginsburg shot himself in the face, unintentionally it appeared, while showing his revolver to his visiting sister-in-law. Even more damaging was the death of Mrs. W. Auderer, mysteriously shot at her home in mid-July. During her autopsy, medical examiners extracted a steel-jacketed bullet suspiciously similar to the ones used in the guardsmen's high-powered rifles. The spilling of blood added another dimension to what many already viewed as a shameful crime perpetrated against Galveston. Numerous commentators questioned the competency of the state troops and their ability to maintain law and order on the island. Instead of seasoned police officers, "green, untrained, irresponsible youths of the Texas National Guard, bearing loaded army rifles and pistols, have been charged with the maintenance of order and the enforcement of the law," claimed the *Houston Press*. In light of

these three incidents, more and more people began to doubt the ultimate useful-
ness of martial law in Galveston.[61]

The military presence incurred further public disfavor through the high-
handed actions of its soldiers and officers throughout the month of August.
Eyewitnesses began reporting that contrary to Wolters's orders, many of the
guardsmen were partaking in vice rather than ridding the city of it.[62] Shortly
after this, Wolters received a visit from a representative of Fox Film News wanting to use the guardsmen to shoot a picture about the Galveston strike. The
general obliged and provided his soldiers as actors while cameras caught the action in a staged "battle" between strikers and guardsmen at Union Station. Such
transparent propaganda did not amuse city officials. After condemning the film
for its misrepresentation of their city, the commissioners quickly received word
from the studio that the film had been canceled. Even the Galveston Commercial Association and the Young Men's Progressive League, both of whom favored
the presence of state troops, joined the commissioners in denouncing the picture.[63] Besides upsetting prominent Galvestonians, including some of his most
adamant supporters, Wolters's decision to allow the filming again indicated his
lack of neutrality in the strike.

The National Guard's most spectacular and damaging indiscretions involved
the *Houston Press* and its editor, G. V. Sanders. Since the declaration of martial law, almost every issue of this progressive newspaper carried news of the
Galveston strike. Although the paper reported many exaggerated and obviously
propagandistic stories, Sanders's criticisms of Wolters and Hobby were often
quite perceptive. He rarely missed an opportunity to skewer either of them for
their actions. In one particularly incendiary front-page article, the paper compared Wolters to General Ludendorff, the German army's supreme commander
in World War I.[64] Remarks such as these aroused anger among military officials
and made the *Houston Press* unwelcome in the martial law zone. Vendors were
arrested for selling the paper, and on at least one occasion, a member of the
National Guard attacked one of the paper's correspondents.[65] The most serious
incident took place on the night of August 30, when three men attempted to
abduct Sanders as he left the Houston Country Club. With the aid of bystand-
ers, many of them prominent Houston city officials and businessmen, the editor escaped. Upon interrogation, the would-be abductors revealed their identities: all three held commissions as lieutenants in the National Guard stationed
at Galveston. Before returning to their proper jurisdiction on the island, Lt.
J. A. Dempsey presented an order from Colonel Mayfield that read, "You are
ordered to arrest Sanders, editor of the *Houston Press*, for writing and circulating

highly incendiary literature calculated to precipitate serious trouble in the zone of military law, both among civilians and soldiers."[66]

This bungled seizure was almost universally condemned. Attempting to shield himself from criticism, Wolters declared that although he had issued instructions to arrest Sanders, the guardsmen acted on their own in taking the matter outside Galveston. Houston city attorney Kenneth Krahl turned his anger toward Hobby, saying "I have been convinced for some time Texas had a fool for governor. If he doesn't take proper action to clean out the whole bunch guilty of [this] outrage, I will be convinced that we have a knave for governor." The mayor of Houston, A. E. Amerman, called the affair "a very foolish stunt" and wired his objection to Austin. Many pro-business newspapers joined in denouncing the high-handed action. "Even if the military authorities had attempted to execute their warrant in the military zone of Galveston," the *Houston Post* editorialized, "it would have been an unwarranted abuse of military authority. . . . [T]here is or ought to be no military despotism in this State."[67]

Perhaps on the orders of his commanding officer, Colonel Mayfield attempted to control this damage and Sanders's allegations of false imprisonment by announcing on September 1 that he accepted full responsibility for the failed arrest. Wolters immediately relieved Mayfield of his duty as provost marshal. A subsequent court martial cleared the three lieutenants of all charges, but Mayfield, proclaiming his guilt, stood by his belief that the arrest lay within his jurisdiction since Sanders's articles aroused tension among both soldiers and citizenry. After three days of testimony from witnesses, including Sanders, the court martial reached a verdict. Before making their decision public, however, the officers sent sealed copies to Austin for Hobby to approve. The *Houston Press* cried foul, labeling the trial a farce. Two weeks later, Hobby proved these suspicions correct, announcing the colonel's acquittal and recommission in the Guard.[68]

Although the evidence is scant, it seems that the bad press garnered by Mayfield's actions and the National Guard's indiscretions gave Hobby reasons to consider withdrawing the troops. A cryptic statement carried in the *Dallas Dispatch* and reprinted by the *Houston Press* quoted the governor as saying that "a crisis is expected in Galveston soon [and] there may be no further need of troops there." Hobby also had to consider the mounting costs of the expedition. Since June, the state had spent $150,000 on the troops. This $50,000 shortfall had forced the notoriously stingy legislature to obtain deficiency warrants from private banks. On the afternoon of September 18, as abruptly as he had declared it three and a half months before, Hobby and city officials made public the terms of an agreement to end martial law.[69]

Since the beginning of September, a committee consisting of religious leaders, local businessmen, labor representatives, and the mayor and commissioners had been in meetings to formulate a plan for removing troops. On September 16, Hobby received a copy of their suggestions signed by committee president Jacob Singer and Mayor Sappington. The citizens' committee requested that the governor send an experienced Ranger officer to command the police department and exercise authority over all peace officers in the city. To assuage anxieties about police neglect, the commissioners pledged "to suspend temporarily and remove from office permanently . . . any officer of the city of Galveston who attempts in any way to impede, obstruct, or interfere with the protection of workers and the enforcement of the law." In addition, the citizens' committee was to continue in an advisory capacity with the purpose of bringing about "a more amicable understanding between employers and employees in the city."[70]

Embarrassed perhaps by the National Guard's recent actions, Hobby announced his satisfaction with the plan and ordered Ranger Capt. Joe Brooks to Galveston, where he would assume police control once martial law ended on October 1. All troops would leave the island between October 5 and 10. Hobby carefully qualified both announcements, however, stating that he would not hesitate to reimplement martial law if the situation once again deteriorated. Keeping these words in mind, the displaced mayor and city commissioners abruptly regained their executive authority at midnight on October 1. That same night, Captain Brooks and thirty-five Texas Rangers replaced General Wolters and the National Guardsmen as Galveston's police authority. In a final indication of the motives behind martial law, local businessmen hosted a banquet for the remaining soldiers at the luxurious Hotel Galvez. These "representative citizens" presented Wolters with a silver loving cup inscribed with the words "An Unpleasant Duty Well Performed." Each of the soldiers also received medals thanking them for their service. On the morning of October 8, the remaining five hundred troops left the island without further ceremony, officially ending Galveston's four-month-long encounter with military occupation. Although they were no longer physically present, the memory of the National Guard lingered in the shipping companies' negotiations with the strikers.[71]

On August 15, the members of Locals 385 and 807 had contacted their respective shipping agents and offered to return to work immediately if the companies discharged all strikebreakers. The response they received demonstrated the Morgan and Mallory lines' new commitment to the open shop as well as the power that the presence of the troops afforded them. In order to gain eligibility for rehire, the members of the striking unions first had to agree to three conditions: (1) the employment of clerks and foremen at the discretion of the company, rather than the union (2) the prohibition of all union delegates from the docks, and (3) nondiscrimination in hiring.[72] This final condition was the most onerous. It meant that no man—union or nonunion, black or white—would receive preference on Galveston's coastwise docks. Not only would this overturn the ILA's ability to control hiring in the port, but it would also destroy the uneasy biracialism that existed between black and white longshoremen by bringing them into direct competition for jobs. The men immediately rejected these conditions. One union official declared, "I, for one, will never open my mouth in favor of agreeing to such un-American terms as those submitted by the steamship companies, which would displace American citizens in favor of alien peons who are absolutely without any desire for a decent standard of living, and who pass their lives huddled together under their filthy ponchos when they are not at work." Neither company, however, paid attention to these protests. On August 25, Mallory officials issued an ultimatum to the strikers. The conditions for reemployment would remain on the table, they declared, but no more negotiations would take place. If the men wanted their jobs, they would have to accept the open-shop conditions without further debate.[73] Although biracial solidarity had managed to withstand the slings and arrows of its opponents for over five months, in Texas's racially charged atmosphere, this alliance could only endure so much pressure before it eventually broke.

The feared split finally occurred on December 13, 1920. Following two months of negotiation, representatives of Local 807 signed an agreement allowing their members to resume work on the Mallory line. The Galveston citizens' committee, which had acquired significant standing in September after devising a plan for the removal of troops, stood at the heart of this resolution. Most of the terms in the new agreement mirrored those offered by the shipping companies in August. Pending their acceptance of nondiscrimination in hiring, the prohibition of union delegates, and the employment of foremen and clerks at company discretion, the strikers could return to work at a rate of sixty-seven cents an hour regular time and one dollar overtime. The settlement also established new grievance procedures, directing all future disagreements to the attention of the citizens' committee for arbitration. Two days later, more than one hundred of the striking longshoremen returned to their jobs at the Mallory docks for the first time since March. Another large group of men followed this example the next day, prompting Mallory shipping agent F. T. Rennie to declare that "Conditions . . . are practically restored to normal."[74]

Shortly after the Mallory settlement, Morgan shipping agent H. M. Wilkins offered his striking workers identical terms. In exchange for a small increase in wages, the men of Local 385 had to agree to open-shop conditions if they wanted to be rehired. It is likely that had Wilkins followed Rennie's example and restored his company's former policy of employing only whites, a settlement would have been easily forthcoming. There seemed to be little hope that Local 385 alone could bring about a successful conclusion of the strike. Wilkins, however, entertained different ideas. Instead of offering to discharge its force of black and Mexican strikebreakers, the Morgan line stood firm on its policy of nondiscrimination. Formerly the exclusive domain of white longshoremen, the Southern Pacific docks suddenly became a potential arena for racial mixing.[75]

This challenge sounded the death knell of biracial waterfront unionism in Galveston. Willing to accept all the company's other terms for reemployment, the members of Local 385 adamantly refused to return to work until they received a guarantee that blacks and whites would not be integrated. Wilkins offered a similarly stubborn response. "It was to our great regret that the white men left us as they did," he declared, "but the present situation is one brought on by themselves." He claimed that at the Southern Pacific docks in New Orleans and the shops in Houston, black and white worked together without trouble. The Morgan line did not intend to mix the races but reserved the right to do so if conditions made it necessary. "Our present dockworkers, numbering several hundred men, less than ten percent of whom are white, voluntarily came to the rescue of the Morgan line and its patrons when the company was in distress," Wilkins continued. Negotiating a contract that excluded either race from employment would be not only a violation of laws upholding the free pursuit of one's business but also an insult to the company's recent saviors.[76]

The Morgan line's racial policies received strong denunciations from Local 385 and the citizen's arbitration committee. Challenging Wilkins's claim, O. A. Anderson declared that Texas's Jim Crow laws prohibited whites from working side by side with blacks. "The laboring men have agreed to every proposition asked by the Morgan line," he announced, "but are not going to shoulder a truck with the negroes." Other white union men argued that 80 percent of Galveston's dockworkers would be black if the Morgan line opened its docks to all races. Such an imbalance threatened to overturn the port's racial hierarchy. At a conference held January 22, a representative of Local 385 declared that "we pleaded with Mr. Wilkins, not as union men, but as white men" to reconsider the company's position. The citizens' committee also expressed its disapproval of the Southern Pacific's actions, saying that it would be wrong for the people of Texas and Galveston to further protect the company if it insisted on mixing the races, "a fundamentally wrong and unsound practice." "There can be no condition of harmony existing here by the mixing of the races," the committee declared.[77]

Wilkins's intransigence also drew the public's wrath. The *Daily News* editorialized that the Morgan line should recognize the impracticality of race-mixing and end the strike by employing one group or the other exclusively. Because whites formerly worked the docks, "The *News* ventures to offer the hope that white men will be reemployed." County Judge E. B. Holman argued that "the mixing of blacks and whites on the dock is bound to lead to trouble later on." Blacks belonged in the cotton field, not "the white man's town" of Galveston. Police chief Sedgewick agreed with Holman, declaring ominously that "to have negroes in a subordinate position will probably work to advantage, but to mix the whites in positions similar to those held by negroes and to work the gangs intermixed is a sure sign of racial trouble that will never be stamped out in the South." The concern for this situation reached all the way to Austin, where the state's newly inaugurated governor, Pat Neff, decided not to withdraw Captain Brooks and his force of Texas Rangers until the Morgan line completely settled the strike and, ostensibly, the racial questions it had raised.[78]

Despite the public opposition that this blatant disregard for contemporary racial standards caused, the Morgan line did not fear reprisal. Even after the members of Local 385 appealed to Governor Neff for assistance, the company stood steadfast behind Wilkins and its open-shop policy of nondiscrimination. This unprecedented turn of events dumbfounded the white longshoremen. None of them ever seriously expected that the waterfront's racial order would be completely overturned. The only leverage these men enjoyed—their whiteness—meant little to company officials eager to end the strike. By allowing African Americans to dominate the coastwise workforce, the Morgan and Mallory lines successfully played the black and white longshore locals off one another and divided the strike along racial lines. Without this solidarity, Galveston's longshoremen had no hope of success against their powerful opponents. Local 385 realized this at the end of January 1921 and grudgingly accepted the Morgan line's conditions for reemployment. On the morning of February 1, a small number of white coastwise longshoremen returned to their jobs alongside the nonunion black workers who replaced them for the past ten months.[79]

In the end, martial law had its intended effect. With the help of the National Guard and Governor Hobby, local and statewide business interests threw open the doors on Galveston's closed shop. In the conflict's aftermath, Texas's most strongly organized city and its waterfront became a hotbed of open-shop employers and antilabor sentiment. By the end of the year, the members of Galveston's Marine Checkers Union, the Machinists Union, and the Cooks and Waiters Union, as well as workers in the island's thirteen cotton compress companies, were all forced into open-shop agreements.[80]

Exactly how much the strike had weakened the longshoremen became obvious shortly after the troubles ended in February 1921. At the ILA's annual convention in July, recovery occupied an important position on the union's list of priorities. Early in the proceedings, the executive council received a request from M. J. Gahagan of Local 385 recommending remittance of his union's taxes for the previous year, presumably because the strike had emptied the local's coffers and its remaining members could not support the added financial burden. Following this, union members from across the South joined representatives from Galveston and asked ILA officials to take action against the Southern Pacific line. Their resolution read as follows:

> Resolved, That the incoming Executive Council of the Longshoremen's Association be instructed to take this matter up with the General Officers of the Southern Pacific Steamship Company at New York and use their best efforts in remedying this practice to the end that *all discrimination against the members of our organization cease, and they be given an equal opportunity in the hiring of men employed on the docks and piers of said Company, both at Galveston, Texas and New Orleans, Louisiana.*[81]

Disregarding the terms it had dictated for reemployment, the shipping company refused to hire union members. This was a significant reversal from the time before the strike when the ILA locals had been largely responsible for rotating their members in and out of the regularly employed gangs on the coastwise docks.[82] No sooner had the men placed this problem before the convention than word of another setback arrived from Galveston. On July 14, 1921, Mallory officials announced that they would lower wages to the prestrike levels of sixty cents an hour regular and ninety cents overtime. They also intended to increase the workday from eight to ten hours. Dissatisfied with this arrangement, the president of Local 807 asked what course of action he should take. He received a disheartening response. Although the ILA strictly opposed the increase in hours, the Mallory workers should accept the pay cut without debate. Having already lost one dispute over wages, the union could not afford to initiate a new battle.[83] Racially divided and subject to the open shop, Galveston's coastwise locals eventually yielded their charters in 1922. Through employee loans and planned social functions, both of which became mandatory conditions of one's continued employment, the companies successfully used welfare capitalism to prevent their workers from organizing again. The formation of company unions in 1924 provided Galveston's coastwise longshoremen with their only form of workplace organization until well into the 1930s. As late as 1936, ILA member Nick Macela claimed that neither the Mallory nor the Morgan line workers had organized independently since the end of the strike.[84]

The longshoremen were not the only Texans affected by the strike—its impact was felt far beyond Galveston Island. Throughout the so-called prosperity decade, workers and their unions all across Texas came under attack from business interests and the state government. On October 4, 1920, a special session of the state legislature practically institutionalized the open shop throughout Texas with its passage of the notorious Hobby-inspired Open Port Law, which made strikes illegal for workers engaged in the common carrying of freight or passengers. Ostensibly written to prevent further troubles in Galveston, the law had much broader implications and hung like a sword over the heads of all working-class Texans who entertained ideas of fighting for their economic rights, at least until it was declared unconstitutional in 1924.[85] Even then, unions did not recover their strength: by 1927 the once-powerful Texas State Federation of Labor had lost nearly 50 percent of its membership.[86] The Galveston troubles had accomplished much more than simply throwing open the doors on the closed shop of the island's waterfront. More fundamentally, it had shifted the terrain beneath the feet of *all* the state's organized workers, helping to place them on the same precarious footing as their fellows throughout the nation. In the words of O. A. Anderson, the outspoken and unusually astute president of Local 385, Texas had become "a corporation representative, ruled by a corporation governor."[87] With appropriate substitutions, such statements were to be echoed from coast to coast for the remainder of the decade.

Notes

This chapter originally appeared in *Southwestern Historical Quarterly* 110 (January 2007): 317–47, and is reprinted with permission.

1. *Union Review* (Galveston), June 25, 1920.
2. For other accounts of the strike, see James C. Maroney, "The Galveston Longshoremen's Strike of 1920," *East Texas Historical Journal* 16 (Spring 1978): 34–38; William D. Angel Jr., "Controlling the Workers: The Galveston Dock Worker's Strike of 1920 and its Impact on Labor Relations in Texas," *East Texas Historical Journal* 23 (Fall 1985): 14–27; Hulen Knox, "Galveston: An Exercise in Aristocratic Control, 1838–1921" (master's thesis, University of Houston–Clear

Lake, 1983), 87–169; Robert Stuart Shelton, "Waterfront Workers of Galveston, 1838–1920" (PhD diss., Rice University, 2000), 1–9; Clifford Farrington, "Biracial Unions on Galveston's Waterfront, 1865–1925" (PhD diss., University of Texas at Austin, 2003), 186–99; and Joseph Abel, "Opening the Closed Shop: The Galveston Longshoremen's Strike, 1920–1921" (master's thesis, Texas A&M University, 2004).

3. *Galveston Daily News*, March 20, 21 (quotation), 1920; *Union Review*, March 26, May 21, 1920; International Longshoremen's Association, *Proceedings of the Twenty-Sixth Convention* (1921), 45–46. On organized labor's struggles during the years of World War I, see Joseph McCartin, *Labor's Great War: The Struggle for Industrial Democracy and the Origins of Modern American Labor Relations, 1912–1921* (Chapel Hill: University of North Carolina Press, 1997). For a fuller account of the strike's causes, see Abel, "Opening the Closed Shop," 49–51; and Knox, "Galveston," 89–90.

4. See, for example, *Galveston Daily News*, April 26, 1920. The paper contained details of a small "affray" between two whites, a black, and a Mexican near the Mallory docks on April 25. Although the reporting police officer felt the fight was strike-related, the combatants were not apprehended and this suspicion was never proven.

5. *Galveston Daily News*, May 12, 1920; *Houston Post*, May 12, 13, 1920; *Union Review*, May 21, 1920.

6. *Galveston Daily News*, June 4, 1920.

7. James C. Maroney, "The International Longshoremen's Association in the Gulf States during the Progressive Era," *Southern Studies* 16 (Summer 1977): 228–30. My analysis of biracial unionism in Galveston draws heavily upon the definitions put forward by Eric Arnesen. See Arnesen, *Waterfront Workers of New Orleans: Race, Class, and Politics, 1863–1923* (New York: Oxford University Press, 1991); Arnesen, "Biracial Waterfront Unionism in the Age of Segregation," in *Waterfront Workers: New Perspectives on Race and Class*, ed. Calvin Winslow (Urbana: Illinois University Press, 1998), 19–22, 32–37; and Daniel Rosenberg, *New Orleans Dockworkers: Race, Labor, and Unionism, 1892–1923* (Albany: SUNY Press, 1988). Daniel Letwin makes many of the same arguments about Alabama coal miners. See Letwin, *The Challenge of Interracial Unionism: Alabama Coal Miners, 1878–1921* (Chapel Hill: University of North Carolina Press, 1998). For a more thorough examination of race and the strike, see Abel, "Opening the Closed Shop," chapter 5.

8. Figures taken from Ernest Obadele-Starks, *Black Unionism in the Industrial South* (College Station: Texas A&M University Press, 2000), 45.

9. *Houston Press*, June 7, 1920. Also see *Union Review*, June 11, 16, 1920; *Houston Labor Journal*, June 12, 1920. Other historians have reached this same conclusion in their studies of the strike. For examples, see Angel, "Controlling the Workers"; and Knox, "Galveston."

10. Robert Justin Goldstein, *Political Repression in Modern America: From 1870 to 1976* (Urbana: Illinois University Press, 2001), 13–14, 184.

11. Jay Littman Todes, "Organized Employer Opposition to Unionism in Texas, 1900–1930" (master's thesis, University of Texas at Austin, 1949), 50–78; Allen M. Wakstein, "The Origins of the Open-Shop Movement, 1919–1920," *Journal of American History* 51 (December 1969), 460–75; David Montgomery, *The Fall of the House of Labor: The Workplace, the State, and American Labor Activism, 1865–1925* (Cambridge, UK: Cambridge University Press, 1987), 269–75, 438–39; James C. Maroney, "Organized Labor in Texas, 1900–1929" (PhD diss., University of Houston, 1975), 207–9.

12. *Galveston Daily News*, May 6, 7, 14, 16 (quotation), 17, 1920. Also see *Houston Post*, May 13, 1920.

13. *Houston Post*, May 14, 1920; *Galveston Daily News*, June 1, 1920. According to Robert Zeigler, Houston's laborers were decidedly unsatisfied after 1914. He argues that the values of Houstonians—conservatism and law and order—worked against organized labor. See Robert E. Zeigler, "The Workingman in Houston, Texas, 1865–1914" (PhD diss., Texas Tech University, 1972), 233.

14. On the position of organized labor in Galveston, see James V. Reese, "The Evolution of an Early Texas Union: The Screwmen's Benevolent Association of Galveston, 1866–1891," *Southwestern Historical Quarterly*, 75 (October 1971), 158–85; Allen Clayton Taylor, "A History of the Screwmen's Benevolent Association from 1866 to 1924" (master's thesis, University of Houston, 1968); Shelton, "Waterfront Workers of Galveston"; Farrington, "Biracial Unions on Galveston's Waterfront"; Lester Rubin, *The Negro in the Longshore Industry* (Philadelphia: University of Pennsylvania Press, 1974), 119–25; Arnesen, "Biracial Waterfront Unionism," 32–37; Maud Russell, *Men Along the Shore* (New York: Brussel and Brussel, 1966), 84–88; and Abel, "Opening the Closed Shop," 25–47.

15. Todes, "Organized Employer Opposition," 77–78; *Galveston Daily News*, May 23, 30, June 2, 3 (quotation), 1920; *Union Review*, June 16, 1920.

16. *Galveston Daily News*, June 2, 3, 1920; *Union Review*, June 4, 1920.

17. *Galveston Daily News*, June 3, 1920 (quotation); *Union Review*, June 16, 1920.

18. James A. Clark, *The Tactful Texan: A Biography of Governor Will Hobby* (New York: Random House, 1958), 56, 79–81, 117–20.

19. William Lee Greer, "The Texas Gulf Coast Oil Strike of 1917" (master's thesis, University of Houston, 1974); Maroney, "Organized Labor in Texas," 186–99; George B. Tindall, *The Emergence of the New South, 1913–1945* (Baton Rouge: Louisiana State University Press, 1967), 334–36.

20. Clark, *Tactful Texan*, 120–21.

21. *Galveston Daily News*, June 3 (1st quotation), 4, 5, 1920; Hobby to Adjutant General Cope, June 3 (quote), 1920, Letterpress Books, Records of William P. Hobby, Texas State Library and Archives Division, Austin, TX (hereafter cited as TSLAD); *Houston Post*, June 3, 4, 1920; *Houston Press*, June 3, 4, 1920; *Houston Labor Journal*, June 5, 1920.

22. *Galveston Daily News*, June 4, 5, 1920.

23. *Galveston Daily News*, June 4, 5, 1920.

24. *Galveston Daily News*, May 4, 5, 1920; Thomas Barker, "Partners in Progress: The

Galveston Wharf Company and the City of Galveston, 1900–1930" (PhD diss., Texas A&M University, 1979), 108, 111–13; David G. McComb, *Galveston: A History* (Austin: University of Texas Press, 1986), 166. Perhaps the best account of this electoral coup and the amendment battle is contained in Knox, "Galveston," chapter 4.

25. Knox, "Galveston," 87.
26. *Galveston Daily News*, June 5, 1920; *Houston Post*, June 5, 1920; *Houston Press*, June 4, 1920.
27. *Houston Press*, June 5, 1920.
28. *Galveston Daily News*, June 6, 1920; *Houston Post*, June 6, 1920.
29. *Galveston Daily News*, June 7, 1920.
30. C. J. Blackwell to Adjutant General Cope, June 2, 1920, Adjutant General's Correspondence, TSLAD.
31. *Galveston Daily News*, June 4, 1920.
32. *Galveston Daily News*, January 1, 1921, Year-end Business Supplement.
33. *Galveston Daily News*, June 8, 1920 (quotation); *Houston Press*, June 7, 1920; Harry Krenek, *The Power Vested: The Use of Martial Law and the National Guard in Texas Domestic Crisis, 1919–1932* (Austin: Presidial Press, 1980), 7–8.
34. *Galveston Daily News*, June 12, 1920; *Houston Post*, June 15, 1920; *Union Review*, June 11, 1920 (quotation); Neil Foley, *The White Scourge: Mexicans, Blacks, and Poor Whites in Texas Cotton Culture* (Berkeley: University of California Press, 1997), 62–63.
35. *Galveston Daily News*, June 9, 1920; *Union Review*, June 11, 1920 (quotation). Although it is likely this meeting included representatives of the African American strikers, there is no direct evidence to support this conclusion.
36. *Union Review*, June 11, 1920; *Houston Labor Journal*, June 12, 1920; *Galveston Daily News*, June 17, 1920.
37. *Galveston Daily News*, June 8, 1920.
38. *Galveston Daily News*, June 8, 1920 (quotation); *Houston Post*, June 8, 9, 1920; *Houston Press*, June 7, 8, 1920; Krenek, *Power Vested*, 11.
39. *Galveston Daily News*, June 12, 1920.
40. *Houston Press*, June 7, 1920.
41. *Houston Post*, June 11, 1920.
42. *Galveston Daily News*, June 11, 1920.
43. Jacob F. Wolters, *Martial Law and Its Administration* (Austin: Gammel's Book Store, 1930), 58, 60.
44. Wolters, *Martial Law*, 59. On June 8, 1920, the *Galveston Daily News* published General Order No. 1 in its entirety.
45. *Galveston Daily News*, June 16, 1920; *Houston Post*, June 15, 1920; *Houston Press*, June 14, 15, 16, 1920.
46. *Galveston Daily News*, June 17, 29, 1920; *Houston Post*, June 17, 19, 29, 1920; *Houston Press*, June 17 (quotation), 29, 1920. Machem's report provides an outstanding example of the ambiguous racial position of Mexican workers in Texas. While the black and white coastwise longshoremen saw them as an inferior race

of cheap, foreign labor, the shipping companies and their supporters showed the Mexican strikebreakers much more respect. For example, Machem's report places a great deal of emphasis on violence against Mexicans and whites, but it mentions almost nothing about attacks on the African American workers who comprised the nonunion workforce on the Morgan Line docks. The court of inquiry tried to equate the two races with one another by making them superior to blacks, an acceptable strategy because of the Mexicans' "in-between" status. See Foley, *The White Scourge*, 40–42.

47.   *Union Review*, July 2, 1920; Goldstein, *Political Repression*, 14-16.

48.   Wolters, *Martial Law*, 67–68; Krenek, *Power Vested*, 15–16.

49.   *Galveston Daily News*, June 20, 25, 1920; *Houston Post*, June 26, 1920; *Houston Press*, June 22, 25, 1920; Herbert Gutman, "Class, Status, and Community Power in Nineteenth-Century American Industrial Cities," in *Work, Culture, and Society in Industrializing American: Essays in American Working-Class and Social History* (New York: Random House, 1976), 234–60.

50.   *Houston Press*, June 19 (quotation), 20, 1920; *Houston Post*, June 19, 1920; *Union Review*, June 18, 1920.

51.   Knox, "Galveston," 62, 114–15; Barker, "Partners in Progress," 36–39, 108–13; Susan Wiley Hardwick, *Mythic Galveston: Reinventing America's Third Coast* (Baltimore: Johns Hopkins University Press, 2002), 109–11; McComb, *Galveston*, 134–35, 166.

52.   *Galveston Daily News*, July 5, 1920; *Houston Post*, July 5, 1920; *Houston Press*, July 5, 1920 (quotation).

53.   *Houston Press*, June 30, July 2, 1920; *Houston Post*, July 3, 1920; E. F. Tinsley, "Race Riots, Texas 1920," in *Federal Surveillance of Afro-Americans, 1917–1925: The First World War, the Red Scare, and the Garvey Movement*, ed. Theodore Kornweibel (microfilm, University Publications of America, 1986), Case File OG387830, reel 13; J. V. Bell, "Purchase of Firearms by Negroes, 1920," *Federal Surveillance of Afro-Americans*, Case File BS203677, reel 7.

54.   See Knox, "Galveston," 111.

55.   *Galveston Daily News*, July 16, 1920; *Houston Post*, July 16, 1920; Wolters, *Martial Law*, 71–72.

56.   *Houston Press*, July 16, 1920; *Houston Post*, July 16, 1920; *Galveston Daily News*, July 16, 1920; *Houston Labor Journal*, July 17, 1920; Krenek, *Power Vested*, 17.

57.   *Galveston Daily News*, July 16 (quotations), 17, 1920; *Houston Post*, July 17, 1920; *Houston Press*, July 16, 17, 1920.

58.   *Galveston Daily News*, July 31, August 11, 1920; *Houston Post*, August 1, 11, 1920; *Houston Press*, July 31, August 10, 11, 1920; Knox, "Galveston," 122–23.

59.   *Galveston Daily News*, July 20, 22 (quotation), 1920; *Houston Post*, July 22, 1920; *Houston Press*, July 21, 22, 1920; *Houston Labor Journal*, July 24, 1920.

60.   *Galveston Daily News*, July 31, Aug. 1, 3, 1920; *Houston Post*, July 31, August 2, 3, 4, 6, 7, 1920; *Houston Press*, July 30, 31, August 2, 3, 4, 6, 1920.

61.   *Houston Post*, July 27, 1920; *Houston Press*, July 30, 1920.

62.   *Houston Press*, August 6, 9, 1920.

63. *Houston Press*, August 19, 20, 1920; *Houston Labor Journal*, August 28, 1920.

64. *Houston Press*, August 6, 9, 1920.

65. *Houston Press*, July 31, August 23, 1920; *Galveston Daily News*, August 26, 1920; *Houston Post*, August 23, 27, 1920.

66. *Galveston Daily News*, August 31, 1920 (quotation); *Houston Press*, August 31, 1920.

67. *Houston Press*, August 31, 1920; *Houston Post*, September 1, 1920.

68. *Houston Press*, August 31, September 1, 2, 4, 6, 7, 9, 1920; *Galveston Daily News*, September 2, 8–10, 1920; *Houston Post*, September 2, 3, 4, 9, 10, 19, 1920; *Houston Labor Journal*, September 25, 1920.

69. *Houston Press*, September 8, 1920; *Galveston Daily News*, August 4, 1920.

70. Jacob Singer to Hobby, September 16, 1920 (quotations), Adjutant General's Correspondence, TSLAD; *Galveston Daily News*, September 19, 1920; *Houston Post*, September 19, 1920; *Houston Press*, September 20, 1920.

71. Letter, Hobby to Adjutant General Cope, September 21, 1920, Adjutant General's Correspondence, TSLAD; *Galveston Daily News*, September 19, 30, Oct. 1, 3, 9, 1920; *Houston Post*, September 19, 30, October 5, 9, 1920; *Houston Press*, September 19, 30, October 1, 8, 1920; Wolters, *Martial Law*, 79; Krenek, *Power Vested*, 25–27.

72. *Galveston Daily News*, August 1, 4, 16, 19, 20, 21, 1920; *Houston Press*, August 21, 1920; *Union Review*, August 27, 1920; *Houston Labor Journal*, August 7, 28, 1920; International Longshoremen's Association, *Proceedings of the Twenty-Sixth Convention* (1921), 52.

73. *Galveston Daily News*, August 21, 1920 (quotation). For the companies' response to union proposals, see *Galveston Daily News*, August 22, 1920; *Houston Post*, August 21, 22, 25, 1920; *Union Review*, August 20, 27, 1920; *Houston Labor Journal*, August 28, 1920. The companies' proposal is especially radical in light of other studies that argue for southern business's total acceptance of racism and Jim Crow up to the 1960s. Stanley Greenberg argues that "[w]here commercial farmers and dominant workers insist on the traditional race lines businessmen will take the course of least resistance . . . dependent on the good-will of dominant consumers and the state, [they] will learn to tolerate prevailing ideas on political practice and the utilization of labor." The behavior of the Morgan and Mallory lines stands in direct contrast to Greenberg's conclusion. Although in practice both companies (especially the Mallory line) proved somewhat less than dogmatic in their call for nondiscrimination in hiring, the mere fact that they articulated this demand at all demonstrates a willingness to go against prevailing attitudes about racial segregation. See Greenberg, *Race and State in Capitalist Development: Comparative Perspectives* (New Haven, CT: Yale University Press, 1980), 146. For an interesting account of how southern employers consciously used race to divide black and white workers, see Brian Kelly, *Race, Class, and Power in the Alabama Coalfields, 1908–1921* (Urbana: Illinois University Press, 2001).

74. *Galveston Daily News*, December 14, 15, 16, 1920; *Houston Post*, Dec. 15, 1920; *Houston Press*, Dec. 14, 1920; "Results of a Meeting Held in the Office of Mr. J. H. W. Steele, Galveston, Texas, Dec. 13, 1920, Between Citizens' Sub-

Committee and Representatives of Mallory Line Local #807," Adjutant General's Correspondence, TSLAD. The settlement agreement between the Mallory line and its former employees also stipulated that the company would henceforth provide ice water at no charge. This was the only clear cut "victory" the men attained in the strike.

75. *Galveston Daily News*, January 6, 1921; *Houston Post*, January 6, 1921. Although there is no direct evidence of cooperation or communication, it seems likely that Morgan officials collaborated with Mallory officials in making this decision.

76. *Galveston Daily News*, January 6, 12 (quotations), 1921; *Houston Post*, January 6, 1921; *Houston Press*, January 12, 1921. The Morgan line's intransigence provides further evidence contradicting the conclusions Greenberg reached. He argues that businessmen were quick to reproduce socially acceptable segregation on the shop floor, formally recognizing "colored jobs" and "white jobs" and imposing Jim Crow on the workplace. See Greenberg, *Race and State*, 227–30.

77. *Galveston Daily News*, January 6, 7, 23, 1921. Surprisingly, the local labor press refused to comment on Wilkins's policies. Although there is no direct evidence to support this conclusion, the *Union Review* may have been attempting to salvage a relationship between the black and white locals. Also see Greenberg, *Race and State*, 282–86.

78. *Galveston Daily News*, January 9 (1st quotation), 12 (2nd quotation), 20, 1921; *Houston Post*, January 20, 1921, *Houston Press*, January 19, 1921.

79. *Houston Post*, January 21, 1921; *Houston Press*, January 21, 1921; International Longshoremen's Association, *Proceedings of the Twenty-Sixth Convention* (1921), 52. On the place of whiteness in the American labor movement, see David R. Roediger, *The Wages of Whiteness: Race and the Making of the American Working Class* (London: Verso, 1991); and Noel Ignatiev, *How the Irish Became White* (New York: Routledge, 1995).

80. *Houston Press*, June 15, 1920; *Union Review*, August 27, 1920; *Houston Labor Journal*, August 7, 1920; *Galveston Daily News*, August 1, 4, 1920; Knox, "Galveston," 133–36.

81. International Longshoremen's Association, *Proceedings of the Twenty-Sixth Convention* (1921), 183. Emphasis added.

82. Rubin, *Negro in the Longshore Industry*, 123–25; Arnesen, "Biracial Waterfront Unionism," 32–33.

83. ILA, *Proceedings of the Twenty-Sixth Convention*, 139, 215–16.

84. Albert Anderson, "Interview by Anonymous," July 13, 1936, Labor Movement in Texas Collection, Box 2E306, Center for American History, University of Texas at Austin; Doc Hamilton, "Interview by Anonymous," July 8, 1936, Labor Movement in Texas Collection, Box 2E306; Nick Macela, "Interview by Anonymous," July 8, 1936, Labor Movement in Texas Collection, Box 2E306. Macela also claimed that the Galveston longshoremen's wage scale had declined—although the regular pay rate remained at sixty cents an hour, overtime pay had fallen to only seventy cents an hour. On the corporate strategy of welfare capitalism, see

Lizabeth Cohen, *Making a New Deal: Industrial Workers in Chicago, 1919–1939* (Cambridge: Cambridge University Press, 1990).

85. The Open Port Law was invoked only once, by Gov. Pat Neff, in the Railroad Shopmen's Strike of 1922, where it proved decisive in breaking the conflict. On the Open Port Law, see *Galveston Daily News*, September 16, 21, 24–26, 28, 30, October 2, 3, 1920; *Houston Press*, September 18, 21, 22, 23, 27, 28, 29, 30, October 3, 1920; *Houston Post*, September 21, 24, 26, 29, October 3, 1920; *Houston Labor Journal*, September 25, 1920; Clark, *Tactful Texan*, 136–37; Abel, "Opening the Closed Shop," 150–53, 156–57

86. Maroney, "Organized Labor in Texas," 222–23, 229–31.

87. *Houston Press*, June 15, 1920.

ZARAGOSA VARGAS

Tejana Radical

Emma Tenayuca and the San Antonio Labor
Movement during the Great Depression

In the 1930s Mexican Americans fought their first major battles for worker rights and racial equality when they joined the revitalized labor movement.[1] In many instances of labor upheaval on farms, at mine sites, and in factories in the United States, Spanish-speaking workers took the lead. They created separate labor unions that were rooted in the tradition of mutual aid societies and workers' leagues, joined unions of mixed racial-ethnic composition, or sought national union affiliation. What emerged was a style of unionism that drew not just on the courage and militancy of Mexicans but also on their rich historical and cultural traditions, refashioned to fit the immediate labor struggle. From these shared social and cultural experiences emerged a collective identity and class-consciousness. Immersion in labor activism broadened the political horizons of Mexicans. They linked their struggles to those of other American workers by joining causes that embraced national and international issues such as the campaign to free the Scottsboro Boys, the CIO-sponsored Labor's Non-Partisan League, the Congress of Spanish-Speaking Peoples, and the Communist Party's American League Against War and Fascism.[2]

New Deal labor legislation became the impetus for the first phase of Mexican American labor insurgency in 1933–34. The creation of the Congress of Industrial Organizations (CIO) in 1935 ushered in another wave of rank-and-file labor organizing that embraced the democratic principle of racial equality. In the Southwest and Midwest, unions targeted Mexican workers in mining, metal mills, agriculture, food packing, steel, and auto work.[3] An important factor in union campaigns was the integral leadership and commitment of left-wing organizers. Lacking a formal directive about working with Mexicans, like the Southern strategy outlined for blacks, the Communist Party realized that it would have to accommodate the interests and needs of these wary workers. Communist organizers soon discovered that dry Marxist doctrine and lofty revolutionary aims counted less than their antiracist stance and willingness to lend their organizing abilities to the Mexicans' cause.[4]

Grassroots activism brought Mexican and Mexican American women to the forefront of labor struggles as rank-and-file organizers, and these minority women comprised the main ranks of some local unions. Such acts of solidarity transformed their lives and consciousness, just as gender, racial-ethnic, and class identities in turn shaped the various working-class movements that unfolded among the larger Mexican population.[5] As workers and strike leaders, Tejanas (Texas Mexicans) like Manuela Solis Sager, Minnie Rendon, and Juana Sanchez all played prominent roles in the depression-era union effort in San Antonio, Texas. A key activist was Emma Tenayuca. She had a magnetic personality and possessed extraordinary organizing abilities honed by years of active struggle on behalf of San Antonio's Mexican community. Under the banners of the Unemployed Councils and the Workers' Alliance of America, she helped Mexicans organize hunger marches, protests, and demonstrations to gain relief, obtain jobs on public works projects, and fight against racial injustice and harassment by the US Immigration Service.[6]

Tenayuca is best known as a leader of the 1938 pecan shellers' strike. With over ten thousand participants, it was the largest labor strike in San Antonio history and the most massive community-based strike waged by the nation's Mexican population in the 1930s. Tenayuca challenged the Southern Pecan Company, a major Texas industry, and the city government of San Antonio when she demanded an end to race-based wage differentials between "white" workers and lower-paid Mexicans. In calling for equal pay for equal work for the entire San Antonio market, the Tejana sought nothing less than a restructuring of the compensation system on the basis of racial and gender equity. Tenayuca's efforts thus shared a common purpose with those of ethnically diverse women who struggled for justice during the 1930s.

As Tenayuca grew in the belief that the workplace required radical revision to achieve equality, she joined a small group of Mexican Americans who turned to the Communist Party. She belonged to communist-led organizations and married an avowed communist; she finally joined the party in 1937, only to leave it in disillusionment two years later following the signing of the Nazi-Soviet nonaggression pact. She found Marxism especially persuasive in intellectual terms. She coauthored a polemic for the Communist Party that discussed Mexicans, Mexican Americans, and the national question. In 1938 she ran for office as a party candidate. But like many other communists, Tenayuca never proclaimed her membership nor did she recruit Mexicans to join the party. Marxist ideology motivated the Tejana less than did her strong attachment to her working-class community. According to Tenayuca, she joined the party because no one else but the communists expressed any interest in helping San Antonio's dispossessed Mexicans. A former strike leader who worked closely with her confirmed this assessment: "I never got the feeling that [Tenayuca] was in the least interested in Russia or in the Internationale except in a mild academic way. . . . Her interests were with the people."[7]

She was not without enemies. San Antonio's middle-class Mexican American community did not appreciate the Tejana's pursuit of worker rights or her challenge to the city's long established racial caste system. Driven by anticommunist obsession, San Antonio's city bosses and the Roman Catholic Church condemned Tenayuca and launched a red-baiting campaign to discredit her. They most feared that she was undermining their authority by instilling confidence and teaching leadership among the city's Mexican workers.

The issue of communism would play a central role in the San Antonio pecan shellers' strike. Accusations of communist subversion altered the public perception of the strikers and their cause and thus inhibited potential strike support. These allegations diverted action from the strike issues toward fighting the strike's negative aspects. The alleged threat of communism offered city officials and the police the pretext to unleash a reign of violence against the strikers and their leaders. Undaunted, Emma Tenayuca remained firm in her commitment to gain social justice for Mexicans through collective self-organization.[8]

To date, historians have published very little about the crucial role of women in the Mexican American labor movement.[9] This study attempts to fill a portion of that gap in the existing literature by following the work of Emma Tenayuca as labor organizer and political radical in San Antonio, Texas, through four phases in the 1930s: as strike organizer during the years 1933 and 1934; as activist in Unemployed Councils and the Workers' Alliance of America from 1935 through 1937; as leader of the pecan shellers' strike in 1938; and as Communist Party activist in 1939.

Unemployed Councils and the Workers' Alliance

Organizing San Antonio's Spanish-speaking labor force in the 1930s proved a huge endeavor. Forty percent of the nation's Mexican population resided in Texas, and large numbers lived in cities. The Spanish-speaking population consisted of Tejanos and Mexican nationals. The latter assimilated the culture and language of the Tejanos so that differences between the two became imperceptible to Anglos. The vulnerability of Mexican nationals to abuse and exploitation, however, irrevocably influenced their fate. They gained no sympathy from organized labor and its rank-and-file membership. As with blacks, total exclusion, confinement to segregated locals, and racially prescribed employment quotas characterized the treatment of Mexicans. Farm workers comprised nearly half of the state's 236,000 gainfully employed Tejanos, who were overwhelmingly locked by old-time Texas racism into seasonal migration patterns. The Texas Farm Placement Service controlled the intrastate and interstate movement of Tejano migratory workers, handling, organizing, and routing laborers from farm to farm, season to season. Another problem the Spanish-speaking population faced was decentralized New Deal programs that were controlled locally by employers, unions, and city officials.[10]

Along with the rural culture that migrant workers reproduced in San Antonio, Jim Crow practices prevailed in the city. Semi-industrial firms and skilled labor had established patterns of Anglo and Mexican work. This entrenched dual-wage labor market had denied Mexican workers equal pay for equal work for almost fifty years.[11] Along with race, gender-based employment patterns compounded the sweatshop conditions of the factories. Mostly young and single, Tejana women made up 79 percent of San Antonio's low-paid garment, cigar, and pecan-shelling labor force. Much like the pattern among the nation's African American women, the high labor force participation rate of Spanish-speaking women in San Antonio obscured their largely temporary and unsatisfactory work experiences. New Deal wage and hour legislation essentially ignored the needs of women. One-fourth of the National Recovery Administration (NRA) codes adopted a lower wage rate for women. Not only did women earn less than men, but minority women earned less than white women. Regardless of their skills or occupations, women of color were generally classified as unskilled by the NRA and hence received the lowest wage rates. Occupational segregation along racial and gender lines, combined with San Antonio's discriminatory work relief program policies, decided the nature of subsequent labor struggles.[12]

Deprived of equal wages because of racial and sexual discrimination and given their inequality in society, it is not surprising that Tejanas were at the forefront of labor demonstrations in San Antonio in the 1930s. Emma Tenayuca and a small group of labor and community activists took up their cause. The young woman's growing radicalism and her challenge to the established racial and social order would have repercussions, leading to her denunciation as a communist by city officials and criticisms by the middle-class Mexican American community.[13]

Tenayuca first met with labor organizing in 1933 when several hundred San Antonio women cigar workers walked out of the Fink Cigar Company, demanding increased pay, better working conditions, and union recognition. Then age sixteen, she went to jail with the strikers the second time that police arrested the women cigar workers for protesting against the NRA's discriminatory wage rates and bad working conditions, which gained the strikers an arbitration hearing. The Tejana high school student had joined the labor movement. The following year she helped organize garment workers when the women struck Dorothy Frocks, an infants' and children's wear company. Impressed with Tenayuca's leadership abilities, Tejana working women in their newfound militancy looked to her for leadership, and she responded willingly. Tenayuca's active presence and refusal to be intimidated by white men soon earned her a reputation on San Antonio's West Side as a devoted organizer. Tenayuca recalled that when she walked down the working-class streets, she often heard the comment: "Here comes the little girl who confronts men."[14]

Another important undertaking for Tenayuca was battling the powerful political machine of Mayor C. K. Quinn and chief of police Owen W. Kilday. Poll tax and citizenship requirements had disenfranchised most of the city's Mexicans. By buying what remained of the Mexican vote, the political machine maintained its power. Quinn and Kilday colluded with employers in the exploitation and oppression of Mexicans. Fearing that Mexican empowerment might accompany the labor movement, these city bosses employed force, violence, and red-baiting to break any strike threat.[15]

Much of this hostility was directed at Tenayuca, who was advocating community action in her determination to do something about poverty on the West Side. Here, compressed in a four-square-mile area, two-thirds of the city's one hundred thousand Tejanos lived in rundown shacks. Tenayuca's hometown had some of the worst slums in the United States, and because of rampant disease and malnutrition, the nation's highest tuberculosis and infant mortality rates. The continued influx of migrant families compounded the problems of overcrowding and poor health. Clearly, San Antonio's Mexican heritage was valued only for tourist consumption, primarily through the federal government's encouragement of a revival of Spanish colonial arts. The Tejana teenager began her work with the West Side's voiceless and powerless Mexicans through the Unemployed Councils, which were sponsored by the communist-led Trade Union Unity League. As an Unemployed Council relief worker, Tenayuca promptly introduced jobless Mexicans to organized social and economic protest.[16]

In 1935, as the secretary of the West Side Unemployed Council, Tenayuca held mass meetings to protest the elimination of thousands of Mexican families from the city's relief rolls because of the new eligibility standards of the Works Progress Administration (WPA) work relief programs. The next year she set up chapters of the Workers' Alliance, following this organization's merger with the Unemployed Councils. The Tejana activist devoted much of her time to the Workers' Alliance and was eventually elected the general secretary of at least ten chapters in San Antonio. Oriented toward issues pertinent to women and their families, Tenayuca appealed to working-class Mexicans to join the progressive organization to assure the equitable distribution of WPA job and wage assignments and to improve the quality of food relief. Speaking for the Workers' Alliance, she explicitly called for a revision of WPA minimum-wage guidelines; she wanted to raise the rate to fifty cents an hour. She helped Mexicans formulate other demands, such as the restoration of WPA projects and a thirty-hour work week for unskilled labor. Mexicans also demanded that children of all relief recipients receive clothing, school supplies, and free school lunches.[17]

Tenayuca launched a writing and telegram campaign to New Deal officials in Washington, timed to coincide with congressional appropriation decisions in June. She immersed her self in door-to-door, street-by-street organizing. Without much sleep or food to sustain her, Tenayuca suffered from nervous exhaustion and became ill with tuberculosis. Though weakened by her failing health, she daily confronted the San Antonio police force and the US Immigration Service to protest their suppression of workers' rights. Employers used the police and the Immigration Service to intimidate and discourage Mexican WPA workers from joining the Workers' Alliance.[18] Knowing she would face intimidation and arrest, Tenayuca nonetheless staged marches and demonstrations for the Workers' Alliance to protest the repatriation of Mexican-born workers engaged in labor activity. Given the scope of the repatriation program begun in Texas in 1928, this was a major accomplishment. Over one-fourth of the estimated half-million Mexicans repatriated during the Great Depression had been living in the Lone Star state. Through rousing speeches, Tenayuca instilled confidence in the Mexicans, prodding them to organize. She repeatedly told them, "Even though you are not US citizens, you have the right to join the union." She worked to eliminate strikebreaking by Mexican nationals, and she led the campaign to unionize the pecan shellers. She left a lasting impression on Mexican workers—men and women who were not accustomed to either a Mexican or a woman confronting the police over violations of civil rights.[19]

In 1937 Tenayuca was appointed to the National Executive Committee of the Workers' Alliance. She served on the National Executive Board with African American Frances Duty, the leader of the Harlem Workers' Alliance. The appointments of these two women exemplified the attempt at multiracial solidarity by the Workers' Alliance, and more generally, by communist-led mass movements. That June, Tenayuca attended the Workers' Alliance convention in Milwaukee, where she supported a bill for relief work and a resolution against war and fascism. At the Workers' Alliance convention Tenayuca learned, probably from mountain states delegates, of the poor treatment of Mexicans in Colorado. There the governor's declaration of martial law had led to the roundup and arrest of Mexican nationals and Mexican Americans. Her thinking about class struggle was shifting as she rode the train home from the Workers' Alliance convention. She aimed to connect the plight of San Antonio's Mexicans to that of other American workers and to international events.[20]

Under the leadership of the twenty-year-old Tenayuca, the Workers' Alliance of San Antonio numbered fifteen branches with three thousand members, making it one of the strongest such organizations in the country. The Tejana's call for WPA relief workers to stage sit-ins and mass demonstrations against WPA cutbacks and racist relief policies created trouble with city officials. Red-baiting became a potent weapon in Texas; in San Antonio it seriously undermined community activism and labor insurgency. This tactic was effectively used to isolate Tenayuca from the workers. Moreover, anticommunism similarly became a weapon that city officials used to repress Mexicans, thus gaining public favor and winning votes.[21]

Communists had been active in San Antonio since 1930, although the Texas Communist Party was quite small. In 1937 there were 409 members; a year later membership had grown to perhaps 500, essentially a smattering of college students, professionals, workers in CIO locals, and poor and jobless Mexicans and blacks. Forty communists were active in San Antonio, with Jewish immigrants forming the majority of the members.

In 1937 Tenayuca joined the Communist Party and also married fellow communist Homer Brooks, whose influence drew her deeper into the party. The Tejana would be ostracized by members of San Antonio's Anglo and Mexican communities because of her political affiliation, as well as for crossing the acknowledged social barrier of race through her marriage to Brooks. Known in local party circles as the "Blue-eyed Boy," Brooks had a reputation as an indefatigable organizer. The party sent him from New York to Texas as part of its southern strategy to recruit and support new members. Brooks's effectiveness was confirmed when he was appointed secretary of the Texas Communist Party.[22]

Tenayuca and other Workers' Alliance organizers continued to stage protests against relief conditions and the abuse of Mexican-born workers. A degree of apprehension gripped the mainstream political leadership of San Antonio; city officials feared a genuine challenge to domestic peace. Suspecting that communist agitators were inciting Mexicans to revolt, police chief Kilday stepped up his attacks on the Workers' Alliance. On June 29, 1937, Kilday led a raid on the Workers' Alliance hall. Police armed with axes wrecked the meeting place, confiscated literature, and arrested Tenayuca and five Workers' Alliance grievance committee members on charges of unlawful assembly and disturbing the peace. When hundreds of angry alliance members protested the arrests, Kilday seized the opportunity to smear Tenayuca as a communist subversive. The police chief boasted that the material captured in the police raid "just proves my former contention that the Tenayuca woman is a paid agitator sent here to stir up trouble among the ignorant Mexican workers." Presiding judge W. W. McCrory had little sympathy for Tenayuca and dutifully added his voice to the condemnation of her as a Tejana radical who was allegedly plotting revolution. Still defiant after serving her jail time, Tenayuca vowed that she would continue her activities on behalf of the Mexicans by visiting the WPA offices again. Her next opportunity came during the pecan shellers' strike.[23]

The 1938 Pecan Shellers' Strike

Forty percent of the nation's pecans came from Texas in the 1930s. The Southern Pecan Company owned by "Pecan King" Julius Seligmann annually shelled fifteen million pounds of pecans valued at more than 1 million dollars. The machine shelling of pecans had been phased out in 1926 in favor of less expensive handwork performed by Mexicans. Working on a contract basis under sweatshop conditions, approximately twelve thousand Mexicans shelled pecans during the season that ran from November to March. Pecan shelling was performed in four hundred work sheds scattered throughout the West Side's working-class neighborhoods. Women comprised over 90 percent of the poorly paid workforce. A Mexican family working together earned five to six cents per pound for shelled pecans and averaged one dollar to four dollars a week, or $192 annually, among the lowest wages in the nation. In actuality, most pecan shellers made even less, because payment depended on the quality of the nuts cracked. Whole halves paid more than broken halves: nut fragments and poor-quality nuts paid nothing, since the latter were discounted from the total weight of pecans shelled. Pay was frequently in food; the impoverished workers of the

Southern Pecan Company received allotments of coffee, flour, rice, or beans drawn from the company commissary for their week's work. With the onset of the depression, the already low wages of pecan shellers plummeted further. New Deal policies multiplied the severe problems workers faced. San Antonio's pecan-shelling industry was designated an agricultural enterprise by the Agricultural Adjustment Administration (AAA). Therefore, employers like Seligman did not need to recognize government codes that fixed pay scales for nonfarm work at a higher rate. Meanwhile, the local labor force mushroomed with the arrival of jobless farmworkers desperate for work. Out of work and struggling daily to survive, Mexicans had few alternatives but relief.[24]

San Antonio's Mexican pecan shellers first walked out in 1934 to protest low wages. That strike was settled through arbitration but gained only company union representation for the workers. The issues of meager wages and unfair labor practices remained unresolved for almost four years. A wage reduction, coinciding with the economic recession in 1937 and increased unemployment, seriously worsened the shellers' plight. Government monies dried up. Across Texas, relief rolls dropped precipitously from 1.2 million to 46,616, and the first to be discontinued were Mexican clients. A tempest was brewing among workers in San Antonio's West Side, and the sentiment for action spread. The organizational groundwork for the upcoming battle had been put in place by Tenayuca and other key Tejana and Tejano Workers' Alliance members. Previous strikes had taught hard lessons. Only through collective action, Tenayuca insisted, would the workers achieve victory. Along with the other activists, she urged a walkout. Militancy spread quickly through the crowds of pecan shellers; their ranks increased with the steady arrival of migrant families pushed out of the Rio Grande Valley by low wages and crops destroyed by an early frost.[25]

On Monday, January 31, 1938, between six thousand and eight thousand workers from more than 170 of the small pecan-shelling plants walked out to protest a pay cut, bad working conditions, and the illegal homework. The walkout shut down the plants so that fewer than one thousand workers showed up for work. Linked by strong bonds of kinship and community, the pecan shellers prepared to challenge their employer through picketing and demonstrations. Each confrontation swelled the size of the crowds, producing fear of a mass uprising. Tenayuca's was a major voice, convincing the pecan shellers that it was in their best interest to strike for higher pay and better working conditions. More workers responded and joined the picket lines. Many were Workers' Alliance members, unfailing in their support of the Tejana organizer. The workers unanimously elected her the honorary strike leader, but she had opposition as well. Police quickly arrested her and several other organizers from the United Cannery, Agricultural, Packing, and Allied Workers of America (UCAPAWA) on charges of communist agitation.[26]

While Tenayuca sat in jail, demonstrations took place at nearby parks and downtown at Milam Plaza. Workers on the West Side held meetings in lots next to the pecan-shelling sheds. Women formed the majority of strikers, just as they comprised a significant proportion of the membership in the Workers' Alliance. The strike brought many women out of their homes and into the streets for the first time. Adapting to their new role as strikers, the empowered women persuaded their husbands and children to come to the rallies, where they could be educated about the issues. The strike's Mexican leadership reflected a diverse range of men and women activists that included various mutual-aid society members, anarchists, socialists, and communists. These ardent crusaders provided a voice with which Mexican workers could identify. The organizers were not outsiders. Like Tenayuca, Manuela Solis Sager, Minnie Rendon, and Willie Gonzalez, they were Mexicans and Tejanos from the local West Side barrio. Support for the striking pecan shellers also came from across the Mexican border, from Vicente Lombardo Toledano's Confederacion de Trabajadores de Mexico (Confederation of Mexican Workers, or CTM).[27]

The Mexican Communist Party had prodded US communists to address the problems of Mexican workers within US borders. Mexican communists similarly pushed the CTM to take the initiative in a joint organizational effort with the CIO. The CTM supported the militant labor uprisings in South Texas, and its activities extended outside the Southwest. The CTM also trained Mexican American labor organizers at its Universidad Obrera (Workers' University) and helped educate their ill-informed American counterparts about the plight of Mexicans, lecturing the national federation that it needed to do more to benefit the growing Spanish-speaking population.[28]

The pecan-sheller labor disturbance amplified the already strong sentiment against the Mexican-based labor movement. The large communist element within its ranks was particularly distressing to Anglo and Mexican American middle-class interests and the Catholic Church. The city's two biggest newspapers, the *San Antonio Light* and the *San Antonio Express*, assailed anyone who lent support to the strike. The timid and relatively weak middle-class Mexican American establishment was represented by the conservative League of United Latin American Citizens (LULAC). This self-styled "loyal and patriotic" organization professed sympathy for the pecan shellers' deplorable working conditions and dismal wages, but it condemned the strike because of its communist leadership. LULAC supported the repatriation campaigns by the US Border Patrol and called for the suppression of the pecan shellers' strike by the police.[29]

The Catholic Archdiocese's response to the strike grew out of its paternalism toward Mexicans, but it was also driven by the desire to battle communist influences that threatened to seize the union's leadership. While embracing labor's cause, the Catholic Church also vilified the CIO for allowing communists into its leadership ranks.[30] At the end of the first week of the strike, the church's focus was on communist control of the strike. The Catholic Church sought to prevent the spread of communism among its one hundred thousand Spanish-speaking parishioners in San Antonio. It was determined to protect Mexicans from the red menace, especially from its "lying promises that through communism all their ills will come to an end and an earthly paradise will be established for them." More important than battling communism, priests worried about the consequent erosion of their influence on and control of Mexican Catholics.[31]

The church leaders particularly resented a challenge from a Mexican woman and an admitted communist to the patriarchal power structure. Beyond offering a prayer that living conditions would improve for the pecan shellers, the church's response to the strikers was to dislodge dangerous radicals like Tenayuca, to stifle her voice in the community, and to restore its own power over Mexican parishioners' lives. Like LULAC, the church refused to support the strike until its leaders signed a statement renouncing communism. It tried every tactic to discourage the workers from joining the red union UCAPAWA, including publicly slandering the jailed Tenayuca.[32] These sentiments were shared by a small group of Mexican Catholics who resented her overstepping the traditional boundaries governing the behavior of Mexicans—not to challenge the rule of discrimination. The men denounced the Tejana in the Catholic newspaper *LaVoz*: "In the midst of this community exists a woman by the name of Emma Tenayuca who wants to spread disorder and hatred. This woman has all the appearances of a communist. . . . Don't give your names to her when she comes around to solicit them. Warn people when she comes around. Mrs. Tenayuca de Brooks is not a Mexican, she is a Rusofile, sold out to Russia, communist. If she were a Mexican she would not be doing this type of work."[33]

Released from jail, Tenayuca resumed her work with the strikers. Field representatives of the national CIO had taken an interest in the strike, as had those of UCAPAWA who had arrived in San Antonio several months earlier. The CIO took charge as soon as its field representatives arrived. The UCAPAWA unionists who helped in the strike included Clyde Johnson, James Sager, and John Beasley; they were veteran labor organizers of the union drives by, respectively, black workers in the South, Mexican onion workers in South Texas, and Mexican beet workers in Colorado. Local leadership remained in the hands of San Antonio's West Side Mexicans, who had already been organized by the Workers' Alliance. The CIO and UCAPAWA moved to settle the labor dispute through arbitration. Meanwhile, the strike spread.[34]

Predictably, the Texas branch of the American Federation of Labor (AFL) and its locals disapproved of the picketing by Mexicans, and in various labor newspapers they branded the CIO leadership as communist agitators. CTM's efforts the previous year to gain agreement from the state federation for the admission of Mexicans to local affiliates were apparently ignored. The explicit practice of racial unity within union organizing by the UCAPAWA and the national Communist Party (CPUSA) was strongly resisted in Texas, a state that displayed many of the Dixie South's Jim Crow peculiarities of race hatred and discrimination.[35] Most of organized labor's criticism of, and contempt for, radical agitation focused on Tenayuca precisely because she brought the race issue into the open by calling for the unionization of Mexicans.

In Texas the issue of race served to undermine gender alliances between Anglo and Mexican women. In its efforts to crush the communist plot, the Texas AFL had an ally in Rebecca Taylor of the International Ladies' Garment Workers Union (ILGWU). The ILGWU leader, though a fellow Texan, had poor rapport with San Antonio's Mexicana workers. She remained outspoken in her criticism of Tenayuca's radicalism, helping to fuel organized labor's suspicions of the Tejana's intentions. At the same time, Taylor's indictment of Tenayuca further alienated the Mexican pecan shellers. Devoted to their community leader, they became more watchful of the Anglo ILGWU representative, whom they suspected of being a stooge for the police. Concerned with UCAPAWA's communist ties and needing to regain and align public support, the Texas CIO sent its own representatives to San Antonio to stay apprised of developments and provide assistance. This reflected a new strategy within the CIO, as collective bargaining began to replace militancy, confrontation, and the wide scope of issues that characterized earlier strikes in which Tenayuca had participated. This bargaining would ultimately affect her capacity and effectiveness as a community organizer.[36]

In the 1930s, scholars have noted, communists placed revolutionary world communism above the needs of the local communities and used abstract slogans in addressing the jobless. Homer Brooks, who had taken initial control of strike operations, did not hide his Communist Party affiliation. In his role as a party functionary, Brooks's primary concern was forming and maintaining cells. According to one former strike participant, the dogmatic Brooks "would give the pecan shellers lectures on the Communist Party . . . and the great things the party had done in Russia. . . . There would be a meeting in the morning . . . at eight o'clock, and Brooks would still be lecturing at eleven o'clock with no strike business having transpired."[37] Brooks created considerable consternation among the strikers when he removed all the incipient strike leaders who had not officially identified with the Communist Party by signing a card and agreeing to attend meetings. Brooks's marriage to Tenayuca had provided direct access to the West Side Mexican community. Privately, Tenayuca did not hide her disapproval of her husband's zealousness. Although reflecting her own radical tendencies, his tactics went against her concept of how the strike should progress. The veteran Tejana organizer remained confident, however, that Mexican workers would dismiss much of her husband's communist propaganda in favor of issues that applied directly to their concerns.[38]

Intracommunist political conflicts periodically surfaced. Subservience to party directives and discipline nevertheless prevailed. Notwithstanding UCA-PAWA president Donald Henderson's own communist membership, the federation demanded, as a condition for continued support, that Tenayuca (and other communists) not participate in further strike activities on the grounds that too much attention had been focused on her open ties to communism. She remembered becoming infuriated by this demand. "I organized that strike, led it, and then Don Henderson came in, a left winger. I was never consulted. I was given a paper to sign removing myself from the leadership of the strike so workers could get support of the people here." Headstrong, Tenayuca still held daily meetings, produced and distributed circulars, and sent strikers to picket lines.[39]

Big city politicians did not maintain neutrality in the strike. Chief of police Kilday carried on a campaign of harassment. City police, at the request of employers, kept the pecan-shelling plants open and protected those few workers who crossed the picket lines. Kilday repeatedly refused the striking pecan shellers the right to picket and remained firm in labeling the strike an illegal action. Ever vigilant and believing that he was protecting the West Side from a communist takeover, Kilday boosted morale among his forces with anticommunist exhortations. On at least six occasions during the pecan shellers' walkout, strikers confronted San Antonio police officers. More than one hundred firemen served as a supplementary police force. What unfolded was an unusual instance of a Mexican and Anglo confrontation—a 1930s version of the proverbial Mexican standoff.[40]

Following Tenayuca's instructions, picket captains told the pecan shellers not to make eye contact with the police, and they ordered those strikers sick with tuberculosis not to spit on the ground. Such acts could be construed as violations of city ordinances and would result in arrests during this state of virtual martial law. The picketers instead devised methods of resistance that exploited weaknesses in police surveillance and enforcement, including blowing out the tires of police cars by throwing tacks on the streets and vandalizing shipments of unshelled pecans. Police intensified their efforts to crush the working-class protest. Men, women, and children were run down and clubbed by hostile police, and many officers were armed with three-foot-long axe handles, in keeping with the notorious Texas style of justice for dealing with "bad" Mexicans. The police teargassed picketers eight different times, sending women and children running from the fume-filled air. Police arrested hundreds of strikers and jailed them on such minor charges as obstructing sidewalks. The US Immigration Service joined in the fray and began arresting Mexicans. The government dragnet stopped only when the Mexican consul filed a formal protest. Women strikers went to jail accompanied by their children, who were also arrested in the sweeps. Because of rampant hunger, some shellers went to jail willingly in order to be fed. When the incarcerated strikers protested against overcrowded conditions, jail keepers turned fire hoses on them. Such acts failed to break the strikers' spirits. At night the jailed but jubilant strikers sang Spanish renditions of "We Shall Not Be Moved" and "Solidarity Forever," along with Mexican labor songs.[41]

Tenayuca devoted much time and effort in helping to feed the families of the jailed strikers and continued to do so even after their release. She remained adamant about the union. Repeatedly explaining to Mexicans how their lives could be improved through unionization, her message urged direct action through organizational efforts. San Antonio's West Side Mexicans filled the streets to hear her rail angrily against the Southern Pecan Company and the city bosses. The open-air meetings drew an average attendance of five thousand pecan shellers.[42]

News that the strike had assumed the dimensions of a popular uprising soon reached the state capital in Austin. The governor warned that he might call in the Texas Rangers and possibly the National Guard to restore order in San Antonio. The Texas Industrial Commission began public hearings on the strikers' grievances. At issue was the possible violation of Mexicans' civil rights after witness after witness testified before the commission about widespread police repression. The police continued to blame the Workers' Alliance and Tenayuca for the labor disturbance.[43]

The strike's momentum eroded within a few months, however. The newly passed Fair Labor Standards Act created a national minimum wage of twenty-five cents per hour, but the companies refused to pay it. Instead, the industry mechanized, displacing thousands of pecan shellers. No longer was off-season employment in the pecan-shelling sheds available to the migrant farmworkers in San Antonio. Moreover, because of their low wages in agricultural work, shellers who lost their jobs did not receive benefits under the Texas Unemployment Compensation Act. Impoverished, these men and women had to rely on charity from the Catholic Church and the CIO.[44]

An important goal besides union organizing still remained for Tenayuca: expounding the communist philosophy of class struggle and its relation to the Mexicans of the Southwest. During the height of the pecan shellers' strike, Tenayuca and Brooks formulated and wrote a treatise on Mexicans and the question of nationalism. They provided the first discussion of the historical relationship between Mexican nationals and the Mexican American experience and of how the commonalities of the two groups had shaped the social and cultural identity of the Spanish-speaking community of the Southwest.[45]

"The Mexican Question in the Southwest" and Other Party Activities

Mexican American men and women joined the Communist Party in the 1930s because the party sought to eliminate racial barriers from trade unionism. As party members or sympathizers, Mexican Americans provided leadership for the jobless by leading marches on city halls, calling for an end to racial discrimination, engaging in union drives, land disputes, and relief bureau sit-ins, and rallying against discrimination in WPA cutbacks and other New Deal programs. In the late 1930s the CPUSA altered its organizing strategy from work among the unemployed to trade unionism, which placed a few Mexican Americans in positions as officers of some unions. The party's tactics likewise changed from mass confrontation and protest to electoral politics. For Tenayuca, this policy shift encouraged her to seek national office on the Communist Party slate. She was the only Mexican American who held this distinction in the 1930s.[46]

In 1938 the Texas Communist Party nominated Tenayuca at its state convention in Houston as candidate for the US Congress from San Antonio. The party also nominated Brooks as its candidate for governor, while the lieutenant governor's nomination went to African American civil rights activist Cecil B. Robinet from Houston. This multiracial ticket reflected the party leadership's advocacy of racial equality; however, it was nothing more than a symbolic gesture in the context of Anglo Texan prejudice and politics.[47]

Tenayuca put theory into practice in 1939 when she and Brooks coauthored "The Mexican Question in the Southwest." Conceived and written in a span of two weeks, at the height of the pecan shellers' strike, the polemic expressed her interpretation of the Marxist concept of national minorities. It also reflected her extensive reading in Texas history and her firsthand knowledge of the experiences of Mexican residents of Texas. Tenayuca and Brooks stated that the Southwest's Mexican Americans and Mexican nationals were one people who represented an oppressed working class and shared a common history, culture, and language. Mexican Americans were a conquered population as a result of the Mexican War In the nineteenth century. Mexican nationals who had entered the United States served as exploited, unskilled workers. Racial, cultural, and political discrimination indissolubly bound all Mexicans. Nonetheless, the Spanish-speaking people of the Southwest did not represent an "oppressed national group" within the United States, nor did Mexican Americans constitute a border segment of the nation of Mexico. Rather, the two communists argued, Mexican Americans and Mexicans had historically evolved separate communities in the Southwest. Tenayuca and Brooks explicitly added that the distinct Spanish-speaking communities were linked to the Anglo working-class populations of the Southwest as a result of the region's economic and political integration with the rest of the United States. Liberation for Mexicans and Mexican Americans could come only by connecting their struggle to a wider movement. This goal required that the party consider the language, culture, and day-to-day needs of this oppressed racial minority. The authors believed its goals should include eliminating the dual-wage labor system, preventing the confiscation of small landholdings, promoting bilingualism in the public schools, and eradicating Jim Crow segregation (connected to the "Negro" struggle) and political repression through a revision of government regulations regarding citizenship.[48]

Probably the key aim of "The Mexican Question in the Southwest" was to educate the party about the Spanish-speaking population of the region. The authors tried to explain the importance of expanding the work of the Communist Party by promoting a Popular Front definition of an oppressed national minority that was part of the American working classes. During this Popular Front period, the party undertook extra efforts to improve and expand its influence and membership among mostly second-generation Americans, including Mexican Americans. By doing so, party leaders hoped to rally support for the Soviet Union as the prospect of war loomed over Europe.[49]

Tenayuca's fate was inextricably tied to the policies of the national Communist Party. The party's declining militancy in the late 1930s, its increasing emphasis on international relations, and its desire to become part of the lobbying and electoral mainstream placed in the background many of the local issues that she had embraced. The Texas Communist Party planned to hold its state convention in San Antonio in late August 1939. The city's new mayor, Maury Maverick, was a staunch believer in civil rights and gave Tenayuca permission to use the city auditorium on behalf of the Communist Party. Tenayuca was a friend of Maverick's, and behind the scenes she supported his reelection. The Catholic Archbishop immediately protested the city's decision to agree to "a bold and brazen harangue of Communism from the platform of our auditorium." Other area churches and veterans' groups registered their own strong protests against the upcoming conference. In the wake of the anticommunist hysteria in San Antonio, Tenayuca and fellow party member Elizabeth Benson decided not to hold the meeting. Brooks, recently returned from the party's district headquarters in Houston, decided otherwise. The timing could not have been worse.

On the night of August 25 a near riot ensued at San Antonio's Municipal Auditorium when the Texas Communist Party convened its meeting. A rock-throwing mob of around five thousand stopped the proceedings. In the name of "Americanism," the crowd destroyed public property and battled police, on the pretext that they were defending the US Constitution against a Kremlin conspiracy. As the angry swarm wrecked the auditorium, police escorted Tenayuca, Brooks, and the rest of the rally participants out of the auditorium. The previously defeated city machine used this highly controversial event to regain control of San Antonio, oust Maverick from office, and finally bring about the downfall of Emma Tenayuca.[50]

What proved most destructive to the Tejana's credibility was the announcement that the Soviet Union and Nazi Germany had signed a nonaggression pact, ushering in the German invasion of Poland on September 1 and the start of World War II. Brooks had never shown his wife and other party members the telegram from the CPUSA's National Executive Committee announcing the signing of the pact and the start of the war. Tenayuca learned of this later from newspaper reports. Like many devoted American communists who had steadfastly opposed the spread of fascism, she was stunned by the news. She recalled, "It was a very peculiar situation. I think every communist in the country was confused because a few days earlier [Earl] Browder had said Stalin would never do anything like that." It took the Tejana several weeks to recover emotionally from the betrayal.[51]

Tenayuca and Brooks separated, and he was eventually arrested for draft eva-
sion. When the war spread to the Soviet Union, the National Executive Committee of the Communist Party expelled him. Disillusioned with CPUSA policy, Tenayuca quit the party in 1941. One of her brothers was in the US Army,
like thousands of other San Antonio Mexican Americans, and she could not
uphold the party's stance that World War II was an imperialist conflict. Tenayuca found herself isolated with few friends. Ostracized because of her recent
activism, she could not find work. A Jewish garment manufacturer of US Army
officer uniforms who had sympathized with her community work finally gave
her a job as secretary and bookkeeper.[52]

Tenayuca later learned of the "Great Terror"—Joseph Stalin's arrest, torture,
and murder of Bolsheviks. This news was extremely upsetting because most of
these Soviet crimes had occurred during the years 1937–39, the heyday of her
activism. She later lamented, "[Nikita] Khrushchev's announcement horrified
the world, it horrified me." The Tejana learned the hard lesson that Marxist doctrine and unwavering allegiance to party principles counted more to the party
than promoting the welfare of Mexican workers. The actions of her ex-husband,
Homer Brooks, emphasized this quandary. Tenayuca had suffered condemnation by city officials, church leaders, and members of the San Antonio Mexican community for her left-wing views. This rejection was a cruel blow to her
dreams of helping Mexicans make economic progress.[53]

Conclusion

In six years of labor organizing and political protest from 1933 through 1938,
Emma Tenayuca helped Mexicans in San Antonio achieve an unparalleled sense
of confidence and group pride as a racial minority. Her work also helped Mexican American women gain a sense of self-worth and prominence.[54] Her efforts
brought Tejana workers to the forefront of the demonstrations, marches, and
picketing, as well as bringing the issues of wages, relief services, and civil rights to
the attention of the public. At the beginning of the pecan shellers' walkout, just
fifty women were union members. By the end of the strike, Tenayuca had helped
increase their membership in the pecan shellers' union to about ten thousand.
The Tejana organizer also earned the respect of local workingmen, and she successfully led and organized men as well as women during the pecan shellers'
strike.[55]

The contributions of Tenayuca are an essential part of this history of Mexican Americans identifying their rights as workers. She challenged an important

corporate enterprise and the power structure of San Antonio city government, she called for equal pay for equal work in an era of wage differentials, and she articulated the integral issue of Mexican American identity. Her career illuminates our understanding of the interaction between labor movements and political radicalism in the 1930s. Moreover Tenayuca's community and union activism is an example of how women of this era redefined and gendered the American labor movement.[56] The Tejana became a key catalyst for subsequent worker actions by Mexicans in Texas and the rest of the Southwest. Mexican Americans, as an American people, were prepared to continue their struggles for civil rights in the 1940s.[57]

Notes

This chapter originally appeared in *Pacific Historical Review* 66, No. 4 (1997): 553–80, and is reprinted with permission.

1. In this article I use Mexican, Tejano, and Mexican American as terms of self-reference and group reference. In Texas in the 1930s the preferred term of self-reference was Mexican or Tejano (Texas Mexican). The term "Mexican" refers to both Mexican nationals and Tejanos. On the other hand, the terms "Mexican" and "Mexican American" emphasize group identity. "Mexican American" also emphasizes US citizenship.

2. Cletus E. Daniel, *Bitter Harvest: A History of California Farmworkers, 1870–1941* (Berkeley, 1981), 106, 108; Lizabeth Cohen, "Tradition and the Working Class, 1850–1950," *International Labor and Working Class History* 42 (1992): 86–87; "Mexican Radical Activities," March 18, 1936, in US Military Intelligence Division Files, File 2657-G-657–186, Records of the War Department General and Special Staffs, Record Group 165, National Archives, Washington, DC (hereafter cited as RG 165, NA). Several recently unpublished and published works address certain aspects of the experiences of Mexican workers in the 1930s. Among the articles, monographs, and dissertations, see Luis Leobardo Arroyo, "Industrial Unionism and the Los Angeles Furniture Industry, 1918–1954" (PhD diss., University of California, Los Angeles, 1979); Luis Leobardo Arroyo, "Chicano Participation in Organized Labor: The CIO in Los Angeles, 1938–1950: An Extended Research Note," *Aztlan* 6 (1975): 277–303. Recently published books include Sarah Deutsch, *No Separate Refuge: Culture, Class, and Gender on an Anglo-Hispanic Frontier in the American Southwest, 1888–1940* (New York, 1987); Devra Weber, *Dark Sweat, White Gold: Farm Workers, Cotton, and the New Deal* (Berkeley, 1994); George J. Sanchez, *Becoming Mexican American: Ethnicity, Culture, and Identity in Chicano Los Angeles, 1900–1945* (New York, 1993).

3. James C. Foster, "Mexican Labor and the Southwest," in *American Labor in the Southwest: The First One Hundred Years*, ed. James C. Foster (Tucson, 1982),

160–61; Robert H. Zieger, *The CIO, 1935–1955* (Chapel Hill, NC, 1995), 112–13; Lizabeth Cohen, *Making a New Deal: Industrial Workers in Chicago, 1919–1939* (Cambridge, UK, 1990), 338–39; Zaragosa Vargas, *Proletarians of the North: Mexican Industrial Workers in Detroit and the Midwest, 1917–1933* (Berkeley, 1993), 194–99.

4. Daniel, *Bitter Harvest,* 278; Douglas Monroy, "Anarquismo y Comunismo: Mexican Radicalism and the Communist Party in Los Angeles during the 1930s," *Labor History* 24 (1983): 52–53. For information on the CIO's response to racial minority rank and file, see the special issue "Race and the CIO" in *International Labor and Working Class History* 44 (1993).

5. Sarah Deutsch, "Gender, Labor History, and Chicano/a Ethnic Identity," *Frontiers* 14 (1994): 1–2. Recent studies of 1930s women include Elizabeth Faue, *Community of Suffering and Struggle: Women, Men, and the Labor Movement in Minneapolis, 1915–1945* (Chapel Hill, NC, 1991), and Dolores E. Janiewski, *Sisterhood Denied: Race, Gender, and Class in a New South* (Philadelphia, 1985). Women historians are continuing to document the contributions of Anglo and multiracial women to the history of the American West and of the southwestern region. For other representative examples of the recent scholarship, see Susan Johnson, "'A Memory Sweet to Soldiers': The Significance of Gender in the History of the American West," *Western Historical Quarterly* 24 (1993): 495–517; Antonia I. Castaneda, "Women of Color and the Rewriting of History," *Pacific Historical Review* 61 (1992): 501–33.

6. Green Peyton, *San Antonio: City in the Sun* (New York, 1946), 169; David Lewis Filewood, "Tejano Revolt: The Significance of the 1938 Pecan Shellers Strike" (master's thesis, University of Texas, Arlington, 1994), 23; Richard Croxdale, "The 1938 San Antonio Pecan Shellers' Strike," in *Women in the Texas Workplace*, ed. Richard Croxdale and Melissa Hield (Austin, TX, 1979), 30; George and Latane Lambert Papers, p. 25, Collection 127, Labor History Archives, University of Texas at Arlington Library; Harry Koger Papers, p. 2, Collection 66, ibid.

7. Lambert Papers, p. 19.

8. Filewood, "Tejano Revolt," 85.

9. Among the articles and books on the role of Mexican American women in the labor movement, see, for example, Victor Nelson-Cisneros, "UCAPAWA Organizing Activities in Texas, 1930–1950," *Aztlan* 9 (1978): 7–84; Clementina Duron, "Mexican Women and Labor Conflict in Los Angeles: The ILGWU Dress-makers' Strike of 1933," *Aztlan* 15 (1982): 145–61; Vicki L. Ruiz, *Cannery Women, Cannery Lives: Mexican Women, Unionization, and the California Food Processing Industry, 1930–1950* (Albuquerque, 1987); Mario T. Garcia, *Mexican Americans: Leadership, Ideology, and Identity, 1930–1960* (New Haven, CT, 1989).

10. David Montejano, *Anglos and Mexicans in the Making of Texas, 1836–1986* (Austin, TX, 1987), 164–65, 189–90; Robert Thomas, *Citizenship, Gender, and Work: The Social Organization of Industrial Agriculture* (Berkeley, 1985), 148; Texas State Employment Service, *Origins and Problems of Texas Migratory Farm Labor* (Aus-

tin, TX, September 1940), 20, 42; Richard A. Garcia, *Rise of the Mexican American Middle Class: San Antonio, 1929–1941* (College Station, TX, 1991), 58; Weber, *Dark Sweat, White Gold*, 112, 114–15.

11. Montejano, *Anglos and Mexicans in the Making of Texas*, 265.

12. Jacqueline Jones, *Labor of Love, Labor of Sorrow: Black Women, Work, and the Family from Slavery to the Present* (New York, 1985), 199; J. R. Steelman, Commissioner of Conciliation, San Antonio, TX, to H. L. Kerwin, US Department of Labor, Washington, DC, April 20, 1935, US Mediation and Conciliation Service, Case File 182/326, Records of the US Mediation and Conciliation Service, Record Group 280, National Archives (hereafter cited as RG 280, NA); Department of State, American Consul Romeyn Wormuth, Nuevo Laredo, Mexico, to Secretary of State, Washington, DC, May 4, 1935; 811.5045/179, Box 5112, Records of the Department of State, Record Group 59, National Archives (hereafter cited as RG 59, NA); Sharon Hartman Strom, "Challenging 'Women's Place': Feminism, the Left, and Industrial Unionism in the 1930s," *Feminist Studies* 9 (1980): 301–62; Mary Loretta Sullivan and Bertha Blair, *Women in Texas Industries: Hours, Wages, Working Conditions, and Home Work* [Department of Labor, Women's Bureau Bulletin No. 126] (Washington, DC, 1936), 47–48, 57; Nancy E. Rose, *Workforce or Farm Work: Women, Welfare, and Government Work Programs* (New Brunswick, NJ, 1995), 48.

13. Filewood, "Tejano Revolt," 27.

14. Julia Kirk Blackwelder, *Women of the Depression: Caste and Culture in San Antonio, 1929–1939* (College Station, TX, 1984), 103–4; Roberto Calderon and Emilio Zamora, *Chicana Voices: Intersections of Race, Class, and Gender* (Austin, TX, 1986), 33; R. A. Garcia, *Rise of the Mexican American Middle Class*, 60.

15. Raul Ramos, "Asi Fue: La Huelga de los Nueceros de San Antonio, Texas, Febrero 1938" (unpublished senior thesis, Princeton University, 1989), 9; Blackwelder, *Women of the Depression*, 144–45; Filewood, "Tejano Revolt," 41–42; Irene Ledesma, "Texas Newspapers and Chicana Workers' Activism, 1919–1974," *Western Historical Quarterly* 26 (1995): 318; WPA Central Files, Texas 1935–1936, Box 2618, Folder 641,199/1189, No. 3168–5A, Records of the Works Progress Administration, Record Group 69, National Archives (hereafter cited as RG 69, NA).

16. Peyton, *San Antonio*, 147; Filewood, "Tejano Revolt," 29, 32–33, 37–39; Ramos, "Asi Fue," 6; Blackwelder, *Women of the Depression*, 145; George O. Coalson, *Development of the Migrant Farm Labor System in Texas, 1900–1954* (San Francisco, 1977), 58; *San Antonio Light*, September 17, 1938; Jane Warner Rogers, "WPA Professional and Service Projects in Texas" (master's thesis, University of Texas, Austin, 1976), 52–53; Deutsch, *No Separate Refuge*, 187–96; Harvey Klehr, *The Heyday of American Communism: The Depression Decade* (New York, 1984), 50–56; Emma Tenayuca, interview by author May 4, 1990. For works on the Unemployed Councils, see Daniel Leab, "'United We Eat': The Creation and Organization of the Unemployed Councils," *Labor History* 8 (1967): 300–315,

and Roy Rosenzweig, "Organizing the Unemployed: The Early Years of the Great Depression, 1929–33," *Radical America* 10 (1976): 37–60.

17. *People's Press*, January 23, 1937; Tenayuca, telephone interview by author, February 20, 1990; Fraser M. Ottanelli, *The Communist Party of the United States: From the Depression to World War II* (New Brunswick, NJ, 1991), 35–36.

18. Tenayuca, interview by author, May 3, 1990; Franklin Folsom, *Impatient Armies of the Poor: The Story of Collective Action of the Unemployed, 1808–1942* (Niwot, CO, 1991), 421–22; "La Pasionaria de Texas," *Time* 31 (February 28, 1938), 17; Klehr, *Heyday of American Communism*, 273; Monroy, "Anarquismo y Comunismo," 55; D. H. Dinwoodie, "Deportation: The Immigration Service and the Chicano Labor Movement in the 1930s," *New Mexico Historical Review* 52 (1977): 193–94; Gilbert Mers, *Working the Waterfront: The Ups and Downs of a Rebel Longshoreman* (Austin, TX, 1988), 122.

19. Tenayuca, interview by author, May 3, 1990; *People's Press*, March 6, 1937; Abraham Hoffman, *Unwanted Mexican Americans in the Great Depression: Repatriation Pressures, 1929–1939* (Tucson, 1974), 120.

20. Folsom, *Impatient Armies of the Poor*, 422–23; *San Antonio Light*, June 30, 1937; Calderon and Zamora, *Chicana Voices*, 33; Tenayuca, interview by author, May 4, 1990; Richard H. Pells, *Radical Visions and American Dreams: Culture and Thought in the Depression Years* (New York, 1973), 259.

21. *People's Press*, July 10, 1937; Robin D. G. Kelley, *Hammer and Hoe: Alabama Communists during the Great Depression* (Chapel Hill, NC, 1990), 191–92.

22. Don Carleton, *Red Scare: Right Wing Hysteria, Fifties Fanaticism, and Their Legacy in Texas* (Austin, TX, 1985), 27–28; Filewood, "Tejano Revolt," 85; Ledesma, "Texas Newspapers," 319; Tenayuca, interview by author, May 5, 1990; Klehr, *Heyday of American Communism*, 273; Mers, *Working the Waterfront*, 122, 124.

23. Ramos, "Asi Fue," 26; Filewood, "Tejano Revolt," 72; Ledesma, "Texas Newspapers," 318; *People's Press*, July 10, 24, 1937; Tenayuca, interview by author, May 5, 1990.

24. Ramos, "Asi Fue," 3–14, 20–22; Ledesma, "Texas Newspapers," 317; R. A. Garcia, *Rise of the Mexican American Middle Class*, 55, 60–62; *Current*, May 22, 1986; Blackwelder, *Women of the Depression*, 141, 148–49; Filewood, "Tejano Revolt," 46–50, 58; Sullivan and Blair, *Women in Texas Industries*, 78; Albert Camarillo, *Chicanos in California: A History of Mexican Americans in California* (San Francisco, 1984), 59. People of Mexican background comprised about 52.2 percent of San Antonio's relief rolls; half of these (22.8 percent or 16,324 individuals) were Mexican nationals and the remainder (about 29.4 percent or 21,032 individuals) were Mexican Americans. Lyndon Gayle Knippa, "San Antonio II: The Early New Deal," in *Texas Cities and the Great Depression*, ed. W. W. Newcomb (Austin, TX, 1973), 87.

25. Filewood, "Tejano Revolt," 70, 72–73; *The Green Rising*, p. 14, Reel 13, Clyde Johnson Papers, Special Collections, University of California, Los Angeles; *People's Press*, August 14, 1937.

26. Ramos, "Asi Fue," 23, 26; Blackwelder, *Women of the Depression*, 141, 148–49; *Current*, May 22, 1986; Filewood, "Tejano Revolt," 79–80; Lambert Papers, pp. 19, 29; US Mediation and Conciliation Service, Report of District 3, *UCAPAWA Year Book 1938*, 22, Case File 195/114, RG 280, NA; R. A. Garcia, *Rise of the Mexican American Middle Class*, 62.

27. Tenayuca, interview by author, May 3, 1990; Ramos, "Asi Fue," 26.

28. Gigi Peterson, "Compañeros across the Border: The Mexican Labor-Left and its US Connections, 1936–1940" (unpublished seminar paper, Department of History, University of Washington, Spring 1992), 18–19.

29. Montejano, *Anglos and Mexicans in the Making of Texas*, 244; Filewood, "Tejano Revolt," 80–88.

30. The call for Catholic clergy to join an anticommunist crusade against international communism was the result of a 1937 papal encyclical *Divini Redemptoris*. Gary Gerstle, *Working Class Americanism: The Politics of Labor in a Textile City, 1914–1960* (New York, 1989), 250.

31. Blackwelder, *Women of the Depression*, 141; Peyton, *City in the Sun*, 170; Filewood, "Tejano Revolt," 85–86.

32. Tenayuca, interview by author, May 4, 1990; R. A. Garcia, *Rise of the Mexican American Middle Class*, 169–73.

33. Ramos, "Asi Fue," 57–58.

34. Filewood, "Tejano Revolt," 76–77; Ramos, "Asi Fue," 33; US Mediation and Conciliation Service, Report of District 3, *UCAPAWA Year Book 1938*, 22.

35. The CTM delegates also got an agreement from Texas organized labor to counter anti-Cardenas propaganda in the United States. Peterson, "Compañeros across the Border," 20; WPA Central Files, Texas 1935–1936, Box 2618, Folder 641, 199/1189, No. 3168–5A, RG 69, NA; *Houston Labor Journal*, January 27, 1939.

36. R. A. Garcia, *Rise of the Mexican American Middle Class*, 63; Blackwelder, *Women of the Depression*, 141–49; Filewood, "Tejano Revolt," 82–83; Strom, "Challenging 'Women's Place,'" 368–69; Ramos, "Asi Fue," 25; Elizabeth Faue, "Paths of Unionization: Community, Bureaucracy, and Gender in the Minneapolis Labor Movement of the 1930s," in *Work Engendered: Toward a New History of American Labor*, ed. Ava Baron (Ithaca, NY, 1991), 296–301.

37. Filewood, "Tejano Revolt," 106; Lambert Papers, pp. 18–19.

38. Lambert Papers, pp. 18–19; Ramos, "Asi Fue," 55; Tenayuca, interview by author, May 3, 1990.

39. Roger Papers, p. 6; Tenayuca, interviews by author, May 3, 5, 1990.

40. Ramos, "Asi Fue," 73; Filewood, "Tejano Revolt," 90–93; Tenayuca, interview by author, May 4, 1990.

41. Ramos, "Asi Fue," 71–74; Blackwelder, *Women of the Depression*, 141; Filewood, "Tejano Revolt," 93–96; Ledesma, "Texas Newspapers," 318; Roger Papers, p. 2; Lambert Papers, pp. 23–24, 28–29; Tenayuca, interview by author, May 4, 1990. On the infrapolitics of subordinate groups, see James C. Scott, *Domination and the Arts of Resistance: Hidden Transcripts* (New Haven, CT, 1990).

42. R. A. Garcia, *Rise of the Mexican American Middle Class*, 63.

43.   Blackwelder, *Women of the Depression*, 142; Filewood, "Tejano Revolt," 114–15.

44.   Ramos, "Asi Fue," 85–86; Filewood, "Tejano Revolt," 120.

45.   For an excellent elaboration of this theme, see David G. Gutierrez, *Walls and Mirrors: Mexican Americans, Mexican Immigrants, and the Politics of Ethnicity* (Berkeley, 1995).

46.   Monroy, "Anarquismo y Comunismo," 52; Suzanne Forrest, *The Preservation of the Village: New Mexico's Hispanics and the New Deal* (Albuquerque, 1989), 154–55; Mark Naison, *Communists in Harlem during the Depression* (New York, 1983), 256–57.

47.   Carleton, *Red Scare*, 29.

48.   Emma Tenayuca and Homer Brooks, "The Mexican Question in the Southwest," *The Communist* 18 (March 1939): 257–68; Monroy, "Anarquismo y Comunismo," 42–44; Tenayuca, interview by author, May 3, 1990; Calderon and Zamora, *Chicana Voices*, 34–35; M. T. Garcia, *Mexican Americans*, 153–54. For an overview of the literature on the issue of Chicanos and the national question, see Antonio Rios Bustamante, *Mexicans in the United States and the National Question: Current Polemics and Organizational Positions* (Santa Barbara, CA, 1978).

49.   M. T. Garcia, *Mexican Americans*, 154.

50.   Naison, *Communists in Harlem*, 256–57; Richard B. Henderson, *Maverick: A Political Biography* (Austin, TX, 1970), 214–16; Roger Papers, p. 3; Lambert Papers, pp. 21–22; Ledesma, "Texas Newspapers," 321; Tenayuca, interview by author, May 3, 1990.

51.   Tenayuca, interview by author, May 3, 1990; Dorothy Healey and Maurice Isserman, *Dorothy Healey Remembers: A Life in the Communist Party* (New York, 1990), 80–82; Ottanelli, *Communist Party of the United States*, 183–85.

52.   Homer Brooks later died of a heart attack in Los Angeles. Tenayuca, interview by author, May 4, 1990.

53.   Ottanelli, *Communist Party of the United States*, 182–83.

54.   Deutsch, *No Separate Refuge*, 170; Deutsch, "Gender, Labor History, and Chicano/a Ethnic Identity," 16.

55.   Filewood, "Tejano Revolt," 102; *People's Press*, March 19, 1938.

56.   Faue, *Community of Suffering and Struggle*, 71.

57.   Rebuffed by the San Antonio community for her affiliation with radicalism, Tenayuca moved to San Francisco, where she enrolled at San Francisco State College (now San Francisco State University) and in a few years graduated magna cum laude. Fifteen years later, Tenayuca returned to San Antonio, enrolled in St. Mary's University, and received a master's in education while following a career as an elementary school teacher.

     Emma Tenayuca still lives in San Antonio. In her eighties and in ill health, the ex-communist and retired schoolteacher has not lost the boundless resistance to injustice that in the 1930s won her the nickname of "La Pasionaria." [**Editors' note: Emma Tenayuca died in 1999.**] Interest in her importance to the Mexican American labor movement resurfaced during the 1970s. Recalling the obstacles she faced while organizing San Antonio's Mexicans, Tenayuca passionately recollected the events that won her a respected place in Chicano history: "I had every damn right to be apprehensive. Was I in a state of panic or fear? No. I was pretty defiant. [I fought] against poverty, actually starvation, high infant death rates, disease and hunger and misery. I would do the same thing again" (Tenayuca, interview by author, May 4, 1990).

GREGG ANDREWS

Unionizing the Trinity Portland Cement Company in Dallas, Texas, 1934–1939

In 1934–35 Pres. Franklin D. Roosevelt's administration confronted a direct challenge to Section 7(a) of the National Industrial Recovery Act (NIRA) in Dallas, Texas. A local panel of the National Labor Relations Board—established by the president through power given him by a congressional resolution in June 1934—ruled that the Trinity Portland Cement Company had to recognize the overwhelming desire of workers at the company's plant in Dallas to name Portland Cement Workers Union No. 19310 as their exclusive bargaining agent. Portland Cement Workers Union No. 19310 was affiliated with the Texas State Federation of Labor (TSFL) and the American Federation of Labor (AFL). On December 10, 1934, however, the company notified the board that it refused to comply with the ruling.[1]

Although Trinity's workers had voted in favor of the union by a nearly unanimous margin of 150 to 2, company officials held out in defiance of the NIRA's labor provisions, hoping to retain their company union and reaffirm exclusive control over labor policies. Until January 1939, Trinity's workers battled an array of antiunion measures in an attempt to force the company to recognize their union and sign a collective bargaining agreement. After a tenacious campaign to assert their rights under the New Deal, the workers achieved a victory whose ramifications extended beyond the Dallas plant. Trinity signed joint labor agreements at all three of its Texas plants—the first such labor agreements signed with a cement corporation in the United States.

Trinity's first plant—located near the west fork of the Trinity River on a five-hundred-acre bed of limestone and shale reserves in Eagle Ford, a small community on the western edge of Dallas County—began producing cement in 1909. The company built a plant in Fort Worth in 1924 and another in Houston in 1926.[2] The campaign to organize workers at Trinity's Eagle Ford plant also was tied to unionization efforts at the Lone Star Cement Company in the

245

nearby community of Cement City. In fact, Eagle Ford was so close that Dallas residents at the time commonly referred to both communities as Cement City.[3]

The Eagle Ford and Cement City mills were the first cement plants in Dallas, the state's largest city in 1910. Clustered together, the two plants converted West Dallas into a focal point of cement manufacturing to service the growing demands of an increasingly urbanized area. The Trinity plant took advantage of good rail facilities via the Texas and Pacific Railway and the Texas Northern Railroad to ship barrels and jute bags of cement. The cement was used to pave Dallas-area streets and sidewalks, build viaducts and bridges, encase artesian wells drilled by area farmers for irrigation purposes, build highways, and facilitate other construction and oil drilling projects in Texas, New Mexico, Louisiana, Arkansas, and Oklahoma.[4]

Trinity had no difficulty attracting a cheap labor force. Many of the plant's initial unskilled production workers were Mexican immigrants uprooted by the Mexican Revolution and drawn by the lure of industrial jobs to Dallas. Thanks to family ties and community networks, word of jobs at the Trinity plant, which employed between 300 and 325 workers during peak times, often spread through villages such as San Felipe in the state of Guanajuato, the origins of many Eagle Ford families. Trinity's plant often employed three generations of families—fathers, sons, and grandsons—thanks in part to the company's hiring policy that gave preference to family members. In addition, the company employed African American and Anglo workers from poor neighborhoods in nearby West Dallas.[5]

Because of inadequate transportation, the plant's rather remote location at the time, and racial segregation and Jim Crow social customs, company officials built two segregated villages nearby to meet the needs of many of its workers. In one village lived the general manager of the division, the plant manager, and other white supervisors with their families in houses that contained five or six rooms. Many of the Trinity plant's production workers, mostly Mexicans, Mexican Americans, and African Americans, lived in the other village in two rows of approximately twenty-four to thirty houses separated by a dirt street. These houses, which lacked electricity or gas, likewise contained five or six rooms and rented for two dollars per month per room.[6]

Throughout the history of Trinity's Eagle Ford plant, company paternalism shaped labor relations. Trinity operated a grocery store and meat market in the village and issued food coupons redeemable only at its store, deducting these coupons from the workers' wages. It also furnished cement, labor, and other materials to build a new two-story concrete school in Eagle Ford, and the company supplied a doctor to attend to the medical needs of Trinity workers and their families for a small fee. On a hillside northwest of the plant, a cemetery provided a burial spot, mainly for Mexican workers and their families. In addition to sponsoring an employee representation plan, or company union, to give workers a voice, at least in theory, in the production process, Trinity also sponsored a baseball team, picnics, barbecues, and other recreational activities in the community.[7]

Trinity officials touted this paternalism as an expression of the company's goodwill and concern for its workers, but such paternalism disguised underlying forms of autocratic control. In particular, officials emphasized that during the Great Depression, the use of company food stamps during slack times provided workers with protection against hunger. Trinity's management downplayed the rate of profit at the company store and meat market, but the use of food coupons reinforced workers' indebtedness and dependence on the company. Control over housing and subsequent fear of evictions provided Trinity with an important club against potential labor agitators in Eagle Ford. The use of a company guard to patrol the community, ostensibly to provide protection to residents, also made it more difficult for union organizers to hold meetings without detection by plant officials.[8]

For many Mexican immigrants and Mexican American and African American workers, jobs at the Eagle Ford plant provided at least a partial escape from an even more marginal, dreary life of lower-paying, often transitory work in Texas agriculture, but working conditions in the cement industry were very dangerous, hours were long, and pay was low. The physical demands of working a thirteen-hour night shift were so great, for example, that shift foremen at Trinity's plant ignored or consented to the common practice in which a worker's buddy would relieve him for about one hour each night so that he could take a short nap. In many cases, a workweek of ninety-one hours prevailed. According to a 1929 study of 102 portland cement plants in the United States, male workers in Texas averaged 67.9 hours on the job per week—the highest number compared to their counterparts elsewhere. Moreover, they averaged only 37.3 cents per hour in wages, the lowest average pay among any of the cement workers included in the study. Trinity's Eagle Ford plant operated around the clock, seven days per week, requiring workers on the day shift to put in eleven hours per day, and night workers to endure shifts of thirteen hours. In 1925 and 1926, wages at Trinity's Eagle Ford plant bottomed out at 15 cents per hour for laborers, and at 18 cents per hour for foremen.[9]

The cement industry had one of the highest work-related accident rates in the United States. If a worker became sick or temporarily unable to work, he had to rely on the buddy system; that is, in order to keep his job, he had to find someone to take his place until he could return to work. Of course, fatigue increased the likelihood of accidents in plants where a single careless slip might cause workers to suffer a grisly accident and be crushed, ground up, mangled, suffocated, or otherwise mutilated by machinery used to manufacture cement.[10] A state-administered Industrial Accident Board (created in 1913) that was heavily biased in favor of insurance companies made it nearly impossible for accident victims and their families to receive adequate, timely compensation. As Judge E. W. Napier of Wichita Falls told the Texas State Federation of Labor's annual convention in 1930, he had seen too many insurance companies "rob ignorant men and women. . . . The Workmen's Compensation Law, instead of doing a lot of things you were told it would do to better your condition, has been the opening wedge for the influx of hordes of foreign corporations who are taking your money, and every dollar of it represents the blood of some injured man."[11]

Except for company paternalism, workers at Trinity's plant had few options until 1933, when Section 7(a) of the NIRA required employers to recognize the rights of workers to join trade unions and engage in collective bargaining. Because of the deep, nasty racism and antilabor sentiments that saturated Texas, workers—particularly Mexican immigrants, Mexican Americans, and African Americans—had few allies among Texas politicians, state officials, or even members of the labor movement itself in the 1920s. Charles McKay, state labor commissioner, complained in 1930 that he represented "the most unpopular branch" of government in Austin. Referring to himself as "the most unpopular public official in the State of Texas," he bitterly denounced the state legislature's lack of concern for working people.[12]

Neither could Trinity's workers expect much, if anything, from the TSFL, whose ranks had been decimated in the antilabor atmosphere of the 1920s. The TSFL's policies and practices mirrored those of the AFL, which before the 1930s had made only sporadic and largely unsuccessful efforts to organize unskilled workers in the portland cement industry. The TSFL was made up almost exclusively of Anglo skilled workers and was racist in its craft orientation. Thus, it provided anything but a hospitable climate for unskilled minority workers, even though the organization badly needed members. For years, the state labor body had fought to curb immigration from Mexico, preferring to condemn immigrants rather than try to organize them. A handful of black members of the TSFL had worked diligently but unsuccessfully throughout its history to combat the racism that underlay the state labor body's neglect and disregard for organizing black workers.[13]

Passage of the NIRA in 1933 provided a stimulus to labor organizing in the cement industry, which until then had largely kept unions out of its plants. In keeping with the provisions of the NIRA, the cement industry established a "code of fair competition" to limit hours, regulate working conditions, and set wages in an effort to prevent unbridled competition from contributing to further layoffs, price wars, strikes, and cuts in wages and production. As in other industries, the largest cement companies, represented by the Cement Institute, were authorized to devise the industry's code and hold public hearings with input from government-appointed representatives of labor, industrial, and consumer boards. The National Recovery Administration (NRA) allowed regional, or racialized, wage differentials, despite protests from organized labor and from its own Labor Advisory Board. As a result, the cement code, finalized on September 15 and signed by President Roosevelt on November 27, 1933, called for an hourly wage rate of only thirty cents for workers in Texas and other southern states, compared to a rate of forty cents for most workers in the industry.[14]

According to the Trinity Portland Cement Company's publications, the 1934–35 period was the most critical one in the Dallas plant's history as the result of high energy costs and "extremely low" cement prices. Although New Deal construction projects stimulated demand for cement, Texas's nine active cement plants operated at only 32.4 percent of utilized capacity in 1934, and at only 34.2 percent in 1935. To increase profitability at the Dallas plant, Trinity officials turned to an alternative source of fuel. Cy E. Caron, general superintendent of the company's three Texas plants, worked out arrangements to buy cheap waste coke from a nearby oil refinery in the Eagle Ford–Cement City area. The company then built new coke burners to fuel the Dallas plant's kilns.[15]

Contrary to company complaints about low cement prices, the US Bureau of Mines reported that industry prices in Texas were far above the national average. In 1934, for example, the average net mill price for cement in Texas was $1.75, compared to a national average of $1.54 per barrel. In 1935, the average price in Texas was $1.73, compared to a national average of $1.51 per barrel. Cement prices in Texas, which itself comprised one of nine districts created by the Bureau of Mines, were in fact higher than in any other district in the nation.[16]

Trinity's company publications do not mention labor problems during this period, but its workers became part of a wave of labor militancy that immediately swept Dallas, which was dubbed by organized labor as the capital of the open shop, after passage of the NIRA. The Dallas Central Labor Council received numerous letters from area workers requesting information and assistance in unionizing. One of the leading, although unpaid, organizers was John

B. Schulte, a member of the executive board of the Dallas Central Labor Council and president of the AFL's Retail Clerks International Protective Association. "Not even during the War period," he told AFL president William Green on September 27, 1933, "have so many new charters been issued in Dallas, as at the present time, many groups who have never had a charter before in the city of Dallas."[17]

Workers at the plants owned by Trinity and the Lone Star Cement Company in Eagle Ford–Cement City decided to create a union composed of members from both plants. On February 27, 1934, L. E. Gulledge, who worked at Lone Star's plant, contacted NRA administrator Hugh S. Johnson to get a clarification of workers' rights under the NRA. He asked Johnson if the law provided "any means of requiring or compelling the company to meet with a committee duly elected as their representative for the purpose of negotiating a wage scale and working agreement for the employees." Gulledge noted that the "employees here are willing to organize," but he told Johnson that they would first like to know if the code required employers to meet with workers' representatives.[18]

With voluntary assistance and coordination provided by Schulte, workers from these two plants organized Portland Cement Workers Local 19310. The AFL granted a charter to the local on March 13, 1934. The new local, which comprised approximately three hundred members, affiliated with the TSFL a month later and set out to test labor's rights under the NRA.[19]

At Trinity, officials hoped in vain that its company union, or employee representation plan, would satisfy workers long dependent on company paternalism. When Trinity refused to recognize a committee elected by Local 19310, the union called on the regional labor board to supervise an election. On May 10, 1934, the board supervised an election in which Trinity's workers voted overwhelmingly across ethnic lines by a margin of 150 to 2 to choose Local 19310 as their bargaining representative.[20]

Soon after the election, the local again sent a committee to request a conference with Trinity officials, who at first agreed to meet but abruptly changed course. The company refused to meet again with the union unless it furnished the names of the 150 men who had voted for the AFL.

Organizer Schulte complained that Trinity officials "virtually agreed to meet and recognize the committee and then overnight they forgot all they promised and even refused to produce the minutes of that meeting, saying that it mysteriously disappeared." The local's committee, fearing retaliation, refused to provide Trinity with the 150 names.[21]

Officials at the Lone Star plant in Cement City showed a more flexible attitude, however, recognizing and meeting with a committee representing Local 19310. The company warned foremen not to discriminate against or try to intimidate members of the union. Lone Star workers immediately won a wage increase ranging from 10 to 40 percent, but the company held out against signing a written agreement with the union. Instead, Lone Star officials promised to abide by an oral agreement for three months.[22]

Lone Star officials feared that fledgling unions in the cement industry would lead to standardized labor rates in the state. When officers of the Southwestern Portland Cement Company's plant in El Paso, where workers had formed Local 19533, sought a more coordinated approach to combat the unions by exchanging information on wage rates and job classifications, Lone Star refused. William R. Blair, sales manager at the El Paso plant, sent a schedule of Southwestern Portland's labor rates to L. R. Ferguson, vice president of the Lone Star Cement Company in Dallas, requesting that Ferguson in turn share Lone Star's pay rates and job classifications with him. "We are having some question with our men as to classification of Labor and rates of pay," wrote Blair, "and would like very much to check your rate schedules on labor, if agreeable." After consulting with executives in New York, Ferguson refused, arguing that to exchange such information "would result in standardization of wages, at least in districts where the various manufacturers have common interests. . . . Should this occur, it would we believe be a strong weapon in the hands of the union organizers and would strengthen the arguments which they are at present advancing to have the cement industry unionized."[23]

AFL and NLRB officials tried to convince Trinity's management to recognize the union and respect the collective bargaining wishes of its workers. At Schulte's request, the AFL sent organizer W. R. Williams to Dallas in June, but a meeting with Trinity officials failed to break the impasse. Although collective bargaining negotiations with the workers' committee began, Trinity withdrew abruptly from the conference on June 21. The regional labor board, which at that time was located in San Antonio, tried but failed to get the company to comply with the election results and participate in collective bargaining. Frustrated by the unprecedented challenge to the board's authority, Roger M. Busfield, secretary of the San Antonio regional labor board, complained to NLRB headquarters in Washington, DC, that "the company continues to ignore all efforts of this Board to arrange a collective bargaining conference. . . . As far as I know, no instructions have ever been received by this Board relative to the handling of a situation such as that at the Trinity Portland Cement plant."[24]

In an attempt to disrupt the union, Trinity instead supervised its own plant election on July 15, 1934, "to put over their company union idea." The company continued to ignore all communications from the regional labor board. Schulte and Williams hoped to prevent further strife, but Williams warned AFL president Green that "from all indications we are heading for a battle."[25]

A lack of resources hampered the local union. L. E. Gulledge, financial secretary of Local 19310, expressed frustration to AFL president Green that the AFL provided only one organizer for the entire state of Texas. Emphasizing that only three of the state's nine cement plants were organized, Gulledge pressed Green to add Schulte to the AFL's staff of paid organizers to help Williams, who had already left Dallas. Green told Gulledge that the AFL would love to hire Schulte but lacked the resources to do so.[26]

Trinity continued to refuse to meet with representatives of the union, insisting that the workers' committee furnish proof that they in fact represented a majority of the plant's employees. On August 8 Trinity general superintendent Caron met with AFL organizer Williams and the secretary of the regional labor board, promising to bargain with the union if a check of the union membership rolls against the company payroll of April 15 proved that a majority of Trinity's workers had indeed voted for the union.[27]

Trinity's stalling tactics continued throughout the fall of 1934. On October 16, Caron, along with Jim Curtis, general manager of the Cowham Engineering Group (which had built the plant), and William Ganser, plant superintendent, finally met with Williams and a committee representing Local 19310. After two meetings to discuss a wage scale and working agreement, labor representatives believed that they were making at least tentative progress, but then company officials abruptly changed course in the middle of a third meeting. According to L. M. Fisher Jr., president of the Dallas local, "On the third day of the conference the management repudiated the things to which they had previously agreed and at the same time presented the committee with a proclamation addressed 'To Our Employees' completely out of line." Management then issued a take-it-or-leave-it offer, but the committee refused. As Fisher bitterly reported, "The management has broken its word so many times before this meeting that our faith in it has been broken. Attempts to break up this union, cases of discrimination, and the unfair and unethical tactics used by and on the part of company officials have forced this local to take drastic action."[28]

Although the plant was still shut down, members of the union voted unanimously at a special meeting on October 19, 1934, to strike in order to fight for their rights under Section 7(a) of the NIRA. AFL president Green expressed regret that they had been forced to take such desperate steps and expressed hope for an early, peaceful resolution of the conflict. The union apparently dropped plans to call a strike, however, after Green reminded them that according to the AFL's constitution and bylaws, they would not be eligible for strike benefits until March 13, 1935.[29]

On November 12, Portland Cement Workers Union No. 19310 presented its case against Trinity in Dallas's city hall auditorium before a panel of the National Labor Relations Board presided over by Dr. Edwin A. Elliott, the new director of the Texas-Oklahoma regional labor board (now headquartered in Fort Worth). On the panel were August W. Schultz, who represented labor, R. W. Van Valkenburgh, who represented industry, and L. M. Rice, who represented the public. After both sides agreed to eliminate a large amount of irrelevant information that included personality conflicts, charges, and counter-charges, the board ruled on three main unsettled issues. First, the Dallas panel ruled that Trinity was bound to recognize the union as the exclusive bargaining agent for all of the plant's workers. Second, the board concluded that although one of the objectives of Section 7(a) was that employees and employers should reach a collective bargaining agreement in matters submitted by either party, the law did not compel such an agreement as long as both parties could substantiate a good faith effort in the negotiations. Finally, the panel ruled that the law did not require a written collective-bargaining agreement.[30]

The ruling gave Trinity fifteen days to recognize Local 19310 as the sole bargaining agent of eligible employees at its Dallas plant, but the company challenged the authority of the National Labor Relations Board, which lacked power to enforce its rulings. In what was the most important labor-related question of the year in the nation's cement industry, Trinity notified the board on December 10, 1934, that it refused to comply with the ruling and that it would not recognize the union as the exclusive bargaining agent of its workers: "We must protest . . . against an order which would require us to deal exclusively with any single agency regardless of whether or not all of our employees are members of the group which it represents. . . . [W] e must remain free to treat with them, severally and collectively, as their and our emergencies, needs and best interests may require."[31]

Workers at the Lone Star plant also hit a snag in their efforts to unionize. Like Trinity, the Lone Star Cement Company put forth a company-sponsored union committee to challenge the AFL union's committee. In mid-October, Elliott, director of the regional labor relations board in Fort Worth, reported that an executive of the Lone Star Cement Company suggested to him at a meeting that the company had already recognized a plant committee for the purposes of collective bargaining. A plant election on December 19, 1934, resulted in a tie vote in which eighty workers voted for Portland Cement Workers Union No. 19310, and eighty voted for the company's committee. One vote was ruled void. The AFL contested the election, however, and requested that the regional board force the Lone Star Cement Company to recognize its union.[32]

To complicate matters for Trinity workers, the Dallas County Relief Board, mired in controversy and riddled with political problems, had purged them from the relief rolls in September, even though the plant had been shut down for all but about three months during the year. After an investigation, Adam R. Johnson, director of the Texas Relief Commission, warned the board, which was headed by the Lone Star Gas Company's president, L. B. Denning, that "something is radically wrong." Johnson urged the board to undertake an intensive review of the "entire relief set-up, including the personnel," in Dallas County.[33]

As the local relief board took workers off the rolls, Trinity took steps to strengthen workers' dependence on company paternalism in an effort to undercut the union. To those who applied, the company issued coupon books worth fifteen dollars per month in groceries at its commissary. Of course, this would put workers deeper into debt, since they would ultimately have to repay the company through future earnings.[34]

Desperate, Trinity's workers asked union officials to discuss their plight with the county relief board and company officials and to request aid "from such a drastic and un-American policy." Union president L. M. Fisher Jr. met with members of the board and company officials in an attempt to secure relief but to no avail. According to Fisher, the board and company were acting in tandem. Emphasizing that Trinity's policy had been to operate the plant at full capacity for about two months and then to shut down for several months, he criticized the use of food coupons to exploit the desperate circumstances that encouraged workers' indebtedness. "When they do work," he complained, "the company takes practically their entire earnings for such indebtedness."[35]

The National Labor Relations Act (also known as the Wagner Act), passed in the summer of 1935 after the US Supreme Court ruled on May 27 that the NIRA was unconstitutional, strengthened the hand of workers in their efforts to unionize, but Trinity's laid-off workers continued to experience problems as they sought relief from the state. AFL organizer W. R. Williams, who met with county, state, and federal officials about the continued denial of relief, reported that state relief commission officials had conducted investigations into the matter, "but because of certain political conditions they never amounted to anything." In his view, Trinity officials had reached an understanding with

E. L. Earp, a caseworker who soon became relief administrator in Dallas, to deny relief to laid-off workers in order to force them to accept company food coupons. Williams concluded that a thorough investigation by someone outside the state of Texas "without political connections" should be conducted into the affairs of the Dallas County Relief Board: "I have thought several times that I would ask a federal grand jury to investigate this case, but I have not done this because I have felt that the company, in this open shop town, would have influence even with the grand jury, and the District Attorney who is unfavorable to organized labor."[36]

On November 13, 1935, Trinity posted a notice that it would discontinue the use of food coupons after December 1, inviting laid-off workers to apply for a final ten-dollar coupon booklet in the meantime. The president of Local 19310 complained to the director of the regional National Labor Relations Board in Fort Worth about the desperate circumstances confronting Trinity's workers. "The employees and their families at the Trinity Plant at Dallas are faced with starvation and much suffering unless they can obtain temporary aid until the plant resumes operation some time next year," L. M. Fisher Jr. said in a request for help through private charity or government aid. "Being on the payroll of the company is a detriment to those employees in obtaining work elsewhere. Relief from the Government has been denied them from time to time."[37]

By January 1936, the men laid off at Trinity's Eagle Ford plant had been employed on WPA projects, but it would be nearly three more years before they negotiated a collective bargaining contract. By then, workers at the company's Fort Worth and Houston plants had also unionized, providing added leverage against Trinity.[38] In addition, as we shall see, Trinity and other cement companies faced an important threat from state and federal officials determined to end a long-standing pricing system in the industry that disguised price-fixing and antitrust violations. At a time when Trinity continued to thwart the National Labor Relations Act and resist unionization at its Texas plants while the law's constitutionality was being tested in the federal courts, prosecutors put added pressure on cement companies to abandon pricing practices that gouged taxpayers and strained the budgets of already-strapped state and federal programs.

In 1937 the Texas State Board of Control and Highway Department, which used more than 1 million barrels of cement annually, turned to the legislature for help against the artificially inflated prices of Trinity and other cement companies. An investigative committee composed of Texas House of Representatives members Ben Sharpe, Ross Hardin, Cecil Rhodes, Fred Noritz, and Fred Felty held hearings into cement prices but filed no official report. The chair of the committee gave the testimony and documents to the attorney general, however, requesting prosecution of the cement firms under antitrust statutes. Representative Sharpe expected the firms to seek a compromise settlement in order to stop the prosecution, but he emphasized to the attorney general's office that he opposed a settlement, "for I want them brought before justice and exposed to the entire state of Texas for their unfair trade practices."[39]

In March 1938 the Texas attorney general filed suit against cement companies in the state, shortly after the Federal Trade Commission began hearings on the entire cement industry. Ralph W. Yarborough, a Texas district judge at the time, appointed former attorney general W. A. Keeling to take testimony and gather evidence in preparation for a trial in the case. Investigations revealed that in bids submitted to the WPA for the purchase of cement on WPA projects in Texas, more than 95 percent of sealed cement bids were identical, often to the fourth decimal of a penny per barrel. An official of the Southwestern Portland Cement Company in El Paso, in response to a question from the Texas attorney general's office about what he regarded as a "reasonable profit," replied, "All you can get. . . . The sky is the limit, just so we do not go beyond the point where other products that compete with cement interfere with us."[40]

While the suit against cement companies was in progress, the Texas Board of Control and Highway Department began to import a large amount of foreign cement for highway construction and maintenance work. So did small lumber companies. Cement companies complained about inadequate tariff protection and the growing importation of foreign cement, even though the use of foreign cement in part was a by-product of the industry's own monopolistic structure. For example, cement firms refused to sell cement to small lumber companies that did not belong to the Lumbermen's Association. Frustrated because they were denied access to cement at special dealers' prices, small lumber companies therefore had to buy from large domestic dealers at higher prices, or from foreign sources. W. D. Mosley of the Five Points Lumber and Wrecking Company in El Paso complained to the Texas attorney general on January 17, 1939, that out of necessity he had imported and sold cement manufactured in Mexico because the Southwestern Portland Cement Company refused to sell cement to him. Likewise, the owner of the West End Lumber Company in Houston threatened to import Belgian cement and expose the Trinity and Lone Star Cement companies for their refusal to sell him cement from their plants.[41]

Despite the cement industry's opposition to unionization, the Texas State Federation of Labor sided with the companies on the tariff question and the growing reliance on foreign cement. At its 1938 annual convention, the TSFL adopted a resolution endorsed by the Texas State Council of Cement Mill Workers and Allied Industries, protesting the use of foreign cement at a time when several cement plants in Texas were shut down.[42]

Inflated cement prices not only encouraged the importation of foreign cement but also strengthened the hand of those who had long favored a state-run cement plant operated by prison labor. The legislative committee set up to investigate the industry in Texas, in fact, recommended the creation of such a plant with labor provided by the state penitentiary to manufacture cement exclusively for state buildings and highway construction. For the general manager of Southwestern Portland Cement Company, this made it especially important to conceal the rate of profit at its Texas plant: "I dislike to show what we can make cement for at El Paso, as it would only add fuel to the fire of the advocates of the state cement plant."[43]

The Trinity Portland Cement Company, which tried to stonewall the Texas attorney general office's efforts to examine the company's files, continued to employ intimidation tactics in its ongoing campaign to maintain an open shop. In the fall of 1938 the company fired many members of the union at its Eagle Ford plant, along with several members of Local 21337 in Fort Worth, including the union president.[44]

Trinity's workers benefited, however, from the growing internal split within the ranks of organized labor when John L. Lewis and others unhappy with the AFL's outdated organizing strategy led a rebellion inside the AFL in the mid-1930s. Mavericks on the AFL's Committee on Industrial Organization criticized the AFL's philosophy of organizing skilled workers along craft lines. In 1937 the TSFL suspended ten unions affiliated with the committee after W. R. Williams, the AFL's sole organizer in Texas, met with the TSFL Executive Board. The following year, after the AFL expelled its rebellious unions, the Congress of Industrial Organizations (CIO) was formally established as a rival organization. However, the Texas State Industrial Union Council, an affiliate of the CIO, had begun organizing work in Texas the year before.[45]

The AFL, in response to critics of its craft orientation, did adopt a more aggressive industrial union strategy to bring more unskilled workers into its ranks. The Texas State Federation of Labor endorsed this shift in strategy. In 1936 the TSFL's Committee on Organization called on unions to launch a systematic campaign to organize unskilled workers, criticizing "clannish attitudes taken by the members of organizations who enroll only skilled workmen toward the common laborer and his efforts to organize."[46]

The CIO, more open to radical elements, challenged the racist practices and attitudes that had limited organized labor in the past. In some cases, companies' fears of the CIO's radicalism and more egalitarian racial attitudes led to an alliance with the AFL in order to keep the CIO out of their plants. A good example is the Lone Star Cement Company, which after being unionized by the AFL in 1937, worked with local unionists to head off CIO incursions into its plant in New Orleans. The anti-CIO hysteria reached a particularly feverish pitch among open-shop forces in Dallas, where it led to extralegal violence against organizers that went unpunished by local authorities. In 1937 Gov. James Allred sent Texas Rangers to Dallas in response to the failure of local officials to take action against the Ford Motor Company's use of thugs against CIO organizers.[47]

On August 15, 1938, the AFL's National Council of United Cement Workers, created in 1936, called for chartering an industrial union of international cement, lime, and gypsum workers. William Schoenberg, a member of the International Association of Machinists who headed the National Council of United Cement Workers, spearheaded the campaign to unionize the portland cement industry. He soon became an instrumental figure in coordinating the negotiations with Trinity and securing an AFL charter for the United Cement, Lime, and Gypsum Workers International Union on September 11, 1939.[48]

Schoenberg contacted Trinity's headquarters in Chicago and persuaded the company's general superintendent to direct Cy E. Caron to meet with an AFL representative in the company's Fort Worth office on October 19, 1938. He also asked AFL president Green to send a salaried organizer to the meeting to help find a way to avert a possible strike.[49]

At Schoenberg's request, E. L. Gibson, Trinity's general superintendent in Chicago, also came down to attend this meeting. Also in attendance were AFL representative William H. Knott, as well as company officials and a union committee from each of Trinity's three Texas plants. At the meeting, they hammered out a collective bargaining contract not only for workers at the Dallas plant but also for those employed at the company's mills in Fort Worth and Houston.[50]

On January 6, 1939, Caron and J. W. Ganser, manager of Trinity's Dallas plant, signed a one-year contract with H. N. Staley, T. V. Jordan, and H. Barker, representatives of Local 19310, which governed industrial relations at the mill. Trinity recognized the union, established grievance and arbitration procedures, and granted numerous benefits, including vacation, holiday, and overtime pay. In addition, the company provided holiday pay for black workers on June 19 rather than on July 4.[51]

Even more significantly, Trinity agreed to similar terms with the union at all three of its Texas plants. As Schoenberg pointed out, "These are the first joint agreements with any cement corporation in the United States." Furthermore, the contract contained a clause in which Trinity agreed to deduct union dues from workers' paychecks—"the first check-off of Union dues clause in any cement plant in the South."[52]

It is unclear what accounts for the policy shift on the part of Trinity officials at this time, but a couple of important considerations must be emphasized. First, given the anti-CIO hysteria in Dallas, it is reasonable to assume that in meetings with Trinity, AFL officials exploited fears of the CIO's radicalism and challenges to established racial practices. In short, Local 19310, which did not represent a threat to the racial pecking order, was a safer bet for the company.

Until late 1938 and early 1939, Trinity had pursued an antagonistic relationship with the Roosevelt administration, state of Texas, and the AFL over control of labor and pricing practices. As Trinity and other cement companies neared the end of the state of Texas's antitrust suit against them, they fully expected to lose the case. After the election of conservative Gov. W. Lee O'Daniel in 1938, in particular, they sought a more cooperative relationship with state officials. The new governor, fiercely opposed to organized labor, tapped into public fears of the CIO as he set out to destroy the new labor organization in Texas. By November 1939, the Texas attorney general's office, which had trouble getting special funds from the new legislature to pay the costs of the cement lawsuit, was more willing to accept a settlement with Trinity and the state's other cement companies.[53]

Whatever the factors that underlay Trinity's capitulation to the AFL, the struggle of workers at the Dallas plant to win recognition of their union and a collective bargaining contract had significance that went beyond their own particular case. The company's unprecedented joint agreements with workers in Dallas, Fort Worth, and Houston represented an opening wedge by unions in their drive to establish a nationwide pattern for bargaining in the industry. However, not until the nationwide strike of 1957 did cement companies drop their insistence on plant-by-plant negotiations and regional wage patterns, and accept the United Cement, Lime, and Gypsum Workers Union's demands for uniformity of wages and working conditions.[54]

Notes

This chapter originally appeared in *Southwestern Historical Quarterly* 111 (July 2007): 31–49, and is reprinted with permission.

1.   A. E. Hjerpe, Trinity Portland Cement Company, to B. H. Rader, Chairman,

Code Authority of the Portland Cement Industry, December 11, 1934, Box 320, Records of the National Recovery Administration (NRA), RG 9, National Archives (NA). On the earlier, weaker versions of the National Labor Relations Board that preceded the 1935 National Labor Relations Act, see Arthur M. Schlesinger Jr., *The Coming of the New Deal* (Boston: Houghton Mifflin, 1958), 136–51.

2. The company began its operations in Dallas as the Southwestern States Portland Cement Company. As the result of a lawsuit by the attorney general of Texas, the company was found guilty of violating antitrust laws in 1914, and subsequently reorganized and changed its name to the Trinity Portland Cement Company in 1915. The name change was a way to avoid confusion with the Southwestern Portland Cement Company, which operated mills in El Paso, TX, and Victorville, CA, and which also had been found guilty of antitrust violations in 1914. Trinity, headquartered in Chicago, used the dry process of manufacturing with fuel oil to power three kilns at its mill in Dallas, whose capacity was forty-five hundred barrels in the mid-1920s. See Ernest F. Burchard, "Cement Industry in the United States in 1910," in US Geological Survey, *Mineral Resources of the United States, Calendar Year 1910*, pt. 2: *Nonmetals*, 524–25; Robert W. Lesley, John B. Lober, and George S. Bartlett, *History of the Portland Cement Industry in the United States* (1924; repr., New York: Arno Press, 1972), 299, 300; Sidney A. Davidson Jr., *General Portland, Inc.: The Dallas Plant Story* (Dallas: General Portland, Inc., 1987), 5; "Memorandum: Anti-Trust Suit Against Cement Manufacturers," undated, 1, *State of Texas v. Lone Star Cement Corporation et al.*, Litigation Files, Records, Texas Attorney General's Office, Texas State Library and Archives Commission, Austin (hereafter cited as TSLAC). Brief sketches of the history of the Trinity plants in Texas are in Box 1, Folder "Barney C. Jones," Alex M. Troup Cement City Research Collection 2000–43 (unprocessed), Special Collections Division, University of Texas at Arlington Libraries, Arlington (hereafter cited as Special Collections Division, UTA).

3. Lesley, Lober, and Bartlett, *History of the Portland Cement Industry*, 290, 299; *Texas, Cornerstone of an Enterprise Which Serves the Heart of the Western Hemisphere: The Story of Lone Star Cement* (n.p., 1936); International Cement Corporation, *Annual Report*, 1928; Federal Trade Commission, *Report of the Federal Trade Commission on Price Bases Inquiry, the Basing-Point Formula, and Cement Prices* (Washington, DC: US Government Printing Office, 1932), 152–53. Texas Portland, which incorporated in Texas in 1914 and changed its name to Lone Star Cement Company, Texas, in 1928, owned a west Dallas plant very close by in the small sister community of Cement City, as well as a plant in Houston. Lone Star's Texas company was one of eight domestic subsidiaries of the International Cement Corporation, which also had foreign cement manufacturing subsidiaries in Argentina, Cuba, and Uruguay.

4. Claudia M. Jones and Barney C. Jones, "The History of General Portland, Inc.," 43, 45, Box 2, Folder "Barney C. Jones Information," and Sidney A. Davidson, "General Portland, Inc.: The Dallas Plant Story," 25, 29–30, Box 3, Folder "Gen-

eral Portland Story," both in Cement City Research Collection, Special Collections Division, UTA.

5. Davidson, "General Portland," 25–26, 27, 28, Box 3; Jones and Jones, "History of General Portland," 43–45, Box 2; A. M. Troup Research Associates, "Beginnings and Evolution of the Mexican American Hispanic Communities in Dallas County: People, Places and Folklore," 21–22, Box 1. All in Cement City Research Collection, Special Collections Division, UTA. On the Guanajuato origins of many Trinity workers, see also "Migration Study Finds Roots," *Dallas Morning News*, August 9, 1998. For recent studies of Mexican and African American labor in Texas during the late nineteenth and early twentieth centuries, see especially Michael R. Botson Jr., *Labor, Civil Rights, and the Hughes Tool Company* (College Station: Texas A&M University Press, 2005); Michael Botson, "Jim Crow Wearing Steel-Toed Shoes and Safety Glasses: Dual Unionism at the Hughes Tool Company, 1918–1942," *Houston Review* 16, No. 2 (1994): 101–16; Neil Foley, *The White Scourge: Mexicans, Blacks, and Poor Whites in Texas Cotton Culture* (Berkeley: University of California Press, 1997); Ernest Obadele-Starks, *Black Unionism in the Industrial South* (College Station: Texas A&M University Press, 2000); and Emilio Zamora, *The World of the Mexican Worker in Texas* (College Station: Texas A&M University Press, 1993).

6. Davidson, "General Portland," 27, Box 3, and Jones and Jones, "History of General Portland," 43–44, Box 2, both in Cement City Research Collection, Special Collections Division, UTA.

7. Ibid. Trinity's paternalism was part of the broader growth of welfare capitalism among the nation's largest corporations in the 1920s. For a discussion, see Stuart D. Brandes, *American Welfare Capitalism, 1880–1940* (Chicago: University of Chicago Press, 1970).

8. Davidson, "General Portland," 27–28, Box 3, and "Beginnings and Evolution," 243, Box 1, both in Cement City Research Collection, Special Collections Division, UTA.

9. "Wages and Hours of Labor in the Portland Cement Industry, 1929," *Monthly Labor Review* 31 (August 1930), 157–60; Davidson, "General Portland," 26, 28, Box 3, Cement City Research Collection, Special Collections Division, UTA.

10. Davidson, "General Portland," 27–28, Box 3, Cement City Research Collection, Special Collections Division, UTA. On the dangerous nature of work in the cement industry, see, for example, *Monthly Labor Review* 9 (November 1919): 261–62; Earl J. Hadley, *The Magic Powder: History of the Universal Atlas Cement Company and the Cement Industry* (New York: G. P. Putnam's Sons, 1945), 244; Gregg Andrews, *City of Dust: A Cement Company Town in the Land of Tom Sawyer* (Columbia: University of Missouri Press, 1996), 67–84.

11. Texas State Federation of Labor, *Proceedings*, 1930, 35, 37. Compensation claims by cement workers are scattered throughout the records of the Industrial Accident Board, RG 453, Archives and Information Services Division, TSLAC.

12. TSFL, *Proceedings*, 1930, 52.

13. Ibid., 66–71; Obadele-Starks, *Black Unionism*, 13–15; Zamora, *World of the*

Mexican Worker, chapter 7; American Federation of Labor, *Proceedings*, 1911, 202, 342; American Federation of Labor, *Proceedings*, 1913, 165, 168, 324, 344; Gary M. Fink, ed., *Labor Unions* (Westport, CT: Greenwood Press, 1977), 51–52. See also Andrews, *City of Dust*, 115.

14. National Recovery Administration, "Code of Fair Competition for the Cement Industry as Approved on November 27, 1933, by President Roosevelt" (Washington, DC: US Government Printing Office, 1933), 326–30; "Statement on Behalf of the Workers in the Cement Industry Affiliated with the American Federation of Labor Presented at the Public Hearing before the National Recovery Administration," July 11, 1934, Box 1318, Folder 12, NRA Records, RG 9, NA.

15. To make matters worse, Trinity officials, already strapped with heavy indebtedness because of recent investments in the Fort Worth and Houston plants, had experienced internal upheaval and costly litigation to fight off an attempted hostile corporate takeover by the highly monopolistic Ideal Cement Company. See Davidson, "General Portland," 27, and Box 1, Folder "Barney C. Jones," both in Cement City Research Collection, Special Collections Division, UTA; B. W. Bagley, "Cement," US Department of the Interior, Bureau of Mines, *Minerals Yearbook*, 1936, 801. In 1925 the Ideal Cement Company, incorporated in Colorado, had taken over all of the assets of the Cement Securities Company, which had been the subject of prosecution by the US Department of Justice in 1922 because of antitrust violations. See Federal Trade Commission, *Report of the Federal Trade Commission on Price Bases Inquiry, the Basing-Point Formula, and Cement Prices* (Washington, DC: US Government Printing Office, 1932), 148–52. William H. Sackett, clerk of the National Recovery Administration's office in El Paso, reported that the sales manager for the Southwestern Portland Cement Company, which had a plant in El Paso, "frankly stated that the NRA was a wonderful aid in putting business back on its feet," but favored voluntary arrangements with labor rather than clear-cut laws. See William H. Sackett, Clerk, El Paso Office, "Report on Attitude of Employers toward NRA Legislation," October 26, 1935, NRA Records, RG 9, NARA-SW Region, Fort Worth.

16. "Memorandum: Anti-Trust Suit Against Cement Manufacturers," undated, 6–7, *State of Texas v. Lone Star Cement Corporation et al.*, Litigation Files, Records, Texas Attorney General's Office, TSLAC.

17. John B. Schulte, President, Retail Clerks International Protective Association, to Wm. Green, President, American Federation of Labor, September 27, 1933. See also Schulte to Frank Morrison, Secretary, AFL, August 22, 1933. Both in American Federation of Labor, *Records: The Samuel Gompers Era* (microfilming edition, 1979), Reel 36 (hereafter cited as AFL *Records*), and *Dallas Morning News*, January 21, 1933.

18. L. E. Gulledge, Dallas, to Gen. Hugh S. Johnson, Administrator, NRA, February 27, 1934, Box 1320, Folder 16, NRA Records, RG 9, NA.

19. President, American Federation of Labor, to L. M. Fisher, October 29, 1934, American Federation of Labor, *Records, Part 1: Strikes and Agreements File, 1898–1953* (Frederick, MD: University Publications of America, 1985), Reel

18 (hereafter cited as AFL Strikes and Agreements File); TSFL, *Proceedings*, 1934, 64.

20. John B. Schulte, organizer, A. F. of L., Dallas, to Wm. Green, May 29, 1934, AFL Strikes and Agreements File, Reel 18; San Antonio Regional Labor Board, Weekly Report, July 7, 1934, 4, Box 1, San Antonio Regional Labor Board General Correspondence, April 1934–September 1934, Records of the National Labor Relations Board, Fort Worth Region, RG 25, NARA-SW Region, Fort Worth.

21. Schulte to Green, May 29, 1934, AFL Strikes and Agreements File, Reel 18.

22. Ibid.

23. Wm. R. Blair to L. R. Ferguson, August 28, 1934, and Ferguson to Blair, September 20, 1934, *State of Texas v. Lone Star Cement et al.*, Litigation Files, Records, Texas Attorney General's Office, TSLAC. El Paso Cement Workers Local 19533 affiliated with the Texas State Federation of Labor on May 7, 1934. See TSFL, *Proceedings*, 1934, 65. As of April 1, 1937, the lowest hourly wage rate at the Trinity plant was thirty-eight cents for common labor in the sack house, compared to forty-two cents for the same work in Lone Star's plants. See "Texas Cement Plants Wage Rates as of April 1, 1937," Litigation Files, Records, Texas Attorney General's Office, TSLAC.

24. Schulte to Green, May 29, 1934, AFL Strikes and Agreements File, Reel 18; Roger M. Busfield, Secretary, San Antonio Regional Labor Board, to Lloyd Garrison, Chairman, National Labor Relations Board, Washington, DC, July 26, 1934, Box 1, Folder 3, "Subject Files 1934–1937," Records of the National Labor Relations Board, Fort Worth Region, RG 25, NARA-SW Region, Fort Worth.

25. Schulte to Green, May 29, June 16, 1934, and Green to Schulte, June 1, 1934, AFL Strikes and Agreements File, Reel 18; San Antonio Regional Labor Board, Weekly Report, July 7, 1934, 4, Box 1, San Antonio Regional Labor Board General Correspondence, April 1934–September 1934, RG 25, NARA-SW Region, Fort Worth.

26. L. E. Gulledge to Wm. Green, August 1, 1934, and Green to Gulledge, August 23, 1934, AFL Strikes and Agreements File, Reel 18.

27. San Antonio Regional Labor Board, Weekly Report, August 9, 1934, 3, Box 1, San Antonio Regional Labor Board General Correspondence, April 1934–September 1934, RG 25, NARA-SW Region, Fort Worth.

28. L. M. Fisher, Secretary, Portland Cement Workers Union Local #19310, to Frank Morrison, Secretary, AFL, October 23, 1924, AFL Strikes and Agreements File, Reel 18.

29. Fisher to Morrison, October 23, 1924, and President, American Federation of Labor, to L. M. Fisher, October 29, 1934, AFL Strikes and Agreements File, Reel 18.

30. *Portland Cement Workers Union No. 19310, Dallas, v. Trinity Portland Cement Company, Dallas*, Aug. 12, 1934, Box 1, Decisions, November 1934–April 1935, RG 25, NARA-SW Region, Fort Worth. The San Antonio region of the National Labor Relations Board was abolished in September 1934. After that date,

the region was divided between New Orleans (District 7) and Fort Worth (District 13).

31.   Ibid.; "Summary: The Portland Cement Industry," 92–93, Box 1319, and A. E. Hjerpe, Trinity Portland Cement Company, to B. H. Rader, Chairman, Code Authority of the Portland Cement Industry, December 11, 1934, Box 320, both in NRA Records, RG 9, NA.

32.   "Report to National Labor Relations Board, Week of October 7–13, 1934," "Weekly Report of the Fort Worth Regional Labor Board, Thirteenth District, Week of December 16–22, 1934," both in folder "Correspondence September 1934–December 1934"; and "Report to the NLRB from Regional Labor Board, Thirteenth District, Ft. Worth, Texas," Folder "Correspondence January 1935–June 1935." All in Box 1, Records of the National Labor Relations Board, Fort Worth Region, RG 25, NARA-SW Region, Fort Worth.

33.   L. M. Fisher Jr., President, to Dr. Edwin A. Elliott, Director, National Labor Relations Board, Fort Worth, November 14, 1935, AFL Strikes and Agreements File, Reel 18; Adam R. Johnson to Dallas County Relief Board, January 18, 1935, Adam R. Johnson Papers, 1934–1938, 1985/165, TSLAC.

34.   Fisher to Elliott, November 14, 1935, AFL Strikes and Agreements File, Reel 18.

35.   Ibid.

36.   W. R. Williams to Wm. Green, January 23, 1936, AFL Strikes and Agreements File, Reel 18. At the time, Dallas was also the scene of a highly publicized strike by women in the garment industry that led to violence and the arrests of strikers. Gov. James Allred appointed a committee to investigate the underlying problems and recommend legislation. See, for example, *Dallas Morning News*, July 7, 8, 1935, and George N. Green, "ILGWU in Texas, 1930–1970," *Journal of Mexican American History* 1 (Spring 1971): 144–69.

37.   Fisher to Elliott, November 14, 1935, AFL Strikes and Agreements File, Reel 18.

38.   Williams to Green, January 23, 1936, AFL Strikes and Agreements File, Reel 18.

39.   Ben H. Sharpe to Victor W. Bouldin, July 17, 1937; "Memorandum: Anti-Trust Suit Against Cement Manufacturers," undated, 1–2; "Report of Legislative Committee Appointed by 45th Legislature to Investigate the Cement Industry in Texas," undated, 1; "Memorandum," enclosed in Victor W. Bouldin to Honorable Alfred Petsch, January 13, 1939; all in *State of Texas v. Lone Star Cement et al.*, Litigation Files, Records, Texas Attorney General's Office, TSLAC.

40.   "Report of Legislative Committee," 2, and "Memorandum," 2–3, both in *State of Texas v. Lone Star Cement et al.*, Litigation Files, Records, Texas Attorney General's Office, TSLAC. The quote is in the "Memorandum," p. 13. For a discussion of the industry's multiple basing-point system, which had been upheld by a business-friendly US Supreme Court in 1925, see Samuel Loescher, *Imperfect Collusion in the Cement Industry* (Cambridge, MA: Harvard University Press, 1959), 181–85, 243–63, and David Lynch, *The Concentration of Economic Power* (1946; repr.; New York: Johnson Reprint Corporation, 1970), 182–83, 340. The Cement Institute, to which most cement companies belonged, policed its members to discourage them from charging lower prices that undercut the industry's

pricing system, which the FTC and the US Supreme Court forced the industry to abandon in 1948. See *Federal Trade Commission v. Cement Institute et al.*, October term, 1947, *United States Supreme Court Reports*, book 92 (Rochester, NY: Lawyers Co-operative Publishing Company, 1948), 1010–55, and Andrews, *City of Dust*, 268–72.

41. W. D. Mosley to Attorney General, January 17, 1939, and report filed by Loran L. Adkins, a Lone Star Cement Company salesman, on July 1, 1931, enclosed in Lewis R. Ferguson, Vice President, Lone Star Cement Company, Texas, to H. C. Koch, July 28, 1931, *State of Texas v. Lone Star Cement et al.*, Litigation Files, Records, Attorney General's Office, TSLAC. Foreign cement imports into the United States nearly tripled between 1935 and 1937, rising from 618,043 to 1,792,018 barrels. See Lone Star Cement Corporation, "Report of the President," March 29, 1939, *Annual Report*, 1938.

42. TSFL, *Proceedings*, 1938, 152–53.

43. "Memorandum," 11, *State of Texas v. Lone Star Cement et al.*, Litigation Files, Records, Texas Attorney General's Office, TSLAC. According to the *Houston Labor Journal*, April 14, 1933, a bill to create a state cement plant was introduced in the Texas legislature during every new session.

44. William Schoenberg to William Green, October 17, 1938, AFL Strikes and Agreements File, Reel 18. On the strained contacts between Trinity and the Texas attorney general's office, see, for example, A. E. Hjerpe to Victor Bouldin, Assistant Attorney General, December 16, 1937, Victor Bouldin to A. E. Hjerpe, December 18, 1937, William H. Flippen to Vick Bouldin, December 21, 1937, all in *State of Texas v. Lone Star Cement et al.*, Litigation Files, Records, Attorney General's Office, TSLAC.

45. TSFL, *Proceedings*, 1937, 37. On the CIO, see especially Robert H. Zieger, *The CIO, 1935–1955* (Chapel Hill: University of North Carolina Press, 1995). See Murray Polakoff, "The Development of the Texas State CIO Council" (PhD diss., University of Texas, 1955).

46. TSFL, *Proceedings*, 1936, 61–62.

47. Schoenberg to Green, January 8, 1942, AFL *Records*, pt. 2, ser. A, 1934–1952, Reel 25. Just a few years later, the CIO took advantage of the AFL's poor relations with black workers to snatch away the Lone Star Cement Company's plants in Dallas, Houston, and New Orleans. See TSFL, *Proceedings*, 1946, 63–67. On the Ford violence, see, for example, Carl Brannin, "Anti-Union Terror Reigns in Dallas as Police Ignore Beatings," *Federated Press*, August 13, 1937, Box 1, Folder 2, Carl Brannin Papers, Collection No. 91, UTA. On the liberal orientation and policies of Governor Allred, see, for example, George Norris Green, *The Establishment in Texas Politics: The Primitive Years, 1938–1957* (Westport, CT: Greenwood Press, 1979), 14, and Seth Shepard McKay, *Texas Politics, 1906–1944* (Lubbock: Texas Tech University Press, 1952), 290–93.

48. AFL, *Proceedings*, 1939, 46–47. On the creation of the National Council of United Cement Workers, see William Schoenberg, "The National Council of United Cement Workers," *American Federationist* 44 (April, 1937): 396–99.

49. Schoenberg to Green, October 17, 1938, AFL Strikes and Agreements File, Reel 18. Union on September 11, 1939.

50. Green to Schoenberg, October 18, 1938; Green to Schoenberg, January 18, 1939; both in AFL Strikes and Agreements File, Reel 18.

51. Schoenberg, National Council of United Cement Workers, to Green, January 7, 1939, AFL, Strikes and Agreements File, Reel 41.

52. Ibid. Copies of all three agreements are in this file.

53. "Memorandum: Anti-Trust Suit against Cement Manufacturers," 3–4; Victor W. Bouldin, Assistant Attorney General, to Honorable Homer Thornberry, April 4, 1939; Bouldin to Honorable Paris Smith, April 6, 1939; Bouldin to Ethel E. Fisher and Associates, Inc., May 10, 1939; Bouldin to J. P. Early, October 5, 1939; Bouldin to Walter Koch, November 2, 1939. All in *State of Texas v. Lone Star Cement et al.*, Litigation Files, Records, Texas Attorney General's Office, TSLAC.

54. On pattern bargaining in the industry, see Herbert R. Northrup, "From Union Hegemony to Union Disintegration: Collective Bargaining in Cement and Related Industries," *Journal of Labor Research* 10 (Fall 1989): 337–76.

GEORGE N. GREEN

Discord in Dallas

Auto Workers, City Fathers, and the Ford
Motor Company, 1937–1941

As auto workers and other factory laborers joined the Congress of Industrial Organizations (CIO) by the millions in the late 1930s, the workforce at the Ford Motor Company in Dallas was not involved in the process—even though local headlines in 1937 indicated that there were considerable labor difficulties at the plant. United Automobile Workers' unionization efforts were virtually nil in Dallas, and the city's autoworkers were unresponsive, if not hostile, to unions anyway. Yet the city and the Ford company went to great lengths to prevent the men from organizing. Why, in the face of so little threat, did so many people act against unions? An account of Dallas's labor troubles in 1937 and the unusual context in which they occurred may ultimately reward us with fresh insights into the story of American unions.

Along with many other industries at the time, the Dallas assembly plant at 5200 East Grand abused its workers in order to maintain a rate of production that would maximize profits. The most oppressive practice was the speedup, which forced workers to strain themselves to the limit of endurance in order to keep up. The same production was expected for the day even if the line had stopped for a few hours or some men had been laid off. Consequently, the men often toiled twelve or more hours a day but were paid for only eight. Men often worked with injuries and illnesses, prodded by the foremen's constant threats in the 1930s to give their jobs "to a one-armed nigger" or "a guy living on a cracker." The plant also fired most workers when all orders had been fulfilled for the year. Three or four months later, when it was time for production of the new model, no one was guaranteed employment. The plant shut down for over a year in 1932–34, and no one in Dallas knew if it would ever reopen. Besides the lack of job security, there was no seniority or grievance machinery. Some foremen would fire good hands and replace them with friends and relatives. There were no rest periods, no relief from extreme heat in the summer, and often no time for a drink of water or a visit to the restroom. Half the thirty-minute lunch break was spent in preparing to go back on the line.[1]

Even more debasing to the employees was the company's spy system and policy of persecution, spawned by Henry Ford's paranoia about unions. Ford tested the system at the main plant in Dearborn, then began to install it in all company plants—under the Service Department—with the express purpose of preventing unionization. The branch management at Dallas, after watching the United Auto Workers (UAW) take root in Ford's Kansas City plant in the spring of 1937, took some twenty husky workers off the line (along with one sent especially from Dearborn) and assigned this "outside squad" to cruise around Dallas and neighboring areas to ferret out possible information about efforts to organize the Dallas plant. Some were assigned to bus and airline terminals and the rail stations. There is some evidence that they had a network in all the larger cities of Texas and hoped to smash unionism, especially the CIO, throughout the state. Anyone suspected of union sympathies was, generally speaking, to be beaten senseless.[2]

In May 1937 the US Supreme Court upheld the Wagner Act, which legitimized collective bargaining and, among other provisions, forbade employers from coercing employees in the exercise of their right to organize. In June 1937, two UAW representatives from Kansas City appeared outside the factory and began talking to some of the men who were leaving, some of whom reported everything to the company. Both were soon pummeled in broad daylight, one so severely that he had several broken ribs. Anticipating more action, the plant's maintenance department then manufactured blackjacks, whips, and rubber hoses for the outside squad. The company also formed the "inside squad"—mostly a spy network listening for union sentiments or just job dissatisfaction—to prevent the possibility of secret organization from within. Antiunion literature was widely distributed in the plant, and a mass meeting of Dallas Ford workers in July denounced strikes and any need for the CIO.[3]

On July 10 the outside squad searched for attorney W. J. Houston, who had been retained by the UAW, and beat him up in daylight at the corner of Elm and Akard Streets in the heart of downtown Dallas. He was sent to the hospital. For good measure, a client who happened to be with him was also slugged. Later that month the outside squad managed to tap Houston's home phone in a vain attempt top intercept UAW strategy talks. Houston closed his law office and moved from Dallas.[4]

The next victims were twin brothers who were in business together and who were never connected with any union. One of them, however, often discussed labor matters with a Ford employee and openly stated his support of unions. After the failure of an attempt to draw the businessman into a phony scheme of signing up Ford workers for the UAW, the outside squad thought they had successfully lured him to a rendezvous, where he was bashed from behind and kicked repeatedly while lying on the ground. They had the wrong brother. Remaining under a doctor's care for the next four months, the man died from pneumonia developed while recuperating from his injuries.[5]

Other assaults in the summer and fall included the whipping and kicking of an autoworker from Kansas City, who was not a member of any union, the slugging into unconsciousness (and whipping with a cat-o'-nine-tails) of a former autoworker from Kansas City who applied for a job at the Dallas Ford plant, and the beating of three tourists from California at the fairgrounds parking lot because of a CIO sticker on their car. Dallas Ford workers were also victimized: one was blackjacked because he was suspected of not being a diligent spy against an alleged CIO man, two were kidnapped and roughed up for supposed pro-union remarks, and two were beaten for alleged pro-union sympathies.[6]

The most spectacular attacks occurred in August. On August 9 the outside squad was tipped off by Dallas police that an American Federation of Labor (AFL) organizer was attempting to unionize the local millinery industry. Veteran organizer George Baer was assaulted in daylight and his face was repeatedly smashed with blackjacks until most of his teeth were missing and an eye was knocked out of its socket. Dumped into a field, he later crawled to a highway and a passing motorist took him to a hospital. He lost the teeth and the sight of one eye.[7]

That same evening of August 9, 1937, the inside and outside squads collaborated in an attack at a Textile Workers Organizing Committee meeting in a public park, where a couple of labor movies were being shown. One CIO organizer, George Lambert, was beaten severely, while the other, Herbert Harris, was knocked unconscious, tarred and feathered, and dumped on the doorstep of the *Dallas Morning News*, where a photographer awaited. Even the tar, feathers, and brush were supplied by the local Ford plant.

The Baer and Harris incidents were widely publicized around the country; Harris's picture was carried in *Look* magazine. Gov. Jimmie Allred, over the protests of the chief of police, promptly dispatched Texas Rangers to Dallas, and the outside squad slowed its activities and shut down a few months later. The outside squad did not seem to be intimidated by the Rangers, however, since more assaults occurred in October. The squad shut down because the Rangers had forestalled some attacks and because the violent antiunion strategy had succeeded and was no longer necessary. In all, there were eighteen known victims of beatings, with perhaps as many as twice that number that went unreported.[8]

Nonviolent discrimination was also practiced. One Ford worker was fired and threatened with a beating because his wife was a member of the milliners' union. Another lost his job and came very close to being battered after being surrounded by six thugs, because he had joined an independent electricians' association, one not affiliated with the AFL or the CIO.[9]

On the face of it, there is nothing unusual about these events. They appear typical of the management-inspired maimings of the time. Perhaps the mistaken murder and the tarring and feathering were a shade more bizarre than most, but these Dallas beatings nevertheless resemble others in 1937 in San Francisco, Chicago, Minneapolis, Detroit, Aliquippa, the Yakima and Imperial Valleys, and other industrial and agrarian centers—with one glaring difference. There was no union movement at the Dallas Ford plant!

It does not appear that Ford's erratic policy completely explains the absence of union activity in the Dallas plant. The majority of those beaten in the eighteen documented assaults were not union organizers or members of the UAW, and seven were not members of any union. The five known attacks on Dallas Ford workers, none of whom was attempting to form a union, were the least violent and spectacular assaults. Technically, nearly all the workers at the assembly plant were members of the inside squad. The worker who was fired because of his wife's union membership immediately persuaded her to resign from the union, which the company deemed an insufficient response. The other one who was discharged quickly resigned his membership in the independent electrical union, but again the Ford management was unimpressed. After taking hundreds of thousands of words of testimony, the National Labor Relations Board determined that only these two out of a fifteen-hundred-man workforce were unjustly fired; their jobs, of course, were restored.

To be sure, Dallas Ford management intimidated the workers and played upon community fears with threats that Ford would abandon the Dallas plant before it would recognize the CIO or (somewhat contradictorily) that the CIO would bring many blacks into the factory. But these and similar charges were spread all over the country without preventing the stirrings of unionism. One might be tempted to explain the dearth of Dallas Ford unionism on the grounds that the workforce was composed of provincial Anglo-Saxon Protestants, ignorant and gullible southern and southwestern country boys. They were trekking to the city, making more money than they had ever known before, and were all too ready to believe whatever the company told them. But this composite picture would match those of most Sunbelt workers—mill hands throughout the Southeast, oil refinery workers in California, Oklahoma, and Texas, rubber workers in Los Angeles and Gadsden, Alabama, sugar refinery hands in Texas and Louisiana—all of whom were forming unions, sometimes without much help from outside.[10]

Much of the explanation for the absence of a union spirit undoubtedly rests with the city of Dallas. At the time Dallas was more of a distributing than a manufacturing center, and most Dallas businesses were in the hands of first-generation owners who greatly feared the possible loss of absolute control over their companies. The chamber of commerce and the Dallas Open Shop Association sought to induce industries to move to the city by advertising its cheap labor. Even a fleeting visitor in 1940 noted the city's "passionate devotion to the open shop," and in labor circles Dallas was generally recognized as the worst open-shop bastion in the United States. The building and construction trades represented the bulk of AFL membership, while only the Typographers and International Ladies' Garment Workers Union represented the CIO.

The Dallas Open Shop Association, formed in 1919, remained as one of the strongest, most tightly knit organizations in the country twenty years later. It boasted that it kept the city free from strikes and labor disturbances in general. In 1937, National Labor Relations Board hearings on a garment strike revealed that one of the Dallas Open Shop Association's rules held that any business holding membership in the association that knowingly hired a union member was subject to a three-thousand-dollar fine. The association guaranteed that no member firm would be permitted to go bankrupt as result of a strike, and it reputedly had two or three million dollars to back up the promise.[11]

That same year of 1937, Dallas's leading bankers and merchants organized the Dallas Citizens' Council, purportedly the nearest thing to a mercantile oligarchy since the Italian Renaissance cities. Described by a sympathizer as a "super-elite Chamber of Commerce and advisory board to the city council," many of its members served on the city council, as officials in the chamber of commerce, and as leaders in the Dallas Open Shop Association (whose office was in the Chamber of Commerce Building). The chamber staff actually implemented Citizens' Council projects, and it was the chamber's board of directors that secured a charter and incorporated the Dallas Open Shop Association in 1919.

In the midst of the labor assaults, in October 1937, the chamber reaffirmed its commitment to the open shop association and its principles. These "decision makers" were good friends who almost never argued and who all thought alike on almost every subject. Certainly the interlocking directorate of these three organizations and the Ford Motor Company all thought alike on the subject of unions, and none took any public notice of the beatings. One spokesman did. Dale Miller, associate editor of Dallas's conservative *Texas Weekly* (later hired by the chamber of commerce as its lobbyist in Washington, DC), reported that the various beatings were "unrelated incidents," that they had nothing to do with the Ford company, that the only (slight) labor disorder in the city was in the millinery industry, and that unions were "unnatural curtailments" of capitalism.[12]

While the Citizens' Council did not completely capture city hall in the 1937 municipal elections, the city was firmly in the hands of businessmen. The upper class and business community were split in the mid-1930s over such issues as sewer taxes, the rigidity of law enforcement during the Texas Centennial, and the extent of city involvement in the levee improvement district. There is certainly no evidence that they were divided on currying the favor of the Ford company.[13]

Few in Dallas expected the police to make more than a perfunctory gesture toward apprehending the terrorists. Various policemen abandoned the sites of beatings where they were normally on duty, tipped off the outside squad on the presence of labor organizers, connived with Ford officials in farcical arrests, and on one occasion, when three of the outside squad were arrested, advised them to dispose of the blackjacks if they had them. Just after the tarring and feathering incident the police chief announced that he was going to stop such violence by closing the parks to meetings that were likely to cause trouble. He canceled the order after the *Dallas Journal* suggested that—following the same line of reasoning—the chief might prevent auto accidents in the city by closing all the streets to traffic. The only person arrested on that occasion was George Lambert, a victim of the mob.[14]

Dallas mayor George Sprague denied Governor Allred's charge that nothing was done about the violence until the Rangers arrived. The mayor claimed that the police had done "a lot of good work" and that "Police Chief Bob Jones . . . had the guilty men about cornered." Jones agreed and added that the grand jury had the facts before it. Two days later the grand jury noted that it had no tangible evidence regarding the identity of Harris's kidnappers. Five men were arrested after some of the assaults, but bail was paid by Ford supervisor J. B. Moseley and there were never any trials.[15]

After the assaults on August 9 one of the victims, socialist CIO organizer Lambert, tried to persuade local liberals to stage a mass protest. Led by an Episcopalian minister, they refused to call a meeting on account of the hot weather and the fear of being identified with socialism. Dallas's small band of socialists—led by George Clifton Edwards, Carl Brannin, and Lambert—appeared to be labor's leading defenders in the city. The only other group that spoke out were forty CIO printers, whose letter to the editor was published by the *Dallas Morning News* on August 24, 1937, though the men identified themselves only as "taxpaying citizens."[16]

In such an atmosphere the split within the house of labor was painfully obvious. The AFL's *Dallas Craftsman* never even mentioned the Ford terror. The local trades' assembly offered the open shop association and the chamber of commerce its services in keeping the CIO out of Dallas. The assembly vainly tried to prevent several local clothing manufacturers from signing or renewing CIO contracts by threatening to boycott their products. AFL president William Green spoke in Dallas on Labor Day and consorted openly with members of the chamber of commerce while lambasting the CIO. He neglected to mention that one of his organizers had almost been killed in Dallas three weeks earlier.[17]

Dallas newspapers, very much part of the city's establishment, denounced the beatings and defended free speech on occasion, but they consistently played down the violence and rarely identified it with the Ford company. The city's most prestigious paper, the *Dallas Morning News*, presented a picture of Harris, tarred and feathered, and stated that the incident was carried out by twenty unidentified men. Three years later the NLRB hearings revealed that Ford's outside squad had made plans with a *News* photographer to dump the victim near the newspaper building so the photographer could get the picture. The *News* account of the assault on Baer on the same day stated that the attackers were unidentified and implied that the incident resulted from trouble between the AFL and the CIO. At least five of the assaults, including four against Ford employees, were not even mentioned by the *News*. After the governor sent Rangers to Dallas, the *News* published seventeen telegrams criticizing him for the action, accusing him of being a socialist and a stooge of John L. Lewis. The leader of the protestors, F. M. Salas, described himself as an uninterested party. The *News* was evidently unconcerned about the veracity of these claims. Salas was the owner of the Ford plant service station next to the company. The story also reported that Leon Armstrong had called the paper to criticize the move and had sent a telegram to the governor. The paper did not point out that he was the personal secretary to the Ford plant superintendent and that his telegram was signed by Ford's inside squad.[18]

The Dallas establishment's coverup and the Ford company's terrorism might have succeeded had the company realized that gunmen cannot easily be fired from their jobs. Ford's outside squad returned to work in the plant in October

1937, but in the spring and summer of 1939 four of them were fired, two because of thefts they had committed in the plant. One of them began to talk to the NLRB, and the seamy story reached a wider audience. The revelations, predictably, received scant coverage in the Dallas media.[19]

When the NLRB began holding hearings on charges against the Ford Motor Company of Dallas, the *New York Times* sent its best labor reporter to cover the trial, and he remained over a week. The *Times* carried his detailed stories about the proceedings, and after the trial was over, a complete account of the trial and the NLRB decision. The *Wall Street Journal* excerpted some of the testimony in several front-page stories. Through more than a million words and over a month of testimony the *Dallas Morning News* gave its readers 112 column inches of space, counting headlines. The minute coverage was accompanied by a continuous failure to give accurate information on the charges against the company. Not a line of testimony was presented until the twelfth day, and then much of the story was devoted to attacks on labor board procedures as being unfair to Ford. The longest account to appear in the *News* came March 10, 1940, and opened: "One of the most bitterly criticized federal agencies created by the New Deal is conducting a hearing in Dallas." After this article the *News'* coverage trailed off. The *Dallas Journal* started with better coverage than the *News*, but soon slacked off to a few small stories that were buried in the back and that ignored testimony that was damaging to the Ford company. The *Dallas Times-Herald* gave more coverage than either of the other two dailies, but just used Associated Press reports and tended to stress the Ford attorneys' complaints about the trial and their insistence that the violence was not connected to the company.[20]

There is absolutely no reason to doubt that Dallas publishers were sincere in clinging to the same attitudes toward the New Deal and the NLRB that were held by the Ford company. In any event, no one in the city's power elite was inclined to criticize local manufacturers. Had there been any contrary notion, however, it doubtless would have been crowded out by the advertising of car dealers. The Ben Griffin and Ed Maher Ford dealers were consistent advertisers in the *Dallas News*, often placing three or four ads per day. They sometimes combined with other area Ford dealers to buy almost a full-page ad. Griffin and Maher also advertised in the *Times-Herald*.[21]

To a degree, the Dallas Ford tactics were emulated in other branch plants (and in Dearborn itself). In Memphis the threat of removing the huge Ford payroll was sufficient to make the city officials cooperate in the suppression of unionism, but they managed to do so without precipitating much violence. Much the same was true in Kansas City, where the company closed its plant and announced that it would not reopen until the city could guarantee "proper protection" to Ford employees. The Kansas City plant reopened only after the city manager journeyed to Dearborn and gave the guarantee. Thereafter, the city police were used as strikebreakers, though apparently there was little or no violence there either. At the mighty River Rouge plant in Dearborn the local outside squad ambushed and slugged Walter Reuther and another UAW organizer at the famous Battle of the Overpass in 1937, while the company fired at least twenty-nine workers for union activity. In 1941 the River Rouge management fired more union activists and deliberately fomented racial violence between groups of white picketers carrying baseball bats and black strikebreakers armed with knives and bars. Even this violence did not quite equal that in Dallas, and of course the assaults in Dearborn occurred in the midst of strong and successful unionization efforts.[22]

Historians, particularly those of the "new left," have asked what it was that led four million people to join the CIO and half a million to stage sit-down strikes in 1936 and 1937. Some of them believe that hidden in the labor history of the 1930s is a strain of rank-and-file militancy with a genuine, if unfulfilled, revolutionary potential. More conventional labor historians have noted that even in the great strikes in the mass production industries only a minority of rank-and-file workers were involved.[23] What can either camp say about the Dallas Ford workers? Clearly there was no revolutionary sentiment whatever. More surprising, as of 1937, not even a minority of the workers—beyond perhaps a few individuals who certainly kept their thoughts to themselves—favored unionism at all, much less militancy.

One of Henry Ford's biographers concluded that the Dallas tactics "approached a degree of savagery that was extreme even for Ford Service."[24] Yet the public revelations of the Dallas terror in August 1940 did not have a national impact. Dallas Ford workers played no role in forcing unionism on the company. It was the hearings and orders of the NLRB in the River Rouge case, the rulings of various courts, and the actions of Michigan autoworkers that brought the unions into Ford plants nationwide.[25] To be sure, Ford's Dallas employees voted for UAW representation in 1941 by the customary thumping majority, but the men were told that their jobs depended on it. It was more in keeping with the heritage of Dallas and Ford that the first local union chairman was a "chamber of commerce type" who opposed the UAW until Ford signed the national contract.[26]

Once the Dallas Ford workers were in a union, however, the men soon perceived the advantages of it. The UAW had an effective education program. In three months the original chairman was replaced by an elected president, executive board, and committeemen. Well-attended departmental meetings informed the entire membership about grievance procedures. Wages and working conditions soon improved. Within six months, in December 1941, Local 870 was dispatching a telegram to Speaker of the House Sam Rayburn noting its opposition to all antistrike and antilabor legislation. Over the years the local produced two southwest area directors of the UAW and played a vigorous role in community, CIO, and UAW politics until Ford closed the aging plant in 1970.[27]

Clearly, though, the particular combination of Dallas and Ford was a poisonous blend for workingmen until 1941. It was a unique situation in some ways but also an illustration of the obstacles faced by Texas unionism. In 1941 Texas unions represented less than 15 percent of the workforce, while the US average was 23 percent.[28] Certainly the Dallas-Ford intermixture was one reason for the weakness of unions in Texas, even while they were expanding in most of the rest of the nation in the late 1930s.

Notes

This chapter originally appeared in *Labor's Heritage* 1, No. 3 (July 1989): 21–33, and is reprinted with permission.

1. United Auto Workers Local 870 brochure and Hiram Moon, Area Director of UAW, interview by Travis Polk, July 16, 1965, cited in Travis Polk, "The Ford Motor Company's Resistance to the Labor Movement in Dallas, Texas" (master's thesis, North Texas State University, 1966), 8–10; Allan Nevins and Frank Hill, *Ford: Decline and Rebirth* (New York: Charles Scribner Sons, 1963), 153; Robert Dunn, *Labor and Automobiles* (New York: International Publishers, 1929), 88–91, 108, 136–37; Dallas Ford workers of the 1930s, Roy Alexander, Claude Cawthon, R. C. Stubbs, E. H. Veach, Rufus Fleming, Earl Edwards, Jim Gathings, and W. M. Shields, interviews by author, April 1–29, 1988, Dallas, TX.

2. National Labor Relations Board v. the Ford Motor Company, No. 9679, Transcript of Testimony, 1:173–75, and 4:2603–4 (5th Circuit, 1940), Dallas Ford Motor Company Collection, 89-1-5 and 89-4-1, Texas Labor Archives, University of Texas at Arlington; Edwin Elliot, Regional Director, NLRB, interview by author, April 7, 1975, Oral History Project, Texas Labor Archives; Irving Bernstein, *Turbulent Years* (Boston: Houghton Mifflin, 1971), 735–40.

3. Transcript of Testimony, 1:180–82, and 3:1673–80; in re Ford Motor Company, *Decisions and Orders of the National Labor Relations Board*, 26 (hereafter *NLRB Decisions*), 338; Edwin Elliot, interview by author; H. C. McGarity, Ford worker, interview by author, April 22, 1987, Oral History Project, Texas Labor Archives; Nat Wells, "The NLRB at the Dallas Ford Plant," unpublished manuscript, 5–7,

Dallas Ford Motor Company Collection, 89-1-1; Dale Miller, "Message to the CIO," *Texas Weekly*, July 3, 1937, 9; Lloyd Morris, *Not So Long Ago* (New York: Random House, 1949), 366–67.

4. Transcript of Testimony, 1:197–201, 227–29; Wells, "NLRB at the Dallas Ford Plant," 12.

5. *NLRB Decisions*, 62; Transcript of Testimony, 1:208–13.

6. *NLRB Decisions*, 353–54, 361062; Transcript of Testimony, 1:195–97, 237–50.

7. *NLRB Decisions*, 363–65; Transcript of Testimony, 1:214, and 3:1710–13.

8. *NLRB Decisions*, 366; Transcript of Testimony, 1:191, 219–20; Miller, "Message to the CIO," 4; George Clifton Edwards Jr., *Pioneer-at-Law* (New York: W. W. Norton, 1974), 170, 172–73; Wells, "NLRB at the Dallas Ford Plant," 9; George Lambert, union organizer, interview by author, February 6, 1972, Oral History Project, Texas Labor Archives; Carl Brannin, socialist journalist, interview by author, April 12, 1967, Oral History Project, Texas Labor Archives; Doug Flamming, "Labor and the Press in Dallas, Texas, 1937 and 1940," *Essays in History*, E. C. Barksdale Student Lectures, 7 (Arlington: University of Texas at Arlington Press, 1982), 131–36; *Look*, October 12, 1937, 9.

9. *NLRB Decisions*, 385–86; Transcript of Testimony, 1:273–78; Nat Wells, labor lawyer, interview by Polk, July 9, 1965, in Polk, "Ford Motor Company's Resistance," 57; Wells, "NLRB at the Dallas Ford Plant," 8.

10. Nevins and Hill, *Ford: Decline and Rebirth*, 142; *NLRB Decisions*, 386; Transcript of Testimony, 1:275–76; Moon interview; *UAW Citizen*, 5; UAW brochure quoted in Polk, "The Ford Motor Company's Resistance," 26; Alexander, Cawthon, Stubbs, Veach, Fleming, Edwards, Gathings, Shields, and McGarity interviews; Edwards, *Pioneer-at-Law*, 163, 173.

11. George Lambert interview; George Lambert, "Dallas Tries Terror," *Nation* 145 (October, 9 1937): 376–78; Miller, "Message to the CIO," 5; *Dallas Typographical Union,* No. 173, *Minutes*, July 25, 1937, 41–43, in 41-3-2, Texas Labor Archives; "open shop" quote in David Cohn, "Dallas," *Atlantic Monthly* 166 (October 1940): 454; "cheap labor" quote in Wells, "NLRB at the Dallas Ford Plant," 1; Andrew DeShong, Dallas Chamber of Commerce, interview by author, April 23, 1987, Oral History Project, Texas Labor Archives. DeShong, who edited the chamber's magazine in the late 1930s, denied that either the Chamber or the Open Shop Association recruited cheap labor.

12. George Lambert and Andrew DeShong interviews; John Rogers, *The Lusty Texans of Dallas* (New York: E. P. Dutton, 1965), 346–50; *Southwest Business*, October 1937, 25; Miller, "Message to the CIO," 4–5; E. C. Wallis, "After Dallas Threw Off the Shackles of the Closed Shop," *Manufacturers Record*, February 13, 1930, 53. The lack of public notice was apparent in the chamber's magazine, *Southwest Business*, in the minutes of the city council, and in the newspapers for 1937.

13. Harold Stone, Don Price, and Kathryn Stone, *City Manager Government in Dallas* (Chicago: Public Administration Service, 1939), 52–57, 64–71, 79, 81.

14. Transcript of Testimony, 1:199–201, 213–20, 414, 652, 655, 658; *NLRB Decisions*, 370; *Dallas Morning News*, August 23–25, 27, 1937; Lambert, "Dallas Tries Terror," 377; Carl Brannin interview; Edwards, *Pioneer-at-Law,* 169. The *Dallas Police Department Time Book, 1937–1939*, No. 103, Dallas Police Archives, Dallas Public Library, shows that a traffic policeman was on duty at Elm and Akard and Main and Akard throughout every day in October 1937, but this is the earliest time that such records were kept. There are no records for July 10, when W. J. Houston and his client were beaten there. A policeman did arrive to break up the assault, but only after Houston was reeling.

15. *Dallas Morning News*, August 23, 25, 1937; Edwards, *Pioneer-at-Law*, 157–67, 169.

16. *Dallas Morning News*, August 24, 1937; Flamming, "Labor and the Press in Dallas," 133–34; Edwards, *Pioneer-at-Law*, 157–67, 169; George Lambert to American Civil Liberties Union and Workers Defense League, August 19, 1937, in Workers Defense League Papers, Series 1, Box 40, File 2, Walter P. Reuther Library of Labor and Urban Affairs, Wayne State University, Detroit (hereafter Reuther Library).

17. Carl Brannin to Workers Defense League, n.d., and George Lambert to American Civil Liberties Union and Workers Defense League, August 19, 1937, Workers Defense League Papers, Series 1, Box 40, File 2, Reuther Library; Lambert, "Dallas Tries Terror," 377; *Dallas Morning News*, July 1–3, 1937. There is no indication, however, of the extent to which Green actually knew of the Ford terror. No correspondence on the matter appears to exist in the pertinent extant files of the George Meany Memorial Archives.

18. *Dallas Morning News*, August 10–11, 15, 20–22, and October 7, 27, 1937; Flamming, "Labor and the Press in Dallas," 128–29, 132–33; Polk, "Ford Motor Company's Resistance," 46–47; Vance Sumner, "Labor Policy of the Ford Motor Company at Dallas, Texas" (master's thesis, North Texas State University, 1942), 67–75.

19. Polk, "Ford Motor Company's Resistance," 68–73.

20. Carl Brannin to Roger Baldwin, March 5, 1940, American Civil Liberties Union Papers, Vol. 2246, Seeley Mudd Library, Princeton, NJ; Carl Brannin column, *Emancipator*, April 1940; Sumner, "Labor Policy of the Ford Motor Company at Dallas, Texas," 75–86; Flamming, "Labor and the Press in Dallas," 138–42.

21. Flamming, "Labor and the Press in Dallas," 143.

22. George Lambert, "Memphis Is Safe for Ford," *Nation* 146 (January 22, 1938), 93–94; Bernstein, *Turbulent Years*, 570–71, 740–45.

23. See David Brody, *Workers in Industrial America* (New York: Oxford University Press, 1980), 134–35, 157, 165.

24. Keith Sward, *The Legend of Henry Ford* (New York: Rinehart, 1948), 398.

25. John Forsythe, "The Effect of Federal Labor Legislation on Organizing Southern Labor during the New Deal Period" (master's thesis, North Texas State University, 1962), 147–48; Walter Galeson, *The CIO Challenge to the AFL* (Cambridge: Harvard University Press, 1960), 180–81.

26. Lambert interview.

27. *United Auto Workers #870 Minutes,* July 24, September 2, October 16, November 11, December 22, 1941, in 15-1-1, Texas Labor Archives (originals in Reuther Library); UAW International Representatives Garland Ham and Roy Kinney, interview by author, Arlington, TX, February 12, 1988; Alexander, Cawthon, Stubbs, Veach, Fleming, Edwards, Gathings, and Shields interviews.

28. Robert Christopher, "Rebirth and Lost Opportunities: The Texas AFL and the New Deal, 1933–1939" (master's thesis, University of Texas at Arlington, 1977), 106.

13

JULIA KIRK BLACKWELDER

Texas Homeworkers in the Depression

During the 1930s Texas homeworkers spent long hours bent over tedious tasks that earned them mere pennies a day. In San Antonio, described by a local labor paper as a "pesthole of low-paid labor," social and economic conditions interacted to encourage the growth of industrial homework before and during the Great Depression. Deploring the exploitative aspects of home labor, the paper's editor complained, "The New Deal glorified the fact that the sweat shop of the home had been abolished. The sweat shop in the home still continues in this city, and if anything is on the increase." Laredo was another Texas city where homework flourished in the 1930s. Two federal studies preserved the stories of Texas homeworkers. In 1932 the US Women's Bureau completed survey research on the wages and working conditions of women in Texas industries. The study included 123 personal interviews with homeworkers in San Antonio and Laredo. In the late 1930s Selden Menefee and Orin C. Cassmore collected data on the pecan-shelling industry in San Antonio. Their research, published by the Works Progress Administration, documented the emergence of homework where factory employment had once prevailed.[1]

Hand sewing and pecan shelling were the two major areas of industrial employment for San Antonio homeworkers, with approximately four thousand persons deriving income in each of these areas during the mid-1930s. In 1937 it was estimated that some fifteen thousand to twenty thousand families in and around San Antonio existed on homework.[2] There were fewer homeworkers in Laredo and they were principally garment workers. Although the sewing trades were exclusively female, men as well as women worked as pecan shellers. The vast majority of industrial homeworkers were Chicano, a situation that reflected ethnic discrimination in the labor market and the dislocation of Mexican agricultural workers. In San Antonio the geographic segregation of Chicanos on the city's West Side further encouraged Chicana domination of garment work.

World War I labor shortages and the overall decline of immigration to the

281

United States encouraged mechanization in many sectors of the American economy. However, a dramatic rise in immigration from Mexico offset wartime labor shortages for farmers in the Southwest. In Texas manual labor persisted as the backbone of production. The extremity of economically depressed conditions in Mexico in the 1920s guaranteed that Mexican immigrants would undercut Anglo or black workers in unskilled labor just as "illegal aliens" undercut other US workers in the 1980s. The eagerness of Mexicans to cross the border likewise guaranteed that Chicanos could not withhold their labor to bargain for higher wages. As the oldest and largest city in the United States with a distinctively Mexican heritage and identity, San Antonio acted as a magnet for those immigrants who chose not to return to Mexico after the harvests had ended. Consequently, San Antonio emerged as the national marketing point for migrant workers with labor agents from as far away as Michigan maintaining recruitment offices in the city. Many other immigrants adopted border towns like El Paso and Laredo, Texas, as their permanent homes. Chicanos in Texas were an internal colony of laborers. Driven from their homeland by the intense poverty of the 1920s, migrants from rural Mexico had become the harvesters of our nation's crops. As migrant workers, Chicanos earned lower wages than any other occupational grouping. During the late fall and early winter, little if any agricultural work could be found, and Texas Chicanos returned to San Antonio and many smaller cities and towns along the Mexican border. In their winter homes, Chicanos took work when and where they could find it.[3]

The presence of thousands of low-paid, temporarily unemployed migrant families in San Antonio encouraged the expansion of nonmechanized industrial work in the city while the national economy was moving away from hand labor. Similar developments occurred on a smaller scale in Texas border towns like Laredo. The shelling of pecans was one area of winter employment. Pecans gathered in late summer could be shelled later, after migrant workers had returned from harvests elsewhere. During the depression much of the pecan-shelling activity in Texas moved from organized plants into workers' homes.[4] In greater San Antonio pecan shelling emerged as a significant occupation of Chicano men as well as women.

Texas Chicanas also presented the unique attraction that lured manufacturers to Texas in the 1920s. Taught by nuns, grandmothers, and mothers over generations, many Chicanas had practiced embroidery and fine sewing since early childhood. The artistry of these women and the cheapness of their labor encouraged the establishment of garment factories in many Texas cities. In San Antonio and in Laredo and other border towns, the infants' and children's wear industry grew especially strong. The small dresses, gowns, and other items of children's clothing had little machine sewing and featured fine embroidery. Such skills were readily available in few US locations and virtually no US labor market was cost-competitive with the Texas towns. While larger, machine-sewn garments were produced mostly in sweatshops or factories, infants' and children's wear was produced just as easily at home as in a plant. In San Antonio and Laredo, homeworkers also hemmed handkerchiefs. The garment industry became the major employer of homeworkers in the 1920s. This homework persisted through the depression.

During the 1930s industrial homework flourished in Texas despite the existence of federal policies to eliminate it. High unemployment and federal preoccupation with broad economic issues undermined policies intended to restrict home production.[5] In San Antonio and Laredo, National Recovery Administration (NRA) regulations that controlled the wages and conditions of homework were flagrantly violated, and homework conditions in the late 1930s mirrored a situation that the NRA had tried to eradicate. The NRA homework provisions required certification that workers were free of contagious disease and that they maintained sanitary surroundings. The failure of the San Antonio health department to ensure these standards among workers led to a local ban on industrial homework in 1940. The NRA codes also stipulated that "all material and findings must be supplied by the employer and delivered and returned without expense to the worker. No deductions may be made for spoiled work. The homeworker must pledge himself not to allow other persons to assist in any part of the homework. The assignment of more work than it is possible to complete in the applicable code hours is prohibited."[6] When interviewed by representatives of the Women's Bureau in 1932, San Antonio and Laredo workers consistently complained of the continuance of exploitative conditions that the NRA would outlaw. Not only were the NRA codes unenforceable because compliance was voluntary, but an authority to oversee the code for the shelling industry was never selected.

Although the abundance of cheap Chicano labor gave rise to both home shelling and home sewing, the pattern of growth for the two industries in San Antonio was somewhat different. As pecans are native to East Texas, commercial shelling had existed in the state long before the 1920s. By the early 1920s machinery to crack the nuts and separate the shells from the meats had been developed. The introduction of shelling machines led to an expansion of the pecan trade in San Antonio, where the largest plants operated. However, by 1926 the large number of Mexican immigrants in the city had depressed the wages of unskilled labor to the point that hand labor was cheaper than machine shelling, so owners of shelling plants gradually replaced the shelling machines with hand labor.[7] In St. Louis, the other major pecan-shelling location in the United States, the reconversion to hand labor did not occur. As hand shelling required a lower level of capital outlay than the mechanized plants, cheap labor attracted many marginal entrepreneurs to the industry. The adoption of the contract system of shelling, which could be initiated with even less capital than the hand-shelling plants, brought still further expansion of the industry in San Antonio and its hinterland. In the 1920s contractors frequently delivered pecans to the workers' homes and returned for the shelled nuts.

During the years of expansion in the shelling industry, piece rates of six to eight cents per pound prevailed. In the 1920s a single worker might average six to seven dollars per week, engaging in such labor at home or in the shelling plants, but wages fell rapidly during the depression. By the late 1930s wages had fallen as low as four cents per pound with work available less regularly. Whole families working together could not earn enough for the barest level of subsistence. Weekly shelling incomes fell to an average of $2.50 for adult workers.

Chicanos in San Antonio initially entered into pecan shelling and provided an attractive labor supply for shellers because the work was seasonal and could be taken up after the agricultural harvest. Shelling plants were concentrated on the West Side, where Mexican American residence centered and where high population density allowed workers to walk to the sheds. As few Anglos or blacks lived in the area, few had much knowledge of the shelling industry and fewer still sought employment in pecans. As the contract system was adopted, pecan shelling became less centralized. Individual contractors used workers in points distant from the West Side, frequently outside Bexar County (San Antonio), but the pattern of Chicano dominance persisted.

During the 1920s some shelling was conducted throughout the year, but most of the shelling was done from October through May, providing opportunities for steady employment for many agricultural workers who wintered in San Antonio. With the onset of the depression, opportunities for migrant employment dwindled, enlarging the importance of income from shelling. At the same time, however, the price of pecans fell, driving some shellers out of business and compelling others to cut wages. The use of the contract system, which cut overhead by eliminating the costs of maintaining a plant, became more attractive as prices fell. An El Paso man who operated a shelling plant stated in 1932 that he had cut wages 20 percent, but that he could no longer maintain even the lower wage level because of falling prices. He told a Women's Bureau agent that he planned to close his plant and sell unshelled pecans to home shellers and buy back the meats because he saw no other way to compete with San Antonio shellers who were driving down rates and prices through this arrangement. The plant owner said he had complained of the situation to the federal government and received a reply that the prohibition of homework was a state matter.[8] In 1934 a strike against the shelling plants dramatized the plight of pecan workers. The striking workers sought the support of home shellers and endeavored to prevent contractors' distribution of pecans to homeworkers. While the 1934 strike and the more protracted and violent strike of 1938 did close down several plants, they were ineffective in curtailing home shelling.[9] The persistence of the homeworkers encouraged plant owners to adopt the contract system.

The children's wear and handkerchief industries were not as seasonal in their labor demands as was pecan shelling. Garment workers did not and generally had not followed the crops, although their male relatives may have done so. They were available for garment employment because of their permanent residence in Laredo, San Antonio, or other urban centers. Although they needed to work, a variety of factors had discouraged Chicana garment workers from other employments. Inadequate education and ethnic prejudices excluded Mexican American women from most sales and clerical jobs, and Mexican familial values discouraged Chicanas from accepting domestic employment in Anglo homes. San Antonio and Dallas emerged as major garment centers that drew largely on underemployed Chicana labor. In Laredo, which offered even fewer employment opportunities for Chicanas than the major Texas cities, the children's wear and handkerchief industries did not have to compete with sectors of the garment industry that were mainly factory based.

The farming out of garment sewing from pieces cut in New York City, either to homeworkers or workshops, was not unique to Texas. Connecticut, New Jersey, and Pennsylvania all received such work from the New York garment district before and during the depression. In the 1920s the passage of New York state labor laws governing hours and conditions of female and child employment—laws stricter than those in other states—had encouraged the decentralization of hand sewing. Sending the work as far as Texas clearly reflected the lower wage levels among Mexican American workers. An Anglo handworker interviewed by the Women's Bureau in 1932 stated that the Chicanas set the pace for speed and quality of work and that it was up to the Anglos to keep up or look for other work.[10]

While the low wages in Texas made the decentralization of New York's industries feasible, the expansion of the garment industries in the 1920s also rested on the belief that Mexican American women represented a peculiar combination of skills and attitudes. These factors were an ideal situation for investment in the 1920s, and as late as the 1960s the sociologist Robert G. Landolt reported that "Mexican American women were found characteristically to have the dexterity and temperament for being adept at both hand and machine needlework. Their ability to work well on highly repetitious jobs was attributed to their Indian ancestry. Their particular proficiency in the skills of garment making was attributed to the centuries-old practice of the Catholic nuns of teaching Mexican and Indian women to sew, and the emphasis on excellence in needlework was handed down from mothers to daughters."[11]

The sewing and embroidering done by Texas handworkers was extremely exacting. In addition to the fine stitching required for infants' clothing, the women often smocked, appliquéd, and embroidered the garments. The Women's Bureau reported that "the articles usually were of so fine and delicate a texture that the utmost care was required in handling so as to preserve their freshness and daintiness."[12]

Employers supplied materials for workers that included patterns, cut fabric, and thread. Workers then returned the finished garments or handkerchiefs, but contractors paid only for those products that met their satisfaction. The work was then pressed at the shops and sent on to buyers or to the home offices. Although the work was precut, none of the designs or smocking patterns was stamped on the materials. The worker had to be extremely skillful to get the exact amount of tautness in smocking or drawn work that the employer desired and had to have a well-practiced knowledge of embroidery to copy the intricate designs from the patterns.

As all homeworkers, except a privileged few who sewed designers' samples, were required to call for and deliver their work, the vast majority of workers lived near the manufacturers' offices or plants. Wage levels were too low to accommodate carfare for the weekly trip that most of the women made to the plants. In San Antonio employers located plants on the West Side because they calculated their profits on employing skilled Chicanas for whom few employment alternatives existed. The Women's Bureau survey of 1932 revealed that a few Anglo women living in north San Antonio had taken up home sewing because of depression emergencies, but the West Side location of the industry discouraged both black and Anglo women from seeking such work, even if they would accept the low pay. None of the manufacturing concerns surveyed by the Women's Bureau employed black women to do sewing.

The Women's Bureau interviewed one hundred San Antonio home sewers, eighty-four of whom were Chicana, sixteen Anglo, and none black. The women ranged in age from sixteen years to sixty-five, with the majority being over the age of thirty. That the majority of the women were currently married or had been married supports the view that homework appealed primarily to women who were homebound by child care or other household responsibilities. That all of the single homeworkers were Chicana may reflect either the Mexican prefer- ence for keeping daughters at home whenever possible or the relative lack of alternative employment options for Mexican women. Certainly Anglo women had access to better jobs that were denied Mexican Americans, but occasionally an interviewee commented on her preference for homework over alternatives. One Chicana reported that her daughter had been working as a maid for three dollars per week but that she quit that job because she could "make that much at home without killing herself." A young Mexican American girl stated that sewing paid poorly but that housework was the only other job that she could get and that she "would not feel right staying in another house." Two of the San Antonio workers told bureau representatives that home sewing was prefer- able to factory work. One of these workers questioned the interviewer as to the Women's Bureau's intentions because the "foreman of [the] factory told her that the Labor Department women were going around trying to get information to be used in discontinuing homework for Mexicans." Another worker said factory wages were no better and that workers were fired for talking on the job.[13]

The conditions under which women entered and continued homework dif- fered significantly between Anglos and Chicanas. A number of the Chicanas reported that they had learned needlework from other homeworkers in their families, but none of the Anglo women commented on acquiring their skills in this way and none of the Anglos had relatives who assisted them in fine sewing. Many of the Chicanas had done the work for several years, while the Anglos were mostly newcomers who had taken up handwork because of sudden changes in economic conditions. One Anglo told the interviewer she had previously been a seamstress and milliner but that this was the only work she could get at present. Another Anglo had taken up homework after her husband and daughter had lost their jobs. The family was able to get by temporarily by moving in with her mother and sharing expenses with a brother who also lived in the house. Unlike virtually all the Chicana workers, the Anglos did not walk to the factory but drove or rode the bus to the plant periodically to deliver and collect their work.

The Women's Bureau interviewed twenty-three homeworkers, all Chicanas, in Laredo. Proportionally more of the Laredo workers than the San Antonio Chicana subjects were under thirty years of age, and ten of the twenty-three were single. The significant difference between the San Antonio and Laredo respondents is the conditions under which they accepted homework. Unlike the San Antonio women, none of the Laredo workers said that she did homework because other employment options were unsuitable. Most of the women pursued homework because it was the only employment they could find. Laredo workers who were not homebound by child care or other equally confining situations often expressed a preference for other work.

Not all Chicana homeworkers came from the lowest socioeconomic brackets, but they generally did. Two young Chicanas were supported by their fathers but did sewing in order to have spending money. A single woman from an educated family was engaged in homework because she wanted to be of some assistance in getting through the hard times of the depression. The family finally made her give up the work, claiming that she was expending a greater cost in shoe leather walking back and forth to the factory than she was earning.[14]

As in the case of shellers, pay for hand sewers was extremely low. One worker reported that she was paid forty-two cents for twelve hours' work on a single dress that the Women's Bureau reported could be purchased in an eastern shop for eight dollars. Fifty-three of the 123 homeworkers in Laredo and San Antonio reported hourly earnings under five cents. Outside Texas, wages reported by homeworkers were markedly higher. A 1936 Women's Bureau study documented wages in New Jersey and Pennsylvania that ranged from five cents to eleven cents per hour for inexperienced homeworkers, while the most skilled needle workers averaged twenty-one cents per hour.[15]

Based on the estimated wages workers reported to the interviewers, the *average* wage per person among home sewers in San Antonio and Laredo was approximately $2.20 per week for anywhere from a few hours per day part of the week to a sixty-hour week. The highest wage reported by any of the workers was $5.53 and the lowest was $.83. In contrast, the study found the *median* wage of workers in four San Antonio garment factories to be $5.70 per week. Of one worker who claimed to earn only one dollar per week as the sole supporter of children and an unemployed spouse, the interviewer noted, "Mystery to me how they live."[16] Many families like this one got by from day to day only through the charity of friends and relatives. Only two of the workers stated that they had received any relief assistance. Other families got by only through the combined efforts of two or more homeworkers. While some reported that the work was steadily available, others found sewing work only periodically.

Although some of the women were not at their sewing tasks full-time, most claimed to work in excess of eight hours per day at least six days a week. Many

Laredo workers alternated homework with factory work but this rarely happened in San Antonio, where the factory work differed from homework. San Antonio garment factories produced machine-sewn women's clothing, and the garment factories offered higher wages than the handworkers could earn. For Laredo workers, factory employment was not essentially different from home sewing. The Kewpie Juvenile Manufacturing Company, which was the major employer in the industry and operated in Laredo and San Antonio, paid the same piece rates in both cities. There was little if any machine sewing in the manufacture of these garments. A few of the Laredo workers had their own machines and did this work at home.

While San Antonio workers were hostile to the garment companies, the Laredo workers did not feel that the firms exploited them. However, the Laredo women saw the subcontractors, who distributed and collected the work and who paid them, as being responsible for many of their employment complaints. Two of the Laredo workers believed that the subcontractor skimmed off part of the wage that the firms paid workers. One of the interviewees told the bureau representative that her supervisor was opposed to the interviews because she feared the bureau would discover that she had cheated the workers.[17]

One San Antonio homeworker complained that the manufacturers exploited the sewers, paying them almost nothing while the garments sold for high prices. Another woman stated that her employer had started as a garment cutter himself and "now they've got a big factory, own big cars, have a beautiful home, and pay the workers very little. Their factories get bigger and bigger and they pay us less and less. We make very little and work so much." One employer countered that he was not exploiting workers more than he was being exploited. A San Antonio manager, who contracted hand-embroidered garments for a New York employer, complained of the low rates after the home office had instituted a number of cuts in 1931 and 1932. He was informed by New York that San Antonio "must compete with cheap Puerto Rican labor or lose the contract." The Women's Bureau cited a 1932 report, issued by the governor of Puerto Rico, that listed handwork rates ranging from $2.67 to $2.77 per week per worker with more than 12 million women's and children's garments and 1.5 million handkerchiefs entering the United States from Puerto Rico from July 1931 through June 1932.[18]

Some employers of homeworkers, like the Texas Infant Dress Company and the Randolph-Kohlman Company, were locally owned concerns that operated factories to supplement the labor of homeworkers. Other companies, like the Juvenile Manufacturing Company, were branches of New York firms that sent bundles of cut work to San Antonio and Laredo for distribution to the workers. Women who worked for this category of firm frequently complained of long delays in receiving their wages, as requisitions for payment came from New York after the San Antonio office had certified the amount of work completed.

However, individuals were anxious not to make themselves conspicuous to employers as complainers or troublemakers. They believed they would be fired if they complained, and many had no other work experience. In the 1930s, when the repatriation movement flourished, the fear of "voluntary" deportation was an ever-present concern to all Mexican Americans. And the experience of workers in San Antonio, even at wage levels well below subsistence, was that employers could pick and choose among workers because of the abundance of labor. Many believed, not always without knowledge of conditions in Mexican and border communities, that there were people earning even less than they.

In fact, the workers had fairly clear notions of the rates offered by various local employers. The most consistent complaint of the Laredo and San Antonio sewers was that the rates had been cut 50 percent since the onset of the depression. A characteristic comment was that a garment maker "used to earn more and didn't work so hard."[19] But despite the cuts the sewers kept on with their jobs. The lower the rates, the harder they drove themselves. Of the 123 workers whom the Women's Bureau investigated, only two had quit work because of the wage cuts.

As San Antonio's lowest-paid workers, pecan shellers and home garment workers endured some of the nation's worst living conditions. Many of the workers lived in the "corrals" of the West Side of San Antonio—one- or two-room shacks without plumbing or electricity. Housing conditions among the Laredo workers were comparable. An interviewer for the Women's Bureau, asked to describe the housing of one respondent, commented simply, "indescribable." This house was a one-room structure renting for four dollars per month. The renter had no light and cooked all of her meals outside the house. She shared central water and toilet facilities with fifteen other families. Despite these difficulties, the interviewer noted, the garment maker was "herself immaculate."[20]

Early in the depression the low wages and poor working conditions in the San Antonio garment industry attracted the attention of national labor organizations. Labor leaders reasoned that improvements had to be achieved in San Antonio to prevent cheap labor there from driving down wages or destroying jobs in eastern garment-making centers. In 1934 the International Ladies' Garment Workers' Union (ILGWU) began organizing in San Antonio. Emily Jordan of the United Garment Workers (UGW) also began similar work in the city earlier in the same year. Unlike the UGW, the ILGWU undertook, as a considered aspect of organizational strategy, to include hand sewers and embroiderers as well as machine workers in their drive. Meyer Perlstein of the ILGWU, who was in San Antonio after the first local had been organized, explained that "the problem of organization in [Texas] cities is very complicated because of the nationality question, and also because the Mexican border is open for immigration, and at any time that the Mexicans who reside in this country want to organize or ask for any improvement, they are let out and new Mexicans brought in to take their place."[21] The reality of the situation in San Antonio was that very few immigrants were arriving from Mexico, but the staggering unemployment among the city's Mexican Americans made the replacement of troublesome workers a simple matter. Perlstein reported that a group of Anglo women and Chicanas had formed a local affiliated with the ILGWU about a year before his visit but that manufacturers began to blacklist the women and that only the local charter remained by the end of 1934. Before Perlstein left the city, the garment workers had succeeded in resurrecting their local. In subsequent weeks the ILGWU obtained a contract with a local firm. The agreement brought some improvement to the handworkers covered, but the vast majority of homeworkers were not covered and the union's success was short lived.

In 1936 Perlstein returned to San Antonio. With Perlstein came one of the ILGWU's chief organizers, David Dubinsky, who would remain there for several months. However, most of the 1936 labor activity centered around a strike at the Dorothy Frocks factory, which was not a contractor of homework, and the ILGWU secured no subsequent contracts involving homeworkers. From 1937 to 1938 the ILGWU made the Texas Infant Dress Company, a major employer of homeworkers, its primary target. The International members struck and picketed in May 1937 and again in March 1938, but by this time the split between San Antonio's factory-based machine workers and home-based hand sewers was an accomplished fact. Although union organizers had wanted to unite the two groups, the pickets' demands included a minimum wage for machine operators, a forty-hour week, and the termination of homework. Thus, the cottage laborers were deprived of the one voice that had spoken for the improvement of their situation as opposed to the destruction of their jobs.

In 1938 Congress passed the Fair Labor Standards Act, which mandated a fifteen-cents-per-hour minimum wage. The Fair Labor Standards Act eventually guaranteed a living wage for shellers and garment workers, but in the process the majority of jobs in both industries disappeared in San Antonio and Laredo. The initial response of employers to the legislation was avoidance, accomplished partly through the replacement of plant labor with homework. Some pecan plant owners as well as contractors for home shelling sold the unshelled nuts to workers and bought back the meats, asserting that the shellers were independent businessmen, not employees, and that the Fair Labor Standards Act therefore did not apply. Although the majority of plant owners did not convert to home shelling, the number of home shellers reportedly increased in 1938 and continued to increase in areas surrounding San Antonio through 1939.[22] Although the reintroduction of machine shelling was well underway before the end of 1939, home shellers were still operating in the city in 1940.

In San Antonio the Women's Bureau's 1932 investigation of conditions in pecan shelling and garment making rallied organized labor, women's groups, and a number of public officials behind a movement to eliminate homework. In September 1936, L. P. Bishop, head of the San Antonio health department, appeared before the city council to request passage of an ordinance that would appropriate funds for the health department to enforce sanitation standards in the shelling industry. Bishop testified that the health department destroyed any pecans that it knew had been shelled in homes but that the bulk of the nuts escaped health department notice. Although the city had initiated a system of issuing health cards to food handlers and food processors in May of the same year, it was simply beyond the health department's capacities to administer physicals to San Antonio's many thousands of food workers. The physicals therefore were perfunctory, and home shellers were most certainly ignored.

The release of the Women's Bureau's findings sparked an alliance of middle-class club women and working-class men who set out to reform homework in San Antonio. In December 1936, William B. Arnold, editor of the trades council's *Weekly Dispatch*, reported that he had interviewed a number of home sewers in their homes and that he "found in one instance the worker sitting along the side of the bed where her husband was lying (he had a case of tuberculosis) sewing infants' garments and the garments were spread out on the bed. . . . In another hole in the wall two women were sewing garments and by the side of one were piled several pieces of goods and a small mangy dog was sleeping on them."[23]

The following February, Bexar County representative William Carssaw introduced a bill in the Texas legislature to regulate homework in the garment industry. The initial goal of Carssaw, the *Dispatch*, and women's groups was to establish systems of health cards for workers and to require sterilization of the finished products. Clearly the predicament of thousands of exploited workers was not the central concern. In the succeeding months the *Dispatch* carried a series of articles supporting Carssaw's bill that carried scare headlines about disease-infected products.

Carssaw's bill failed to pass, but in 1940 the San Antonio city council adopted an ordinance forbidding both the home shelling of pecans and the sale of garments manufactured by homeworkers. The council had been embarrassed by a 1938 *Focus* magazine article about home shelling.[24] *Focus* condemned local officials for endangering public welfare by not eradicating unhealthful conditions among the city's homeworkers. The institution of a ban rather than a set of controls on homework was enforceable, and homework declined precipitously after 1940. In addition, the Fair Labor Standards Act had begun to be enforced against shelling. Puerto Rican workers had already undercut the pitifully low wages of Texas home needleworkers, and the children's and infants' wear industries declined in Laredo as well as San Antonio. By 1940, then, there was little reason for managers in either the pecan or garment industries to oppose a ban on homework.

The history of Texas home shellers and hand sewers illustrates both the grimmest consequences of the economics of discrimination and the vested interest of employers in maintaining occupational segregation. The abundance of locally noncompetitive workers in San Antonio and Laredo encouraged employment expansion in the 1920s, but the expansion was calculated on minimal capital investment or the replacement of capital with labor. As the depression deepened, the trend toward increasing labor intensity continued. There appeared to be no wage level below which shellers and garment workers would overwhelmingly refuse employment. The Fair Labor Standards Act destroyed Texans' competitive edge over other garment and pecan producers. Consequently, sewing machine operators replaced hand sewers and cracking and sorting machines replaced hand shellers. For the garment industry the change meant that hand embroidery and other fine sewing would be given over to foreign producers. The guaranteed wage meant fewer jobs for Chicanas because it destroyed their advantage in the national market without affecting the pattern of discrimination that excluded them from other jobs. After the depression ended, many handworkers moved into the garment factories, but these women remained disadvantaged because occupational segregation persisted and a continued influx of labor into Texas held wages down.

Notes

This chapter originally appeared in *Homework: Historical and Contemporary Perspectives on Paid Labor at Home*, edited by Eileen Boris and Cynthia R.

Daniels (Urbana: University of Illinois Press, 1989), 75–90, and is reprinted with permission.

1.   *San Antonio Weekly Dispatch*, July 20, 1934; Mary Loretta Sullivan and Bertha Blair, *Women in Texas Industries*, Women's Bureau Bulletin No. 126 (Washington, DC: GPO, 1936). The interview materials in this essay come largely from the survey materials for this study. The materials are part of the records of the Women's Bureau National Archives, Washington, DC; Selden Menefee and Orin C. Cassmore, *The Pecan Shellers of San Antonio*, Works Progress Administration (Washington, DC: GPO, 1940).

2.   *San Antonio Weekly Dispatch*, January 15, 1937.

3.   Neither scholar nor government statistician has attempted more than a rough estimate of Mexican immigration to the United States for any decade. Careful records were not kept on immigrants who returned to Mexico, and illegal immigration was heavy during the 1920s. Robert G. Landolt estimated that legal immigration from Mexico numbered 49,642 persons from 1901 to 1910; 219,004 from 1911 to 1920; 459,259 from 1921 to 1930; and 22,666 from 1931 to 1940. Landolt, *The Mexican-American Workers of San Antonio, Texas: The Chicano Heritage* (New York: Arno, 1976), 32.

4.   "Working Conditions of Pecan Shellers in San Antonio," *Monthly Labor Review* 45 (March 1939): 549–50.

5.   US Bureau of Labor Statistics, "Homework and Sweatshops," in *Handbook of Labor Statistics*, 1936, Bulletin No. 615 (Washington, DC: GPO, 1936), 196–204; Bertha M. Nienberg, *A Policy Insuring Value to Women Buyers and a Livelihood to Apparel Makers*, Women's Bureau, Bulletin No. 146 (Washington, DC: GPO, 1936), 18–21.

6.   National Recovery Administration, Press Release No. 9861, January 28, 1935.

7.   Menefee and Cassmore, *Pecan Shellers of San Antonio*, 16; "Working Conditions of Pecan Shellers," 549–50.

8.   T. Azar, interview, Materials Relating to Bulletin No. 126, Records of the Women's Bureau, National Archives, Washington, DC.

9.   Menefee and Cassmore, *Pecan Shellers of San Antonio*, 23–26; "Working Conditions of Pecan Shellers," 549–50.

10.   San Antonio homeworker, interview no. 77, Materials Relating to Bulletin No. 126, Records of the Women's Bureau.

11.   Landolt, *Mexican-American Workers*, 184–85.

12.   Sullivan and Blair, *Women in Texas Industries*, 72.

13.   San Antonio homeworkers, interviews nos. 5, 71, 34, Materials Relating to Bulletin No. 126, Records of the Women's Bureau.

14.   Laredo homeworker, interview no. 16, San Antonio homeworker, interview no. 23, Materials Relating to Bulletin No. 126, Records of the Women's Bureau; Carmen Perry, interview by author, May 22, 1979.

15.   Nienberg, *A Policy Insuring Value*, 17–18.

16.   San Antonio homeworker, interview no. 36, Materials Relating to Bulletin No. 126, Records of the Women's Bureau.

17. Laredo homeworker, interview nos. 4 and 20, Materials Relating to Bulletin No. 126, Records of the Women's Bureau.

18. Typescript report on homeworkers, Materials Relating to Bulletin No. 126, Records of the Women's Bureau.

19. San Antonio homeworker, interview no. 25, Materials Relating to Bulletin No. 126, Records of the Women's Bureau.

20. San Antonio homeworker, interview no. 96, Materials Relating to Bulletin No. 126, Records of the Women's Bureau.

21. Meyer Perlstein, quoted in Menefee and Cassmore, *Pecan Shellers of San Antonio*; *San Antonio Weekly Dispatch*, December 21, 1934.

22. *San Antonio Weekly Dispatch*, April 26, 1940; Menefee and Cassmore, *Pecan Shellers of San Antonio*, 21–22.

23. William B. Arnold, quoted in *San Antonio Weekly Dispatch*, December 4, 1936.

24. "Disease and Politics in Your Food: The Case of San Antonio," *Focus*, April 1938, 3.

ERNEST OBADELE-STARKS

Black Texans and Theater Craft Unionism

The Struggle for Racial Equality

The evolution of the small, craft-oriented, black-led labor union in an urban-industrial setting is one of the more understudied aspects of American labor history. The struggle for black workplace rights was not unique to the unskilled, and the pervasiveness and influence of black labor extended beyond the ranks of prominent labor organizations to penetrate the circles of urban craft unions. The experiences of two urban-based black craft unions in the International Alliance of Theatrical Stage Employees and Moving Picture Operators (IATSE)—a union consisting of stagehands, projectionists, motion picture craft workers, and technicians—provide such an example. Although small and somewhat obscure, the trajectories of IATSE Locals 279-A of Houston and 249-A of Dallas intersected many important issues in American labor, cultural, political, and social history. The unique responses of the black workers in each of these two major metropolitan centers toward the communications industry, conservative unionism, workplace inequities, corruption, technological advances, mergers, government labor policy, and social reform resulted in both similarities and differences. A look at the origins and the development of each local reveals the labor-movement values held by the members of each union as they struggled to define their place among the skilled working class. Although studies on the labor movement have focused primarily on the unskilled labor force with racial and ethnic in-fighting as a central theme, the racialization of craft unions, which based their union strength and power on the physical abilities and skills of their workers, holds a special place in the historiography of American labor.[1]

The chartering of Locals 279-A and 249-A resulted from more than half a century of racial and economic subordination in an industry that from its inception demonstrated little movement toward racial inclusion. IATSE emerged during the 1890s as a labor organization focused primarily on redressing workplace grievances of white theater workers, and as it grew its development continued hand in hand with racial exclusion, black workers being consistently marginalized. At the 1895 IATSE national convention in Boston, white-controlled union locals affiliated with the American Federation of Labor (AFL) were granted sole authority to determine whether blacks would be offered membership in their unions. Most white unionists refused to accept biracial unionism and only reluctantly made concessions to black workers who desired union membership or wished to participate in their union activities and gatherings. This opposition to black unionization, which persisted throughout much of the first half of the twentieth century, stemmed in part from white unionists' belief that blacks were not deserving of union representation.[2]

Not until delegates for the Texas Federal Labor Union (TFLU) crashed the 1904 AFL convention in Fort Worth did Texas's black theater workers gain a voice in the conservative union policies of the IATSE, which typically viewed black workers as "a serious menace to the white union men." Reaction among white theater workers to black workers' demands was virtually nonexistent. IATSE Local 330 in Fort Worth, for example, remained indifferent to racial outcries, directing its interests toward ensuring its longevity and securing the jobs of its white workers while ignoring its pronounced racially discriminatory policies. This was a pattern that persisted throughout the industry for the next three decades.[3]

Local 330 was just one of many IATSE locals targeted by nonunionized black theater workers from the turn of the twentieth century through labor's most critical decade, the 1930s. Serious challenges to the insensitivity of white IATSE workers in Texas started when black stagehands and motion picture operators in Houston, eager to start a union of their own, began picketing white-owned theaters in the city's predominantly black districts and staging protests outside the luxurious homes of theater owners. Andrew Lee Lewis, founder of Local 279-A, the "negro auxiliary," pointed out that these open acts of rebellion were provoked by white workers from Local 279 and their theater employers who often collaborated to "intimidate" black workers. Lewis was forced to hire full-time security to protect himself and his family after the manager of the Washington Theater held the labor activist at gunpoint for his role in organizing the city's black theater workers. "They . . . just weren't bothered about us," said Lewis, who after migrating from Des Moines, Iowa, to Houston during World War I, had worked in many of the white-owned theaters in the black sections of town. To his chagrin, he had discovered that white unionists had no intention of assisting blacks in organizing their own union locals.[4]

The gangster-like behavior of obstinate theater employers and their equally bullheaded white employees compelled Lewis and his people to turn to the Congress of Industrial Organizations (CIO), a labor federation formed during the mid-1930s as an alternative to the more conservative labor organizations. Prior to Lewis and his men joining the CIO in 1937, the federation had sent a labor organizer to Houston's black theaters "practically every day." Armed with its racial equality plan, which condemned discrimination, the CIO had emerged as a viable option for a wide range of black workers in Texas.[5] In April 1937 the Oil Workers International Union (OWIU) through the leadership of the CIO initiated an aggressive drive to unionize black oil-workers at the major refineries along the Texas Gulf Coast. When the Texas chapter of the CIO held its first convention in Beaumont, Texas, in July 1937 it voiced its support for racial equality and pledged to work particularly hard to increase its membership among black longshoremen, steelworkers, laundry workers, cooks, bakers, confectionery workers, barbers, brewery workers, auto mechanics, meatcutters, retail clerks, garment workers, tailors, and musicians. It also made clear its intention to pursue skilled black labor, which included black stagehands and motion picture operators.[6]

Black theater workers struggled for recognition throughout the 1930s, and by the early 1940s they faced yet a new set of problems. Allegations and investigations linking the IATSE with organized crime and systematic corruption overshadowed many of the workplace and labor concerns that had heretofore comprised so much of the dialogue within the industry. Court records indicate that motion picture industry executives had dispensed funds totaling 2.5 million dollars to syndicate leaders and mobsters. Company executives protested such charges, denying any collaboration with the mob, and accused IATSE union officials of extorting the money by threatening nationwide strikes. It was later learned that industry executives were indeed operating in league with syndicate leaders, who they believed were best suited to direct what the industry saw as its long-term interests—risk-free growth and a large, underpaid workforce.[7]

The 1940s posed an array of new challenges for black IATSE workers. For one thing, the gangster-like reputation of the movie industry persisted as an issue, and many blacks refused to occupy their time and energy with it, particularly during World War II when most workers balanced their labor struggles with the call for patriotism. Black IATSE workers responded to an appeal to fight America's enemies through the Office of War Information (OWI), an agency formed in June 1942 to, among other things, disseminate wartime propaganda. The OWI mobilized black theater workers by contracting neighborhood theaters to show government films designed in part to bolster the American war effort by minimizing racial consciousness and counteracting the distorted images of black Americans as portrayed by film makers and the theater community.

The romanticized film versions of cordial and harmonious race relations were as exaggerated as the depiction of black Americans in two of the most popular black musicals of the 1940s, *Cabin in the Sky* and *Stormy Weather*, which portrayed blacks as simple, ignorant, and superstitious Sambo-like people, capable of performing only menial tasks.[8]

Black unionists from Local 279-A came together to protest various forms of workplace inequities at a time when many blacks across the nation—and especially in the South—reluctantly accepted racial separation as a fact of life. Under the banner of the NAACP and from its inception in 1937, Local 279-A's workforce eschewed the traditional black intellectual's goal of separate equality, and favored instead a direct assault on the Jim Crow culture. While the NAACP did not directly challenge the separate-but-equal dictum, it did provide an example for black activists and unionists as they set out to eradicate discrimination within the IATSE. Despite the NAACP's best efforts, however, Local 279-A could not rely solely on that organization's meager resources and its limited staff to resolve the vast issues confronting them. Government intercession, particularly the investigative actions of federal agencies into the racial labor affairs of their industry, provided perhaps the most viable prospect for change.[9]

Acting on behalf of black workers from Local 279-A, Arthur J. Mandell, one of the principal partners of the well-known Houston law firm Mandell and Wright, presented a simple ultimatum to the Federal Mediation and Conciliation Services (FMCS), a government body that focused on resolving or minimizing wartime labor disputes. Anything less than the "equalization in pay," he insisted, was unacceptable for Local 279-A's thirteen black motion picture operators. Although the FMCS recommended a 25 percent wage increase for black unionists, it failed to meet their minimum expectation of equal pay for equal work. Moreover, white theater owners also cried foul and wasted little time rejecting the proposal, claiming that the wage differences between the races was a result of the conditions under which black and white unionists worked. In the case of Local 279, they insisted, higher wages were justified for those who worked at the larger and more extravagant suburban theaters, which served a large number of white patrons.[10]

Many white theater owners denied all accusations of racial discrimination and considered their conduct to be in compliance with wage scales set for Locals 279 and 279-A "in accordance with a contract executed by representatives of the . . . union." In reality though, they paid higher wages to whites who worked at the more prestigious theaters and found reasons to underpay black workers, who allegedly "caused more damage to the machinery entrusted to them."[11]

The FMCS could do only so much for Local 279-A, and when it appeared that the agency had reached the limits of its authority, Lewis and his colleagues turned toward the Fair Employment Practices Commission (FEPC) for further action. Lewis appealed to the FEPC on behalf of his union mates when he filed a wage complaint in 1943. His demand for retroactive pay stemmed from a 1941 contract with theater owners that paid blacks thirty dollars a week while whites earned seventy. After examining their complaint, Carlos Castaneda, acting regional director of the FEPC, notified Tom Clemons, proprietor of the Dowling Street Theater, Albert and Harold Farb of the Rainbow Theater, and Victor Barraco of the Roxy Theater, advising them that their refusal to pay equal wages constituted discrimination and violated the mandates of the FEPC. The fact that the IATSE did not appear on the government's list of "essential industries" contributed greatly to the FEPC's failure to abolish wage discrimination within the union.[12]

Postwar technological advances thrust the motion picture industry and the union into yet another realm of complicated circumstances. Economic pressures brought on by the advent of television and the resulting trend of declining employment in the movie industry created new tensions. The formative years for television became a near-desperate period for the theater industry, which lost many of its patrons while IATSE workers saw many in their ranks leave their jobs for newer and less restrictive opportunities in television. By 1946 box office receipts had peaked, and then steadily decreased during the last years of the decade. Despite the transition from movie and theater houses to television and a decline in membership, white members of IATSE remained reluctant to relinquish their elitist ideals and adopt more racially inclusive policies.[13]

The advent of television and the changing nature of the labor movement had discernible effects on the movie industry's race relations. The 1947 Taft-Hartley Act, which regulated and limited interunion collaboration and the scope of labor strikes, represented an open attack on the labor movement, declaring closed shops to be illegal and allowing employers to circumvent work stoppages by hiring replacement workers. Conservative policy makers resented the enormous powers that New Dealers had granted labor unions during the depression, and in the light of post–World War II conditions—such as reduced industrial production and recurring labor difficulties—many of these resentments were rekindled. The restrictive guidelines imposed by Taft-Hartley on large labor unions worked to the advantage of employers, who enjoyed loosened restrictions. The act outlawed closed shops and allowed states to deny protection to striking workers and unions through right-to-work laws. Taft-Hartley did not destroy the labor movement as many workers and labor leaders had predicted, but it did undermine weaker unions, particularly those in small and loosely organized industries.[14]

Racketeering convictions during the 1940s tempered the thuglike raids masterminded by phobic union heads on union locals and curtailed the flow of money between industry executives, union officials, and syndicate loyalists. Although the cozy relationship between IATSE leaders and executives in the motion picture industry did not kill the IATSE, it gave it such a blow that splinter groups of dissident IATSE workers proliferated. The Conference of Studio Unions (CSU), for instance, challenged many of the rules and working conditions set by the IATSE. By the time CSU had won a government-sanctioned election in 1949 for representation on behalf of theater- and movie-set decorators—a group that in the past had offered its loyalties to the IATSE—the violence against picketers and the accusations of communist infiltration had become so intense that few CSU members were willing to openly declare their membership in the union. Many of those who did were driven from their jobs.[15]

The allegation of communist infiltration was no frivolous matter. The communist movement along the upper Texas coast generated concern among Texas lawmakers and union organizers who regarded its appearance as an indication of the organization's commitment to a bold recruiting campaign in the region. When communists announced the formation of a Harris County commission on "Negro work" in November 1938, it drew a sharp response from Texas congressman Joe H. Eagle who contended that the aggressive organizing strategy of the communists was an issue to be reckoned with and remedied. The mere thought of some eight hundred "Reds" in Harris County alone was enough to make Houston mayor Oscar Holcombe denounce the Teamsters Union in 1939 and insist that it rid its organization of communists. Holcombe made his demand after members of the union, along with local leaders of the CIO, showed up to hear an anticommunist speech given by city attorney Sewall Myer, who charged that "imported communist agitators and communist lawyers" were responsible for the tense labor climate along the upper Texas coast.[16]

Black communists attracted much attention when they criticized government officials, unions, and employers for their treatment of black workers. Most were linked to James W. Ford, an internationally renowned communist leader who often addressed large crowds in Texas. His Houston speech in October 1940 demonstrated the seriousness of communist efforts to organize black workers, who would be given a vital role in the unions in the struggle for racial equality. As a critic of labor unions, Ford, a native of Alabama and US vice presidential candidate for the Communist Party during the 1930s, avowed that the redistribution of wealth was the only solution to the disparities that existed in the labor movement between the races.[17]

Black unionists from Local 279-A, on the other hand, went all out to protect their interests. The uncertain state of organized labor compelled them to act on new and creative alternatives for addressing their labor concerns. Local 279-A joined forces with the Texas Federation Club (TFC), a statewide black political and labor organization founded by Moses LeRoy, president of Local 1534 of the Brotherhood of Railway and Steamship Clerks, and Freeman Everett, president of the International Longshoremen's Association Local 872. In May 1949 Lee Lewis, executive secretary of the TFC, spoke to a gathering of black workers from across the state who had assembled in Houston to establish a collaborative network and to open up intraracial dialogue among a cross section of the state's black workforce. One point of contention centered on pressuring white labor unions into breaking a pattern of blatant racism by boycotting convention hotels that discriminated against black patrons by allowing whites to enjoy certain privileges unavailable to blacks.[18]

The TFC made concerted efforts to connect itself to the black political community, and it often invited prominent members of the black elite to attend its scheduled meetings. When R. A. Cavitt, executive secretary of the Houston Negro Chamber of Commerce, and Lulu B. White of the NAACP spoke to the organization at its October meeting in 1949, they drew attention to the deteriorating racial conditions in Houston. Strained relations between the black community and the local police, in particular, made it incumbent upon each black citizen, White exclaimed, to bring an end to such behavior. It was clear that both White and Cavitt understood the significance of having a politically and socially active labor community as opposed to an organization that catered solely to labor issues. The far-reaching camaraderie established between black labor and the black middle class was evidenced when C. E. Edwards of Dallas rose to his feet and invited the entire group in attendance to a November labor banquet in Dallas.[19]

Edwards's invitation may have had much to do with the need of black workers in Dallas to be exposed to the assertive character and experience of those from Houston. Indeed, the pioneering efforts of Local 279-A helped blaze a trail for black stagehands in Dallas who, prior to getting help from their contemporaries in Houston, received much of their direction from the all-white Local 249, also of Dallas. Before receiving their union charter in November 1949, Dallas's black stagehands negotiated contracts directly with theater managers and white unionists. Their primary focus was centered on the working conditions and the placement of "competent men . . . as operators on jobs in each theater in Dallas . . . patronized by Negro patrons." By 1949 black theater workers in Dallas had come together to protect the interests of just about every black employee affiliated with the theater industry. Although many were not official union members, black carpenters, propertymen, electricians, and others affiliated in some capacity with the theater business all benefited from the bargaining efforts of Local 249-A. The local was able to establish clear guidelines for working conditions, job responsibilities, and pay.[20]

Much of the progress that members of Local 249-A enjoyed can be attributed to the tireless work of LeRoy Hawkins and S. R. Tankersley. Hawkins first came into contact with theater work while moonlighting after his full-time job with a Dallas insurance company. Having previously worked in theaters in Abilene, Texas, during World War II, he maintained his association with the industry and encouraged his good friend and insurance coworker Tankersley to join him in his late afternoon and weekend endeavor. Within two years of learning the craft of operating moving pictures, Tankersley found himself immersed in the union affairs of motion picture operators and became one of the union's principal voices of protest against the unfair treatment of black workers. While working at Dallas's Star Theater Tankersley discovered discrepancies in the standings of blacks and whites. For one thing, Local 249 denied full membership privileges to blacks but required an initiation fee of five hundred dollars for each black worker who desired to join their local. The union ignored most of the concerns of black workers, usually through the dissenting votes of the white majority. Although many whites worked at theaters patronized by blacks, no theater would employ a nonwhite to operate equipment at exclusively white theaters. Yet, theater owners and white unionists fully expected Tankersley and Hawkins to fill job vacancies with union workers at urban theaters, where the supply of available blacks had dwindled to an all-time low.[21]

Confronted with the uncertain state of unionism and the evaporating prospects of fair work, Tankersley and Hawkins set out to organize their own local. With the help of the Dallas Negro Chamber of Commerce and Local 279-A the two men struggled to attain the seven-worker minimum required to charter a union local. Surprisingly, ten workers showed up in October 1949 at an organizational meeting arranged by Tankersley. One of the first things the group agreed upon was the establishment of a modest twenty-dollar initiation fee for its members. After receiving their charter, members of Local 249-A tried unsuccessfully to obtain labor contracts from theater owners. Tankersley and his fellow union members brought about dramatic changes in the Dallas theater industry after they engaged in a series of successful strikes that allowed them to negotiate new contractual terms between themselves and theater managers. These included a reassessment of workplace sanitation, overtime employment, job responsibilities, wage scales, hourly pay, vacation time, staffing, conflicts of interest, and workplace turpitude.[22]

Initially, strikes and pickets served Local 249-A well, but ultimately they exacerbated many of the existing problems the industry was experiencing. With more members than available jobs and the closing of several theaters by the early 1950s, frustration began to set in, and some disgruntled workers refused to pay their membership dues. Declining work opportunity was not solely the fault of assertive and rebellious black theater workers, however. The growing popularity of television continued to pose grave threats to the survival of movie and stage houses. Between 1947 and 1951, a large number of shoestring operations in the Los Angeles area began producing films for television. Vallee Video, Bonded Television Producers, and Telepak, although working with inferior resources, ushered in a new era of film entertainment that threatened to dominate the consumer and employment market. The growing profitability and prospects of telefilm expanded the IATSE's organizing strategies to include the pursuit of unorganized workers in the television industry. The precipitous decline in motion picture employment compelled the organization to seek new jurisdiction for unionization, particularly of workers in television production.[23]

While the IATSE accelerated its efforts to acquire television production workers and to establish a congenial relationship with them, black workers within the union still agonized over unfair treatment. "We ran all over the state of Texas—got put up in the pokey for trying to organize" black theater workers and "to keep them up with the different laws being passed," Lee Lewis stated. Their campaigns throughout East Texas drew sharp reactions from townsfolk and white workers, who often intimidated black organizers with their "big Texas hats—pistol and sidearms sagging down" alongside their bodies. "They were so hostile toward us," Tankersley lamented, that they "wouldn't let us see their contracts." Tankersley and his crew continued to walk picket lines—particularly at theaters in predominantly black neighborhoods that hired white workers and excluded black ones—even at the risk of confrontation with local police and business owners. Shop owners made their position toward striking black theater workers known by displaying guns and other weapons. Protest demonstrations and civil disobedience were becoming a way of life for black Americans, but Tankersley and his group made certain they followed the letter of the law to avoid confrontation with local police.[24]

Signs of relief did not emerge until 1955 when the AFL and the CIO merged into a single labor federation. George Meany, a New York building-trades unionist, led the organization for the next twenty-four years, with the goal of securing for labor its share of postwar profits. In exchange for labor peace and stability—fewer strikes—corporate managers often cooperated with unions, agreeing to contracts that gave many workers secure, predictable, and steadily rising income. The integration of these two labor bodies was inspired by government apathy and the continuing decline in union membership. The move necessarily required the AFL-CIO, and unions in general, to reassess racial policies.[25]

The following year, for instance, AFL-CIO president Meany appeared at the forty-third annual IATSE convention in Kansas City. He preached to an audience of delegates, which included E. J. Miller and Frank Coogler of Local 279 and Harvey D. Hill of Local 249, about the importance of labor unions rallying around the cause of civil rights. "We in the trade union movement," Meany articulated, "have to consider . . . as part of our duties . . . to see that people are not discriminated against." Meany's speech carried particular importance because it was delivered in a state that possessed at least two segregated IATSE locals. Kansas City Local 170-A and St. Louis Local 143-A were among several all-black locals that struggled against the deferential treatment enjoyed by their white counterparts. Others included Locals 8-A and 307-A of Philadelphia, 163-A of Louisville, 181-A of Baltimore, 224-A of Washington, DC, 236-A of Birmingham, 249-A of Dallas, 279-A of Houston, 293-A of New Orleans, 316-A of Miami, 327-A of Cincinnati, 370-A of Richmond, 550-A of Norfolk, and 589-A of Jackson, Mississippi. Meany's captivating speech did more than just earn him a hearty and lengthy applause—it moved the IATSE to pass a resolution eliminating the "A" suffix from the identification of its black locals. The "A" suffix, delegates agreed, carried a stigma that hindered black unionists during their contractual talks. Theater owners held little respect for members of the "A" locals and often expressed their disrespect through lower wages and poor working conditions.[26]

The IATSE's new attitude toward its racial practices coincided with the rise of the modern civil rights movement in which black IATSE workers, ironically, became the beneficiaries of televised civil unrest during the late 1950s and for much of the 1960s. The technology that had threatened their job security was now poised to play a part in preserving it. Indeed, the televised struggles of the civil rights movement had a profound impact on the IATSE's labor practices. Challenges to segregation in public accommodations filtered over into the labor ranks and engendered discussions about equal employment opportunities. The peak of union financial assistance to the civil rights movement was reached during the period between 1961 and 1964. During the 1963 Birmingham campaigns, the United Auto Workers met the bail-bond needs of thousands of protesters. Union donations to the Congress of Racial Equality exceeded forty thousand dollars. Labor contributions to the Southern Christian Leadership Conference, the Urban League, and the NAACP also increased during this period. Ironically, reports of persistent charges of discrimination levied by black workers against labor unions were widely circulated among civil rights activists. Five years after its merger, the AFL-CIO had failed to eradicate racial discrimination and segregation.[27]

This is not to suggest that the federation made no effort to accommodate black workers. To the contrary, its approach to racial inclusion had permeated labor circles throughout the country, and many labor organizations worked to revamp their constitutions and bylaws, which for years had deferred to the wishes and demands of white workers. The IATSE initiated efforts to modify its racial labor policies. In November 1963 it set up biracial merger committees, and by January 1964 merger talks between black and white workers from Locals 249 and 279 were under way. It was the IATSE's new outlook on unionization that energized black workers from both black-led locals to a new level of activism. While neither black nor white workers preferred merger, blacks were particularly concerned that racial amalgamation would be a greater threat to their job security than segregated unionism was. "We were afraid that we would lose what little jobs we had," said Tankersley.[28]

Although each took five years to come to fruition, the merger histories of Locals 279 and 249 present an interesting dichotomy. While the amalgamation of black and white workers from Local 279 went forward with little turmoil, the consolidation of the races from Local 249 took place amid bitter conflict. Lee Lewis and his crew protected the stability of their jobs and secured their seniority rights by having local labor-law attorneys thoroughly examine the content and language of their agreement. Deep-seated animosities, Lewis alleged, which neither black nor white members of Local 249 could seem to overcome, were responsible for much of the discord in Dallas. We had people with "common sense" who were willing to "sit down and work out our problems." In the end, blacks from Local 249 lost out on their seniority to white workers, who refused to grant black workers seniority based on their date of employment.[29]

Tankersley took matters into his own hands when he filed a complaint in 1969 with the Equal Employment Opportunity Commission (EEOC) against Local 249, alleging that their merger agreement discriminated against blacks by demanding that they come into the union as new members, thus denying them some nineteen years of seniority. Basing his discriminatory claim on the Civil Rights Act of 1964, which established the EEOC, Tankersley demonstrated his willingness to use federal agencies to remedy the workplace concerns of his workers. Following an investigation and the regional director's written findings, the EEOC voiced its support for Tankersley's claim, and white members began to rethink their position. The EEOC's initial ruling provided the impetus for Tankersley's group to demand a written agreement protecting the seniority rights of his workers. Tankersley followed up the EEOC decision with a class-action lawsuit that he filed in federal court in April 1972. Despite the EEOC decision, the federal court offered a different interpretation regarding the merger dispute. Discrimination did not present as much of a concern to the court as did the issues of "coercion," "deception," and "voluntary negotiations." When Tankersley signed the original merger agreement in January 1969, Judge W. M. Taylor ruled, he did so willingly and of sound mind and judgment. Because the seniority system had been negotiated and agreed upon by both parties, "the rights the Plaintiffs might have had were voluntarily waived" when they signed the agreement. The court's decision was a bitter pill to swallow for Tankersley and his crew. Throughout much of their careers, racism had played a key role in the travails of black workers in the IATSE and as far as Tankersley was concerned racism played a part in the merger agreement.[30]

Despite the fate of black workers from Local 249, the examination of skilled black labor contributes much to the field of American labor history. The struggles endured by blacks within the IATSE are worthy of historical consideration in that they are very much a part of the storied experiences of working-class blacks and the American labor movement. The corrective responses of black IATSE workers toward a film industry in rapid flux, and a labor movement that sanctioned black subordination, were bold, focused, and strategic. In the face of extreme internal and external circumstances, these two small unions held to their convictions and to a clear sense of purpose—full and equal opportunity within an industry that threatened to mechanize both black and white workers out of existence and in which racial polarization undermined the unions' economic power. With this in mind, it is time for historians to give due consideration to the vital role that African American skilled labor played in facilitating changes in the American labor movement and to address the distinctive contours of their experiences and the consequences of their efforts to topple racial inequities in craft unions.

Notes

This chapter originally appeared in *Southwestern Historical Quarterly* 106 (2003): 533–50, and is reprinted with permission.

1. C. M. Fox and S. A. Austin, "A Brief History of Motion Picture Operators: Local Union 330," *Twenty-Fifth Anniversary Banquet and Dance of MPO Local No. 330*, International Alliance of Theatrical and Stage Employees Collection (IATSE Collection), Texas Labor Archives, University of Texas at Arlington, (cited hereafter as TLA). Most labor studies that have reevaluated the role of African American labor in the union movement agree that black labor, particularly in the South, developed a tradition of activism that helped shape the labor-union identity. The historical literature on the black working-class has been dominated by discussion of unskilled black workers and of those belonging to the larger and more powerful unions and federations. For studies on the role of black workers in the American labor movement, see Eric Arnesen, *Waterfront Workers of New Orleans: Race, Class, and Politics, 1863–1923* (New York: Oxford University Press, 1991); Michael Goldfield, *The Color of Politics: Race and the Mainsprings of American Politics* (New York: New York Press, 1997); Keith Grittier, *What Price Alliance? Black Radicals Confront White Labor* (New York: Garland, 1994); William H. Harris, *The Harder We Run: Black Workers since the Civil War* (New York: Oxford University Press, 1982); Michael Honey, *Southern Labor and Black Civil Rights: Organizing Memphis Workers* (Urbana: University of Illinois Press, 1993); Robin Kelley, *Hammer and Hoe: Alabama Communists during the Great Depression* (Chapel Hill: University of North Carolina Press, 1990); Tera Hunter, *To Joy My Freedom: Southern Black Women's Lives and Labors after the Civil War* (Cambridge: Harvard University Press, 1997); Daniel Letwin, *The Challenge of Interracial Unionism: Alabama Coal Miners, 1878–1921* (Chapel Hill: University of North Carolina Press, 1998); Ernest Obadele-Starks, *Black Unionism in the Industrial South* (College Station: Texas A&M University Press, 2000); Joe William Trotter Jr., *Coal, Class, and Color: Blacks in Southern West Virginia, 1915–32* (Urbana: University of Illinois Press, 1990).

2. The first organization of stage employees began in New York in the late 1880s as a fraternal organization but soon became identified with the Knights of Labor and later the American Federation of Labor (AFL). While it is generally accepted that the IATSE modeled itself on unions of similarly sized industries, inadequate records prevent a full understanding of the early development of many of the first IATSE locals. Locals were initially organized in the larger cities to ensure a large membership. The National Union was formed to facilitate control over the industry and to address grievances. After two previous attempts, the IATSE was finally organized in 1893, complete with its own constitution and bylaws.

It was chartered as an international union in 1902. For more on the history and early years of the IATSE, see Michael C. Nielsen, "Motion Picture Craft Workers and Craft Unions in Hollywood: The Studio Era, 1912–1948" (PhD diss., University of Illinois at Champaign-Urbana, 1985), 26–36; Robert Osborne Baker, "The International Alliance of Theatrical Stage Employees and Moving Picture Machine Operators in the United States and Canada" (PhD diss., University of Kansas, 1933); Michael C. Nielsen, "Toward a Worker's History of the US Film Industry" in *Labor, the Working Class, and the Media*, ed. Vincent Mosco and Janet Wasco (Norwood, NJ.: Ablex Publishing, 1983); Janet Wasko, "Trade Unions and Broadcasting: A Case Study of the National Association of Broadcast Employees and Technicians," in Mosco and Wasco, *Labor, the Working Class, and the Media*; Alfred L. Bernheim, *The Business of the Theater: An Economic History of the American Theater, 1750–1932* (New York: B. Blom, 1964).

3.   *Proceedings of the Texas State Federation of Labor*, 1904, Texas Labor Archives, University of Texas at Arlington (cited hereafter as *TSFL Proceedings*); *TSFL Proceedings*, 1913, 88 (quotation); "Local 330 Anniversary Speech," IATSE Collection, TLA; *Twenty-Fifth Anniversary Banquet and Dance of MPO Local No. 330*, IATSE Collection, TLA.

4.   Lee A. Lewis, interview by George N. Green, October 4, 1971, transcription, TLA, #14.

5.   *Negro Labor News*, September 11, 1937; Lewis interview (quotation); *Texas State Industrial Council Convention Proceedings*, Texas Labor Archives, University of Texas at Arlington (cited hereafter as *TSCIO Proceedings*). For the CIO organizing campaign in Texas, see Murray E. Polakoff, "The Development of the Texas State CIO Council" (PhD diss., Columbia University, 1955). For discussions of the CIO's racial equality program, see Michael Goldfield, "Race and the CIO: The Possibilities for Racial Egalitarianism during the 1930s and 1940s," *International Labor and Working-Class History* 44 (Fall 1993): 1–32; Judith Stein, "The Ins and Outs of the CIO," ibid., 53–63; Gary Gerstle, "Working-Class Racism: Broaden the Focus," ibid., 33–40; Robert Korstad, "The Possibilities for Racial Egalitarianism: Context Matters," ibid., 41–44. For general accounts of the CIO's organizing struggles for industrial unions, see Robert H. Zieger, *The CIO, 1935–1955* (Chapel Hill: University of North Carolina Press, 1995); Melvyn Dubofsky and Warren Van Tine, *John L. Lewis: A Biography* (Urbana: University of Illinois Press, 1977); and Irving Bernstein, *Turbulent Years: A History of the American Worker, 1933–1941* (Boston: Houghton Mifflin, 1969).

6.   *Negro Labor News,* September 11, 1937; Lewis interview; Chris Dixie, interview by Ernest Obadele-Starks, April 22, 1995, Houston; 1938 *TSCIO Proceedings*, 6.

7.   Denise Hartsough, "Crime Pays: The Studios' Labor Deals in the 1930s," *Velvet Light Trap* 23 (Spring 1989): 49–63; Harold Seidman, *Labor Czars: A History of Labor Racketeering* (New York: Liveright, 1938), 173–82, 243–45; Carey McWilliams, "Racketeers and Movie Makers," *New Republic* 27 (October 1941): 533–35. The *New York Times* provided compelling details of the testimony during trials in 1941 and 1943.

8. Clayton R. Roppes and Gregory D. Black, "Blacks, Loyalty, and Motion-Picture Propaganda in World War II," *Journal of American History* 73 (September 1986): 383–406. For additional studies on blacks in American film, see Manthia Diawara, ed., *Black American Cinema* (New York: Routledge, 1993); G. William Jones, *Black Cinema Treasures: Lost and Found* (Denton: University of North Texas Press, 1991); John Kisch, *A Separate Cinema: Fifty Years of Black-Cast Posters* (New York: Farrar, Straus, and Giroux, 1992); John Gray, *Blacks in Film and Television: A Pan-African Bibliography of Films, Filmmakers, and Performers* (New York: Greenwood Press, 1990).

9. Amilcar Shabazz, "An Ideological Shootout in Texas: Separate Equality versus Racial Integration, 1940–1950" (paper presented at the Southern History Conference, Birmingham, AL, 1998). Jim Crow here refers to the racial discrimination resulting from a system of laws that segregated the races and sanctioned the social, political, and economic domination of whites over blacks. See James Martin Sorelle, "The Darker Side of Heaven: The Black Community in Houston, Texas, 1917–1945" (PhD diss., Kent State University, 1980); James Melvin Banks, "The Pursuit of Equality: The Movement for First Class Citizenship Among Negroes in Texas" (PhD diss., Syracuse University, 1962); Michael L. Gillette, "The NAACP in Texas, 1937–1957" (PhD diss., University of Texas, 1984); Steven A. Reich, "Soldiers for Democracy: Black Texans and the Fight for Citizenship, 1917–1921," *Journal of American History* 82 (March 1996), 1478–1504; Howard N. Rabinowitz, *The New South, 1865–1920* (Arlington, IL: Harlan Davidson, 1992); Neil McMillan, *Dark Journey: Black Mississippians in the Age of Jim Crow* (Urbana: University of Illinois Press, 1989); George B. Tindall, *The Emergence of the New South, 1913–1945* (Baton Rouge: Louisiana State University Press, 1967); C. Vann Woodward, *Origins of the New South, 1877–1913* (Baton Rouge: Louisiana State University Press, 1951).

10. Arthur J. Mandell to John R. Steelman, December 9, 1943 (quotation), File #301–9749, Federal Mediation and Conciliation Service Case Files, 1913–1948, RG 280, National Archives, Washington, DC (cited hereafter as FMCS); Progress Report, February 11, 1944, File #301–9749, FMCS; Joseph Meyers to Howard T. Colvin, March 20, 1944, File #301–9749, FMCS; Mandell and Wright to Colvin, December 9, 1944, File #301–9749, FMCS.

11. Castaneda to Clemons, October 6, 1943, Disposition Report, 10-BR-41, IATSE File, Records of the Fair Employment Practices Commission, RG 228, National Archives, Suitland, MD (cited hereafter as FEPC Records).

12. The FEPC was a government agency established by Franklin Roosevelt to investigate discrimination among defense contractors during World War II. The FEPC began preliminary investigations of Texas defense industries in 1942 and continued until the closing of the Dallas FEPC office in 1945. This resulted in the discovery of pervasive discrimination against black workers throughout Texas. Generally, the FEPC experienced more difficulties in industries where a lower percentage of workers were blacks and achieved greater successes in workplaces where blacks comprised a significant portion of the worker population. Final

Disposition Report, February 14, 1944 (quotation), IATSE File, FEPC Records; Final Disposition Report, November 5, 1943, ibid.; "Statement of Position By Local No. 279-A," File # 301–9749, FMCS; Castaneda to Farb, October 6, 1943, IATSE File, FEPC Records; Castaneda to Barraco, October 6, 1943, ibid.; Castaneda to Lewis, October 12, 1943, ibid. Also see Ernest Obadele-Starks, "The Road to Jericho: Black Workers, the Fair Employment Practice Commission, and the Struggle for Racial Equality in the Upper Texas Gulf Coast, 1941–1947" (PhD diss., University of Houston, 1996); Emilio Zamora, "The Failed Promise of Wartime Opportunity for Mexicans in the Texas Oil Industry," *Southwestern Historical Quarterly* 95 (January 1992), 323–50. For specific discussions on the origins and development of the FEPC, see Merl Reed, *Seedtime for the Civil Rights Movement: The President's Committee on Fair Employment Practice* (Baton Rouge: Louisiana State University Press, 1991); Louis C. Kesselman, *The Social Politics of the FEPC: A Study in Reform Pressure Movements* (Chapel Hill: University of North Carolina Press, 1948); Louis Ruchames, *Race, Jobs and Politics: The Story of FEPC* (New York: Columbia University Press, 1953); Herbert Garfinkel, *When Negroes March: The Organizational Politics of FEPC* (Glencoe, IL: Atheneum Press, 1959).

13.   Denise Hartsough, "Film Union Meets Television: IA Organizing Efforts, 1947–1952," *Labor History* 33 (Summer 1992): 357–71; Tino Balio, ed., *The American Film Industry*, rev. ed. (Madison: University of Wisconsin Press, 1985), 401.

14.   Irving McCann, *Why the Taft-Hartley Law?* (New York: Committee for Constitutional Government, 1950), 1–5.

15.   Hartsough, "Film Union Meets Television," 361.

16.   *Negro Labor News*, November 12, 1938 (quotations), June 10, 1939, July 27, October 19, 1940. It should be noted that C. W. Rice, owner and editor of the *Negro Labor News*, maintained an antilabor union and anticommunist agenda in his community activities and newspaper editorials. Company unions, as far as Rice was concerned, offered black workers the best alternative to biased labor unions.

17.   *Negro Labor News*, November 12, 1938, July 27, October 19, 1940.

18.   "Minutes of the Texas Federation Club," May 15, 1949, Box 154, File 1, Folder 2, Lee A. Lewis Papers, Houston Area Metropolitan Archives and Research Center (cited hereafter as Lewis Papers).

19.   "Minutes of the Texas Federation Club," October 23, 1949, Lewis Papers; Lewis interview; Ernest Obadele-Starks, "Black Labor, the Black Middle-Class, and Organized Protest along the Upper Texas Gulf Coast, 1883–1945," *Southwestern Historical Quarterly* 103 (July 1999): 53–65.

20.   Contract between Park Theater and MPMO Local No. 249-A, October 27, 1949 (quotation), IATSE Collection, TLA; "Dallas Moving Picture Machine Operators Union Local 249-A," ibid.

21.   S. R. Tankersley, interview by George Green, July 23, 1971, transcribed, OH Collection No. 9, TLA.

22.   Lewis interview; Tankersley interview; "Dallas Moving Picture Machine Operators Union Local 249A," IATSE Collection, TLA; "Contract between the Park Theater and Local No. 249A," 1949, ibid.

23. Tankersley interview; Dennis Joseph Dombrowski, "Film and Television: An Analytical History of Economic and Creative Integration" (PhD diss., University of Illinois, 1982); Hartsough, "Film Union Meets Television," 362–65.

24. "Minutes of the Texas Federation Club," April 20, 1952, Lewis Papers; Lewis interview (1st and 2nd quotations); Tankersley interview (3rd and 4th quotations).

25. Paul Buhle, *Taking Care of Business: Samuel Gompers, George Meany, Lane Kirkland, and the Tragedy of American Labor* (New York: Monthly Review Press, 1999); Taylor E. Dark, *The Unions and the Democrats: An Enduring Alliance* (Ithaca, NY: ILR Press, 1999); Ray M. Tillman and Michael S. Cummings, eds., *The Transformation of US Unions: Voices, Visions, and Strategies from the Grassroots* (Boulder: Lynne Rienner Publishers, 1999); Archie Robinson, *George Meany and His Times: A Biography* (New York: Simon and Schuster, 1981).

26. 1956 Proceedings of the International Alliance of Theatrical Stage Employees and Moving Picture Machine Operators of the United States and Canada, in *Combined Convention Proceedings of the International Alliance of Theatrical State Employees and Moving Picture Machine Operators of the US and Canada* (New York: IATSE, 1960), 1152, 1154, 1196.

27. On the relationship between the broadcast media and the civil rights movement, see Taylor Branch, *Parting the Waters: America in the King Years* (New York: Simon and Schuster, 1988), 51, 203, 367, 381, 420, 425, 445, 621, 633, 720, 763, 872, 881, 888. Recent literature that touches on some aspect of the civil rights movement and its specific link to labor includes Herbert H. Haines, "Black Radicalization and the Funding of Civil Rights: 1957–70," *Social Problems*, 1984, 32–36; Robert Korstad and Nelson Lichtenstein, "Opportunities Found and Lost: Labor, Radicals, and the Early Civil Rights Movement," *Journal of American History* 75 (December 1988): 786–811; Jack E. Davis, ed., *The Civil Rights Movement* (Malden, MA: Blackwell Publishers, 2001); Jonathan Birnbaum and Clarence Taylor, *Civil Rights since 1787: A Reader on the Black Struggle* (New York: New York University Press, 2000); Timothy J. Minchin, *Hiring the Black Worker: The Racial Integration of the Southern Textile Industry, 1960–1980* (Chapel Hill: University of North Carolina Press, 1999); Rod Bush, *We Are Not What We Seem: Black Nationalism and the Struggle in the American Century* (New York: New York University Press, 1999); Melvyn Stokes and Rick Halpern, *Race and Class in the American South since 1890* (Providence, RI: Berg, 1994); Alan Draper, *Conflict of Interests: Organized Labor and the Civil Rights Movement in the South, 1954–1968* (Ithaca, NY: ILR Press, 1994); Michael K. Honey, *Southern Labor and Black Civil Rights: Organizing Memphis Workers* (Urbana: University of Illinois Press, 1993); Jack Bloom, *Class, Race and the Civil Rights Movement* (Bloomington: Indiana University Press, 1987).

28. Tankersley interview (quotation); Herbert Hill, "Racism within Organized Labor: A Report of Five Years of the AFL-CIO," *Journal of Negro Education* 30 (Spring 1961): 109–18.

29. Lewis interview.

30. Memorandum of Opinion of the US District Court for the Northern District

of Texas–Dallas Division, *Samuel R. Tankersley vs. IATSE Local No. 249*, TLA, (quotations); Tankersley interview; "Operators Union Faces Racial Suit," *Dallas Morning News*, December 30, 1971. For discussions on the EEOC and black workers, see Benjamin W. Wolkinson, *Blacks, Unions, and the EEOC: A Study of Administrative Futility* (Lexington, MA: Lexington Books, 1973); Equal Employment Opportunity Commission, *Making a Right a Reality: An Oral History of the Early Years of the EEOC, 1965–1972, in Celebration of the Twenty-Fifth Anniversary, July 2, 1990* (Washington, DC: EEOC, 1990).

EMILIO ZAMORA

15

The Failed Promise of Wartime Opportunity for Mexicans in the Texas Oil Industry

Mexicans came out of the Great Depression facing an unprecedented opportunity to improve their traditional position as low-wage labor and to alter the generational effects of prior occupational discrimination. The wartime rhetoric of democracy, public policy measures that prohibited discrimination by defense industries, government employers and labor unions, and above all, dramatic job growth in high-wage firms led Mexicans to believe that their time had indeed arrived. The occupational gains made during the war may have raised their hopes further. Obstacles continued, however, to deny Mexican workers equal employment opportunities. Most Mexican workers still worked for low-wage employers, and those that secured jobs in high-wage firms assumed the least-skilled and lower-paying ones.[1]

This study examines wartime discrimination as an obstacle to Mexican workers in the oil-refining industry of the Texas Gulf Coast, a region bounded by Texas City, Houston, and Beaumont. Oil refineries normally denied Mexicans equal occupational, wage, and upgrading opportunities. Unionized and non-unionized Anglo workers played an important role in sustaining inequality primarily by opposing the adoption of a nondiscrimination policy in the oil industry. This opposition was cast in racial terms, though it was fundamentally motivated by economic and political concerns over the issue of job control. Although more work is required before we can properly gauge the effects of persistent discrimination, this study supports the conventional yet rarely substantiated view that Mexican workers continued to face formidable barriers when they entered high-wage firms during the war.[2]

The primary focus here is the role played by the Fair Employment Practices Commission (FEPC), the agency responsible for implementing President Roosevelt's Executive Orders 8802 and 9346 prohibiting various forms of discrimination by defense industries, government employers, and labor unions.[3] The FEPC waged a two-and-a-half-year challenge against discrimination in twelve oil refineries.[4] FEPC examiners focused on group complaints submitted by Mexican workers against three of the twelve refineries (Humble, Sinclair, and Shell), a company union at Humble named the Baytown Employees' Federation and two Congress of Industrial Organizations (CIO) unions, Locals 227 and 367. FEPC officials sought favorable settlements in the three refineries as a first step in pushing for a policy of nondiscrimination in the entire regional industry. Anglo worker opposition was so strong, however, that the FEPC was unable to assure Mexicans the wartime promise of full and unobstructed job opportunities. The agency's failure to effectively combat discrimination in three major refineries underscored its powerlessness; it also demonstrated the durable strength of a system of racial inequality.[5]

The experience of Mexican oil workers reflected a pattern of employment discrimination in other war-related industries. As the wartime expansion of the southwestern economy opened up new job opportunities, Mexicans for the first time began to obtain employment in urban-based War Industries such as garment, meatpacking, construction, shipping, aircraft repair, and oil. The newfound opportunities, however, soon dried up as high-wage firms filled up their laborer positions, the jobs that were normally available for Mexicans. As a result, War Industries reached an employment level of only about twenty-five thousand Mexicans during the war, which represented a low utilization rate of 5 percent. The wartime gains, therefore, accompanied persistent inequality. This inconsistency was especially evident in growth industries such as oil. Employers usually assigned Mexicans unskilled jobs that paid the lowest wages and denied them the opportunity to advance into the better-paying skilled positions. They shared this condition with African American workers. Moreover, when the war ended and industrial production decreased, they were generally denied further access and displaced from the jobs they had recently acquired.[6]

The booming oil industry in the Gulf Coast offered some of the more attractive job opportunities since it claimed one of the highest wage rates for skilled and unskilled workers in the state. The sheer fact that oil refineries offered a large and growing number of jobs also attracted the attention of workers. Also, by the mid-1940s the CIO-affiliated Oil Workers International Union (OWIU) had organized eleven of the twelve major refineries in the Gulf Coast and claimed some of the most favorable contractual agreements won by labor in Texas.[7] Despite the attractiveness of oil, only between 1,041 and 1,388, or less than 5 percent of the 25,000 Mexicans in the state's War Industries, were drawn into the refineries by the time of Pearl Harbor. They also represented a small portion—between 6 and 8 percent—of the industry's workforce.[8]

A significant number of the Mexican oil workers may have been born in Mexico. The only known source of information on nativity characteristics, a survey conducted by the FEPC in one of the refineries in 1943, indicated that 59 percent were born in Mexico and 41 percent in the United States. According to one observer, the US-born Mexicans were underrepresented because they were better informed about the discrimination that awaited them in oil and preferred to search for jobs elsewhere.[9] Mexican nationals presumably had fewer options and tended to accept the low-paying jobs. The presence of a large number of Mexican nationals explains why Anglo workers may have been especially sensitive to the possibility of a wage-cutting threat from below. It also reveals why the Mexican consul from Houston assumed an important role in representing the Mexican complaints before the FEPC.

Mexicans rarely found employment in the pipeline and production branches of the industry. Management usually assigned them common-laborer jobs in the refineries, paid them less than Anglos that were similarly classified, and denied them opportunities to advance into better-paying skilled occupations. When Mexican and African American workers assumed skilled jobs also held by Anglos, their job classification and pay normally remained unchanged. Rarely would management promote them to such jobs as mechanics, truck helpers, truck drivers, and bottle washers.[10]

The practice of placing minorities in the common-laborer positions and denying them upgrading opportunities created a ceiling on hiring that was often maintained through contractual agreements or informal understandings with labor unions. Organized labor was thus instrumental in defining the occupational hierarchical order, a fact that became clearer when unionists openly pressured the refineries to resist FEPC directives to end discrimination. Popular anti-Mexican-immigrant feelings that resulted from fears of increased job competition had previously influenced labor's defensive posture and the industry's hiring practices regarding both Mexican nationals and US-born Mexican workers. The widespread anti-Mexican agitation by Anglo workers during the tight market days of the depression, for instance, resulted in decisions by Humble, Sinclair, and Shell to temporarily halt the employment of Mexican workers. The result was a gradual depletion of their Mexican workforce. More importantly, these early tensions and protests coincided with union campaigns and contractual negotiations that formally and informally defined the Mexican's bottom position in the industry.[11]

Despite the express displeasure of national CIO officers who publicly supported the president's executive orders, the local unions and the leadership of the OWIU rarely challenged the discriminatory practices of the companies or the racially exclusive organizing policies of company unions and AFL locals. In fact, in at least four refineries CIO locals negotiated collective bargaining agreements that established dual wage systems, segregated work areas, separate occupational categories, and upgrading procedures that effectively barred minority workers from the skilled occupations. These agreements, as well as numerous informal understandings established at other refineries, were negotiated with the knowledge and support of the OWIU. The OWIU and local union leaders presumably shared the sentiments of their local membership or thought that it was less than worthwhile to disturb widespread and deeply ingrained racial customs.[12]

Although it may be impossible to know to what degree racial thinking motivated the union leadership, it is clear that both the unions and company representatives resisted compliance on the grounds that widespread opposition by Anglo workers threatened to disrupt production. This was a recurring claim that seriously hampered the FEPC throughout the war period. There was ample evidence and good reason to believe this claim. Some FEPC officials, however, suspected that management and union leaders were concealing their own opposition to integration and seeking to encourage dissent by stalling the compliance process. Although company representatives may have shared racial views with the Anglo workforce or even entertained the idea of promoting racial thinking to ingratiate themselves with labor or to encourage divisions among the workers, their stated position was credible to an extent given the economic losses they could incur as a result of a disruption in production. The unions, on the other hand, were responding to more than just fears of possible Anglo workers' reactions. Underneath their claims of possible disruptions lay an interest in protecting the privileged position of their constituency from the FEPC threat.

Although the refineries often publicly complained of FEPC compliance pressures, they usually appeared to be projecting an image of disinterested players rather than actively provoking a reaction. Local unionist leaders, however, at times openly encouraged workers to see the intervention of the federal government as a threat to racial privilege and job control. This was evident when union leaders representing the company union at Humble and the CIO locals at Sinclair and Shell openly defied FEPC directives and defended discrimination, particularly against blacks, as the prevailing custom in the South. Among the ideas entertained by unionists and the rank and file was the notion that if concessions were made to Mexicans, blacks would follow with similar allegations, competition would intensify, and management would decrease wages and release Anglo workers.[13]

Although opposition to FEPC directives significantly undermined compliance, other factors constrained the agency's work. These included the short life span of the FEPC, the lack of enforcement powers, and internal divisions that periodically surfaced on the question of whether to challenge discrimination in the entire industry or on a plant-by-plant basis. These problems, however, did not seem to seriously impair the FEPC in its work in other industries. In fact, what most often appeared to be the case is that opposition to the FEPC in oil magnified internal constraints.[14]

Mexican workers began submitting their complaints in 1941 to the Office of Production Management in San Antonio and the FEPC office in Washington, DC. Problems associated with distance and a lack of personnel kept government officials from servicing these complaints adequately until the president's Executive Order 9346, issued on May 26, 1943, made it possible to establish the Region X office in Dallas. FEPC examiners began their oil investigations almost immediately. Although the Dallas office recorded a continuous stream of settlements in other industries throughout the state, the oil refineries, especially Humble, Sinclair, and Shell, kept it occupied until the agency ceased its operations in 1945.[15]

Dr. Carlos Castaneda, the University of Texas history professor who directed the Dallas office, was an especially important figure in FEPC work in part because of his membership in a national network of Mexican American civil rights leaders that was actively testing the sincerity of the wartime rhetoric of world democracy and Pan-Americanism. His battles against the oil refineries, particularly the fight against Shell, thus became focal points of concern in the civil rights movement and drew attention to the importance of discrimination against Mexicans in Mexico–United States relations.[16]

Castaneda processed Mexican complaints against eight of the twelve major refineries between May 1943 and December 1944. He adopted a dual strategy that first focused on complaints against Humble, Sinclair, and Shell hoping that favorable adjustments in these refineries would compel the entire industry to enforce the president's executive orders. The second part of the strategy involved a decision to challenge the general practice of racial discrimination with complaints by Mexican workers. Since he feared stronger Anglo opposition to African American complaints, Castaneda decided first to establish the existence of racial discrimination on the basis of Mexican complaints and then direct the refineries to adopt a policy of nondiscrimination that would benefit all minority workers.[17]

W. Don Ellinger became the director of the Dallas office in December 1944, while Castaneda assumed new duties as special assistant to the FEPC director on Latin American affairs and as director of a new regional office in San Antonio. Although Castaneda was no longer officially involved in the oil cases, he continued to advise the Dallas office. Ellinger handled the cases against the oil companies until the FEPC ceased operations in Texas during 1945.[18]

Castaneda and Ellinger normally coordinated the preparation and submission of complaints with local groups of workers, officials from the Mexican consulate at Houston, and community leaders associated with the well-known civil rights organization, the League of United Latin American Citizens (LULAC). Preliminary fact-finding meetings also included workers and civil rights leaders from the African American community. Meetings with local minority leaders and investigations conducted immediately after the opening of the Dallas office revealed that the most blatant cases of discrimination were occurring at Humble, Sinclair, and Shell. Moreover, there were a sufficient number of Mexican workers in each plant willing to formally challenge their employers.[19] Although the FEPC handled cases against the three refineries simultaneously, Castaneda obtained the first settlement at Humble.

Humble owned four oil refineries in Texas, including the one at Baytown that became the center of early controversy for the FEPC. The Baytown plant employed approximately three thousand workers during the war, including about seventy-five Mexicans and four hundred blacks. The complaint against Humble occurred while the CIO-led Oil Workers' Organizing Campaign (OWOC) was joining the issue of unionization with the cause of minority workers. The CIO's national leadership initially directed the OWOC and thus injected a more progressive view on minority rights than was normally the case in the area. The OWOC leadership endorsed the claim of discrimination by Mexican complainants in part because it was actively soliciting the support of minority workers for the CIO union, Local 333, in the upcoming union election. This touched off a near-violent and racially inspired reaction by the company union, the Baytown Employees' Federation (BEF).[20]

In the midst of this highly controversial organizing campaign, a group of six Mexican workers charged Humble with six forms of discrimination. According to the complaint, Mexican laborers received seventy-six and one-half cents per hour for performing the same tasks as Anglo laborers who were paid eighty-nine and one-half cents an hour. While Mexican orderlies in the company hospital received a wage of $137 per month, Anglo janitors received $180 per month. Mexican and Anglo workers doing the same work in and around the acid tanks received seventy-nine and one-half cents per hour and ninety-two and one-half cents per hour, respectively. Although Mexicans cut, bent, and tied steel for seventy-six and one-half cents per hour, Anglos working for contractors on refinery property earned $1.34 for doing the same work. Mexicans were usually assigned to the labor department without opportunities for promotion, and Humble had refused to hire Mexicans since at least 1937.[21]

The company superintendent, Gordon L. Farned, responded to the complaint with a lengthy justification of Humble's record with its Mexican workers. He also broached the issue of Anglo worker opposition that was to loom over compliance negotiations in the industry. Farned cautioned the FEPC about disrupting the deep-rooted custom of discrimination against Mexicans in the state and urged a strategy of gradual change to minimize Anglo hostility.[22]

> Unless and until there is a change in public feeling and sentiment, regardless of what we as one employer may do about the matter, it is an undeniable fact that Anglo American workmen and the public generally, exclusive of the Mexicans themselves, do set themselves apart and do consider themselves to be superior mentally, physically and socially to the Mexicans. . . . [I]t probably would be to the best interests of the Mexicans to "make haste slowly"; to make social and economic gains gradually, to educate the populace at large gradually, and to promote their acceptance of the principles aimed at, rather than to take action intended to accomplish the ends you seek, which in actuality, if carried out, would most certainly start serious hostilities and lead to a harmful conflagration.[23]

Farned added a second related reason for resisting compliance that was to plague the FEPC's work in the industry. He suggested that the FEPC seek industry-wide compliance rather than plant-by-plant settlements. Otherwise, each company that complied presumably would be made the focus of the community's wrath with the resulting disruption of production.

Subsequent investigations revealed a glaring inconsistency in the company's claims that Mexican workers were not hired or promoted because they did not meet the company's educational requirements. Company officials admitted that Anglos were frequently hired without meeting the requirements and that Mexicans were denied employment even when they met them. Moreover, the officials failed to demonstrate a lack of ability by the Mexican workers since they often performed the same tasks as Anglos. As a result of the investigation, the complaint was expanded to include charges of discriminatory skill classifications and segregated drinking and toilet facilities.[24]

While Castaneda negotiated with Humble representatives, the company union began to openly declare that Local 333 was threatening the livelihood of Anglo workers by welcoming Mexicans and blacks into the union and by supporting claims of racial discrimination in the refinery. Leaders of the BEF stepped up their race-baiting activities against both Local 333 and the FEPC during the following weeks through a widely distributed organ, *The Bulletin*.[25] The paper consistently warned that compliance would result in granting equal treatment to blacks.[26]

At one point, *The Bulletin* pointed to the association between Local 333 and the FEPC with the following observation: "A vote for the CIO is a vote for absolute equality between the white and colored races on every job in the Baytown Refinery from labor gang to Department head."[27] When the FEPC wired the BEF to cease making inflammatory statements, *The Bulletin* responded that it did not "intend to be swayed from our purpose by any telegraphed reprimands from any of the CIO-owned and operated Fair Labor Practices Committees in Washington, DC, so this is a notice to them to save stamps and telegraph costs."[28]

Despite the findings of the initial investigation, the FEPC decided to delay action on the joint complaint and an additional complaint in which Local 333 alleged discrimination in the hiring, tenure, and compensation of Mexican and African American workers. This decision to withdraw from the conflict was made pending the outcome of the union election and FEPC deliberations in Washington regarding a proposed hearing to investigate complaints of discrimination against Mexicans in the Southwest. Also contributing to the postponement was the FEPC's indecision on whether to seek compliance on an industry or plant-by-plant basis.[29]

A renewed interest in the oil companies became evident when Castaneda obtained permission for a second investigation at Humble. By this time, the union had failed to secure certification and the FEPC had decided that the proposed hearing be confined to the mining industry in the Arizona–New Mexico–West Texas region and that action against the oil companies be pursued on an individual basis.[30] The second investigation generated complaints by three Mexican workers alleging wage discrimination. By the time Castaneda met with company officials, however, Humble had settled the complaints. A subsequent inquiry confirmed that Humble had granted the complainants a raise. The settlement, however, accompanied a decision by Humble to rid itself of its minority workforce by contracting out to the Brown and Root Company all of its laboring work.[31]

One can only conjecture on the almost sudden reversal of opinion by Humble. Officials had been insistent on adhering to the local custom of denying employment opportunities to Mexican workers on the grounds that it would invite trouble. Moreover, company officials had been reluctant to fully admit the existence of discrimination or to correct past abuses supposedly because of the feared reaction by Anglo workers. Humble officials, however, may have concluded that compliance was inevitable given the FEPC's belated yet determined decision to consider one refinery at a time. The union election, on the other hand, was probably the single most important factor that opened the way for resolving the impasse.

Humble had kept the FEPC at bay while it did battle with the OWOC on its successful march through the rest of the industry. Once the union lost the election the company was free to confront the problem that it faced with the FEPC. By introducing changes in the plant that exceeded the FEPC's directives, the company rid itself of a potentially difficult conflict with the agency. Although Humble may have appeared overly compliant, it had also begun to dispose of its minority workforce. With this move, the company also avoided a conflict with its Anglo workforce and nullified one of Local 333's most important organizational and ideological bases of operations.

Local 333 was the only union in the region known to have cooperated fully with the FEPC. This was due largely to the influence of the CIO-run OWOC, which embraced the cause of the Mexican complainants. After a successful campaign that resulted in election victories in approximately six refineries, the CIO organizers in the OWOC boldly confronted racial discrimination. Supporting the cause of the Mexican complainants, however, resulted in the OWOC's only defeat in the early 1940s. The defeat also reinforced local fears of an Anglo workers' reaction to compliance and revealed a serious division between members of the national CIO and local and state leadership around the issue of race.

The OWIU and local CIO leaders had opposed the OWOC's progressive racial policy, including its endorsement of Mexican complaints during the organizing campaign at Humble. Pressure on the national CIO office eventually led to the removal of its organizers and an end to labor's express concern for minority workers. Prior to the election, the OWIU renegotiated its organizing agreement with the local and state CIO unionists, which resulted in the replacement of the organizers with personnel selected by the OWIU. The experience at Humble thus demonstrated that the OWIU and local leadership preferred to avoid the race issue for fear of antagonizing Anglo workers, a view that also found expression during the compliance battle at Sinclair.[32]

The Sinclair refinery located in Pasadena employed a workforce of approximately fifteen hundred, which included approximately one hundred Mexicans and 250 blacks.[33] At least three joint complaints were submitted on behalf of Mexican workers. J. O. Gray, secretary-treasurer of Local 227, submitted the first complaint in April 1942 to the Office of Production Management in San Antonio. He indicated that a foreman had unfairly issued warnings to the men and that the union's Workmen's Committee had submitted a request to transfer them to another department.[34] There is no evidence that the FEPC acted on the initial complaint, perhaps because around that same time a group of Mexican workers was also seeking the assistance of the FEPC with a more comprehensive complaint that charged the company as well as the union with discrimination.

The forty Mexican complainants secured the assistance of consul Adolfo G. Dominguez in alleging a historical pattern of discrimination by the company and Local 227.[35] One of their major allegations was that Sinclair had stopped hiring Mexicans since the early 1930s. The workers also claimed that Sinclair routinely hired blacks to replace departing Mexican workers. The complainants further charged that the company, in collaboration with union leaders, maintained a job classification system that placed Mexicans in the laboring positions at an approximate wage of seventy-eight and one-half cents. Many performed the same tasks as skilled Anglo workers though they were given job classifications as helpers at an hourly wage of ninety-eight and one-half cents. Four of them received eighty-three and one-half cents an hour. They worked as janitors along with nine African American workers, and they could transfer to other departments only if they kept their classification as common laborers. Moreover, skilled and semiskilled vacancies were never posted, and only Anglo unionists were allowed to bid for these jobs. Only one of the workers had ever been promoted; he was a naturalized citizen who worked as a foreman for a crew of black workers.

The Mexican workers also complained about the company's segregation practices. They were required to punch the time clock in a separate line shared with African American workers. Also, the company kept separate lockers and bathing facilities for minority workers. During the lunch hour, Mexican workers were given the choice of eating outdoors or joining the African American workers in a segregated section. Lastly, Mexicans and blacks were transported to work in two crowded buses while the Anglos traveled in a separate, less-crowded bus.

Once Castaneda had confirmed the allegations through on-site investigations, he submitted the joint complaint to Sinclair and Local 227. When neither responded, Castaneda visited the complainants at the Mexican consul's office to further substantiate the charges. On the basis of this inquiry, the FEPC once again forwarded a complaint and requested a response to specific allegations of discrimination against both Mexican and African American workers in wages and upgrading opportunities.[36]

The superintendent of the refinery, D. A. Young, responded with a denial of the charges. He added that despite the fact that few Mexican and African American workers qualified for the better-paying jobs, Sinclair had upgraded three Mexican workers to semiskilled and skilled positions. Probably because he anticipated a finding in favor of the Mexican complainants, Young resorted to placing the burden of compliance on Local 227. He warned FEPC officials that the union would not "permit the commingling of the different races employed at this plant."[37] To demonstrate that this was not a ploy to evade compliance, Young furnished Cochran with correspondence in which the union expressly opposed the promotion or reclassification of Mexican workers.

During a subsequent meeting with Castaneda, Young expressed a willingness to provide upgrading opportunities to Mexican as well as African American workers if the union could be made to guarantee support for compliance. Local 227 representatives, on the other hand, admitted that the union had opposed upgrading but promised to seek the cooperation of the entire membership for a policy of nondiscrimination. Company and union representatives, however, denied that discrimination existed regarding wages, the posting of vacancy notices, and the use of transportation facilities.[38]

Two months later Castaneda was reporting that the upgrading case against Sinclair had been adjusted. The company had kept its word and the union membership had grudgingly decided not to contest what Castaneda admitted were "minor advances given Latin Americans" at Sinclair.[39] A major factor in the settlement was Castaneda's decision to settle the complaint on the basis of the admissions made by the company and union representatives. Castaneda's conciliatory approach was clearly intended to capitalize on the single admission of upgrading discrimination in order to proceed with a directive calling for the adoption of a general policy of nondiscrimination.

Although Castaneda had initially filed the case alleging discrimination against Mexicans at Sinclair, he sought a settlement that favored the entire minority workforce. Consequently, when he confirmed the settlement, he made binding an agreement that benefited both Mexican and black workers. In a letter to an officer of the union, he stated: "I am pleased to note that as the result of the meetings held your union has agreed to permit the company to abandon its discriminatory practices and to give all employees an equal opportunity for promotion in accord with their experience, ability and aptitude, regardless of race, creed, color or national origin."[40]

Although the company and the union may have been cooperative during the final settlement negotiations, they did not satisfy the concerns of the Mexican workers who continued to informally complain of discrimination. One year after Castaneda had secured the settlement, the same Mexican complainants were again formally contesting Sinclair's discriminatory practices. They claimed that Sinclair was refusing to hire qualified Mexican applicants and denying them upgrading opportunities. The company had allegedly refused employment to three Mexican applicants at the same time that it had been hiring African American and Anglo workers. Moreover, Sinclair had refused to upgrade at least three Mexican workers. On the basis of this complaint, Ellinger informed Sinclair that despite the recent settlement, the FEPC had determined that discrimination against Mexicans was continuing.[41]

The company responded to the complaint by denying the charges while the union simply chose to disregard it. The FEPC, on the other hand, did not press the issue even though additional complaints continued to arrive. This was probably due to the fact that mounting political opposition to the FEPC in Washington was already signaling the end of the agency and thus discouraging forthright action. Also, the FEPC was then waging its most trying battle at Shell, which may have drawn its resources and attention from the fight at Sinclair.[42]

The case against Sinclair once again demonstrated the FEPC's difficulty in securing permanent settlements. One obvious problem was the discontinuance of the agency's operations at a time when settlements were still pending. Additionally, indecision regarding the compliance strategy that the FEPC wished to pursue contributed to the initial delays. Other more important factors included the opposition of the union and the refusal of the company to comply until it could be guaranteed that Local 227 would not strike in protest. Also, the company failed to live up to its promise to comply with the FEPC directives and continued to challenge allegations of discrimination confirmed by the FEPC. The union was generally indifferent to the second complaint, preferring instead to leave the minority workers to fend for themselves against Sinclair.

Reminiscent of the fight at Humble, the FEPC often appeared to back away as if it was facing an opponent too formidable to confront. Despite the large amount of evidence accumulated in support of the complaints, the FEPC exhibited a conciliatory attitude in the settlement process. It may have been expedient, however, for Castaneda to seek a speedy settlement in light of the trouble that the agency was having at the time with Shell. This willingness to settle allowed Castaneda to correct one case of upgrading discrimination and to justify a directive calling for the adoption of a policy of nondiscrimination. Rushing into a settlement that conceded ground on key charges, however, no doubt left the impression that the FEPC lacked the confidence and enforcement power to challenge employment discrimination, a perception that plagued the agency in its dealings with Shell.

Shell Oil Company maintained a large refinery at Deer Park with a workforce of approximately twelve hundred workers that included at least one hundred Mexican and African American workers.[43] Mexican workers faced the same problems evident in the Humble and Sinclair refineries. Widespread discrimination restricted them as well as African American workers to the lowest-paying unskilled positions. Moreover, both groups of workers were limited to segregated transportation, eating, and restroom facilities. Mexican complaints against Shell resulted in one of the most bitter fights over the issue of discrimination. It involved open defiance by the union and the continuing embarrassing ineffectiveness of the FEPC.

The FEPC initiated its case against Shell in May 1943 with a complaint submitted by consul Dominguez on behalf of thirty-four Mexican nationals who had tried unsuccessfully to settle their claims with the company during the previous two years. They had also failed to convince Local 367 to intervene on their behalf. As a result, they had quit the union and were now appealing to the Mexican consul and local LULAC leaders as an act of last resort. The workers made the familiar charges of occupational, wage, and upgrading discrimination, a hiring ceiling, and segregated facilities.[44]

During a meeting at the Mexican consulate attended by company, union, and Mexican workers' representatives, an FEPC investigator confirmed the allegations, though he was unable to settle the complaint. When Dominguez asked that Mexican workers be granted a just wage and the promotional guarantees enjoyed by Anglos, management and union representatives responded that they could not give assurances because of the all too prevalent fear of antagonizing Anglo workers. They claimed that there was a widespread belief among Anglo workers that a concession to the Mexicans would encourage complaints by blacks seeking similar guarantees and that this would result in depressed wages and their eventual replacement by minority workers.[45]

The company and the union maintained that the only way to avoid a disruption was for the FEPC to hold an industrywide hearing and order all the refineries in the area with CIO union contracts to adopt a policy of nondiscrimination. The union offered to communicate the plan to the other locals. Seeing no other option, Dominguez expressed his support for the plan and recommended that the FEPC initiate such a settlement in a meeting with O. A. Knight, president of the Oil Workers International Union, and D. W. Hobey, president of the Gulf Coast Refiners Association.[46]

The FEPC may have allowed Shell and the union to independently implement their proposed plan because there is no evidence that Castaneda participated in it. When months passed without any news about the implementation of the plan from Shell, the local, or the OWIU, Castaneda called on the FEPC to grant him the authority to proceed with the case. He was particularly concerned that consul Dominguez and other Mexican leaders would become more disillusioned with the FEPC. Castaneda also expressed the view that the company and the local had called for an industrywide hearing for the sole purpose of delaying the compliance process. He felt that the most reasonable and promising measure to take was individual action based on the findings of discrimination that Shell and Local 367 officers openly admitted.[47]

A worsening situation at Shell underscored the need for immediate action. On November 3, the manager suspended seven Mexican workers for insubordination. According to the workers, he had instructed them to do a temporary job for eighty-seven cents an hour in the segregated pipe-fitting department though the prevailing wage for pipe fitters ranged between ninety-seven cents and $1.39 an hour. When they refused to do the work at the disputed wage, he fired them. The company subsequently advertised vacancies for these same jobs at ninety-seven cents an hour. The workers once again sought the help of Mexican consul Dominguez. This time, however, Dominguez convinced his superiors to intercede in the matter—an indication of growing concern in Mexican government circles. The Mexican ambassador to the United States, Rafael de la Colina, expressed his government's displeasure to the chairman of the FEPC by stating that continuing defiance at Shell violated the Good Neighbor Alliance and undermined the US government's wartime pledge of international solidarity against racial injustice. The issue of discrimination in oil thus reached international proportions, a development that pressured the FEPC to redouble its efforts.[48]

Meanwhile, to support his contention for a hearing that would address the complaints against Shell, Castaneda called for an additional investigation, which later confirmed the prior findings. He also recommended immediate action, particularly because Shell again admitted practicing discrimination.[49] The subsequent conference that Castaneda held with Shell and Local 367 representatives in December ended on a familiar note. The manager of the refinery and the president of Local 367 admitted discrimination but insisted that they would not agree to any changes until a general hearing was held or a directive was issued by the FEPC ordering the entire industry to implement a policy of nondiscrimination.[50] When FEPC officials requested a formal statement documenting this response, the union officer answered defiantly, "The Union at this time does not propose to change without first having a hearing or order, as we consider ourselves and the company both in violation of the Executive Order."[51] The company representative added, "The position of the Management of the company is that the consequences of any change in this respect are so far-reaching and would have such detrimental results that we do not see any reason for change."[52]

Shell defended its bid for an industrywide hearing and directive with the argument that a unilateral settlement would place the company in an unfair position with its competitors. With this argument, Shell placed the burden of change on the union, while the union officers openly admitted that the membership would strike if the company complied.[53] The deadlock seemed unbreakable especially since the FEPC had delayed action while its personnel debated on the proper strategy to pursue. While Castaneda insisted on an individual hearing with Shell, other officials in the Dallas office were urging an industrywide hearing. A decision was finally reached to proceed with Castaneda's recommendation and to schedule a hearing for December 1944.[54] On the day that the public hearing was to take place, Shell officials finally conceded. They requested a private conference and promised to abide by the decision to be rendered by the trial examiner and a committee of four FEPC representatives that included Castaneda.[55]

In his opening statement before the committee, an FEPC official accused the company and the union of disregarding the skills and experience of Mexican workers and of restricting them to the menial jobs at wages that were lower than those paid to Anglo workers performing the same tasks. This had been accomplished through a formal contract that defined the discriminatory rates of pay, hours of work, and other terms of employment operating in the plant. Since discrimination at Shell had been directed against both Mexicans and blacks, the FEPC called for an end to all forms of discrimination.[56]

The opening statement included other observations that acknowledged the importance that the Shell case had acquired in the international arena, particularly with the major ally of the United States in the hemisphere, Mexico.[57] In calling for an end to racial and national origin discrimination, the FEPC described the denial of opportunities as a problem that undermined the war effort because it harmed relations with Latin American nations: "The eyes of our neighbors to the south are watching with keen interest. The denial of equal opportunities for full participation in the war effort, and for advancement to workers of Latin-American extraction, negatives [*sic*] our professions of good neighborliness and reflects upon our moral leadership in the family of nations."[58] The committee appeared to have settled the issue once and for all when it ordered the company and the union to eliminate all forms of discrimination. The company and the union agreed to expunge from the collective bargaining agreement all basis for discrimination and to stop denying Mexican and African American workers hiring and upgrading opportunities. The committee also gave specific instructions directing Shell to submit a separate wage complaint to the War Labor Board for adjustment and to upgrade two Mexican complainants to carman's helper and truck driver. The FEPC followed by rendering a decision on January 27 that directed the company and the union to comply with the president's executive order within ninety days.[59] The stage was now set to determine if compliance could proceed to its logical conclusion without setting off a reaction by Anglo workers.

The compliance process quickly became burdened with difficulties that tested the FEPC's ability to influence the ensuing course of events. When several Mexican workers, including the complainants who had been assured promotions, signed up for available jobs, a foreman and the personnel manager informed them that Shell did not intend to abide by the FEPC directive until the April 27 deadline. FEPC officials rightfully saw this as a direct challenge against the spirit, if not the letter, of the settlement. Pressure was again brought to bear on Shell.[60]

In response to the FEPC's requests for support, other government agencies reminded the company that it was obligated to honor the president's executive order or risk losing lucrative federal contracts. The FEPC had mixed results, however, in convincing labor leaders to pressure Local 367. While the national CIO office declared support for a policy of nondiscrimination, key state leaders such as O. A. Knight and Timothy Flyn, state CIO director, claimed that the parent organizations did not dictate policy to their locals. Nonetheless, pressure from government agencies finally convinced Shell to cooperate. The first upgrading occurred on March 8 when Shell appointed a Mexican worker to a carman's helper position. A week later, a second Mexican worker was upgraded to a truck driver's job.[61]

Increased pressure by the FEPC eventually forced Shell to upgrade additional minority applicants. This, however, did not occur without Shell first announcing that the FEPC was forcing the company to integrate the workforce against its will. Two vice presidents of the local added to the growing tensions by resigning from their positions as a sign of disapproval of the FEPC directives. On March 22 the company nevertheless upgraded one Mexican and seven blacks to general helpers in each of the eight separate craft departments. An incident followed that raised the developing conflict to a higher level.[62]

A company foreman who obviously sought to disassociate himself from the issue of compliance convened Anglo workers from each department and asked them to publicly state if they would work alongside the upgraded minority workers. Although some of the Anglo workers may have been inclined to accept this proposition, the fear of reprisals from coworkers was probably too great because none agreed to work with them. In opposing the upgrading decision the Anglo workers were absolving the company from any blame in the compliance conflict and accepting the major responsibility for defending the status quo. Soon after the vote, an undetermined number of Anglo workers and the two union officers that had resigned threatened to stage a strike if the minority workers were placed in their new positions. The company quickly returned the workers to their previous jobs. Emboldened by this immediate response, the protesting Anglo workers then demanded that the previously upgraded Mexican workers also be returned to their former jobs. The company again capitulated.[63]

FEPC officials called a series of conferences with company and union representatives to try to remedy the situation that had clearly gotten out of hand. The company maintained that it was forced to concede to the demands of the Anglo workers. Union representatives, on the other hand, expressed an interest in complying with the FEPC directives but requested time to convince a portion of their membership that was opposed to integration. Matters deteriorated further as Shell officials continued to publicly present the company as a helpless victim and as the union membership began to more forcefully express its opposition to the issue of integration.[64] Although the union did not guarantee support for compliance, continued FEPC pressure led the company to upgrade two Mexican workers on April 27. The results were predictable.[65]

Anglo workers in the automotive department responded by walking off their jobs. Negotiations followed between the union, Shell, and a conciliator from the Department of Labor. When negotiations failed to produce any results, the FEPC brought in the assistant disputes director from the Dallas office of the War Labor Board to help resolve the issue. The result was a six-day hearing that affirmed the FEPC directive and the Smith-Connally Act, which required workers to issue a petition before waging a strike in wartime. As part of the settlement, the workers agreed to remain on the job and not insist on the removal of the upgraded Mexicans without first filing a strike petition with the National Labor Relations Board (NLRB). In granting the union the right to hold a vote on what was essentially a compliance matter, however, the War Labor Board undermined the FEPC directives and provided the segregationists the opportunity to legitimately defy the FEPC at a future date.[66]

The tenuous settlement involved important concessions by FEPC officials who by now seemed to be desperately seeking to regain their influence. First of all, they failed to dispute the decision by the War Labor Board that granted the union the right to challenge the compliance directive. In fact, the FEPC granted Shell and the local a thirty-day extension on the compliance order to accommodate the scheduling of the election. Moreover, a general understanding was reached whereby no more upgrading actions were to be taken until the strike ballot was cast. Although the FEPC was essentially forced to back down, the prospect of losing complete control led Ellinger to declare with a sense of relief, "[W]e have won a tremendous victory by the skin of our teeth in the agreement of the men to work with the Latin-Americans on the job."[67]

Mexican government officials and Mexican civil rights leaders from Texas did not share Ellinger's enthusiasm. They began to more openly view the Shell case as a stark demonstration of deep-rooted racism and ineffective government intervention. Mexico's foreign minister, Ezequiel Padilla, for instance, commented while attending the first United Nations conference at San Francisco that nothing less than the hemispheric prestige of the United States as a democratic nation was at stake. Also, Castaneda reported that Mexican leaders from throughout the state expressed "strong resentment" against Shell and felt that the FEPC was not sufficiently aggressive.[68]

Minority workers remained steadfast in support of compliance. Mexican workers called for full integration, while African American workers supported the idea of a segregated workforce on a separate but equal basis. In other words, both Mexican and African American workers sought guarantees of equal access to all jobs at the same pay while the latter group did not insist on working side by side with Anglo workers. Minority workers also agreed that the FEPC should continue to press the company and the union with claims of discrimination by Mexican workers since they had the best chance of succeeding and setting the necessary precedent for the complete integration of the workforce.[69]

Anglo workers refused to concede despite the urgings of the FEPC and the negative publicity that the case brought the oil industry and the labor movement. This became openly evident when a majority of them voted in favor of a strike on June 6, 1945. The NLRB-sanctioned election not only affirmed the segregationist posture of the union; it also demonstrated the union's newfound talent for legitimately defying the president's executive order. As a result of the election, the FEPC scuttled its compliance directive and endorsed a settlement proposed by the union. The union's plan designated a small number of skilled jobs for minority workers to be set aside in still-segregated departments. Shell representatives, on the other hand, washed their hands of the whole matter. They declared a willingness to adopt whatever plan the FEPC and the union favored.[70]

Minority workers expressed deep resentment over the strike vote and were adamant in demanding that the FEPC not relent in its dealings with the company and the union despite efforts by Anglo workers to divide them. Mexicans were told that if African American workers had not been included in the directive, Anglos would have complied. Blacks, on the other hand, were told that the Mexicans ought not be supported because they were pretentious and claimed to be better than blacks. With matters still unresolved, the FEPC first restricted and then closed its operations in Texas when Congress decided to deny the agency the needed appropriations for the postwar period. There is no record of the FEPC being able to negotiate a settlement acceptable to the minority workers. Presumably, they were left to fend for themselves against continued occupational and wage discrimination.[71]

The Shell case once again demonstrated the agency's weakness. The case underwent numerous delays primarily because the company and Local 367 consistently refused to comply with the president's executive order. The Shell local acted much like the Baytown Employees' Federation and Local 227 in reinforcing racial inequality. Local 367 collaborated with management in restricting minority workers to the laboring occupations and in denying them the opportunity to advance into the higher-paying and skilled jobs in the refinery. Unlike Local 227, the Shell union was steadfast in its refusal to support compliance. This refusal, coupled with the FEPC's setbacks at Humble and Sinclair, underscored the significance of discrimination in denying Mexicans equal employment opportunities in the Texas Gulf Coast oil industry.

The problem of discrimination in the oil industry had special importance when one considers that there may never have been a better time than the period World War II for Mexicans from Texas to have altered their occupational standing relative to Anglos. The wartime demand on the economy had expanded job opportunities to unprecedented levels. Increased job growth coupled with labor shortages occasioned by conscription resulted in immediate occupational gains that seemed to presage a new era of equality. Accompanying these promising developments was the rhetoric of world democracy that encouraged even higher expectations of racial justice and equality at the home front. Lastly, with the establishment of FEPC regional offices in Texas, the federal government promised Mexican workers protection against employment discrimination.

Mexican oil workers were part of the relatively small yet important wave of upwardly mobile workers making the transition from low-wage employers to high-wage and well-organized firms during the war. Their disproportionate representation in the lesser-skilled and lower-paying jobs, however, defined the limits that discrimination placed on them. The twelve oil refineries located in the Gulf Coast generally maintained low hiring quotas for Mexicans, assigned them laborer occupations, paid them a lower wage than Anglos, denied them upgrading opportunities, and restricted them to segregated work, eating, and restroom areas. A key element in maintaining a racial order in the refineries was the race-conscious Anglo workers, including members of CIO-affiliated unions. Anglo workers and their representatives also assumed an important role in defending the segregated order by pressuring the companies against complying with FEPC directives. Fearing the loss of their hard-won gains during the 1930s, they claimed job prerogatives and reacted defensively toward the FEPC.

Although some improvements for minority workers resulted from the intercession of the FEPC, the agency was not able to challenge discrimination and inequality effectively at Humble, Sinclair, and Shell. Since the FEPC directed most of its attention to these three companies, and other refineries do not seem to have been compelled to implement nondiscrimination policies, we can conclude that the FEPC did not make an appreciable impact in the oil industry. Its work was a positive yet minor contribution next to the demand for labor that provided Mexican workers the initial limited opportunity for employment. The FEPC's lack of enforcement powers, its short duration in Texas, its internal divisions, and management's ambivalence in the face of a threatened Anglo workers' reaction no doubt contributed to the failure of governmental intervention in the oil industry. The most decisive factor in the fight over compliance, however, was the opposition of Anglo workers. The most striking result was yet another delay in the full incorporation of Mexican workers into the Texas occupational structure.

Notes

This chapter originally appeared in *Southwestern Historical Quarterly* 95 (1992): 323–50, and is reprinted with permission.

1.　Carlos Castaneda, "Statement on Discrimination against Mexicans in Employment," in *Are We Good Neighbors?*, ed. Alonso S. Perales (San Antonio: Artes Graficas, 1948), 59–63; Carlos Castaneda, Testimony before the US Senate Subcommittee of the Committee on Education and Labor Hearings, 79th Cong., 1st sess., March 12–14, 1945 (Washington, DC: Government Printing Office, 1945), 131–35 (Y4.Ed8/3:Em7/3); Pauline R. Kibbe, *Latin Americans in Texas* (Albuquerque: University of New Mexico Press, 1946), 157–66. Readings on Mexicans during the War Include Mario Garcia, "Americans All: The Mexican American Generation and the Politics of Wartime Los Angeles, 1941–1945," *Social Science Quarterly* 65 (June 1984): 279–89; Raul Morin, *Among the Valiant: Mexican-Americans in WW II and Korea* (Los Angeles: Borden Publishing Co., 1966); Gerald Nash, "Spanish-Speaking Americans in Wartime," in *The American West Transformed: The Impact of the Second World War* by Gerald D. Nash (Bloomington: Indiana University Press, 1985), 107–27; and Robin F. Scott, "Wartime Labor Problems and Mexican-Americans in the War," in *An Awakened Minority: The Mexican-Americans*, ed. Manuel P. Servin (Beverley Hills: Glencoe Press, 1974), 134–42. The term Mexican refers to both Mexican nationals and US-born Mexicans for two reasons. Incomplete nativity and citizenship data made it impossible in most cases to make such a distinction. Also, the use of the term Mexican seems appropriate since they shared the experiences of occupational, wage, and upgrading discrimination.

2.　Publications that treat the subject of the Mexican worker and the FEPC are rare. These include the previously cited works by Garcia and Nash as well as two studies, one by a CIO organizer involved in the Oil Workers' Organizing Campaign of 1942–43 and the other by a former head of the FEPC: Clyde Johnson, "The Battle for Baytown," June 1984 (copy of unpublished book-length manuscript in author's possession); and Malcolm Ross, "Those Gringos," in *All Manner of Men* by Malcolm H. Ross (New York: Greenwood Press, 1948), 265–78. A study by Ray Marshall examines racial discrimination against black workers in the Texas Gulf Coast oil industry and the successful 1955 challenge against it by the government and the NAACP: "Some Factors Influencing the Upgrading of Negroes in the Southern Petroleum Refining Industry," *Social Forces* 42 (December 1963): 186–95.

3.　President Roosevelt established the FEPC on June 25, 1941, with Executive Order 8802, a measure intended to end discrimination by unions, defense industries, and government employers. On May 26, 1943, the president issued Executive Order 9346 that reorganized the agency and strengthened its effectiveness with an improved budget and regional offices in such places as Dallas and San Antonio. Book-length studies of the FEPC include Herbert Garfinkel, *When Negroes March: The March on Washington Movement in the Organizational Policies for FEPC* (Glencoe, IL: Free Press, 1959); Louis C. Kesselman, *The Social Politics of FEPC: A Study in Reform Pressure Movements* (Chapel Hill: University of North Carolina Press, 1948); and Louis Ruchames, *Race, Jobs, and Politics: The Story of FEPC* (Westport, CT: Negro Universities Press, 1953).

4.   The twelve refineries were Sinclair (Houston), Shell (Houston), Texas Company (Houston), Texas Company (Port Neches), Pure Oil (Port Neches), Republic (Texas City) Southport (Texas City), Pan American (Texas City), Texas Company (Port Arthur), Gulf (Port Arthur), Humble (Baytown), and Magnolia (Beaumont). Fair Employment Practice Committee, *Final Report* (Washington, DC: US Government Printing Office, 1947), 23; W. Don Ellinger, "Complete Report on Shell Situation, May 1, 1945," 1–5, Division of Field Operations, Records of the Fair Employment Practice Committee, National Archives (cited hereafter as FEPC Records).

5.   The FEPC conducted preliminary investigations in the Southwest in 1942 that resulted in the discovery of widespread discrimination against Mexican workers in the oil companies of the Texas Gulf Coast. The cases against the refineries and the workers' organizations lasted until the closing of the Dallas office in 1945. Report of Clay Cochran to Dr. Castaneda, October 25, 1943, Administrative Division, FEPC Records; John Morton Blum, *V Was for Victory: Politics and American Culture during World War II* (New York: Harcourt Brace Jovanovich, 1976), 198; Lawrence W. Cramer to M. C. Gonzales, November 26, 1941, Division of Field Operations, FEPC Records; Will Alexander to W. G. Carnahan, December 26, 1941, Division of Field Operations, ibid.; Carlos Castaneda to Will Maslow, January 26, 1944, Administrative Division, ibid.

6.   Castaneda, "Statement on Discrimination against Mexicans in Employment," 59–63; Castaneda, Testimony, 1945, p. 131–35; Carlos Castaneda, "The Second Rate Citizen and Democracy," in Perales, *Are We Good Neighbors?*, 17–20; and C. L. Golightly, "Wartime Employment of Mexican Americans, 1943," Division of Review and Analysis, FEPC Records. The Mexican population, both US- and Mexico-born, was at least 1 million, or 11.5 percent of the total population in the state. Approximately 500,000 Mexicans were gainfully employed. The 25,000 figure was calculated on the basis of a 5 percent utilization rate reported by Casteneda.

7.   For readings on the oil industry, see Carl Coke Rister, *Oil: Titan of the Southwest* (Norman: University of Oklahoma Press, 1949); Joseph A. Pratt, *The Growth of a Refining Region* (Greenwich, CT: JAI Press, 1980); and C. A. Warner, "Texas and the Oil Industry," *Southwestern Historical Quarterly* 50 (July 1946): 7–24. For an account by a participant in the 1941–43 Oil Workers' Organizing Campaign, see Johnson, "The Battle for Baytown." Other studies that treat the subject of labor organizing in Texas, include Harvey O'Conner, *History of the Oil Workers' International Union* (Denver: Oil Workers' International Union, 1950); F. Ray Marshall, *Labor in the South* (Cambridge: Harvard University Press, 1967), 194–99, 230–33; Herbert Werner, "Labor Organizations in the American Petroleum Industry," in *The American Petroleum Industry: The Age of Energy, 1899–1959*, ed. Harold F. Williamson, Ralph L. Andreano, Arnold R. Daum, and Gilbert C. Klose (Evanston: Northwestern University Press, 1963), 827–45.

8.   The figure for the Mexican workforce was estimated based on a total of 17,350

workers in the twelve refineries reported by the FEPC. Kibbe suggests a lower figure of less than 3 percent. Kibbe, *Latin Americans in Texas*, 159–61.

9. Golightly, "Wartime Employment of Mexican-Americans," 2; G. L. Farned to Lawrence Cramer, January 26, 1943, 4–5, Personal Collection of Clyde Johnson, Berkeley, CA (cited hereafter as Johnson Collection). The nativity figures suggested by the survey have to be taken with caution. They differ substantially from the overall ratio of one Mexico-born to six US-born Mexicans in the state.

10. One important FEPC finding in the Texas Gulf Coast oil industry involved the use of a dual classification system. According to one FEPC report, all refineries in the area with the exception of the Texas Company maintained a wage differential that segregated two types of common laborers. The first group was composed of Anglos who received the higher rate of pay, which was approximately eighty-nine cents an hour. The second group was made up of Mexican and African American workers who received around seventy-nine and one-half cents an hour. Ernest G. Trimble to Francis J. Haas, July 9, 1943, Region X Files, FEPC Records.

11. This summary of conditions has been gleaned from numerous FEPC documents cited throughout the paper.

12. See Johnson, "The Battle for Baytown," for criticism of the union leadership. A CIO organizer assigned to the oil industry in the Gulf Coast, Mr. Johnson was especially critical of the inconsistent support that the OWIU gave the CIO-backed Oil Workers' Organizing Campaign (OWOC), 1941–43, of which he was a part. Much of the conflict that occurred between the staff of the OWOC and the OWIU hinged on the general reluctance of the latter organization to support the OWOC's strong civil rights planks that called for an end to discrimination in the refineries. Clyde Johnson, interview by author, February 9, 1988; Clyde Johnson, "CIO Oil Workers' Organizing Campaign in Texas, 1942–1943," in *Essays in Southern Labor History: Selected Papers, Southern Labor History Conference, 1976*, ed. Gary M. Fink and Merl E. Reed (Westport, CT: Greenwood Press, 1977), 173–87. See the following for copies of these contracts or references to them: Carlos Castaneda to Will Maslow, September 17, 1943, Region X Files, FEPC Records; Leonard M. Brin to Will Maslow, May 24, 1944, ibid.; "Application of Seniority for Selecting Men for Jobs in New Operating Units Not Replacing Other Units," July 23, 1943, ibid.; "Mechanical Seniority," October 1, 1936, ibid.; and President's Committee on Fair Employment Practice, Stipulation, in the Matter of Shell Oil Company, Incorporated, and Oil Workers' International Union, Local 367, CIO, December 30, 1945, 3–4, Legal Division, FEPC Records.

13. The leadership of the OWIU freely admitted widespread discrimination by its locals in the Gulf Coast, though they claimed that it was for the most part "company inspired" and, to an extent, reflective of local prejudices. Oil Workers' International Union, Report of the Oil Workers' International Union Concerning Experiences in the Field of Racial and Religious Discrimination, 1944, Division of Review and Analysis, FEPC Records. There were exceptions to the general

rule of discrimination by the unions. CIO Local 449 from the Southport refinery in Texas City is a case in point. When the refinery refused to end its practice of wage discrimination, the union successfully challenged the company before the War Labor Board in 1943. The WLB ordered the company to end its dual classification system and pay African American workers equal wages. Another example occurred at the Gulf refinery of Port Arthur in 1945. When 250 members of the Black CIO Union, Local 254, went on a wage strike, the president of the white CIO union announced the support of his membership. National War Labor Board, in the Matter of Southport Petroleum Company of Delaware and Oil Workers' International Union Local 449, Case No. 2898-CS-D, June 5, 1943, Johnson Collection; Castaneda to Maslow, June 16–31, 1945, Region X Files, FEPC Records.

14.   International divisions regarding the proper strategy to pursue when challenging the oil industry was an especially debilitating problem that reflected wider political concerns within the FEPC. Such differences, which contributed to important delays, usually appeared when management and union leaders proposed industry-wide hearings on the grounds that it was unfair to single out individual refineries. Differences of opinion also coincided with a related ambivalence in Washington. For instance, the FEPC entertained the idea of a general hearing that would investigate the issue of discrimination against Mexicans in the Southwest as early as 1942 but dropped its plans at the insistence of secretary of state Sumner Welles who was concerned that revelations of discrimination against Mexicans would damage relations with Latin America. Lawrence Cramer, the executive secretary of the FEPC in 1943, on the other hand, considered a general hearing involving the oil industry but remained noncommittal because he feared that it could provoke a racial reaction much like one that occurred after the FEPC hearings in Alabama. Preparations were made once again in 1944 to hold general hearings at El Paso to investigate discrimination against Mexicans in the mining industry of Arizona, New Mexico, and West Texas. These plans were also rescinded as a result of objections raised by the State Department. Blum, *V Was For Victory,* 199; Kesselman, *The Social Politics of FEPC,* 17–18; Edwin Smith to Clyde Johnson, November 6, 1942, Johnson Collection; Carlos Castaneda to Maslow, September 1, 1944, Legal Division, FEPC Records.

The FEPC delayed its investigation of the oil industry on two occasions. The first delay coincided with the aborted 1943 plans for a general hearing. The second one occurred during the latter part of 1944 while Castaneda was heading an investigation of the mining industry. Although there is no evidence that these decisions against holding general hearings contributed to similar decisions in oil, the FEPC personnel in Texas, however, did express similar reservations on which strategy to pursue. Castaneda to Maslow, January 26, 1944; Brin to Maslow, June 24, 1944, Division of Field Operations, FEPC Records; Stanley I. Metzger to Clarence M. Mitchell, July 11, 1944, ibid.

15.   Manuel Gonzales to Sidney Hillman, November 17, 1941, Division of Field Operations, FEPC Records; Lawrence Cramer to Gonzales, Nov. 26, 1941, ibid.;

W. G. Carnahan to Will W. Alexander, December 1, 1941, Legal Division, FEPC Records; Carnahan to Alexander, December 9, 1941, Division of Field Operations, ibid.; Gonzales to Trimble, July 29, 1942, Administrative Division, ibid. See Region X Weekly Reports, ibid., beginning in August 1943 for complaint summaries.

16. See articles by Felix D. Almaraz Jr. on Castaneda's highly successful career as a historian and archivist: "Carlos Eduardo Castaneda, Mexican-American Historian: The Formative Years, 1896–1927," *Pacific Historical Review* 42 (August 1973): 319–44; "The Making of a Boltonian: Carlos E. Castaneda of Texas—The Early Years," *Red River Valley Historical Review* 1 (Winter 1974): 329–50; and "Carlos E. Castaneda and *Our Catholic Heritage*: The Initial Volumes (1933–1943)," *Social Science Journal* 13 (April 1976): 27–37. Mario T. Garcia devotes a chapter to the life of Castaneda in his book *Mexican Americans: Leadership, Ideology, and Identity, 1930–1960* (New Haven, CT: Yale University Press, 1989). See the following for insightful views on Mexican civil rights and labor politics, and its international ramifications during the 1940s: Juan Gomez-Quinones, *Chicano Politics: Reality and Promise, 1940–1990* (Albuquerque: University of New Mexico Press, 1990). Almaraz and Garcia generally ignore the work that Castaneda did with the FEPC and his active associations with other civil rights leaders of the period, preferring instead to focus on his career as a historian. This, despite the voluminous amount of information that records his civil rights work. See, for example, Carlos E. Castaneda Papers, Mexican American Archival Collection, Nettie Lee Benson Latin American Collection, University of Texas at Austin; Eleuterio Escobar Papers, ibid.; Perales, *Are We Good Neighbors?*; and his various testimonies in congressional hearings, cited elsewhere in this article.

17. Ross, *All Manner of Men*, 273–74. Castaneda's strategy can be gleaned from his weekly reports on the meetings. See Castaneda's Weekly Reports, FEPC Records. The decision by Castaneda to focus on complaints by Mexican workers was based on consultations with Mexican and black complainants as well as with the Mexican consul and black and Mexican civil rights leaders from Houston.

18. Fair Employment Practice Committee, *First Report* (Washington, DC: US Government Printing Office, 1945), 107.

19. Although Mexican workers from various refineries submitted complaints, the workers from Humble, Sinclair, and Shell registered the most and best documented ones. Also, these Mexican workers were consistent in resubmitting complaints through the Mexican consul's office when the FEPC periodically requested additional evidence in support of the complaints.

20. "Humble Oil and Refining Company, Baytown, Texas," typed summary of FEPC case against Humble, November 1943, Division of Review and Analysis, FEPC Records. For information on early discriminatory practices, see Henrietta M. Larson and Kenneth Wiggins Porter, *History of Humble Oil and Refining Company: A Study in Industrial Growth* (New York: Harper and Brothers, 1959), 200–201.

21. Statement on Discrimination against Mexican Workers at the Baytown Refinery, Humble Oil and Refining Company, Baytown, Texas, signed by Andres Con-

treras, C. Beltran, J. Santana, Onofre Gonzalez, L. Herrera, and G. N. Ponce, November 25, 1942, Johnson Collection.

22. Gordon L. Farned to Cramer, Jan. 26, 1943, Johnson Collection; Johnson to Trimble, March 15, 1943, ibid.

23. Ibid. The summary of Farned's response is drawn from his letter to Cramer, January 26, 1943, and from the FEPC report titled "Humble Oil and Refining Company, Baytown, Texas."

24. Ibid.

25. "Humble Oil and Refining Company, Baytown, Texas," 4; Victor Rothen, Memorandum for the Solicitor General, 1–2, Region X Files, FEPC Records.

26. See issues of the *CIO Campaigner*, the OWOC's organ in the Gulf Coast, for critiques of discrimination in the industry. Also, see copies of *The Bulletin* for examples of the Federation's criticisms of the union. Both are in the Johnson Collection.

27. *The Bulletin*, May 6, 1943.

28. *The Bulletin*, April 27, 1943.

29. Castaneda, Final Disposition Report, Humble, February 9 and 10, 1944, Administrative Division, FEPC Records; Rothen, Memorandum for the Solicitor General, 1–2; "Humble Oil and Refining Company, Baytown, Texas," 2–3.

30. Castaneda to Maslow, October 16 and 23, 1943, Region X Reports, FEPC Records.

31. Castaneda, Final Disposition Report, Humble, February 9 and 10, 1944, FEPC Records; Castaneda to Maslow, January 26, 1944, 2, Administrative Division, ibid.

32. See Johnson, "The Battle for Baytown," for a description of the OWOC and the conflict with the OWIU leadership, 3

33. Brin, Final Disposition Report, Sinclair, February 11, 1944, FEPC Records.

34. J. O. Gray to Carnahan, April 15, 1942, Region X Files, FEPC Records; Affidavit, A. S. Sanchez, February 15, 1945, ibid.

35. The discussion on the complaint is based on the following documents: Minutes of the Conference Held with Management and Labor of Sinclair Refinery, Houston, December 28, 1943, 2–6, Region X Files, FEPC Records; Adolfo G. Dominguez, Memorandum on Discrimination of Mexican Workers at the Refinery of the Sinclair Refining Company in Houston, Texas, June 8, 1943, Division of Review and Analysis, FEPC Records; Affidavits of J. R. Flores and Teodosio Gutierrez, November 20, 1943, ibid.; and Cochran to Sinclair Refining Company, November 26, 1943, ibid.

36. Castaneda to Maslow, December 25, 1943, 3–4, Region X Reports, FEPC Records; Minutes of the Conference, December 28, 1943.

37. Young to Cochran, December 7, 1943, 1–2.

38. Minutes of the Conference, December 28, 1943, 1–6.

39. Castaneda, Final Disposition Report, Sinclair, February 11, 1944, FEPC Records.

40. Castaneda to Clyde Ingram, March 1, 1944, Region X Files, FEPC Records.

41. Ellinger to Sinclair Refining Company, March 15, 1945, Region X Files, FEPC

Records; Affidavits dated February 1945 and signed by A. S. Sanchez, A. V. Salinas, Juan Robledo, S. Rodriguez, Jesse Lozano Caballero, Henry S. Mendez, and M. de la Garza, ibid.

42. Ellinger to Sinclair Refining Company, March 15, 1945; Affidavits, February 1945, signed by A. S. Sanchez A. V. Salinas, Juan Robledo, S. Rodriguez, Jesse Lozano Caballero, Henry S. Mendez, and M. de la Garza.

43. Summary of Shell Oil Case, May 5, 1945, 1, Legal Division, FEPC Records. A precise figure for the number of Mexican workers at Shell is not available.

44. Dominguez, Memorandum on Racial Discrimination at the Shell Refining Company, Houston, Texas, April 26, 1943, and Memorandum on Conference Held Friday, May 14, 1943, at Mexican Consulate in Houston, Texas, Relative to Discrimination of Mexican Workers at Shell Oil and Refining Company, May 15, 1943, Division of Review and Analysis, FEPC Records. The discussion that follows on the complaint is based on the Dominguez documents.

45. Dominguez, Memorandum on Conference, May 14, 1943, 1–4.

46. Ibid.; Trimble to Haas, July 9, 1943, 1–2, Region X Files, FEPC Records.

47. Castaneda to Maslow, September 18, 1943, Region X Reports, FEPC Records.

48. Castaneda to Maslow, December 4, 1944, Region X Files, FEPC Records; Castaneda to Dominguez, September 16, 1943, ibid.; Castaneda to John J. Herrera, October 7, 1943, ibid.; Castaneda to Dominguez, October 7, 1943, ibid.

49. Castaneda to Maslow, October 16, 23, 1943, ibid.

50. Castaneda to O. A. Knight, January 1, 1944, Region X Files, FEPC Records.

51. Castaneda to Maslow, December 31, 1943, ibid.

52. Ibid.

53. Castaneda to Maslow, December 31, 1943, January 1, 1944, ibid.

54. Castaneda to Maslow, January 26, 1944, Region X Files, FEPC Records; Castaneda to Brin, May 17, 1944, ibid.

55. Opening Statement, December 28, 1944, Legal Division, FEPC Records; Ellinger to Maslow, December 30, 1944, Region X Reports, FEPC Records.

56. Ibid. Also see President's Committee on Fair Employment Practice, Statement of Charges and Order for Hearing, in the Matter of Shell Oil Company, Incorporated, and Oil Workers' International Union, Local 367, CIO, December 11, 1945, FEPC Records; FEPC, Statement of the Case, January 27, 1945, ibid.; and FEPC, Stipulation, December 30, 1945, Legal Division, ibid.

57. Opening Statement, December 28, 1944, 1, 9.

58. Ibid.

59. Statement of the Case, January 27, 1945; Stipulation, December 30, 1945.

60. Castaneda to Maslow, March 24, 1945, 5, Region X Reports, FEPC Records; Mitchell to Ellinger, April 11, 1945, Region X Files, FEPC Records.

61. Summary of Shell Oil Case, May 5, 1945, 1.

62. Summary of Shell Oil Case, May 5, 1945, 1–2.

63. Ibid.; Ellinger to Ross, May 1, 1945, 1–5, Region X Files, FEPC Records. The following description of events is based on information from these two reports.

64. Also see Mitchell to Emanuel Bloch, April 12, 1945, Legal Division, FEPC Records.

65. Ellinger to Ross, Re: The Attached Memorandum, May 1, 1945, 1–3, Region X Files, FEPC Records; Ellinger to Ross, Re: Complete Report on Shell Situation, May 1, 1945, 1–5, Division of Field Operations, ibid.

66. Ibid.

67. Ellinger to Ross, Re: The Attached Memorandum, May 1, 1945, 2, ibid.

68. Castaneda to Maslow, May 16, 1945, 4, Region X Reports, FEPC Records.

69. Ellinger to Knight, May 24, 1945, Region X Files, FEPC Records; Knight to Ellinger, June 2, 1945, ibid. See Ellinger to Ross, May 20, 1945, Legal Division, FEPC Records, for proposal by union on segregated workforce.

70. George Weaver to Ellinger, June 19, 1945, Region X Files, FEPC Records; Ellinger to Mitchell, July 14, 1945, ibid.; J. J. Hickman to Ellinger, July 24, 1945, Division of Review and Analysis, FEPC Records; Castaneda to Maslow, June 1–15, 1945, 4–5, Region X Reports, ibid.

71. Castaneda to Maslow, June 16–30, 1945, 4, Region X Reports, FEPC Records.

MICHAEL R. BOTSON JR.

No Gold Watch for Jim Crow's Retirement

The Abolition of Segregated Unionism at Houston's Hughes Tool Company

On July 1, 1964, the National Labor Relations Board (NLRB) decertified the racially segregated Independent Metal Workers Union as the collective bargaining agent at Houston's Hughes Tool Company. In a unanimous decision, the five-member board determined that the union had failed to fairly represent all workers at the company and systematically had discriminated against African Americans. The ruling ended nearly fifty years of Jim Crow unionism at Hughes Tool, one of Houston's premier manufacturing plants.[1]

Ivory Davis, a black material handler and longtime employee at Hughes Tool Company, filed the discrimination charge against the union that ultimately led to its decertification. Davis's action against the union stemmed from the white leadership's refusal to file a grievance on his behalf after the company's management denied him an apprenticeship because of his race. The union's labor agreement with Hughes Tool reserved apprenticeships for whites only. In 1962 Davis and the black union leaders decided to challenge the validity of the racially biased labor contract between Hughes Tool and the Independent Metal Workers Union (IMW). Davis's action was the beginning of a two-year struggle that combined the efforts of the federal government, the National Association for the Advancement of Colored People (NAACP), and African American unionists in the IMW to break Jim Crow's grip over Hughes Tool's workforce.[2]

Ivory Davis's struggle for shop-floor racial equality at Hughes Tool Company, however, has a deeper meaning when placed within the context of the early 1960s and the growing militancy of black workers nationwide who demanded justice and equality in industrial America. Black workers capitalized on the country's growing commitment to civil rights and desegregation to launch an assault against institutionalized racism in organized labor.[3] They received help from new federal policies such as Pres. John F. Kennedy's Executive Order 10925, which required fair employment practices in companies awarded government contracts; from the NAACP's increased attacks on racism within

343

organized labor; and from the willingness of individual black workers to fight racism within unions.[4]

This study examines an important episode in the struggle of black workers to abolish Jim Crow segregation in labor unions. The IMW's refusal to process Davis's grievance presented the union's black leaders with an opportunity to put an end to the IMW's racism. With the help of the NAACP, they pushed the NLRB to decertify the IMW for discriminating against Davis. The crusade against the IMW is important because it marked a major turning point in the NLRB's policy in protecting the rights of black workers. For the first time in its history, the NLRB ruled that racial discrimination by labor unions is an unfair labor practice prohibited by the National Labor Relations Act. The NLRB's decision was of great significance not only because it purged Jim Crow unionism from Hughes Tool but also because it created the legal means to desegregate all labor unions.[5]

Segregated labor organizations had been part of Hughes Tool Company's history. In the 1920s, the management established two employee welfare organizations, segregated by race. Whites belonged to the Employees Welfare Organization and blacks were restricted to the Hughes Tool Colored Club. The NLRB disbanded both groups in 1940 when it was determined that they were management-dominated unions, which became illegal under the National Labor Relations Act of 1935. In 1941 former members of the defunct welfare groups responded to the NLRB's decision by organizing the Independent Metal Workers Union (IMW). The IMW spurned affiliation with either the AFL or CIO, and instead acted as a single-employer union that represented only workers at Hughes Tool. It established two locals and segregated them by race; Local No. 1 was exclusively for whites and Local No. 2 was for blacks. Except for a brief period between 1943 and 1946 when the CIO-backed United Steelworkers of America wrested their bargaining rights away, the IMW remained the dominant union at the plant.[6]

To a significant degree, Hughes Tool Company promoted racial segregation in order to capitalize on racism's divisive effects within the unions. Beginning with its segregated welfare organizations and then its relationships with the IMW and CIO unions, management remained committed to segregating the workforce. Experience demonstrated that Hughes Tool's color barrier had helped management undermine union solidarity along racial lines and also provided the company with a relatively cheap and submissive pool of black workers reserved for the hottest, dirtiest, and most menial jobs in the plant.[7]

The company defended its segregationist policy against calls for integration of the workforce. During World War II, the Fair Employment Practices Commission (FEPC), a federal agency that investigated discrimination against minorities employed in defense industries, determined that Hughes Tool encouraged discriminatory arrangements at its main facility, at Dickson Gun Plant, and at Aircraft Strut Plant, all of which manufactured war material for the federal government. During the war, a few black workers leveled charges with the FEPC against Hughes Tool alleging that management had denied blacks promotions and access to whites-only jobs. Company officials did not deny the charges and said that blacks never had been allowed to perform whites-only jobs and suggested that opening whites' jobs to blacks would cause trouble, even possible rioting by white employees who supported segregation. The FEPC pressured Hughes Tool to put an end to its discriminatory employment and job practices, but the company successfully resisted integrating its workforce.[8]

The company later turned down a 1953 proposal submitted by the presidents of the IMW's two locals that called for a biracial grievance committee to replace the existing procedure, which required each local to handle grievances for its own membership. The new grievance committee would consist of seven representatives from each local and was intended to strengthen the union's bargaining position in settling grievances with management. The proposal specifically excluded any further calls for racial solidarity and left segregated jobs and lines of promotion intact. Nonetheless, the initiative represented the only departure from the IMW's constitution, which called on each local to conduct its own labor relations with management. Hughes Tool rejected the proposal, based on the argument it used with the FEPC during World War II, and refused to negotiate with biracial committees.[9] Except for this one limited attempt at racial solidarity, the company and the IMW cooperated to institutionalize Jim Crow unionism between 1946 and 1961. Jim Crow flourished, in part, because of the NLRB's joint certification of the IMW's two locals.

The IMW defeated the United Steelworkers of America and the AFL-backed International Association of Machinists in several union certification elections between 1946 and 1961. Following each election, the NLRB jointly certified both IMW locals as the collective bargaining agent at Hughes Tool Company.[10] The National Labor Relations Act of 1935 (NLRA) empowered the NLRB to conduct union certification elections so workers could choose either a collective bargaining agent or no union, and also to certify unions as exclusive collective bargaining agents. The act also guaranteed that employers could recognize and bargain with unions their employees chose. Though the NLRA increased and institutionalized the collective bargaining strength of organized labor, black workers enjoyed few of its benefits. The act specifically ignored racial discrimination in unions and contained no provisions for protecting minority interests from the majority rule.[11] Consequently, the IMW's certification by the National Labor Relations Board enabled the union's racially segregated locals to appear to be coequal partners in a unified labor organization while in practice allowing the white majority to dominate the black members. Technically, according to the NLRB's joint certification of the IMW's two locals, any collective bargaining agreement between the union and Hughes Tool needed the approval of both locals to be valid. But in practice, the minority membership of Local No. 2, approximately 25 percent of the union, ensured that it could not vote down any contract approved by Local No. 1.[12]

The IMW's constitution and its contracts with Hughes Tool Company expanded and defined white control over black unionists. Section 1 of the constitution contained seven articles, which formulated the union's organizational structure and established general principles for governing the IMW. The articles in section 1 created two segregated locals, with Local No. 1 for whites and Local No. 2 for "colored members." They also set membership requirements, granted each local the authority to handle its own affairs independently, and stipulated, even though Hughes Tool rejected this provision, that the locals "may form a joint committee to handle grievances and to engage in collective bargaining." Amending the IMW's constitution required that three-fourths of the combined membership from both locals approve proposed amendments. The articles enabled Local No. 1 to exploit its numerical superiority, impose racial segregation, control amendments to the constitution, and decide whether or not to include Local No. 2 in contract talks with the management.[13]

The constitution's second section contained the IMW's bylaws, which established the union's hierarchy and operating procedures. Though the constitution only listed the bylaws for Local No. 1, the statutes established the offices of president, vice president, treasurer, secretary, a governing council, and the standing committees for both locals. The bylaws also contained procedures for electing officers and councilors and appointing committee members. Consequently, the second section of the constitution established barriers that racially segregated the union's leadership in much the same way that the constitution's first section separated the rank and file.[14]

Contracts negotiated between the IMW and Hughes Tool Company between 1946 and 1961 perpetuated black subordination. The agreements generally covered two-year periods and were renegotiated before they expired. The negotiating procedure called for the officers of each local to prepare proposals before they met with the management. Prior to actual talks with the company, the leadership from both locals would meet to review the proposals and decide which ones to present to the management. After agreeing on specific proposals, the presidents of both locals then met with company officials to negotiate the contract. The president of Local No. 1 customarily served as the IMW's only spokesman during the actual talks with Hughes Tool. The process put Local No. 2 at a disadvantage since all proposals prior to contract talks were subject to a vote by the rank and file, which carried an implicit threat that any initiatives from the black leadership that called for an end to their Jim Crow status quo could be voted down by the majority white membership. Additionally, the president of Local No. 1 could either refuse to accept Local No. 2's proposals, demand revisions that rendered the proposals impotent, or simply refuse to introduce the other proposals during the bargaining sessions with management.[15]

The contracts also established a segregated job classification system with twelve hourly labor grades. The classifications were subdivided into two groups with Group I for whites and Group II for blacks. The grouping system created segregated lines of promotion and demotion that prevented members of Group II from being promoted or demoted to jobs in Group I.[16] Blacks hired on at the lowest level in labor grade 1 and could not advance higher than grade 5, while whites hired on at the highest scale in labor grade 5 and customarily did not hold any classification lower than that. The highest level in labor grade 12 paid 32 percent more than the highest level available to blacks in labor grade 5.

During the cutbacks caused by business downturns, whites received preferential treatment, since the contracts allowed whites who faced layoffs in their classification system to bump blacks holding jobs in labor grades 4 and 5 who had less seniority. But even during periods of layoffs, whites refused to accept jobs in labor grades 1, 2, and 3 because those had always been "Negro" jobs. Additionally, the contracts reserved unskilled menial jobs for blacks and specifically excluded them from all occupations that required operating any machinery other than material-handling equipment. All skilled-trades classifications and apprenticeships for various crafts, such as electricians, machinery repairman, and millwright, were in Group I and reserved for qualified white applicants from within the plant.[17] Management's traditional support of segregation, labor agreements between IMW and Hughes Tool, the union's constitution, bylaws, and majority white membership, and the NLRB's joint certification all allowed Jim Crow to flourish at the company.

Smothered by the Jim Crow environment that dominated labor relations at Hughes Tool and in Houston, African American workers had no alternative but to accept segregation because there were few ways for them to redress the unequal and unfair conditions imposed on them.[18] Federal agencies offered little hope in reforming the status quo. The NLRB and the federal courts heard cases from black workers in other industries that accused unions of racial discrimination, but both the NLRB and the federal judiciary refused to recognize racism within unions as an unfair labor practice subject to punitive action. Between 1945 and 1962, the NLRB and federal courts justified their position by arguing that black workers who voluntarily placed themselves under the bargaining authority of discriminatory white-controlled unions could choose to leave those unions.[19] The NLRB's daily contact with labor problems enabled it to define a union's duty of fair representation, but rather than concerning itself with racial discrimination as well as its normal duties of protecting workers from employer discrimination based on union activity or inactivity, for nearly twenty years following World War II, the NLRB contended that unions in which blacks were segregated, such as the IMW, did not unfairly represent their African American membership. Consequently, the NLRB continued to issue joint certifications that permitted segregated locals to represent workers in the same bargaining unit.[20]

The IMW's black leadership kept abreast of NLRB decisions and court rulings concerning racial discrimination in labor. They understood that to purge Jim Crow from Hughes Tool Company, two things would be necessary: first, the right set of conditions had to be present to mount a challenge to segregation, and second, the NLRB had to recognize racial discrimination as an unfair labor practice.[21] In 1961 deteriorating economic conditions at Hughes Tool and the federal government's increasing commitment to civil rights presented Local No. 2's black leadership with an opportunity to challenge Hughes Tool's segregationist tradition.

During the late 1950s, when the demand for its drilling products dropped dramatically, Hughes Tool significantly reduced its workforce in order to offset the financial losses it suffered.[22] From a peak of approximately six thousand workers in World War II, by 1961 Hughes Tool had trimmed its number of hourly employees to two thousand, of which sixteen hundred were white and four hundred black.[23] Additionally, Hughes Tool diversified. One of its new ventures involved subcontracting machine repair and rebuilding work for government contractors involved in the space program. Hughes Tool management hoped that securing government subcontracts would allow the company both to maintain its workforce and to provide more opportunities in the future, but federal work required that Hughes Tool carry out a policy of nondiscrimination in employment practices, which stemmed from President Kennedy's Executive Order 10925, signed in 1961.[24]

The executive order mandated the elimination of "racial discrimination in employment [because it injured] both its victims and the national economy." The order forced every government contractor to promise that it would "not discriminate against any employee or applicant for employment because of race, creed, color, or national origin."[25] The order also required all government contractors to provide equal employment opportunities, and created President Kennedy's Committee on Equal Employment Opportunity (PCEEO) to enforce its directives. The PCEEO functioned in much the same way that the FEPC had done during World War II but with one critical difference—the PCEEO had the power to require contractors to submit compliance reports concerning their racial practices while the FEPC had not. Kennedy's order also pressured the NLRB to take firmer action against discriminating unions, such as the IMW, and required the NLRB to reconsider its unwillingness to regard racial discrimination as an unfair labor practice.[26] Under Executive Order 10925, Hughes Tool Company faced disqualification from much-needed federal work because of its Jim Crow tradition and racially segregated labor agreements with the IMW. The changing conditions overshadowed the contract talks that took place in the autumn of 1961.

Several months prior to the opening of negotiations, the leadership of Locals 1 and 2 accepted proposals from the rank and file at regularly scheduled union meetings. Officers and councilors of each local studied its members' proposals and selected ones to introduce in negotiations with Hughes Tool. In October and November 1961, the officers of both locals met several times to make final decisions on which proposals to present. Lorane Ashley, president of Local No. 2, made an unprecedented proposal that called for the IMW to eliminate racial segregation in the new contract. Encouraged by Executive Order 10925 and Hughes Tool's desire to secure government contracts, Ashley, the black local's treasurer, Ivory Davis, and councilors Columbus Henry and Alison Alton, all decided that the right set of circumstances were in place for Local No. 2 to challenge Jim Crow.[27] T. B. Everitt, Local No. 1's president, had anticipated the proposal, and though he did not accept Local No. 2's assertion that the IMW discriminated against blacks, agreed to consider the issue if Local No. 2 submitted a formal written proposal that outlined a procedure for integrating.[28]

On December 14, 1961, Ashley presented Everitt with the black local's petition, which stated: "The Parties, Locals 1 and 2, herein agree that part one and part two of the current contract has created in its interpretation a problem between the Locals as to advancement opportunities for all employees. Therefore the parties agreed that they will within a period of two years or sooner correct the above matter, and provide a greater and more equitable opportunities for all employees."[29] Everitt disliked the proposal's contention that problems existed between the two locals over job promotions and refused to be bound by its two-year time limit.[30] Supported by the white leaders, he refused to include Local No. 2's proposal with the twenty-three already submitted, claiming that there had not been enough time for the IMW's joint bargaining committee to review the petition and agree on its provisions. Everitt did offer to meet with Local No. 2's leadership to discuss the union's segregation, but not until after the new contract was signed.[31] Without telling Ashley and before he met with management to sign a new contract, Everitt unofficially notified Jimmy Delmar, Hughes Tool Company's director of industrial relations, that a confrontation was brewing between the IMW's two locals over segregation.[32]

Jimmy Delmar, who received a copy of Local No. 2's proposal before the new contract was signed, refused to have the company take a stand in the IMW's battle over desegregation and placed the onus for integration on the union. In a meeting with Lorane Ashley prior to the opening of formal negotiations on the new contract, Delmar made it clear that the racial dispute between the two locals was their own business. Management reasoned that the contractual provisions that segregated workers by race was rooted in the IMW's constitution and bylaws, and therefore it was the union's responsibility to abolish them.[33]

Nonetheless, Everitt and Ashley met with Delmar and other Hughes Tool Company officials on December 18, 1961, to sign a new contract. The major provisions of the agreement included across-the-board wage increases in all twelve labor grades, acceptance of the twenty-three proposals submitted by the union's joint bargaining committee, and an expanded apprenticeship program that included three more trades.[34] Everitt served as the IMW's spokesman during the meeting and signed the contract as the representative of Local No. 1. Lorane Ashley refused to sign the new agreement. Supported by Ivory Davis, Columbus Henry, and Alison Alton, Ashley withheld Local No. 2's approval because Local No. 1 had refused to include a clause calling for the elimination of discrimination based on race, creed, or color.[35] Though this marked the first time in Hughes Tool's history that a Jim Crow labor organization had refused to rubber-stamp a racist contract, the company and Local No. 1 put it into effect without Local No. 2's approval. Local No. 2's stand raised three critical legal questions concerning the IMW's role as the collective bargaining agent at Hughes Tool. One question involved the NLRB's joint certification of the

IMW's two locals, the second was the IMW's obligation under its certification to fairly represent all employees in the bargaining unit, and the third was Hughes Tool's acquisition of federal work.

The NLRB jointly recertified the IMW's two locals in October 1961, and the certification prohibited either local from consummating a separate agreement with the management.[36] The new contract, signed only by Local No. 1, violated the provisions of the IMW's certification and was grounds for punitive action by the NLRB. Local No. 2 had exercised its power under the IMW's certification by refusing to sign the new contract because it violated the union's NLRB mandate to fairly represent all hourly workers in the plant regardless of whether they were unionized, nonunionized, black, or white. Shortly after the new contract was signed, the black leadership and Ivory Davis planned to force the IMW to honor its duty of fair representation, or face sanctions from the federal government.

On February 15, 1962, Hughes Tool Company posted a bid notifying workers that the company was accepting applications for the newly created machinist tool-and-die-maker apprenticeship. Ivory Davis decided to bid on the job even though the 1961 contract denied blacks admission into apprenticeship programs.[37] Davis signed the bid, in part, to force Local No. 1 to reconsider the discriminatory contract, but his desire to learn a skilled trade and improve his occupational status was equally important. The following week, the company posted the list of workers chosen for the apprenticeship and, as expected, Davis's name did not appear. Davis, Henry, and Ashley met with management to discuss Davis's rejection in light of Hughes Tool's pledge to integrate its workforce. The management explained that Davis could bid on the apprenticeship but that Hughes Tool was bound to honor its contract obligations with the IMW that limited apprenticeships to white employees in Group I.[38] Dissatisfied with Hughes Tool's response, Davis filed a grievance over the issue. Since Local No. 2 was not under contract with Hughes Tool, and technically could not file a grievance on his behalf, Davis took the unprecedented step of asking the white local to represent him and file the grievance.

The black leadership knew that the IMW's NLRB certification required Local No. 1 to file the grievance, even though doing so would violate its racially segregated contract with Hughes Tool. They reasoned that the management would not support Local No. 1's continuing commitment to segregation as it had in the past, since the company faced pressure from the federal government to integrate its workforce in order to secure government contracts. Ashley, Davis, Henry, and Alton knew that the white leadership would never represent a black member, but it had never been their intention to have Local No. 1 file Davis's grievance. As part of their strategy to abolish Jim Crow at Hughes Tool, they anticipated that the white local would refuse to process the grievance. Local No. 1's refusal would give the blacks the opportunity to file an unfair labor charge against Local No. 1 with the NLRB, and force an official investigation into the union's racial discrimination and unfair representation of black workers.[39] With the support of Ashley, Alton, and Henry, Davis wrote to Everitt on April 17, 1962, and asked him for representation in the apprenticeship dispute.[40]

Davis waited over a month for Everitt to respond, and when it became clear that an answer was not forthcoming, Local No. 2 lodged a formal complaint with the NLRB's Houston office against the white local on May 23, 1962. The complaint accused Local No. 1 of violating Davis's rights under the National Labor Relations Act by refusing to file a grievance on his behalf. The NLRB's regional director notified Hughes Tool Company and Local No. 1 of the charge, reviewed it, and assigned an NLRB agent to investigate the complaint.[41]

The investigation lasted until August, and the agent assigned to the case determined that Davis's complaint had merit, since it appeared that Local No. 1 had violated Davis's rights by not processing the grievance. The investigator did not implicate Hughes Tool because he accepted the company's position that the IMW's constitution and bylaws were responsible for the firm's segregation. His report concluded that the NLRB should appoint a trial examiner to conduct a formal hearing to determine if the white local had broken the law and abused its NLRB certification. The NLRB's regional director affirmed the report's findings and scheduled a hearing for October 3, 1962, at the Federal Building in Houston.[42]

Local No. 1's attorney, Tom Davis, responded to the NLRB's report on September 12, 1962, when he defended Local No. 1's refusal to process Ivory Davis's grievance and denied any wrongdoing. Tom Davis's brief argued that, based on the union's constitution and bylaws, Ivory Davis's grievance was the responsibility of the black local. Additionally, it pointed out that in the past, Hughes Tool had insisted that Local No. 1 handle grievances for whites and Local No. 2 those for blacks. The brief's last point stated that the black leadership had rejected a contract amendment proposed by Local No. 1 that would have attempted to create equal opportunities in the plant. The arguments in Tom Davis's brief were unsuccessful and did not persuade the NLRB's regional director to drop the complaint against Local No. 1.[43]

Local No. 2 also took action during the period leading up to the hearing. In September, the black leadership asked the NAACP to represent Local No. 2 and to act as its attorney in the case. Since the black local could not afford legal representation, the NAACP readily agreed to take the case. Robert Carter, general counsel for the NAACP, who worked out of the civil rights group's New York office, requested that the NLRB postpone the hearing so he could gather facts and draft an argument in support of Ivory Davis's complaint.[44] The NLRB's regional director granted a postponement and rescheduled the hearing for November 7, 1962.

After researching the case, Carter concluded that the only way to guarantee that blacks received equal opportunities at Hughes Tool Company was for the NLRB to rescind its certification of the IMW. Carter based his conclusion on the IMW's tradition of discrimination and its long record of black inequality. He theorized that the NLRB could force the IMW, under threat of decertification, to handle Ivory Davis's grievance but also speculated that if Davis was offered the apprenticeship, his white coworkers could easily disqualify him by insisting that he could not perform the duties he was assigned. Carter wanted to protect Davis from that kind of retribution, and he also wanted to use the case to establish a precedent so that in the future, qualified blacks who sought whites-only jobs would not have to fight their cases individually. If the NLRB merely forced the IMW to process Davis's grievance and left the union in place, all blacks seeking whites-only jobs would face the same daunting process that confronted Ivory Davis. Carter concluded that the only way to prevent that, and to guarantee equal opportunity for black workers in the future, was to persuade the NLRB to revoke the IMW's certification.[45] Convincing the NLRB to decertify the IMW because it racially discriminated against Ivory Davis would establish a legal precedent that the NLRB could use in the future to outlaw racial discrimination throughout organized labor. Carter felt confident that the NAACP could win the case, and on October 24, 1962, submitted his brief, which requested that the NLRB decertify the IMW as the collective bargaining agent at Hughes Tool.[46]

In an attempt to avoid an NLRB hearing and possible decertification, attorney Tom Davis advised Everitt that a merger of the two locals might be a solution. Davis's plan called for disbanding Local No. 2, opening up membership in Local No. 1 to blacks, and amending the IMW's constitution and bylaws to include a pro forma commitment to eliminate discrimination based on race, color, or creed.[47] Everitt agreed, and subsequently Tom Davis asked the NLRB for another postponement of the hearing so the leadership and attorneys for both locals could meet and negotiate a merger agreement that would resolve the charges against Local No. 1. The NLRB looked favorably on the proposal, agreed to postpone the hearing until December 11, 1962, and urged Carter and the black leadership to seek a settlement before the hearing.[48]

The NLRB's joint certification empowered Local No. 2 to reject the proposed merger in the same way that it had blocked ratification of the 1961 contract. Additionally, a merger needed the NLRB's approval, since it required amending the IMW's certification to stipulate that the union would consist of only one local. NAACP attorney Carter and the black leaders opposed the merger because it did not spell out in detail how the consolidated IMW would carry out its obligation of fair representation, eliminate separate lines of promotion, and facilitate the admission of blacks into training programs, and they intended to use Local No. 2's leverage to block the proposal.[49] Jim Crow's "separate but equal" doctrine came back to haunt Local No. 1, since the NLRB's certification allowed Local No. 2 to veto any merger offer from the white local that fell short of full racial equality.

During November 1962 the white leaders and their attorney pressed for a meeting between the officers of both locals.[50] Carter met with Ashley, Henry, and Ivory Davis in mid-November 1962 and cautioned them not to accept any provisions outlined in the merger proposal that did not include specific guarantees for equal job opportunities and the elimination of existing discrimination in the plant.[51] Everitt and Tom Davis expressed their desire to consummate the merger quickly, but Carter suspected their intentions because they blamed blacks for the IMW's segregation in their communications with him and the black leaders. Everitt and Tom Davis echoed a widely held white belief that when the union was first organized in 1941, blacks had insisted on segregated locals because they felt that such an arrangement was necessary to protect their interests and would give them full voice in managing their affairs in the IMW.[52] The argument proved fallacious for several reasons. For example, Local No. 2 emanated from the Hughes Tool Colored Club, which was steeped in the company's segregationist tradition; Houston's oppressive Jim Crow tradition precluded widespread white support for integration and racial equality in the IMW; and lastly, when the CIO reneged on its promise of racial equality and integration in the mid-1940s, blacks had withdrawn their support and the CIO had suffered a devastating defeat at the hands of the IMW in a 1946 union certification. Blacks had never demanded that they be segregated and relegated to an inferior status in the IMW, it was a position imposed on them by tradition and white unionists.[53]

Moreover, aware that blacks suffered similar and often worse discrimination in integrated unions, Carter speculated that the consolidation of the two locals was a ruse to create a seemingly integrated union, which would actually purge blacks from leadership positions and make the IMW's discrimination worse.[54] Carter feared that the merger would abrogate the need for a hearing and would allow the IMW's racism to escape NLRB scrutiny. Carter insisted that an NLRB hearing was vital if the black leaders hoped to decertify the IMW and persuade the NLRB to issue a binding proclamation that outlawed racial discrimination in any union that represented workers at Hughes Tool Company.[55] Carter advised the black leaders to avoid meeting with representatives from Local No. 1, but the white leaders pressed hard, and against Carter's advice, Ashley agreed to a meeting between the officers of both locals.[56]

On November 13, 1962, Ashley, Ivory Davis, and Henry met with Everitt and the other officers of Local No. 1, vice president Len McDonald, treasurer Bob McDonald, and secretary R. G. Neel. During the meeting, Henry and Davis prevented Ashley and the white leaders from disbanding Local No. 2 and forming one local by insisting that a biracial subcommittee be organized to meet at a later date to draft wording changes in the union's constitution and bylaws, which in turn would be presented to the rank and file of each local for approval. Before the meeting concluded, the white leaders proposed giving blacks four seats on the new local's twelve-member executive council, three places each on the eight-member grievance and nine-member negotiating committees, and one of the three positions on the job-evaluating committee.[57] Davis, Henry, and Ashley acknowledged the proposals without accepting them and agreed to meet with the subcommittee's white representatives on November 26.

The subcommittee consisted of Ashley, Davis, Henry, Everitt, and seven members of Local No. 1's governing council. They revised the constitution and bylaws to reflect the biracial nature of the governing council and committees that had been proposed at the previous meeting but stopped short of including a declaration, though the black leadership proposed one, banning discrimination based on race, color, or creed.[58] The white negotiators voted the motion down but offered to include one in future contracts the union negotiated with the management of Hughes Tool Company. The meeting concluded on that note, and Ashley, Davis, and Henry told Everitt that any further movement on the merger would have to wait until Carter and Local No. 2's membership examined the revisions and offered their opinions. Due to prior commitments, Carter could not return to Houston from New York until December 8, and he advised the black leaders to take no action until he arrived.[59]

Following the subcommittee meeting, Everitt and Tom Davis increased their pressure on Local No. 2 to adopt the amended constitution, merge the locals, and drop the charges pending against Local No. 1. Their efforts seemed to have affected Ashley, who expressed a willingness to resolve the dispute by accepting the constitutional revisions and creating one local.[60] In a strongly worded letter to Ashley after the meeting and prior to his arrival in Houston, Carter warned him not to accept Local No. 1's offer since it would destroy their case with the NLRB and leave racial segregation and inequality in place. Carter cautioned Ashley that it would be the fault of the black union leaders, and no one else, if the case did not abolish racial discrimination at Hughes Tool Company and establish a precedent to prevent its reoccurrence in the future.[61] Davis and Henry agreed with Carter's recommendation to reject any compromise settlement before the NLRB hearing, and persuaded Ashley to ignore Everitt and Tom Davis's overtures until the hearing date.[62] On December 11, 1962, NLRB trial examiner Frederick Reel opened the hearing and took testimony for two days. Witnesses called during the hearing included Ivory Davis, Ashley, Henry, Everitt, Neel, and J. P. Thompson, Hughes Tool Company's superintendent of tool manufacturing.

Arthur Safos, the NLRB general counsel who presented Ivory Davis's charges to the trial examiner, and Carter built their case against Local No. 1 on two issues: the IMW's duty to fairly represent all employees in the bargaining unit at Hughes Tool and the union's racial discrimination, which prevented it from fulfilling that duty. Their witnesses, Ivory Davis, Ashley, and Henry, testified that the IMW's segregation created an unequal, race-based job classification and promotional system that discriminated against black employees in the bargaining unit. In the course of their testimony and their responses to Tom Davis's cross-examinations, it became clear that Local No. 1, despite the NLRB's joint certification of both locals, dominated the IMW and used its power to subordinate the black membership. Carter presented the case against the merger and argued that the IMW's tradition of inequality would carry over into the consolidated union even if the NLRB issued an order banning racial discrimination. Carter remained staunchly convinced that the decertification of the IMW was the only solution to breaking down the color barrier at Hughes Tool.[63]

Tom Davis did not dispute Local No. 1's history of segregation or dominance over the IMW. Davis and the witnesses he called, Everitt, Neel, and Thompson, all defended Local No. 1 by testifying that when the IMW was organized in 1941, blacks demanded that the union be segregated and insisted that segregationist clauses be included in the union's constitution and bylaws. Therefore, they claimed, black-approved union statutes, not race, had influenced Everitt's refusal to process Ivory Davis's grievance. Secondly, Tom Davis argued vigorously throughout the hearing that the white leaders' merger proposal demonstrated a good faith effort on their part to eliminate Jim Crow, and though Local No. 2 had not responded to the offer, white officials remained willing to desegregate the IMW using the plan.[64]

Trial examiner Frederick Reel played a critical role in the proceedings. The NLRB in Washington had empowered him to conduct the hearing, gather testimony and evidence, and use the data to determine if the IMW had violated the law when it refused to represent Ivory Davis. If Reel determined that it did, he was required to recommend appropriate punitive action against the union. During the two days of testimony, Reel queried Tom Davis, Carter, and Safos at length concerning the IMW's joint certification as the collective bargaining agent and their interpretation of Local No. 1's obligation under that certification to fairly represent all employees in the bargaining unit regardless of union membership or race. Reel took particular interest in Tom Davis's admission that race had exerted a small measure of influence over Everitt's refusal to process Ivory Davis's grievance, though Everitt never wavered in his testimony that Davis's race had nothing to do with the complaint.[65]

Reel also pointed out to the attorneys that the merger was not an issue in the case, since the pending charges would have to be resolved before the NLRB could consider reissuing a new certification reflecting the merger of the IMW's two locals. He considered the merger an issue that both locals and their attorneys would have to resolve before it became an issue for the NLRB. When Reel concluded the hearing on December 13, 1962, he instructed the attorneys representing the parties in the case to submit their briefs to him in Washington, DC, by January 14, 1963.[66] Reel's conclusions, based on the evidence gathered, briefs received, and his own research into the legalities of the case, would all influence his recommendation to the NLRB involving the future of the IMW at Hughes Tool Company.[67]

Frederick Reel presented his report to the NLRB in Washington, DC, on February 28, 1963. He determined that Local No. 1 had violated its certification by discriminating against Ivory Davis and that it had been bound to process Davis's grievance regardless of his race. When it failed to do so, the union violated its obligation to fairly represent all employees in the bargaining unit, and consequently Reel recommended that the NLRB should rescind the IMW's certification because the union "discriminated on the basis of race in determining eligibility for full and equal membership, and segregated [its] members on the basis of race." Reel also suggested that in the future, any union seeking to become the bargaining representative at Hughes Tool be required to post notices throughout the plant that it would not ratify any contract that discriminated against employees because of race.[68]

The NLRB's decision on Reel's recommendation would take time, and during the interim period, the IMW's position as collective bargaining agent at Hughes Tool became muddled. Technically, there was no labor agreement between Hughes Tool and the IMW since Local No. 2 had refused to sign the 1961 contract. Secondly, since the IMW still held the collective bargaining rights at Hughes Tool, it was required to be under contract with the company or face NLRB charges of dealing in bad faith with management. The officers of both locals and company officials met in January 1963 and agreed to a new contract that called for eliminating discrimination based on race, color, creed, or national origin, although the contract contained no enforcement provisions to ensure racial equality. Hughes Tool Company signed the contract as an imperative to keep operating, but the company's legal counsel cautioned Jimmy Delmar, director of industrial relations, that the force of the agreement was suspect due to the pending NLRB decision and in light of the fact that although the contract called for eliminating dual job classifications, the IMW itself had not purged itself of discrimination.[69] Neither had Hughes Tool.

Despite the contract's integrationist intent, after its ratification the company imposed new restrictions on blacks seeking whites-only jobs that effectively kept Jim Crow in place. One regulation required all blacks, but not whites, who sought apprenticeships to take an aptitude test. And as late as October 1964, several months after Pres. Lyndon B. Johnson signed the Civil Rights Act, Hughes Tool still maintained racially segregated restrooms, dining areas, and drinking fountains.[70]

Also during the interim period, Local No. 1, with Ashley's support, continued to press for merging the IMW's two locals. Ashley's lobbying efforts in support of the merger alienated him from the other black leaders and Local No. 2's rank and file. Henry successfully challenged Ashley's presidential reelection bid in January 1963 and under Henry's leadership the black local successfully resisted the proposed merger until the NLRB handed down its decision.[71]

The NLRB rendered its decision in Washington, DC, on July 1, 1964. The five-member NLRB voted unanimously in favor of decertifying the IMW as recommended in Reel's intermediate report. It affirmed Reel's findings that Local No. 1 had violated its duty of fair representation when it refused to process Ivory Davis's grievance, though two board members did disagree with Reel's conclusion that the union's action was racially motivated. Nonetheless, the majority agreed that racism was the basis of the IMW's unfair treatment of Ivory Davis.

The decision established a legal precedent whereby unions that hold NLRB certifications must take affirmative measures to eliminate racial discrimination and provide fair representation or face punitive action from the NLRB.[72]

Everitt responded to the NLRB's decision by saying that the IMW had been unfairly cast as a "bunch of racists" and was made the "scapegoat" in the drive to integrate Hughes Tool and undo the company's history of discrimination. From the beginning, he blamed the NAACP for causing the rift between Locals No. 1 and 2 by insisting that decertification, not merger, was the only way to purge the IMW of discrimination.[73] The NLRB's ruling did not disband the IMW or prevent it from trying to recertify itself through another election. Indeed, the NLRB had postponed a certification election requested by the United Steelworkers of America (USWA) until it had announced the decision in the case. Following the announcement, Local No. 1 petitioned the NLRB for a new election, and Everitt confidently predicted that the IMW would once again defeat its traditional opponent.[74] The NLRB scheduled an election for August 4, 1964, and in a surprise upset, the USWA defeated the IMW by a very thin margin of sixty-nine votes. The IMW polled 917 votes to the USWA's 986, which suggests that the IMW still enjoyed considerable popularity in spite of its recent ordeal.[75]

Throughout Jim Crow's long history at Hughes Tool Company, organized labor and management contributed, in varying degrees, to the firm's racial segregation. In the end, it took agitation by black workers such as Ivory Davis and Columbus Henry, who were disgusted with the indignities they suffered under Jim Crow, to purge segregation from the company. Their struggle resulted in an unprecedented victory that represented a milestone in the American labor movement. In the years that followed, organized labor was forced to abandon its color barriers and to provide African American workers the full benefits of trade unionism.[76]

Notes

This chapter originally appeared in *Southwestern Historical Quarterly* 101 (April 1998): 497–521, and is reprinted with permission.

1. National Labor Relations Board, *Decisions and Orders of the National Labor Relations Board*, 147 (Washington, DC: US Government Printing Office, 1965), 1578 (cited hereafter as *Decisions*); *Monthly Labor Review* 87 (September 1964): 1061–62 (cited hereafter as *MLR*). For a brief history of the Hughes Tool Company, see Walter Rundell Jr., *Early Texas Oil: A Photographic History, 1866–1936* (College Station: Texas A&M University Press, 1977), 80–88; Charles R. Hamilton, "Images of an Industry: The Hughes Tool Company Collection," *Houston*

Review 15, No. 1 (1993): 45–54; Adele Hast, ed., *International Directory of Company Histories* (Chicago: St. James Press, 1991), 3:428–29.

2.   "NLRB to Act in Local Union Case: Race Discrimination to be Charged on Hughes Tool Union," *Houston Post*, August 21, 1962, sec. 1, p. 1; "Hughes Tool Local Claims Racial Discrimination," *Houston Chronicle*, August 20, 1962, sec. 1, p. 1; "NLRB to Probe Hughes Labor Rift," *Houston Press*, August 21, 1962, sec. 1, p. 1; *Informer* (Houston), August 22, 1962, sec. 1, p. 1.

3.   For a survey of blacks in organized labor, see William H. Harris, *The Harder We Run: Black Workers since the Civil War* (New York: Oxford University Press, 1982). Earlier studies of racial practices in labor unions in the United States can be found in Herbert Northrup, *Organized Labor and the Negro* (New York: Harper and Brothers, 1944); and Horace R. Cayton and George S. Mitchell, *Black Workers and the New Unions* (Chapel Hill: University of North Carolina Press, 1939). Current scholarship that questions the effectiveness of labor unions in promoting racial equality can be found in August Meier and Eliot Rudwick, *Black Detroit and the Rise of the UAW* (New York: Oxford University Press, 1979); Robert J. Norell, "Caste in Steel: Jim Crow Careers in Birmingham, Alabama," *Journal of American History* 73 (December 1986): 669–94, 988; and Bruce Nelson, "Organized Labor and the Struggle for Black Equality in Mobile during World War II," *Journal of American History* 80 (December 1993): 952–88. For an excellent examination of black labor historiography, see Joe William Trotter Jr., "Afro-American Workers: New Directions in US Labor Historiography," *Labor History* 35 (Fall 1994): 495–523.

4.   Ray Marshall, "Unions and the Negro Community," *Industrial and Labor Relations Review* 17 (January 1964): 193–94; Herbert Hill, "Racism Within Organized Labor: A Report of Five Years of the AFL/CIO," NAACP Labor Department (1960), reprinted in *Journal of Negro Education* 30 (Spring 1960): 109; *MLR* 85 (December 1962): 1406.

5.   Herbert Hill, *Black Labor and the American Legal System: Race, Work, and the Law* (Madison: University of Wisconsin Press, 1985), 22–26, 131–33; Harris, *The Harder We Run,* 137–43, 156–58.

6.   Michael Botson, "Jim Crow Wearing Steel-Toed Shoes and Safety Glasses: Duel Unionism at the Hughes Tool Company, 1918–1942," *Houston Review* 16, No. 2 (1994): 101–16.

7.   "Official Report of Proceedings before the National Labor Relations Board: In the Matter of Hughes Tool Company and Independent Metal Workers Union, Locals Nos. 1 and 2, and United Steelworkers of America," AFL-CIO, Docket No. 23-CB-429, 23-RC-1758, 33–36, 256–58, RG 025, National Archives, cited hereafter as "NLRB Proceedings"; Ivory Davis and Columbus Henry, interview by Michael R. Botson Jr., May 3, 1994, RG 329, Texas Labor Archives, University of Texas at Arlington.

8.   Ernest Obadele-Starks, "The Road to Jericho: Black Workers, The Fair Employment Practice Commission, and the Struggle for Racial Equality on the Upper Texas Gulf Coast, 1941–1947" (PhD diss., University of Houston, 1996),

173–79. See Emilio Zamora, "The Failed Promise of Wartime Opportunity for Mexicans in the Texas Oil Industry," *Southwestern Historical Quarterly* 95 (January 1992): 323–50, for a study of the FEPC's failure to abolish discrimination against Mexican American workers in the upper Texas Gulf Coast oil industry.

9.   "NLRB Proceedings," 33–36, 256–58; Columbus Henry, interview by Michael R. Botson Jr., May 9, 1997, handwritten notes in Botson's possession.

10.   "Independents, Steelworkers at Hughes Vie for Bargaining Rights," *Informer* (Houston), July 20, 1946, sec. 1, p. 1; "IMW Winner at Hughes Plant," *Houston Post*, August 2, 1946, sec. 1, p. 1; "Personal Message from Those Who Quit IMWU," *Steelworker News*, n.d., RG 329, Texas Labor Archives; National Labor Relations Board, *Decisions*, 104:318–20; National Labor Relations Board, *Decisions*, 147:1595.

11.   Hill, *Black Labor*, 100–106; Harris, *The Harder We Run*, 110; Robert L. Carter and Maria L. Marcus, "Trade Union Practices and the Law," in *The Negro and the American Labor Movement,* ed. Julius Jacobson (Garden City: Anchor Books, 1968), 385–86. The NAACP and the National Urban League vigorously opposed the National Labor Relations Act. At the time of its passage in 1935, unions affiliated with the American Federation of Labor, except for the United Mine Workers, enforced rigid racial segregation. Black opponents of the NLRA argued that the law would be used by AFL-affiliated unions to establish closed-shop contracts with employers and effectively bar blacks from employment opportunities. The AFL successfully lobbied against including an antidiscrimination clause in the NLRA. Sen. Robert Wagner of New York, who authored the bill and privately supported the inclusion of a nondiscrimination amendment, bowed to AFL pressure out of fear that the entire bill would be defeated over the issue of racial discrimination.

12.   "NLRB Proceedings," 274, RG 025, National Archives; Botson, "Jim Crow Wearing Steel-Toed Shoes," 102–3.

13.   "NLRB Proceedings," 4–5, Exhibit R-1 ; 274–75, RG 025, National Archives.

14.   Ibid., 6–12, RG 025, National Archives; Ivory Davis, interview by Michael Botson Jr., May 1, 1997, handwritten notes in Botson's possession. The segregated structure of the IMW's elected offices and councils were patterned after the Employees Welfare Organization and HTC Club. See *Summary of Agreement Arrived at by the Hughes Tool Company and Its Hourly Employees,* October 1, 1937, 1-11, RG R-1 (Houston Metropolitan Research Center, Houston Public Library, Houston).

15.   "NLRB Proceedings," 76, RG 025, National Archives; Davis and Henry interview, May 3, 1994.

16.   National Labor Relations Board, *Decisions*, 147:1595.

17.   Davis and Henry interview, May 3, 1994; "NLRB Proceedings," 10–20, Exhibit GC-2, RG 025, National Archives.

18.   Jim Crow segregation characterized all facets of Houston's race relations during the first six decades of the twentieth century. See James M. SoRelle, "Race Relations in Heavenly Houston, 1919–1945," in *Black Dixie: Afro-Texan History and*

Culture in Houston, ed. Howard Beeth and Cary Wintz (College Station: Texas A&M University Press, 1992), 175–91; and Robert Fisher, "Organizing in the Private City: The Case of Houston, Texas," in Beeth and Wintz, *Black Dixie*, 253–77.

19. Hill, *Black Labor*, 109–21.

20. Carter and Marcus, "Trade Union Practices and the Law," 385–86.

21. Davis and Henry interview, May 3, 1994.

22. Hughes Tool Bulletin No. 671, August 4, 1958; Bulletin (no number), February 9, 1959; Bulletin No. 679, February 26, 1959, RG 329, Texas Labor Archives. According to the Hughes Rig Count, between August 1957 and July 1958 the number of rigs operating throughout the world dropped from 2,716 to 1,957. In 1957 the company manufactured 2,500 drilling bits a day and in 1959 the number fell to 1,600.

23. National Labor Relations Board, *Decisions*, 45:824–25; "NLRB Proceedings," 275, RG 025, National Archives.

24. "NLRB Proceedings," Exhibit CP-3, RG 025, National Archives.

25. US Department of Justice, *Amicus Curie in US before the NLRB*, 1–2, RG 329, Texas Labor Archives.

26. Ray Marshall, *The Negro and Organized Labor* (New York: John Wiley and Sons, 1965), 226–31; *MLR* 84 (May 1961): 530.

27. "NLRB Proceedings," 54–63, 145–48, 178–84, RG 025, National Archives; Henry interview, May 9, 1997.

28. "NLRB Proceedings," 241, RG 025, National Archives.

29. Ibid., Exhibit GC-4.

30. Ibid., 284–86, 298–300.

31. The joint bargaining committees of Locals No. 1 and No. 2 did meet on March 28, 1962, to reconsider the proposal. The white leadership offered a watered-down counterproposal that merely asked the union to attempt to eliminate discrimination. Local No. 1's counterproposal stated: "The parties agree that they will, within a period of two (2) years or sooner, attempt to provide a greater and more equitable opportunity for all employees." The black leadership rejected the counterproposal because it found the language too weak and believed it would leave the union's inequitable racial status quo in place. See "NLRB Proceedings," 108–9, 209–19, 239–44, Exhibit R-3, RG 025, National Archives.

32. Ibid., 64, 148.

33. National Labor Relations Board, *Decisions*, 147:1596; "NLRB Proceedings," 61–65, 147–50, 232–34, RG 025, National Archives.

34. "NLRB Proceedings," Exhibits GC-3, GC-8, RG 025, National Archives.

35. Ibid., 138–42, Exhibits CP-2, CP-2A; National Labor Relations Board, *Decisions*, 147:1596.

36. National Labor Relations Board, *Decisions*, 147:1593.

37. "NLRB Proceedings," Exhibits GC-3, GC-5, GC-6, RG 025, National Archives.

38. Ibid., 65–72, 158–67, Exhibits GC-8, GC-9, GC-10, GC-11, GC-12. Officials

from Hughes Tool responded that it was following the provisions of the 1959 contract and used that agreement to determine what employees were eligible for the bid.

39. Ibid., 228–29; Davis and Henry interview, May 3, 1994.
40. "NLRB Proceedings," Exhibit GC-7, RG 025, National Archives.
41. Ibid., 292–94, Exhibits GC-1A, GC-1B, GC-1C. Lorane Ashley filed the complaint as president of Local No. 2 and his name appeared on the complaint along with Ivory Davis's.
42. Ibid., Exhibit GC-1D.
43. Ibid., Exhibit GC-1F.
44. L. A. Ashley to Robert Carter, letter, September 23, 1962; L. A. Ashley to Robert Breaux, letter, September 23, 1962; Robert Carter to L. A. Ashley, letter, September 27, 1963, RG 329, Texas Labor Archives; "NLRB Proceedings," Exhibit GC-1G, RG 025, National Archives.
45. Robert Carter to L. A. Ashley, letter, October 24, 1962; Robert Carter to L. A. Ashley, letter, October 25, 1962, RG 329, Texas Labor Archives; "NAACP Takes Sides Here in Labor Hearing Dispute," *Houston Chronicle*, October 18, 1962, sec. 1, p. 1; "NAACP Seeks to Oust Hughes Union," *Houston Chronicle*, October 26, 1962, sec. 1, p. 12.
46. "NLRB Proceedings," Exhibit GC-1K, RG 025, National Archives; Robert Carter to L. A. Ashley, letter, October 24, 1962, RG 329, Texas Labor Archives. Prior to Carter's petition to decertify the IMW, Hughes Tool had also contributed to the building momentum against Local No. 1. On October 9, 1962, Hughes Tool posted a notice throughout the plant announcing that it had secured federal subcontracting work for the NASA space program. One of the requirements in the contracts called for the posting and carrying out of a policy of nondiscrimination in employment practices, including the selection of apprentices. Signed by M. E. Montrose, Hughes Tool's president, and posted without first consulting Local No. 1, the notice created a furor throughout the plant because the company had publicly declared its intention to integrate the workforce in order to secure government contracts. In response to the commotion caused by the notice and in an effort to clarify Local No. 1's position, Everitt issued an announcement declaring that Local No. 1 and Hughes Tool were bound by the collective bargaining agreement signed on December 18, 1961, and that the company's announcement did not alter the contract's segregationist provisions. Hughes Tool did not respond to Local No. 1's proclamation. See "NLRB Proceedings," 260–61, Exhibits CP-3, CP-4, RG 025, National Archives.
47. Tom Davis to Robert Carter, letter, November 1, 1962; Robert Carter to Tom Davis, letter, November 9, 1962, RG 329, Texas Labor Archives.
48. "NLRB Proceedings," Exhibit GC-1I, GC-1L, GC-1M, RG 025, National Archives; Robert Carter to Ivory Davis, letter, October 31, 1962; Robert Carter to Tom Davis, letter, November 1, RG 329, Texas Labor Archives; Bob Tuft, "Hughes Racial Labor Hassle Nears Accord," *Houston Chronicle*, November 1, 1962, sec. 1, p. 12.

49. Robert Carter to Lorane Ashley, letter, October 30, 1962; Lorane Ashley to T. B. Everitt, letter, October 31, 1962, RG 329, Texas Labor Archives.

50. "NLRB Proceedings," Exhibits R-11, R-12, RG 025, National Archives.

51. Robert Carter to Lorane Ashley, letter, November 28, 1962, RG 329, Texas Labor Archives.

52. "NLRB Proceedings," Exhibit R-6, R-8, RG 025, National Archives.

53. Bill Stewart, interview by Michael R. Botson Jr., March 25, 1997, RG 329, Texas Labor Archives; Davis and Henry interview, May 3, 1994; Michael R. Botson Jr., "Organized Labor at the Hughes Tool Company, 1918–1942: From Welfare to the Steel Workers Organizing Committee" (master's thesis, University of Houston, 1994), 105–7.

54. White unionists belonging to United Steelworkers of America Local No. 2708, which represented workers at Armco Steel Corporation's massive Houston works, successfully kept a segregated system of job promotions in place within an integrated local. Similar cases of racial discrimination in integrated USWA locals occurred at the Atlantic Steel Company in Atlanta, GA, and the Tennessee Coal and Iron Company in Birmingham, AL. The USWA and the steel companies instituted aptitude tests for blacks that effectively kept lines of promotion segregated and the federal courts upheld the legitimacy of the tests. See Ray Marshall, *The Negro and Organized Labor* (New York: John Wiley and Sons, 1965), 185–88; Whitefield v. United Steelworkers, *Race Relations Law Reporter* 3 (February 1958): 55–63; Whitefield v. United Steelworkers, *Race Relations Law Reporter* 4 (Spring 1959): 122–26.

55. "NLRB Proceedings," 38–43, RG 025, National Archives; Robert Carter to L. A. Ashley, letter, November 8, 1962; Robert Carter to L. A. Ashley, letter, November 9, 1962, RG 329, Texas Labor Archives.

56. "NLRB Proceedings," Exhibit R-11, R-12, RG 025, National Archives; Robert Carter to L. A. Ashley, letter, November 28, 1962, RG 329, Texas Labor Archives; Davis interview, May 1, 1997. Lorane Ashley never fully agreed with the NAACP's effort to decertify the IMW, a position that put him at odds with Robert Carter, Columbus Henry, and Ivory Davis. Ashley's original objective in filing Ivory Davis's complaint had been for Local No. 2 to gain parity with the white local, but keep the IMW intact. Ashley remained committed to working within the IMW despite its segregation because he believed that the union's joint certification allowed it to block any local proposals that it opposed. Technically, this was true, but it had not prevented Local No. 1 from discriminating against blacks by creating separate lines of promotion, establishing white-only jobs, and excluding blacks from apprenticeships. Ashley submitted the motion to decertify the IMW at the urging of Henry and Ivory Davis, who threatened to do it themselves if Ashley would not.

57. "NLRB Proceedings," 94, 266, Exhibit R-13, RG 025, National Archives. Henry now served as Local No. 2's vice president due to the death of Charles Benson, who had held that office when the charges were filed. Local No. 2's secretary, Pinkston Bell, was on vacation at the time and unable to attend the meetings.

58. "NLRB Proceedings," 268, Exhibits R-2, R-6, R-7, RG 025, National Archives.

59. Davis and Henry interview, May 3, 1994; Robert Carter to L. A. Ashley, letter, December 3, 1962; Robert Carter to Tom Davis, letter, December 3, 1962, RG 329, Texas Labor Archives; "Hughes Tool White, Negro Unions Merge," *Houston Chronicle*, December 11, 1962, sec. 2, p. 1; "Negro Local Cautious on Merger Move," *Houston Chronicle,* December 12, 1962, sec. 1, p. 1.

60. "NLRB Proceedings," 193, 226–27, 264–69, 311–13, RG 025, National Archives.

61. Robert Carter to L. A. Ashley, letter, November 28, 1962, RG 329, Texas Labor Archives.

62. "NLRB Proceedings," 98–99, 318–21, RG 025, National Archives.

63. Ibid., 12–22, 37–41; Charles Culhane, "Negro Charges Hughes Tool Withheld Training," *Houston Post*, December 12, 1962, sec. 1, p. 9.

64. Charles Culhane, "Represents Whites, Hughes Union Chief Says as NIRB [*sic*] Ends Hearing," *Houston Post*, December 13, 1962, sec. 1, p. 23; Bob Tuft, "Hearing Ends: Hughes Ready to Halt Job Discrimination," *Houston Chronicle*, December 13, 1962, sec. 1, p. 18; "NLRB Proceedings," 26–37, 293–96, RG 025, National Archives; National Labor Relations Board, *Decisions*, 147:1602–3.

65. "NLRB Proceedings," 20–24, 174–75, 313–17, 325–35, RG 025, National Archives; "Negro Seeks Equal Hughes Union Rights," *Houston Chronicle*, February 11, 1963, sec. 1, p. 4.

66. "NLRB Proceedings," 313–17, RG 025, National Archives.

67. Ibid., 293–97, 324.

68. National Labor Relations Board, *Decisions*, 147:1577, 1605–7; Robert Carter to Columbus Henry and Ivory Davis, letter, February 28, 1963, RG 329, Texas Labor Archives; Bob Tuft, "NLRB Asks Union Removal in Hughes Row," *Houston Chronicle*, February 28, 1963, morning edition, sec. 1, p. 6; "NLRB Asks Removal of Union in Racial Row," *Houston Chronicle*, February 28, 1963, final edition, sec. 1, p. 1; David Allred, "NLRB Is Asked to Oust All Hughes Tool Unions," *Houston Post*, March 1, 1963, sec. 1, p. 2.

69. National Labor Relations Board, *Decisions*, 147:1598; W. M. Streetman to Jimmy Delmar, letter, March 13, 1963, RG 329, Texas Labor Archives.

70. Hobart Taylor to Ivory Davis, letter, April 29, 1963; Ivory Davis to Hobart Taylor Jr., letter, May 28, 1963; Hughes Tool Bulletin (no number), October 30, 1964, RG 329, Texas Labor Archives.

71. Columbus Henry to Robert Carter, letter, December 11, 1963, RG 329, Texas Labor Archives; "Negro Seeks Equal Hughes Union Rights," *Houston Chronicle*, February 11, 1963, sec. 1, p. 4.

72. National Labor Relations Board, *Decisions*, 147:1574; Hill, *Black Labor*, 131–33; "NLRB Penalizes Union at Hughes: Says Local Failed to Follow Up Negro Worker's Complaint," *Houston Chronicle,* July 2, 1964, sec. 1, p. 1; Doug Freelander, "NLRB Says Union Guilty of Race Discrimination," *Houston Post*, July 3, 1964, sec. 1, p. 1.

73. Doug Freelander, "NLRB Action Against More Unions Is Hinted," *Houston Post*,

July 4, 1964, sec. 1, p. 12; "NAACP Takes Sides Here in Labor Hearing Dispute," *Houston Chronicle*, October 18, 1962, sec. 2, p. 1.

74.   Alvin DuVall, "Hughes Union Seeks New NLRB Election," *Houston Post*, July 8, 1964, sec. 3, p. 14.

75.   "Hughes Workers Vote Switch," *Houston Chronicle*, August 5, 1964, sec. 5, p. 18; "USW Wins Election at Hughes," *Houston Post*, August 6, 1964, sec. 3, p. 6.

76.   Hill, *Black Labor*, 133–40; Carter and Marcus, "Trade Union Practices and the Law," 387–97.

MARY MARGARET MCALLEN AMBERSON

"Better to Die on Our Feet than to Live on Our Knees"

United Farm Workers and Strikes in the Lower Rio Grande Valley, 1966–1967

On June 29, 1967, four United States senators—Harrison Williams of New Jersey, Edward Kennedy of Massachusetts, Paul Fannin of Arizona, and Ralph Yarborough of Texas—arrived at the steamy, isolated delta of the Lower Rio Grande Valley to hold hearings on recent farmworker strikes and resulting violence that had made national headlines for over a year.[1] Their arrival marked the first time a Kennedy had traveled to Texas since Pres. John F. Kennedy's assassination four years earlier, adding to the drama of the occasion.[2] Valley residents, intrigued, puzzled, and worried about the arrival of this prestigious lineup of legislators, watched the proceedings as the media covered the culmination of over a year of strife and violent conflict between growers and farm strikers.[3]

The senators queried growers and union organizers about farmworkers' wages and their thoughts on unionization. For decades, labor analysts' calls for improvements in working conditions and pay had plagued corporate farms, but the owners refused to yield ground. Sensing the time was right for legislation to advance reforms, the senators heard testimony on work conditions and questioned the hegemonic relationship between growers and workers. Pending were Senate Bill 8, requiring agricultural workers to belong to a union; Senate Bill 195, to establish a National Advisory Council on Migratory Labor; Senate Bill 197, extending child labor rules to workers thirteen years of age and younger; and Senate Bill 198, to improve voluntary services to migrant workers, including health care and transportation.[4] The senators also wanted to examine the recent actions and jurisdictional limits of the Texas Rangers in controlling strikers. However, as the hearings progressed, activists' statements and affidavits revealed that more incendiary issues involving civil rights, politics, and organized labor had splintered their movement to aid the farmworker.[5]

Within a few months of the senatorial subcommittee hearings, two major factors silenced the outcry, scattered the players, and ceased most of the national scrutiny on Lower Rio Grande Valley farmworkers: the advent of Hurricane

Beulah and the Cabinet Committee Hearings on Mexican American Affairs held simultaneously with the hearings on the Chamizal Treaty of 1967.[6] On September 20, 1967, Hurricane Beulah would cause an immediate cessation of all agricultural activities for months. Thirty-seven days later, the hearings signified Pres. Lyndon B. Johnson's acquiescence to work with Hispanic-American civil rights activists and opened the door to La Raza Unida in Texas. By 1967 the strike in the Lower Rio Grande Valley, which had been weakening for some time, suffered from lack of money and interest, as Hispanics gaining political ground galvanized behind civil rights.[7]

The workers, who had neither organized the strikes nor realized much positive benefit from them, became extraneous once Hispanic civil rights achievements began to accrue. It was yet another episode in the Lower Rio Grande Valley's 220-year history in which groups with larger political agendas came to find the area, its people, and proximity to the border useful, until certain ends were met.[8] In order to understand how local incidents resonated nationally and propelled change through the 1970s, it is important to understand the network of players and sequence of events that transpired between the summers of 1966 and 1967.

In May 1966, encouraged by recent progress toward farmworker unionization in California, Eugene Nelson, representing the National Farm Workers Association (NFWA) under Cesar Chavez, traveled to Houston to advance a nationwide grape boycott.[9] Chris Dixie, a Houston lawyer for the AFL-CIO and the Political Association of Spanish-Speaking Organizations (PASO), advised Nelson to investigate the conditions in the Lower Rio Grande Valley fields, in particular La Casita Farms, a subsidiary of Harden Farms of California and one of the union's main targets. Dixie and others in the AFL-CIO feared that unionization would occur in the valley under the Teamsters, since truckers were involved in shipping produce out of the Lower Rio Grande Valley. However, some in the AFL-CIO doubted that farmworkers along the border could be unionized, as the workers were highly mobile and the region's proximity to Mexico offered an endless supply of workers, which could keep wages low.[10]

Undaunted by such concerns, Nelson mobilized other association members, like former farmworker Gilbert Padilla, Bill Chandler, and Chandler's wife, Irene, to recruit strikers and planters, convinced that the time for unionization had arrived in deep South Texas.[11] Dolores Rodriguez Serna, who would become the secretary of the Rio Grande City outpost of the union, remembered how she came to be involved. Eugene Nelson spoke one June evening in the center plaza of Rio Grande City. Serna, pregnant and in mourning for her recently deceased father, strolled to the town square and came upon Nelson's recruitment oratory accompanied by accordion music. He convinced her to join "La Causa."[12]

Nelson quickly captured the attention of the farming community. At mass meetings in Rio Grande City and Roma, farmworkers vented their frustrations, and approximately seven hundred enlisted in the hastily formed Independent Workers Association (IWA), though the number of reported supporters remained inflated throughout the entire tenure of Nelson's campaign. To provide immediate assistance for the workers, Nelson asked for donations of clothing and food, and for volunteers to conduct classes in English.[13] They rented the abandoned Mexico Theatre in the town center of Rio Grande City and made it a headquarters where they held meetings and rallies, fed volunteers, and provided child care for strikers.[14] Nelson relied heavily on local union supporters, especially Margil Sanchez, a used-car dealer from nearby Mission. Though a Teamster supporter, Sanchez aligned himself with the farmworkers' cause and eventually became a vice president of the Rio Grande City chapter.[15]

Nelson's efforts attracted a number of idealistic student organizers from California—a development that made some locals nervous. The experience of student striker Kathy Lynch Murguia exemplifies the reason why. "Politically, I considered myself a mainstream Democrat," Murguia recalled. "However . . . Marxism seemed to provide a fresh interpretation on understanding the dynamics of the political reality. . . . I was barreling down a path of activism based on a belief that social change within our constitutional framework was a moral imperative."[16]

While the activities in the Lower Rio Grande Valley attracted idealistic students, Nelson and the others understood that the strikes had national implications for labor unions. As "La Huelga" broiled in the summer of 1966, so too did the struggle between the AFL-CIO and the Teamsters Union as they competed for new members. A feud between the Teamsters' Jimmy Hoffa and the Senate's Migratory Labor Subcommittee's Sen. Robert Kennedy accelerated the AFL-CIO's membership drive. While Kennedy called the Teamsters a "corrupt, gangster-ridden union," the Teamsters pressured small local organizations to come under their umbrella.[17] The stridently anticommunist John Birch Society meanwhile alleged that subversives had infiltrated the unionized farmworkers, and Teamsters organizers found the red-baiting techniques useful in recruiting new members.[18]

The AFL-CIO retaliated by accusing the Teamsters of frequently intimidating and selling out their members. Teamsters, on the other hand, allowed leniency in dues to those who frequently returned to Mexico, while the AFL-

CIO-aligned National Farm Workers Association charged back dues to their members.[19] Despite disagreements between the United Automobile, Aerospace, and Agricultural Implement Workers of America (UAW) and the AFL-CIO, together they agreed to aggressively recruit agricultural workers to win them from the Teamsters. At the end of 1965, the UAW's president and AFL-CIO advocate Walter Reuther pledged ten thousand dollars, with a promise for another five thousand dollars per month, to the farmworkers' unions in California through 1966.[20] Meanwhile, Harrison Williams and Robert Kennedy of the Senate Subcommittee on Migratory Labor traveled to California in early 1966 over the possibility of legislation on unionizing the farmworkers.[21]

On June 1, the Independent Workers Association in Rio Grande City called its first strike against six large farms and area packing sheds. The strikers demanded recognition of their right to collectively bargain, a wage of $1.25 per hour, the replacement of crew bosses with IWA representatives, and curiously, a five-cent-per-crate fee for an organization called the "JFK Memorial Fund." Owners of packing sheds, however, were particularly concerned with the walkout of 150 valley employees loyal to the United Packinghouse Food and Allied Workers Union of the AFL-CIO, who sympathized with the farmworkers' strike.[22]

Outraged local law enforcement called in Texas Rangers for assistance. That evening the strikers blocked the Missouri Pacific Railroad to stop an eastbound train hauling melons and other produce. Rangers Jerome Priess and Frank Horger instructed the strikers to vacate the tracks, and Nelson, in his flair for the dramatic, responded that his foot was caught in the rails. Nelson asked the crowd, "Que dices amigos?" The rangers untied his shoe, pulled him off the track, and arrested him for disturbing the peace. The court later released him on bond.[23] Reportedly, that evening someone sprayed the picketers with DDT fog from a machine routinely used to control mosquitoes.[24]

Not ready to lose eight thousand acres of cantaloupes worth over 2 million dollars, on June 6 the growers sought judicial remedy. Breaking the strike with a ten-day restraining order from the Seventy-Ninth State District Court in Falfurrias, the growers then sent trucks to the Roma international bridge to recruit "green card" Mexican workers.[25] In relying on Mexican workers who lived south of the border—some only hundreds of yards away in riverside settlements—the growers were using methods resorted to since the 1940s.[26] Normally, Hispanic American crew bosses recruited laborers north of the river, often trucking them to nearby work sites for a fee.[27] But additional "green-carders" or "*viseros*" also regularly crossed the Rio Grande from Mexico to work as day labor, often creating a surplus of workers that helped depress wages.[28]

Ignoring the restraining order, Nelson and California union officer Dolores Huerta organized a strike at Garciasville and a picket line at the Roma bridge, pleading with "green card" scabs not to work at the farms. Starr County deputy sheriff Raul Pena accused the group of violating the restraining order and arrested Nelson, who spent a few hours in jail.[29] Later that month, the IWA voted to merge with the National Farm Workers Association, which almost simultaneously was renamed the United Farm Workers Organizing Committee (UFWOC).

National allegations of the UFWOC's ties to communism haunted local participants, causing valley farmworkers to worry about joining forces with the California union. Margil Sanchez, the local IWA vice president, had read a recent John Birch Society pamphlet charging the California union with communist ties.[30] Consequently, Sanchez never felt comfortable relinquishing control to Nelson and the Californians, even though the charges cited in the Birch article remained unproven.[31]

Nelson defended himself. "I'm not a communist and don't know of any communists here. . . . If there are communists in the Rio Grande Valley it is because there are conditions here that are conducive to their activity. I don't like communists any more than the Birchers do. That's why I'm here—to set conditions right before the communists get here," he said, in a wholesale renunciation of communism.[32]

By joining UFWOC, workers in the Lower Rio Grande Valley received immediate national attention.[33] A few local growers found the acronym change advantageous, calling the strikers "U-F**K" and other pejoratives. Generally, the growers questioned the union's motives, assuming they had ties to either organized crime or socialist organizations. The notions of collectivism, workers' rights, and collective bargaining were frightening to many residents who had grown up during the Cold War.[34]

Around the nation, through May and June 1966, Students for a Democratic Society (SDS), the Committee on Racial Equality, and the American Friends Service Committee held strikes and sympathy demonstrations for valley farmworkers and Delano grape pickers.[35] A flurry of endorsements for the Texas farmworkers began, starting with the Political Alliance of Spanish-Speaking Organizations, the Teamsters, and the League for United Latin American Citizens, and followed by the GI Forum based in San Antonio and the Texas AFL-CIO and its Industrial Union Department. Support arrived when Albert Penia, a Bexar County commissioner and formerly of PASO, and Teamster Ray Schafer arrived with two truckloads of food.[36] On June 26, the Texas chapter of the Amalgamated Meat Cutters and Butchers Workmen of North America donated five hundred dollars to the Texas UFWOC. Father Phillip Byron of Immaculate Conception Catholic Church at Brownsville also attended, demonstrating support from at least one religious body.[37]

Seeking to capitalize on the national recognition, and in an effort to revitalize the strikers demoralized by local legal injunctions, Nelson and other UFWOC workers announced a major march to Austin, departing on July 4 and culminating in Austin on Labor Day. Clergy members were some of the first to aid the event, with the Reverends Sherrill Smith and William Killian announcing that they would accompany the marchers.[38]

Religious groups became an important source of support for the farmworkers. Because Cesar Chavez's philosophy called for nonviolence, the UFWOC gained the support of the Catholic Church to assist workers in getting better wages, pointing out that these were not workers for poor unviable operations, but massive agribusiness corporations.[39] Archbishop Robert E. Lucey at San Antonio was one of the most vocal supporters for farmworkers, and he embraced policies to assist the poor and uneducated. He also attempted to include all Hispanics, not just the urbanized, in order to expand the ministry further. Reverend Smith, acting as an agent for Lucey, investigated allegations of discrimination and became involved in the Rio Grande City labor dispute.[40] Rev. Jack Alford of the National Council of Churches also offered his endorsement of "La Causa," noting that it benefited from the African American civil rights movement and the War on Poverty programs passed under the Johnson administration. However, church involvement presented complexities deriving from lingering traditional attitudes of priests and their imposing superiority over congregations, especially Hispanics, even by priests of Hispanic origin.[41]

On July 4, Nelson led some one hundred UFWOC marchers from Rio Grande City east toward the Catholic shrine at San Juan, Texas, a distance of forty-five miles. Other marches set out the next day from Edinburg and ended at the San Juan shrine where priests from San Antonio conducted a special mass, the local padres wanting to stay out of the controversy.[42] On July 8, at another mass, conducted by Father Humberto Medieros, the new archbishop of Brownsville, the archbishop revealed that he supported the strike, a sign perhaps that the UFWOC was becoming more accepted by established religious institutions.[43]

When the then thirty-five marchers approached Mission on July 7 under the hot Texas sun, Rev. James Navarro and Father Antonio Gonzalez of Houston took positions at the head of the group. Gonzalez proclaimed himself cochairman of the march. Suddenly, strikers from Rio Grande City saw a minister with a Christian flag and a priest in a cowboy hat sporting a sign reading "migrant priest" at the front of the line. This did not read well to Nelson, or to many of the marchers, who recognized that four hundred miles lay between them and Austin.[44]

Ultimately, at some point during the UFWOC march, Navarro, Gonzalez, Smith, and other priests, enthusiastic in their missionary zeal, were asked to walk beside, not ahead of the farmworkers, due in part to the legacy of domination priests had over Hispanic parishioners and the inconsistency of their support for the farmworkers.[45] The march belonged to the farmworkers, but other agendas began to fragment the purity of "La Causa."

The marchers took on an east–west zigzag pattern between Highways 281 and 77, as they made their way north to Austin. The numbers marching varied widely depending on the stretch of road. On July 20, nineteen marchers set out from Rachal by bus for Falfurrias where they anticipated the support of the Knights of Columbus and the local Catholic Church. Upon their arrival, however, the priests turned them away. "They would not even give us water," recalled marcher Juan Rocha, who viewed this as a sign of fear and ambivalence by many old-line clergy regarding the new radical thinking sweeping the country.[46]

By way of Kingsville, they reached Mathis, where Hiram Moon of the UAW of Dallas presented one thousand dollars to Nelson. By August 27, the strikers reached San Antonio and were greeted by Archbishop Lucey, who held a mass and candlelight vigil.[47]

During the march, it became apparent to some farm strikers that religious leaders had transformed "La Huelga" into a broader fight for social justice and against poverty and prejudice. At San Antonio, the workers' demand for $1.25 per hour seemed ancillary to the other agendas, especially evident when Father Gonzalez informed Nelson that they could not endorse "every program [the unions] recommended."[48] Nevertheless, the priests supported justice and equal political status for Hispanics in Texas.

Cesar Chavez joined the marchers for a week in late July. Seeing the difficulties in the Texas strike by its proximity to the Mexican border, he flew to Mexico City to seek the cooperation of Mexican labor unions to help stop the flow of green-carders who habitually broke strike lines.[49] Meanwhile, Nelson threatened a hunger strike if Gov. John Connally did not call a special legislative session to consider a minimum wage for farmworkers. He hinted that the strikers might take the march all the way to Washington, DC. The governor refused to acknowledge Nelson's threats.[50]

When the marchers, numbering about fifty, reached New Braunfels on August 31, Governor Connally, Atty. Gen. Waggoner Carr, and House Speaker Ben

Barnes were awaiting them. At first the protestors celebrated, thinking they had at last obtained the support of the governor. However, as Connally addressed them, it became apparent that they would not receive a warm reception in Austin. He informed them that there would be no special legislative session to consider the $1.25 minimum wage, nor would he appear with them in Austin. "I don't want to lend the prestige and dignity of the governor's office to dramatize the march," said Connally.[51] Attorney General Carr added that the only people waiting for the strikers in Austin were agitators and extremists who would spur violence and rioting.[52] While Connally may have believed his New Braunfels meeting would cause the *huelguistas* to abandon their march, it only stiffened their resolve and created a memory that would come back to hurt Connally later.

Upon reaching Austin, thousands of supporters joined the *huelguistas* at the Capitol. Ralph Yarborough, Henry B. Gonzalez, Franklin Spears, Aaron R. "Babe" Schwartz, Chet Brooks, Oscar Mauzy, and Barbara Jordan spoke on behalf of the cause, as did numerous state representatives. Big names in labor, such as William Kircher, national director of the AFL-CIO, and Hank Brown, president of the Texas AFL-CIO, congratulated the marchers, as did Cesar Chavez, flush from recent victories against Schenley and Di Gregorio Farms in California. Booker T. Bonner of the Southern Christian Leadership Conference (SCLC) brought a number of black sympathizers from East Texas.[53] The Valley Workers Assistance Committee under Erasmo Andrade pledged to lobby statewide support.[54] Marchers carried signs reading, "Bobby can deliver a $1.25 wage."[55]

The rally lasted into the night with a *conjunto* band, singing, and prayer. A burro named "Uno Veinte-Cinco" ($1.25), which came with the marchers from Rio Grande City, was let loose on the Capitol grounds. "He ate the flowers and pecans," said Dolores Serna. "It was a very beautiful time."[56]

At the rally's conclusion, the farmworkers appointed two of their members to maintain a vigil as sentries at the Capitol, until the $1.25 hourly minimum passed into law. The marchers then returned to Rio Grande City. Chavez accompanied them to reconnoiter the region and to help boost morale. With associate and lawyer William Kircher, Chavez held a rally at the Texas Theatre.[57]

After the march, growers reportedly began to pay higher wages but refused to enter into any contracts with the UFWOC.[58] The march had broadened the meaning of "La Causa" to include civil rights, but it also resulted in increased militancy. UFWOC continued to protest the infiltration of Mexican workers, adopting Delano tactics of coaxing workers from the fields by use of verbal intimidation and loudspeakers.[59] Farmworkers used "mischief" to annoy their employers and upset the balance of power. Through the late 1960s into the 1970s, as the leadership of organized labor became more ethnically diverse because of civil rights efforts, militancy helped to make gains in the labor movements, a phenomenon that Cesar Chavez admired and found useful, despite his philosophy of nonviolence.[60] In Rio Grande City, strikers acquired equine syringes to inject melons with old motor oil.[61] They also threatened to soak the crops with kerosene.[62] In an effort to provoke into rash actions that could be exploited via the media, the UFWOC employed a strategy of creating inflammatory situations that could be then used to levy charges of civil rights violations.[63] Texas Rangers commander Alfred Y. Allee and other Rangers knew little about dealing with organized labor tactics in the remote, antilabor, patron-driven system of South Texas.

Mexican "scab" labor crossing lines on a routine basis continued to frustrate Nelson and his small team. In desperation, during the predawn hours of October 24, Nelson, Bill Chandler, Antonio Orendain, and twelve other strikers blocked transports of Mexican workers by lying down on the international bridge between Roma and Ciudad Miguel Aleman. Warned by officials on both sides of the river, the local sheriff and his deputies physically removed and arrested them, with the cooperation of Mexican authorities.[64] One week later, despite another restraining order, some of the same group closed and locked the steel gates on the bridge. They, too, were arrested and imprisoned, this time for ten days in Ciudad Miguel Aleman by Tamaulipecan authorities.[65]

Simultaneous to these October conflicts, in Washington, Lyndon Johnson and his key advisors saw that Robert Kennedy preparing for a presidential bid courted the farmworkers and in turn listened to Hispanic civil rights advocates. Under pressure to take similar action, Johnson invited approximately sixty Hispanic Americans to plan a symposium. The participants wholeheartedly agreed that a White House summit had become essential and they aimed for a date in late spring 1967. However, to strengthen its legitimacy, Johnson needed the support of the southwestern governors, especially John Connally, who remained entirely unresponsive to requests by White House staff members and conference planners.[66]

In the Lower Rio Grande Valley on November 3, shortly after unionized railroad conductors honored picketers on the rail line, a switching crew from Harlingen reported a fire at the railroad trestle spanning the Arroyo de Los Olmos creek bed. The fire destroyed the midsection of the 450-foot bridge. Though some implicated the farmworkers union, the case was never solved.[67] Later that month, the Starr County grand jury issued a statement condemning the strike, calling it "unlawful and un-American." Citing Nelson and others as "hard-core" individuals who engaged in activities "incident to their wage demands, interlaced with threats, violence and breaches of the law . . . [to] attempt to terrify and force the true farm laborers from their work," they requested federal and state police protection, fearing for their safety and way of life.[68]

Meanwhile, through the fall of 1966 and spring of 1967 caravans involving hundreds of students and supporters brought two tons of food and clothing to Rio Grande City at Thanksgiving, Christmas, and Easter. Retracing the steps of the July 4 march, they also collected funds to support the farmworkers. Gilbert Padilla, then based out of Delano, worked to get grocers to boycott La Casita Farms produce, with dubious results.[69]

By February 1967, after long delays and indecisiveness, the White House dropped the idea of a Hispanic American conference in Washington, despite calls from major Hispanic organizations and the press. Rep. Kika de la Garza appealed to Johnson for the conference to go forward. However, in the absence of support from southwestern governors and under pressure from Kennedy appointees whom he did not trust, Johnson tentatively abandoned the Washington conference.[70] But in Texas, shifts in attitude began to occur. At Easter, on the eve of a rally in Austin, the Texas legislature debated a minimum wage bill into the night.[71] Almost simultaneously sensing growing political momentum in *La Causa*, which he equated to increasing power for Mexican Americans, Hector Garcia, founder of the GI Forum in San Antonio, publicly warned that if a Hispanic appointment to the Equal Employment Opportunity Commission (EEOC) was not imminent, President Johnson would not carry Texas in a reelection bid in 1968.[72]

Meanwhile, civil unrest and violence continued in Starr County. On February 2, 1968, the sheriff arrested San Antonio priests Sherrill Smith, William Killian, Harry W. Hayes, D. J. Hefferman, and Ismael Diaz of Rio Grande City for shouting intimidating language from private property near La Casita Farms. When Jim Rochester, one of the managers of La Casita, ordered them to leave his land, the pickets began to dispute the ownership of the property. Deputized and armed, Rochester fired his gun in the air as a warning, though the protesters later claimed that he had aimed the gun at them. Starr County deputy sheriffs found the group in violation of picketing rules and arrested them, including the five priests.[73]

Prior to their arrests, Archbishop Lucey, who had recently reversed his prolabor stance along with his anti-Vietnam position, proclaimed himself against picketing and had warned the priests not to reenter the UFWOC picket. Afterward, he exiled Smith and Killian to Via Coelli, a remote mountain aerie near Jemez Springs, New Mexico, a place of reflection and reform for fallen priests.[74]

The 1967 May harvest loomed in the horizon. In a speech, Ralph Ross of La Casita Farm presciently said, "The coming melon deal will 'make or break' the strike that is not a strike."[75] However, UFWOC members saw the benefits of their negotiations with Mexican unions when the next day, Mexican green-card workers refused to cross a picket line. These members of the Confederation of Mexican Workers (CTM) waved their red flag as they formed their line.[76] This only lasted a day, according to one law enforcement group, but enthusiastic UF-WOC members said it lasted three days.[77]

In preparation for the May harvest, both the UFWOC organizers and the Texas Rangers girded themselves for battle. Some called in reinforcements. Chapters of the Student Nonviolent Coordinating Committee and the SDS from Houston and Austin planned to travel to Rio Grande City, especially encouraging African American students to attend.[78] At a Rio Grande City rally, Gilbert Padilla stated that growers had two choices, to enter into "reasonable negotiations or [endure] the stench of rotting melons."[79] Ray Rochester of La Casita Farms assessed the underlying pressures facing the UFWOC strikers. "This is the second melon harvest since they have been here, and they will have to do something. They will lose too much face if they don't."[80] The managers commented that the 1967 spring crop was the best in five years. "We'll be shipping 50 to 60 (rail) carloads of melons a day at the peak harvest season," said Ralph Ross. It would prove to be the showdown predicted in the press.[81]

The next day, forty pickets at La Casita Farms watched two busloads of Mexican laborers harvest a record yield of 40,000 boxes of cantaloupes and 340,000 boxes of honeydew melons.[82] Two days later, on May 11, strikers gained a small measure of success when the Confederation of Mexican Workers' brick-making union prevented about 150 laborers from crossing the bridge at Ciudad Miguel Aleman. However, the green-carders crossed later in the day after the picket line dispersed.[83] Under mounting tensions, David Lopez of the AFL-CIO alleged that Texas Ranger Jack Van Cleve shoved him during a confrontation at a picket line.[84] On May 12, Nelson stormed into the Starr County Courthouse looking for Alfred Y. Allee, the newly arrived commander of the Rangers. Unable to find Allee, Nelson shouted at the constable on duty, "You tell that son of a bitch that he had better lay off [the pickets] or there's going to be some dead rangers." The local justice of the peace ordered Nelson's arrest and assessed his bond at two thousand dollars. The UFWOC leader spent three nights in jail.[85] Allee, who resembled a caricature of a Texan rural law enforcement officer, with a low-slung gun belt under an overhanging belly, a slanted Stetson, boots, and a cigar, presented at once a tough yet humorous figure. As the antithesis of the Californian strikers who considered themselves enlightened and progressive, Allee played into their hands because he was quick to anger and act in an unprofessional manner.[86]

In subsequent state congressional hearings, Sen. Joe Bernal of San Antonio adopted the popular *grito*, "*¡Abajo los Rinches!*" or "Down with the Rangers!" He sensed the timing was right to limit Ranger power in labor disputes.[87] It was a point of pride among the strikers that they challenged the jurisdiction of the Texas Rangers, who had been used to protect strikebreakers since the 1920s.[88] But the legacy of the Rangers extended back further in history for some Hispanics. Although Rangers of Mexican descent served on the force, many Tejanos associated the Texas Rangers with racial intimidation and unequal treatment. The governor could call upon them as a special force as needed, and strikers viewed them as the establishment's "thugs" or "enforcers."[89]

Though one smaller farmer in Rio Grande City, Joe Guerra, agreed to negotiate with the United Farm Workers, organizers made no headway with the six corporate farms under strike. In the spotlight of the national media, frustrations between pickets and law enforcement officials grew over the following two weeks until it reached its crescendo in early June.[90]

Arrests continued on May 18 at Trophy Farm when Othal Brand filed a complaint of secondary picketing within fifty feet of his property, resulting in the arrest of twenty-two strikers, including five women. Eight days later, Rangers escorting a Missouri Pacific train laden with melons arrested sixteen picketers for unlawful assembly. Starr County deputy Roberto Pena, who assisted in the arrests, said they shouted vulgarities at the officers. They were held in the Hidalgo County jail at Edinburg for two days until a representative of the UAW made the cash bond of eight thousand dollars.[91]

By the end of May, total arrests for the year stood at 117, and tempers reached new heights.[92] On May 26, Texas Rangers protecting a railroad shipment traveling through Mission roughed up Rev. Edward Kruger and confiscated his camera. One allegedly slapped UFWOC striker Magdaleno Dimas, knocking a hamburger out of his mouth, and forced him close to the passing train, threatening to push him onto the rails. Texas Rangers denied that brutalities occurred.[93] That same evening, the Rangers confiscated the movie camera of UAW representative Pancho Medrano as he shot film of the Rangers arresting and forcing a young volunteer, Kathy Baker, into a police car. Medrano struggled against the Ranger, who also arrested him, pushed him in the squad car, and punched him in the nose. Later, when the picketers complained about their treatment, the Rangers said they made much ado about nothing.[94]

Allee, a former military officer and career Texas Ranger, attempted to defend his men's actions. "This thing has gotten plumb out of hand as far as law enforcement is concerned. We've been involved in . . . [other strikes]. We're not prejudiced against organized labor. If they want to organize, let 'em go ahead, . . . but let 'em do it in a way favorable to all the people of the country and not just favorable to the union." He added that none of the workers had walked off the job, and that they did not want to unionize. Outside agitators (Nelson, Chandler, and Padilla) had caused the disturbance.[95]

Despite the Rangers' enforcement of state law, the UFWOC appealed to federal labor leaders to persuade President Johnson and Governor Connally to have them removed. Roy Reuther of the UAW in Detroit, the brother of Walter P. Reuther, called the president and the governor to complain that Medrano's arrest was unprovoked and without cause.[96] On May 31, the Rangers arrested twelve more pickets, each held on four hundred dollars' bond.[97]

On June 1, tensions came to a head. At 11:00 p.m., Allee and his men went looking for Magdaleno Dimas and another striker, Ben Rodriguez, who were reportedly armed with rifles. The Rangers asked several union members, including Bill Chandler, about their location, but nobody knew the men's whereabouts. Rangers then went into a house adjacent to Chandler's and found Dimas and Rodriguez. According to the UFWOC members, the Rangers severely beat the two men, arrested them, and hauled them to jail.[98] Later, evidence presented to the Senate subcommittee revealed that the first doctor to examine the men, Mario Ramirez, found the men conscious, oriented, and not complaining of any malaise. Another, Dr. Ramiro Casso, found just the opposite, that Dimas had suffered a concussion and damage to his spine as the result of a severe beating.[99]

Texas Rangers Col. Homer Garrison, director of the Department of Public Safety, said the charges of brutality were totally unfounded. Starr County district attorney Randall Nye said the Rangers needed to subdue Dimas to confiscate his weapon. Meanwhile, the truth remained a mystery, and the incident pushed any negotiations between farmers and strikers further apart.[100]

By mid-June, the harvest had almost ended. The UFWOC called a rally on June 6, simultaneous to the visit of Texas senators Oscar Mauzy, Don Kennard, and A. R. ("Babe") Schwartz, who concluded that the Texas Rangers had indeed been needed to control violence arising from the labor dispute. Citing the damage to railroad tracks, the stoning of the trains, and the expensive bridge repairs blamed on farm strikers, the Missouri Pacific Railroad also brought political pressure to control the strikers' behavior.[101]

Nonetheless, a week later the Rangers were ordered from Starr County. But the damage was done. Union members wrote to US attorney general Ramsey Clark to send in federal marshals, but moreover, they knew that the matter would be examined further at the Senate Subcommittee on Migratory Labor hearings, planned only two weeks hence.[102]

That June in Washington, President Johnson appointed Texan Vicente Ximenes, a former World War II veteran, Panama Canal administrator, and Democratic Party leader, to the EEOC.[103] The Hispanic Americans, at least the old guard, were making political gains, a goal dreamed of for decades. Governor Connally, meanwhile, finally met with UFWOC's Gilbert Padilla and the UAW's Pancho Medrano, who requested union votes and arbitration on corporate farms. Connally, however, maintained his neutrality in loyalty to agribusiness supporters.[104]

Growers won another victory when district judge C. W. Laughlin issued a temporary injunction on June 8 that broke the strike for most of the month.[105] Meanwhile the leadership of the UFWOC team in South Texas began to show signs of vulnerability. At a hearing to consider a permanent injunction against strikes on June 27, Eugene Nelson testified that since the beginning of summer, the farmworkers union no longer employed him. When asked about union shenanigans against growers, such as burning cars and slashing tires, Nelson remained passive and neutral on the issue.[106]

Despite this, there were signs that some growers were willing to negotiate with union officials. While most produce packers remained strongly resistant to any union contracts, when labor lawyer Chris Dixie, on behalf of the National Labor Relations Board (NLRB) and the AFL-CIO, requested that Starr Produce workers be allowed to vote whether to unionize, Starr capitulated. The vote ended in a fourteen–fourteen tie, which under NLRB rules constituted a loss, though the UFWOC considered it a moral victory.[107]

On June 26, Chris Dixie, joined by lawyers Jerry Cohen and James D. McKeithan representing the UFWOC, filed a civil rights lawsuit against the Texas Rangers and the county officials of Starr County. On behalf of Francisco "Pancho" Medrano, David Lopez, Gilberto Padilla, Magdaleno Dimas, Benjamin Rodriguez, and Kathy Baker, the suit against Allee, Jack Van Cleve, Jerome Preiss, Ray Rochester, deputies Raul and Robert Pena, and others cited civil rights and jurisdictional violations by Texas Rangers.[108] Medrano swore they would fight it all the way to the US Supreme Court. Almost simultaneously, the Texas Council of Churches also filed a suit for a temporary injunction against the Rangers and Rio Grande City police.[109] The Texas Advisory Committee to the US Commission on Civil Rights released a report of a hearing condemning the persistent arrests of UFWOC protestors. It also found that Texas Rangers encouraged farmworkers to cross picket lines, and that Starr County officials intimidated workers, making them fearful of joining a union.[110]

On June 29 the Senatorial Subcommittee on Migratory Labor opened dialogue in Rio Grande City. Commenced by Senator Williams, accompanied by Edward Kennedy, Paul Fannin, and Ralph Yarborough, Williams declared, "We have come to Texas in response to considerable requests, and also because we have before the Senate of the United States legislation that would, under law, permit people to organize in unions, and if they do agree to organize in unions, they would be protected under the law to bargain collectively." The subcommittee was also considering legislation that would give agricultural labor similar certification and collective bargaining rights as industrial labor. Unfortunately, without formal endorsement, the bills' chances of passage remained negligible.[111]

The *Texas Observer* termed the government proceeding "Little People's Day," with approximately 350 participants and spectators gathered at the courthouse.[112] Williams chaired the hearings and directed much of the dialogue, allowing what he wished and interrupting what opinions he did not want to have entered on the record. A seasoned labor proponent and former steelworker, Williams's reputation was that of a legislative bulldog. It soon became apparent that the coterie of Williams, Kennedy, and Yarborough favored the new legislation, while Fannin invited dialogue and input from the planters, implying that he opposed the bills.[113]

One by one, the farmers, the union members, the clergy, students, and law enforcement officials gave their testimony. Though Williams and Yarborough allowed attorneys, such as Morris Atlas, a local lawyer representing La Casita Farms, to speak, they blocked most negative dialogue about union organizers. Sometimes the tensions flared. When Marvin Schwarz, president of the Texas Citrus and Vegetable Growers, complained that one proposed law amounted to compulsory unionism, Yarborough interrupted him. Local Head Start educator and strawberry grower, Marjorie Stites snapped at Yarborough, "Do you represent all of Texas?" "Yes, I represent all Texans; you too," said Yarborough. "Please wait then till you hear both sides all the way through," said Stites.[114] Most growers testified along the lines of the Farm Bureau's representatives, who repeated that the volatility of agriculture made most unions nonviable, though special agreements between farmers and farmworkers would be acceptable, including secret balloting to determine representation.[115]

Williams allowed discussion of alleged violations of civil liberties by Gilbert Padilla and other union representatives. A long condemnation of Ranger jurisdiction and brutality provided little new information other than that reported in the press. When some senators evinced outrage, others began to question their concern. Senator Fannin interrupted to defend a point by an agricultural leader, and he questioned his colleagues on the fairness of various questions posed to growers.[116] Two things became clear during the testimony: the senators came to get evidence supporting their bills, and more importantly than the farm-worker issue, Hispanics wanted an audience on civil rights and political issues.

When Erasmo Andrade, state chairman of the Valley Workers Assistance Committee, spoke about migrant workers, he insisted on addressing their draft deferrals. "Seventy-eight percent of those drafted are Mexican Americans in some south Texas counties. The green card carrier, they beat the draft by . . . staying out of the country during [the time] . . . they are eligible for the draft. . . . So somebody has to . . . carry the burden, and it's been heavily put on the Mexican American."[117] Andrade continued to testify on the numbers of Hispanics serving in the military and insisted that the Department of Agriculture needed more Mexican American employees. Yarborough defended the government, citing the recent appointment of Vicente Ximenes to the EEOC.[118]

Andrade continued, "But then the President appointed the head of that Commission yesterday, and you know who he was. He was . . . the young attorney who was on LBJ's staff, . . . [an African American] from New Jersey."

Senator Williams said, "Cliff Alexander."

"Alexander, right. And then Thurgood to the Supreme Court. So we get Ximenes and they get Thurgood and then get Alexander," said Andrade.[119]

After a discussion of the numbers of each minority represented at the federal level and quotas of appointees—few at best—Yarborough informed Andrade, "I think the figures [statistics] are against you."

Andrade concluded, "I think the figures that I have were given to me by your Labor Department."[120]

Henry Munoz Jr. testified along the same lines but with more vinegar. As a representative of the Texas AFL-CIO, he discussed its role in the Head Start programs and cited their work, getting the limited cooperation of the Mexican unions. Stating that the greenbacks had more influence over the green carder, he called Mexico an island named the "Republic of Misery" run by Juan Tortilla, and he admonished the United States for not doing more to help the people, inferring that if Mexico was controlled by Communists, a war would be launched, as he made indirect references to Russia and Vietnam.[121]

"I think that the people have made up their minds that they rather die on their feet than die on their knees, and that you are kidding yourselves that with the bill S. 8 you are going to solve all of those problems," said Munoz.[122] He continued to say that only political power would solve the problems of the Mexican Americans. "How long do you think that you can keep them down with the Rangers?"[123]

At the end of the day, the senators packed up and went back to Washington. On August 2 they convened again in Washington to hear testimony mostly from Texas planters who prevailed upon Sen. John Tower for another audience with the subcommittee, feeling that their testimony was not taken seriously on June 29. Tower's intervention set the stage for rising acrimony between labor and Texas conservative factions. At the hearing, Morris Atlas testified that La Casita Farms paid their workers more than $1.25 per hour and made their books available for senatorial scrutiny, but no one showed up. Tempers flared when Atlas stated there was no dispute between the workers and the growers. Sen. Robert Kennedy, also a subcommittee member, shouted at Atlas that the farms failed to let the workers vote whether to unionize.[124]

Despite the examination of the evidence for new laws for farmworkers, the UFWOC effort in the Lower Rio Grande Valley began to die. Cesar Chavez halted all strikes, choosing to fight the strikebreakers in the courts.[125] Chavez likely recalled Nelson because of the hasty launching of the valley effort.[126] Nelson called the first protests only two weeks after arriving on the border.

In Delano, Chavez planned for three years before organizing workers in the first strike. Though successes began to accrue in California, the ethos and philosophy of union organization would not so readily translate to South Texas farm fields. Nelson woefully underestimated the backlash of Texas conservatives and their support for their right-to-work statutes.[127]

In the meantime, President Johnson ordered a complete briefing from the FBI on the UFWOC strikes in the valley, demonstrating a renewed focus on Hispanic affairs.[128] In Bexar County, Commissioner Albert Pena publicly called for the removal of the Rangers, threatening Johnson and Connally: "If you are not going to listen to us in 1967, we are not going to listen to you in 1968."[129] But this had deeper meaning and relevance than just preventing Ranger interference, which Johnson understood. He was at work with Ximenes to plan hearings somewhere in the Southwest, to reach out to grassroots Hispanics, who they felt could not reach Washington.[130]

Meanwhile, Mexican authorities arrested and imprisoned Magdaleno Dimas in Torreon, Mexico, on drug possession charges. Police alleged he was transporting twenty-six packages of marijuana. Gilbert Padilla and the UFWOC, who had only recently based so much of their argument against the Texas Rangers on "the Dimas incident," disassociated themselves, saying that the union considered his situation "a personal matter."[131]

Toward the end of the summer, Andrade organized a rally in New Braunfels for September 1, followed by a Labor Day march to Austin to commemorate the 1966 march. Andrade felt the need to remind citizens that the fight was still on to improve Texas farmworker wages. Despite his expectations, only one hundred supporters attended the New Braunfels rally and a scant twelve marchers set off for Austin.[132]

Undaunted by the low number of marchers, Andrade arrived in Austin in the soaking rain, picking up another two dozen supporters on the way. As they made their way to the Capitol chanting "Viva La Marcha, Viva La Huelga," Andrade did not anticipate the lapse in interest for the farmworkers' cause. He expressed shock at the dearth of political supporters who failed to attend from the year previous. Joe Bernal and Franklin Spears of San Antonio, who he expected to join him, did not attend, nor did Hector Garcia, a new appointee in Washington. No one from the GI Forum, LULAC, or the Texas AFL-CIO came to Austin. Most of the Roman Catholic authorities, with the exception of Rev. James Navarro, failed to support the march. Mostly, Andrade was glad to see about two hundred supporters show up on that rainy Labor Day. He unveiled two granite markers, one reading, "Here Lies the Arrogance of the Texas Governor, September 1, 1966," and the other said, "*Es Mejor Morir de Pie que Vivir de Rodillas.*"[133]

The day after, an angry Andrade and others called their brethren "sellouts" to "Big John" Connally, searching for reasons why the coalition from 1966 did not come together again. Someone made a flippant remark that all the others stuck to their new political agendas—a direct jab at politicians hoping for a 1968 bid.[134]

Within the next few days, the UFWOC expelled Magdaleno Dimas and Horacio Carillo. Also, the Valley Farm Workers State Assistance Committee voted to remove Andrade, citing the failure of the Labor Day march and his allowance of a radical group leader from New Mexico to participate in the rally.[135]

On September 20, Hurricane Beulah, the third largest hurricane of the twentieth century, made landfall at the mouth of the Rio Grande with winds topping 140 miles per hour and dumping between twenty and thirty inches of rain across the Lower Rio Grande Valley. The hurricane spawned 115 tornados, and record high floods caused nine thousand refugees from Mexico to seek shelter in Rio Grande City. Another sick or injured of the same number sought assistance from Valley health facilities. The waterlogged delta, paralyzed for months, saw little agricultural activity until the following spring. Farmers limped along to produce a 1968 crop. Agricultural worker figures for the valley dropped from a normal level of approximately ten thousand to twenty-one hundred.[136]

Nine days later, President Johnson appeared in San Antonio and felt the sting of angry Hispanic protesters calling out "Box Thirteen, Box Thirteen" at his appearance at La Villita Assembly Hall. Around La Villita, farmworker advocates and antiwar protestors bore signs and shouted at the president.[137]

At El Paso on October 23, President Johnson convened the Cabinet Committee Hearings on Mexican American Affairs. Some Hispanics felt the event was meant to make up for the former plans of a White House conference. Chavez, who waited for the administration to act on collective bargaining and to control the Texas Rangers, complained that the hearings would do nothing for farmworkers' rights. Simultaneously, Johnson formalized the long-pending agreement with Mexican president Gustavo Diaz Ordaz known as the Chamizal Treaty, ceding 366 acres of land in the middle of the Rio Grande to Mexico.[138] More importantly, at the Cabinet Committee Hearings, representatives of La Raza Unida held an ad hoc rally to raise interest in starting a Texas chapter. They cobbled together a plan of action and revolution, termed the "Plan de La Raza Unida," echoing the World War I–era "Plan de San Diego." The Chicano movement in Texas, budding from the farmworkers' strikes and marches the year earlier, found purchase in a newly emerging political climate.[139]

The El Paso hearings served to crystallize Chicano philosophies, as illustrated in "El Plan Espiritual de Aztlan," a separatist vision of reclaiming cultural pride and power deriving from the preconquest days of the Aztec civilization. While some old-line Mexican Americans dismissed the youth-based Chicano movement as egocentric, together the factions blended radical ideas with older conservative doctrines to plan a civil rights movement.[140]

In the UFWOC arena, Chavez's skill at traditional union organization, brilliant public relations moves, and reliance in religion and nonviolence broadened his support base. In California and in the East, "La Causa" had taken on a cachet as sympathizers organized "radical chic" fundraisers, cocktail parties, public speeches, and marches. Political elites felt that by participating in produce boycotts and other acts of economic resistance, they had created a new political environment for Hispanic power. Although they did not necessarily remain focused on agricultural labor, the farmworker remained the vanguard of the Chicano movement.[141]

In Washington, Senate Bills 8, 195, 197, and 198 favoring agricultural labor unions made it out of committee with dissenting votes from Senators Fannin of Arizona and George Murphy of California. As evidence of withering support, the bills failed to pass. Despite eight hearings, hours of testimony, much travel, and reams of newsprint, the Subcommittee on Migratory Labor did not make a compelling case for legislation to force farms to deal with unionized workers.[142]

The following January, La Raza Unida, joined by the Mexican American Republicans, venerated LULAC members, and young radicals of the Mexican American Youth Organization (MAYO), convened in San Antonio. The fifteen hundred delegates designed a plan of action with the help of a $630,000 grant from the Ford Foundation to create the Southwest Council of La Raza for voter education and registration. The conference made a major statement about growing Hispanic political power.[143]

In the ongoing buildup to the 1968 elections, Robert Kennedy took mass with Cesar Chavez at the end of his hunger strike in Delano. Seeing his popularity rising among liberals and Hispanics, Kennedy announced his candidacy for president, against the advice of some of his advisors. Almost simultaneously, Ronald Reagan astutely named William Orozco as his personal representative in Los Angeles, as politicians begin to recognize that many Hispanics were not in alignment with unions and Chavez, but with the growers and industry. President Johnson, acknowledging he was in the center of many controversies, including the farmworker debacle, prevailed on Connally to help draft a statement declining a run for reelection. Johnson renounced any candidacy for office on March 31, 1968.[144]

With Richard Nixon's presidency, the mood of the administration and the country began to change toward many of Johnson's programs, including the War on Poverty.[145] In the fall of 1968, students and activists in the Lower Rio Grande Valley began protesting anew, but the focus emphasized personal and civil liberties. The US Commission on Civil Rights condemned farmworkers' living and wage conditions as peonage or close to slavery.[146] With organizing assistance from La Raza Unida, students staged protests and walkouts for gay pride, miniskirts, discrimination, and other causes supported by PASO, and Volunteers in Service for America (VISTA) which lobbied for local bus drivers and longer class hour changes. Observers in the FBI asserted that these students previously aligned themselves with produce boycotts.[147]

In 1974 a new organization, the Southwest Voter Registration Education Project, began an aggressive effort to educate and register voters, especially relying on women volunteers. However, Chicano tactics continued to divide the old and new guard. Hispanics appointed to major positions at the national level began to negotiate approaches between various factions, a process that would last into the next decade.[148]

Though some called the Texas UFWOC strike a failure, participants on both sides disagreed with that conclusion. Bill Chandler said, "It was a victory in the broadest sense. Others like the Meat Cutters and Lone Star Steel gained better leverage during the farmworker strikes. It also resulted in La Raza Unida and the Southwest Voter Registration, as well as other economic justice events around the state and nation."[149] Joe Bernal added that jurisdictional limits set by the Supreme Court on the Texas Rangers in controlling labor disputes marked the greatest gain from the strikes and marches. "They've never again gotten in the way of worker and employee relations. Their role changed, really forever," Bernal said.[150] Valley grower Othal Brand said the strikers, despite their illegitimate approach, did some good "to focus attention upon the lack of education, the low level of income from seasonal work."[151]

A review of the reports of the farmworkers, union organizers, planters, legislators, and legal representatives suggests that the inability to unionize workers in the lower Rio Grande Valley stemmed from a variety of reasons. The UFWOC representatives' assumption that the ethos of labor tactics in California would translate to deep South Texas, an isolated, right-to-work region, did not anticipate such strong popular and institutional resistance. The threat of hasty imposition of regulated farming rates and hours did not sit well with growers who already felt besieged by a government that had turned its back on the domestic farmer, willing instead to allow prices paid per unit to drop as foreign produce and raw materials flooded the American market. The union organizers, who continued to use basic techniques developed in the 1930s industrial settings, lacked intimate knowledge of the social system and transient labor pool prevalent along the border.[152]

Fearing for their safety and that of their crops, against a liberal and semi-organized labor protest transplanted from California, the growers requested that authorities call in the Texas Rangers. Businessmen across Texas viewed the services and methods of the Rangers as a quick and effective defense against outside influence, for good or bad. Historically, Rangers contained chaos along the border until the United States installed permanent law enforcement in 1916 with its entry into World War I.[153]

Multiple levels of economic need and emotion drove the protestors. Strikers commonly described the pathos of working in the fields, subject to the vagaries of weather, crop plagues, and wage and market conditions, all the while feeling marginalized by the corporate machine. Moreover, this cry of discontent not only expressed the angst of the strikers but also served a metaphor symbolizing the deep feelings of injustice among Hispanic Americans about their comparatively meager social, political, and economic gains—particularly when set against recent strides of African Americans. Many Mexican Americans felt that they had been relegated to the lowest depths, while the black population appeared to enjoy recognition and incremental social progress. While this gloomy outlook was accurate in some respects, the Hispanic community was making significant gains.[154]

Activists for Texas farmworkers both in Texas and Mexico carried hope that Antonio Orendain could continue the fight for workers' rights and better pay. Some Mexican intellectuals felt the only humane treatment for *campesinos* who worked in US farm fields would come from governmental and philanthropic support, and Orendain seemed to be one of the few remaining who cared about their brethren north of the border.[155] Many within the UFWOC agreed, wanting to place Orendain in control as early as April 1967, but the power remained in the hands of Chavez in California. In 1969 Orendain would emerge as the leader of the remaining faithful as the Delano union cut its ties to Texas. Upon his return to the valley, Orendain faced a number of obstacles, including the virtual suspension of financial support from the Texas AFL-CIO.[156]

Orendain spearheaded the Texas Farm Workers' Union through 1975, focusing mostly on strikes, boycotts, and health care for workers.[157] Though the Catholic Church gave him financial support, he remained cynical about their loyalty, as well as that of Chicano activists. When the group began to disintegrate under allegations of mismanagement, Rebecca and Jim Harrington assumed the control of the Seasonal Farm Workers' Service Center, previously run by Orendain.[158] Refusing to end his crusade, Orendain carried on as leader of the union, castigating the factions among the local labor leaders. He wrote that the Hispanic movement contained many self-seeking agendas:

More Chicano leaders will follow their brilliant paths, but some will lose in the end . . . some will no longer be in contact with the sad reality of the severe poverty of the farm workers, but this shouldn't be motive for us to quit. . . . The Texas Farm Workers' Union will continue to struggle, because we think that it is better to die on our feet that to live on our knees. We are strategizing not how we are going to come across with pretty phrases for the Chicanos ... instead ... our goals are long range and dedicated to a struggle which will not lose in the midst of egoism and false patriotism ... we use as excuses for our economical benefit.[159]

To many onlookers in South Texas, the campaign for farmworker rights in the Lower Rio Grande Valley during the late 1960s was a losing effort. The sieve created by the farms' proximity to the Mexican border, as well as conservative historical and societal attitudes, made unionization difficult. Without permanent advocates to endorse regular work ethics for the transitory laborer, there was little hope that growers and workers could cooperate or compromise. The planters and the workers lived in two distant galaxies, one as transitory and perpetual outsider and the other as landholder, planter, and salesman. Though union organizers envisioned the workers being part of the community, the two groups never successfully unified.[160] The growers used the readily available farm labor supply to create wealth for their families and stockholders. Conversely, the farmworkers collected their meager pay and watched and waited for news of better times ahead. Though one world felt they helped the other, the two would remain separate, despite the best efforts of the United Farm Workers to bring them together.

Notes

This chapter originally appeared in *Journal of South Texas* 20, No. 1 (2007): 56–103, and is reprinted with permission.

1. Hearings before the Subcommittee on Migratory Labor of the Committee on Labor and Public Welfare, *Migratory Labor Legislation*, US Senate, 90th Cong., 1st sess. (Washington, DC: US Government Printing Office, 1968), ix–x (hereafter cited as Senate Subcommittee Hearings on Migratory Labor.)

2. "Washington Report," UAW Citizenship-Legislative Department, vol. 7, No. 28 (July 10, 1967), 3, United Farm Worker Organizing Committee (UFWOC) Collection, Walter Reuther Library, Wayne State University, Detroit (hereafter cited as Reuther Library).

3. *Texas Observer*, July 21, 1967.

4. Sociologists Lyle Saunders and Olen Leonard tabulated growers' profits against wages paid to illegal immigrant workers. *New York Times*, March 26, 1951. Senate Subcommittee Hearings on Migratory Labor, 5–31. Minimum wage legislation passed in 1966 included farm labor for operations with seven or more full-time employees. It did not extend to migrant workers. *Dallas Morning News*, September 8, 1966.

5. Senate Subcommittee Hearings on Migratory Labor, 381–83, 524–25, 621, 658.

6. Gladys Gregory and Sheldon B. Liss, "Chamizal Dispute," in *The New Handbook of Texas*, ed. Ron Tyler, Douglas E. Barnett, Roy R. Barkely, Penelope C. Anderson, and Mark F. Odintz (Austin: Texas State Historical Association, 1996), 2:35–36; Julie Leininger Pycior, "From Hope to Frustration: Mexican Americans and Lyndon Johnson in 1967," *Western Historical Quarterly* 24 (November 1993): 483.

7. Pycior, "From Hope to Frustration," 483–86; Kristen Boeke, "Organized Religion Meets Organized Labor in the Civil Rights Movement in Texas, 1966–1975," *E. C. Barksdale Essays in Texas History*, 3 (University of Texas at Arlington, 2002) 1, http://barksdale.uta.edu/rabun3.htm (accessed September 23, 2006).

8. "Larger political agendas" refers to the Plan de San Diego. The 1915 pronunciamento called for the reclamation of Texas, Arizona, and most of the Southwest, and the formation of a new republic, accomplished by killing all Anglo men over the age of sixteen. This added to border chaos, part of the lead-up to the US involvement in World War I. Mary Margaret McAllen Amberson, James A. McAllen, Margaret H. McAllen, *I Would Rather Sleep in Texas: A History of the Lower Rio Grande Valley and the People of the Santa Anita Land Grant* (Austin: Texas State Historical Association, 2003), 472–73. Chicano activists used the Plan of San Diego as a civil rights rallying cry in the 1960s and 1970s. Benjamin H. Johnson, *Revolution in Texas: How a Forgotten Rebellion and Its Bloody Suppression Turned Mexicans into Americans* (New Haven: Yale University Press, 2003), 204–5.

9. Richard Ray Bailey, "Farm Labor in Texas and the Starr County Strike" (master's thesis, Texas Christian University, 1969), 34.

10. *New York Times*, February 1, 1967; UFWOC AFL-CIO, "La Casita Farms: A Profile of a 'Small Texas Farmer,'" UFWOC Collection, Reuther Library; Charles Carr Winn, "Mexican Americans in the Texas Labor Movement" (PhD diss., Texas Christian University, 1972), 98–100; Bill Chandler, interview by author, January 16, 2007.

11. Dolores Rodriguez Serna, interview by author, September 11, 2006; Bailey, "Farm Labor in Texas," 4; Senate Subcommittee Hearings on Migratory Labor, 360–61.

12. Dolores Rodriguez Serna interview.

13. Bailey, "Farm Labor in Texas," 36; Winn, "Mexican Americans in the Texas Labor Movement," 101–2.

14. Dolores Rodriguez Serna interview.

15. Winn, "Mexican Americans in the Texas Labor Movement," 101.

16. Kathy Lynch Murguia, "Kathy Lynch Murguia, 1965–1983," 1–2, http://www.farmworkersmovement.org/essays/essays/020%20MurguiaKathy%20Lynch.pdf (accessed November 13, 2006).

17. One of the first unions to help Cesar Chavez fund the NFWA was United Auto Workers under Pres. Walter P. Reuther, who pledged ten thousand dollars per month. Farmworker dues to the NFWA ran $3.50 per month, charged whether they worked or not. In California, and other agricultural communities, the Teamsters

saw successes in getting growers and workers to switch over to their union structure, which was generally more liberal with regard to dues and other stipulations. Chavez generally sided with the AFL-CIO but insisted on his own rules, including the hiring hall and seniority system to dispatch workers. He also believed preparation was key. Ronald B. Taylor, *Chavez and the Farm Workers: A Study in the Acquisition and Use of Power* (Boston: Beacon Press, 1975), 14–16, 21; Taylor, "Chavez and the Farm Workers," 198 (quotation). Through 1977, growers liked Teamster terms mostly on nonwage issues, namely because Teamsters representatives would act as the sole bargaining agent, giving the appearance of union coverage, irrespective of wage and other worker issues. Linda C. Majka, "Labor Militancy among Farm Workers and the Strategy of Protest: 1900–1979," *Social Problems* 28 (June 1981): 543–44.

18. Jacques Levy, *Cesar Chavez: Autobiography of La Causa* (New York: W. W. Norton, 1975), 228, 258; Gary Allen, "The Grapes: Communist Wrath in Delano," 2–3, Texas Farm Workers Union Collection, Benson Latin American Collection, University of Texas at Austin (cited hereafter as BLAC). Sen. Robert Kennedy favored the AFL-CIO because they had made efforts in the 1950s and early 1960s to clean corruption out of its affiliated unions. Robert F. Kennedy, *The Enemy Within: The McClellan Committee's Crusade against Jimmy Hoffa and Corrupt Labor Unions* (New York: Da Capo Press, 1994), 318.

19. Despite that AFL advocate Walter Reuther, through his UAW presidency, continued to challenge George Meany of the CIO, with whom he differed philosophically, they both pledged to aggressively recruit farm labor as part of the "brotherhood." Taylor, "Chavez and the Farm Workers," 198; *New York Times,* November 17, 1968. The UAW and Reuther had a long history of intervention into other unions' fights. Kennedy, *The Enemy Within*, 275–76; Bill Chandler interview, January 16, 2007; Ronald B. Taylor interview, November 10, 2006.

20. Walter Reuther to Paul Schrade, November 24, 1965; clipping from the *Fresno Bee*, December 17, 1965; Al Green to Paul Schrade, August 8, 1966; Al Green to Cesar Chavez, September 12, 1966, United Auto Workers President's Office, Reuther Collection; Jacques Levy, *Cesar Chavez: Autobiography of La Causa* (New York: W. W. Norton, 1975), 204.

21. Levy, *Cesar Chavez*, 204–5. Kennedy demonized the Teamsters and concerned himself with going after them for smuggling, avoiding scales, and other crimes. Additionally, Republicans took a strong stance against the farmworkers and saw benefit in splitting labor unions. After Kennedy's assassination, Nixon used Kennedy's same allegations against the unions. Bill Chandler interview, January 16, 2007.

22. Despite many inquiries, the growers could not get answers from Nelson on the purpose of a five-cent levy per crate, nor any information about the "JFK Memorial Fund." Larry Sheerin, interview by author, September 13, 2006; Bill Robertson, interview by author, September 14, 2006. The six farms were Los Puertos, Santex, Trophy (Griffin and Brand), Negro, Stan Produce, and La Casita. *New York Times,* July 11, 1967; Bailey, "Farm Labor in Texas," 36–37; Winn, "Mexican Americans in the Texas Labor Movement," 103.

23. Bailey, "Farm Labor in Texas," 37 (quotation); Winn, "Mexican Americans in the Texas Labor Movement," 103.

24. Winn, "Mexican Americans in the Texas Labor Movement," 103.

25. Ibid., 104; Bailey, "Farm Labor in Texas," 38.

26. Daniel D. Arreola, *Tejano South Texas: A Mexican American Cultural Province* (Austin: University of Texas Press, 2002), 46–47, 56–57.

27. Bailey, "Farm Labor in Texas," 11; Larry Sheerin, interview by author, September 13, 2006.

28. Bailey, "Farm Labor in Texas," 12.

29. Ibid., 38.

30. In 1966, Chavez reluctantly agreed to join forces with the Agricultural Workers Organizing Committee AFL-CIO representing Filipino workers. The two organizations merged as the United Farm Workers Organizing Committee. Both worked to avoid the term "union" in their titles because of the bloody history of California strikes. Peter Matthiessen, *Sal Si Puedes: Cesar Chavez and the New American Revolution* (Berkeley: University of California Press, 1969), 111; Bailey, "Farm Labor in Texas," 39; Winn, "Mexican Americans in the Texas Labor Movement," 114–15.

31. Winn, "Mexican Americans in the Texas Labor Movement," 114–15.

32. US Department of Justice, FBI memo, June 28, 1966.

33. Bailey, "Farm Labor in Texas," 39.

34. Anonymous, interview by author, September 10, 2006; *Valley Evening Monitor*, June 26, 1967.

35. US Department of Justice, FBI memo, May 23, 26, 1966.

36. US Department of Justice, FBI memo, June 28, 1966; Bailey, "Farm Labor in Texas," 40, 44; Winn, "Mexican Americans in the Texas Labor Movement," 107; *Valley Evening Monitor*, June 12, 1966.

37. Winn, "Mexican Americans in the Texas Labor Movement," 112; US Department of Justice, FBI memo, June 28, 1966.

38. US Department of Justice, FBI memo, June 28, 1966.

39. "Report of the Social Action Department of the Texas Catholic Conference to the Catholic Bishops of Texas," (1967) Texas United Farm Workers Collection, Reuther Library.

40. Stephen A. Privett, "Robert E. Lucey: Evangelization and Catechesis among Hispanic Catholics" (PhD diss., Catholic University of America, 1985), 288–89, 292, 306, 310, 315; Robert E. Lucey, Testimony to the Migratory Labor Committee, Texas United Farm Worker Collection, Office of the President, Reuther Library.

41. Bailey, "Farm Labor in Texas," 39; Winn, "Mexican Americans in the Texas Labor Movement," 109.

42. US Department of Justice, FBI memo, August 5, 1966; Dolores Rodriguez Serna interview.

43. However, Medieros remained an outsider. A native of the Portuguese Azores, Medieros served four and a half years at Brownsville before being transferred to

Boston. Archbishop Humberto Medieros, Roman Catholic Diocese of Browns-ville, http://www.cdob.org/diocese/ (accessed February 10, 2007).

44. Bailey, "Farm Labor in Texas," 42.

45. Joe Bernal, interview by author, February 1, 2007; Juan Rocha, interview by au-thor, November 9, 2006 (quotation).

46. US Department of Justice, FBI memo, July 20, 1966; Juan Rocha interview, No-vember 9, 2006; *Dallas Morning News*, July 17, 1966; Winn, "Mexican Ameri-cans in the Texas Labor Movement," 119.

47. US Department of Justice, FBI memos, July 27, August 10, September 2, 1966.

48. Bailey, "Farm Labor in Texas," 43.

49. Ronald B. Taylor, *Chavez and the Farm Workers: A Study in the Acquisition and Use of Power* (Boston: Beacon Press, 1975), 202–3.

50. *Dallas Morning News*, August 24, 1966.

51. Ibid., September 1, 1966.

52. Ibid.

53. Bailey, "Farm Labor in Texas," 46; *Dallas Morning News*, June 22, September 2, 1966.

54. Winn, "Mexican Americans in the Texas Labor Movement," 125.

55. *Valley Evening Monitor*, September 5, 1966 (quotation); Chavez competed for contracts against the Teamsters-growers coalition in Delano, finally winning a workers contract in 1966 and 1967. The growers would continue to invite Teamster competition, through the 1970s. Rev. Frederick Eyster, "The Western Conference of Teamsters: A Long History of Union-Busting Collusion," UFW President's Collection, Cesar Chavez Files, Reuther Library. The burro symbol-ized the difference between man (Hispanic worker) and beast. Boeke, "Organized Religion Meets Organized Labor," 4.

56. Dolores Rodriguez Serna interview (quotations).

57. *Valley Evening Monitor*, September 8, 1966. Despite the questionable outcome of the march to Austin, Erasmo Andrade and other activists captivated the state and local press. *Daily Texan* (Austin), October 20, 1966, photocopy in Erasmo Andrade Collection, Box 8, Folder 5, BLAC.

58. Dolores Rodriguez Serna interview.

59. *Valley Evening Monitor*, September 6, 1966; Winn, "Mexican Americans in the Texas Labor Movement," 124–25, 129.

60. Larry Isaac and Lars Christiansen, "How the Civil Rights Movement Revitalized Labor Militancy," *American Sociological Review* 67 (October 2002): 740; Michael L. Westmoreland-White, "Cesar Chavez and the Practice of Nonviolent Struggle," http://www.ecapc.org/articles/WestmoW2002.10.27.asp (accessed November 9, 2006).

61. Bill Chandler interview, January 16, 2007.

62. Dolores Rodriguez Serna interview.

63. US Department of Justice, FBI memo, April 25, 1966. In the 1960s and 1970s, activists in South Texas sought techniques to force social reform, and some were sent by various agencies and organizations to the Industrial Area Foundation,

organized by Saul Alinsky, who trained labor organizers to engage in confrontational and radical techniques. Among those with even the most liberal political tendencies, South Texans considered Alinsky's approaches too foreign to their own attitudes. Rolando Cantu, interview by author, November 9, 2006.

64. *Valley Evening Monitor*, October 24, 1966. The FBI contacted US attorney general Mort Sussman to see if the strikers had violated antiracketeering or other laws. Sussman told them to leave it to the local authorities. US Department of Justice, FBI memo, October 24, 1966; Bailey, "Farm Labor in Texas," 58–59; Winn, "Mexican Americans in the Texas Labor Movement," 126. Meanwhile, Eugene Nelson charged county deputies with police brutality. *Valley Evening Monitor*, October 25, 1966.

65. US Department of Justice, FBI memo, October 31, 1966, November 18, 1966; "Sons of Zapata," UFWOC Collection, Reuther Library; Winn, "Mexican Americans in the Texas Labor Movement," 126.

66. Pycior, "From Hope to Frustration," 476.

67. Dolores Rodriguez Serna interview; Winn, "Mexican Americans in the Texas Labor Movement," 127.

68. *New York Times*, November 18, 1966 (1st and 2nd quotations); Bailey, "Farm Labor in Texas," 59 (3rd quotation); Subcommittee on Migratory Labor, 384–97; *New York Times*, November 18, 1966.

69. Winn, "Mexican Americans in the Texas Labor Movement," 125; *New York Times*, November 27, 1966; *San Antonio News*, March 27, 1967, photocopy in Erasmo Andrade Collection, Box 8, Folder 5, BLAC; *New York Times*, February 1, 1967.

70. Pycior, "From Hope to Frustration," 477–78; Julie Leininger Pycior, *LBJ and Mexican Americans: The Paradox of Power* (Austin: University of Texas Press, 1997), 187–88.

71. US Department of Justice, FBI memo, March 15, 1967.

72. US Department of Justice, FBI memo, March 13, 1967.

73. Bailey, "Farm Labor in Texas," 61; Winn, "Mexican Americans in the Texas Labor Movement," 129; UFWOC AFL-CIO, "Harden Farms of California and the Texas Strike," UFWOC Collection, Reuther Library.

74. Winn, "Mexican Americans in the Texas Labor Movement," 129; Saul E. Bronder, "Robert Emmet Lucey," in Tyler et al., *The New Handbook of Texas*, 4:328–29.

75. *Valley Evening Monitor* (McAllen), April 12, 1967 (quotation).

76. US Department of Justice, FBI memo, April 12, 1967.

77. Ibid.; *Texas Observer*, June 9, 1967.

78. US Department of Justice, FBI memo, May 13, 1967.

79. *Dallas Morning News*, May 7, 1967 (quotation).

80. *Valley Evening Monitor* (McAllen), May 9, 1967 (quotation).

81. *Dallas Morning News*, May 7, 1967 (quotation).

82. Winn, "Mexican Americans in the Texas Labor Movement," 133.

83. Ibid.; US Department of Justice, FBI memo, May 16, 1967; *New York Times*, May 12, 1967.

84. Bailey, "Farm Labor in Texas," 63; *Texas Observer*, June 9, 1967.
85. Winn, "Mexican Americans in the Texas Labor Movement," 133–34. Bond was made by UFWOC legal counsel James McKeithan in cash because Starr County would not accept surety bonds, even signed by local citizens. US Department of Justice, FBI memo, May 13, 16, 1967; *Texas Observer*, June 9, 1967 (quotation); Bailey, "Farm Labor in Texas," 64 (same quotation); *New York Times*, May 13, 1967.
86. *Texas Observer*, June 9, 1967; Joe Bernal interview, February 1, 2007.
87. Earlier in June, Bernal sought to have the rangers recalled from the area. US Department of Justice, FBI memos, June 3, 27, 1967. Allee asked Bernal if he was trying to get into the newspapers. Joe Bernal interview, February 1, 2007 (quotation).
88. Murguia, "Kathy Lynch Murguia, 1965–1983," 7; Joseph Abel, "Opening the Closed Shop: The Galveston Longshoremen's Strike of 1920," *Southwestern Historical Quarterly* 110 (January 2007): 326–28, 337.
89. *Texas Observer*, June 9, 1967; *New York Times*, March 10, 1970.
90. Winn, "Mexican Americans in the Texas Labor Movement," 134; *Texas Observer*, June 9, 1967; *New York Times*, May 19, 1967.
91. Winn, "Mexican Americans in the Texas Labor Movement," 134–35; US Department of Justice, FBI memo, May 19, 1967.
92. *Texas Observer*, June 9, 1967.
93. Ibid.
94. *Texas Observer*, June 9, 1967; Senate Subcommittee Hearings on Migratory Labor, 434.
95. *Texas Observer*, June 9, 1967 (quotation).
96. *New York Times*, May 28, 31, 1967.
97. Ibid., June 1, 1967.
98. US Department of Justice, FBI memo, June 1, 1967; *Texas Observer*, June 9, 1967; Winn, "Mexican-Americans in the Texas Labor Movement," 135–37.
99. Ramirez stated that Dimas's wounds were minor and superficial. Casso maintained that Dimas suffered a concussion, sustained bruises, and the loss of a fingernail due to a beating with rifle butts. Senate Subcommittee Hearings on Migratory Labor, 459–60, 466–67; *Texas Observer*, June 9, 1967. Because of Dimas's prior record, Allee regarded him as a hardened criminal. Winn, "Mexican-Americans in the Texas Labor Movement," 137–38.
100. *Texas Observer*, June 9, 1967.
101. Winn, "Mexican-Americans in the Texas Labor Movement," 135–39.
102. US Department of Justice, FBI memos, June 12, 16, 1967.
103. A year later, Hector Garcia of San Antonio's GI Forum also received a presidential appointment. Pycior, "From Hope to Frustration," 481.
104. US Department of Justice, FBI memo, June 27, 1967.
105. *Valley Evening Monitor*, June 26, 1967.
106. Ibid., June 27, 1967. Bill Chandler said that Nelson's withdrawal from active union leadership stemmed from two possible reasons: as an author, Nelson needed to write to make money, as the union paid little, and Nelson also suffered from

bouts of depression, likely immobilizing him for periods of time. Bill Chandler, interview by author, February 20, 2007.

107. *Valley Evening Monitor*, June 26, 1967; Larry Sheerin, interview by author, September 13, 2006; Bill Chandler interview, February 20, 2007; Senate Subcommittee Hearings on Migratory Labor, 432; "United Farm Workers Organizing Committee Newsletter," April 20, 1967, UFWOC Collection, Office of the President file, Reuther Library.

108. Susan Ferris and Ricardo Sandoval, *The Fight in the Fields: Cesar Chavez and the Farm Workers Movement* (San Diego: Harcourt Brace, 1997), 137; *Allee v. Medrano*, US Supreme Court, 416 US 802 (1974).

109. US Department of Justice, FBI memo, June 14, 1967; *Valley Evening Monitor*, June 28, 1967.

110. Winn, "Mexican-Americans in the Texas Labor Movement," 143–44.

111. Senate Subcommittee Hearings on Migratory Labor, 337; *New York Times*, June 7, 1967. Meanwhile, on July 10, under the guidelines of a newly established law to control strikebreakers, Wirtz certified the strikes against the six corporate farms in the valley, thereby making it illegal to employ Mexican national "green-carders." *New York Times*, July 11, 1967.

112. *Texas Observer*, July 21, 1967.

113. Ibid.

114. Senate Subcommittee on Migratory Labor, 503.

115. American Farm Bureau Federation, *The Truth about the Grape Boycott* (1969), 22–23, Texas Farmworkers Collection, Reuther Library. Morris Atlas said the Rangers were invited to testify, but their administrators didn't allow them to, presumably. Morris Atlas, interview by author, January 2, 2007.

116. Senate Subcommittee on Migratory Labor, 352–54, *Texas Observer*, July 21, 1967.

117. Senate Subcommittee on Migratory Labor, 523 (quotation).

118. Ibid., 324.

119. Ibid., 524 (quotations); Pycior, *LBJ and Mexican Americans*, 188.

120. Senate Subcommittee on Migratory Labor, 524 (quotations).

121. Ibid., 615–16 (quotation).

122. Ibid., 616 (quotation).

123. Ibid., 616 (quotation).

124. Ibid., 250–51; *New York Times*, August 3, 1967.

125. US Department of Justice, FBI memo, July 10, 1967; Levy, *Cesar Chavez*, 451.

126. Bowman, "What About Texas? The Forgotten Cause," 17–19; Bill Chandler blamed Nelson's impetuousness on his tendency toward depression. Bill Chandler interview, February 20, 2007.

127. Bowman, "What about Texas? The Forgotten Cause," 17–19.

128. US Department of Justice, FBI memo, July 10, 1967.

129. *San Antonio Express*, August 14, 1967 (quotation).

130. Pycior, *LBJ and Mexican Americans*, 202–203.

131. US Department of Justice, FBI memo, August 29, 1967.

132. Ibid., FBI memos, September 1, 5, 1967.

133. The quote translates to "It is better to die on our feet, than to live on our knees." US Department of Justice, FBI memos, September 1, 5, 1967 (quotations); *Dallas Morning News*, September 4, 1967.

134. US Department of Justice, FBI memo, September 5, 1967.

135. Andrade invited Reies Tijerina, founder of La Alianza, an organization for the reclamation of Spanish land grants in New Mexico. Tijerina had recently been released from prison for an armed raid on a New Mexico courthouse. Pycior, *LBJ and Mexican Americans*, 180–81; US Department of Justice, FBI memo, September 14, 1967; *Valley Morning Star*, September 7, 1967.

136. Hurricane Beulah, http://www.srh.noaa.gov/crv/docs/research/hurrhistory/Beulah/beulah.html; Roy Sylvan Dunn, "Hurricanes," in Tyler et al., *The New Handbook of Texas*, 3:798–99; *Valley Evening Monitor*, September 20–22, 1967; Winn, "Mexican-Americans in the Texas Labor Movement," 144–45.

137. "Box thirteen" referred to Johnson's narrow victory over Coke Stevenson in 1948, when amended returns from box thirteen in George Parr's stronghold of Jim Wells County gave Johnson enough votes to win. During the recount, the ballots went missing or were destroyed by fire. Eldon S. Branda, "Coke Stevenson," in Tyler et al., *Handbook of Texas Online*, http://www.tsha.utexas.edu/handbook/online!articles/SS/fst48.html (accessed March 12, 2007); US Department of Justice, FBI memo, September 29, 1967 (quotation).

138. Pycior, "From Hope to Frustration," 483–84. Simultaneously, the United States received a portion of adjacent Cordova Island, also in the Rio Grande. Gregory and Liss, "Chamizal Dispute," in Tyler et al., *New Handbook of Texas*, 2:36–37. Johnson saw the opportunity to pair the hearings with the already scheduled Chamizal Treaty. Pycior, *LBJ and Mexican Americans*, 203–4.

139. Though this plan did not call for the execution of every Anglo male over the age of sixteen, it did call for a renunciation of all things Anglo. Pycior, "From Hope to Frustration," 486–87.

140. David Gutierrez, "Sin Fronteras?: Chicanos, Mexican Americans, and the Emergence of the Contemporary Mexican Immigration Debate, 1968–1978," in *Between Two Worlds: Mexican Immigrants in the United States*, ed. David Gutierrez (Wilmington, DE: Scholarly Resources, 1996), 185–86.

141. David Gutierrez, "Globalization, Labor, Migration, and the Demographic Revolution: Ethnic Mexicans in the Late 20th Century," in *History of Latinos in the United States since 1960*, ed. David Gutierrez (New York: Columbia University Press, 2004), 54–55; J. Craig Jenkins and Charles Perrow, "Insurgency of the Powerless: Farm Worker Movements (1946–1972), *American Sociological Review* 24 (April 1977): 264–66.

142. "The Migratory Farm Labor Problem in the United States," March 15, 1967, Report No. 71, 1967, *Report of the Committee on Labor and Public Welfare*, 90th Cong., 1st sess., 1967, 69–73; *US Code Congressional and Administrative News*, 90th Cong., 1st sess., 1967 (St. Paul: West Publishing, 1968), 2:3653.

143. Pycior, "From Hope to Frustration," 490–92.

144. Ibid., 492–94.

145. *New York Times*, November 17, 1968.

146. Ibid., December 13, 1968.

147. US Department of Justice, FBI memo, December 1, 1969.

148. Gutierrez, "Sin Fronteras," 185–86; Pycior, *LBJ and Mexican Americans*, 239–40.

149. Bill Chandler interview, January 16, 2007 (quotation).

150. *Allee v. Medrano*, US Supreme Court, 416 US 802 (1974); Joe Bernal interview, February 1, 2007 (quotation).

151. *San Antonio Express-News*, December 12, 2006 (quotation).

152. William H. Friedland and Dorothy Nelkin, "Technological Trends and the Organization of Migrant Farm Workers," *Social Problems* 19 (Spring 1972): 513, 516.

153. Amberson, *I Would Rather Sleep in Texas*, 485–86; Pycior, *LBJ and Mexican Americans*, 204.

154. Joe Bernal, interviews by author, September 27, 2006, February 1, 2007.

155. Carlos Marentes, "El Sindicato de Trabajadores Agricolas de Texas," in *Revista del Mexico Agrario*, Tarsicio Gonzalez, ed., vol. 11, No. 4 (October–December 1978): 145, 161, 164–65, 167–68.

156. Natalie Gross to K. Gross, April 1, 1967, UFWOC Collection, Office of the President, Reuther Library. Although Orendain requested annual support of twenty-five thousand dollars from Hank Brown and the Texas AFL-CIO, the union group only granted him five hundred dollars per month for the year starting July 1, 1970. Antonio Orendain to Hank Brown, September 1, 1970, Hank Brown to Antonio Orendain, October 1, 1970, UFWOC Collection, Tony Orendain File, Reuther Library; Bowman, "What about Texas," 53–56, 58.

157. Former Ranger Jack Dean said that in 1971, Othal Brand bought a field of onions to be harvested. When the farm strikers came to the field to confront the workers with shouting and sticks, Brand and others filmed the scene. A lawsuit filed against the growers was later dismissed. Jack Dean, interview by author, January 29, 2007.

158. Antonio Orendain to Carl Love, undated (through believed to be December 1969); Carl Love to Milton Richardson, March 19, 1970, United Farm Workers of Texas, Reuther Library. After the UFWOC leaders connected to Chavez left in 1967, Orendain and others relocated the farm labor headquarters to San Juan, Texas. Rebecca Flores Harrington to Harry Hubbard, January 12, 1977, United Farm Workers of Texas, Reuther Library.

159. Antonio Orendain, "Farmworkers and the 80's," no date (ca. 1980), Texas Farm Workers Union Collection, BLAC (quotation); Levy, *Cesar Chavez*, 277.

160. Friedland and Nelkin, "Technological Trends," 513–14; Senate Subcommittee on Migratory Labor, 348.

YOLANDA G. ROMERO

Adelante Compañeros

The Sanitation Worker's Struggle in Lubbock, Texas, 1968–1972

The 1960s turned into a decade of active involvement in the areas of politics and labor organization for the Mexican American population in Texas. As early as 1960 Mexican Americans were actively organizing "Viva Kennedy" Clubs throughout Texas. In Northwest Texas such clubs could be found in approximately fourteen towns, among them Lubbock, Lamesa, Amarillo, Muleshoe, Brownfield, Plainview, and Hereford. Union organizers recognized the political power Mexican Americans in Texas were gaining and sought to mobilize these voters. Indeed, Mexican Americans won control of the city council in Crystal City in 1963 with the support of the Teamsters Union as well as the Political Association of Spanish-Speaking People. Then in 1969 a student protest led to more permanent changes in Crystal City and the organization of *La Raza Unida Party*.[1]

Another case of organization in the mid-sixties involved the farmworker movement. The United Farm Workers Organizing Committee of the AFL-CIO worked mostly with Mexican American farm laborers in the Lower Rio Grande Valley of Texas from June 1966 to June 1967. The unionizing efforts led to bitter feelings and violence between the farmworkers and organizers on the one hand, and growers and local and state authorities on the other. Eventually the strike produced the case of *Francisco Medrano et al. v. A. Y. Allee et al.* (1972), a suit against five Texas Rangers, one sheriff, two deputy sheriffs, a justice of the peace, and a special deputy from both Dimmitt and Starr Counties. The district court issued an injunction restraining the defendants from interfering with the plaintiffs, who had suffered illegal arrests, detentions, dispersals, threats, abuse, and prosecutions.[2]

In Northwest Texas, Mexican Americans felt increasingly inspired by the successes of the Hispanic community in the other parts of the state. Spurred on by well-established groups such as LULAC and GI Forum, Mexican Americans in Lubbock took due notice of activism elsewhere. These organizations with the aid of the AFL-CIO sponsored in June 1966 a "War on Poverty and Migrant Labor Conference" at Lubbock's St. Joseph Catholic Church. The conference meant to aid "all people in West Texas interested in helping the poverty-stricken take advantage of various government programs." The campaign continued when in early 1967 Manuel Garza, executive director of LULAC, visited Lubbock to investigate charges of discrimination in the workplace. Without giving specific detail, Garza maintained that Mexican Americans and African Americans received less pay as well as no promotions from Lubbock employers. Garza was probably referring to an earlier strike that occurred in February of 1967. That episode involved AFL-CIO Packinghouse Workers, Local 1202, whose membership included two hundred Mexican Americans, fifteen African Americans, and all white supervisors and foremen. The strike began on February 5, 1967, against Farmers Co-op Gin, Inc., which refused to negotiate seniority rights of Mexicanos. In this case Mexican Americans lost their jobs to local African Americans who were promoted for returning to work, and to all-black crews hired from Dallas. When Local 1202 filed civil rights complaints with the EEOC, the co-op management went to Juarez, Mexico, and hired green-carders.[3]

In this climate of mounting organization, Mexican American sanitation workers went on strike in 1968 and won a partial victory against the city of Lubbock. Tom Lara, a participant in the strike, remembered that sanitation workers had no uniforms, gloves, boots, or drinking water as did other city department workers. Lara remembered that he and fellow employees often went through the garbage looking for clothes to wear in order to avoid ruining their own clothes or boots. The lack of drinking water became a real problem for the workers, and they were forced to drink from water hoses in yards. Some Lubbock homeowners did not like this practice and reported the workers for trespassing. Other city departments had water jugs that hung on the sides of the trucks.

Another major problem the sanitation workers faced became the lack of "johns" at the landfill; thus, they were forced to relieve themselves behind piles of garbage. Still another issue of contention involved the practice of city officials hiring Anglo foremen from the outside and overlooking Mexican Americans for advancement. When the walkout occurred, only the Mexican Americans participated while the Anglos stayed at work. The strike lasted approximately one week, and strikers asked for a 12 percent pay raise, overtime pay, and uniforms. Strikers attained uniforms and drinking water as well as portable toilets. The strikers were organized by Isidro Gutierrez, who would lead the sanitation workers in yet another strike in 1972 before eventually moving to San Antonio to organize for the Construction and Municipal Workers Union Local 1253.[4]

Between 1968 and 1972 the AFL-CIO continued to organize workers. Under the direction of Henry Munoz, a Texas AFL-CIO Permanent Committee on Mexican American Affairs organized the Mexican American Political Action Institute (MAPAI) in March of 1970 at San Antonio. The institute was primarily funded by labor but also utilized resources from other interested groups and individuals. An advisory committee of forty members representing the eleven areas in Texas would direct the work of the institute. Isidro Gutierrez of Lubbock became a member of the advisory committee, and a steering committee was chosen from these forty members. The goal of the MAPAI became year-round political action and political education campaigns to mobilize the Mexican American vote. The MAPAI solicited the help of community leaders who were not necessarily within the ranks of labor but wished to aid in these campaigns. Educational efforts were to ensure that Mexican American votes would best serve and represent Mexican American needs and of course organized labor.[5]

Because of the work of the MAPAI, it should have come as no surprise when on August 28, 1972, Lubbock city sanitation workers walked off the job in "protest of poverty wages." Sanitation workers asked for a 15 percent pay raise, which would increase their monthly salary from $357 to $412. Led by Isidro Gutierrez, MAPAI advisory committee member and fourteen-year veteran of the sanitation department, the workers did not go back to work for a month. The Construction and Municipal Workers Union, Local 1253, represented 75 percent of the employees in the city's public works departments. Membership numbered 350, according to union business manager Robert Mendez. Over half these members worked in the sanitation department.

Earlier, in July 1972, Mendez had appeared before the city council during a preliminary budget meeting. At the hearing Mendez had asked for a 15 percent raise for all city employees, payment for unused sick leave upon termination, and a Monday through Friday workweek. Sam Wahl, director of public works, countered that sanitation workers with seniority could take varying days off, with the first choice of Saturdays and Sundays. It became the consensus of the council that the city could not afford the 1.3 million dollars it would cost to give all city employees a 15 percent pay hike. However, the council did come up with enough money to grant pay raises for 75 percent of all city employees. Some sanitation workers did fall within that category, and if they had worked for more than a year would be eligible for a 5 percent raise.

By the end of the first week, the city of Lubbock had replaced some of the striking workers, although no decision had been made on whether protesting workers were considered terminated. City policy required that an employee be released after three days of missing work if management had not been notified of a sufficient reason for the absence. In a related development, sewage treatment plant workers stayed off their job, two men per shift, in a show of support for the sanitation workers, but despite this momentum, by Thursday, the fourth day of the strike the city council had decided there would be no 15 percent pay raise, and all but thirteen of the strikers' positions had been filled.

Analyzing the situation at the end of the first week, the *Lubbock Avalanche* found that the 154 workers that had walked off the job made from $2.11 to $2.44 an hour. Drivers made the higher wages. The average annual salary per worker was $4,652.88. Fifty-four of the workers claimed between five and nine dependents. The newspaper estimated that one man with six dependents brought home $158.77 every two weeks.[6]

As the strike entered the second week, workers lowered their demand of a raise to 12 percent. This same week Ramsey Muniz, *Raza Unida* nominee for governor, spoke in Lubbock. He urged Mexican Americans to support the striking sanitation workers and argued that "the workers' request was reasonable and calls for a decent salary to provide food and clothes for their families."[7] Support did not stop there. At least thirteen employees from the water, street, and water reclamation departments united with the strikers. Also, by the end of the week the Lubbock Central Labor Council offered financial aid to the workers.

The city continued to fill vacated positions. By September 9 half the workers had been replaced by new permanent employees. The city council refused to agree to any kind of pay raise, and instead pushed for containerization to lower the need for manpower. In the meantime the city encouraged employees like janitors or laborers making less money to move into the higher-paying jobs held by sanitation workers.[8]

In the third week, the city council found replacements for all openings. Sanitation superintendent Jim Weston estimated that from 45 to 50 percent of the new employees were African American, 25 percent were Mexican American, and 25 percent were Anglo American. But the council's action generated an unexpected response from the Catholic clergy in the city. At a council hearing on September 15 lasting four hours, Lubbock priests promised to advocate a boycott among their parishioners against the municipal power service. Father Tom McGovern of Carlisle representing the Priest Senate of the Amarillo Diocese addressed the council, albeit with no success. Then Father Henry Waldo of Our Lady of Grace spoke, "We came with the faith we would be heard. We have had our say but we're not sure you've been listening. We will go to our pulpits Sunday and press for economic sanctions and ask our people en masse to switch from

Lubbock Power and Light to Southwestern Public Service and not to pay the garbage service charge." Father Waldo ended by declaring, "Lubbock Power and Light has said it is people power, let's see where the real power of the people lies." A crowd of at least three hundred, comprised of sanitation workers, families, clergymen, and friends, attended the hearing in support of the strike.[9]

True to their word, on Sunday morning Catholic priests urged their parishioners to boycott Lubbock Power and Light and not pay the garbage fee unless the city council agreed to negotiate with the strikers. They outlined a five-point program, distributed at all Lubbock churches. The program called for a utility boycott, a refusal to pay the garbage fee, a rejection of replacement workers, declarations of individual protest, and finally, making contributions to the employee protest fund, care of American State Bank. At Our Lady of Grace alone, some five hundred of about fifteen hundred people attending mass signed "switchover cards" from Lubbock Power and Light to Southwestern Public Service. That afternoon, as the fourth week of the strike began, door-to-door campaigns began in support of a utility boycott.

By Wednesday of that week Gustavo Gaynett with the US Justice Department's Office of Community Relations arrived from the Dallas office to act as mediator. Gaynett maintained the Justice Department feared "outside agitators" might escalate the problems. He first spoke with city officials, then met with a delegation of priests. Meanwhile, the boycott continued, with a total of 250 actual customer changeovers and approximately 350 new requests. Office manager Carroll McDonald estimated that changeover requests came in at about forty a day. In addition, many customers each day threatened not to pay the two-dollar garbage fee.

At the end of the week the city council invited the sanitation workers to return to their jobs. Sanitation workers rejected the offer and presented their own plan. Finally it came down to two committees from both sides negotiating with Gaynett. The city agreed to create jobs in order to find employment for all strikers. When the positions opened up in the sanitation department, workers could return to their old positions. As to the 12 percent raise, the city would only agree to the already budgeted merit raises of 5 percent.[10] All strikers returned to work on September 26, 1972, at the same pay. The boycott had resulted in 350 changeovers and 428 more orders awaiting the transfer to Southwestern Public Service. Once the city had agreed to put the men back to work, Catholic clergy issued a statement of approval.

The strike may be seen as a partial victory for the sanitation workers in Lubbock, since they failed to receive their demands but at least kept their jobs. In other respects the strike can be deemed as a success. Without a doubt, it united the community. The boycott implemented by the Catholic priests became a powerful force. The strike demonstrated to the entire Lubbock community that a nonviolent protest could be effective. Further, the strike launched a decade of protest and demonstration in the Lubbock *barrios*. Indeed, the sanitation workers succeeded in bringing the message to the Mexican American community that their *compañeros*, rather than looking back, should look *adelante* to the future.[11]

Notes

This chapter originally appeared in *West Texas Historical Association Yearbook* 69 (1993): 82–88, and is reprinted with permission.

1. John Staples Shockley, *Chicano Revolt in a Texas Town* (Notre Dame: University of Notre Dame Press, 1974); *La Voz de Texas,* Lubbock, July 8, 1972; *La Prensa del Suroeste,* Lubbock, January 24, 1960, 1.

2. *Francisco Medrano et al., Plaintiffs v. A. Y. Allee et al., Defendants*, Ct. A, No. 67 B36, US District Court, Southern District of Texas, Brownsville Division, June 26, 1972.

3. *Lubbock Avalanche Journal*, June 6, 1966, March 15, 1967; Texas AFL-CIO, Mexican American Affairs, Records, 1953–1971, Series 11, Committee Hearings, 278-11-1-1, Memo from Henry Munoz to H. S. Hank Brown, October 16, 1967, Special Collections, University of Texas at Arlington.

4. Tom Lara, interview by Yolanda Romero, October 6, 1989, Lubbock, TX, Southwest Collection, Texas Tech University, Lubbock.

5. Texas AFL-CIO, Mexican American Affairs, Records, 1953–1971, Series 11, Mexican American Political Action Institute, 278-11-2-12, Special Collections, University of Texas at Arlington.

6. *Lubbock Avalanche Journal*, August 29–September 2, 1972.

7. *Lubbock Avalanche Journal*, September 4, 1972.

8. *Lubbock Avalanche Journal*, September 5–9, 1972.

9. *Lubbock Avalanche Journal*, September 14, 15, 1972.

10. *Lubbock Avalanche Journal*, September 18–23, 1972; Tom Lara interview.

11. *Lubbock Avalanche Journal*, September 25–October 5, 1972.

Selected Bibliography

Abel, Joseph. "African Americans, Labor Unions, and the Struggle for Fair Employment in the Aircraft Manufacturing Industry of Texas, 1941–1945." *Journal of Southern History* 77 (August 2011): 595–638.

———. "Opening the Closed Shop: The Galveston Longshoremen's Strike, 1920–1921." Master's thesis, Texas A&M University, 2004.

———. "Opening the Closed Shop: The Galveston Longshoremen's Strike of 1920–1921." *Southwestern Historical Quarterly* 110 (January 2007): 317–47.

Acosta, Teresa Palomo. "Texas Farm Workers Union." *Handbook of Texas Online*, http://www.tshaonline.org/handbook.

Adedeji, Moses. "Crossing the Colorline: Three Decades of the United Packinghouse Workers of America's Crusade against Racism in the Trans-Mississippi West, 1936–1968." PhD diss., North Texas State University, 1978.

Allen, Ruth A. "The Capitol Boycott: A Study in Peaceful Labor Tactics." *Southwestern Historical Quarterly* 42 (April 1939): 297–326.

———. *Chapters in the History of Organized Labor in Texas*. Austin: University of Texas Publications, 1941.

———. *East Texas Lumbering Workers: An Economic and Social Picture*. Austin: University of Texas Press, 1961.

———. *The Great Southwest Strike*. Austin: University of Texas Press, 1942.

———. "Irons, Martin." *Handbook of Texas Online*, http://www.tshaonline.org/handbook.

———. "The Labor of Women in the Production of Cotton." PhD diss., University of Chicago, 1933.

———. "Mexican Peon Women in Texas." *Sociology and Social Research* 16 (1931): 131–42.

Allen, Ruth A., George N. Green, and James V. Reese. "Labor Organizations." *Handbook of Texas Online*, http://www.tshaonline.org/handbook/online.

———. "Strikes." In *The New Handbook of Texas* (Austin: Texas State Historical Association, 1996), 6:128–29.

Allen, Ruth A., and James V. Reese. "Union Regulation." *Handbook of Texas Online*, http://www.tshaonline.org/handbook/online.

Alter, Thomas E. "E. O. Meitzen: Agrarian Radical in Texas, 1855–1906." Master's thesis, Texas State University–San Marcos, 2008.

Amberson, Mary Margaret McAllen. "'Better to Die on Our Feet, Than to Live on Our Knees': United Farm Workers and Strikes in the Lower Rio Grande Valley, 1966–1967." *Journal of South Texas* 20, No. 1 (2007): 56–103.

Anderson, Robert. "History of the Farm Labor Union of Texas." Master's thesis, University of Texas at Austin, 1928.

Anderson, Rodney D. *Outcasts in Their Own Land: Mexican Industrial Workers, 1906–1911.* De Kalb: Northern Illinois University Press, 1976.

Andrews, Gregg. "Black Labor Leaders and the Civil Rights Struggle in New Deal Texas: The Cases of Freeman Everett and Thyra J. Edwards." Paper presented at the annual meeting of the Texas State Historical Association, March 7, 2008.

———. "Black Working-Class Political Activism and Biracial Unionism: Galveston Longshoremen in Jim Crow Texas, 1919–1921." *Journal of Southern History* 74, No. 3 (August 2008): 627–68.

———. *Shoulder to Shoulder? The American Federation of Labor, the United States, and the Mexican Revolution, 1910–1924.* Berkeley: University of California Press, 1991.

———. *Thyra J. Edwards: Black Activist in the Global Freedom Struggle.* Columbia: University of Missouri Press, 2011.

———. "Unionizing the Trinity Portland Cement Company in Dallas, Texas, 1934–1939." *Southwestern Historical Quarterly* 111 (July 2007): 31–49.

Angel, William D. Jr. "Controlling the Workers: The Galveston Dock Workers' Strike of 1920 and Its Impact on Labor Relations in Texas." *East Texas Historical Journal* 23, No. 2 (1985): 14–27.

Arnesen, Eric. *Brotherhoods of Color: Black Railroad Workers and the Struggle for Equality.* Cambridge: Harvard University Press, 2001.

———. "'Like Banquo's Ghost, It Will Not Down': The Race Question and the American Railroad Brotherhoods, 1880–1920." *American Historical Review* 99 (December 1994): 1601–33.

Arnold, Frank. "Humberto Silex: CIO Organizer from Nicaragua." *Southwest Economy and Society* 4 (Fall 1978): 3–18.

Ashbaugh, Carolyn. *Lucy Parsons, American Revolutionary.* Chicago: Illinois Labor History Society, 1976.

———. "Parsons, Lucy Eldine," *Handbook of Texas Online*, http://www.tshaonline.org/handbook/online.

Ashburn, Karl E. "Economic and Social Aspects of Farm Tenancy in Texas." *Southwestern Social Science Quarterly* 15 (March 1935): 298–306.

Auerbach, Jerold S. "Southern Tenant Farmers: Socialist Critics of the New Deal." *Labor History* 7 (Winter 1966): 3–74.

Babbington, Lamar J. "Mexican-American Labor Problems in Texas." PhD diss., University of Texas at Austin, 1965.

Bailey, Richard Ray. "Farm Labor in Texas and the Starr County Strike." Master's thesis, Texas Christian University, 1969.

———. "The Starr County Strike." *Red River Valley Historical Review* 4 (Winter 1976): 42–61.

Baker, Susan Belden. "Many Rivers to Cross: Mexican Immigrants, Women Workers, and the Structure of Labor Markets in the Urban Southwest." PhD diss., University of Texas at Austin, 1989.

Baron, Eva, ed. *Work Engendered: Toward a New History of American Labor*. Ithaca, NY: Cornell University Press, 1991.

Beasley, Johnny W. "The History of the Congress of Industrial Organization in Texas." Master's thesis, Stephen F. Austin University, 1950.

Beil, Gail K. "Melvin B. Tolson—Texas Radical." *East Texas Historical Journal* 40, No. 1 (2002): 26–36.

Berry, Lisa. "Cooperation and Segregation: A History of North Central Texas Coal Mining Towns, Organized Labor, and the Mexican Workforce." Master's thesis, University of Texas at Arlington, 2004.

Blackwelder, Julia Kirk. "Emma Tenayuca: Vision and Courage." In *The Human Tradition in Texas*, edited by Ty Cashion and Jesus F. de la Teja, 191–208. Wilmington, DE: Scholarly Resources, 2001.

———. "Texas Homeworkers in the 1930s." In *Homework: Historical and Contemporary Perspectives on Paid Labor at Home*, edited by Eileen Boris and Cynthia R. Daniels, 75–90. Urbana: University of Illinois Press, 1989.

———. "Women in the Work Force: Atlanta, New Orleans, and San Antonio, 1930–1940." *Journal of Urban History* 4 (May 1978): 331–58.

———. *Women of the Depression: Caste and Culture in San Antonio, 1929–1939*. College Station: Texas A&M University Press, 1984.

Borrer, Jennifer. "The Colored Trainmen of America: Kingsville Black Labor and the Railroads." *Journal of South Texas* 11 (1998): 74–103.

Botson, Michael R. Jr. "Jim Crow Wearing Steel-Toed Shoes and Safety Glasses: Dual Unionism at the Hughes Tool Company, 1918–1942." *Houston Review* 16.2 (1994): 101–16.

———. *Labor, Civil Rights, and the Hughes Tool Company*. College Station: Texas A&M University Press, 2005.

———. "The Labor History of Houston's Hughes Tool Company, 1901–1964: From Autocracy and Jim Crow to Industrial Democracy and Civil Rights." PhD diss., University of Houston, 1999.

———. "No Gold Watch for Jim Crow's Retirement: The Abolition of Segregated Unionism at Houston's Tool Company." *Southwestern Historical Quarterly* 101 (April 1998): 497–521.

———. "Organized Labor at the Hughes Tool Company, 1918–1942: From Welfare to the Steel Workers Organizing Committee." Master's thesis, University of Houston, 1994.

———. "Revisiting the Battle for Baytown: Unions, Reds, and Mayhem in a Company Town." *East Texas Historical Journal* 49 (Fall 2011): 9–23.

———. "We're Sticking by Our Union: The Battle for Baytown, 1942–1943." *Houston History Magazine* 8 (Spring 2011): 8–14.

Botter, David. "Labor Looks at Texas." *Southwest Review* 31 (Spring 1946): 111–17.

Bowman, Timothy Paul. "What About Texas? The Forgotten Cause of Antonio Orendain and the Rio Grande Valley Farm Workers, 1966–1982." Master's thesis, University of Texas at Arlington, 2005.

Brandenstein, Sherilyn. "International Ladies' Garment Workers' Union." *Handbook of Texas Online*, http://www.tshaonline.org/handbook/online.

Brewer, Thomas B. "State Anti-Labor Legislation: Texas—A Case Study." *Labor History* 11 (Winter 1970): 58–76.

Briggs, Alton King. "The Archeology of 1882 Labor Camps on the Southern Pacific Railroad, Val Verde County, Texas." Master's thesis, University of Texas at Austin, 1974.

Briody, Elizabeth K. *Household Labor Patterns among Mexican Americans in South Texas: Buscando Trabajo Segura.* New York: AMS Press, 1988.

Brookshire, Margorie S. "The Industrial Pattern of Mexican-American Employment in Nueces County." PhD diss., University of Texas at Austin, 1954.

Brophy, William Joseph. "The Black Texan, 1900–1950: A Quantitative History." PhD diss., Vanderbilt University, 1974.

Byrd, Barbara K. "Chapters in the Struggle for Human Rights in Texas: The Life of Ruth Alice Allen." Paper presented to the meeting of the Southwest Labor Studies Association, University of Texas at Arlington, March 29–31, 1984. Typed copy, dated August 1985.

———. "Labor Education in Texas Colleges and Universities: A Case Study in Adult Education Program Development." PhD diss., University of Texas at Austin, 1988.

———. "Labor's Challenge to Education: The Case of Texas." Proceedings of the Adult Education Research Conference. Raleigh, NC, April 4–7, 1984.

Burran, James, "Violence in an 'Arsenal of Democracy': The Beaumont Race Riot, 1943." *East Texas Historical Journal* 14, No. 1 (Spring 1976): 39–51.

Calderón, Roberto R. *Mexican Coal Mining Labor in Texas and Coahuila, 1880–1930.* College Station: Texas A&M University Press, 2000.

Campbell, Randolph B. *An Empire for Slavery: The Peculiar Institution in Texas, 1821–1865.* Baton Rouge: Louisiana State University Press, 1989.

Carlson, Paul H., and Ellen Schneider. "Gunnysackers, Carreteros, and Teamsters: The South Texas Cart War of 1857." *Journal of South Texas* 1, No. 1 (Spring 1988): 1–9.

Carruthers, John F. "The Influence of the Oil Workers International Union in Port Arthur, Texas." Master's thesis, University of Texas at Austin, 1950.

Case, Theresa A. "Black and White Railroaders Join the Texas Knights of Labor." Paper presented to the meeting of the Texas State Historical Association, March 6, 2003.

———. "Blaming Martin Irons: Leadership and Popular Protest in the 1886 Southwest Strike." *Journal of the Gilded Age and Progressive Era* 8 (January 2009): 51–82.

———. "Free Labor on the Southwestern Railroads: The 1885–1886 Gould System Strikes." PhD diss., University of Texas at Austin, 2002.

———. *The Great Southwest Railroad Strike and Free Labor.* College Station: Texas A&M University Press, 2010.

———. "The Radical Potential of the Knights' Biracialism: The 1885–1886 Gould System Strikes and Their Aftermath." *Labor: Studies in Working Class History* 4 (Winter 2007): 83–107.

Chandler, Jerry Wayne. "The Knights of Labor and the Southwestern Strikes." Master's thesis, Florida State University, 1970.

Christopher, Robert. "Rebirth and Lost Opportunities: The Texas AFL and the New Deal, 1933–1939." Master's thesis, University of Texas at Arlington, 1977.

Chumley, Leo B. "Negro Labor and Property Holdings in Shelby County, Texas, 1870–1945." Master's thesis, Prairie View Agricultural and Mechanical College, 1948.

Cisneros, Victor B. Nelson. "La Clase Trabajadora en Tejas, 1920–1950." *Aztlan: International Journal of Chicano Studies Research* 6 (Summer 1975): 239–65.

———. "UCAPAWA Organizing Activities in Texas, 1935–1950." *Aztlan* 9 (Spring–Summer 1978): 71–84.

Coalson, George. *Development of the Migratory Farm Labor System in Texas, 1900–1954.* San Francisco: R&E Research Associates, 1977.

Cohen, Jan Hart (Jan Hart). "To See Christ in Our Brothers: The Role of the Texas Roman Catholic Church in the Rio Grande Valley Farm Workers' Movement, 1966–1967." Master's thesis, University of Texas at Arlington, 1974.

Cothran, Mary Lessie. "Occupational Patterns of Rural and Urban Spanish-Americans in Two South Texas Counties." Master's thesis, Texas Agricultural and Mechanical University, 1966.

Coyle, Laurie, Gail Hershatter, and Emily Honig. "Farah Strike." In *The New Handbook of Texas*, edited by Ron Tyler, Douglas E. Barnett, Roy R. Barkley, Penelope C. Anderson, and Mark F. Odintz, 2:950. Austin: Texas State Historical Association, 1996.

———. *Women at Farah: An Unfinished Story.* El Paso: Reforma, 1979.

Crain, Forest B. "The Occupational Distribution of Spanish-Name People in Austin, Texas." Master's thesis, University of Texas at Austin, 1948.

Cravens, John N. "Two Miners and Their Families in the Thurber-Strawn Coal Mines, 1903–1918." *West Texas Historical Association Yearbook* 45 (1969): 115–26.

Croxdale, Richard. "The 1938 Pecan Shellers' Strike." In *Women in the Texas Workforce: Yesterday and Today*, edited by Richard Croxdale and Melissa Hield, 24–34. Austin: People's History in Texas, 1979.

———. "Pecan-Shellers' Strike." *Handbook of Texas Online*, http://www.tshaonline.org/handbook/online.

Cullen, David O'Donald, and Kyle G. Wilkison. "'The Right to Work, to Starve, to Die': The Forgotten Radical Heritage of Texas." In *The Texas Left: The Radical Roots of Lone Star Liberalism*, edited by David O'Donald Cullen and Kyle G. Wilkison, 1–15. College Station: Texas A&M University Press, 2010.

De Leon, Arnoldo. "Los Tasinques and the Sheep Shearers' Union of North America: A Strike in West Texas, 1934." *West Texas Historical Association Yearbook* 55 (1979): 3–16.

Dell, Meaghan H. "The Unionization of San Antonio Garment Workers during the Great Depression." Master's thesis, Texas State University–San Marcos, 2005.

Dixon, Donna Sue Beasley. "A History of OCAW Local 4-229, Port Neches, Texas." Master's thesis, Lamar State College of Technology, 1970.

Dulaney, W. Marvin, "The Texas Negro Peace Officers' Association: The Origins of Black Police Unionism." *Houston Review* 12, No. 2 (1990): 59–78.

Esparza, Francisco, and Edith Esparza-Young. "The Eagle Bus Strike: An Immigrant's Recollection of Workers' Voices through Political Satire." *Journal of South Texas* 20, No. 1 (2007): 104–15.

Evans, Roy. *Tragedy at Work*. Houston: Institute of Labor and Industrial Relations, University of Houston, 1979.

Farrington, Clifford. *Biracial Unions on Galveston's Waterfront, 1865–1925*. Austin: Texas State Historical Association, 2007.

———. "The Galveston Waterfront and Organized Labor, 1866–1900." Master's thesis, University of Texas at Austin, 1997.

Ferrell, Jeff. "The Brotherhood of Timber Workers and the Culture of Conflict." *Journal of Folklore Research* 28 (1991): 163–77.

———. "East Texas/Western Louisiana Sawmill Towns and the Control of Everyday Life." *Locus* 3, No. 1 (1990): 1–19.

Ferrell, Jeff, and Kevin Ryan. "The Brotherhood of Timber Workers and the Southern Trust: Legal Repression and Worker Response." *Radical America* 19 (July–August 1985): 55–74.

Fickle, James E. "Early Lumber Trade Associations and the Lone Star State." *East Texas Historical Journal* 8 (October 1970): 149–62.

———. "The Louisiana-Texas Lumber War of 1911–1912." *Louisiana History* 16 (Winter 1975): 59–85.

———. "Management Looks at the 'Labor Problem': The Southern Pine Industry during World War I and the Postwar Era." *Journal of Southern History* 40 (February 1974): 61–76.

Filewood, David. "Tejano Revolt: The Significance of the 1938 Pecan Shellers' Strike." Master's thesis, University of Texas at Arlington, 1994.

Floyd, Willie M. "Thurber, Texas: An Abandoned Coal Field Town." Master's thesis, Southern Methodist University, 1939.

Foley, Neil. "Mexicans, Mechanization, and the Growth of Corporate Cotton Culture in South Texas: The Taft Ranch, 1900–1930," *Journal of Southern History* 62 (May 1996): 275–302.

———. *Quest for Equality: The Failed Promise of Black-Brown Solidarity*. Cambridge, MA: Harvard University Press, 2010.

———. *The White Scourge: Mexicans, Blacks, and Poor Whites in Texas Cotton Culture*. Berkeley: University of California Press, 1997.

Foster, James C. *American Labor in the Southwest: The First One Hundred Years*. Tucson: University of Arizona Press, 1982.

Garcia, Mario T. "The Chicana in American History: The Mexican Women of El Paso, 1880–1920—A Case Study." *Pacific Historical Review* 49 (May 1980): 315–37.

———. *Desert Immigrants: The Mexicans of El Paso, 1880–1920*. New Haven, CT: Yale University Press, 1981.

———. "Obreros: The Mexican Workers of El Paso, 1900–1920." PhD diss., University of California, San Diego, 1975.

———. "Racial Dualism in the El Paso Labor Market, 1880–1920." *Aztlan: Chicano Journal of the Social Sciences and the Arts* 6 (Summer 1975): 197–218.

Garner, Milton. "The Application of the Anti-Trust Laws of Texas to Labor Unions." *Southwestern Law Journal* 2 (Spring 1948): 109–20.

Gentry, Mary Jane. *The Birth of a Texas Ghost Town: Thurber, 1886–1933*. Edited and with an introduction by T. Lindsey Baker. College Station: Texas A&M University Press, 2009.

———. "Thurber: The Life and Death of a Texas Town." Master's thesis, University of Texas at Austin, 1946.

Gibson, Charles Mac. "Organized Labor in Texas from 1890 to 1900." Master's thesis, Texas Tech University, 1973.

Gilmore, Glenda Elizabeth. *Defying Dixie: The Radical Roots of Civil Rights, 1919–1950.* 31–66. New York: W. W. Norton, 2008.

Glasrud, Bruce A., ed. *African Americans in South Texas.* College Station: Texas A&M University Press, 2011.

———. "Literature of Black Labor Unionists in Texas." *Lone Star Legacy: African American History in Texas* 1 (2011): 45–55.

Glasrud, Bruce A., and Archie P. McDonald, eds. *Making East Texas, East Texas: Selections from the* East Texas Historical Journal. Nacogdoches: East Texas Historical Association, 2009.

Glasrud, Bruce A., and Gregg Andrews. "Confronting White Supremacy: The African American Left in Texas, 1874–1974." In *The Texas Left: The Radical Roots of Lone Star Liberalism,* edited by David O'Donald Cullen and Kyle G. Wilkison, 157–90. College Station: Texas A&M University Press, 2010.

Gonzalez, Gabriela. "Two Flags Entwined: Transborder Activists and the Politics of Race, Ethnicity, Class, and Gender in South Texas, 1900–1950." PhD diss., Stanford University, 2004.

Graham, Donald. "Red, White, and Black: An Interpretation of Ethnic and Racial Attitudes of American Radicals in Texas and Oklahoma, 1880–1920." PhD diss., University of Saskatchewan, 1973.

Green, George N. "Anti-Labor Politics in Texas, 1941–1957." In *American Labor in the Southwest: The First One Hundred Years,* edited by James C. Foster, 217–27. Tucson: University of Arizona Press, 1982.

———. "Crucial Decade for Texas Labor: Railway Union Struggles, 1886–96." In *Seeking Inalienable Rights: Texans and Their Quests for Justice,* edited by Debra A. Reid, 17–35. College Station: Texas A&M University Press, 2009.

———. "Discord in Dallas: Auto Workers, City Fathers, and the Ford Motor Company, 1937–1941." *Labor's Heritage* 1, No. 3 (July 1989): 21–33.

———. *The Establishment in Texas Politics: The Primitive Years, 1938–1975.* Norman: University of Oklahoma Press, 1979.

———. "The ILGWU in Texas, 1930–1970." *Journal of Mexican American History* 1 (Spring 1971): 144–69.

———. "Militant Railroad Workers and the Closing of the Frontier, 1870s–1920s." *Red River Historical Review* 2 (Fall 2001): 14–36.

———. "The Texas Labor Movement, 1870–1920." *Southwestern Historical Quarterly* 108 (July 2004): 1–25.

———. "Texas State Industrial Union Council." *Handbook of Texas Online,* http://www.tshaonline.org/handbook/online.

———. "Texas . . . Unions . . . Time: Unions in Texas from the Time of the Republic through the Great War, 1838–1919." In *The Texas Left: The Radical Roots of Lone Star Liberalism*, edited by David O'Donald Cullen and Kyle G. Wilkison, 92–111. College Station: Texas A&M University Press, 2010.

Green, George N., and James C. Maroney. *The Heritage of Texas Labor, 1838–1980.* Pamphlet, Samuel Gompers Celebration, San Antonio, Labor Day 1982. San Antonio: Texas AFL-CIO, 1982.

Green, George N., and Michael R. Botson Jr. "Looking for Lefty: Liberal/Left Activism and Texas Labor, 1920s–1960s." In *The Texas Left: The Radical Roots of Lone Star Liberalism*, edited by David O'Donald Cullen and Kyle G. Wilkison, 112–32. College Station: Texas A&M University Press, 2010.

Green, James R. "The Brotherhood of Timber Workers, 1910–1913: A Radical Response to Industrial Capitalism in the Southern USA." *Past and Present* 60 (August 1973): 161–200.

———. *Death in the Haymarket: A Story of Chicago, the First Labor Movement, and the Bombing That Divided Gilded Age America.* New York: Pantheon, 2006.

———. "Populists, Socialism, and the Promise of Democracy." *Radical History Review* 24 (1980): 7–24.

———. "Tenant Farmer Discontent and Socialist Protest in Texas, 1901–1917." *Southwestern Historical Quarterly* 81 (1977): 133–54.

———. "'We Shall Not Be Moved': Socialists and the Southern Tenant Farmers' Union." In *Grass-Roots Socialism: Radical Movements in the Southwest, 1895–1943*, by James R. Green, 419–32. Baton Rouge: Louisiana State University Press, 1978.

Greer, William Lee. "The Texas Gulf Coast Oil Strike of 1917." Master's thesis, University of Houston, 1974.

Grubbs, Donald H. *Cry from the Cotton: The Southern Tenant Farmers' Union and the New Deal.* Chapel Hill: University of North Carolina Press, 1971.

Gullett, Ryan. "East Texas Theatre of the Timber War: Kirby Lumber Company's War with the Brotherhood of Timber Workers." *East Texas Historical Journal* 68, No. 2 (2010): 58–84.

Hales, Douglas. *A Southern Family in White and Black: The Cuneys of Texas.* College Station: Texas A&M University Press, 2003.

Halpern, Eric Brian. "'Black and White Unite and Fight': Race and Labor in Meatpacking, 1904–1948." PhD diss., University of Pennsylvania, 1989.

Halpern, Rick. "Interracial Unionism in the Southwest: Fort Worth's Packinghouse Workers, 1937–1954." In *Organized Labor in the Twentieth-Century South*, edited by Robert E. Ziegler, 158–82. Knoxville: University of Tennessee Press, 1991.

Hamlett, Samuel. "Labor Legislation in Texas, 1836–1876." Master's thesis, University of Texas at Austin, 1949.

Harper, Marjory. "Emigrant Strikebreakers: Scottish Granite Cutters and the Texas Capitol Boycott." *Southwestern Historical Quarterly* 95 (April 1992): 465–86.

Harris, Townes Malcolm. "The Labor Supply of Texas." Master's thesis, University of Texas at Austin, 1922.

Harvey, Sandra Denise. "Working for Change: Wage-Earning Women in Waco, Texas Defense Industries during World War II." PhD diss., Texas Tech University, 2009.

Helburn, I. B. "The American Federation of Teachers in Texas: Case Study of a Hostile Environment." *Journal of Collective Negotiations* 1 (August 1972): 1.

Henderson, Dwight F. "The Texas Coal Mining Industry." *Southwestern Historical Quarterly* 68 (October 1964): 207–19.

Herrera, Toni Marie Nelson. "Constructed and Contested Meanings of the Tex-Son Strike in San Antonio, Texas, 1959: Representing Mexican Women Workers." Master's thesis, University of Texas at Austin, 1997.

Hield, Melissa. "Union-Minded: Women in the Texas ILGWU, 1933–1950." In *Women in the Texas Workforce: Yesterday and Today*, edited by Richard Croxdale and Melissa Hield, 1–23. Austin: People's History in Texas, 1979.

Hild, Matthew. *Greenbackers, Knights of Labor, and Populists: Farmer-Labor Insurgency in the Late Nineteenth-Century South*. Athens: University of Georgia Press, 2007.

Hill, Charles J. *A Brief History of ILA Local 872*. Houston: Centaur Publishing Company, 1960.

Hill, Patricia Everidge. "Real Women and True Womanhood: Grassroots Organizing among Dallas Dressmakers in 1935." *Labor's Heritage* 5, No. 4 (Spring 1994): 4–17.

Hinze, Virginia Neal. "Norris Wright Cuney." Master's thesis, Rice University, 1965.

Honig, Emily. "Women at Farah Revisited: Political Mobilization and Its Aftermath among Chicana Workers at El Paso." *Feminist Studies* 22, no. 2 (Summer 1996): 425–41.

Hooks, Michael Q. "Thurber: A Unique Texas Community." *Panhandle-Plains Historical Review* 56 (1983): 1–17.

Hunter, Tera W. *To 'Joy My Freedom': Southern Black Women's Lives and Labors after the Civil War*, 77–82. Cambridge, MA: Harvard University Press, 1997.

Industrial Workers of the World. "Lucy Parsons: Woman of Will," IWW Biography, http://www.iww.org/en/history/biography/LucyParsons/1.

Irons, Martin. "My Experiences in the Labor Movement." *Lippincott's Magazine*, June 1886, 618–27.

Johnson, Clyde. "CIO Oil Workers' Organizing Campaign in Texas, 1942–1943." In *Essays in Southern Labor History*, edited by Gary M. Fink and Merl E. Reed, 173–87. Westport, CT: Greenwood Press, 1977.

Jones, Lamar Babington. "Mexican American Labor Problems in Texas." PhD diss., University of Texas, Austin, 1965.

Kemper, Deane A. "Texas Labor in the Thirties: Gilbert Mers and The Corpus Christi Waterfront Strikes." *Houston Review* 3, No. 3 (1981): 308–20.

Lack, Paul D. "Urban Slavery in the Southwest." *Red River Valley Historical Review* 6 (Spring 1981): 8–27.

Lackman, Howard, and George Green. "Origin and Progress of the Texas Labor Archives." *Labor History* 11 (Summer 1970): 341–44.

Landholt, Robert. *Mexican-American Workers of San Antonio, Texas*. New York: Arno Press, 1976.

Leal, Ray Robert. "The 1966–1967 South Texas Farm Workers Strike." PhD diss., Indiana University, 1983.

Ledesma, Irene. "Texas Newspapers and Chicana Workers' Activism, 1919–1974." *Western Historical Quarterly* 26 (Fall 1995): 309–31.

———. "Unlikely Strikers: Mexican American Women in Strike Activity in Texas, 1919–1974." PhD diss., Ohio State University, 1992.

Levenstein, Harvey A. "The AFL and Mexican Immigration in the 1920's: An Experiment in Labor Diplomacy." *Hispanic American Historical Review* 48 (May 1968): 206–19.

Licht, Walter. *Working for the Railroad*. Princeton, NJ: Princeton University Press, 1983.

Lopez, David E. "Cowboy Strikes and Unions." *Labor History* 18 (Summer 1977): 329–40.

Maroney, James C. "Brotherhood of Timber Workers." *Handbook of Texas Online*, http://www.tshaonline.org/handbook/online.

———. "The Galveston Longshoremen's Strike of 1920." *East Texas Historical Journal* 16, No. 1 (1978): 34–38.

———. "Great Southwest Strike." *Handbook of Texas Online*, http://www.tshaonline.org/handbook/online.

———. "International Longshoremen's Association." *Handbook of Texas Online*, http://tshaonline.org/handbook/online.

———. "The International Longshoremen's Association in the Gulf States during the Progressive Era." *Southern Studies* 16 (Summer 1977): 225–30.

———. "Knights of Labor." *Handbook of Texas Online*, http://www.tshaonline.org/handbook/online.

———. "Labor's Struggle for Acceptance: The Houston Worker in a Changing Society, 1900–1929." In *Houston: A Twentieth Century Urban Frontier*, edited by Francisco A. Rosales and Barry J. Kaplan, 34–57, 188–91. Port Washington, NY: Associated Faculty Press, 1983.

———. "Labor's Struggle for Acceptance: The Houston Worker in a Changing Society, 1900–1929." *Houston Review* 6, No. 1 (1984): 5–24. Expanded and revised version.

———. "The Negro and Organized Labor." *Community College Social Science Quarterly* (Spring 1976): 39–41.

———. "Oilfield Strike of 1917." *Handbook of Texas Online*, http://www.tshaonline.org/handbook/online.

———. "Organized Labor in Texas, 1900–1929." PhD diss., University of Houston, 1975.

———. "The Texas-Louisiana Oil Field Strike of 1917." In *Essays in Southern Labor History*, edited by Gary M. Fink and Merl E. Reed, 161–72. Westport, CT: Greenwood Press, 1977.

———. "Texas State Federation of Labor." *Handbook of Texas Online*, http://www.tshaonline.org/handbook/online.

———. "Thurber, Texas." *Handbook of Texas Online*, http://tshaonline.org/handbook/online.

———. "The Unionization of Thurber, 1903." *Red River Valley Historical Review* 4 (Spring 1979): 27–32.

———. "William Knox Gordon." *Handbook of Texas Online*, http://tshaonline.org/handbook/online.

Marshall, F. Ray. "Independent Unions in the Gulf Coast Petroleum Refining Industry—The Esso Experience." *Labor Law Journal* 12 (1961): 823–40.

———. *Labor in the South*. Cambridge, MA: Harvard University Press, 1967.

———. "The Negro in Southern Unions." In *The Negro and the American Labor Movement*, edited by Julius Jacobson, 128–54. Garden City, NY: Doubleday, 1968.

———. *The Negro Worker*. New York: Random House, 1967.

———. "Some Factors Influencing the Upgrading of Negroes in the Southern Petroleum Refining Industry." *Social Forces* 42 (December 1963): 186–95.

———. "Some Reflections on Labor History." *Southwestern Historical Quarterly* 75 (October 1971): 139–57.

Maxwell, Robert S. "Lumbermen of the East Texas Frontier." *Forest History* 9 (April 1965): 12–16.

McCain, Johnny Mac. "Texas and the Mexican Labor Question, 1942–1947." *Southwestern Historical Quarterly* 85 (1981): 45–64.

McCartin, Joseph. *Labor's Great War: The Struggle for Industrial Democracy and the Origins of Modern American Labor Relations*. Chapel Hill: University of North Carolina Press, 1997.

McCord, Charles R. "A Brief History of the Brotherhood of Timber Workers." Master's thesis, University of Texas, 1959.

McLaurin, Melton. *Knights of Labor in the South*. Westport, CT: Greenwood Press, 1978.

Meador, Bruce S. "'Wetback' Labor in the Lower Rio Grande Valley." Master's thesis, University of Texas at Austin, 1951.

Menefee, Selden, and Orin C. Cassmore. *The Pecan Shellers of San Antonio*. Washington, DC: US Government Printing Office, 1940.

Mers, Gilbert. *Working the Waterfront: The Ups and Downs of a Rebel Longshoreman*. Austin: University of Texas Press, 1988.

Montes, Rebecca Anne. "Undermining Segregation: Black Longshore Locals and Community Activism during the 1930s." Paper presented at the annual meeting of the Texas State Historical Association, March 6, 2003.

———. "Working for American Rights: Black, White, and Mexican American Dockworkers in Texas during the Great Depression." PhD diss., University of Texas at Austin, 2005.

Morgan, George T. Jr. "The Gospel of Wealth Goes South: John Henry Kirby and Labor's Struggle for Self-Determination, 1901–1916." *Southwestern Historical Quarterly* 75 (October 1971): 186–97.

———. "No Compromise—No Recognition: John Henry Kirby, the Southern Lumber Operators' Association, and Unionism in the Piney Woods, 1900–1916." *Labor History* 10 (Spring 1969): 193–204.

Mosher, W. S. "Open Shop in the Southwest." *Open Shop Review* 18 (March 1921): 115–17.

Motl, Kevin C. "Under the Influence: The Texas Businessmen's Association and the Campaign against Reform, 1906–1915." *Southwestern Historical Quarterly* 109 (2006): 495–530.

Mullenix, Grady Lee. "A History of the Labor Movement in the Oil Industry." Master's thesis, North Texas State Teachers College, 1943.

———. "A History of the Texas State Federation of Labor." PhD diss., University of Texas, 1955.

Nelson, Bruce. *Workers on the Waterfront: Seamen, Longshoremen, and Unionism in the 1930s.* Urbana: University of Illinois Press, 1988.

Nettleton, Douglas A. "The Growth of Unions in the Waco, Texas, Area." Master's thesis, Baylor University, 1963.

Obadele-Starks, Ernest. "Black Labor, the Black Middle Class, and Organized Protest along the Upper Gulf Coast, 1883–1945." *Southwestern Historical Quarterly* 103 (July 1999): 53–65.

———. "Black Struggle, White Resistance, and Upper Texas Gulf Coast Railroads, 1900–1945." *Houston Review* 18, No. 2 (1996): 104–13.

———. "Black Texans and Theater Craft Unionism: The Struggle for Racial Equality." *Southwestern Historical Quarterly* 106 (2003): 533–50.

———. *Black Unionism in the Industrial South.* College Station: Texas A&M University Press, 2000.

———. "The Road to Jericho: Black Workers, The Fair Employment Practice Commission, and the Struggle for Racial Equality on the Upper Texas Gulf Coast, 1941–1947." PhD diss., University of Houston, 1996.

O'Connor, Harvey. *History of the Oil Workers International Union–CIO.* Denver: Oil Workers International Union, 1950.

Olson, Bruce A., and Jack L. Howard. "Armed Elites Confront Labor: The Texas Militia and the Houston Strikes of 1880 and 1898." *Labor's Heritage* 7 (Summer 1995): 52–61.

Olson, James S., and Sharon Phair. "The Anatomy of a Race Riot: Beaumont, Texas, 1943." *Texana* 11 (1973): 64–72.

O'Rourke, T. P. *A Brief History of the Union Labor Legislative Movement in Texas.* 1909; repr., Ithaca, NY: Cornell University Press, 2000.

Parigi, Sam F. "A Case Study of Latin American Unionization in Austin, Texas." PhD diss., University of Texas at Austin, 1964.

Peace, John. *Selected Cases and Materials on Texas Workmen's Compensation Law.* San Antonio: St. Mary's University Book Store, 1950.

Perales, Monica. *Smelter Town: Making and Remembering a Border Community.* Chapel Hill: University of North Carolina Press, 2010.

Pitre, Merline. "George T. Ruby: The Party Loyalist." In *Through Many Dangers, Toils, and Snares: Black Leadership in Texas, 1868–1900*, 166–73, 238–40. Austin, TX: Eakin Press, 1985.

———. "Ruby, George Thompson." *Handbook of Texas Online*, http://www.tshaonline .org/handbook/online.

Polakoff, Murray E. "The Development of the Texas State CIO Council." PhD diss., Columbia University, 1958.

———. "Inner Pressures on the Texas State CIO Council, 1937–1955." *Industrial and Labor Relations Review* 12 (January 1959): 227–42.

Porter, Kenneth W. "Negro Labor in the Western Cattle Industry." *Labor History* 10, no. 3 (Summer 1969): 346–74.

Privett, John Delmar. "Agricultural Unionism among Chicanos in Texas." Master's thesis, University of Texas at Austin, 1976.

Proctor, Ben H. "The Modern Texas Rangers: A Law Enforcement Dilemma in the Rio Grande Valley." In *Reflections of Western Historians*, edited by John Alexander Carroll, 215–33. Tucson: University of Arizona Press, 1969.

Pycior, Julie Leininger. "La Raza Organizes: Mexican American Life in San Antonio, 1915–1930." PhD diss., University of Notre Dame, 1979.

Quiroz, Anthony. "'We Are Not Wetbacks, Meskins, or Slaves, but Human Beings': The Economy Furniture Company Strike of 1968–1971." In *Tejano Epic: Essays in Honor of Felix D. Almaraz Jr.*, edited by Arnoldo De Leon, 115–29. Austin: Texas State Historical Association, 2005.

Rachleff, Peter. *Black Labor in the South*. Philadelphia: Temple University Press, 1984.

Reese, James V. "The Early History of Labor Organizations in Texas, 1838–1876." *Southwestern Historical Quarterly* 72 (July 1968): 1–20.

———. "The Evolution of an Early Texas Union: The Screwmen's Benevolent Association of Galveston, 1865–1891." *Southwestern Historical Quarterly* 75 (October 1971): 158–85.

———. "The Worker in Texas, 1821–1876." PhD diss., University of Texas, 1964.

Reich, Steven A. "The Making of a Southern Sawmill World: Race, Class, and Rural Transformation in the Piney Woods of East Texas, 1830–1930." PhD diss., Northwestern University, 1998.

———. "Soldiers of Freedom: Black Texans and the Fight for Citizenship, 1917–1921." *Journal of American History* 82 (March 1996): 1478–1504.

Rhinehart, Marilyn D. "A Lesson in Unity: The Houston Municipal Workers' Strike of 1946." *Houston Review* 4.3 (Fall 1982): 137–53.

———. "Robert Dickie Hunter." *Handbook of Texas Online*, http://tshaonline.org/handbook/online.

———. "'Underground Patriots': Thurber Coal Miners and the Struggle for Individual Freedom, 1888–1903." *Southwestern Historical Quarterly* 92 (April 1989): 509–42.

———. *A Way of Work and a Way of Life: Coal Mining in Thurber, Texas, 1888–1926*. College Station: Texas A&M University Press, 1992.

Rhinehart, Marilyn D., and Thomas H. Kreneck. "The Minimum Wage March of 1966: A Case Study in Mexican-American Politics, Labor, and Identity." *Houston Review* 11, No. 1 (1989): 27–44.

Riley, Mary Elizabeth. "The Austin Chicano Huelga." Master's thesis, University of Texas at Austin, 1996.

Romero, Yolanda G. "*Adelante Compañeros*: The Sanitation Worker's Struggle in Lubbock, Texas, 1968–1972." *West Texas Historical Association Yearbook* 69 (1993): 82–88.

———. "Migrant Housing and Labor Camps in Northwest Texas, 1930s–1940s." In *Tejano Epic: Essays in Honor of Felix D. Almaraz Jr.*, edited by Arnoldo De Leon, 87–98. Austin: Texas State Historical Association, 2005.

Samora, Julian, Joe Bernal, and Albert Pena. "John Connally's Strikebreakers." In *Gunpowder Justice: A Reassessment of the Texas Rangers*, 131–56. Notre Dame: University of Notre Dame Press, 1979).

Sandlin, Barry. "The 1921 Butcher Workmen Strike in Fort Worth, Texas." Master's thesis, University of Texas at Arlington, 1988.

Seely, Amber, and Leon Richardson. "Clifton Frederick Richardson Sr." *Handbook of Texas Online*, http://www.tshaonline.org/handbook/online.

Shapiro, Harold. "The Labor Movement in San Antonio, Texas, 1865–1915." *Southwestern Social Science Quarterly* 36 (September 1955): 160–75.

———. "The Pecan Shellers of San Antonio, Texas." *Southwestern Social Science Quarterly* 32 (March 1952): 229–44.

———. "The Workers of San Antonio, Texas, 1900–1940." PhD diss., University of Texas, 1952.

Sharpless, Rebecca. *Fertile Ground, Narrow Choices: Women on Texas Cotton Farms, 1900–1940*. Chapel Hill: University of North Carolina Press, 1999.

Shelton, Robert Stuart. "'Built by the Irishman, the Negro, and the Mule': Labor Militancy across the Color Line in Post-Reconstruction Texas." *East Texas Historical Journal* 46, No. 2 (Fall 2008): 15–26.

———. "On Empire's Shore: Casual Laborers and Enslaved African-Americans in Galveston, Texas, 1840–1860." *Journal of Social History* 40 (Spring 2007): 717–30.

———. "Slavery in a Texas Seaport: The Peculiar Institution in Galveston." *Slavery and Abolition* 8 (August 2007): 155–68.

———. "Waterfront Workers of Galveston, Texas, 1838–1920." PhD diss., Rice University, 2000.

———. "'Which Ox Is in the Mire': Race and Class in the Galveston Longshoremen's Strike of 1898." *Southwestern Historical Quarterly* 110 (October 2006): 219–39.

Simpson, Herman W. *Hands of the Throttle: A Black Man's Struggle on the Road*. Houston: Privately printed, 1995.

Sitton, Thad, and James H. Conrad. *Nameless Towns: Texas Sawmill Communities, 1880–1942*. Austin: University of Texas Press, 1998.

Smallwood, James M. "Perpetuation of Caste: Black Agricultural Workers in Reconstruction Texas." *Mid-America* 61 (1979): 5–23.

SoRelle, James M. "An De Po Cullud Man Is in the Wus Fix uv Awl: Black Occupational Status in Houston, Texas, 1920–1940." *Houston Review* 1, No. 1 (Spring 1979): 15–26.

Sparks, Earle Sylvester. "A Survey of Organized Labor in Austin." Master's thesis, University of Texas at Austin, 1920.

Spero, Sterling D., and Abram L. Harris. *The Black Worker*. New York: Columbia University Press, 1931.

Srinivasan, Sethuraman. "The Struggle for Control: Technology and Organized Labor in Gulf Coast Refineries, 1913–1973." PhD diss., University of Houston, 2001.

Sullivan, Mary Loretta, and Bertha Blair. *Women in Texas Industries: Hours, Wages,*

Working Conditions, and Home Work. Washington, DC: US Government Printing Office, 1936.

Sundstrom, William. "Half a Career: Discrimination and Railroad Internal Labor Markets." *Industrial Relations* 29 (Fall 1990): 423–40.

Taussig, Frank W. "The South-Western Strike of 1886." *Quarterly Journal of Economics* 1, No. 2 (1887): 184–222.

Taylor, Allen Clayton. "A History of the Screwmen's Benevolent Association from 1866 to 1924." Master's thesis, University of Texas, 1968.

Taylor, Hobart T. "C. W. Rice: Labor Leader." BA thesis, Prairie View State Normal and Industrial College, 1939.

Teel, Robert Eli. "Discrimination against Negro Workers in Texas: Extent and Effects." Master's thesis, University of Texas, 1947.

Todes, Jay L. "Organized Employer Opposition to Unionism in Texas." Master's thesis, University of Texas at Austin, 1949.

Urbano, David. "When the Smoke Lifted: The 1857–1858 'Cart War' of South Texas." PhD diss., University of Houston, 2009.

Vargas, Zaragosa. "Emma Tenayuca: Labor and Civil Rights Organizer of 1930s San Antonio." In *The Human Tradition in America between the Wars, 1920–1945*, edited by Donald W. Whisenhunt, 169–84. Wilmington, DE: Scholarly Resources, 2002.

———. *Labor Rights Are Civil Rights: Mexican American Workers in Twentieth-Century America*. Princeton, NJ: Princeton University Press, 2005.

———. "Tejana Radical: Emma Tenayuca and the San Antonio Labor Movement during the Great Depression." *Pacific Historical Review* 66, No. 4 (1997): 553–80.

Vassberg, David E. "The Use of Mexicans and Mexican Americans as an Agricultural Work Force in the Lower Rio Grande Valley of Texas." PhD diss., University of Texas at Austin, 1967.

Wakstein, Allen M. "Origins of the Open Shop Movement, 1919–1920." *Journal of American History* 51 (1964): 460–75.

Walker, Kenneth P. "The Pecan Shellers of San Antonio and Mechanization." *Southwestern Historical Quarterly* 69 (July 1965): 44–58.

Warner, Juliann. "Lambert, George Phillip." *Handbook of Texas Online*, http://www.tshaonline.org/handbook/online.

Webber, Carolyn C. "The Negro in the Texas Industrial Labor Market, 1940–1947." Master's thesis, University of Texas at Austin, 1948.

Weber, Bruce J. "Progressive Mind in Texas: A Survey of Journalistic Response to Labor Radicalism, Violence, and Socialism, 1900–1916." Master's thesis, University of Houston, 1973.

Winn, Charles Carr. "Mexican Americans in the Texas Labor Movement." PhD diss., Texas Christian University, 1972.

———. "The Valley Farm Workers' Movement, 1966–1967." Master's thesis, University of Texas at Arlington, 1970.

Woods, Randall B. "George T. Ruby: A Black Militant in the White Business Community." *Red River Valley Historical Review* 1 (1974): 269–80.

Wortham, John. "Regulation of Organized Labor in Texas, 1940–1945." Master's thesis, University of Texas, 1947.

Young, Andrew H. "Life and Labor on the King Ranch: The Early Years, 1853–1865." *Journal of South Texas* 6, No. 1 (Spring 1993): 54–71.

Zamora, Emilio. "Chicano Socialist Labor Activity in Texas, 1900–1920." *Aztlan: Chicano Journal of the Social Sciences and the Arts* 6 (Summer 1975): 221–36.

———. *Claiming Rights and Righting Wrongs in Texas: Mexican Workers and Job Politics during World War II*. College Station: Texas A&M University Press, 2009.

———. "The Failed Promise of Wartime Opportunity for Mexicans in the Texas Oil Industry." *Southwestern Historical Quarterly* 95 (1992): 323–50.

———. "Labor Formation, Community, and Politics: The Mexican Working Class in Texas, 1900–1945." In *Border Crossings: Mexican and Mexican-American Workers*, edited by John Mason Hart, 139–62. Wilmington, DE: Scholarly Resources, 1998.

———. "Sara Estela Ramirez: Una Rosa Roja en el Movimiento." In *Mexican Women in the United States: Struggles Past and Present*, edited by Magdalena Mora and Adelaida R. del Castillo, 163–69. Los Angeles: Chicano Studies Research Center Publications, UCLA, 1980.

———. *The World of the Mexican Worker in Texas*. College Station: Texas A&M University Press, 1993.

Zeigler, Robert E. "The Cowboy Strike of 1883: Its Causes and Meaning." *West Texas Historical Association Yearbook* 47 (1971): 32–46.

———. "The Limits of Power: The Amalgamated Association of Street Railway Employees in Houston, Texas, 1897–1905." *Labor History* 18 (Winter 1977): 71–90.

———. "The Workingman in Houston, Texas, 1865–1914." PhD diss., Texas Tech University, 1972.

Zieger, Robert H., ed. *Organized Labor in the Twentieth-Century South*. Knoxville: University of Tennessee Press, 1991.

Contributors

JOSEPH ABEL (PhD, Rice University) is a research fellow of the Clements Center for Southwest Studies at Southern Methodist University. He is the author of articles in the *Journal of Southern History* and the *Southwestern Historical Quarterly* on Texas labor and working-class history.

MARY MARGARET MCALLEN AMBERSON, independent historian, is a seventh-generation Texan raised on a South Texas cattle ranch and is author of books and articles on Spanish and Mexican trans-border history, including *I Would Rather Sleep in Texas* and *A Brave Boy and a Good Soldier*, about the 1842 Mier expedition.

GREGG ANDREWS (PhD, Northern Illinois University), distinguished professor emeritus, Texas State University, San Marcos, is author of numerous books and articles on labor history, including *City of Dust: A Cement Company Town in the Land of Tom Sawyer*, *The American Federation of Labor, the United States, and the Mexican Revolution, 1910–1924*, *Thyra J. Edwards: Black Activist in the Global Freedom Struggle*, and articles in the *Journal of Southern History* and the *Southwestern Historical Quarterly*, among others.

JULIA KIRK BLACKWELDER (PhD, Emory University), professor of history at Texas A&M University, has published numerous books and articles on working-class women, including *Women of the Depression: Caste and Culture in San Antonio, 1929–1939*, *Now Hiring: The Feminization of Work in the United States, 1900 to 1995*, and *Styling Jim Crow: African-American Beauty Training during Segregation*.

MICHAEL R. BOTSON JR. (PhD, University of Houston) is a former union steelworker, labor historian, and professor of history at Houston Community

College. He is the author of *Labor, Civil Rights, and the Hughes Tool Company* and articles on civil rights and working-class history in the *Southwestern Historical Quarterly*, *Houston History Magazine*, *East Texas Historical Journal*, and others.

THERESA A. CASE (PhD, University of Texas at Austin), assistant professor of history at the University of Houston–Downtown, is author of *The Great Southwest Railroad Strike and Free Labor* and articles in *Labor: Studies in Working-Class History* and the *Journal of the Gilded Age and Progressive Era*.

BRUCE A. GLASRUD (PhD, Texas Tech University) is professor emeritus of history, California State University, East Bay, and retired dean of the School of Arts and Sciences, Sul Ross State University. A specialist in the history of blacks in the West, Glasrud has published eighteen books and more than seventy articles. A fellow of the Texas State Historical Association and of the East Texas Historical Association, Glasrud currently is president of the West Texas Historical Association.

GEORGE N. GREEN (PhD, Florida State University) is professor emeritus of history at the University of Texas at Arlington, where he was cofounder of the Texas Labor and Political Archives. He is a fellow and past president of the Texas State Historical Association and is author of *The Establishment in Texas Politics* and of numerous articles on Texas labor and political history. He currently is working on a two-volume history of the labor movement in Texas.

JAMES R. GREEN (PhD, Yale University) is professor of history at the University of Massachusetts at Boston. He is a member of the Organization of American Historians' Distinguished Lecture program and is author of numerous books and articles on labor and working-class history, including *Grass-Roots Socialism, Radical Movements in the Southwest, 1895–1943, The World of the Worker*, and *Death in the Haymarket: A Story of the First Labor Movement and the Bombing that Divided Gilded Age America*.

JAMES C. MARONEY (PhD, University of Houston) is professor emeritus of history at Lee College and former visiting scholar at the *New Handbook of Texas*, where he coordinated and wrote a number of the *Handbook*'s labor history articles. He is author of articles on Texas labor history in books and journals, including *Essays in Southern Labor History, Houston Review, Southern Studies, East Texas Historical Journal, Red River Valley Historical Review*, and others.

The late **GEORGE T. MORGAN JR.** (PhD, University of Oregon) was professor of history at the University of Houston. He published books and articles on forest and environmental history, as well as articles on the labor movement in Texas in *Labor History* and the *Southwestern Historical Quarterly*.

ERNEST OBADELE-STARKS (PhD, University of Houston) is professor of history at Texas A&M University and author of *Black Unionism in the Industrial South* and *Freebooters and Smugglers: The Foreign Slave Trade in the United States after 1808*, as well as articles in books and the journals *Southwestern Historical Quarterly*, *Houston Review*, *East Texas Historical Journal*, and others.

The late **JAMES V. REESE** (PhD, University of Texas at Austin) was a history professor and director of the Southwest Collection at Texas Tech University and professor of history and dean of the graduate school at Stephen F. Austin State University. One of the pioneers in Texas labor history, Reese published articles on early Texas unions and on Galveston's Screwmen's Benevolent Association in the *Southwestern Historical Quarterly*.

MARILYN D. RHINEHART (PhD, University of Houston) currently is executive vice president of academic affairs and chief academic officer at Johnson County Community College in Overland Park, Kansas. She is author of *A Way of Work and a Way of Life: Coal Mining in Thurber, Texas, 1888–1926*, and articles on labor and working-class history in the *Southwestern Historical Quarterly*, the *Houston Review*, and others.

YOLANDA G. ROMERO (PhD, Texas Tech University) teaches history at North Lake College in the Dallas County Community College District. She was the first Mexican American woman to receive a PhD in history from a Texas university. She has conducted research and oral histories of migrant workers, the Brown Berets, the Raza Unida Party, and the Southwest Voter Registration Education Project, among others. Her publications include an article in the *West Texas Historical Association Yearbook* on the struggle of sanitation workers for equality of pay and civil rights in Lubbock, Texas, 1968–72.

ROBERT S. SHELTON (PhD, Rice University) is associate professor of history and director of graduate studies at Cleveland State University. He has researched and published articles on race, waterfront workers, slavery, and labor in the *Journal of Social History*, *Slavery and Abolition*, and *East Texas Historical Journal*.

ZARAGOSA VARGAS (PhD, University of Michigan) is professor of history at the University of North Carolina at Chapel Hill. A specialist in nineteenth- and twentieth-century labor, Chicano, and ethnic history, he is author of a number of books and articles, including *Proletarians of the North: A History of Mexican Industrial Workers in Detroit and the Midwest, 1917–1933, Labor Rights Are Civil Rights: Mexican American Workers in Twentieth-Century America*, and "Tejana Radical: Emma Tenayuca and the San Antonio Labor Movement during the Great Depression."

EMILIO ZAMORA (PhD, University of Texas at Austin) is professor of history at the University of Texas at Austin and a fellow of the Texas State Historical Association. He is author of numerous books and articles on Mexican, borderlands, labor, and civil rights history, including *The World of the Mexican Worker in Texas* and *Claiming Rights and Righting Wrongs in Texas: Mexican Workers and Job Politics during World War II.*

ROBERT E. ZEIGLER (PhD, Texas Tech University) is president of San Antonio College. At Texas Tech he studied under James V. Reese. Zeigler is author of articles on "The Amalgamated Association of Street Railway Employees in Houston, Texas, 1897–1905" in *Labor History* and the cowboy strike of 1883 in the *West Texas Historical Association Yearbook.*

Index

workforce, 113–14; strikebreaking tactics of, 122–24; unionization of miners, 124–27; wage scales of miners as grievance, 120–24; working conditions of miners, 109–10. *See also* Thurber, Texas

Texas & Pacific Railway, 86, 88, 92, 110–11, 246. *See also* Gould system railroads

Texas Board of Control, 256

Texas Chamber of Commerce, 189–90

Texas Constitutional Convention of 1845, 29

Texas Council of Churches, 381

Texas Engineers' Association, 35

Texas Farm Placement Service, 222

Texas Farm Workers' Union, 388–89

Texas Federal Labor Union (TFLU), 298

Texas Federation Club (TFC), 303

Texas Federation of Labor, 129–30

Texas Highway Department, 256

Texas Industrial Commission, 232

Texas Infant Dress Company, 289, 291

Texas Joint Labor Legislative Board of Texas, 10, 11

The Texas Left (Cullen and Wilkison), 12

Texas Live Stock Journal (newspaper), 69, 70–71

Texas-Louisiana oil field strike (1917): attempts at union organization, 173–74; conciliation attempt undermined by producers, 174–77; Reed Commission mediation efforts, 177–78; settlement of, 178–80; use of martial law in, 191

Texas National Guard, 192, 194–201, 202–03

Texas Northern Railroad, 246

Texas Observer (newspaper), 381

Texas Open Shop Association (TOSA), 11

Texas Pacific Mercantile and Manufacturing Company, 115–16

Texas Rangers: in antiunion violence in Dallas, 269–70; and civil rights lawsuit, 380–81, 399; in coal strikes, 121–22; in cowboy strike, 69; in farmworkers' strike, 16, 224, 370, 375, 377–80; historic role as law enforcement agency, 387, 388; in longshoremen's strike, 194, 202, 205, 208; as peace keepers, 115, 123–24, 126–27; testimony against in senate hearings, 382

Texas State Convention of Germans (1854), 32

Texas State Council of Cement Mill Workers and Allied Industries, 257

Texas State Federation of Labor (TSFL), 10, 245, 250, 256–57

Texas State Gazette (newspaper), 30, 49

Texas State Industrial Union Council, 257

Texas Typographical Association, 32–34

Texas Weekly (newspaper), 272

TFC (Texas Federation Club), 303

TFLU (Texas Federal Labor Union), 298

theater industry, 299, 301–02, 305

theater owners, 300–301, 306

theater unions. *See* IATSE (International Alliance of Theatrical Stage Employees and Moving Picture Operators)

theater workers. *See* black theater workers; white theater workers

third-party politics, 97, 100–101

Thomas, Henry, 191

Thompson, E. P., 2–3

Thompson, F. O., 189, 190

Thompson, J. P., 356

Thurber, Texas: company paternalism in, 9, 109, 110–11, 114–18, 128–29; departure of mine workers from, 127–28; disruptive labor activity in, 118–23; ethnically diverse population of, 111–13; miners' working conditions in, 109–10; race relations in, 113–14; results of labor activism in, 128–30; strikebreaking attempts in, 122–24; union organizing in, 124–27

timber workers, 1, 9, 143–47, 158. *See also* Kirby Lumber Company

Todes, Jay L., 5–6

Tomson, Don, 95, 98–99, 101

TOSA (Texas Open Shop Association), 11

Tower, John, 383

trackmen, railroad, 79, 83, 85–86, 87

Tradesmen's Club (New Braunfels), 30

Trade Union Unity League, 223

trainmen, railroad, 84, 85–86

Trinidad Weekly Advertiser (newspaper), 71

Trinity Portland Cement Company: antiunionism of, 245; Eagle Ford plant, 245–48; and industry pricing, 249; organizing attempts at, 249–54; and passage of NIRA, 248–49; paternalism, 246–47, 254–55; unfair trade practices and antitrust violations of, 255–57; unionization of workers under AFL, 257–59; working conditions at, 247–48